Medical Surgical Nursing Concepts Made Insanely Easy!

A New Approach to Prioritizing Nursing!

Loretta Manning, MSN, RN, GNP
Lydia Zager, MSN, RN, NEA-BC

I CAN
PUBLISHING® INC.

I CAN Publishing®, Inc. ◆ Duluth, GA
www.icanpublishing.com

I CAN Publishing®, Inc.
2650 Chattahoochee Drive, Suite 100
Duluth, GA 30097
www.icanpublishing.com

Editorial Assistants: Mary Jo Zazueta, Traverse City, MI; Larry Zager, Columbia, SC
Illustrations: Teresa R. Davidson, Greensboro, NC
Cover Design: Teresa R. Davidson, Greensboro, NC
Interior Design: Mary Jo Zazueta, Traverse City, MI
Publishing Service Manager: Jennifer Robinson, Duluth, GA

ISBN: 978-0-9842040-9-0
Library of Congress Control Number: 2014943577

Nursing procedures and/or practice described in this book should be applied by the nurse, or healthcare practitioner, under appropriate supervision according to established professional standards of care. These standards should be used with regard to the unique circumstances that apply in each practice situation. Every effort has been taken to validate and confirm the accuracy of information presented and to describe generally accepted practices. However, the authors, editors, and publisher cannot accept any responsibility for errors or omissions or for consequences from application of the information in this book and make no warranty, express or implied, with respect to the contents of this book.

Every effort has been exerted by the authors and publisher to ensure that drug selection and dosage set forth in this text are in accord with current recommendations and practice at the time of publication. However, in view of ongoing research, the constant flow of information relating to government regulations, drug therapy, and drug reactions, the reader is urged to check the manufacturer's information on the package insert of each drug for any change in indications and dosage and for added warnings and precautions. This is particularly important when the recommended agent is a new or infrequently used drug. This publication is not providing medical advice and is not recommending or endorsing any specific tests, providers of care, procedures, products, processes, or any other information that may be reviewed in this book.

This book is written to be used as a book for learning nursing concepts and linking these to professional standards and the NCLEX-RN®. To the fullest extent of the law, neither the Publisher or the Authors assumes any liability for any injury and/or damage to persons or property coming out of or pertaining to any use of the information contained in this book.

Professional Praise for *Medical Surgical Nursing Concepts Made Insanely Easy!*

"As a nurse educator, I have discovered that two of the most important concepts at the core of entry-level nursing programs are critical thinking and the ability to apply theory to practice. These concepts are interdependent and must be refined as nursing students migrate from novice to the advanced beginner in a constantly evolving profession. Recently, I was challenged with introducing an innovative 'SAFETY' model in our clinical reasoning course that is concept based. Instead of teaching the application and implementation of nursing diagnoses, as we all know it; I was charged with implementing an approach to teaching, using concepts. Our nursing students were very receptive to learning one nursing concept that could represent several NANDA nursing diagnoses. This paradigm shift from nursing diagnoses to concepts helped our students develop a plan of care in the clinical settings with ease and confidence.

After planning and initiating the transition to concepts, I would offer the following advice to nursing programs that are considering moving from nursing diagnoses to concepts. First, nursing faculty, generate enthusiasm with students and with fellow colleagues about teaching and learning conceptually. It is very important that all faculties, especially adjunct clinical faculty, are involved in the planning and implementing processes. It takes a cohesive, united village of faculty to yield positive results in critical thinking enhancements and knowledge application. Second, nursing faculty must be always cognizant of teaching and learning styles and how they contribute and enhance the student's ability to learn simple to complex applications. Finally, I encourage nursing faculty to have fun and enjoy the ride in this transition! Like any groundbreaking, innovative idea, there will be growing pains for faculty and students alike. However, the reward will be preparing nursing students who are knowledgeable and confident in critical thinking and clinical judgment skills necessary to allow them to "hit the ground running" as new graduates."

KAREN WORTHY, MSN, MPH, RN
BSN SUCCESS COORDINATOR/CLINICAL INSTRUCTOR
COLLEGE OF NURSING
UNIVERSITY OF SOUTH CAROLINA, COLUMBIA, SOUTH CAROLINA

"Loretta and Lydia have managed to simplify the most complex topics. This book pulls everything together, linking the pathophysiology of a given disease process to the assessments the RN will make because of the pathophysiology, and on to the prioritized nursing interventions that will reverse or control the pathophysiology. This book is a gift for nursing faculty who open a nursing textbook and think, 'How will I ever get through all of this information?' My advice is to close the textbook, embrace the 'SAFETY' model and use it to guide the instructional design. Loretta and Lydia have provided a brilliant organizing framework covering the most tested NCLEX® activities. They have done the work for us!"

MELISSA GEIST, EdD, APRN-BC, CNE
INTERIM DEAN, COLLEGE OF INTERDISCIPLINARY STUDIES,
TENNESSEE TECHNOLOGICAL UNIVERSITY, COOKEVILLE, TENNESSEE
ASSOCIATE PROFESSOR OF NURSING
WHITSON-HESTER SCHOOL OF NURSING TENNESSEE TECHNOLOGICAL UNIVERSITY

"The transformation of complex information in this book far exceeds expectations. Information is simplified and concepts are connected to pathophysiology through charts, images, mnemonics, songs and other creative strategies that will compliment any nursing curriculum. This book will assist faculty in providing excellent, standard based education that meets the desired program outcome of NCLEX® success for students."

KAREN E. ALEXANDER, PhD, RN, CNOR
PROGRAM DIRECTOR, RN TO BSN PROGRAM
ASSISTANT PROFESSOR NURSING (BSN)
UNIVERSITY OF HOUSTON–CLEAR LAKE, HOUSTON, TEXAS

"I was pleasantly surprised by how efficient and streamlined my lectures became by using the 'SAFETY' model for teaching. Adapting existing slides to the new model was easy to do because of the flexibility of the model. Incorporating system's specific physiology forced me to focus on the 'need to know' material instead of the 'fun to know', thus freeing up at least 30 minutes of lecture time. This additional time allowed me to incorporate NCLEX® style questions into the classroom providing an interactive opportunity to gage the student's understanding of the information and to assess what areas needed additional explanation. Delineating system specific assessments, priorities, and expected outcome measures made the flow of information easier for students to comprehend, particularly at the foundations level."

KIMBERLY A. GLENN, MN, RN, CPN
ASSISTANT DEAN AND CLINICAL ASSOCIATE PROFESSOR
UNIVERSITY OF SOUTH CAROLINA, COLUMBIA, SC

"After teaching in a concept-based curriculum, I can say from first hand experience the 'SAFETY' model and the strategies used in this book have transformed both my teaching and students' learning! In the past, we have struggled with assisting students in understanding the pathophysiology behind concepts. *Medical Surgical Nursing Concepts Made Insanely Easy* is the answer to this challenge! Pathophysiology is linked with concepts, and concepts are linked with NCLEX® and standards. I currently use both books, *Nursing Made Insanely Easy and Pharmacology Made Insanely Easy*, to facilitate the preparation for my lectures and interactive exercises. The images have been very successful with improving scores on both classroom exams and NCLEX®. *Medical Surgical Nursing Concepts Made Insanely Easy* is another resource that that will provide the foundation to assist nursing students in learning how to think like a nurse!"

CAROLINE B. BAIRD, RN, MSN
ASSISTANT PROFESSOR, NURSING DEPARTMENT
ROCKINGHAM COMMUNITY COLLEGE, WENTWORTH, NORTH CAROLINA

"WOW, if only I would have had this book while in nursing school, maybe I would have had a better understanding of the nursing concepts based on the pathophysiology. Even in practice now, I still use my books, *Pharmacology and Nursing Made Insanely Easy*, as a preceptor for junior and senior nursing students during their clinical experience. The pictures and mnemonics used in the books *Pharmacology Made Insanely Easy!* and *Nursing Made Insanely Easy!* do a great job of linking professional standards to clinical practice. In my current role as Director of Nursing Services for a skilled nursing facility, these books by I CAN Publishing benefit our nursing students who are preparing for clinical, new graduates studying for the NCLEX®, and for any nurse involved in an orientation or educational program."

CAROL ANNE BAKER, BSN, MBA/HA, RN
DIRECTOR OF NURSING SERVICES
SENTARA NURSING CENTER, VIRGINIA BEACH, VA

"The concepts help you identify priority care areas that you will learn or have learned in your first nursing courses. The concepts provide a link across courses to help you create connections rather than memorizing lists of symptoms and intervention steps for every content area. For instance, once you recognize priority assessments and interventions for the concept of oxygenation specific to airway obstruction, it is much easier to recognize what the differences are for assessment and care of epiglottitis versus asthma versus aspiration, all of which are alterations in oxygenation. The concepts allow you to see connections with client care no matter what the disease process is. The ability to prioritize the specific needs of the client is essential to nursing practice. The 'SAFETY' model provides a solid foundation to help you develop a 'nursing frame of mind'!"

KATE K. CHAPPELL, MSN, APRN, CPNP
CLINICAL ASSISTANT PROFESSOR
COLLEGE OF NURSING
UNIVERSITY OF SOUTH CAROLINA, COLUMBIA, SOUTH CAROLINA

"This book has renewed my confidence that a concept-based approach to learning for nursing programs will successfully work. I am a firm believer that nursing schools who decide to adopt this book will not only have extraordinary pass rates, but will find their students will become confident & competent in their ability to deliver priority standard based care."

KIMI C. MCMAHAN, MSN-ED, RN
CLINICAL COORDINATOR; INSTRUCTOR
SOUTHWESTERN COMMUNITY COLLEGE, SYLVA, NORTH CAROLINA

"I believe learning should not be hard and that it should be fun! I was first introduced to *Nursing Made Insanely Easy* five years ago and have used the books in medical/surgical and mental health areas. Students express to me how much they learn in a short amount of time when complex information is simplified and presented in a fun and interesting way. One of my students remarked, '*The Nursing Made Insanely Easy* books should be a class requirement because they are more useful than ANY of the textbooks I used this semester'. This is just one of many similar comments I received from my students. I highly recommend faculty use *Medical Surgical Nursing Concepts Made Insanely Easy* with your students."

PENNY MORRISON, MN, BSN, RN
UH-BASED VA NURSING ACADEMY
SCHOOL OF NURSING
UNIVERSITY OF HAWAII AT MANOA, HONOLULU, HI

CONTENTS

Foreword . . . . *xv*

Acknowledgments . . . . *xvii*

Reviewers . . . . *xviii*

Contributors . . . . *xix*

Message to Our Readers . . . . *xxi*

   Hints on How to Effectively Use This Book . . . . *xxii*

   Icons . . . . *xxiii*

Introduction 1

   Safety Model 3

SECTION ONE:
LINKING MULTIPLE SYSTEMS TO PATHOPHYSIOLOGY OF DISEASES

Chapter 1   **Prioritization** **11**

   Algorithm *13*

   Strategies *14*

   Linking Clinical Situations to Prioritization *16*

Chapter 2   **Linking Multiple Systems to Pathophysiology**
               of Fluid Imbalance **21**
               Concept: Fluid and Electrolytes: Fluid Balance

   Fluid Volume Deficit *24*

   Fluid Volume Excess *25*

   Clinical Decision-Making Exercise *27*

   Decision-Making Analysis Form *33*

Chapter 3   **Linking Multiple Systems to Pathophysiology**
               of Sodium Imbalance **35**
               Concept: Fluid and Electrolytes: Sodium Balance

   IV Fluid Types (Replacement) *38*

      Isotonic Solutions *38*

      Hypertonic Solutions *39*

      Hypotonic Solutions *40*

   Hyponatremia *43*

Hypernatremia..*45*

Clinical Decision-Making Exercise.................................*48*

Decision-Making Analysis Form...................................*54*

Chapter 4 Linking Multiple Systems to Pathophysiology of Potassium Imbalance..................................**57**
Concept: Fluid and Electrolytes: Potassium Balance

Hypokalemia..*59*

Hyperkalemia..*60*

Clinical Decision-Making Exercise.................................*63*

Decision-Making Analysis Form...................................*66*

Chapter 5 Linking Multiple Systems to Pathophysiology of Calcium Imbalance..................................**69**
Concept: Fluid and Electrolytes: Calcium Balance

Hypocalcemia...*74*

Hypercalcemia...*76*

Clinical Decision-Making Exercise.................................*79*

Decision-Making Analysis Form...................................*83*

Chapter 6 Linking Multiple Systems to Pathophysiology of Magnesium Imbalance.................................**85**
Concept: Fluid and Electrolytes: Magnesium Balance

Hypomagnesemia...*87*

Hypermagnesemia..*88*

Clinical Decision-Making Exercise.................................*89*

Decision-Making Analysis Form...................................*92*

Chapter 7 Linking Multiple Systems to Pathophysiology of Diseases..........**95**
Concept: Acid-Base Balance

Respiratory Acidosis...*97*

Respiratory Alkalosis..*98*

Metabolic Acidosis..*99*

Metabolic Alkalosis...*100*

Clinical Decision-Making Exercise................................*115*

Decision-Making Analysis Form..................................*121*

Chapter 8 Respiratory System: Linking Concepts to Pathophysiology of Diseases.................................**123**
Concept: Oxygenation

COPD (Emphysema/Chronic Bronchitis)..........................*133*

Asthma...*134*

Cystic Fibrosis...*135*

Epiglottitis/Croup..*136*

Tuberculosis..*137*

Pneumonia 138

Severe Acute Respiratory Syndrome (SARS)......................... 138

Pneumothorax... 139

Hemothorax.. 139

   Tension pneumothorax.................................... 139

Water-Sealed Chest Drainage (Chest Tubes) 140

Pulmonary Emboli..141

Acute Respiratory Distress Syndrome (ARDS)......................142

Acute Respiratory Failure (ARF) 142

   Ventilator Care...143

Anemia..144

Sickle Cell Anemia 145

Clinical Decision-Making Exercise 147

Decision-Making Analysis Form................................*152*

**Chapter 9   Cardiovascular System: Linking Concepts to
                  Pathophysiology of Diseases** **155**
   Concept: Perfusion Cardiac/Peripheral

Risk Factors...*157*

Cardiac Sounds 159

Hypertension..167

   Hypertensive Crisis 168

Atherosclerosis 169

Peripheral Vascular Disease 169

   Arterial and Venous Ulcers................................*171*

   Deep Vein Thrombosis (DVT)...............................*172*

Angina *173*

Acute Myocardial Infarction 174

   Cardiac Catheterization *176*

   Coronary Artery Bypass Graft (CABG) *182*

Heart Failure *183*

Pulmonary Edema..187

Congenital Heart Defects 188

Valvular Heart Disease 189

Cardiogenic Shock 190

Cardiac Monitoring...191

Cardiac Conduction System 192

   Cardiac Arrhythmias 198

   Pacemakers...202

   Cardioversion and Defibrillation 208

Rheumatic Heart Disease....................................*210*

Endocarditis. 211

Myocarditis 211

Pericarditis. 211

    Cardiac Tamponade. 211

Clinical Decision-Making Exercise. 212

Decision-Making Analysis Form. 220

Chapter 10 Linking Multiple Systems to Pathophysiology of Diseases **223**
    Concept: Perfusion/Shock

Cardiogenic Shock 223

Obstructive Shock. 227

Distributive Shock. 227

    Anaphylactic. 227

    Neurogenic. 227

    Septic. 227

Hypovolemic Shock 229

Clinical Decision-Making Exercise 237

Decision-Making Analysis Form. 243

Chapter 11 Neurological System: Linking Concepts to
               Pathophysiology of Diseases **245**
    Concept: Intracranial Regulation

Increased Intracranial Pressure 250

Cerebral Vascular Accident (CVA). 262

Head Injury 264

Spinal Cord Injury. 265

    Autonomic Dysreflexia. 270

Seizures 271

Myasthenia Gravis. 273

Guillain Barré 275

Brain Neoplasm (Tumor). 276

    Craniotomy 277

Dementia (Alzheimer's) 278

Multiple Sclerosis 280

Parkinson's Disease 282

Amyotrophic Lateral Sclerosis (ALS). 283

Meningitis 285

Clinical Decision-Making Exercise. 287

Decision-Making Analysis Form. 292

Chapter 12 Gastrointestinal/Biliary System: Linking Concepts to Pathophysiology of Diseases 295
Concept: Metabolism Gastrointestinal/Biliary

Gastroesophageal Reflux Disease (GERD) 296

Peptic Ulcer Disease (PUD) 307

Gastrointestinal Surgery Post-Op Care............................ 308

   Dumping Syndrome................................... 309

Irritable Bowel Syndrome (IBS).................................310

Hirschsprung's Disease 310

Hernias 311

Infections (Bacteria, Viruses and Parasites) 312

   Diarrhea (Clostridium d-Difficile, Escherichia coli, etc.) 313

Inflammatory Bowel Disease (IBD) 314

   Acute IBD 314

      Gastroenteritis 314

      Appendicitis 314

      Peritonitis 314

   Chronic IBD 316

      Crohn's Disease...............................316

      Ulcerative Colitis 316

      Diverticular Disease 316

Cholecystitis/Cholelithiasis 319

Pancreatitis 320

Intestinal Obstructions 321

Colon Cancer (Colostomy/Ileostomy Care).........................321

Pyloric stenosis...321

   Perforations 323

Clinical Decision-Making Exercise 327

Decision-Making Analysis Form.................................334

Chapter 13 Hepatic System: Linking Concepts to Pathophysiology of Diseases 337
Concept: Metabolism Liver

Liver Failure.. 342

Nutritional Imbalances 343

Hepatitis (A, B, C, D and E).................................. 346

Cirrhosis of the Liver....................................... 350

   Paracentesis......................................353

   Esophageal Varices 353

   Hepatic Encephalopathy 355

Clinical Decision-Making Exercise 356

Decision-Making Analysis Form................................ 363

Chapter 14 Endocrine System: Linking Concepts to Pathophysiology of Diseases **365**
Concept: Metabolism Pituitary, Thyroid, & Adrenal

Pituitary 368

    Diabetes Insipidus (DI) 368

    Syndrome of Inappropriate Antidiuretic Hormone (SIADH) 368

Thyroid 378

    Hyperthyroidism (Graves Disease).....................378

    Hypothyroidism (Myxedema) 378

        Thyroidectomy.............................381

        Thyroid Storm..............................383

        Myxedema Coma 383

Adrenal Gland.......................................384

    Cushing's Disease 384

    Addison's Disease............................. 384

Clinical Decision-Making Exercise 390

Decision-Making Analysis Form.......................397

Chapter 15 Endocrine System: Linking Concepts to Pathophysiology of Diabetes Mellitus **399**
Concept: Metabolism Glucose

Diabetes Mellitus (Type 1) Hyperglycemia.............................403

Hypoglycemia.......................................419

Diabetic Ketoacidosis (DKA) 421

Hyperosmolar Hyperglycemic Nonketotic Syndrome (HHNS).............422

Diabetes Mellitus (Type 2) 427

Gestational Diabetes Mellitus (GDM).....................428

Clinical Decision-Making Exercise.......................431

Decision-Making Analysis Form........................437

Chapter 16 Genitourinary System: Linking Concepts to Pathophysiology of Diseases **439**
Concept: Elimination

Urinary Incontinence/Retention 445

Fecal Incontinence/Constipation 447

Renal Calculi 449

Benign Prostatic Hypertrophy 451

    Continuous Bladder Irrigation (CBI) 452

Lower Urinary Tract Infections 453

    Cystitis 453

    Urethritis.....................................453

Upper Urinary Tract...*453*

    Pyelonephritis..*453*

Clinical Decision-Making Exercise *456*

Decision-Making Analysis Form..................................... *463*

**Chapter 17 Renal System: Linking Concepts to
Pathophysiology of Diseases** **465**
    Concept: Perfusion Renal

Chronic Renal Failure...*467*

    Glomerulonephritis *482*

    Nephrotic Syndrome *483*

Hemodialysis.. *485*

Peritoneal Dialysis *486*

Clinical Decision-Making Exercise *487*

Decision-Making Analysis Form.....................................*493*

**Chapter 18 Musculoskeletal System: Linking Concepts to
Pathophysiology of Diseases** **495**
    Concept: Mobility

Complications of Immobility...*503*

Fractures *505*

    Cast Care... *506*

    Complications (Fat Emboli and Compartment Syndrome)............... *506*

    Traction Care *507*

Amputation *508*

Osteoporosis *509*

Fibromyalgia *510*

Osteoarthritis *511*

    Joint Replacement Care *512*

Osteomyelitis *514*

Gout *515*

Rheumatoid Arthritis *516*

    Hot and Cold Therapy.......................................*516*

Systemic Lupus Erythematosus *517*

Assistive Devices *518*

    Cane..*518*

    Crutches...*520*

    Walker *520*

Clinical Decision-Making Exercise *522*

Decision-Making Analysis Form.....................................*529*

Chapter 19 Linking Multiple Systems to Pathophysiology of Oncology 531
        Concept: Cellular Regulation

Breast cancer 541

Lung cancer. 542

Prostate cancer 543

Lymphomas. 544

Leukemia 545

Cellular Immunity: Human Immunodeficiency Virus (HIV) 546

Clinical Decision-Making Exercise 547

Decision-Making Analysis Form. 553

Chapter 20 Integumentary System: Linking Concepts to
        Pathophysiology of Diseases **555**
        Concept: Tissue/Skin Integrity

Preventative Care 557

Types of Wounds 564

        Wound Care 566

Infections. 567

        Bacterial (Cellulitis). 567

        Fungal (Tinea) 567

        Viral (Herpes Simplex Type 1 and 2) 567

        Infestations (Lice and Scabies) 567

Ulcers (Pressure, Diabetic, Arterial and Venous) .570

        Stages of Ulcers 571

        Ulcer Care 572

Thermal/Radiation Injuries 573

        Burn Care 574

Benign and Premalignant Skin Cancer 578

Clinical Decision-Making Exercise 580

Decision-Making Analysis Form. 587

Chapter 21 Visual and Auditory Systems: Linking Concepts to
        Pathophysiology of Diseases **589**
        Concept: Sensory Perception

Vision 590

Hearing 595

Somatosensory 599

Cataracts 603

Macular Degeneration. 603

Glaucoma 603

Retinal Detachment. 603

Ménière's Disease. 606

Otitis Media (Labyrinthitis) 607

Clinical Decision-Making Exercise 608

Decision-Making Analysis Form. 611

SECTION TWO:
CONCEPTS THAT ARE INTER-RELATED THROUGHOUT THE SYSTEMS:
LINKING MULTIPLE SYSTEMS AND CONCEPTS TO PATHOPHYSIOLOGY OF DISEASES

Chapter 22 Linking Multiple Systems and Concepts:
Safety/Prevention of Injury **615**
Concept: Safety/Prevention of Injury

Components of a Safe Patient Care Environment 616

Safety QSEN Competences for the Nurse 617

Comparison of Patient Safety Standards. 618

Reportable Safety Conditions 621

Resources: References and Websites. 622

Clinical Decision-Making Exercise 623

Decision-Making Analysis Form. 627

Chapter 23 Linking Multiple Systems and Concepts: Infection Control **629**
Concept: Infection Control

Standard Precautions 631

Airborne Precautions 632

Contact Precautions. 632

Droplet Precautions 632

Protective Precautions 635

Clinical Decision-Making Exercise 638

Decision-Making Analysis Form. 642

Chapter 24 Linking Multiple Systems and Concepts: Nutrition..................**645**
Concept: Nutrition Balance

Macronutrients (Protein, Carbohydrates, Fat)........................ 648

Minerals (Sodium, Potassium, Calcium)...............................651

Water Soluble Vitamins (B_6, B_9, B_{12}, C) 654

Fat Soluble Vitamins (A, D, E, K) 657

Therapeutic Diets (Iron, Residue, Purines, Lactose-Free, Gluten-Free)......... 660

System/Diseases Nutritional Diet Needs. 664

Protein Calorie Malnutrition 664

Other Therapeutic Diets (Anorexia Nervosa, Bulimia Nervosa) 665

Clinical Decision-Making Exercise 667

Decision-Making Analysis Form. 670

Chapter 25   Linking Multiple Systems and Concepts: Pain **673**
           Concept: Pain

Pain Assessment, Scales, Interventions *674*

Pharmacological Pain Management. *677*

Nonpharmacological Pain Management *683*

Clinical Decision-Making Exercise 685

Decision-Making Analysis Form. 689

Chapter 26   Linking Multiple Systems and Concepts: Thermoregulation **691**
           Concept: Thermoregulation

Hypothermia 694

Hyperthermia. 696

Clinical Decision-Making Exercise *701*

Decision-Making Analysis Form. *705*

SECTION THREE:
GUIDES TO LINKING MULTIPLE SYSTEMS AND CONCEPTS

Chapter 27   Guides to Linking Multiple Systems and Concepts:
           Health Promotion **709**
           Concept: Health Promotion

Health Promotion *710*

  Primary Prevention. *710*

  Secondary Prevention *710*

  Tertiary Prevention *710*

  Client Teaching *711*

Documentation and Evaluation of Client Teaching *713*

Planning for Discharge *715*

Chapter 28   Guides to Linking Multiple Systems and Concepts: Coping **717**
           Concept: Coping

Coping Behaviors. *718*

  Adaptive *718*

  Maladaptive *718*

Risk Factors for Poor Coping. *719*

Resources to Help with Coping. *721*

        Index **723**

FOREWORD

This book, *Medical Surgical Nursing Concepts Made Insanely Easy: A New Approach to Prioritizing Nursing,* is an innovative approach for teaching and learning what has historically been difficult information for nursing students to learn. Equally it has been a challenge for nursing faculty to determine what was important to teach from this vast information.

The authors have based their **"SAFETY"** Model on what researchers have discovered in the last 15 years about the way the brain learns, organizes and stores information for long-term retention. Thanks to MRIs, we now know that the brain is constantly changing in a process called recontouring. The brain makes very few if any new neurons, but the alignment of the neurons with each other is constantly changing when the brain is recontouring. Neurons align in networks of connections that allow the storage, recall, revision, and application of new knowledge. These neuro-networks are refined and expanded with experience and practice. Novice learners, like nursing students, have simple neuro-networks. The great news is the more students learn, the more complex their networks become. As the complexity of their network increases, novice students become successful graduate nurses and eventually expert nurses.

The authors' goal is to facilitate students' learning and to continue to develop their neuro-networks. Research indicates the brain does not learn information in isolation. The brain learns by clustering information and assigning a name to it. In cognitive learning theory, this is called chunking. These chunks of information begin the process of building a structure for storage. The most common structure used in health care is body systems. The authors of this book have chunked information by systems based on pathophysiology, and then linked it to the concepts as well as to priority of care.

Teaching by concepts is not new, but the way the authors connect concepts certainly is. Using recent research on how the brain learns, the concepts are linked to each other in a variety of ways, which creates the development of more neuro-networks. Using body systems as the structure, the authors make links between concepts based on the pathophysiology of the disease process and the priority nursing care. The genius of their work is that student learning is greatly enhanced through the use of charts, mnemonics, and links to previously learned information. This process of making connections allows information to be organized in the brain and stored for future application. This approach to learning develops clinical reasoning skills and supports nursing students as they engage in safe and efficient clinical decision-making.

This book is a very useful and valuable resource for both faculty and students. Faculty can use the book as a resource and guide to design learning activities for students both in the classroom and in clinical. Students can use the book, with its creative and easy approach, as a resource to help learn the information and more importantly connect knowledge to real-world nursing applications. The book makes use of a variety of strategies to engage students and provide meaningful learning. The questions at the end of each chapter allow students to practice clinical decision-making skills based on what they have learned. The rationales for the questions and the link to the NCLEX® activities provide another crucial link to transfer the information to long-term memory.

JoAnne Herman, Professor Emeritus RN, PhD

ACKNOWLEDGMENTS

We truly appreciate the ongoing support of our families as we wrote, rewrote, and kept adding to the book!

To Randy Manning, Loretta's husband, thank you for your love, support, and sense of humor that keeps life in perspective as we continue to juggle family, business, travel, and writing. Thank you for bringing me special snacks and food during those long hours at the computer!

I truly appreciate the love and flexibility of my daughter, Erica Manning who remained flexible and willing to jump in and provide support at home.

A special thank you to my wonderful mother, Juanita Shera, who always had the right words to say during the middle of chaotic moments.

To Larry Zager, Lydia's husband, thank you for your endless love and for being our constant supporter and motivator. You kept us going while we spent hours and hours at the computer. Thank you for all of those yummy meals you made to help keep us on track. We can now answer your question: "Yes, the book is DONE!" You have supported us emotionally and your objective, analytical reviews and edits of the book were invaluable to us.

Adam (my son) and Lauren (his fiancé), we are happy to report the book is done before you get married! Thank you for your love and all of your words of encouragement and interest in our project.

To my dad, David Huffman, you have always been my inspiration for the kind of educator I wanted to be. I have been in admiration of your style of teaching and the example you set in the classroom, even when you thought I was not listening! Thank you, Dad. This book is for you with all my love.

. . . .

A special thank you to Teresa Davidson, our dear friend, artist, computer guru, and the genius who takes our words and ideas and interprets them into meaningful images. Teresa has been there from the first edition of *Nursing Made Insanely Easy*. No matter how close our deadline for print is approaching, she is always supportive, calm even when we continue to make changes minutes before going to print.

To Mary Jo Zazueta, our book designer and wise friend. You have our sincerest appreciation and gratitude. We are always amazed at how you take our sloppy drafts and transform them into a professional book with style! You have worked night and day on this journey with us to make this project become a reality. We absolutely could not have done it without you, thank you!

Jennifer Robinson, Administrative Director of I CAN Publishing, Inc. who is our friend and lifeline in our project development and distribution center. Even during chaos, she keeps us laughing and organized. Thank you for taking care of the business for these past few months when all we could do was travel and write.

A very special thank you to all of our contributors and reviewers who were very supportive in providing feedback, sharing their expertise and enthusiasm which kept us going these last few weeks.

A special recognition and thank you to the clinical nursing faculty and the curriculum task force at the University of South Carolina, in Columbia, for all of your critiques and contributions to the concepts as we moved forward with the book.

Now, a very important thank you to all of you nursing students and faculty who have been requesting this book for several years! Without each of you reading and using this book while you are in school, there would be no need for the book.

Loretta and Lydia

REVIEWERS

Karen E. Alexander, PhD, RN, CNOR
Program Director, RN to BSN Program
Assistant Professor Nursing
University of Houston–Clear Lake
Houston, Texas

Caroline B. Baird, MSN, RN
Assistant Professor, Nursing Department
Rockingham Community College
Wentworth, North Carolina

Carol Anne Baker, BSN, MBA/HA, RN
Director of Nursing Services
Sentara Nursing Center
Virginia Beach, Virginia

Susan Beverung, MSN, RN
Clinical Assistant Professor
College of Nursing
University of South Carolina
Columbia, South Carolina

Angel Boling, MSN, RN
Assistant Professor
Baptist College of Health Sciences
Memphis, Tennessee

Michelle Staton Briley, BSN, RN
Education Consultant
Greenville, North Carolina

Judy J. Duvall, EdD, RN
Alumnus CCRN
Assistant Professor
Whitson-Hester School of Nursing
Tennessee Technological University
Cookeville, Tennessee

Melissa Geist, EdD, APRN-BC, CNE
Associate Professor of Nursing
Whitson-Hester School of Nursing
Tennessee Technological University

Interim Dean, College of Interdisciplinary Studies
Associate Professor of Nursing
Tennessee Technological University
Cookeville, Tennessee

Cieanna Hairston, MSN, MHA, RN
Director of Clinical Practice and Education
Morehead Memorial Hospital
Eden, North Carolina

Kim Kennel, MSN, CCRN, RN-BC CNE
Assistant Professor
Baptist College of Health Sciences
Memphis, Tennessee

Kimi C. McMahan, MSN-Ed, RN
Clinical Coordinator; Instructor
Southwestern Community College
Sylva, North Carolina

Stephanie Evans-Mitchell, EdD, MSN, RN
Associate Professor
Delaware State University
Dover, Delaware

Penny Morrison, MN, BSN, RN
UH-Based VA Nursing Academy
University of Hawaii at Manoa School of Nursing
Honolulu, Hawaii

Lisa O'Steen, MSN, CNE, RN
Nursing Faculty
Columbus State University
Columbus, Georgia

Karen Worthy, MSN, MPH, RN
BSN Success Coordinator/Clinical Instructor
University of South Carolina College of Nursing
Columbia, South Carolina

Larry Zager, MSN, BSN
Leadership and Education Consultant
Ridgeway, South Carolina

CONTRIBUTORS

Carol Anne Baker, BSN, MBA/HA, RN
Director of Nursing Services
Sentara Nursing Center
Virginia Beach, VA

Katherine K. Chappell, MSN, APRN, CPNP
Clinical Assistant Professor
College of Nursing
University of South Carolina
Columbia, South Carolina

Darlene Franklin, MSN, RN
Assistant Professor of Nursing Emeritus
Whitson-Hester School of Nursing
Tennessee Technological University
Cookeville, Tennessee

Melissa Geist, EdD, APRN-BC, CNE
Associate Professor of Nursing
Whitson-Hester School of Nursing
Tennessee Technological University

Interim Dean, College of Interdisciplinary Studies
Associate Professor of Nursing
Tennessee Technological University
Cookeville, Tennessee

Kimberly A. Glenn, MN, RN, CPN
Assistant Dean and Clinical Associate Professor
College of Nursing
University of South Carolina
Columbia, South Carolina

JoAnne Herman, PhD, RN, CSME
Associate Professor
Faculty Emeritus
College of Nursing
Columbia, South Carolina

Selina Hunt McKinney, PhD, APRN, PMHNP-BC
Clinical Assistant Professor
College of Nursing
University of South Carolina
Columbia, South Carolina

Kimi C. McMahan, RN, MSN-Ed
2nd Nursing Instructor and Clinical Coordinator
Southwestern Community College
Sylva, North Carolina

Penny Morrison, MN, BSN, RN
UH-Based VA Nursing Academy
School of Nursing
University of Hawaii at Manoa
Honolulu, HI

Heather Ruff, MSN, RN-C
Clinical Assistant Professor
College of Nursing
University of South Carolina
Columbia, South Carolina

Sabra H. Smith, DNP, MS, FNP-BC
Clinical Assistant Professor
College of Nursing
University of South Carolina
Columbia, South Carolina

Deborah Bagnasco Stanford, MSN, RN
Clinical Assistant Professor
University of North Carolina in Greensboro
Greensboro, North Carolina

Karen Worthy, MSN, MPH, RN
BSN Success Coordinator/Clinical Instructor
College of Nursing
University of South Carolina
Columbia, South Carolina

MESSAGE TO OUR READERS

It is hard to believe that after this journey, we have finished the last chapter! This journey began after several key events: writing the books *Nursing Made Insanely Easy* and *Pharmacology Made Insanely Easy* and the feedback from students while in school. The response overwhelmingly was a consistent call from both students and faculty to develop a book on *Medical Surgical Nursing Concepts Made Insanely Easy*!

As the healthcare industry becomes more complex, it has become of paramount importance for nursing students to have a resource for simplifying the large volumes of information that they need to learn. After working with thousands of students both during school and after graduation, we were inspired to write this book by consistent statements such as, *"Where were you when I was in nursing school? I am finally getting it! I never really knew how to link concepts to actual nursing care or understood how to prioritize nursing care. I can actually remember the information I read."* Medical Surgical Nursing Concepts Made Insanely Easy* is the answer to these requests.

Our task was to combine the world of medical diagnoses, the human body's systems and the pathophysiology that occurs with complications to the system with the national accrediting organizations' standards and to connect these with nursing concepts based on practice standards. If that was not enough, the book needed to help nursing students to survive nursing school and be successful on the NCLEX®. After all, we are about students' success! There you have it—the framework for *Medical Surgical Nursing Concepts Made Insanely Easy*!

We have organized the material using the "SAFETY" Model. While this model was originally developed for nursing students providing a structure for NCLEX® standards, it has been revised to provide a platform for organizing nursing concepts within the framework of standards. We will use the "SAFETY" Model to link concepts to systems, to pathophysiology and to the NCLEX® standards. This will help you learn how to prioritize and how to "think like a nurse"!

We know from experience, that successful learning requires you to take one step at a time, so we have not attempted to provide all the resources you will need. We will recommend that you use the book *Pharmacology Made Insanely Easy*, by Manning and Rayfield. There will be lists of medications included with the concepts; however, the innovative strategies used in *Pharmacology Made Insanely Easy* will help you remember the pharmacology agents. The diagnostic tests and procedures are also reviewed with creative strategies to assist you in prioritizing necessary-to-know information in the book *Nursing Made Insanely Easy*.

We both have a passion for helping nursing students achieve successful outcomes. We hope that as you read any section in this book, you will experience an "AHA" moment! Now open, the book and begin your journey. You are on the road to becoming a genius in nursing concepts! We had a great time writing this book, and our hope is that you will have a great time reading it!

Loretta Manning and Lydia Zager

HINTS ON HOW TO EFFECTIVELY USE THIS BOOK

This book, as you will discover, is a different type of reference. It was designed to help you become a safe practicing nurse by:

- Thinking and making decisions like a nurse.
- Understanding the why behind the priority of care by linking system specific pathophysiology to the concepts and medical diseases.

We have developed several tools to assist you. The first tool is the mnemonics developed from large volumes of detailed information to help you prioritize nursing care and be skillful at high-level decision-making. Here is a guide for the mnemonics.

The mnemonics:

- Reflect priority information in chunks that reflect the standards (i.e., NCLEX®, client safety, standards of practice, etc.). This is important to know even if you do not learn with mnemonics; the content is the priority chunk of information you need to know!
- Chunk information that is essential to help you learn and store the information into your long-term memory, so you can find it when you are taking care of clients and when you are taking tests!
- Provide a structure for the information and is not necessarily in chronological order, but will change based on the clinical situation.
- Focus the content in this book on "What is necessary to know" versus "What is nice to know"!
- Take large volumes of complex information and simplify it to help you master the most important information. Learning occurs best when you build from simplex to complex!

Here is an example of how we have organized many of the mnemonics to reflect the concept for the disease. In the chapter on *Oxygenation*, we use the mnemonic "DYSPNEA" to represent assessments of hypoxia and "BREATHE" for the priority nursing care for clients with hypoxia. Learning these two mnemonics, you will be able to prioritize the assessments and interventions with any disease that results in hypoxia, such as pneumonia, bronchitis, anemia, etc. We have carefully designed these to assist you with chunking of priority nursing facts. The brain loves organization!

Under the category of *Evaluation of Expected Outcomes* in the "SAFETY" summary of the concepts, you will see "WDL," which stands for "Within Defined Limits."

Exceptions and Additions by Disease is a section in many of the chapters where medical diagnoses are reviewed that require additional assessments and plans of care for the concept. All you have to do is to learn the differences or additions to the plan of care! You will also see that many of the systems involve multiple concepts. Remember it is easier to learn twenty-eight concepts than hundreds of diseases!

The *"PRIORITIZATION ALGORITHM"* on p. 13, is a tool that will be very valuable to you. As you work through the clinical decision making exercises, this tool will assist you in how to prioritize nursing care successfully. The "SAFETY" model described in the introduction is all about prioritization of care. The "Prioritization Algorithm" you will find helpful while you study and when you are preparing for clinical or simulation!

The icons on the adjacent page (i.e. memory tool icon, concept link, etc.) will also assist, direct, and help you reinforce priority information as you study from this reference. Many of the concepts will be linked and connected to other concepts. Remember, this is a journey; you will need to repeat the information over and over again to begin to feel confident and move the information to your long term memory. We want your confidence to grow as you review and learn each of the concepts!

We know YOU can be a Medical Surgical Nursing Concept "GENIUS"! The most important icon is the "GENIUS" within YOU!

ICONS

 This shield links SAFE PRIORITIES OF CARE to NCLEX® and PROFESSIONAL STANDARDS.

 This icon is used to link NCLEX® STANDARDS.

 This icon is used to link PRIORITIES of care.

 This icon is used to represent SAFETY.

 This icon is used to link PATHOPHYSIOLOGY.

 This icon is used to link CONCEPTS.

 This icon is used as a link to GERIATRICS.

 This icon is used as a link to a MEMORY TOOL.

 This icon is used to remind you of the "GENIUS WITHIN YOURSELF"!

INTRODUCTION

Answering the Call for Education Transformation

There has been a call from the Institute of Medicine Report on *The Future of Nursing: Leading Change, Advancing Health* (2010) to transform nursing education. Benner, Sutphen, Leonard, & Day's book, *Educating Nurses: A Call for Radical Transformation* (2010), also recommends similar changes in nursing education. The authors state that "To practice safely and effectively, today's new nurses must understand a range of nursing knowledge and science, from normal pathological physiology ... pharmacology ... patient-therapies, the physics of gas exchange in the lungs, cell-level transport of oxygen for the acutely ill patient, as well as the human experience of illness and normal growth and development and much more" (p. 1).

Because of the explosion of knowledge, nursing faculty have been forced to teach more and more information in the same amount of time. Nursing education has been like a sailboat navigating in a large ocean of information; however, it has been a challenge to redirect the compass to an attainable and manageable body of water. In other words, we need to focus on the information that is "necessary" versus "nice to know." What nursing faculty do know, it is impossible to teach everything and students know they can't learn everything! Most of the available resources continue to add volumes of information that is knowledge based where practice requires the transformation of knowledge to a higher level of application and clinical judgment. The purpose of this book, *Medical Surgical Nursing Concepts Made Insanely Easy*, is to prioritize the vast volumes of information through a systematic, standard-based approach, (National Council Licensure Examination, (NCLEX®), Institute of Healthcare Improvement (IHI), Patient Safety Standards, Quality Safety Education for Nurses (QSEN), National League for Nursing (NLN) Competencies for Nursing Education, American Colleges of Nursing (AACN) Baccalaureate Science of Nursing Essentials, Joint Commission and the Center for Disease Control (CDC)), that is organized around systems, pathophysiology and concepts.

The expectation for the new graduate nurse to think and perform with high-level clinical decision-making and judgment skills has contributed to the complexity of nursing education. The level of competency expected of the new graduate has continued to increase based on the demands of the healthcare industry. This is further compounded by the fact that nursing graduates must perform successfully on the NCLEX®, which has continuously increased in difficulty. Learning how to make high-level judgments about the priority of care must begin in nursing school!

Benner, Sutphen, Leonard, & Day (2010), point out that nursing education requires the following transformations:

- Move from decontextualize knowledge to contextual knowledge.
- Move from complex to simple.
- Move from a long list of competencies to integrated clinical performance based on patient safety standards.
- Move from separation of class and clinical to integrated classroom with clinical.
- Move from critical thinking to clinical reasoning and judgment (p. 89).

This book connects current concepts with systems and standards. Connections are essential for transferring information from short-term to long-term memory in order to apply and prioritize information. This is based on neuroscience that confirms pathways in the brain are essential for connecting newly learned information in order to transform knowledge to application. This must occur before the student can learn and be competent in higher-level decision-making resulting in the ability to prioritize.

Just as neuroscience confirms, nursing education must also make links and connections. Conceptual teaching and learning requires connections to operationalize the information. This book was developed based on neuroscience and cognitive learning theory incorporating traditional systems, the medical model, and pathophysiology with a conceptual approach. The "**SAFETY**" Model has been designed to integrate concepts with medical diagnoses and systems that provide a platform for classroom, clinical, simulation, and testing. The Model represents an integrated approach and will be used as the framework to assist students in becoming competent with prioritization and clinical judgment.

"SAFETY" Model

The following is the description of the format for the **"SAFETY"** Model that has been incorporated throughout the book.

The "SAFETY" Model for Classroom, Clinical and Testing

S System-specific pathophysiology, assessments, labs and diagnostic procedures.

A Analysis of concepts.

F First-Do Priority Nursing Interventions.
First-Do Medications.

E Evaluation of Expected Outcomes.

T Trend For Potential Complications.

Y You Must Manage Care to Prevent **"RISK"** to the Client.

The following explanation will provide examples of how to adapt the **"SAFETY"** Model:

System-Specific Pathophysiology will be addressed in each of the chapters. The diseases are organized around the pathophysiology for the system. The key to linking concepts to other diseases is to understand the physiological changes that are occurring with the client; you must know the "why"!

The NCLEX® activities included are:

- Identify pathophysiology related to an acute or chronic condition (i.e., signs and symptoms).
- Assess and respond to changes in vital signs.

System-Specific Assessments are discussed with a focus on pathophysiology. The journey in nursing school is a process of being able to not only know the assessments but be able to recognize early versus late clinical findings. The good news is you will quickly recognize that, for example, 15 diseases involving the respiratory system will result in the same system specific assessment findings for the concept of oxygenation.

With the **S** in "**SAFETY**" for System-Specific assessments, eight more NCLEX® activities are addressed:

- Perform focused assessment and re-assessment.
- Assess and respond to changes in vital signs.
- Recognize signs and symptoms of complications and intervene appropriately when providing care.
- Recognize trends and changes in client condition and intervene.
- Perform diagnostic testing.
- Evaluate the results of diagnostic testing and intervene as needed.
- Diagnostic testing assessment/intervention.
- Lab values.

The **A** in "**SAFETY**" stands for **Analyzing Priority Concepts**. Once the assessments have been completed as reviewed above, proceed on to analyze the priority care required for this client based on the analysis of the concept(s). Throughout the book, the concepts addressed will be the priority for that particular system and pathophysiology. The NCLEX® activity addressed for this process is:

- Assess/triage clients to prioritize order of care delivery.

The **F** in "**SAFETY**" represents **First-Do Priority Interventions**. The interventions listed in each of the chapters will represent the priority interventions for that specific concept. However, the interventions are not in order of priority because they are based on the clinical situations. The interventions also include medications (refer to the book *Pharmacology Made Insanely Easy*). NCLEX® activities represented include:

- Prioritize workload to manage time effectively.
- Prioritize delivery of client care.
- Recognize signs and symptoms of complications and intervene appropriately when providing care.
- Assess client and respond to changes in vital signs.

The **E** in "**SAFETY**" represents **Evaluation of Expected Outcomes** from nursing care as well as from the administration of medications. In this book, the evaluation of outcomes will represent the return of clinical assessments within the defined limits (WDL). The NCLEX® activities addressed include:

- Evaluate/document response to treatment.
- Evaluate therapeutic effect of medications.
- Evaluate the effectiveness of treatment regime for a client with acute or chronic diagnosis.

The **T** in "**SAFETY**" is **TREND for Potential Complications**. Throughout the chapters, potential complications are addressed. A very important component of clinical judgment is to be competent in comparing, contrasting and trending ongoing system assessments, lab results, and/or changes in the client's condition that require intervention. This is a skill that has to be developed over time. It begins with knowing the normal clinical findings specific to the concept and progressing to the ability to differentiate between early and late clinical findings. This part of the "**SAFETY**" Model was developed to address patient safety standards. The NCLEX® activities reviewed include:

- Recognize trends and changes in client condition and intervene.
- Recognize signs and symptoms of complications and intervene appropriately when providing care.
- Assess and respond to changes in vital signs.

The **Y** in "**SAFETY**" stands for **You Must Manage Care to Prevent "RISK" to the Client**. This represents the NCLEX® client needs of "Management of Care," representing approximately 25% of the NCLEX® exam and is an essential aspect of care for each concept addressed. The mnemonic "**RISK**" is a valuable tool to organize and reflect the priority-management standards. These standards will be reviewed in the NCLEX®-style questions evaluating Clinical Decision Making.

R Room Assignments, Recognize limitations of staff, Restraint safety, Risk for falls, Receive or give report.

I Identify trends, Infection control, Identification of client, Identify accuracy of orders, Informed consent, Interdisciplinary Team Collaboration.

S Skin breakdown, Safe equipment, Scope of Practice for delegation.

K Know Standards of Practice, Know how to document, Know how to prepare for transfer, discharge, Know how to teach and incorporate health-promotion activities.

Two charts are included on the next pages that illustrate different ways to use the "SAFETY" Model. The charts can be used as information organizers, a study guide for exams or as a clinical tool.

Studying with the "SAFETY" Model

S	A	F	E	T	Y
System-Specific Physiology Assessments Labs/Procedures	Analysis of Concepts	First-Do Priority Interventions	Evaluation of Expected Outcomes	Trend Potential Complications	You Must Manage Care to Prevent "RISK" to Clients
Identify the pathophysiology related to the client's condition. Based on the focused assessment, what vital sign changes require a response? What are the signs and symptoms that require intervention and indicate potential complications? What lab values and diagnostic tests require follow-up or intervention?	What are the priority concepts based on the assessment of the client?	What are the priority interventions based on the system-specific assessments for the concepts identified? Which clients should be seen first or what interventions should be done first based on the assessment findings? What medications are ordered for administration and is there a priority based on the client's presenting clinical findings (i.e., serum glucose results, complaint of pain, etc.)?	Was the desired outcome for the client met (i.e., did the bleeding stop, did the breath sounds improve, did vital signs return to within the desired limits for the client, etc.)? Was the therapeutic effect of the administered medications achieved? Are there additional interventions required to meet the expected outcomes?	What are the trends and changes in the client's condition that require intervention? What are the priority interventions needed to prevent complications or prevent further complications? What system-specific assessments require ongoing contrasting, comparing, and trending?	Are the orders accurate and appropriate for this client? What "RISK" does the client have? (Refer to "RISK" in this chapter)

Questions based on the National Council of State Boards of Nursing, Inc. NCLEX-RN® Test Plan Activities, 2012.

Organizational framework for "SAFETY" Model copyrighted by I CAN Publishing®, Inc., 2007.
Questions adapted from Herman, Manning, Zager, 2011, pp. 82–85.

"SAFETY" Tool: Note Taker, Study Guide for Exams, and/or Clinical Tool

Medical Diagnoses_____ System(s) _____				
System-Specific Physiology				
System-Specific Assessments, Labs, Diagnostic Procedures				
Analyze Concept(s)				
First-Do Priority Interventions; Medications				
Evaluation of Expected Outcomes				
Trend Potential Complications				
You Must Manage Care to Prevent "RISKS" to Clients				
Health Promotion and Discharge Planning				

References for Introduction

Benner, P., Sutphen, M., Leonard, V., and Day, L. (2010). *Educating nurses: a call for radical transformation.* San Francisco, CA: Jossey-Bass, A Wiley Imprint.

Herman, J., Manning, L. S., and Zager, L. R. (2011). *The eight-step approach to teaching clinical nursing: Tools for nurse educators.* Duluth, GA: I CAN Publishing, Inc.

Institute of Medicine (2010). *The future of nursing: leading change, advancing health.* Retrieved from http://www.iom.edu/Reports/2010/the-future-of-nursing-leading-change-advancing-health.aspx

Manning, L. and Rayfield, S. (2014). *Nursing made insanely easy* (7th ed.). Duluth, GA: I CAN Publishing, Inc.

National Council of State Boards of Nursing, INC. (NCSBN) 2012. *Research brief: 2011 RN practice analysis: linking the NCLEX RN® examination to practice.* Retrieved from https://www.ncsbn.org/index.htm

Pesut, D. and Herman J. (1999). *Clinical reasoning: The art and science of critical and creative thinking.* Albany, NY: Delmar Publishers.

Zager, L. R., Herman, J., and Manning, L. S. (2011). *The eight-step approach for student clinical success: Tools for students.* Duluth, GA: I CAN Publishing, Inc.

SECTION ONE

Linking Multiple Systems to Pathophysiology of Diseases

CHAPTER 1

Prioritization

A New Approach to Prioritizing Nursing Care

Due to the aging population, the complexity of patient care, the Health Care Reform, the ongoing revisions with standards of care, NCLEX® revisions, and reimbursement criteria, it is of paramount importance for the nurse to be competent in prioritizing nursing care. The nurse must be skillful and proactive in assessing and intervening with clients prior to the development of complications. Prioritizing is an important aspect of all the components in health care including (i.e., acute and/or chronic medical conditions, medication administration, nursing interventions, health promotion activities, as well as an interdisciplinary collaboration in discharging clients from the hospital in preparation for home care).

In the past, the role of the nurse has been to identify and recognize basic symptoms of hypoxia, hemorrhaging, fluid and electrolyte imbalance, etc. Today, however, it is imperative for the nurse to recognize early signs of potential complications by comparing, contrasting, and trending clinical assessment findings. The nurse must be able to prioritize the plan of care based on the analysis of clinical findings and determine which intervention(s) should be implemented. This competency requires a new approach to thinking and processing clinical data. According to Benner, Sutphen, Leonard, & Day (2010), "Today's nurses are expected to know more about interpretation of laboratory findings than simply the normal and abnormal ranges. To use current intravenous drugs, which must be carefully monitored and titrated, nurses need sophisticated knowledge of pharmacokinetics, hemodynamics, and cardiac function" (p. 27) The chart on page 12 reviews and compares basic clinical assessments previously required to the current expectations of nursing students and/or graduates.

This new approach, as outlined in the chart on the following page, requires the nurse to expand the basic assessments to include the critical elements (i.e., client history, medications, equipment, etc.) that may impact these findings. The outcome of these expanded assessments will facilitate the nurse and the health care team to prioritize the plan of care. The GREAT NEWS is that any disease that results in the altered concept of oxygenation (as in the example) can be applied to numerous diseases! The linking of concepts will build your confidence in prioritizing care.

The **new approach to prioritization** has capitalized on the recommendations of Benner, Sutphen, Leonard, & Day, 2010 to develop teaching strategies based on "situated cognition and thinking in action." Benner et. all suggest "a central goal of nursing education is for the learner to develop an attuned, response-based practice and capacity to quickly recognize the nature of whole-situations in terms of most pressing and least pressing concerns" (p. 43). The bottom line is the students must know how to prioritize the plan of care!

Prioritization is to select the client who is most likely to experience ill effects if not taken care of first. The question that nursing students, graduates, and nurses are faced with is *"How can I prioritize care when it seems that all of the clients are a priority?"* In other words, *who is going to croak if they are not seen first?*

BASIC CLINICAL ASSESSMENTS	TREND FOR POTENTIAL COMPLICATIONS
Medical Diagnosis: Disease **Chronic Obstructive Pulmonary Disease**	**System-Specific Pathophysiology** Obstructive airflow that impedes RR Concept: Oxygenation (altered)
1. Respiratory Rate?	1. Respiratory Rate: • Compare, contrast, and trend from previous assessment. (i.e., shallow, nasal flaring present, etc.) • Has client just received a narcotic that may affect the breathing?
2. Breath sounds? Equality?	2. Breath sounds? Equality? • Compare, contrast, and trend from previous assessment (i.e., adventitious sounds, etc.), use of accessory muscles.
3. O$_2$ saturation?	3. O$_2$ saturation: • Is the finger cold? • Is the probe in appropriate place? • Is it connected to monitor? • Does the client have appropriate oxygen on? • Does the client have peripheral vascular insufficiency such as Raynaud's Disease?
4. Hypoxia?	4. Is the client presenting with **early** versus **late** signs of hypoxia? • Early: restless, increase in the HR and RR. • Late: confusion, decrease in the HR and RR.
5. Arterial blood gas values?	5. Arterial blood gas values: • Trending from previous values. • Is the client current experiencing changes (i.e., RR, breath sounds, shallow respirations, etc.)?
6. Which client should be assessed first? (*Answer with basic clinical assessments.*) Any client presenting with an airway issue.	6. Which client should be assessed first? a. A client with COPD who has RR 18/min and in one hour increased to 24/min. b. A client with COPD with RR 22/min. c. A client with asthma who had an acute exacerbation with audible wheezing 30 minutes ago. Answer: In the past, it worked to say the ABCs would get you to the correct answer; however, now it is more complex. You must make a clinical decision based on the client who needs immediate action, which would make the correct answer c. C is the answer due to client requiring immediate intervention. Options a and b are chronic with no immediate distress and option c is an acute problem that mandates immediate assessment and/or intervention. They all have airway complications!
7. Which of these clinical assessment findings indicate a desired outcome from the nursing care for a client with COPD? (*Answer with basic clinical assessments.*) Respiratory rate within defined limits for client.	7. Which of these clinical assessment findings indicate a desired outcome from the nursing care for a client with COPD? a. Client presents with clear breath sounds. b. Client presents with an O$_2$ sat of 94%, which increased from 86% three hours ago. c. Client with COPD participates in physical activity with no shortness of breath. Options a and c are unrealistic for this client. Option b is the answer. Option b is realistic and is a desired outcome for this client with COPD. In order to answer the question, it is imperative to recognize normal findings for a client with COPD. It is not as easy as using the ABCs! It is imperative to compare and review trends in order to make a clinical decision!

"SAFETY": A NEW SYSTEMATIC APPROACH to PRIORITIZE NURSING CARE BASED ON STANDARDS

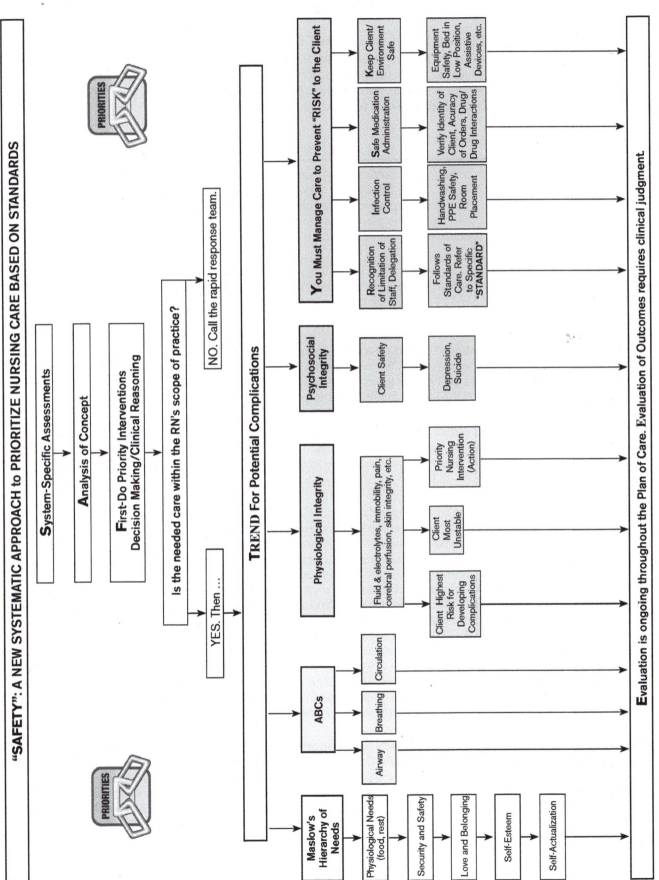

System-Specific Assessments

Analysis of Concept

First-Do Priority Interventions
Decision Making/Clinical Reasoning

Is the needed care within the RN's scope of practice?

NO. Call the rapid response team.

YES. Then …

TREND For Potential Complications

Maslow's Hierarchy of Needs
Physiological Needs (food, rest) → Security and Safety → Love and Belonging → Self-Esteem → Self-Actualization

ABCs
Airway
Breathing
Circulation

Physiological Integrity
Fluid & electrolytes, immobility, pain, cerebral perfusion, skin integrity, etc.
Client Highest Risk for Developing Complications
Client Most Unstable
Priority Nursing Intervention (Action)

Psychosocial Integrity
Client Safety
Depression, Suicide

You Must Manage Care to Prevent "RISK" to the Client
Recognition of Limitation of Staff, Delegation — Follows Standards of Care. Refer to Specific "**STANDARD**"
Infection Control — Handwashing, PPE Safety, Room Placement
Safe Medication Administration — Verify Identity of Client, Accuracy of Orders, Drug/Drug Interactions
Keep Client/Environment Safe — Equipment Safety, Bed in Low Position, Assistive Devices, etc.

Evaluation is ongoing throughout the Plan of Care. Evaluation of Outcomes requires clinical judgment.

PRIORITIES

Process of Prioritization

Below, the mnemonic "**PRIORITY**" will be reviewed to assist you in organizing a systematic approach to nursing care based on standards. As you use the chart, you will recognize the link between prioritization and the "**SAFETY**" Model because both of these structures represent the standards. The priority chart incorporates additional information such as notifying the Rapid Response Team and questions that must be asked to assist in making safe clinical decisions and judgments.

Prioritize: The first step for prioritizing is to begin with system specific assessments. (*Does this sound familiar? This also represents the "S" in the "SAFETY" Model.*) This applies to both clinical practice and in answering test questions. Remember, if the system specific assessments have been made with the client in clinical or is in the stem of the question, then the priority is to proceed forward and analyze the priority nursing concept. If, however, there were no assessments, then indeed the priority would be to assess the client and/or clinical situation.

Review the Analysis of Concept(s): Once the assessments have been completed as reviewed above, proceed on to analyze (*"A" in the "SAFETY" Model.*) the priority care required for this client based on the analysis of the concept(s).

Identify "The Priority Interventions" based on the key concepts: The priority concept(s) will help you decide what the priority actions are to implement. For example if a client is in respiratory distress, the priority nursing intervention may be to elevate the head of the bed. Another example may be if the client is hemorrhaging from a cardiac catheterization, then the priority nursing intervention would be to apply pressure over the site. (*This is the "F" in the "SAFETY" Model.*)

The other question the nurse will need to ask, *"Is the required nursing care within the scope of practice?"* If any of these interventions require care outside the scope of practice such as the need for entubation, chest tube placement, etc., then the priority of care would be to notify the health care provider and/or the Rapid Response Team.

Observe TRENDS, compare and contrast client's response (system-specific assessment findings, priority intervention (s), client's response and/or desired outcomes from medications, diagnostic procedures, etc.). Clinical situations and/or information within the stem of the question or the distracters may require comparing and contrasting current to previous assessments. This comparing and contrasting will assist in determining if there is a trend, and if the trend is towards the desired outcome or a potential complication. For example, if the BP was 176/89 and 60 minutes later it has a change to 135/78 after receiving a beta-blocker, this would indicate a trend towards the desired outcome. In contrast to this, another trend may indicate a potential complication for a post-op client who has a HR of 70 BPM, RR 14/min, and 60 minutes later the HR is 104 BPM and the RR is 24/min. This may indicate bleeding that requires an immediate intervention to prevent further complications. *It is easy to recognize clients are in trouble after they have crashed and present with a low blood pressure and/or heart rate, are cyanotic, etc.; however, the goal is to PREVENT the progression of early to late complications through excellent assessment and wise clinical decision-making skills.* (*"Remember, anyone can recognize a train crash, but it takes an astute nurse to recognize the potential for an impending train crash!"*) (*Does this sound familiar? The "T" is also in the "SAFETY" Model.*)

Review if Maslow's Hierarchy of Basic Needs is the priority. Remember, physiological needs are a higher priority than teaching or psychosocial. The ABCs (airway, breathing, circulation) are the critical physiologic needs, which are also at the base of Maslow's Hierarchy. This also applies to questions evaluating the psychosocial need. While these needs have not changed, remember that the American heart Association has changed the sequence of CPR from "ABC" to "**CAB**;" external **C**ardiac compressions, **A**irway, **B**reathing.

Process of Prioritization (cont'd.)

Identify the client who is unstable or highest risk for developing complications. When the nurse has several clients to provide care for, the ABCs are critical physiological needs. Oxygenation is an immediate concern if physiological changes (i.e., vital signs, skin color, O_2 saturation, or change in the client's mental status such as confusion) indicate hypoxia. Airway may not be the priority of care if there is no physiological basis. This would also apply to answering test questions. For example, if the choice is to see a client who has been depressed, and starts presenting with more energy, giving away favorite possessions, and has a plan to commit suicide versus a client with COPD who is asymptomatic, the priority is to assess the client who is high risk for suicide first because it is an acute safety issue. The client with COPD is chronic and is presenting with no new symptoms. (*Note, this prioritization strategy is adapted from Maslow's Hierarchy of Needs.*)

Some additional strategies to assist in prioritizing the most unstable client is to remember the nurse should assess the **ACUTE clinical presentations before CHRONIC clinical presentations**. One example may be choosing between the client who is actively bleeding or the client who has a chronic pulmonary condition presenting with symptoms such as a barrel chest or sleeps with two pillows at night that may be within defined limits for this client. **EARLY versus LATE** is another strategy to use when you are saying to yourself, "*All of these clients are bleeding or have an infection. How do I prioritize these?*" It is very EASY! Ask yourself, "*If the client is bleeding, is he/she experiencing early or late symptoms of bleeding? OR is the client presenting with early or late signs of shock?*" The priority of care is to evaluate the client with late signs in this situation.

Another component for prioritizing is to identify the client who may the highest risk for developing a complication. For example, an obese client with a history of smoking and is immobilized for several days following a hip replacement may be high risk for developing of a deep vein thrombosis (DVT). In other words, the nurse must always be assessing for those clients who are at risk for developing complications such as infection, bleeding, hypoxia, pain, etc.

Think about risk: You must manage care to prevent "**RISK**" to the client.

Recognize limitations of staff members: Identify standard of practice (scope of practice, wrong orders, interactions, etc.). Scope of practice and standards of practice are often the focus of clinical nursing and/ or test questions. The question may be asking if the standard of practice was met. It may be asking if the nurse needs to intervene or what care is appropriate to delegate. (*This is the "Y" in the "SAFETY" Model.*)

Infection control is very important to the safety of clients and healthcare personnel. Clinical nursing and/ or test questions may present the following: *What are the necessary infection control precautions for prevention and spread of the disease, to include how to avoid communicable diseases or even activities such as room placement, hand washing, steps to donning.*

Safe medication administration in an important step in prioritizing. The book *Pharmacology Made Insanely Easy* by Manning & Rayfield, will be the resource for this book. Clinical nursing and/or test questions may review the protocol for accurate client identification or the need to question an order (i.e., a new prescription order for a nonselective beta blocker to a client with the diagnosis of asthma). Interactions are another component for safe medication administration.

Keep client/environment safe (*falls, equipment, etc.*): ensure client safety. Reduction of hazards in the environment may include fall/accident prevention such as bed position, use of assistive devices, rugs, cords, etc., or could include identifying a client who is at risk for suicide. Clinical and/or questions may ask about safety situations in both the home and the acute care setting.

Your evaluation is an ongoing process. Nursing care requires constant evaluation and reflection regarding clinical outcomes. Ultimately, has the desired outcome been met? If not, what needs to be done differently? Are revisions needed in the plan of care? Or, is the client responding and the plan of care needs to be continued? (*This is the "E" the "SAFETY" Model.*)

Linking Clinical Situations to Prioritizing

You will find sample questions below that represent each of the identified categories in both the mnemonic and the chart titled *"SAFETY: A New Approach to **PRIORITIZE** Nursing Care Based on **STANDARDS**."* These have been developed to assist you in beginning to learn a process for prioritization. We will provide rationales throughout the book for each question; however, the goal here is to provide you with a framework for learning how to prioritize. The initial part of the mnemonic will be reviewed followed by an example of a clinical situation/exam question. The answers will be provided along with the strategy for answering the question and the NCLEX® standard represented. Consider this as a sneak preview for the clinical decision making questions that will be included in each chapter with the exception of the rationale.

Clinical Decision-Making Exercises

Prioritize:	One of the first steps for prioritizing is system-specific assessments.
1. A 30-year-old woman who suffered a head injury and began having seizures is being sent home on phenytoin (Dilantin). What is the priority for teaching the client about this drug? ① "If you stop taking the medication suddenly, an unpleasant, acute withdrawal syndrome is likely along with renal failure." ② "You may stop taking this drug when you have had no seizures for six months." ③ "Let's talk about what kind of contraception you plan to use while you are taking; this medication." ④ "I know it's depressing to face this, but you absolutely must take this drug the rest of your life."	**Answer:** Option 3 **Strategy:** Assessment **NCLEX®: Pharmacological and Parenteral Therapies:** Review data prior to giving med (i.e., lab results, allergies, potential interactions).

Review the Analysis of Concept(s):	Once the assessments have been completed as reviewed on the previous page, proceed on to analyze the priority care required for this client based on the analysis of the concept(s).
2. Which of these clients would be a priority for the nurse to assess immediately following shift report? ① A client with COPD who is presenting with distant breath sounds. ② A client with TB who is complaining of night sweats. ③ A post-op client presents with sudden onset of pleuritic pain and acute dyspnea. ④ A client with pneumonia with a T–100.4°F, HR–90 with a cough.	**Answer:** Option 3 **Strategy:** Analysis of the concept of OXYGENATION and prioritizing the plan of care. **NCLEX®: Management of Care:** Prioritize delivery of client care. **Physiological Adaptation:** Assess client and respond to changes. **Physiological Adaptation:** Recognize signs and symptoms of complications and intervene appropriately when providing care.

Identify "The Priority Interventions" based on the key concepts:	The key concept will help you decide what the priority actions are to implement.
3. What would be the priority nursing intervention for a client with chronic lung disease who is presenting with dyspnea, HR–140 BPM, and labored respirations? ① Administer oxygen at 40% heated mist. ② Assist client to cough and deep breathe. ③ Elevate the head of the bed. ④ Assess breath sounds.	**Answer:** Option 3 **Strategy:** Identify the First-Do Priority Interventions based on the key concepts. **NCLEX®: Management of Care:** Prioritize delivery of client care. **Physiological Adaptation:** Assess client and respond to changes. **Physiological Adaptation:** Recognize signs and symptoms of complications and intervene appropriately when providing care.

Observe TRENDS:	Compare and contrast client's response (system-specific assessment findings; priority intervention(s), and/or desired outcomes from medications, diagnostic procedures, etc.).
4. Which of these clients should be assessed immediately after the nurse comes out of report? ① A client who is vomiting and has diarrhea presenting with a heart rate–88 bpm, BP–134/80. ② A client who has a new diagnosis of heart failure with a new symptom of a moist cough. ③ A client presenting with peripheral edema and a 1 lb. weight gain within 24 hours. ④ A client who has an order for digoxin (Lanoxin) with a heart rate–70 bpm at rest that has decreased from 82 bpm in 24 hours.	**Answer:** Option 2 **Strategy:** Observe TRENDS, compare and contrast client's response (system-specific assessment findings). **NCLEX®: Physiological Adaptation:** Recognize trends and changes in client condition and intervene as needed.

Review if Maslow's Hierarchy of Basic Needs is the priority:	Remember, physiological needs are typically a higher priority than teaching. Physiological needs will most likely be a priority over psychosocial needs; however, if a client presents with the psychosocial complication of depression resulting in a risk for suicide then this may indeed become the priority client.
5. A nurse is admitting a client with a diagnosis of posttraumatic stress disorder to the mental health unit. During this process, the client becomes confused and disoriented. What is the priority intervention? ① Accept the client and help to make client feel safe. ② Orient the client to the unit and introduce to the staff. ③ Review the unit rules and provide a booklet outlining them. ④ Stabilize the client's physical needs.	**Answer:** Option 1 **Strategy:** Review Maslow's Hierarchy of Basic Needs is the priority. **NCLEX®: Psychosocial Integrity:** Provide a therapeutic environment for clients with emotional/behavior issues.

Identify the client who is unstable or highest risk for developing complications:	When the nurse has several clients to provide care for, the ABCs are critical physiological needs. Oxygenation is an immediate concern if physiologic changes (i.e., vital signs, skin color, O_2 saturation, or change in the client's mental status such as confusion) occur, all of which indicate alteration in oxygenation.
6. Which client's assessment findings would alert the nurse that an elderly client may be developing the complication of altered oxygen perfusion? ① An elderly client presenting with a change in functional and mental status. ② An elderly adult client presenting with a congestive and frequent cough. ③ An elderly client presenting with a temperature of 102.4°F. ④ An elderly client with a white blood cell count of 18,000 mm³.	**Answer:** Option 1 **Strategy:** Identify the client who is unstable or highest risk for developing complications. **NCLEX®: Health Promotion:** Provide care for adults over 85 years. **Physiological Adaptation:** Recognize signs and symptoms of complications and intervene appropriately when providing care.

Think about "**RISK**":	You must manage care to prevent "**RISK**" to the client. **R**ecognize limitations of staff members. **I**dentify standard of practice (scope or standard of practice have been broken, wrong orders, interactions, etc.). **S**cope of practice and standards of practice are often the focus of clinical nursing and/or test questions. **K**eep client/environment safe.
7. Which of these nursing actions from an unlicensed assistive personnel (UAP), for a client with a closed head injury, need intervention by the nurse? ① Takes vital signs as ordered and documents. ② Decreases the stimuli in the room. ③ Maintains seizure precautions at the bedside. ④ Places client in the flat, supine position during the bath and back massage.	**Answer:** Option 4 **Strategy:** Recognize limitations of staff members. Identify standard of practice (scope or standard of practice have been broken, wrong orders, interactions, etc.). **NCLEX®: Management of Care:** Supervise/recognize limitation of self/others, seek assist/corrective measures. **Physiological Adaptation:** Manage care with alteration in hemodynamics, tissue perfusion, (cardiac, cerebral).

Your evaluation is an ongoing process:	Nursing care requires constant evaluation and reflection regarding if assessments were correct, was this the priority concept, and is the client responding to the interventions.
8. Which clinical finding would best indicate the expected outcome of fluid replacement for a client who was presenting with hypovolemia? ① Arterial pH 7.34. ② Blood pressure increase from 108/68 to 126/80. ③ Specific gravity–1.030. ④ Urine output 160 mL/5 hours.	**Answer:** Option 2 **Strategy:** Your evaluation is an ongoing process. **NCLEX®: Physiological Adaptation:** Manage the care of the client with a fluid and electrolyte imbalance.

References for Chapter 1

Benner, P., Sutphen, M., Leonard, V., & Day, L. (2010). *Educating nurses: A call for radical transformation.* San Francisco, CA: Jossey-Bass, A Wiley Imprint.

Manning, L. and Rayfield, S. (2014). *Nursing made insanely easy* (7th ed). Duluth, GA: I CAN Publishing, Inc.

Manning, L. and Rayfield, S. (2013). *Pharmacology made insanely easy* (4th ed.). Duluth, GA: I CAN Publishing, Inc.

National Council of State Boards of Nursing, INC. (NCSBN) 2012. *Research brief: 2011 RN practice analysis: linking the NCLEX RN® examination to practice.* Retrieved from https://www.ncsbn.org/index.htm

CHAPTER 2

Linking Multiple Systems to Pathophysiology of Fluid Imbalance
Concept Fluid and Electrolytes: Fluids

A Snapshot of Fluid Balance

Fluid balance is defined as the process of the regulation of the extracellular fluid volume, body fluid osmolality, and plasma concentrations of electrolytes. Fluid is the water and includes the substances dissolved and suspended in it. Two important facts about fluid include the volume characteristics and the osmolality (concentration) (Giddens, 2013). Body fluids are distributed between intracellular (ICF–two thirds of body water) and extracellular (ECF–one third of body water) compartments. Fluids move between compartments through a selectively permeable membranes. This occurs by a variety of methods such as osmosis, diffusion, active transport, and filtration to assist in fluid balance. The two alterations in the fluid balance that are necessary for the nurse to be knowledgeable about are fluid volume deficits and excess.

Fluid volume deficits include hypovolemia-isotonic (loss of water and electrolytes from the ECF) and dehdration—osmolar (water loss with no loss of electrolytes). Dehydration results in hemo-concentration, causing an increase in hematocrit, urine specific gravity, and serum electrolytes. The sympathetic nervous system response of an increase in thirst, release of aldosterone, and/or release of the anitdiuretic hormone (ADH) are compensatory mechanisms for preventing complications from fluid volume deficit. Severe fluid volume deficit can result in hypovolemia leading to shock.

Older adults have an increased risk for dehydration due to the numerous physiological changes that includes a decrease in the total body mass and total body water content.

Fluid overload is overhydration or ECF **volume excess**. Excess fluids are in the vascular system, a problem called hypervolemia, or in the interstitial spaces, a problem usually called third-spacing. The water and sodium are in the same proportions as they exist in other ECF, and this is referred to as iso-osmolar (isotonic) fluid volume excess (Black & Hawk, 2009). Fluid overload can develop from two processes:

1. Administering too much fluid or administering too rapidly.
2. Failure to excrete fluids. Fluid overload many times results from an increase in the total body sodium level.

Fluid and electrolyte balance is a dynamic interplay between three processes: the intake and absorption of fluid and electrolytes; the distribution of the electrolytes; and the output of the fluid and electrolytes. This balance of the fluid and electrolytes is a dynamic interplay since the output of fluid and electrolyte occurs continuously. The intake of fluid and electrolytes influences output to some degree but it can easily become less than or more than output. With change in conditions, fluid and electrolyte distribution can rapidly shift. Optimal balance of fluid and electrolytes maintains the volume, osmolality, and electrolyte concentrations of fluid in the various fluid compartments within their normal physiologic ranges (Hall, 2011).

Let's begin our journey to helping you become a genius at the concept of Fluid Balance!

The Pathophysiology Behind Fluid Imbalance

FLUID IMBALANCE

Extracellular Fluid Volume Deficit				Extracellular Fluid Volume Excess	
↑ Output not Balanced by ↑ Intake of Na⁺ & Water	Third Spacing: Shift from Extracellular Volume into the Third Space	Age-Related Changes	Dehydration: Loss of fluid from Body (not lose Electrolytes)	↓ Output or ↑ Intake of Na⁺ & Water	↓ Output Not Balanced by ↓ Intake of Na⁺ & Water
• Burns • Diabetic mellitus (↑ urination) • Diabetes Insipidus • Diarrhea/ vomiting • Excessive diuretic therapy or laxative use • Draining GI fistula • Nasogastric suctioning • Intestinal decompression • Hemorrhage (i.e., after a procedure, surgery, etc.) • Decrease in aldosterone	• Ascites • Intestinal obstruction • Burns • Hypo-albuminemia • Liver failure • Pleural effusion	• Changes in the kidney and cardio-vascular function as adults age	• Prolonged fever • Excessive sweating • Hyperventilation • Insensible losses from skin and lungs	• IV infusion of Na⁺ containing isotonic solution (i.e., 0.9% NaCl, Ringer's, etc.) in excess with no electrolyte replacement • Interstitial to plasma fluid shifts (i.e., burns, hypertonic fluids) • Sodium intake in excess • Excessive Na⁺ intake from medications such as sodium hypertonic enema solutions, and sodium bicarbonate acids	• Oliguria (i.e., chronic renal disease, etc.) • Excess aldosterone (i.e., chronic heart failure, cirrhosis, etc.) • Syndrome of inappropriate antidiuretic hormone (SIADH) that is an excess of antidiuretic hormone (ADH) • Excessive intake of glucocorticoids (i.e., Cushing's disease)

Labs		Urine Tests	
Serum Sodium:	135–145 mEq/L	**Urine Osmolality–Critical Values:**	
Serum Osmolality:	285–295 mOsm/kg of water	< 100 mOsm/kg of H₂O–overhydration	
BUN:	8–25 mg/dL	> 800 mOsm/kg of H₂O–dehydration	
Hematocrit:	Male: 44–52%; Female: 39–47%	**Urine Sodium: 40–220 mEq/L 24 hr** Random specimen: usually 20 mEq/L **Urine Specific Gravity: 1.003–1.030**	

Insanely Easy Approach:

- Fluid Balance is regulated through the intake and output.
- The intake is maintained through the thirst mechanism.
- The output is regulated by the skin, lungs, GI tract, and kidneys.
- The fluid imbalances you/nurses need to understand include:
  fluid volume deficit and **fluid volume excess**.

Who is at Risk for DEHYDRATION?

D iminished kidney function

E levated temperature

H ighly concentrated tube feedings without enough supplemental water

Y oung infant wearing a diaper – may not get an accurate assessment of output

D iarrhea that is watery; diuretic overuse; diabetes mellitus

R eduction in the body—water content, reduction in LOC, reduction in the temperature, and reduced fluid may result in tachycardia as well (all are signs of dehydration for elderly clients)

A ntidiuretic hormone production decrease may lead to dehydration

T hirst mechanism is reduced

I ncrease in the serum glucose

O ther conditions that accelerates the loss of fluids such as vomiting

N ot able to obtain fluid without help (newborn, infant, elderly)

SAFETY Concept: Fluid and Electrolytes
Fluid Volume Deficit

System-Specific Assessments "The assessments are ↓"	First-Do Priority Interventions "FLUIDS"	Evaluation of Expected Outcomes "The assessments are within defined limits"
↓ moistness of the mucous membranes (dry) ↓ in vascular volume = tachycardia ↓ in postural blood pressure leading to syncope ↓ in neck vein size (flat) ↓ in urine output (oliguria) ↓ too much in BP can lead to shock ↓ in skin turgor (*not valid assessment for elderly client*)	**F**luids po; isotonic; blood **L**evel of consciousness (assess) **U**rine output < 30 mL per hour; report trends ↓ **I**ntake and output; IV fluids as ordered **D**ocument vital signs, weight; monitor for trends **S**afety–Shock position: for ↓ BP, position client on back with legs↑; implement safety precautions to prevent falls **Discharge Teaching:** • Take adequate fluid intake • Monitor urine output • Take daily weight. Report gain or loss > 2 pounds	No ↓ weight (sudden loss) No ↓ moistness of the mucous membranes No ↓ in vascular volume = tachycardia (HR–WDL) No ↓ in postural blood pressure Neck veins not flat No ↓ in urine output No ↓ too much in BP No ↓ in skin turgor (not valid assessment for elderly client)

Fluid Volume Deficit

INSANELY EASY TIP for Comparing Lab Reports with System-Specific Assessments!

Labs (↑s)	System-Specific Assessments (↓s)
↑ Hematocrit ↑ Serum osmolality ↑ protein level ↑ BUN ↑ Sodium ↑ Glucose ↑ Urine specific gravity	↓ weight (sudden loss) ↓ moistness of the mucous membranes (dry) ↓ in vascular volume = tachycardia, ↓ in postural blood pressure leading to syncope ↓ in neck vein size (flat) ↓ in urine output (oliguria) ↓ too much in BP can lead to shock ↓ in skin turgor (not valid assessment for elderly client)
Labs are all increased (↑) with hypovolemia! ⟶	Assessment findings are all ↓(decreased)!

SAFETY Concept: Fluid and Electrolytes
Fluid Volume Excess

System-Specific Assessments "The assessments are ↑"	First-Do Priority Interventions "RESTRICT"	Evaluation of Expected Outcomes "The assessments are within defined limits"
↑ Pulse (may be normal but bounding) ↑ Blood pressure ↑ Confusion ↑ In edema ↑ Weight > 2 lbs/24 hr ↑ In ascites ↑ In crackles in lungs ↑ Respirations and ↑ dyspnea, orthopnea ↑ Swelling neck (jugular vein distention) ↑ Risk for skin breakdown	**R**educe IV flow rate; reposition at least every 2 hrs **E**valuate breath sounds and ABGs, SaO_2, chest x-ray, CBC; edema **S**emi-Fowler's/high-Fowler's position; supplemental O_2 as ordered and needed; support extremities to decrease dependent edema as appropriate **T**reat with oxygen and diuretics as ordered **R**educe fluid and sodium intake **I** & O and daily weight; implement prescriptions for fluid and sodium restrictions and intake **C**irculation, color, and presence of edema **T**urn and position at least every 2 hrs; the diuretics (loop, osmotic) should be given as prescribed	• VS within defined limits for client • No dyspnea, orthopnea • Lungs clear, no wheezing • No cough or pink-tinged frothy sputum • No edema • Weight within 2 pounds of the defined limits • No skin breakdown

Insanely Easy Tip!

17 oz. (0.5 L) of fluid = 1 lb (0.45 kg) weight gain. An increase in weight of 5–10% indicates mild to moderate fluid gain. An increase of more than 10% is a more severe fluid gain.

INSANELY EASY TIP! The nursing care for Fluid Volume Excess is to "**RESTRICT**" the fluids! This will assist you in organizing the **PRIORITY** nursing care for these clients. The **ABCs** will also provide you with another structure to organize the nursing care!

Airway
Breathing=assess breath sounds
Circulation – color, presence of edema
Diuretics as prescribed
Edema- skin care and support
Fluid and sodium reduction

Linking Lab Reports with
System-Specific Assessments for Fluid Volume Excess

Labs (↓s)/Diagnostic Procedures	System-Specific Assessments (↑s)
↓ Hematocrit	↑ pulse (may be normal but bounding)
↓ Serum osmolality	↑ blood pressure, ↑ CVP
↓ Protein level	↑ confusion
↓ BUN	↑ in edema
↓ Sodium	↑ weight > 2 lbs/24 hrs
↓ Glucose	↑ in ascites
↓ Urine specific gravity	↑ in crackles in lungs
	↑ respirations & ↑ dyspnea, orthopnea
(Chest x-ray may show pulmonary congestion.)	↑ swelling neck (jugular vein distention)
	↑ risk for skin breakdown
Labs are all decreased (↓) with hypervolemia! ⟶	Assessment findings are all ↑ (increased)!

Every journey begins with the first step! Remember, one step at a time! Before you know it you will be a GENIUS at Fluid and Electrolytes!

Clinical Decision-Making Exercises

1. Which documentation indicates an understanding of how to position a client who is experiencing fluid overload from too much IV fluid and is presenting with dyspnea, R–38, HR–120 bpm, extremely anxious, and crackles throughout lung fields?

   ① Client positioned in the high-Fowler's position.

   ② Client positioned in the Lithotomy position.

   ③ Client positioned in the supine position.

   ④ Client positioned in the Sim's position.

2. Which system-specific assessment finding for a client who has been vomiting for 24 hours would indicate a need for further intervention?

   ① BP increase from 110/70 to 130/80.

   ② Urine output decrease from 95 mL/hour to 75 mL/hour.

   ③ BUN–15 mg/dL.

   ④ Pulse increased from 68/min to 118/min.

3. What would be the priority of care for an older adult client who is presenting with edema, tachycardia, and acute confusion?

   ① Check for skin turgor and thirst.

   ② Evaluate trends in the daily weight.

   ③ Monitor the I & O.

   ④ Turn and reposition q shift.

4. Which assessment findings would a client present with who has been vomiting and experiencing diarrhea for 48 hours? *Select all that apply.*

   ① Blood pressure increased from 110/80 to 135/85.

   ② Skin temperature hot.

   ③ Complaints of syncope when standing up.

   ④ Heart rate from 88 bpm to 48 bpm.

   ⑤ Decrease in skin turgor.

5. What would be the priority nursing intervention for a client with a BP change from 140/88 to 86/62?

   ① Put client in supine position with legs elevated.

   ② Notify provider of care.

   ③ Put client in Fowler's position.

   ④ Evaluate characteristics of mucous membranes.

6. Which clinical finding is a priority for indicating the client is experiencing fluid volume excess?

   ① BP change from 108/78 to 140/90.

   ② Decreased crackles in lower lung fields.

   ③ Pulse increased from 72/min to 80/min.

   ④ Weight from 150 lbs to 151 lbs.

7. Which of these laboratory values for a febrile client with pneumonia would indicate a complication with dehydration?

    ① Decrease in Serum Osmolarity.

    ② Decrease in Serum Sodium.

    ③ Decrease in BUN.

    ④ Increase in urine specific gravity.

8. Which of these clients would be high risk for fluid overload? *Select all that apply*.

    ① A client who is in chronic renal failure.

    ② A client with cystic fibrosis.

    ③ A client who is in heart failure.

    ④ A client with diabetes mellitus and has Hyperosmolar Hyperglycemic Nonketotic Syndrome (HHNS).

    ⑤ A client with Cushing's Disease.

9. Which nursing action would be the priority for a client with orthopnea, dyspnea, and bibasilar crackles in lungs with auscultation?

    ① Elevate legs to promote venous return.

    ② Decrease the IV fluids and notify the provider of care.

    ③ Orient the client to time, place, and situation.

    ④ Prevent complications of immobility.

10. Which of these nursing actions included in the quality assurance program for clients in heart failure would be most appropriate to delegate to the unlicensed assistive personnel (UAP)?

    ① Assess breath sounds and check for edema daily.

    ② Check charts to make certain clients are receiving verapamil (Calan) as ordered.

    ③ Review all medications with the client every other day.

    ④ Weigh all residents as ordered.

Answers and Rationales

1. Which documentation indicates an understanding of how to position a client who is **experiencing fluid overload** from too much IV fluid and is presenting with **dyspnea, R–38, HR–120 bpm, extremely anxious, and crackles throughout lung fields?**

   ① **CORRECT: Client positioned in the high-Fowler's position. This will assist in optimizing lung expansion and help with O$_2$.**

   ② INCORRECT: Lying on the back with hips and knees flexed and feet in stirrups is going to cause more complications with breathing. This would be used for a perineal or vaginal procedure.

   ③ INCORRECT: This would not help with the dyspnea. It would make it worse.

   ④ INCORRECT: This would be appropriate for a client who is unconscious or getting an enema.

The strategy is to remember to sit client UP for supporting breathing! The good news is that this position is for any client experiencing dyspnea from altered oxygenation no matter the cause (An exception to this would be if a client had a spinal cord injury, or any procedure such as a laminectory that would contraindicate this position). Dyspnea could be from an infection, a chronic lung disease, fluid in the lung, TB, etc. In this situation, the fluid caused the hypoxia, but the care in regards to the positioning would be the same. Any time there is an excess of fluid in the lungs, several of the priorities are to support the oxygenation, restrict fluids, and remove the extra fluids. (*Refer to Concept Oxygenation for more specifics.*)

Reduction of Risk Potential: Manage the care of a client with impaired ventilation/oxygenation.

Physiological Adaptations: Manage the care of the client with a fluid and electrolyte imbalance.

2. Which **system-specific** assessment finding for a **client who has been vomiting for 24 hours** would indicate a **need for further intervention?**

   ① INCORRECT: Blood pressure would be decreased, not increased. There may be less volume to perfuse due to the vomiting.

   ② INCORRECT: This is not a significant trend. While output is important to trend, nurses must use clinical decision making to determine what is the ongoing priority.

   ③ INCORRECT: This is within the normal range of 10–20 mg/dL.

   ④ **CORRECT: Decrease in the vascular volume results in the HR having to pump harder.**

The strategy is to recognize the pulse is compensating for a decrease in the volume. Note, that when studying the concept of oxygenation you will learn that an early sign of hypoxia is tachycardia. With fluid deficit, there is a need for the heart rate to work harder to compensate for the decrease oxygen delivery to the vital organs. With hypoxia, there is also lack of oxygen available to the organs; however, it is from a different etiology. Bottom line, system specific assessment of tachycardia is the SAME! Trending is another strategy that facilitates clinical decision-making.

Physiological Adaptations: Manage the care of the client with a fluid and electrolyte imbalance.

3. What would be the **priority of care** for an **older adult client** who is presenting with **edema, tachycardia, and acute confusion?**

① INCORRECT: Skin turgor and thirst are not accurate assessments for an older adult client. These decrease with aging.

② **CORRECT: The trends with the client's weight is a priority, since it is an objective measurement to determine outcomes from care for client with fluid excess. Acute weight loss/gain may indicate rapid fluid changes.**

③ INCORRECT: This is an important plan for the care; however, it is not a priority over option 2.

④ INCORRECT: Turning and repositioning per protocol (every shift is not enough) to prevent skin breakdown.

The strategy is if a client is presenting with edema, this is a clue that the client is experiencing too much volume. Tachycardia could be a symptom with either fluid volume deficit or excess. If the client is experiencing fluid deficit, the pulse may be thready; however, if the client is experiencing fluid overload the pulse may be bounding. Daily weight is an excellent assessment to evaluate trends in the fluid status of the client. Trending is another strategy that facilitates clinical decision-making. Acute confusion not only indicates a complication with fluid and electrolytes, but can also be indicative of a urinary tract infection, or another type of infection.

Physiological Adaptations: Manage the care of the client with a fluid and electrolyte imbalance.

Management of Care: Prioritize delivery of client care.

4. Which **assessment findings** would a client present with who has been **vomiting and experiencing diarrhea for 48 hours?** Select all that apply.

① INCORRECT: Blood pressure change is not consistent with the client's presentation.

② INCORRECT: Vomiting and diarrhea for 48 hours can lead to hypovolemia. The skin would be cool, clammy, and diaphoretic. The neck veins would be flattened with an absence of tears and decrease in the skin turgor.

③ **CORRECT: This is a concern due to safety issues. Due to volume loss, client should change position slowly to prevent**

complications with hypotension and orthostatic hypotension. The client's gait stability should be evaluated.

④ INCORRECT: The heart rate would be elevated due to volume loss.

⑤ **CORRECT: This is a clinical assessment that can change. Geriatric clients have a change in the elasticity of their skin, so this would not be an accurate assessment for the geriatric client. The client's age, however, would have to be indicated in the question in order for you to incorporate into your decision-making.**

The strategy is to remember that assessments are **DECREASED** with fluid **DEFICIT.** (The exception is the HR which is increased) from the DECREASE in the vascular volume. So BP, skin temperature, urine output, weight, etc. would all be DECREASED. See how EASY this can be when you organize your information!!!

Physiological Adaptations: Manage the care of the client with a fluid and electrolyte imbalance.

5. What would be the **priority nursing intervention** for a client with a **BP change from 140/88 to 86/62?**

① **CORRECT: The client is hypovolemic with this pressure. Lower the head of the bed to a supine position to assist with the declining blood pressure.**

② INCORRECT: This may be important, but a nursing action needs to be implemented immediately with the low pressure.

③ INCORRECT: Putting client in Fowler's position will result in the BP decreasing even more.

④ INCORRECT: This is a subjective assessment and is not a priority with this significant BP change.

The strategy is to know that with low pressure there is a lack of perfusion. Lower the HOB to decrease the declining blood pressure. Elevate the legs to help with perfusion. This is a great link any time there is a blood pressure drop from either bleeding or volume.

Physiological Adaptation: Manage the care of a client with alteration in perfusion.

Reduction of Risk Potential: Recognize trends and changes in client condition and intervene as needed.

6. Which clinical finding is a **priority** for indicating the client is **experiencing fluid volume excess?**

   ① **CORRECT: This change in blood pressure indicates client is experiencing volume excess.**

   ② INCORRECT: Decreased crackles in lower lung fields does not point to fluid volume excess.

   ③ INCORRECT: This is not a significant change.

   ④ INCORRECT: This is not as significant as the rise in the BP. (*Refer to tip below.*)

The strategy with fluid excess is the assessments need to be carefully compared with one another. A clinical judgment is necessary to determine if the assessment is significant enough to be selected as the priority.

INSANELY EASY TIP!

17 oz. (0.5 L) of fluid = 1 lb (0.45 kg) weight gain. An increase in weight of 5–10% indicates mild to moderate fluid gain. An increase of more than 10% is a more severe fluid gain.

Physiological Adaptations: Manage the care of the client with a fluid and electrolyte imbalance.

7. Which of these **laboratory values** for a **febrile** client with **pneumonia** would indicate a **complication with dehydration?**

   ① INCORRECT: This value would be elevated due to the concentration.

   ② INCORRECT: This would be elevated.

   ③ INCORRECT: These would be increased.

   ④ **CORRECT: This would be increased along with the BUN, serum sodium, and serum osmolality.**

The strategy is to recognize that if there is fluid volume deficit as with dehydration, the labs will be increased! The client has less fluid that can result in an increase in the concentration of the BUN, osmolality, sodium, and specific gravity.

Physiological Adaptations: Manage the care of the client with a fluid and electrolyte imbalance.

8. Which of these clients would be **high risk for fluid overload?** Select all that apply.

   ① **CORRECT: A client who is in chronic renal failure. This can lead to overload.**

   ② INCORRECT: A client with cystic fibrosis. These clients will decrease their sodium and would not result in fluid overload.

   ③ **CORRECT: A client who is in heart failure. These clients will have an altered ability to pump blood effectively which could result in overload.**

   ④ INCORRECT: A client with diabetes mellitus and has Hyperosmolar Hyperglycemic Nonketotic Syndrome (HHNS). These clients may experience fluid deficit due to the frequent urination with this HHNS leading to dehydration.

   ⑤ **CORRECT: A client with Cushing's Disease. Due to the sodium retention, the client may experience fluid overload.**

The strategy is that while the etiology for the fluid excess may be different, the outcome is the same with the same changes. For example chronic renal failure can result in client experiencing fluid overload due to the lack of the functioning of the renal system. Heart failure may result in fluid overload due to the inefficiency of the heart, and Cushing's Disease would be a result of increased amounts of adrenal adrenocortical hormones causing the increased sodium which results in fluid retention. You can begin to categorize the diseases that may result in fluid overload. This will assist you in organizing the clinical findings for fluid overload. Even with the different physiological changes in the medical condition, the clinical assessment findings are very similar.

Physiological Adaptations: Manage the care of the client with a fluid and electrolyte imbalance.

9. Which nursing action would be the **priority** for a client with **orthopnea, dyspnea, and bibasilar crackles in lungs with auscultation?**

   ① INCORRECT: Elevate legs to promote venous return. This would result in an increase workload on the cardiopulmonary system.

   ② **CORRECT: Decrease the IV fluids and notify the provider of care. The client is in fluid overload and does not need extra fluid.**

③ INCORRECT: Orient the client to time, place, and situation. This is not the priority over option 2 because no matter how much you orient them to information, if they continue in fluid overload the oxygenation is not going to improve.

④ INCORRECT: Prevent complications of immobility. This is important, but the initial priority would be the complication of oxygenation.

The strategy is to focus on the client assessments. Bottom line is that if there are crackles in the lungs, the client does not need extra fluid. What this is saying to you is that if your client receives extra blood or IV fluid in too short of a period of time or develops pulmonary edema, then the IV fluids must be monitored closely. In most situations, the healthcare provider will be notified and fluids will be decreased.

Physiological Adaptations: Manage the care of the client with a fluid and electrolyte imbalance.

Reduction of Risk Potential: Recognize signs and symptoms of complications and intervene as needed.

Management of Care: Prioritize delivery of care.

10. Which of these nursing actions included in **the quality assurance program for clients in heart failure** would be most appropriate to **delegate to the unlicensed assistive personnel (UAP)?**

① INCORRECT: Assess breath sounds and check for edema daily. UAPs cannot assess.

② INCORRECT: Check charts to make certain clients are receiving verapamil (Calan) as ordered. UAPs cannot administer medications.

③ INCORRECT: Review all medications with the client every other day. UAPs cannot not be involved in the administration of medications.

④ **CORRECT: Unlicensed assistive personnel can weigh clients, which is an appropriate intervention in caring for clients with heart failure.**

The strategy for answering this question is understanding the nursing interventions that are **PRIORITY** in a quality assurance program for clients in heart failure. Monitoring the client's fluid balance, which directly impacts the workload of the heart, is a **PRIORITY**. The nurse would be required to trend the weights to detect any increase in weight indicating an increase in the fluid volume the heart would have to pump, but it is within the scope of practice for the UAP to take the daily weights, report and record the findings.

Management of Care: Assign and supervise care provided by others (i.e., UAP, LPN/VN, etc.) and Participate in performance improvement /quality improvement process.

Did you notice any trends as you were answering the questions? A SNAPSHOT OF THE SUMMARY!

1. With fluid excess, there will be a concern with **fluid in the lungs (oxygenation)** and an increase in the **workload of the heart (perfusion)!**

2. Nursing assessments support this by **monitoring: breath sounds, HR, RR, BP.**

3. Nursing care supports this by **elevating HOB if client is hypoxic from fluid in the lungs, lowering the head of the bed to a supine position if the client is hypotensive from fluid deficit,** monitoring the **weight for evaluation of fluid status.** Fluids will be adjusted if the client is experiencing fluid deficit or excess.

4. **Labs will be in opposite direction of the concept.** If the client is in fluid overload, labs will be decreased. If experiencing fluid deficit, labs will be increased.

5. Management questions such as regarding the scope of practice for UAP/ LPN, etc. will focus on the **concept and appropriate care.** If you have not studied delegation, this will not affect how you answer these questions. The questions will have a focus on the medical surgical concept. If you need a reference book to simplify the concept of delegation, we recommend *Nursing Made Insanely Easy* by Manning & Rayfield, 2014. Our goal for you at this time is to have an understanding of the Standard of Care for the concept Fluid Balance. You have to learn one concept at a time. Once you master the concept(s), then you can add the delegation (Scope of Practice).

Decision-Making Analysis Form

Use this tool to help identify why you missed any questions. As you enter the question numbers in the chart, you will begin to see patterns of why you answered incorrectly. This information will then guide you toward what you need to focus on in your continued studies. Ultimately, this analytical exercise will help you become more successful in answering questions!!!

Questions to ask:

1. Did I have the knowledge to answer the question? If not, what information do I need to review?

2. Did I know what the question was asking? Did I misread it or did I miss keywords in the stem of the question?

3. Did I misread or miss keywords in the distractors that would have helped me choose the correct answer?

4. Did I follow my gut reaction or did I allow myself to rationalize and then choose the wrong answer?

	Lack of Knowledge (Concepts, Systems, Pathophysiology, Medications, Procedures, etc.)	Missed Keywords or Misread the Stem of the Question	Missed Keywords or Misread the Distractors	Changed My Answer (Second-guessed myself, i.e., my first answer was correct.)
Put the # of each question you missed in the column that best explains why you think you answered it incorrectly.				

If you changed an answer because you talked yourself out of the correct answer, or you second-guessed yourself, this is an **EASY FIX: QUIT changing your answers**!!! Typically, the first time you read a question, you are about 95% right! The second time you read a question, you start talking yourself into changing the answer. The third time you read a question, you do not have a clue—and you are probably thinking "Who in the heck wrote this question?"

On the other hand, if you read a question too quickly and when you reread it you realize you missed some key information that would impact your decision (i.e., assessments, lab reports, medications, etc.), then it is appropriate to change your answer. When in doubt, go with the safe route: your first thought! Go with your gut instinct!

As you gain confidence in answering questions regarding specific nursing concepts, you will be able to successfully progress to answering higher-level questions about prioritization. Please refer to the *Prioritization Guidelines* in this book for a structure to assist you with this process.

You CAN do this!

> *"Any fact facing us is not as important as our attitude toward it, for that determines our success or failure."*
>
> NORMAN VINCENT PEALE

References for Chapter 2

Black, J M. and Hawks, J. H. (2009). *Medical surgical nursing: Clinical management for positive outcomes* (8th ed.). Philadelphia: Elsevier/Saunders.

Daniels, R. & Nicoll, L. (2012). *Contemporary medical-surgical nursing*, (2nd ed.). Clifton Park, NY: Delmar Cengage Learning

Ellis, K. M. (2012). *EKG: Plain and simple* (3rd ed.). Upper Saddle Road, NJ: Pearson.

Eliopoulos, C. (2014). *Gerontological nursing* (8th ed.), Philadelphia: Lippincott Williams & Wilkins.

Giddens, G. F. (2013). *Concepts for Nursing Practice*. St. Louis, MO: Mosby, an imprint of Elsevier.

Hall, J. E. (2011). *Guyton and Hall textbook of medical physiology* (12 ed). Philadelphia: Saunders/Elsevier.

Hogan, M. A. (2014). *Pathophysiology, Reviews and Rationales*, (3rd Edition) Boston, MA: Pearson.

Ignatavicius, D. D. and Workman, M. L. (2010). *Medical-Surgical Nursing: Patient-Centered Collaborative Care* (7th ed.). Philadelphia: Elsevier/Saunders.

LeMone, P. Burke, K. M. and Bauldoff, G. (2011). *Medical-surgical nursing: Critical thinking in patient care* (5th edition). Upper Saddle Road, NJ: Pearson/Prentice Hall.

Lewis, S., Dirksen, S., Heitkemper, M., Bucher, L., and Camera, I. (2011). *Medical surgical nursing: Assessment and management of clinical problems* (8th ed.). St. Louis: Mosby.

Manning, L. and Rayfield, S. (2014). *Nursing made insanely easy* (7th ed). Duluth, GA: I CAN Publishing, Inc.

Manning, L. and Rayfield, S. (2013). *Pharmacology made insanely easy* (4th ed.). Duluth, GA: I CAN Publishing, Inc.

National Council of State Boards of Nursing, INC. (NCSBN) 2012. *Research brief: 2011 RN practice analysis: linking the NCLEX RN® examination to practice*. Retrieved from https://www.ncsbn.org/index.htm

Nettina, S. L. (2013). *Lippincott manual of nursing practice* (10th ed.). Philadelphia, PA: Walters Kluwer Health/Lippincott Williams & Wilkins.

North Carolina Concept Based Learning Editorial Board. (2011). *Nursing a Concept Based Approach to Learning.* Upper Saddle Road, NJ: Pearson/Prentice Hall.

Osborn, K. S., Wraa, C. E., Watson, A. S., and Holleran, R. S. (2014). *Medical surgical nursing: preparation for practice* (2nd ed.). Upper Saddle Road, NJ: Pearson.

Pagana, K. D. and Pagana, T. J. (2014). *Mosby's manual of laboratory and diagnostic tests* (5th ed.). St. Louis, MO: Mosby, an imprint of Elsevier.

Porth, C. (2011). *Essentials of pathophysiology* (3rd edition). Philadelphia, PA: Lippincott Williams ad Wilkins.

Porth, C. M. and Grossman, S. (2013). *Pathophysiology, Concepts of altered health states* (9th edition). Philadelphia, PA: Lippincott Williams & Wilkins.

Potter, P. A., Perry, A. G., Stockert, P., and Hall, A. (2013). *Fundamentals of nursing* (8th ed). St. Louis, MO: Pearson/Prentice Hall.

Smeltzer, S. C., Bare, B. G., Hinkle, J. L., and Cheever, K. H. (2010). *Brunner & Suddarth's Textbook of medical-surgical nursing* (12th ed.). Philadelphia: Lippincott Williams & Wilkins.

Wagner, K. D. and Hardin-Pierce, M. C. (2014). *High-Acuity nursing* (6th ed.). Boston: Pearson.

CHAPTER 3

Linking Multiple Systems to Pathophysiology of Sodium Imbalance

Concept Fluid and Electrolytes: Sodium Balance

A Snapshot of Sodium Balance

Sodium is the most abundant electrolyte in the extracellular fluid (ECF) compartment and is the main determinant of serum osmolality. Imbalances of ECF sodium concentration are assumed to cause an overall osmolality imbalance. Appropriate ECF concentration of sodium is necessary to regulate the balance of fluid between the ECF and intracellular fluid (ICF) compartments. Sodium, as part of sodium bicarbonate, has a role in acid-base balance and is necessary for normal transmission of neurological impulses and membrane excitability. Sodium is obtained through gastrointestinal intake and often far exceeds nutritional needs. The kidneys are the efficient main regulator of sodium reabsorption or excretion. Sodium loss through sweat is normally minimal unless the person is exposed to a hot environment or exercise for an extended period of time.

Hyponatremia is a net gain of water or a loss of foods rich in sodium. Hyponatremia refers to a serum sodium level that is below normal (<135 mEq/L). The depolarization of membranes is delayed and slows down in hyponatremia. The water moves from ECF in the ICF, resulting in a swelling of the cells (cerebral edema). Serious complications can result if hyponatremia is left untreated. Several of these include respiratory arrest, seizures, and/or coma.

Link to the Endocrine Section "Syndrome of Inappropriate Antidiuretic Hormone": Low serum sodium concentration does not necessarily mean that the total body sodium is less than normal. In reality, numerous clients may experience hyponatremia as a result of an excess of total body fluid (which may occur with syndrome of inappropriate antidiuretic hormone, heart failure, cirrhosis of the liver, or renal failure) (Metheny, 2012).

Syndrome of Inappropriate Antidiuretic Hormone Secretion (SIADH) produces a special kind of hyponatremia that results in an excessive amount of water retention. Medical conditions may result in the complication of SIADH from either the release of too much antidiuretic hormone or the renal response to the hormone being intensified (Metheny, 2012). This release of the antidiuretic hormone (ADH) is termed inappropriate, since in typical situations a low serum sodium level would depress the ADH activity.

Hypernatremia refers to a serum sodium level that is greater than 145 mEq/L. Hypernatremia can be very serious resulting in cardiac, endocrine, and neurological distrubances. The serum (ECF) becomes hypertonic resulting in the water shifting out of the cells, causing them to be dehydrated.

Link to the Endocrine Section "Diabetes Insipidus": Due to the lack of the antidiuretic hormone (ADH), the client may experience water diuresis. Hypernatremia may result if sufficient water is NOT replaced orally or by IV.

The Pathophysiology Behind Sodium Imbalance

SODIUM IMBALANCE (NORMAL 135–145 mEq/L)

Hyponatremia (< 135 mEq/L) ECF becomes hypotonic; fluid shifts into ICF will occur.		Hypernatremia (> 145 mEq/L) ECF becomes hypertonic; fluid shift out of ICF will occur. True cellular "dehydration."	
• Decrease in the ECF volume • Diuretics (loops, thiazides) • Renal disease • Edematous states–cirrhosis, heart failure, nephrotic syndrome • Fluid replacement with isotonic fluids/pure water during extended vomiting, diarrhea, or sweating • Skin losses–burns, wound drainage, GI obstruction, peripheral edema, ascites	• Infusion with excess rate and/or amount of D_5W • Fluid gain • Inadequate sodium intake (NPO) • Excessive use of tap water enemas or solutions for hypotonic irrigating • Increased antidiuretic hormone (SIADH)–Hyponatremia is caused from the Na^+ being diluted • Addison's Disease–Adrenal insufficiency which leads to low sodium absorption (no mineral corticoid, which is aldosterone = do not hold sodium or water. Instead these two are "wasted" in the urine)	• Fluid replacement with concentrated fluids after extended vomiting or diarrhea • Tube feeding with no extra water intake • Bicarbonate intake • Infusion with excess hypertonic IV fluids–3% saline solutions	• Lack of ability to respond to or communicate thirst (i.e., infancy, dementia, etc.)  • Age-related changes such as a decrease in thirst response/reduction in the body–water content in older clients • Diabetes insipidus (lack of antidiuretic hormone) • Excessive water loss from very high fever, burns, hyperglycemia, watery diarrhea • Excessive intake of sodium • Excessive sodium retention such as with Aldosteronism, Cushing's syndrome, kidney failure, and some meds such as glucocorticosteroids

Fluid & Electrolytes
(Sung to the tune of "Jingle Bells")

Sodium, sodium is found OUTSIDE the cells
Low levels come from pooping, puking, peeing!!

Verse 2

Sodium, sodium is found OUTSIDE the cells
High levels come from too much salt and Not drin……king!

Verse 3 (Discussed in next chapter)

Potassium, potassium is found INSIDE the cells.
Low levels come from Lasix and laxatives.

Verse 4

Potassium, potassium is found INSIDE the cells.
High levels come from some meds and renal fail…..ure!

Verse 5

Electrolytes, electrolytes like sodium and potassium
Don't have to be that hard when you sing our song!

Fluid Types

Fluids in the body typically are not found in the pure forms. There are three types of solutions: isotonic, hypotonic, and hypertonic. During the review of fluid and electrolyte concepts, we will be reviewing recommended IV fluids. It is helpful to have an understanding of the concentration of these fluids.

1. Isotonic Dehydration: Definition is *equal tension*. If a client experiences isotonic dehydration, then the client is losing sodium and water in equal proportions. The outcome is intravascular volume depletion. This would require an isotonic IV fluid which means that is has **the same solute** (particles dissolved in a solution) concentrations as another solution. If both fluids that are next to each other in compartments are equal in concentration, then each area can say to the other, *"Stay in place; there is no need for moving!"* No fluid shift will take place. Osmotic pressure is the same in and out of the cells, so they will not shrink or swell with fluid movement.

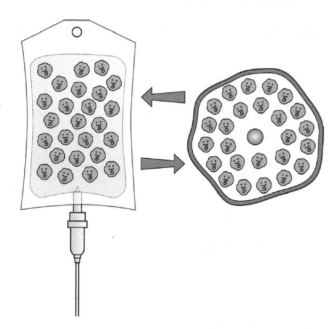

What does this mean to you when learning this information? An example of an IV fluid may be **0.9% Sodium Chloride (Normal Saline solution)**. This is an isotonic fluid, since the concentration of sodium in the solution is close to equal to the concentration of sodium in the blood. Another other example would be **Lactated Ringer's**. There will be no fluid shifts due to concentration being similar to blood!

How do you know if this Isotonic fluid was effective? What would be the expected outcomes? With fluid deficits and hyponatremia, these values would be decreased. After receiving isotonic fluid, these values below would all increase. Monitoring the trends and the changes with these clinical findings are of paramount importance for evaluating the effectiveness of the care.

Expected Outcomes from Isotonic Fluids

1. **CVP** (central venous pressure) (normal range: 2–6 mm Hg) Trend for **increases** to normal range

2. **PAWP** (pulmonary artery wedge pressure) (normal range: 8–12 mm Hg) Trend for **increases to normal range**

3. **BP**–Trend for **increases to normal range**

4. **Urinary output**–Trend for **increases to normal range**

Now let's move on and review hypotonic dehydration.

2. Hypotonic Dehydration: If a client has a low serum osmolality, then fluid leaks from the vascular space into the interstitial spaces and the cells. The outcome is swelling of the cells!

INSANELY EASY TIP! "Hypo" rhymes with "**Low**" osmolality. These clients require **HYPERTONIC IV SOLUTIONS!** "**HY**" PERTONIC has "**HIGH**" Solutes (more than blood)!!! Can lead to a complication with **SHRINKING CELLS**!

Clients can develop ascites, edema, and present with an alteration in the level of consciousness. These changes can be seen in clients with **hyponatremia**, **hypoalbuminemia**, and **SIADH**. This would require a **hypertonic** solution.

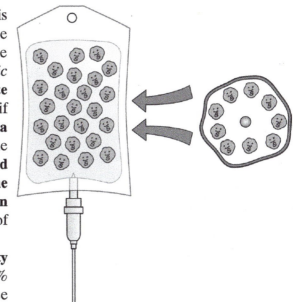

What does this mean to you when learning this information? For this type of dehydration, it will be important to administer a hypertonic solution. You may be asking yourself, *"Why hypertonic solution for a hypotonic dehydration?"* A hypertonic solution has a **higher solute concentration than another solution**. For example, if one solution contains a **large amount of sodium and a second solution has significantly less sodium**, then the **first solution is hypertonic in comparison to the second solution**. The response will be for the **fluid from the second solution to shift into the hypertonic solution in order to begin equalizing** the concentrations in each of the solutions.

Hypertonic solutions are those that have an **osmolality greater than 340 mOsm/kg**. These include Dextrose 5% in 0.45% or half-strength NaCl (Normal Saline), Dextrose 5% in 0.9% NaCl (Normal Saline), 3% sodium chloride solution, Dextrose 10% in Normal Saline solution. Other hypertonic solutions include albumin, Hespan, and TPN. These IV fluids will draw fluids from the intracellular space resulting in **shrinking cells** and **expansion of the extracellular space**. Since hypertonic solutions pull fluids from the cells, clients are at risk for **dehydration of the cells**. Due to this complication, clients with diabetic ketoacidosis (DKA) should not receive these fluids.

How do you know if the hypertonic fluids were effective? (Refer to chart below.)

Expected Outcomes from Hypertonic Fluids

1. **Daily weight** WDL
2. **Vital signs** WDL
3. **LOC** WDL
4. **Cardiac:** Normal heart sounds, no signs of failure
5. **Respiratory:** Breath sounds clear and equal

3. Hypertonic Dehydration: The osmolality of the blood is elevated. With this dehydration, fluid is drawn into the vascular space from the interstitial spaces and the cells to assist in maintaining homeostasis. The outcome can be cellular dehydration. Clients with diabetic ketoacidosis with the ketones and the glucose may experience this type of dehydration.

INSANELY EASY TIP! "**HY**" pertonic dehydration rhymes with "**HIGH**" osmolality. These clients require HYPOTONIC IV SOLUTIONS! HY "**PO**" TONIC has "**LOW**" Solutes (less than blood)!!! A complication can be the **CELLS SWELL!**

What does this mean to you when learning this information? For this type of dehydration, it will be important to administer a hypotonic solution. You may be asking yourself, *"Why hypotonic solution for a hypertonic dehydration?"* A hypotonic solution has a lower solute concentration than the other solution. For example, if one solution contains one part of sodium and the other contains several parts, then the first solution would be hypotonic in comparison with the second solution. The result would be the fluid from the hypotonic solution would shift into the second solution until the two solutions had equal shift and the two solutions had equal concentrations of sodium. The goal of the body is always to remain in balance or homeostasis. Hypotonic solutions have an osmolality less than 240 mOsm/kg. These IV fluids would include: 0.45% NaCl (normal saline solution) or any solutions containing more water with less basic electrolytes. The osmotic pressure draws water into the cells from the extracellular fluid.

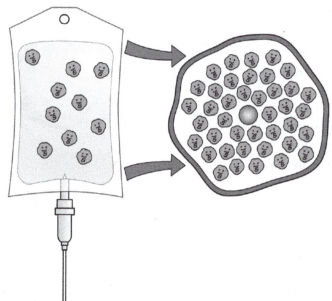

How do you know if the hypotonic fluids were effective? (Refer to chart below.)

Expected Outcomes from Hypotonic Fluids

1. **Urine output WDL**

2. **HR WDL**

3. **Daily weights WDL**

Hypotonic solutions should NOT be administered to clients at risk for increased intracranial pressure such as clients who had a CVA, neurosurgery, or headache. Signs of increased ICP include alterations in the LOC of the client, motor or sensory deficits, alterations in the pupil size and response to light. Hypotonic fluids should NOT be used if a client has suffered from abnormal shifts of fluid into the interstitial space or body cavities. Examples of these include a burn, liver disease or trauma.

INSANELY EASY TIPS for review!

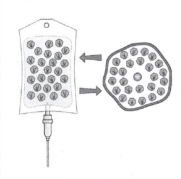

Isotonic IV Fluid = Same concentration as in the cell.

An example of an **Isotonic fluid** IV fluid is **0.9% Sodium Chloride (Normal Saline solution)**. This is an isotonic fluid, since the concentration of sodium in the solution is close to being equal to the concentration of sodium in the cell. Another example of Isotonic fluid would be **Lactated Ringer's**. There will be NO fluid shifts due to concentration being similar to the blood.

Hypertonic IV Fluid = Higher solute concentration than in the cell.
"SHRINKS THE CELL."

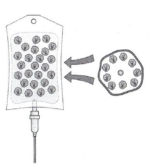

An example of a **Hypertonic** IV fluid is **3% Sodium Chloride (Normal Saline solution)**. This is a hypertonic fluid, since the concentration of sodium in the IV fluid will draw fluid from the intracellular space resulting in **SHRINKING cells** and **expansion of the extracellular space**. The response will be for the **fluid from the second solution to shift into the hypertonic solution in order to begin equalizing** the concentrations in each of the solutions.

Hypotonic IV Fluid = Lower solute concentration than in the cell.
"SWELLS THE CELL."

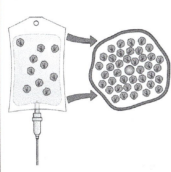

An example represents a **Hypotonic** IV fluid is **0.45% NaCl (normal saline solution)** or any solutions containing more water with less basic electrolytes. For example, if one solution contains one part of sodium and the other contains several parts, then the first solution would be hypotonic in comparison with the second solution. The result would be the fluid from the hypotonic solution would shift into the second solution until the two solutions had equal shift and the two solutions had equal concentrations of sodium. The goal of the body is always to remain in balance or homeostasis.

IV Solution Review

IV Solution	Indications	Priority Clinical Considerations/Assessments
Isotonic: 0.9% Sodium Chloride (Normal Saline solution) Lactated Ringer's Solution	• Hyponatremia • Fluid Challenges • Shock • Fluid replacement in diabetic ketoacidosis • Fluid loss • Dehydration	Since this replaces extracellular fluid, do not use in clients with edema, cardiac failure, or hypernatremia; this could lead to overload. Isotonic fluid is filling the vascular space. Expected outcomes: • CVP (central venous pressure) (normal range: 2–6 mm Hg) Trending for increasing to normal range • PAWP (pulmonary artery wedge pressure) (normal range: 8–12 mm Hg) Trending for increasing to normal range • BP–Trend for increasing • Urinary output–Trend for increasing
Hypertonic: D5.45 Normal Saline 3% Sodium Chloride Dextrose 10% in Normal Saline solution	• DKA after the initial treatment with normal saline solution and half-normal saline solution, hypertonic fluid prevents cerebral edema and hypoglycemia • Severe dilutional hyponatremia • Conditions where some glucose is necessary	Clients with DKA, use when glucose is < 250 mg/dL. Administer cautiously to prevent pulmonary edema. It is imperative to assess neurological assessments closely. Clients with cardiac or renal disease may be unable to handle extra fluid. Monitor serum glucose levels. Observe infusion site closely for signs of infiltration. Expected outcomes: • Daily weight WDL. • Vital signs WDL. • LOC WDL. • Cardiac: Normal heart sounds, no signs of failure. • Respiratory: Breath sounds clear and equal.
Hypotonic: 0.45% NaCl (normal saline solution)	• Gastric fluid loss from nasogastric suctioning or vomiting • Hypertonic dehydration • DKA after (normal saline solution and before dextrose infusion) • Sodium and chloride depletion • Water replacement	Expected outcomes: • Urine output WDL. • HR WDL. • Daily weights. • May cause cardiovascular collapse or increased intracranial pressure, so use cautiously. Do not use for clients with burns, hepatic disease, or trauma.

Snapshot of the Review of IV Fluids!

We do NOT expect you to be an expert at these fluids, but we do want you to be able to have an understanding of what category the IV fluids are in. This will provide you with the necessary information to *"Verify the accuracy or appropriateness of an order"* for IV fluid. The key to nursing is SAFE care! Remember, Isotonic fluids are = to the sodium concentration of the blood. **Hypo**tonic fluids have a **low**er sodium concentration than the blood. **Hyper**tonic fluids have a **high**er sodium concentration than the blood. Isotonic should be used for intravascular volume depletion. Hypertonic fluids **"SHRINK CELLS"**. Hypertonic fluids have a higher osmolality > 340 mOsm/kg. Hypotonic fluids **"SWELLS THE CELL"**. Hypotonic fluids have a **low**er osmolality < 240 mOsm/kg.

INSANELY EASY TIP!
High Serum Sodium = Administer Hypotonic Fluids initially
Low Serum Sodium = Isotonic or Hypertoinc Fluids if severe

Note: Nurses do not prescribe, but nurses do "Verify the accuracy or appropriateness of an order" for IV fluid!

SAFETY Concept: Fluid and Electrolytes **Hyponatremia (< 135 mEq/L)** **Sodium 135–145 mEq/L**		
System-Specific Assessments ****Assessments in both causes!** **(Assessments vary based on a normal, decreased, or increased ECF volume.)**	**First-Do Priority Interventions** **"SODIUM"**	**Evaluation of Expected Outcomes**

Solution Deficit (Na⁺ loss)
 	
• ↓ Serum Na⁺ < 135 mEq/L**
• ↓ in cerebral function**
• ↓ LOC; risk for seizures**
• ↓ Muscle strength**
• ↓ Deep Muscle Reflexes (DTR)**
• ↓ Volume = fast HR (thready pulse)
  ↓ Blood Pressure; orthostatic hypotension
  ↓ Urine output
  ↓ Weight
  ↓ Sodium intake
 	
Dilutional Hyponatremia (Water excess) "HIGH Fluid Retention"
• ↓ Serum Na⁺ < 135 mEq/L**
• ↓ Impaired cerebral function**
• ↓ LOC; risk for seizures**
• ↓ Muscle strength**
• ↓ Deep Muscle Reflexes (DTR)**
 	
↑ Blood Pressure
↑ Urine output
↑ Weight
↑ HR (tachycardia)
	Seizure precautions**
	
	Occurs in Addison disease, Diabetic acidosis, and Renal disease; clients who are NPO; SIADH; perspiring, vomiting, diarrhea; burns or excessive administration of D₅W
	
	Daily weight**; diet foods high in Na⁺ if cause is low Na⁺ intake (i.e., milk, condiments, cheese, etc.)
	
	If retaining fluids, restrict fluids; irrigate NG tube with normal saline
	
	Understand the cause: use hypertonic fluids if severe; isotonic if moderate (0.9% Sodium Chloride) or if need to restore ECF volume.
	
	Monitor vital signs (T, HR, RR, BP, I & O); weight is one of the best indicators of fluid status; skin turgor; monitor for GI changes (ie., hyperactive bowel sounds, increased GI motility, abdominal cramping, anorexia, nausea, vomiting) and Neurological assessments (pupils, LOC, headache); safety (fall precautions; change positions slowly)**
	
	**Both causes of hypernatremia include these interventions!
		Solution deficit (Na⁺ loss)
		
		• Serum Na⁺ 135–145 mEq/L
		• Impaired cerebral function improved
		• LOC normal for client; no seizures
		• Muscle strength normal
		• Deep Muscle Reflexes (DTR) WDL
		• Volume = fast HR (thready pulse)–HR now WDL
		  Blood Pressure WDL
		  Urine output WDL
		  Weight WDL
		  Sodium intake WDL
		
		Dilutional Hyponatremia (Water excess) "HIGH Fluid Retention"
		  Serum Na⁺ 135–145 mEq/L
		• Impaired cerebral function improved
		• LOC normal for client; no seizures
		• Muscle strength WDL
		• Deep Muscle Reflexes (DTR) WDL
		  Blood Pressure WDL
		  Urine output WDL
		  Weight WDL
		  HR WDL

INSANELY EASY TIP for "Hyponatremia"!

1. If the sodium is **high or low, SEIZURE precautions** are important for SAFE care!

2. If the client is hypervolemic, then the sodium is low due to being diluted. This is why the fluids may be restricted.

3. If the client is **NOT** hypervolemic, but is not taking in enough sodium, then the sodium intake should be increased.

4. Notice in dilutional hyponatremia the client's **weight and blood pressure may increase** due to the extra fluid.

The BOTTOM LINE is that the sodium is low either from a decrease in sodium intake or from too much fluid causing a diluted or low value. *Let's look at this another way. Do you remember when you were younger and played in the sandbox. You may have put the same amount of sand in 3 containers, but different amounts of water in each of these. Which one was more diluted? Of course, the one with the most fluid! You have taken another step in mastering this concept of hyponatremia secondary to fluid retention!!*

SAFETY Concept: Fluid and Electrolytes
Hypernatremia (> 145 mEq/L)
Sodium (135–145 mEq/L)

System-Specific Assessments	First-Do Priority Interventions	Evaluation of Expected Outcomes
"DRIED" (hemoconcentrated) **"EDEMA"** (Fluid Excess from Na⁺ Retention)	**"RESTRICT"**	**"DRIED"** (hemoconcentrated) **"EDEMA"** (Fluid Excess from Na⁺ Retention)

System-Specific Assessments	First-Do Priority Interventions	Evaluation of Expected Outcomes

FLUID DEFICIT "DRIED" (Hemoconcentration of Na⁺, water loss)
 	
Dryness of mucous membranes ↑
  ↑ Concentration in urine due to decrease in urine output
  ↑ Deep muscle reflexes
Red, flushed skin ↑
  ↑ restless (irritable)progressing to confusion
  ↑ Serum Na⁺ > 145 mEq/L
Increased temperature; I & O
  ↑ concentration in urine output due to decrease in urine output
  ↑ thirst (may be ↓ in elderly!)
  ↑ risk for seizures
Elevated HR
Decreased weight; decreased blood pressure; decreased CVP, decreased urine output
 	
Fluid Excess from Na⁺ retention occurs from excessive salt intake, increased renal retention, etc.
 	
"EDEMA"
Edema (pitting)
Decrease in the hematocrit; diet ↑ in Na⁺
Elevated weight; elevated BP and HR
Mentation decreased (lethargic)
A flushing of the skin; assess lab Serum Na⁺ > 145 mEq/L
	Restrict fluid intake if experiencing fluid retention.
	  Remember oral hygiene!
	  Restrict foods high in sodium.
	
	Evaluate for cerebral changes such as headache, nausea; evaluate for seizures and initiate seizure precautions.**
	
	Strict intake and output; Safety (falls).**
	
	The blood pressure is elevated (fluid excess); the blood pressure is low for hemoconcentrated Na+ (fluid deficit); VS need to be monitored.
	
	Review origin of hypernatremia.**
	
	If there is a fluid deficit, administer Hypotonic IV fluids for fluid loss (ie., hypertonic dehydration). If client is in shock or requires fluid challenges administer (Isotonic fluids). These will be prescribed by the health care provider. **Encourage fluid intake and discourage sodium intake.**
	
	Check daily weight** ; neurological assessments.**
	
	The excess fluid may be removed by diuretics.
	
	**Both causes of hypernatremia include these interventions!*
		(Hemoconcentration of Na⁺, water loss)
		
		Dry mucous membranes are not a problem (moist); urine output WDL for client.
		Deep muscle reflexes WDL for client.
		Red, flushed skin not present; restless (irritable), progressing to confusion not a problem (alert/oriented).
		Review lab: Serum Na⁺ 135–145 mEq/L (WDL).
		Increased temperature not a problem (afebrile).
		I & O WDL; no increase in urine concentration; no increase in thirst; no seizures.
		Elevated HR not a problem. HR WDL for client.
		Decreased weight not a problem (within normal range for client); decreased CVP not a problem (normal:1–8 mm Hg).
		
		(Fluid Excess from Na⁺ Retention)
		
		Edema (pitting)–No pitting edema
		Decrease in the hematocrit– WDL
		Elevated weight; elevated BP; HR– not a problem; WDL
		Mentation decreased (lethargic) (Not a problem) alert/oriented
		A flushing of the skin (not a problem) assess lab serum Na⁺ 135–145 mEq/L

Foods High in Sodium

Any food in a bag, box, can, or a bottle, condiments, processed meats, ham, any food with salt added (i.e., salted nuts) should be avoided for clients with hypernatremia, hypervolemia, and medical conditions that require fluid restriction.

"SODIUM"

Salt limit, eating and cooking

Omit salty snacks

Do use spices/herbs to enhance taste

Include fresh fruits and vegetables

Use lemon juice for flavor

Minimize canned foods, ketchup, sodas

Salty Six: The Foods Most Frequently Eaten

Breads and rolls

Cold cuts and cured meats

Pizza (*Oh no!! This is sad!* :(*We have eaten a lot of pizza while writing this book!*)

Poultry

Soup

Sandwiches

Reference: American Heart Association (2014)

Labs and Diagnostic Tests/Procedures	
Labs = Hyponatremia	Labs = Hypernatremia
Serum Sodium < 135 mEq/L	Serum Sodium > 145 mEq/L
Serum Osmolarity < 280 mOsm/kg	Serum Osmolarity > 300 mOsm/kg

Questions evaluating knowledge. Need to know information before you can apply information. (Answers below.)

1. What is the normal serum sodium level? _____

2. What is one example of an isotonic IV fluid? _____

3. What is one example of a hypertonic IV fluid? _____

4. What is one example of a hypotonic IV fluid? _____

5. What is an easy way to remember system specific assessments when the client has hypernatremia secondary to fluid deficit? _____

6. What is an easy way to remember system specific assessments when the client has hypernatremia secondary to fluid retention? _____

7. What is an easy way to remember the "First Do Priority Nursing Interventions" for a client with hyponatremia? _____

8. What is an easy way to remember the "First Do Priority Nursing Interventions" for a client with hypernatremia? _____

9. List two foods high in sodium. _____

10. List three interventions that apply to both hyper and hyponatremia. _____
_____

INSANELY EASY TIP for "Hypernatremia"!

1. If the sodium is **high or low, SEIZURE** precautions are important for SAFE care!

2. If the client has fluid volume deficit, then the sodium is high due to being concentrated. Notice **all of the arrows are going** ↑ (with the system specific assessments) except the BP, CVP, weight, and urine output.

3. This is why fluids will be encouraged and sodium intake will be discouraged for clients who are hypernatremic and have a fluid deficit.

4. If the client is taking in too much sodium or has a medical condition that retains sodium, then the priority of care will be restrict fluids and administer diuretics (loop diuretics) to assist in removing the extra fluid.

5. Notice in fluid excess with the high sodium, the client's **weight and blood pressure may increase** due to the extra fluid. (*The exact opposite from the hypernatemia caused by fluid deficit.*)

Answers:
1. 135–145 MEq/L
2. 0.9% Sodium Chloride (Normal Saline solution). Lactated Ringer's Solution
3. D5.45 NS, 3% Sodium Chloride
4. 0.45% NaCl
5. "DRIED"
6. "EDEMA"
7. "SODIUM"
8. "RESTRICT"
9. Milk, condiments, cheese
10. Seizure precautions, daily weight, and intake and outputs

Clinical Decision-Making Exercises

1. Which of these assessment findings would be most important to report to the healthcare provider for a client with a serum sodium of 147 mEq/L?

    ① Dry mucous membranes.

    ② Complaints of being thirsty.

    ③ Urine output drop from 95 mL/hour to 40 mL/hour.

    ④ Skin warm to touch.

2. Which of these orders is the priority plan for a client who has a sodium level of 148 mEq/L?

    ① Adminintster sodium polystyrene sulfonate (Kayexalate).

    ② Administer sodium bicarbonate as prescribed.

    ③ Administer 3% Sodium Chloride as prescribed.

    ④ Administer 0.45 Normal Saline IV fluids as prescribed.

3. Which of these assessment findings would be most consistent with a serum sodium level–128 mEq/L? *Select all that apply.*

    ① Hypotension.

    ② Constipation.

    ③ Weight increase.

    ④ Decreased DTRs.

    ⑤ Hyperactivity.

4. What is the priority of care for a client with a sodium level of 132 mEq/L, BP–150/90; weight gain of 2 lbs in last 24 hours and has an order to push PO fluids?

    ① Review the plan with the UAP.

    ② Develop a plan for the UAP to administer 60 mL of oral fluids per hour.

    ③ Notify the provider of care and verify order.

    ④ Review the importance of recording weight every 48 hours.

5. Which nursing intervention would be most appropriate to delegate to the unlicensed assistive personnel (unlicensed personnel or CNA) for a client with a serum sodium of 148 mEq/L?

    ① Restrict PO water intake.

    ② Evaluate effectiveness of diuretic.

    ③ Provide oral hygiene every 2–4 hours.

    ④ Provide a snack of crackers and cheese.

6. Which nursing intervention is the priority for a client with a serum sodium of 152 mEq/L?

    ① Administer IV fluids 0.9 % Sodium Chloride as ordered.

    ② Place suction at the bedside.

    ③ Monitor I & O.

    ④ Limit water intake.

7. What is the priority nursing intervention for a client with a serum sodium level 128mEq/L?

    ① Have suction at the bedside.

    ② Encourage water intake to 2000 mL/day.

    ③ Question order for IV for Normal Saline.

    ④ Restrict cheese and condiments.

8. What would be the priority lab value to report to the healthcare provider for a client who has an IV infusing of 0.9% NaCL at 115 mL/hour; has a nasogatric tube to suction, a colostomy, and is becoming restless?

    ① Creatinine–1.2 mg/dL.

    ② Hemoglobin–14 g/dL, Hematocrit 58%.

    ③ Specific gravity of urine–1.029.

    ④ Serum sodium–153 mEq/L.

9. What lab report would indicate that an elderly client with dementia has not been drinking enough fluids?

    ① Creatinine–1.5 mg/dL.

    ② Hemoglobin–14 mg/dL, Hematocrit 42%.

    ③ Serum sodium–153 mEq/L.

    ④ Urine specific gravity–1.003.

10. Which of these actions by the LPN would require intervention by the charge nurse to further educate LPN about appropriate standard of care for a client with a serum sodium of 133 mEq/L?

    ① Irrigates the nasogastric tube with tap water.

    ② Assists the UAP in obtaining the daily weight.

    ③ Due to poor sodium intake, reviews food good for snacks such as milk and cheese.

    ④ Discusses with the client the importance of changing positions slowly when getting up from lying down.

Answers and Rationales

1. Which of these **assessment findings** would be **most important to report** to the healthcare provider for a client with a **serum sodium of 147 mEq/L?**

    ① INCORRECT: This would be important, but not the most important to report.

    ② INCORRECT: Being thirsty is an early compensatory mechanism and would not be most important.

    ③ **CORRECT: Urine output drops from 95 mL/hr to 40 mL/hr. The urine is trending down. When the sodium starts increasing due to a decrease in volume, the thirst is stimulated, antidiuretic hormone is stimulated along with aldosterone release, there may be a complication with hypernatremica (fluid deficit). All of these will contribute to a decrease in the urination resulting in an increase in the concentration. This would be the most important to report.**

    ④ INCORRECT: This is a concern, but not the most important, since the urine output is trending down.

The strategy for answering this question is to compare and contrast the options and link to the sodium level. While each of these assessments do indicate a complication with hypernatremia, the correct option 3 is the most important due to the physiological changes that have taken place to result in the downward trend of the urine output.

Physiological Adaptation: Recognize signs and symptoms of complications and intervene appropriately when providing care.

Physiological Adaptation: Manage the care of the client with a fluid and electrolyte imbalance.

Physiological Adaptation: Monitor trends and changes in client condition and intervene appropriately when providing care.

2. Which of these orders is the **priority plan** for a client who has a **sodium level of 148 mEq/L?**

    ① INCORRECT: This would be correct if a client had hyperkalemia.

---

    ② INCORRECT: This would be unsafe for a client with a sodium level that is already elevated.

    ③ INCORRECT: This would be unsafe for this client. Hypotonic fluids would be appropriate then isotonic. Hypertonic fluids would be if sodium was very low.

    ④ **CORRECT: Administer 0.45 Normal Saline IV fluids as prescribed. This is appropriate for this situation. These IV fluids will draw fluids from the intracellular space and may result in shrinking the cells in order to expand the extracellular space. Since hypotonic solutions pull fluids from the cells, clients are at risk for dehydration of the cells. Hypotonic solutions have an osmolality less than 240 mOsm/kg. 0.45% Normal Saline (Normal Saline) is an example of this solution which contains more water with less basic electrolytes. The key is to keep monitoring the serum sodium level in order to provide safe care**

The strategy is to understand that a hypotonic solution has a lower solute concentration than the other solution. For example, if one solution contains one part of sodium and the other contains several parts, then the first solution would be hypotonic in comparison with the second solution. The result would be the fluid from the hypotonic solution would shift into the second solution until the two solutions had equal shift and the two solutions had equal concentrations of sodium. The goal of the body is always to remain in balance or homeostasis. While you are learning this concept, the memory tool that will assist you is the following:

High Serum Sodium = Hypotonic Fluids initially

Low Serum Sodium = Isotonic or Hypertonic Fluids if severe

Physiological Adaptation: Manage the care of the client with a fluid and electrolyte imbalance.

3. Which of these **assessment findings** would be most consistent with a **serum sodium level–128 mEq/L**? Select all that apply.

    ① **CORRECT: Hyponatremia can result in a low blood pressure.**

    ② INCORRECT: Constipation is not consistent with hyponatremia.

    ③ INCORRECT: The assessment findings for a client with hyponatremia would be weight loss.

    ④ **CORRECT: Decreased DTRs is correct for a client with hyponatremia.**

    ⑤ INCORRECT: The client would have decrease in muscle strength and/or a decrease in DTR's, but not hyperactivity.

The strategy for answering this question is to remember the assessment findings for the Solution deficit (Na⁺ loss) are decreased. (*Serum Na⁺ < 135 mEq/L, LOC, risk for seizures, Muscle strength, Deep Muscle Reflexes (DTR), Volume ↓ = fast HR (thready pulse), Blood Pressure, Orthostatic Hypotension, Urine output, Weight, and/or Sodium intake are all ↓.*) Any type of client who presents with hyponatremia may present with these decreased assessments. See how easy this can be! You CAN do it! This covers a lot of information with just one strategy linked to hyponatremia.

Physiological Adaptation: Manage the care of the client with a fluid and electrolyte imbalance.

4. What is the **priority of care for a client with a sodium level of 132 mEq/L, BP–150/90; weight gain of 2 lbs in last 24 hours** and has an order to **push PO fluids**?

    ① INCORRECT: This plan is inappropriate for this client, so there is not a need to review the plan.

    ② INCORRECT: This client should not have extra fluids.

    ③ **CORRECT: Notify the provider of care and verify order. The client has a low sodium with other assessments indicating fluid excess, so if the client continues to take in more fluids, the sodium level will continue to decrease as a result of being too dilutional.**

    ④ INCORRECT: This nursing action should be done daily versus every 48 hours.

The strategy for this question is to recognize the sodium level is low, but the other vital signs indicate fluid retention, so the low sodium may be secondary to being hemodilutional. Another strategy you could use if you had no idea, is that options 1 and 2 are similar in that they are encouraging fluids, so you could delete these since they are similar. Option 4 is not frequent enough, so then you could use the process of elimination to get to the correct answer. (*We did not write this book for basic test taking strategies. We wrote this to help you connect, apply and remember the concepts and become proficient at clinical decision-making! When it comes to your SUCCESS; however, we want to help you in any way we can!*)

Physiological Adaptation: Manage the care of the client with a fluid and electrolyte imbalance.

Management of Care: Verify appropriateness and/or accuracy of treatment order.

5. Which nursing **intervention would be most appropriate to delegate to the unlicensed assistive personnel (unlicensed personnel or CNA)** for a client with a **serum sodium of 148 mEq/L**?

    ① INCORRECT: This would be inappropriate nursing care for a client with hyper-natremia. Fluid is important. Fluids would be restricted if there was evidence of fluid retention; however, there are no assessments indicating fluid excess in this clinical situation.

    ② INCORRECT: No diuretic should be given due to client already having an elevated sodium.

    ③ **CORRECT: Provide oral hygiene every 2-4 hours. This would be very important for a client with hypernatremia due to dry mouth.**

    ④ INCORRECT: Crackers and cheese are high in sodium and should not be given to client.

The strategy is to remember First-Do Priority Interventions, "**RESTRICT,**" will assist you organizing the nursing care. If a client is hypernatremic, they are dry and if they dry they need oral hygiene. This is also within the scope of practice for the UAP.

Physiological Adaptation: Manage the care of the client with a fluid and electrolyte imbalance.

Management of Care: Assign and supervise care provided by others (i.e., LPN/VN, assistive personnel, other RNs).

6. Which **nursing intervention** is the **priority** for a client with a **serum sodium of 152 mEq/L?**

    ①   INCORRECT: The correct fluids for hypernatremia would be hypotonic such as 0.45% NS.

    ②   **CORRECT: A complication of hypernatremia is seizures. It is important to have equipment at bedside for a seizure. Additional equipment may include an ambu bag, an airway, suction equipment, etc.**

    ③   INCORRECT: While this is important, it is not the priority over option 2.

    ④   INCORRECT: With this sodium level, the client should drink fluids with no additional sodium added.

The strategy is to recognize if the client has either hypo/hypernatremia and in this situation it is hypernatremia. With either, you will be concerned with seizures. Safety is a priority, so equipment at the bedside to support client if a seizure occurred would be a priority.

Physiological Adaptation: Manage the care of the client with a fluid and electrolyte imbalance.

Management of Care: Prioritize Delivery of Care.

Safety and Infection Control: Facilitate appropriate and safe use of equipment.

7. What is the priority nursing intervention for a client with a **serum sodium level 128mEq/L?**

    ①   **CORRECT: Have suction at the bedside. This would be a priority due to risk for seizures.**

    ②   INCORRECT: Encourage water intake to 2000mL/day would be inappropriate for this client since it would contribute to Na⁺ being more dilutional.

    ③   INCORRECT: There is no need to question. It is isotonic and may be the drug of choice.

    ④   INCORRECT: Cheese and condiments are high in sodium and would be appropriate for client to eat.

The strategy is to recognize that with either hypo/hypernatremia and in this situation it is hyponatremia, there may be a risk for seizures. With either alterations in the sodium level, seizure precautions are important. Safety is a priority, so equipment at the bedside to support client if a seizure occurred would be a priority. Notice on question 6, the answer is the same. Seizures can result from hyper or hyponatremia. *Repetition is the mother of learning! We want to make certain you have this concept in your memory!*

Physiological Adaptation: Manage the care of the client with a fluid and electrolyte imbalance.

Management of Care: Prioritize Delivery of Care.

Safety and Infection Control: Facilitate appropriate and safe use of equipment.

8. What would be the **priority lab value to report** to the healthcare provider for a client who has an **IV infusing of 0.9% NaCL at 115 mL/hour; has a nasogatric tube to suction, a colostomy, and is becoming restless?**

    ①   INCORRECT: There is no need to report this value. The normal is 0.6–1.2 mg/dL.

    ②   INCORRECT: While the hematocrit does indicate a fluid deficit, this would not be the priority over 4.

    ③   INCORRECT: Specific gravity of urine– 1.029 does indicate client is not well hydrated; however, the Na⁺ is still priority.

    ④   **CORRECT: This is the priority. The client is losing fluids; however, the replacement is only with sodium. The lab indicates client has hypernatremia. This may result in fluid retention causing an increase in the workload on the heart.**

The strategy for answering this question is to review the key assessments in the stem of the question and then to review the options. Ask yourself which of these options would create the highest risk for this client. Yes, the hematocrit and specific gravity are increased, but the sodium presents the highest risk to the client.

Reduction of Risk Potential: Monitor the results of the diagnostic testing (labs) and intervene as needed.

Physiological Adaptation: Manage the care of the client with a fluid and electrolyte imbalance.

9. What lab **report would indicate** that an **elderly client with dementia** has **not been drinking enough fluids?**

① INCORRECT: As the client ages, the renal creatinine will increase. This value does not indicate client is not getting enough fluids.

② INCORRECT: These values do not indicate a problem with lack of fluids. The hematocrit would be elevated if there was a complication.

③ **CORRECT: Due to the loss of some of the fluid in the serum resulting in dehydration, the serum sodium level may elevate.**

④ INCORRECT: This value actually indicates diluted urine. It would be increased if there was a fluid deficit.

The strategy is to understand that when clients do not take in enough fluids these lab values are elevated (i.e., hematocrit, sodium, specific gravity, and BUN). This will assist you in answering any question or taking care of any client who develops dehydration from not drinking fluids, vomiting, diarrhea, diuretics, etc. Refer to the mnemonic "**DEHYDRATION**" in the Concept Fluid Balance to assist you in reviewing which clients may develop hypernatremia due to fluid deficit

Reduction of Risk Potential: Monitor the results of the diagnostic testing (labs) and intervene as needed.

Physiological Adaptation: Manage the care of the client with a fluid and electrolyte imbalance.

10. Which of these **actions by the LPN would require intervention** by the charge nurse to **further educate LPN about appropriate standard of care for a client with a serum sodium of 133 mEq/L?**

① **CORRECT: NG Tube should be irrigated with Normal Saline.**

② INCORRECT: There is no need for intervention, since this is the standard of care.

③ INCORRECT: Due to poor sodium intake, reviews and reinforces food good for snacks such as milk and cheese. This is appropriate for the client.

④ INCORRECT: Discussing the importance of changing positions slowly when getting up from a supine position is important due to the risk of orthostatic hypotension. This can occur from hyponatremia, and does not require further intervention.

The strategy is to connect the concept of hyponatremia with the option that would require intervention due to not following standard of care. If you did not know that tap water would lead to hyponatremia, then look at the other options. Each of these are appropriate interventions for this client and do not require further intervention by the charge nurse.

Physiological Adaptation: Manage the care of the client with a fluid and electrolyte imbalance.

Management of Care: Recognize limitations of others and intervene.

Decision-Making Analysis Form

Use this tool to help identify why you missed any questions. As you enter the question numbers in the chart, you will begin to see patterns of why you answered incorrectly. This information will then guide you toward what you need to focus on in your continued studies. Ultimately, this analytical exercise will help you become more successful in answering questions!!!

Questions to ask:

1. Did I have the knowledge to answer the question? If not, what information do I need to review?

2. Did I know what the question was asking? Did I misread it or did I miss keywords in the stem of the question?

3. Did I misread or miss keywords in the distractors that would have helped me choose the correct answer?

4. Did I follow my gut reaction or did I allow myself to rationalize and then choose the wrong answer?

	Lack of Knowledge (Concepts, Systems, Pathophysiology, Medications, Procedures, etc.)	Missed Keywords or Misread the Stem of the Question	Missed Keywords or Misread the Distractors	Changed My Answer (Second-guessed myself, i.e., my first answer was correct.)
Put the # of each question you missed in the column that best explains why you think you answered it incorrectly.				

If you changed an answer because you talked yourself out of the correct answer, or you second-guessed yourself, this is an **EASY FIX: QUIT changing your answers**!!! Typically, the first time you read a question, you are about 95% right! The second time you read a question, you start talking yourself into changing the answer. The third time you read a question, you do not have a clue—and you are probably thinking "Who in the heck wrote this question?"

On the other hand, if you read a question too quickly and when you reread it you realize you missed some key information that would impact your decision (i.e., assessments, lab reports, medications, etc.), then it is appropriate to change your answer. When in doubt, go with the safe route: your first thought! Go with your gut instinct!

As you gain confidence in answering questions regarding specific nursing concepts, you will be able to successfully progress to answering higher-level questions about prioritization. Please refer to the *Prioritization Guidelines* in this book for a structure to assist you with this process.

You CAN do this!

"You measure the size of the accomplishment by the obstacles you had to overcome to reach your goals."

BOOKER T. WASHINGTON

References for Chapter 3

American Heart Association. (2014). Retrieved from http://www.heart.org/HEARTORG/Conditions/Conditions_UCM_001087_SubHomePage.jsp

Black, J M. and Hawks, J. H. (2009). *Medical surgical nursing: Clinical management for positive outcomes (8th ed.)*. Philadelphia: Elsevier/Saunders.

Daniels, R. & Nicoll, L. (2012). *Contemporary medical-surgical nursing*, (2nd ed.). Clifton Park, NY: Delmar Cengage Learning.

Ellis, K. M. (2012). *EKG: Plain and simple* (3rd ed.). Upper Saddle Road, NJ: Pearson.

Eliopoulos, C. (2014). *Gerontological nursing* (8th ed.), Philadelphia: Lippincott Williams & Wilkins.

Giddens, G. F. (2013). *Concepts for nursing practice*. St. Louis, MO: Mosby, an imprint of Elsevier.

Hogan, M. A. (2014). *Pathophysiology: Reviews and rationales* (3rd ed.) Boston, MA: Pearson.

Ignatavicius, D. D. and Workman, M. L. (2010). *Medical-surgical nursing: Patient-centered collaborative care* (6th ed.). Philadelphia: Elsevier/Saunders.

LeMone, P., Burke, K. M., and Bauldoff, G. (2011). *Medical-surgical nursing: Critical thinking in patient care* (5th ed.). Upper Saddle Road, NJ: Pearson/Prentice Hall.

Lewis, S., Dirksen, S., Heitkemper, M., Bucher, L., and Camera, I. (2011). *Medical surgical nursing: Assessment and management of clinical problems* (8th ed.). St. Louis: Mosby.

Manning, L. and Rayfield, S. (2014). *Nursing made insanely easy* (7th ed.). Duluth, GA: I CAN Publishing, Inc.

Manning, L. and Rayfield, S. (2013). *Pharmacology made insanely easy* (4th ed.). Duluth, GA: I CAN Publishing, Inc.

Metheny, Norma M, (2012) *Fluid and Electrolyte Balance: Nursing Considerations*, (5th Edition), Sudbury, MA: Jones and Bartlett Learning.

National Council of State Boards of Nursing, INC. (NCSBN) 2012. *Research brief: 2011 RN practice analysis: linking the NCLEX RN® examination to practice*. Retrieved from https://www.ncsbn.org/index.htm

Nettina, S. L. (2013). *Lippincott manual of nursing practice* (10th ed.). Philadelphia, PA: Walters Kluwer Health/Lippincott Williams & Wilkins.

North Carolina Concept Based Learning Editorial Board (2011). *Nursing a concept based approach to learning*, Upper Saddle Road, NJ: Pearson/Prentice Hall.

Osborn, K. S., Wraa, C. E., Watson, A. S., and Holleran, R. S. (2014). *Medical surgical nursing: Preparation for practice* (2nd ed.). Upper Saddle Road, NJ: Pearson.

Pagana, K. D. and Pagana, T. J. (2014). *Mosby's manual of laboratory and diagnostic tests* (5th ed.). St. Louis, MO: Mosby, an imprint of Elsevier.

Porth, C. (2011). *Essentials of pathophysiology* (3d ed.). Philadelphia, PA: Lippincott Williams ad Wilkins.

Porth, C. M. and Grossman, S. (2013). *Pathophysiology: Concepts of altered health states* (9th ed.). Philadelphia, PA: Lippincott Williams & Wilkins.

Potter, P. A., Perry, A. G., Stockert, P., and Hall, A. (2013). *Fundamentals of nursing* (8th ed.). St. Louis, MO: Pearson/Prentice Hall.

Smeltzer, S. C., Bare, B. G., Hinkle, J. L., and Cheever, K. H. (2010). *Brunner & Suddarth's Textbook of medical-surgical nursing* (12th ed.). Philadelphia: Lippincott Williams & Wilkins.

Wagner, K. D. and Hardin-Pierce, M. C. (2014). *High-Acuity nursing* (6th ed.). Boston: Pearson.

NOTES

Linking Multiple Systems to Pathophysiology of Potassium Imbalance
Concept Fluid and Electrolytes: Potassium Balance

A Snapshot of Potassium Balance

Potassium is the most abundant intracellular electrolyte. It is the major cation in the intracellular fluid. It is vital in cell metabolism; transmission of nerve impulses; functioning of the heart, lung, and muscle tissues, and acid-base balance. Total body potassium is related to mass, and most of the body's potassium is contained in muscle tissue. Adequate dietary intake of potassium and adequate kidney excretion are necessary to maintain potassium balance. Several factors, such as ECF pH, can cause potassium shifts into or out of the cells. Potassium has reciprocal action with sodium. Appropriate ECF/ICF potassium distribution is essential to have normal excitability of cellular membranes, including muscle, cardiac and neural tissues.

Hypokalemia is the result of an increased loss of potassium from the body or a movement of potassium into the cells. This would result in a potassium level < 3.5 mEq/L.

Hyperkalemia is the result of an increased potassium intake. This could also occur from potassium moving out of the cells, or a decrease in the renal excretion, resulting in an elevated potassium level greater than 5.0 mEq/L.

What is the Pathophysiology behind Potassium Imbalance?

The Pathophysiology Behind Potassium Imbalance

POTASSIUM IMBALANCE (NORMAL 3.5–5.0 mEq/L)

Hypokalemia (< 3.5 mEq/L)			Hyperkalemia (> 5.0 mEq/L)		
Normal Output But ↓ K⁺ intake	↑ Output Not Balanced by ↑ K⁺ Intake	Rapid K⁺ Shift from ECF into ICF	↓ K⁺ output or ↑ K⁺ Intake	↓ Output Not Balanced by ↓ K⁺ Intake	Rapid K⁺ Shift from ICF Into ECF
• Prolonged anorexia • Decrease in K⁺ rich foods • Prolonged use of IVs such as D₅W containing non-electrolytes	• Vomiting and/or acute or chronic diarrhea • Nasogastric suction without replacement • Increased aldosterone • Overuse of laxatives • K⁺ wasting diuretics (i.e., Loop Diuretics) • Steroid therapy in excess amounts	• Alkalosis • Excessive beta-adrenergic stimulation • Diabetics: Insulin and glucose move K⁺ into cell	• IV K⁺ infusion in excess • Excess in transfusion (> 8 units) of stored blood	• Urinary excretion is decreased (i.e., oliguria from renal failure, hypovolemia, etc.) • Potassium sparing diuretics, angiotensin-converting enzyme (ACE) inhibitors • IV potassium administered in excess • Salt substitutes • Adrenal insufficiency • Addison's disease	• Lack of insulin • Metabolic acidosis • Massive tissue injury (i.e., burns, fever, trauma)

SAFETY Concept: Fluid and Electrolytes
Hypokalemia (< 3.5 mEq/L)
Potassium (3.5–5.0 mEq/L)

System-Specific Assessments "CRAMPS"	First-Do Priority Interventions "POTASSIUM"	Evaluation of Expected Outcomes "CRAMPS"
Complications with GI losses (i.e., vomiting, NG suctioning) **C**onstipation	**P**otatoes, avocados, bananos, broccoli, etc. (↑K⁺)	**C**omplications with GI losses–not present; no constipation
Reflexes ↓, Respirations shallow and ↓	**O**ral potassium supplements	**R**eflexes WDL, Respirations not shallow = RR–WDL
Arrhythmias–ECG changes: **Inverted/flat T waves** (no K⁺ for repolarization) **A**bdominal distention; alkalosis; anxiety followed by confusion and eventually a coma	**T** waves depressed or flattened–monitor **A**rrhythmias–monitor **S**hallow ineffective respirations–monitor **S**ounds of breathing diminished–monitor **I**V supplement is **NEVER an IV push**!!! Never IM or SQ	**A**rrhythmias–Inverted T waves not present; NSR; abdomen soft with normoactive bowel sounds; alkalosis = NOT Present; LOC with no confusion
Muscle Cramps; muscles weak; skeletal muscles weak; monitor I & O	**U**rine output and intake–monitor **M**uscle cramping, muscle weakness (fall precautions), motility (GI) ↓, monitor K⁺ and digitalis level (low serum K⁺ can potentiate digitalis toxicity)	**M**uscle Cramps not present; muscles not weak; I & O WDL for client
Pulse–irregular and weak, ↓ BP		**P**ulse–Normal Sinus Rhythm (NSR) with no ECG changes with the T wave–not present
Serum K⁺ < 3.5 mEq/L		**S**erum K⁺–3.5–5.0 mEq/L; no falls; digitalis level WDL if client taking Digitalis

---

Drugs Associated with the Risk for Developing Hypokalemia

(For specifics, refer to the book *Pharmacology Made Insanely Easy*)

Adrenergics, such as epinephrine and albuterol
Amphotericin B
Corticosteroids
Diuretics, such as furosemide (Lasix) and Thiazides
Insulin

INSANELY EASY TIP! for Remembering Foods High in Potassium!
Remember they end in "**TOES**"!

Pota**TOES**

Toma**TOES**

Avocad**TOES**

Banana**TOES** (Bananas)

Orange**TOES**

Salt substitutes are high in potassium.

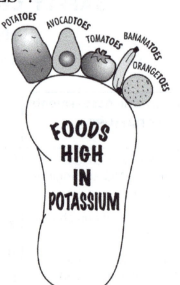

FOODS HIGH IN POTASSIUM

SAFETY Concept: Fluid and Electrolytes
Hyperkalemia (> 5.0 mEq/L)
Potassium (3.5–5.0 mEq/L)

SAFETY

System-Specific Assessments "DEATH"	First-Do Priority Interventions "STOPS"	Evaluation of Expected Outcomes "No DEATH"
Dysrhythmias–Irregular rhythm, bradycardia	**S**top infusion of IV potassium	**D**ysrhythmias–Irregular rhythm, bradycardia = NSR
ECG Changes–Tall Peaked T Waves	**T**all T waves (peaked), widened QRS, prolonged PR interval–(Monitor ECG); monitor K⁺ levels ongoing; take VS with a focus on HR and BP	**E**CG Changes–tall peaked T Waves = NSR
Abdominal cramping; diarrhea	**O**rders: Kayexalate or dextrose with regular insulin	**A**bdominal cramping; diarrhea = NOT Present
The muscles twitch	**P**rovide potassium restricted foods, Potassium-losing diuretics (Lasix)	**T**he muscles twitch, cramp = NOT Present
Hypotension; has irritability/ restlessness	**S**alt substitutes NOT allowed	**H**ypotension; has irritability/ restlessness = NOT Present

Drugs Associated with the Risk for Developing Hyperkalemia

(For specifics, refer to the book Pharmacology Made Insanely Easy)

Angiotensin–Converting Enzyme Inhibitors
Digoxin
Heparin
Nonsteroidal Antiinflammatory Drugs
Potassium Sparing Diuretics (i.e., spironolactone)

Hyperkalemia in Elderly Clients

Renal function deteriorates with the aging process

Elimination (urinary output) is decreased due to decrease in oral fluid intake

Note that plasma renin activity and aldosterone levels also decrease with age

Alteration in the renal blood flow

Likely to take meds that interfere with potassium excretion (*Refer to list prior to this mnemonic.*)

Questions evaluating knowledge.

Need to know information before you can apply information. (Answers below.)

1. What is the normal serum potassium level? _____

2. What is an easy way to remember system specific assessments when the client has hypokalemia? _____

3. What is an easy way to remember system specific assessments when the client has hyperkalemia? _____

4. What is an easy way to remember the "First Do Priority Nursing Interventions" for a client with hypokalemia? _____

5. What is an easy way to remember the "First Do Priority Nursing Interventions" for a client with hyperkalemia? _____

6. List two foods high in potassium: _____

7. List two medications that can cause hyperkalemia: _____

8. List two medications that can cause hypokalemia: _____

9. List two reasons the elderly can develop hyperkalemia: _____

10. What will happen to the T wave if a client is presenting with hypokalemia? _____

Answers:

1. 3.5-5.0 mEq/L
2. "CRAMPS"
3. "DEATH"
4. "POTASSIUM"
5. "STOPS"
6. Potatoes, bananas (Refer to image reviewing foods high in potassium)
7. Angiotensin-converting enzyme inhibitors, potassium sparing diuretics spironolactone (Aldactone)
8. Diuretics, corticosterioids
9. Plasma renin activity and aldosterone levels decrease with age; there may also be an alteration in the renal blood flow; renal function deteriorates with age.
10. Flatten out or becomes inverted.

Clinical Decision-Making Exercises

1. What assessment finding should be reported to the provider of care for a client who is taking bumetanide (Bumex) who has a serum potassium level of 3.0 mEq/L?

   ① A flattened or inverted T wave.

   ② An elevated ST segment.

   ③ A prolonged PR interval.

   ④ Hyperreflexia.

2. What would be the priority lab value to report for a client with food poisoning and is presenting with abdominal pain, cramping, palpitations, and muscle weakness?

   ① Magnesium–1.5 mEq/L.

   ② Sodium–145 mEq/L.

   ③ Potassium–3.1 mEq/L.

   ④ Calcium–9.4 mg/dL.

3. Which documentation indicates the nurse understands how to provide safe care for a client with a serum potassium of 3.3 mEq/L?

   ① Administers potassium chloride IV push.

   ② Holds oral potassium supplement due to level.

   ③ Discusses including oranges, bananas, and potatoes in diet.

   ④ Administers bumetanide (Bumex) as prescribed.

4. Which one of these actions by the new graduate indicates an understanding of how to safely manage the care for a client with a K⁺–5.2 mEq/L?

   ① Monitors for flat T waves on the ECG monitor.

   ② Encourages client to use a salt substitute with food.

   ③ Administers the ace inhibitor after assessing the client's blood pressure.

   ④ Verifies with the healthcare provider the appropriateness of a new order to add potassium to IV bag.

5. Which of these statements made by the client indicates a need for further teaching to a client with a potassium level of 5.2 mEq/L?

   ① "I will drink orange juice each time I take my medications throughout the day."

   ② "I will stop using any salt substitutes with my meals."

   ③ "I can continue to take my bumetanide (Bumex) as prescribed."

   ④ "I will not continue taking my NSAIDs as prescribed until I get my next blood work back."

Answers and Rationales

1. What assessment finding should be **reported to the provider** of care for a **client who is taking bumetanide (Bumex) who has a serum potassium level of 3.0 mEq/L?**

    ① **CORRECT: A flattened or inverted T wave. This client has lost potassium with the diarrhea and the result would be a change in the T wave.**

    ② INCORRECT: An elevated ST segment. This would be depressed.

    ③ INCORRECT: A prolonged PR interval. This would be a change in a heart block.

    ④ INCORRECT: The reflexes would be decreased with hypokalemia.

The strategy is to link the assessments for a client with hypokalemia with this client. Review the assessments of this electrolyte imbalance by reviewing "**CRAMPS**". The normal potassium is 3.5 – 5.0 mEq/L. Review the pathophysiology chart for the causes of this imbalance. For example, any clinical situation that the client vomits, has diarrhea, has a nasogastric suction without replacement, takes steroid therapy, etc. may experience complications of hypokalemia. The assessments are the same, but the causes are different! You have now reviewed a concept that will assist you to answer many questions throughout nursing with this strategy. "**POTASSIUM**" will assist you in remembering the nursing care for these clients.

Physiological Adaptation: Manage the care of the client with a fluid and electrolyte imbalance.

2. What would be the **priority lab value to report** for a client with **food poisoning and is presenting with abdominal pain, cramping, palpitations, and muscle weakness?**

    ① INCORRECT: Magnesium 1.5 mEq/L is a normal level and does not need to be reported.

    ② INCORRECT: Sodium 145 mEq/L is a normal level and does not need to be reported.

    ③ **CORRECT: Potassium 3.1 mEq/L is a low level and needs to be reported due to risk for cardiac dysrhythmias.**

    ④ INCORRECT: Calcium 9.4 mg/dL is a normal level and does not need to be reported.

The strategy for this clinical situation is to recognize that these assessment findings can result in hypokalemia. Also, the other options are within the normal ranges, which can also assist you in answering questions correctly by clustering the normal values.

Physiological Adaptation: Manage the care of the client with a fluid and electrolyte imbalance.

3. Which **documentation indicates** the nurse understands how to **provide safe care** for a client with a **serum potassium of 3.3 mEq/L?**

   ① INCORRECT: Administers potassium chloride IV push. This is NEVER appropriate. This can lead to death.

   ② INCORRECT: Holds oral potassium supplement due to level. The level is low and may require potassium supplement.

   ③ **CORRECT: Discusses eating oranges, broccoli, bananas. This is appropriate. Client needs to eat foods high in potassium.**

   ④ INCORRECT: Administers bumetanide (Bumex) as prescribed. This could lead to a lower potassium level.

The strategy for answering this question is to link the care to **"POTASSIUM"**. An easy way to remember foods high in potassium is to remember the mnemonic **"TOES"**: pota**TOES**, toma**TOES**, avocad**TOES**, banana**TOES**, and orange**TOES**!

Physiological Adaptation: Manage the care of the client with a fluid and electrolyte imbalance.

Basic Care and Comfort: Manage the client's nutritional intake (i.e., adjust diet).

4. Which one of these actions by the **new graduate indicates an understanding of how to safely manage the care for a client with a K⁺–5.2 mEq/L?**

   ① INCORRECT: Monitors for flat T waves on the ECG monitor. The T waves would not be flat for this high level. They would be peaked.

   ② INCORRECT: Encourages client to use a salt substitute with food. This would result in level going higher, since the salt substitute is high in K⁺.

   ③ INCORRECT: Administers the ace inhibitor after assessing the client's blood pressure. These can contribute to hyperkalemia.

   ④ **CORRECT: Verifies with the healthcare provider the appropriateness of a new order to add potassium to IV bag. The level is high and the new order for potassium needs to be verified in order to prevent additional complications with hyperkalemia.**

The strategy is to link the elevated potassium level to the appropriate nursing action. The other options address hypokalemia. You could even cluster the similar options for hypokalemia and option 4 would be odd man out. This could also point you to the correct answer. We do, however, want you to know the nursing care and be confident with your knowledge versus depending on this type of strategy. *As you are learning to answer questions though, our goal is to help you adapt both decision-making strategies with your newly learned information about the concept. We are in this with you, and want you to succeed!*

Physiological Adaptation: Manage the care of the client with a fluid and electrolyte imbalance.

Reduction of Risk Potential: Monitor the results of the diagnostic testing (lab reports) and intervene as needed.

5. Which of these statements made by the client indicates a need for **further teaching** to a client with a **potassium level of 5.2 mEq/L?**

   ① **CORRECT: "I will drink orange juice each time I take my medications throughout the day." Orange juice is high in potassium.**

   ② INCORRECT: "I will stop using any salt substitutes with my meals." This is a good thing, since these are high in potassium.

   ③ INCORRECT: "I can continue to take my bumetanide (Bumex) as prescribed." This would continue to decrease the K⁺ level.

   ④ INCORRECT: "I will not continue taking my NSAIDs as prescribed until I get my next blood work back." This is a good thing, since these meds could lead to a further increase in the K⁺ level.

The strategy is to review "Foods High in Potassium". Orange juice is high in potassium and would be unsafe for this client due to the level.

Physiological Adaptation: Manage the care of the client with a fluid and electrolyte imbalance.

Health Promotion and Maintenance: Educate client about treatment.

Decision-Making Analysis Form

Use this tool to help identify why you missed any questions. As you enter the question numbers in the chart, you will begin to see patterns of why you answered incorrectly. This information will then guide you toward what you need to focus on in your continued studies. Ultimately, this analytical exercise will help you become more successful in answering questions!!!

Questions to ask:

1. Did I have the knowledge to answer the question? If not, what information do I need to review?

2. Did I know what the question was asking? Did I misread it or did I miss keywords in the stem of the question?

3. Did I misread or miss keywords in the distractors that would have helped me choose the correct answer?

4. Did I follow my gut reaction or did I allow myself to rationalize and then choose the wrong answer?

	Lack of Knowledge (Concepts, Systems, Pathophysiology, Medications, Procedures, etc.)	Missed Keywords or Misread the Stem of the Question	Missed Keywords or Misread the Distractors	Changed My Answer (Second-guessed myself, i.e., my first answer was correct.)
Put the # of each question you missed in the column that best explains why you think you answered it incorrectly.				

If you changed an answer because you talked yourself out of the correct answer, or you second-guessed yourself, this is an **EASY FIX: QUIT changing your answers**!!! Typically, the first time you read a question, you are about 95% right! The second time you read a question, you start talking yourself into changing the answer. The third time you read a question, you do not have a clue—and you are probably thinking "Who in the heck wrote this question?"

On the other hand, if you read a question too quickly and when you reread it you realize you missed some key information that would impact your decision (i.e., assessments, lab reports, medications, etc.), then it is appropriate to change your answer. When in doubt, go with the safe route: your first thought! Go with your gut instinct!

As you gain confidence in answering questions regarding specific nursing concepts, you will be able to successfully progress to answering higher-level questions about prioritization. Please refer to the *Prioritization Guidelines* in this book for a structure to assist you with this process.

You CAN do this!

"Effort is the key, but direction and loyalty are paramount."
AUTHOR UNKNOWN

References for Chapter 4

Black, J M. and Hawks, J. H. (2009). *Medical surgical nursing: Clinical management for positive outcomes (8th ed.).* Philadelphia: Elsevier/Saunders.

Daniels, R. & Nicoll, L. (2012). *Contemporary medical-surgical nursing,* (2nd ed.). Clifton Park, NY: Delmar Cengage Learning.

Ellis, K. M. (2012). *EKG: Plain and simple* (3rd ed.). Upper Saddle Road, NJ: Pearson.

Eliopoulos, C. (2014). *Gerontological nursing* (8th ed), Philadelphia: Lippincott Williams & Wilkins.Giddens, G.F. (2013). Concepts for nursing practice. St. Louis, MO: Mosby, an imprint of Elsevier.

Hogan, M. A. (2014). *Pathophysiology: Reviews and rationales* (3rd ed.) Boston, MA: Pearson.

Ignatavicius, D. D. and Workman, M. L. (2010). *Medical-surgical nursing: Patient-centered collaborative care* (6th ed.). Philadelphia: Elsevier/Saunders.

LeMone, P., Burke, K. M., and Bauldoff, G. (2011). *Medical-surgical nursing: Critical thinking in patient care* (5th ed.). Upper Saddle Road, NJ: Pearson/Prentice Hall.

Lewis, S., Dirksen, S., Heitkemper, M., Bucher, L., and Camera, I. (2011). *Medical surgical nursing: Assessment and management of clinical problems* (8th ed.). St. Louis: Mosby.

Manning, L. and Rayfield, S. (2014). *Nursing made insanely easy* (7th ed.). Duluth, GA: I CAN Publishing, Inc.

Metheny, Norma M, (2012) *Fluid and electrolyte balance: Nursing considerations,* (5th Edition), Sudbury, MA: Jones and Bartlett Learning.

National Council of State Boards of Nursing, INC. (NCSBN) 2012. *Research brief: 2011 RN practice analysis: linking the NCLEX RN® examination to practice.* Retrieved from https://www.ncsbn.org/index.htm

Nettina, S. L. (2013). *Lippincott manual of nursing practice* (10th ed.). Philadelphia, PA: Walters Kluwer Health/Lippincott Williams & Wilkins.

North Carolina Concept Based Learning Editorial Board (2011). *Nursing a concept based approach to learning,* Upper Saddle Road, NJ: Pearson/Prentice Hall.

Pagana, K. D. and Pagana, T. J. (2014). *Mosby's manual of laboratory and diagnostic tests* (5th ed.). St. Louis, MO: Mosby, an imprint of Elsevier.

Porth, C. (2011). *Essentials of pathophysiology* (3d ed.). Philadelphia, PA: Lippincott Williams ad Wilkins.

Porth, C. M. and Grossman, S. (2013). *Pathophysiology: Concepts of altered health states* (9th ed.). Philadelphia, PA: Lippincott Williams & Wilkins.

Potter, P. A., Perry, A. G., Stockert, P., and Hall, A. (2013). *Fundamentals of nursing* (8th ed.). St. Louis, MO: Pearson/Prentice Hall.

Smeltzer, S. C., Bare, B. G., Hinkle, J. L., and Cheever, K. H. (2010). *Brunner & Suddarth's Textbook of medical-surgical nursing* (12th ed.). Philadelphia: Lippincott Williams & Wilkins.

NOTES

CHAPTER 5

Linking Multiple Systems to Pathophysiology of Calcium Imbalance
Concept Fluid and Electrolytes: Calcium Balance

A Snapshot of Calcium Balance

Calcium balance: Ninety nine percent of calcium in the body is located in the matrix of the bone. The ECF levels of Ca^{++} are a small amount of total body calcium. Parathyroid hormone (PTH) is the main regulator and distributor of calcium levels in the body. PTH stimulates release of Ca^{++} from the bone into the ECF and causes the kidneys to reabsorb Ca^{++}. Activated Vitamin D (calcitrol) is also necessary for adequate serum levels. Calcium is obtained through the diet, although less than half of dietary intake is absorbed. Calcium is stored in the bones where adequate mineralized calcium is needed for bone density and strength; it is also found in the body's cells and teeth. Ionized calcium in the ECF participates in many enzyme reactions, contributes to membrane excitability, is necessary for contraction in all muscle types (i.e., endocrine, cardiovascular, and neuromuscular) and for blood clotting and teeth formation. Calcium is excreted by the kidneys.

What is the Pathophysiology behind Calcium Imbalance?

 **The Pathophysiology Behind Calcium Imbalance**

CALCIUM IMBALANCE (NORMAL 9–10.5 mg/dL)

Hypocalcemia (< 9 mg/dL)			Hypercalcemia (> 10.5 mg/dL)		
Normal Output But ↓ Ca⁺⁺ Intake/ Absorption	↑ Output Not Balanced by ↑ Ca⁺⁺ Intake & Absorption	Ca⁺⁺ Shift from ECF into Bone or Physiologically Unavailable Form	Normal Output But ↑ Ca⁺⁺ Intake & Absorption	↓ Output Not Balanced by ↓ Ca⁺⁺ Intake	Rapid Ca⁺⁺ Shift from Bone Into ECF
• Low Ca⁺⁺ rich foods in diet • Vitamin D deficiency resulting in poor absorption of calcium • Malabsorption syndromes, such as Crohn's disease	• Binds calcium in GI secretions in addition to the intake of calcium in diet–Steatorrhea	• Post-thyroidectomy • Hypoparathyroidism • Hyperphosphatemia • Alkalosis • Multiple blood transfusions due to the large amount of citrate (binds with Ca⁺⁺) • Pancreatitis • Calcium bound to excess phosphate in renal failure	• Vitamin D or Ca⁺⁺ overdose	• Thiazide diuretics	• Hyperpara-thyroidism • Metastatic malignancy that secretes bone-resorbing factors • Paget's disease • Chronic immobility

Labs and Diagnostic Tests/Procedures

Labs	Tests checking for Trousseau and Chvostek's Signs helps diagnose tetany and hypocalcemia.
Serum calcium level: 9.0-10.5 mg/dL	**Trousseau:** *(usually indicates late tetany)* Apply a blood pressure cuff to upper arm of the client and inflate it to a pressure 20 mm Hg above the systolic pressure. After 1 to 4 minutes, Trousseau's sign may appear. The thumb will be adducted thumb, wrist will be flexed along with metacarpophalangeal joints, and extended interphalangeal joints (with the fingers together). This is known as a *carpopedal spasm*. This indicates tetany, a major sign of hypocalcemia.
Ionized calcium level : 4.5–5.5 mEq/L (Children: 4.4–6.0 mEq/L)	**Chvostek's sign:** Tapping the facial nerve adjacent to the ear of the client can induce this sign. If the upper lip, nose, or side of the face experiences a brief contraction, this indicates the Chvostek's sign.

An INSANELY Easy Approach to the Body's Regulation of Calcium

Parathyroid hormone (PTH) "Pulls" from the bones promoting the transfer of calcium along with phosphorus into the plasma, increasing calcium levels. PTH also promotes kidney reabsorption of calcium and stimulates the intestines to absorb the mineral. Phosphorus is excreted at the same time. In hypercalcemia where too much calcium exists in the body, the body suppresses the release of PTH.

As you can see in the image on the right, the "**PTH**" is "**PULLING**" the calcium and phosphorus from the bone!

CalcitONIN says, "Come On In!" (Keeps calcium in the bone. Come ON IN and do not leave!) Calcitonin a hormone in the thyroid gland that acts as an antagonist to PTH and helps regulate the calcium levels. When calcium is too high the thyroid gland releases calcitonin. High levels of the hormone inhibit bone resoprtion which causes a decrease in the amount of calcium available from bone. This causes a decrease in serum calcium levels. Calcitonin also decreases absorption of calcium and enhances excretion by the kidneys.

As you can see in the image on the right, "**Calcit ON IN**" is opening the door for the calcium and inviting CA in the bone!

Vitamin D "delivers calcium" Vitamin D in the active form promotes calcium absorption through the intestines, calcium resorption from bone, and kidney reabsorption of calcium all of which will raise the serum calcium level. Vitamin D is ingested with foods, especially dairy products. When skin is exposed to ultraviolet light, it synthesizes vitamin D.

The "**CALCIUM DELIVERY SERVICE**" on the right will help remind you that Vitamin D promotes calcium absorption, so it can be taken to the designated destination (i.e., intestines, resorption from bone, etc.)

These facts no longer have to remain tedious; just remember the teeter tauter and you will have this concept remembered FOREVER! The "TEETER TAUTER" applies to both phosphorus and calcium and the pH and calcium! Simply stated, they BOTH (phosphorus and pH) have an inverse relationship with calcium.

Phosphorus: "When phosphorus (P) is high, **CALCIUM FALLS**" or **when Phos Falls then Calcium is high.**" "Phosphorus decreases calcium absorption in the intestines. When Calcium level increases, phosphorus drops."

pH also has an inverse relationship with ionized calcium. When the serum pH level rises (blood becomes alkaline) more calcium binds with protein and the ionized calcium level drops. A client with alkalosis typically has hypocalcemia. When the pH level drops, less calcium binds to protein and the ionized calcium level rises.

SAFETY Concept: Fluid and Electrolytes
Hypocalcemia (Ca^{++} < 9 mg/dL)
Calcium (9–10.5 mg/dL)

System-Specific Assessments "TWITCH"	First-Do Priority Interventions "SAFE"	Evaluation of Expected Outcomes "No TWITCH"
Trousseau's Sign (hand finger spasms) with sustained BP cuff inflation; tingling (numbness) (extremities, circumoral)	**S**eizure precautions	**T**rousseau's Sign–NOT Present
Watch for dysrhythmias (↓ pulse, prolonged QT and ST segments–ECG)	**A**dminister calcium supplements	**W**atch for dysrhythmias NO (↓ Pulse, ↑ ST–ECG)
Increase in bowel sounds; diarrhea	**F**oods high in calcium,(i.e., dairy, green); educate client	**I**ncrease in bowel sounds NOT Present; NO diarrhea
Tetany, twitching, tingling (circumoral, extremities), seizures; spasms at rest than can progress to tetany	**E**mergency equipment on standby; monitor	**T**etany, twitching, seizures; spasms at rest–NOT Present
Chvostek's sign (facial twitching)		**C**hvostek's sign–NOT Present
Hypotension, Hyperactive DTR		**H**ypotension, Hyperactive DTR–NOT Present

©2014 I CAN Publishing®, Inc.
Concept developed by Dr. Melissa Geist

"**SKINNY CA^{++}T**" is on the edge, and "**WOW!**" he is so irritable that he has a "**TWITCH**"! He may be very hungry from not having much milk (Ca^{++}).

Drugs Associated with Hypocalcemia "ABCs"

(For specifics, refer to the book *Pharmacology Made Insanely Easy.*)

Aluminum-containing antacids
Anticonvulsants (i.e., phenytoin and phenobarbital)
Beta-adrenergic blockers
Caffeine
Corticosteroids
Diuretics (Loop) (i.e., furosemide {Lasix})

Hypocalcemia in Elderly Clients

Elderly clients are unable to run a **RACE** during this developmental period of life.

Reduced activity or inactivity

Absorption of calcium is poor (especially in postmenopausal women lacking estrogen)

Calcium intake is inadequate

Excretes calcium from the bones due to inactivity (serum levels may be normal, but bone stores of the mineral are depleted)

SAFETY Concept: Fluid and Electrolytes
Hypercalcemia (Ca^{++}>10.5 mg/dL)
Calcium (9–10.5 mg/dL)

System-Specific Assessments "CALCIUM"	First-Do Priority Interventions "The 7 Fs"	Evaluation of Expected Outcomes "CALCIUM"
Cardiac dysrhythmias; (↓ QT interval and ↓ or shortened ST segment); CNS ↓	**F**luids (0.9% NS IV) to promote excretion; acid-ash fluids (prune, cranberry juice) to reduce risk for renal calculi formation	**C**ardiac dysrhythmias; CNS ↓–NOT Present
Anorexia, nausea; constipation	**F**urosemide (Lasix)	**A**norexia, nausea; constipation–NOT Present
LOC ↓	**F**oods low in calcium	**L**OC ↓–NOT Present
Calcium level > 10.5 mg/dL	**F**iber	**C**alcium level 9–10.5mg/dL NORMAL Level
Increase in drowsiness	**F**ocus on VS, neurological assessment; safety precautions due to confusion	**I**ncrease in drowsiness–NOT Present
Underactive reflexes	**F**all prevention	**U**nderactive reflexes–NOT Present
Muscle weakness	**F**ractures (monitor for pathologic)	**M**uscle weakness–NOT Present

©2014 I CAN Publishing®, Inc.
Concept developed by Dr. Melissa Geist

"FAT CA^{++}T" will help you remember the signs and symptoms of hypercalcemia forever! He drank all of the milk (calcium) and now he is drowsy, like we are after eating a large meal!

INSANELY EASY TIP!
The nursing care for clients with hypercalcemia is to organize care to prevent **STONES** renal (calculi), **BONES** (bone pain, especially if PTH is elevated), **GROANS** (constipation), **MOANS** (psychotic noise, bone pain), and Psychotic OverTONES (depression and confusion). Monitor ongoing for cardiac **DYSRHYTHMIAS**, and implement **SAFETY precautions** due to confusion!

Drugs Associated with Hypercalcemia

(For specifics, refer to the book *Pharmacology Made Insanely Easy*)

Antacids containing calcium
Any calcium preparations (PO or IV)
Vitamin A
Vitamin D
Diuretics (Thiazide)
Lithium

INSANELY EASY TIP to remember foods high in calcium!

Cheese

dAiry (yogurt)

Leafy green vegetables

Cottage cheese

Intake of whole grains

tUna and salmon

Milk

Questions evaluating knowledge.

Need to know information before you can apply information. (Answers below.)

1. What is the normal serum calcium level? _____

2. What is the Trousseau's Sign? _____

3. What is the Chvostek's sign? _____

4. What is an easy way to remember system-specific assessments when the client has hypocalcemia? _____

5. What is an easy way to remember system-specific assessments when the client has hypercalcemia? _____

6. What is an easy way to remember the First-Do Priority Nursing Interventions for a client with hypocalcemia? _____

7. What is an easy way to remember the First-Do Priority Nursing Interventions for a client with hyperkcalcemia: _____

8. List two causes of hypocalcemia: _____

9. List two causes of hypercalcemia: _____

10. List two foods high in calcium: _____

Answers:
1. 9–10.5 mg/dL.
2. Trousseau's Sign (hand/finger spasms) with sustained BP cuff inflation.
3. Chvostek's sign (facial twitching).
4. "The SKINNY CAT: TWITCH"
5. "The FAT CAT: CALCIUM"
6. "SAFE."
7. "The 7 Fs."
8. Low Ca++ rich foods in diet; renal failure; hypoparathyroidism (*Refer to Pathophysiology Chart*).
9. Hyperparathyroidism, chronic immobility.
10. Leafy green vegetables, and salmon.

Clinical Decision-Making Exercises

1. Which of these clinical findings should be reported for a client with a diagnosis of parathyroid disease and presenting with calcium level of 6.0 mg/dL?

   ① Depressed patellar reflex.

   ② Paresthesia in the hand is produced when tapping over the median nerve at the wrist crease.

   ③ Foot extension of the big toe while fanning the other toes when stimulating the outside of the sole of the foot.

   ④ Carpopedal spasm after BP cuff is inflated above systolic pressure.

2. Which one of these clinical findings is the priority to report to the healthcare provider for a client with a calcium level of 7.1 mg/dL?

   ① Constipation.

   ② Facial twitching with tapping on the facial nerve.

   ③ Hypoactive bowel sounds.

   ④ Lethargy with weakness.

3. What would be the priority plan for a client with a calcium level of 11 mg/dL?

   ① Decrease client activity level.

   ② Discourage the intake of fiber.

   ③ Encourage milkshakes for snacks.

   ④ Encourage fluids.

4. Which of these statements by the client indicates an understanding of how the parathyroid hormone (PTH) assists in the body's regulation of calcium?

   ① "The parathyroid hormone works by increasing the release of PTH when the calcium in the blood is high."

   ② "The parathyroid hormone works by keeping the calcium in the bones and decreases the absorption."

   ③ "The parathyroid hormone pulls out calcium from the bones and promotes the transfer of calcium into the plasma."

   ④ "The parathyroid hormone works by releasing PTH in response to the serum pH."

5. Which of these medications should be questioned regarding the appropriateness for a client who has a calcium level of 6.1 mg/dL?

   ① furosemide (Lasix).

   ② hydrochlorothiazide (HCTZ).

   ③ Vitamin A.

   ④ Vitamin B.

6. Which of these clinical findings should the nurse report to the healthcare provider for a client with a calcium level of 7.4 mg/dL?

   ① Drowsy.

   ② Depressed reflexes.

   ③ Prolonged ST segment.

   ④ Decreased QT interval.

Answers and Rationales

1. Which of these **clinical findings** should be reported for a client with a **diagnosis of parathyroid disease** and presenting with **calcium level of 6.0 mg/dL?**

    ① INCORRECT: Depressed patellar reflex. This would be hyper-reactive instead of depressed for a client with hypocalcemia. This assessment would indicate too much of a CNS depressant such as Magnesium Sulfate or a sign of hypernatremia.

    ② INCORRECT: Paresthesia in the hand is produced when tapping over the median nerve at the wrist crease. This is the tinel's sign which is least sensitive, but most specific for carpal tunnel syndrome.

    ③ INCORRECT: Foot extension of the big toe while fanning the other toes when stimulating the outside of the sole of the foot. This is the Babinski reflex which is used to assess adequacy of the higher (central) nervous system.

    ④ **CORRECT: Carpopedal spasm after BP cuff is inflated above systolic pressure. The client has hypocalcemia (normal range is 9-10.5 mg/dL.) The is how the nurse would check the Trousseau sign. The Trousseau's sign of latent tetany is a sensitive sign in hypocalcemia. When the BP cuff is inflated and held in place for 3 minutes, this results in the occlusion of the brachial artery, and the hypocalcemia and subsequent neuromuscular irritability may induce a muscle spasm of the hand and forearm of the client's hand.**

The strategy is to remember "**TWITCH**" for the signs of hypocalcemia. With any client who has hypocalcemia, this clinical assessment could occur. The other findings did not apply to the hypocalcemia. Any medical condition that causes hypocalcemia may result in the client presenting with the Trousseau's sign. Instead of memorizing each disease, just remember this concept, and it will assist in remembering these findings.

Reduction of Risk Potential: Perform focused assessment.

Physiological Adaptation: Manage the care of the client with a fluid and electrolyte imbalance.

2. Which one of these **clinical findings** is the priority to **report to the healthcare provider** for a client with a **calcium level of 7.1 mg/dL?**

    ① INCORRECT: Constipation would be a finding for hypercalcemia.

    ② **CORRECT: Facial twitching with tapping on the facial nerve. This is Chvostek's sign and is a sign of hypocalcemia.**

    ③ INCORRECT: Hypoactive bowel sounds would be a finding for hypercalcemia.

    ④ INCORRECT: Lethargy with weakness would be a finding for hypercalcemia.

The strategy is to remember "**TWITCH**" for the signs of hypocalcemia. With any client who has hypocalcemia, this clinical assessment could occur. The other findings did not apply to the hypocalcemia. Any medical condition that causes hypocalcemia may result in the client presenting with the Chvostek's sign. Instead of memorizing each disease, just remember this concept, and it will assist in remembering these findings.

Reduction of Risk Potential: Perform focused assessment.

Physiological Adaptation: Manage the care of the client with a fluid and electrolyte imbalance.

3.   What would be the **priority plan** for a client with a **calcium level of 11 mg/dL?**

① INCORRECT: Client activity level should be increased.

② INCORRECT: Fiber should be increased to assist with bowel elimination.

③ INCORRECT: Encourage milkshakes for snacks. Calcium should be decreased. This is high in calcium.

④ **CORRECT: Encourage fluids. Fluids should be increased to assist with urinary excretion.**

The strategy is to remember the First-Do Priority Interventions: "The 7 Fs". These apply to any situation that causes hypercalcemia.

Physiological Adaptation: Manage the care of the client with a fluid and electrolyte imbalance.

4.   Which of these **statements by the client** indicates an understanding of how the **parathyroid hormone (PTH)** assists in the body's **regulation of calcium?**

① INCORRECT: "The parathyroid hormone works by increasing the release of PTH when the calcium in the blood is high." The correct physiology is that when the serum calcium levels are low, the PTH is released by the parathyroid glands, which draws and pulls calcium from the bones promoting the transfer of calcium (along with phosphorus) into the plasma.

② INCORRECT: "The parathyroid hormone works by keeping the calcium in the bones and decreases the absorption." This is not done by the PTH; it is done by calcitonin. Calcitonin is produced in the thyroid gland that acts as an antagonist to PTH. High levels of the hormone inhibit bone resorption, which causes a decrease in the amount of calcium available from the bone.

③ **CORRECT: "The parathyroid hormone pulls out calcium from the bones and promotes the transfer of calcium into the plasma."**

④ INCORRECT: "The parathyroid hormone works by releasing PTH in response to the serum pH." This is incorrect. If the serum pH level increases (becomes alkaline), then calcium will bind with protein and the ionized calcium level will drop.

The strategy is to understand the physiology of how the body regulates calcium.

Physiological Adaptation: Identify the pathophysiology related to an acute or chronic condition.

5.   Which of these **medications should be questioned** regarding the **appropriateness for a client who has a calcium level of 6.1 mg/dL?**

① **CORRECT: Furosemide (Lasix). This would contribute to the calcium being more decreased, so should be questioned.**

② INCORRECT: Hydrochlorothiazide (HCTZ). This would be appropriate, since it would contribute to hypercalcemia and would not need to be questioned.

③ INCORRECT: Vitamin A. This would be appropriate, since it would contribute to hypercalcemia and would not need to be questioned.

④ INCORRECT: Vitamin B. This would be appropriate, since it would contribute to hypercalcemia and would not need to be questioned.

The strategy is to link to the medications that lead to hypocalcemia and hypercalcemia. In this question, the calcium level was low which would require the nurse to question an order that would further lead to hypocalcemia.

Physiological Adaptation: Manage the care of the client with a fluid and electrolyte imbalance.

Management of Care: Verify appropriateness and/ or accuracy of medication order.

6. Which of these **clinical findings should the nurse report** to the healthcare provider for a client with a **calcium level of 7.4 mg/dL?**

    ① INCORRECT: Drowsy. Signs of hypercalcemia.

    ② INCORRECT: Depressed reflexes. Signs of hypercalcemia.

    ③ **CORRECT: Prolonged ST segment. This is correct and is consistent with this low calcium level.**

    ④ INCORRECT: Decreased QT interval. Signs of hypercalcemia.

The strategy is to refer to "**TWITCH**" for clinical findings for hypocalcemia. The other options all focused on hypercalcemia; if the ST segment had been from hypercalcemia it would be decreased versus prolonged. "**CALCIUM**" reviews clinical findings for hypercalcemia. The "**Fat and Skinny Ca⁺⁺t**" will assist you in remembering this information!

Physiological Adaptation: Manage the care of the client with a fluid and electrolyte imbalance.

Decision-Making Analysis Form

Use this tool to help identify why you missed any questions. As you enter the question numbers in the chart, you will begin to see patterns of why you answered incorrectly. This information will then guide you toward what you need to focus on in your continued studies. Ultimately, this analytical exercise will help you become more successful in answering questions!!!

Questions to ask:

1. Did I have the knowledge to answer the question? If not, what information do I need to review?

2. Did I know what the question was asking? Did I misread it or did I miss keywords in the stem of the question?

3. Did I misread or miss keywords in the distractors that would have helped me choose the correct answer?

4. Did I follow my gut reaction or did I allow myself to rationalize and then choose the wrong answer?

	Lack of Knowledge (Concepts, Systems, Pathophysiology, Medications, Procedures, etc.)	Missed Keywords or Misread the Stem of the Question	Missed Keywords or Misread the Distractors	Changed My Answer (Second-guessed myself, i.e., my first answer was correct.)
Put the # of each question you missed in the column that best explains why you think you answered it incorrectly.				

If you changed an answer because you talked yourself out of the correct answer, or you second-guessed yourself, this is an **EASY FIX: QUIT changing your answers**!!! Typically, the first time you read a question, you are about 95% right! The second time you read a question, you start talking yourself into changing the answer. The third time you read a question, you do not have a clue—and you are probably thinking "Who in the heck wrote this question?"

On the other hand, if you read a question too quickly and when you reread it you realize you missed some key information that would impact your decision (i.e., assessments, lab reports, medications, etc.), then it is appropriate to change your answer. When in doubt, go with the safe route: your first thought! Go with your gut instinct!

As you gain confidence in answering questions regarding specific nursing concepts, you will be able to successfully progress to answering higher-level questions about prioritization. Please refer to the *Prioritization Guidelines* in this book for a structure to assist you with this process.

You CAN do this!

> *"When a happy person comes into the room, it is as if another candle has been lit."*
>
> RALPH WALDO EMERSON

References for Chapter 5

Black, J M. and Hawks, J. H. (2009). *Medical surgical nursing: Clinical management for positive outcomes* (8th ed.). Philadelphia: Elsevier/Saunders.

Daniels, R. & Nicoll, L. (2012). *Contemporary medical-surgical nursing*, (2nd ed.). Clifton Park, NY: Delmar Cengage Learning.

Ellis, K. M. (2012). *EKG: Plain and simple* (3rd ed.). Upper Saddle Road, NJ: Pearson.

Eliopoulos, C. (2014). *Gerontological nursing* (8th ed.), Philadelphia: Lippincott Williams & Wilkins.

Giddens, G. F. (2013). *Concepts for nursing practice.* St. Louis, MO: Mosby, an imprint of Elsevier.

Hogan, M. A. (2014). *Pathophysiology, reviews and rationales*, (3rd Edition) Boston, MA: Pearson.

Ignatavicius, D. D. and Workman, M. L. (2010). *Medical-Surgical nursing: Patient-Centered collaborative care* (7th ed.). Philadelphia: Elsevier/Saunders.

LeMone, P. Burke, K. M. and Bauldoff, G. (2011). *Medical-surgical nursing: Critical thinking in patient care* (5th edition). Upper Saddle Road, NJ: Pearson/Prentice Hall.

Lewis, S., Dirksen, S., Heitkemper, M., Bucher, L., and Camera, I. (2011). *Medical surgical nursing: Assessment and management of clinical problems* (8th ed.). St. Louis: Mosby.

Manning, L. and Rayfield, S. (2014). *Nursing made insanely easy* (7th ed). Duluth, GA: I CAN Publishing, Inc.

Manning, L. and Rayfield, S. (2013). *Pharmacology made insanely easy* (4th ed.). Duluth, GA: I CAN Publishing, Inc.

Metheny, Norma M, (2012) *Fluid and electrolyte balance: Nursing considerations*, (5th Edition), Sudbury, MA: Jones and Bartlett Learning.

National Council of State Boards of Nursing, INC. (NCSBN) 2012. *Research brief: 2011 RN practice analysis: linking the NCLEX RN® examination to practice.* Retrieved from https://www.ncsbn.org/index.htm

Nettina, S. L. (2013). *Lippincott manual of nursing practice* (10th ed.). Philadelphia, PA: Walters Kluwer Health / Lippincott Williams & Wilkins.

North Carolina Concept Based Learning Editorial Board. (2011). *Nursing a concept based approach to learning.* Upper Saddle Road, NJ: Pearson/Prentice Hall.

Osborn, K. S., Wraa, C. E., Watson, A. S., and Holleran, R. S. (2014). *Medical surgical nursing: preparation for practice* (2nd ed.). Upper Saddle Road, NJ: Pearson.

Pagana, K. D. and Pagana, T. J. (2014). *Mosby's manual of laboratory and diagnostic tests* (5th ed.). St. Louis, MO: Mosby, an imprint of Elsevier.

Porth, C. (2011). *Essentials of pathophysiology* (3rd edition). Philadelphia, PA: Lippincott Williams ad Wilkins.

Porth, C. M. and Grossman, S. (2013). *Pathophysiology, Concepts of altered health states* (9th edition). Philadelphia, PA: Lippincott Williams & Wilkins.

Potter, P. A., Perry, A. G., Stockert, P., and Hall, A. (2013). *Fundamentals of nursing* (8th ed). St. Louis, MO: Pearson/Prentice Hall.

Smeltzer, S. C., Bare, B. G., Hinkle, J. L., and Cheever, K. H. (2010). *Brunner & Suddarth's Textbook of medical-surgical nursing* (12th ed.). Philadelphia: Lippincott Williams & Wilkins.

Wagner, K. D. and Hardin-Pierce, M. C. (2014). *High-Acuity nursing* (6th ed.). Boston: Pearson.

CHAPTER 6

Linking Multiple Systems to Pathophysiology of Magnesium Imbalance
Concept Fluid and Electrolytes: Magnesium Balance

A Snapshot of Magnesium Balance

Magnesium is the second intracellular cation behind potassium. Most of the magnesium in the body is found in the bones. A smaller amount is found in the body cells. About 2% of magnesium in the body is located in the ECF. Magnesium intake is through the diet. The main method of elimination is through the kidneys. Magnesium is necessary for cellular metabolism, maintaining membrane stability, nerve conduction, and all cellular functions that require adenosine triphosphate (ATP). Magnesium is also essential for parathyroid hormone function. Magnesium and potassium levels are interdependent: a decrease in one can lead to a decrease in the other.

What is the Pathophysiology behind Magnesium Imbalance?

The Pathophysiology Behind Magnesium Imbalance

MAGNESIUM IMBALANCE (NORMAL 1.3–2.1 mEq/L)

Hypomagnesemia (< 1.3 mEq/L)			Hypermagnesemia (> 2.1 mEq/L)	
Normal Output But ↓ Mg++ intake	↑ Output Not Balanced by ↑ Mg++ Intake	Mg++ Shift from ECF into Physiologically Unavailable Form	Output < ↑ Mg++ Intake and Absorption	↓ Output Not Balanced by ↓ Mg++ Intake

• Low Mg++ rich foods in diet
• Malabsorption of Magnesium
  • Excessive alcohol intake
  • Diarrhea that is chronic
	• Binds calcium in GI secretions in addition to the intake of magnesium in diet–Steatorrhea
	• Prolonged gastric suction
	• Vomiting
	• Use of drugs/diuretics that increase Mg++ excretion
		• Alkalosis
		• Multiple blood transfusions due to the large amount of citrate (binds Mg++)
			• Mg++ overdose containing laxatives or antacids	• Adrenal insufficiency
				• Chronic renal disease

Labs	Tests checking for Trousseau and Chvostek's Signs helps diagnose tetany and hypomagnesemia.
Serum magnesium level: 1.3–2.1 mEq/L	**Trousseau:** *(usually indicates late tetany)* Apply a blood pressure cuff to upper arm of the client and inflate it to a pressure 20 mm Hg above the systolic pressure. After 1 to 4 minutes, Trousseau's sign may appear. The thumb will be adducted thumb, wrist will be flexed along with metacarpophalangeal joints, and extended interphalangeal joints (with the fingers together). This is known as a *carpopedal spasm*. This indicates tetany, a major sign of low magnesium.
	Chvostek's sign: Tapping the facial nerve adjacent to the ear of the client can induce this sign. If the upper lip, nose, or side of the face experiences a brief contraction, this indicates the Chvostek's sign.

SAFETY Concept: Fluid and Electrolytes
Hypomagnesemia (Mg⁺⁺ < 1.3 mEq/L)
Magnesium (1.3–2.1 mEq/L)

System-Specific Assessments "TWITCH"	First-Do Priority Interventions "SAFE"	Evaluation of Expected Outcomes "No TWITCH"
Trousseau's Sign (hand finger spasms)	**S**eizure/fall precautions	**T**rousseau's Sign–NOT Present
Watch for dysrhythmias, depressed ST–ECG, prolonged QT	**A**dminister Magnesium Sulfate IV per order	**W**atch for dysrhythmias NO (Normal Sinus Rhythm–ST WDL on ECG)
Increase neuromuscular excitability; **I**nspiratory laryngeal stridor	**F**oods high in magnesium (i.e., dark green vegetables, whole grains, etc.)	**I**ncrease in bowel sounds–NOT present (normal sound); normal bowel
Tetany, twitching (seizures), tachycardia, tremors	**E**mergency equipment on standby Electrocardiogram; eliminate drugs that decrease Mg⁺⁺; evaluate deep-tendon reflexes	**T**etany, twitching, seizures–NOT Present
Chvostek's sign (facial twitching)		**C**hvostek's sign NOT Present
Hypoactive bowel sounds; constipation Hyperactive DTR; hypertension		**H**ypertension subsided, Hyperactive DTR–NOT Present

Foods High in Magnesium

SAFETY Concept: Fluid and Electrolytes
Hypermagnesemia (Mg⁺⁺ > 2.1 mEq/L)
Magnesium (1.3–2.1 mEq/L)

System-Specific Assessments "MAGNESIUM"	First-Do Priority Interventions "DOME"	Evaluation of Expected Outcomes "No MAGNESIUM"
Mg⁺⁺ level > 2.1 mEq/L **A**rrhythmias (dysrhythmias) **G**ets flushed, diaphoretic **N**euromuscular excitability decreased; N/V **E**valuate for ↓ BP, ↓ HR, ↓ RR **S**ensorium (LOC) ↓, lethargy **I**ncrease in the trends for RR depression **I**ncrease in diarrhea **U**nderactive reflexes **M**uscle weakness	**D**ecrease magnesium intake **O**rder for diuretics if stable renal function **M**onitor closely for seizures, neurological, VS, etc. **E**valuate VS, level of consciousness, reflexes per protocol **E**lectrocardiogram, Emergency treatment: IV calcium gluconate or dialysis	**M**g⁺⁺ level 1.3–2.1 mEq/L– NORMAL **A**rrhythmias (dysrhythmias)– NOT Present **G**ets flushed, diaphoretic– NOT Present **N**euromuscular excitability ↓; N/V–NOT Present **E**valuate for ↓ BP, ↓ HR, ↓ RR–Not Present and WDL **S**ensorium (LOC) ↓–NOT Present **I**ncrease in the trends for RR depression–NOT Present; NO diarrhea **U**nderactive reflexes–NOT Present **M**uscle weakness–NOT Present

Notice the many similarities between calcium and magnesium. Both of these are predominantly found in the bone! Of course, the levels are different, but system-specific assessments for both hypocalcemia and hypomagnesemia are quite similar. They both can "**TWITCH**" and both the Trousseau's and Chvostek's Signs are indicative of low values! If the values are elevated, they will both experience the following:

Drowsiness

Decrease in muscle tone

Dysrhythmias

Differences: *Diarrhea* would occur for too much magnesium and *constipation* would occur for too much calcium!

Clinical Decision-Making Exercises

1. Which of these foods should be discussed with a client who has a magnesium level of less than 1.3 mEq/L? *Select all that apply.*

   ① Milk.

   ② Orange juice.

   ③ Sandwich on whole-grain bread.

   ④ Nuts.

   ⑤ Seafood.

2. Which of these clinical findings indicate a client has a magnesium level of 3.0 mEq/L?

   ① Hyporeflexia.

   ② Tetany.

   ③ Trousseau's.

   ④ Twitching.

3. Which of these statements made by the client indicates an understanding of the physiology of magnesium?

   ① "Magnesium is mostly found in bones."

   ② "Magnesium is responsible for regulating calcium in the body."

   ③ "Magnesium stimulates the production of the parathyroid hormone."

   ④ "Magnesium plays a vital role in the functioning of the cardiac and muscle tissue."

4. What would be the priority of care for a client with a magnesium level of 3.0 mEq/L and receiving an IV infusion with Magnesium Sulfate?

   ① Stop the infusion if client presents with an absent patellar reflex.

   ② Stop the infusion if client presents with Chvostek's Sign.

   ③ Monitor for tetany and twitches and stop the infusion.

   ④ Monitor for hypertension.

5. Which of these findings should the nurse report for a client with a magnesium level of 1.1 mg/dL?

   ① Depressed reflexes.

   ② Drowsiness.

   ③ Hypotension.

   ④ Depressed ST segment.

Answers and Rationales

1.   Which of these **foods should be discussed** with a client who has a **magnesium level of less than 1.3 mEq/L**? Select all that apply.

① INCORRECT: Milk is high in calcium but not magnesium.

② INCORRECT: Orange juice is not high in magnesium.

③ **CORRECT: A sandwich on whole-grain bread is high in magnesium.**

④ **CORRECT: Nuts are high in magnesium.**

⑤ **CORRECT: Seafood is high in magnesium.**

The strategy for answering this question is to remember the foods high in magnesium: "**NESIUM**" will assist you in remembering these foods.

Physiological Adaptation: Manage the care of the client with a fluid and electrolyte imbalance.

Basic Care and Comfort: Manage the client's nutritional intake (i.e., adjust diet).

2.   Which of these **clinical findings** indicate a client has a **magnesium level of 3.0 mEq/L**?

① **CORRECT: Hyporeflexia is a finding that can happen with an elevated magnesium level.**

② INCORRECT: Tetany would occur with a low magnesium level.

③ INCORRECT: Trousseu's would occur with a low magnesium level.

④ INCORRECT: Twitching would occur with a low magnesium level.

The strategy is to organize the nursing assessments for elevated magnesium levels around "**MAGNESIUM**". "**TWITCH**" will assist you in remembering the signs for a low magnesium level.

Physiological Adaptation: Manage the care of the client with a fluid and electrolyte imbalance.

3.   Which of these **statements made by the client** indicates an **understanding of the physiology of magnesium**?

① **CORRECT: "Magnesium is mostly found in bones" is a true statement.**

② INCORRECT: "Magnesium is responsible for regulating calcium in the body." PTH, Calcitonin level, Vitamin D, pH, and Phosphorus do this.

③ INCORRECT: "Magnesium stimulates the production of the parathyroid hormone." Calcium does this.

④ INCORRECT: "Magnesium plays a vital role in the functioning of the cardiac and muscle tissue." Potassium does this.

The strategy is to link the physiology specific to the electrolyte.

Physiological Adaptation: Identify pathophysiology related to an acute or chronic condition (i.e., signs and symptoms).

Physiological Adaptation: Manage the care of the client with a fluid and electrolyte imbalance.

4. What would be the **priority of care** for a client with a **magnesium level of 3.0 mEq/L** and receiving an **IV infusion with Magnesium Sulfate**?

① **CORRECT: Stop the infusion if client presents with an absent patellar reflex. This indicates the client is receiving too much magnesium.**

② INCORRECT: Chvostek's Sign does not indicate too much magnesium, but too little.

③ INCORRECT: Tetany and twitches do not indicate too much magnesium, but too little.

④ INCORRECT: Hypertension does not indicate too much magnesium, but too little.

The strategy is to link the nursing care to the elevated magnesium levels. "DOME" will assist you in organizing the nursing care for clients With high magnesium levels. "MAGNESIUM" will assist you in organizing the assessment findings for clients with high magnesium levels.

Physiological Adaptation: Manage the care of the client with a fluid and electrolyte imbalance.

5. Which of these **findings** should the **nurse report** for a client with a **magnesium level of 1.1 mg/dL?**

① INCORRECT: Depressed reflexes would be assessed for an elevated level.

② INCORRECT: Drowsiness would be assessed for an elevated level.

③ INCORRECT: Hypotension would be assessed for an elevated level.

④ **CORRECT: Both a depressed ST, and prolonged QT segment may occur with a client who has a low magnesium level. These would need to be reported.**

The strategy is to organize the clinical findings within the framework of a low or elevated magnesium level. "**TWITCH**" will assist you with assessments for a low level and "**MAGNESIUM**" will assist you with assessments for elevated levels. Remember, with low levels of magnesium, the cardiac changes are prolonged or depressed.

Physiological Adaptation: Manage the care of the client with a fluid and electrolyte imbalance.

Physiological Adaptation: Recognize signs and symptoms of complications and intervene appropriately when providing care.

Decision-Making Analysis Form

Use this tool to help identify why you missed any questions. As you enter the question numbers in the chart, you will begin to see patterns of why you answered incorrectly. This information will then guide you toward what you need to focus on in your continued studies. Ultimately, this analytical exercise will help you become more successful in answering questions!!!

Questions to ask:

1. Did I have the knowledge to answer the question? If not, what information do I need to review?

2. Did I know what the question was asking? Did I misread it or did I miss keywords in the stem of the question?

3. Did I misread or miss keywords in the distractors that would have helped me choose the correct answer?

4. Did I follow my gut reaction or did I allow myself to rationalize and then choose the wrong answer?

	Lack of Knowledge (Concepts, Systems, Pathophysiology, Medications, Procedures, etc.)	Missed Keywords or Misread the Stem of the Question	Missed Keywords or Misread the Distractors	Changed My Answer (Second-guessed myself, i.e., my first answer was correct.)
Put the # of each question you missed in the column that best explains why you think you answered it incorrectly.				

If you changed an answer because you talked yourself out of the correct answer, or you second-guessed yourself, this is an **EASY FIX: QUIT changing your answers**!!! Typically, the first time you read a question, you are about 95% right! The second time you read a question, you start talking yourself into changing the answer. The third time you read a question, you do not have a clue—and you are probably thinking "Who in the heck wrote this question?"

On the other hand, if you read a question too quickly and when you reread it you realize you missed some key information that would impact your decision (i.e., assessments, lab reports, medications, etc.), then it is appropriate to change your answer. When in doubt, go with the safe route: your first thought! Go with your gut instinct!

As you gain confidence in answering questions regarding specific nursing concepts, you will be able to successfully progress to answering higher-level questions about prioritization. Please refer to the *Prioritization Guidelines* in this book for a structure to assist you with this process.

You CAN do this!

> *"A hero is an ordinary individual who finds the strength to persevere and endure in spite of overwhelming obstacles."*
>
> CHRISTOPHER REEVE

References for Chapter 6

Daniels, R. & Nicoll, L. (2012). *Contemporary medical-surgical nursing,* (2nd ed.). Clifton Park, NY: Delmar Cengage Learning.

Ellis, K. M. (2012). *EKG: Plain and simple* (3rd ed.). Upper Saddle Road, NJ: Pearson.

Eliopoulos, C. (2014). *Gerontological nursing* (8th ed.), Philadelphia: Lippincott Williams & Wilkins.

Giddens, G. F. (2013). *Concepts for Nursing Practice.* St. Louis, MO: Mosby, an imprint of Elsevier.

Hogan, M. A. (2014). *Pathophysiology, reviews and rationales,* (3rd Edition) Boston, MA: Pearson.

Ignatavicius, D. D. and Workman, M. L. (2010). *Medical-Surgical nursing: Patient-Centered collaborative care* (7th ed.). Philadelphia: Elsevier/Saunders.

LeMone, P. Burke, K. M. and Bauldoff, G. (2011). *Medical-surgical nursing: Critical thinking in patient care* (5th edition). Upper Saddle Road, NJ: Pearson/Prentice Hall.

Lewis, S., Dirksen, S., Heitkemper, M., Bucher, L., and Camera, I. (2011). *Medical surgical nursing: Assessment and management of clinical problems* (8th ed.). St. Louis: Mosby.

Manning, L. and Rayfield, S. (2014). *Nursing made insanely easy* (7th ed). Duluth, GA: I CAN Publishing, Inc.

Metheny, Norma M, (2012) *Fluid and electrolyte balance: Nursing considerations,* (5th Edition), Sudbury, MA: Jones and Bartlett Learning.

National Council of State Boards of Nursing, INC. (NCSBN) 2012. *Research brief: 2011 RN practice analysis: linking the NCLEX RN® examination to practice.* Retrieved from https://www.ncsbn.org/index.htm

North Carolina Concept Based Learning Editorial Board. (2011). *Nursing a concept based approach to learning.* Upper Saddle Road, NJ: Pearson/Prentice Hall.

Pagana, K. D. and Pagana, T. J. (2014). *Mosby's manual of laboratory and diagnostic tests* (5th ed.). St. Louis, MO: Mosby, an imprint of Elsevier.

Porth, C. (2011). *Essentials of pathophysiology* (3rd edition). Philadelphia, PA: Lippincott Williams ad Wilkins.

Porth, C. M. and Grossman, S. (2013). *Pathophysiology, Concepts of altered health states* (9th edition). Philadelphia, PA: Lippincott Williams & Wilkins.

Potter, P. A., Perry, A. G., Stockert, P., and Hall, A. (2013). *Fundamentals of nursing* (8th ed). St. Louis, MO: Pearson/Prentice Hall.

Smeltzer, S. C., Bare, B. G., Hinkle, J. L., and Cheever, K. H. (2010). *Brunner & Suddarth's Textbook of medical-surgical nursing* (12th ed.). Philadelphia: Lippincott Williams & Wilkins.

NOTES

Linking Multiple Systems to Pathophysiology of Diseases
Concept Acid-Base Balance

A Snapshot of Acid-Base Balance

Acid-base balance is the process of regulating the pH, bicarbonate concentration, and partial pressure of carbon dioxide in body fluids (Giddens, 2013). The definition of *acid* is a substance that releases hydrogen (H^+) ions. A *base*, on the other hand, is a substance that accepts H^+. In solutions, the higher the H^+ concentration, the more acidic it is. An inverse relationship exists between pH and H^+ concentration. Increased pH indicates fewer H^+ ions and a more alkaline solution; decreased pH indicates more H^+ ions and an acidic solution.

The pH of a solution is a measure of its degree of acidity. A low pH means the solution is acidic; a high pH means it is basic (alkaline). This is the balance between carbon dioxide (CO_2) that is regulated by the lungs, and the bicarbonate (HCO_3) that is a base regulated by the kidneys.

Three processes: **acid production** or intake, **acid buffering**, and **acid excretion** assist in maintaining the acid-base balance.

The two systems that are effective buffers are the respiratory and renal systems.

The arterial pH is an indirect measurement of hydrogen ion concentration, which is the outcome of how the renal and respiratory systems are functioning. Arterial pH is used to evaluate acid-base balance.

Acid-base balance is a dynamic interplay because acid production never stops. The body's fluids constantly have cellular acids added to them which must be buffered to preserve function; likewise acid-excretion mechanisms must function nonstop to prevent acid from accumulating in the body's fluids and tissues. With a healthy acid-base balance, the pH of the blood and body fluids will remain within the normal physiologic range (7.35–7.45).

Acid-Base Imbalances

Respiratory Acidosis: Excessive retention of CO_2 from hypoventilating. With an increase in carbonic-acid concentration, there will be an increase in H^+ ions and a decrease in the pH (< 7.35).

Respiratory Alkalosis: Excessive loss of CO_2 from hyperventilating. This will result in a decrease in the H^+ concentration and an increase in the pH (> 7.45).

Metabolic Acidosis: Decrease in HCO_3 levels in the serum. This results in an increase in H^+ concentration and a decrease in the pH (< 7.35).

Metabolic Alkalosis: Increase in HCO_3 levels in the serum. This results in a decrease in H^+ concentration and an increase in the pH (> 7.35).

 **The Pathophysiology Behind Acid-Base Imbalance**

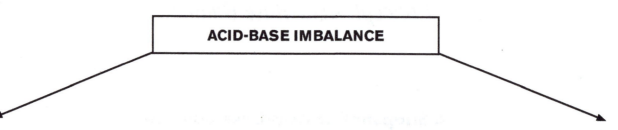

Respiratory Acidosis (Too Much Carbonic Acid)	**Respiratory Alkalosis** (Too Little Carbonic) Acid)	**Metabolic Acidosis** (Too Much Metabolic Acid)	**Metabolic Alkalosis** (Too Little Metabolic Acid)
Alveolar Hypoventilation	Hyperventilation	Excessive Production or Intake of Metabolic Acid	Increase of Base (Bicarbonate)
Conditions that affect pulmonary function: • Obstructive pulmonary disease • Pneumonia • Atelectasis **Depression of the respiratory system:** • Opioid overdose • Head injuries **Post-op pain** **Conditions that alter the chest wall excursion:** • Mechanical hypoventilation • Diseases affecting innervation of thoracic muscle (Guillain-Barré syndrome, polio, etc.) • Thoracic trauma; flail chest	**Primary stimulation of the CNS:** • Apprehension, anxiety, fear • Encephalitis (infection of the CNS) • Salicylate poisoning **Stimulation (Reflex) of the CNS:** • Hypoxia stimulates hyperventilation (i.e., CHF, respiratory infection, etc.) • Temperature **Mechanical hyperventilation:** • "Over breathing" with the ventilator	**Increased production or intake of Metabolic Acid:** • Aspirin overdose • Alcoholic ketoacidosis • Diabetic ketoacidosis • Lactic acidosis (from tissue anoxia) • Starvation • Thyroid Storm **Decrease in the excretion of Metabolic Acid:** • Oliguria from any cause **Bicarbonate Loss:** • Diarrhea that is prolonged • Intestinal drainage or pancreatic fistula	**Base (Bicarbonate) excess:** • Diuretic therapy • Excessive intake of bicarbonate (baking soda) **Excessive loss of Metabolic Acid:** • Vomiting for periods of time • Prolonged nasogastric suctioning without adequate replacement of electrolytes • Excess intake of mineralocorticoid

SAFETY Concept: Acid-Base Balance
Respiratory Acidosis

Respiratory Acidosis: Excessive retention of CO_2 from hypoventilating. With the increase in the carbonic-acid concentration, there will be an increase in H^+ ions and a decrease in the pH (< 7.35).

SAFETY Respiratory Acidosis pH < 7.35; $PaCO_2$ > 45 mm Hg		
System-Specific Assessments "HYPO"	**First-Do Priority Interventions** "BREATHES"	**Evaluate Outcomes** "HYPO"
Hypoventilation; hyperkalemia **Y**es, LOC is decreased **P**ressure (blood) decreased **O**xygen in blood is low; early signs of acidosis (restless and ↑HR)	**B**reath sounds assess, VS, SaO_2, mucous color. **R**eposition in semi/high-Fowler's to facilitate deep breathing and q 2 hrs to prevent atelectasis; turn, cough and deep breathe (TC & DB) post-op; use minimum narcotics due to depression of the RR. **E**ncourage incentive spirometry per protocol; excessive pulmonary secretions should be removed with postural drainage and percussion followed by suction. **A**dminister 0_2 with caution, because it may precipitate CO_2 narcosis. Airway maintain (suction), ABG values. **T**he meds available: bronchodilators, humidity for O_2. **H**ydration maintenance (oral care q 2 hours). **E**valuate for hyperkalemia (ECG for spiked T waves); educate; emotional support. **S**upport renal system to promote adequate compensation; support respiratory system with mechanical ventilation if client does not respond to pulmonary hygiene.	**H**ypoventilation– not present; hyperkalemia–not present **Y**es, LOC is WDL **P**ressure (blood) WDL **O**xygen in blood WDL; no signs of acidosis; ABGs WDL

INSANELY EASY TIP! Clients who **HYPO**ventilate retain CO_2. Remember this and you can organize assessments around the major clinical findings for this condition of Respiratory Acidosis. The **PRIORITY** is to get the client to "**BREATHE**"!

SAFETY Concept: Acid-Base Balance
Respiratory Alkalosis

Respiratory Alkalosis: Excessive loss of CO_2 from hyperventilating. This will result in a decrease in the H^+ concentration and an increase in the pH (> 7.45).

SAFETY Respiratory Alkalosis pH > 7.45; $PaCO_2$ < 35 mm Hg		
System-Specific Assessments "HYPER"	**First-Do Priority Interventions "SLOWER"**	**Evaluate Outcomes "HYPER"**
Hyperventilation; hyperreflexia **Y**es, muscles are weak with tingling of extremities **P**otassium level low: potential for arrhythmias Pulse ↑ **E**valuate for CNS stimulation (i.e., confusion, irritability, anxiety, seizures) **R**apid and deep respirations	**S**hould always begin with determining the cause; slow down the rate of client breathing. **L**ower ventilation by adjusting ventilator rate settings and tidal volume per HCP order. **O**xygen administered if hypocapnia is secondary to hypoxemia. Use objective criteria to evaluate pain and medicate. **W**ith psychological hyperventilation, reassure, remain calm, and ↓ stress. Monitor ABGs; focus on $PaCO_2$. **E**valuate need for sedation. **R**eview breathing mask (such as a rebreather) or techniques (paper bag).	**H**yperventilation; hyperreflexia—none. **Y**es, muscles are weak with tingling of extremities—none. No weakness or tingling of extremities. **P**otassium level 3.5–5 mEq/L; Pulse WDL for client and no trending noted. **E**valuate for CNS stimulation (i.e., confusion, irritability, anxiety, and seizures)—None. **R**apid and deep respirations—Not present. ABGs WDL.

INSANELY EASY TIP! Respiratory Alkalosis is a result of hyperventilation and blowing off the CO_2.

The priority nursing care is for the breathing to be **"SLOWER,"** which will decrease the loss of CO_2 and help retain it.

SAFETY Concept: Acid-Base Balance
Metabolic Acidosis

The **renal system** is also very effective as a buffer, but it is the slowest. The kidneys reabsorb sodium (Na^+) and produce and conserve sodium bicarbonate ($NaHCO_3^-$). In *acidosis*, the H^+ ions are excreted before the potassium (K^+) ions, thereby precipitating hyperkalemia. The potassium moves back into the cell after the acidosis has been corrected. In *alkalosis*, the H^+ concentration is decreased; there is an augmented excretion of the K^+ ions, precipitating hypokalemia. If the renal system is the cause of the pH alteration, then it is not able to correct the problem.

Metabolic Acidosis: Decrease in HCO_3 levels in the serum which results in an increase in H^+ concentration and a decrease in the pH (< 7.35).

SAFETY Metabolic Acidosis pH < 7.35; $HCO_3 < 22$ mEq/L		
System-Specific Assessments "Ds"	**First-Do Priority Interventions** "RESPIRATE"	**Evaluate Outcomes** "Ds"
Deep, rapid respirations (Kussmaul breathing) compensatory action by the lungs **D**iarrhea, nausea, vomiting **D**ecreased BP and HR; decrease and weak peripheral pulses **D**ysrhythmias related to hyperkalemia **D**rowsiness, disorientation, headache, seizures **D**iabetes Mellitus (ketones in urine) **D**ecrease in muscle strength, ↓ reflexes **D**ry, flushed skin	**R**eview initially to determine underlying problem in order to manage. Review weight ongoing. Rehydrate with IV fluid (start IV). If related to GI losses, administer antidiarrheal (as long as the problem is not from food poisoning). **E**valuate RR and support to promote compensation. **S**aO$_2$, pH, and HCO$_3$ levels should be monitored; seizure precautions. **P**lace on ECG monitor and evaluate for dysrhythmias from hyperkalemia. **I**ntake and output records should be maintained. **R**eview weight of client. **A**ssess renal function and hydration status; administer sodium bicarbonate in severe acidosis. If client has diabetes mellitus, evaluate for ketoacidosis, and administer insulin accordingly. **T**each client rationale for nursing care and meds. **E**valuate lab values for hyperkalemia; renal function; ketones.	**D**eep, rapid respirations (Kussmaul breathing)–none **D**iarrhea, nausea, vomiting–none **D**ecreased BP–no; (WDL) **D**ysrhythmias related to hyperkalemia–none **D**rowsiness, disorientation, headache, seizures–none present

INSANELY EASY TIPS!

When **assessing** remember if anything comes out of the **B**ottom, the client loses **BASE** and can result in **ACIDOSIS**.

To help **PRIORITIZE** Care Help the client "**RESPIRATE**" to assist in blowing off the CO_2 to begin compensating for the metabolic acidosis.

SAFETY Concept: Acid-Base Balance
Metabolic Alkalosis

Metabolic Alkalosis: Increase in HCO_3 levels in the serum which results in a decrease in H^+ concentration and an increase in the pH (> 7.45).

SAFETY Metabolic Alkalosis pH > 7.45; HCO_3 > 26 mEq/L		
System-Specific Assessments "EMESIS"	**First-Do Priority Interventions** "WEIGHT"	**Evaluate Outcomes** "EMESIS"
Elevated heart (dysrhythmias, due to hypokalemia) and hypomagnesemia, respiratory rate (shallow-hypoventilate); decrease in BP; labs for ↓ in serum K^+ levels and ↓ Mg^{++} level	**W**eigh daily. **E**valuate VS, cardiac rhythm, and RR; LOC; Labs for ↓ serum K^+ and Mg^{++} levels. **I**rrigate an NG tube with normal saline solution instead of tap water, I & O, IV fluids should have electrolyte replacement.	**E**levated heart (dysrhythmias)–none present; K^+ and Mg^{++} levels WDL
Muscle weakness, numbness, tingling	**G**ive antiemetics to control vomiting.	**M**uscle weakness, numbness, tingling– none
Evaluate weight; emesis, anorexia	**H**ave equipment for seizure precautions; foods high in potassium for clients receiving diuretics.	**E**valuate weight (WDL); emesis, anorexia–none
Sign-Chvostek's and Trousseau's (due to ↓ Mg^{++} level)	**T**hiazide, loop diuretics; corticosteroid antacids (sodium bicarbonate, calcium carbonate); drugs associated with metabolic alkalosis; administer potassium supplement to these clients as required and prescribed.	**S**ign–Chvostek's and Trousseau's–none
Irritability, anxiety, increase N & V		**I**rritability, anxiety, increase N&V–none
Sensorium–confusion, seizures		**S**ensorium, confusion, seizures–none; ABGs WDL

INSANELY EASY TIPS!

When **assessing** metabolic alkalosis, associate **vomiting** with the loss of **hydrochloric acid**. When excess acid is lost either through "EMESIS" or an NG tube, then there is a risk for metabolic alkalosis.

To help **PRIORITIZE** Care. If the client is **vomiting large amounts**, they may lose "WEIGHT." Organize nursing care around **stopping the vomiting**, irrigating the NG with normal saline versus tap water, and replace the K^+.

The Procedure for Arterial Blood Gases

Indications	Pre-Procedure "EDUCATE"	Post-Procedure "RADIAL"
Conditions that require an understanding of the status of oxygenation and acid-base balance of the blood (i.e., oxygen therapy, respiratory diseases, mechanical ventilation, etc.).	**E**ducate regarding procedure. **D**etermine if ABG is going to be obtained with arterial puncture or arterial line. **U**se of anticoagulants. **C**ollection sample: heparinized syringe available. **A**llen's Test prior to arterial puncture. Verify radial and ulnar circulation. Review "T and E" for procedure. **T**he nurse: 1) compresses ulnar and radial arteries simultaneously while instructing client to form a fist. 2) Have client relax hand while releasing pressure on radial artery. **E**valuate hand to determine if it turns pink quickly, indicating patency of radial artery. Repeat process for ulnar artery.	**R**emind client to be still. **A**rterial puncture: use aseptic technique. **D**o collect specimen in heparinized syringe. **I**mmediately put capped specimen into basin of ice to preserve pH levels & O_2 pressure. Take IMMEDIATELY to lab. **A**rterial puncture must have direct pressure for at least 5 minutes, 20 minutes if receiving anticoagulants. Ensure bleeding has stopped prior to removing direct pressure. **L**ook at site for bleeding, loss of pulse, swelling, changes in temperature or color. Look at arterial waveform after completion if arterial line used. Flush line with pre-connected flushing system.

PRIORITY SAFETY TIP

Verify patent radial and ulnar circulation by performing ALLEN's TEST!

After the arterial puncture, direct pressure should be over site for at least 5 minutes.

If client is receiving anticoagulants, apply pressure for 20 minutes.

Terms for Arterial Blood Gas (ABG) Interpretation

Decompensation: pH is either below 7.35 or above 7.45.

Partial Compensation: Partial compensation occurs when the pH is out of the normal limits but is moving toward the normal range. If the client has respiratory acidosis, the HCO_3 is retained to assist in compensation. In respiratory alkalosis, the HCO_3 is excreted to assist in compensation. If the client is presenting with metabolic acidosis, CO_2 is blown off to decrease the acid in the body and the client will present with Kussmaul's respirations. If there is a problem with metabolic alkalosis, CO_2 is retained (hypoventilation).

Compensation: The system (either the respiratory or metabolic) that is not affected is responsible for returning the pH to a more normal level.

Full Compensation: The problem is corrected and the pH has now returned to a normal level but the pH is usually closer to the alkalosis or acidosis range (i.e., acid side = pH < 7.40 or alkalosis side = pH > 7.40). The HCO_3 and CO_2 will still remain out of the normal range but the system that is on the same acid or alkalosis side of the pH will determine if it was metabolic or respiratory originally.

$PaCO_2$ Imbalance: Origin is the respiratory system or it is compensating for the metabolic problem.

Kussmaul's respirations are a deep and labored breathing pattern often associated with metabolic acidosis, particularly diabetic ketoacidosis but also with renal failure.

HCO_3 Imbalance: Origin is primarily metabolic, or it is compensating for a respiratory problem. The normal ratio of HCO_3 to $PaCO_2$ is 20:1; when this ratio is maintained, the outcome is a normal pH.

ABG	Definitions	Normal Range
pH	The chemical abbreviation for negative logarithm of hydrogen ion concentration	7.35–7.45
PaO_2	Pressure of dissolved oxygen in the blood	80–100 mm Hg
$PaCO_2$	Pressure of dissolved CO_2 in the blood	35–45 mm Hg
HCO_3	Bicarbonate	22–26 mEq/L
SaO_2	Percentage of oxygen bound to Hgb as compared to amount that can be carried	95–100%
Mm Hg	Millimeters of mercury	
H^+	Hydrogen ion concentration	
Blood pH level < 7.35 reflects acidosis; pH level > 7.45 reflects alkalosis.		

Insanely EASY TIP!
Start with the pH.
Drop the 7 to get the $PaCO_2$ value (35–45); then divide 45 by 2 to help calculate HCO_3 (22–26) value!
See how EASY this is!

THE BOTTOM LINE GOAL OF THE BODY:
Maintain homeostasis in acid-base balance.

The respiratory system regulates pH by hypo or hyperventilating; the kidneys regulate pH by excreting or retaining hydrogen ions or bicarbonate.

Balancing ABG	pH	$PaCO_2$	HCO_3
Respiratory Acidosis	Decreased pH	Increased $PaCO_2$	WDL
Respiratory Alkalosis	Increased pH	Decreased $PaCO_2$	WDL
Metabolic Acidosis	Decreased pH	WDL	Decreased HCO_3
Metabolic Alkalosis	Increased pH	WDL	Increased HCO_3

The "EASY" 1, 2, 3 Approach to the Interpretation of Arterial Blood Gases (ABGs)

With the process of ABG interpretation, there are several questions you will want to ask yourself! The first step is to memorize the normal pH, $PaCO_2$, and HCO_3.

1. **Is pH normal? (7.35–7.45)? If it is abnormal, analyze if it is representing acidosis (< 7.35) or alkalosis (> 7.45).**

2. **Analyze $PaCO_2$. (Normal 35–45 mm Hg). Is it high or low? Origin is respiratory system.**

3. **Analyze HCO_3. (Normal 22–26 mEq/L. Is it high or low? Origin is primarily metabolic.**

pH	7.35–7.45
$PaCO_2$	35–45
HCO_3	22–26

STRATEGY 1!

The "EASY" 1, 2, 3 Approach to the Interpretation of Arterial Blood Gases (ABGs)

There will be several strategies reviewed in this section to assist in learning how to interpret ABGs.

This **first strategy** will use an "**Easy 1, 2, 3**" method as a guide in learning how to interpret uncompensated, partially compensated, and fully compensated ABGs.

The **second strategy** for interpreting ABGs will be using "**ROME**" (Respiratory Opposite and Metabolic Equal). The **third strategy** will review a "**Referee who is calling the shots.**"

UNCOMPENSATED (Note: The chart on the next page is your tool to simplify this process. Note: <7.40> is being referred as being the mid-range for the normal pH.) Let's begin with Strategy 1!

1. For an uncompensated ABG, the pH is abnormal! The $PaCO_2$ or the HCO_3 are either acidic or alkaline and will be in the column with the pH. *Two key points to remember:*

   • *If the $PaCO_2$ is not within the defined limits, the origin is the respiratory system.*

   • *If the HCO_3 is not within the defined limits, the origin is primarily metabolic.*

2. Place the client's values for both the $PaCO_2$ and HCO_3 in the correct box on the chart.

3. The interpretation is so very easy! If both the pH and the HCO_3 are in the same column (let's say the acid column and the $PaCO_2$ is normal, the interpretation would be an uncompensated metabolic acidosis).

The next page is simply a blank chart for you to review the normal ABG values and start to become familiar with these. After you review the chart, turn to Exercise 1. Place the ABG values in the designated boxes, and then make the decision if this client's report is metabolic or respiratory in origin and if it is acidic or alkaline.

After you have made your decision, refer to the bottom of the page for the actual interpretation and rationale. After you have reviewed this Exercise 1, proceed to Exercise 2.

Use this Chart to Interpret ABGs

Client's ABG Report is:			
	Acid	**Normal Range**	**Alkaline**
pH **Compensated**	< 7.35 < 7.35–7.40	7.35–7.45 < 7.40 >	> 7.45 > 7.40–7.45
Client Value			
HCO₃	< 22	22–26	> 26
Client Value			
PaCO₂	> 45	35–45	< 35
Client Value			
Interpretation:			

Let's try one ...

Exercise 1: *Client's ABG Report is pH–7.26, HCO₃–17, PaCO₂–42*			
	Acid	**Normal Range**	**Alkaline**
pH Compensated	< 7.35 < 7.35–7.40	7.35–7.45 < 7.40 >	> 7.45 > 7.40–7.45
Client Value			
HCO₃	< 22	22–26	> 26
Client Value			
PaCO₂	> 45	35–45	< 35
Client Value			
Interpretation:			

Answers to Exercise 1:

Exercise 1: Client's ABG Report is pH–7.26, HCO₃–17, PaCO₂–42

	Acid	**Normal Range**	**Alkaline**
pH Compensated	< 7.35 < 7.35–7.40	7.35–7.45 < 7.40 >	> 7.45 > 7.40–7.45
Client Value	7.26		
HCO₃	< 22	22–26	> 26
Client Value	17		
PaCO₂	> 45	35–45	< 35
Client Value		42	

Interpretation: Acute Metabolic Acidosis–Uncompensated. Rationale: Both pH and the HCO₃ are in the acid column. PaCO₂ is normal.

Here's another ...

Exercise 2: *Client's ABG Report is pH–7.49, HCO₃–23, PaCO₂–30*			
	Acid	**Normal Range**	**Alkaline**
pH Compensated	< 7.35 < 7.35–7.40	7.35–7.45 < 7.40 >	> 7.45 > 7.40–7.45
Client Value			
HCO₃	< 22	22–26	> 26
Client Value			
PaCO₂	> 45	35–45	< 35
Client Value			
Interpretation:			

Answers to Exercise 2:

Exercise 2: *Client's ABG Report is pH–7.49, HCO₃–23, PaCO₂–30*			
	Acid	**Normal Range**	**Alkaline**
pH Compensated	< 7.35 > 7.35–7.40	7.35–7.45 < 7.40 >	> 7.45 > 7.40–7.45
Client Value			7.49
HCO₃	> 22	22–26	> 26
Client Value		23	
PaCO₂	> 45	35–45	< 35
Client Value			30
Interpretation: Acute Respiratory Alkalosis – Uncompensated. **Rationale:** Both pH and PaCO₂ are in the alkaline column. The HCO₃ is normal.			

Strategy 1, continued!

The "EASY" 1, 2, 3 Approach to the Interpretation of Arterial Blood Gases (ABGs)

PARTIALLY COMPENSATED

1. For a partially compensated ABG the pH is abnormal.
2. For a partially compensated ABG, either the $PaCO_2$ and the HCO_3 are opposite of each other (neither will be within the defined limits).
3. The interpretation is so very easy! If both the pH and the $PaCO_2$ are in the same column, (let's say the acid column and the HCO_3 is not within the defined limits and is in the alkaline column, then interpretation would be a partially compensated respiratory acidosis).

After you have processed these steps,

proceed to Exercise 3 and work through this.

Yea! I bet you got it!

Remember, this is a process! Be kind to yourself as you learn! No one is perfect when they begin learning a new concept! The key to your success is **practice**, **practice**, **practice**!! *We have two more strategies to help you learn—after we practice some more exercises!*

Here's another ...

Exercise 3: *Client's ABG Report is pH–7.26, HCO₃–34, PaCO₂–52*			
	Acid	**Normal Range**	**Alkaline**
pH Compensated	< 7.35 < 7.35–7.40	7.35–7.45 < 7.40 >	> 7.45 > 7.40–7.45
Client Value			
HCO₃	< 22	22–26	> 26
Client Value			
PaCO₂	> 45	35–45	< 35
Client Value			
Interpretation:			

Answers to Exercise 3:

Exercise 3: *Client's ABG Report is pH–7.26, HCO₃–34, PaCO₂–52*			
	Acid	**Normal Range**	**Alkaline**
pH Compensated	> 7.35 < 7.35–7.40	7.35–7.45 < 7.40 >	> 7.45 > 7.40–7.45
Client Value	7.26		
HCO₃	< 22	22–26	> 26
Client Value			34
PaCO₂	> 45	35–45	< 35
Client Value	52		

Interpretation: Partially Compensated Respiratory Acidosis. **Rationale:** Both pH and the PaCO₂ are in the same acid column. The HCO₃ is opposite the PaCO₂ trying to compensate but only partially because the pH is still acidic.

Strategy 1, continued!

The Interpretation of Arterial Blood Gases (ABGs)—Continued

FULLY COMPENSATED

1. Now the pH is normal (7.35–7.45)!
2. The $PaCO_2$ and HCO_3 are opposite of each other and are not within the defined limits.
3. The origin can be determined by:
   - pH < 7.35–7.40 = acidosis (Respiratory= $PaCO_2$)
   - pH > 7.40–7.45 = alkalosis (Metabolic= HCO_3)
   - The value of the $PaCO_2$ or the HCO_3 that is on the same side as the adjusted pH will determine if the ABG is respiratory or metabolic.
   - The interpretation would be if the pH is normal and $PaCO_2$ and the HCO_3 are opposite and adjusted pH is < 7.40 and $PaCO_2$ were in the acid column, then this would indicate a fully compensated respiratory acidosis.

After you have processed these steps,
proceed to Exercises 4 and 5 and work through them.

Yea! I bet you got it!

Do you need to take a break before moving on?

Here's another ...

Exercise 4: *Client's ABG Report is pH–7.36, HCO₃–34, PaCO₂–50*

	Acid	Normal Range	Alkaline
pH Compensated	< 7.35 < 7.35–7.40	7.35–7.45 < 7.40 >	> 7.45 > 7.40–7.45
Client Value			
HCO₃	< 22	22–26	> 26
Client Value			
PaCO₂	> 45	35–45	< 35
Client Value			
Interpretation:			

Answers to Exercise 4:

Exercise 4: *Client's ABG Report is pH–7.36, HCO₃–34, PaCO₂–50*

	Acid	Normal Range	Alkaline
pH Compensated	< 7.35 > 7.35–7.40	7.35–7.45 < 7.40 >	> 7.45 > 7.40–7.45
Client Value		7.36	
HCO₃	> 22	22–26	> 26
Client Value	34		
PaCO₂	> 45	35–45	< 35
Client Value	50		

Interpretation: *Fully Compensated Respiratory Acidosis.* **Rationale:** pH is normal and the PaCO₂ and HCO₃ are opposite. **Fully compensated:** It is respiratory acidosis in origin because the adjusted pH < 7.40 and PaCO₂ are in the acid column.

One more ...

Exercise 5: *Client's ABG Report is pH–7.43, HCO₃–30, PaCO₂–49*

	Acid	Normal Range	Alkaline
pH Compensated	< 7.35 < 7.35–7.40	7.35–7.45 < 7.40 >	> 7.45 > 7.40–7.45
Client Value			
HCO₃	< 22	22–26	> 26
Client Value			
PaCO₂	> 45	35–45	< 35
Client Value			
Interpretation:			

Answers to Exercise 5:

Exercise 5: *Client's ABG Report is pH–7.43, HCO₃–30, PaCO₂–49*

	Acid	Normal Range	Alkaline
pH Compensated	> 7.35 < 7.35–7.40	7.35–7.45 < 7.40 >	> 7.45 > 7.40–7.45
Client Value		7.43	
HCO₃	< 22	22–26	> 26
Client Value			30
PaCO₂	> 45	35–45	< 35
Client Value	49		

Interpretation: Fully Compensated Metabolic Acidosis. *Rationale:* pH is normal and the PaCO₂ and HCO₃ are opposite. **Fully compensated:** It is metabolic alkalosis in origin because the adjusted pH > 7.40 and HCO₃ are in the alkaline column.

STRATEGY 2!

Another EASY Approach to Interpreting the Acid-Base Status

Refer to "**ROME**" below for an easy way to remember how to determine if the client is presenting with metabolic or respiratory acidosis/alkalosis.

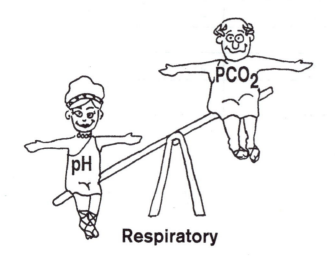

Respiratory

Another approach is to remember if it is a **Respiratory** problem, the pH and PCO_2 will Be in OPPOSITE directions from the normal.

Metabolic

Reprinted with permission ©1994 Creative Educators

If, however, both the pH and the HCO_3 are in the **SAME** (both up or both down), then it is a metabolic problem.

Respiratory

Opposite

Metabolic

Equal

STRATEGY 2—continued

Another EASY Approach for Interpreting the Compensatory Status

Respiratory

Kidneys begin to hold on to bicarbonate to compensate for the respiratory problem. Compensation is not complete until the pH has returned to the normal value of 7.35–7.45.

Notice the HCO_3 will also be in **OPPOSITE** direction of the pH as compensation begins.

Metabolic

Respiratory system begins to compensate for the metabolic problem when the lungs hold on to PCO_2.

Now, instead of the values being in **OPPOSITE** directions like they are in the respiratory interpretation, these values will be in the **SAME** direction. In other words, if the client is experiencing metabolic acidosis and each of the values are low, eventually the lungs will blow off the CO_2 and this value will also be low as compensation begins. Once again, compensation is not complete until the pH returns to the normal range.

STRATEGY 3!

Another EASY Approach to Interpret If the Client is Losing ACID or BASE

The referee calls the shots in Acid-Base. He will help you remember if **ACID** or **BASE** is lost. Above the waist **A**cid is lost. **B**elow the waist **B**ase is lost.

The stomach, above the waist, contains HCl (H⁻ is an acid). HCl acid is lost during vomiting or when the client has a nasogastric tube. As a result, the client may develop a problem with alkalosis. When the client is hyperventilating, he increases the loss of carbonic acid which will result in alkalosis.

The bowel, below the waist, contains alkaline substances that are lost during diarrhea. If alkali are lost, then the client may become acidotic. See how easy this is!

Above the waist—lost acid. Below the waist—base is lost.

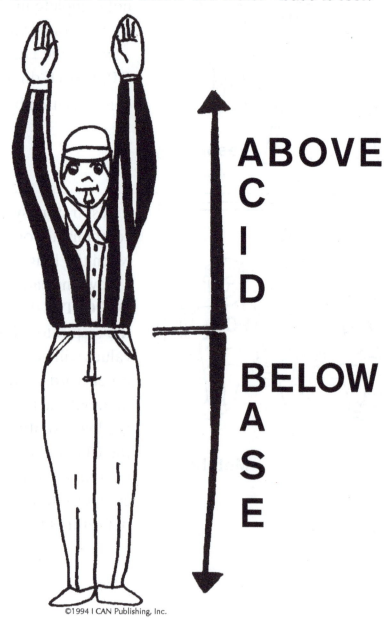

©1994 I CAN Publishing, Inc.

Clinical Decision-Making Exercises

1. What is the priority of care for a client who presents with the following ABG report: pH–7.48; PaCO$_2$–33 mm Hg; HCO$_3$–23 mEq/L?

    ① Assist client to slow down breathing and assist with rebreathing device.

    ② Notify the healthcare provider about the arterial blood gas report interpreted as respiratory acidosis.

    ③ Place in high-Fowler's and encourage deep breathing and coughing.

    ④ Place in the prone position to prepare for respiratory therapy.

2. What is the priority of care for a young female client in her 37th week of pregnancy who continues to breathe at 32/minute and is presenting with this ABG report: pH–7.47; PaCO$_2$–32 mm Hg; HCO$_3$–24mEq/L?

    ① Administer the oxygen supplement per protocol.

    ② Assist client to slow down breathing and assist with rebreathing device.

    ③ Reposition every 2 hours and encourage coughing and deep breathing.

    ④ Notify the healthcare provider about the arterial blood gas report interpreted as respiratory acidosis.

3. What is the priority of care for a client who had a thoracotomy 12 hours ago and is on 40% humidified oxygen with the following ABG results: PaO$_2$–90%; pH–7.30; PaCO$_2$–48 mm Hg; HCO$_3$–26mEq?

    ① Position in high-Fowler's and encourage coughing and deep breathing.

    ② Place in the prone position to prepare for respiratory therapy.

    ③ Notify the healthcare provider about the report and expect an order to increase oxygen percentage.

    ④ Administer anti-anxiety agent, and assist the client with a rebreathing device to increase oxygen levels.

4. Which one of these clinical findings would the nurse document and report, indicating a problem with a client who has Guillain-Barré and who developed a respiratory infection 48 hours ago?

    ① pH–7.45; PaCO$_2$–36 mm Hg; HCO$_3$–25 mEq/L.

    ② pH–7.50; PaCO$_2$–31 mm Hg; HCO$_3$–23 mEq/L.

    ③ pH–7.52 PaCO$_2$–35 mm Hg; HCO$_3$–28 mEq/L.

    ④ pH–7.32; PaCO$_2$–49 mm Hg; HCO$_3$–26 mEq/L.

5. What clinical finding is a priority to report to the healthcare provider for a client who has been presenting with diarrhea for the last 48 hours from an unknown etiology?

    ① Arterial Blood Gas of pH–7.31; PaCO$_2$–35 mm Hg; HCO$_3$–20mEq/L.

    ② Arterial Blood Gas of pH–7.46; PaCO$_2$–45 mm Hg; HCO$_3$–27 mEq/L.

    ③ Trousseau's sign.

    ④ Shallow breathing.

6. Which of these assessment findings are important to monitor for a post-op client who is presenting with a pH–7.32; $PaCO_2$–35 mm Hg; HCO_3–21mEq/L? ***Select all that apply.***

   ① BP–160/100.
   ② Diarrhea.
   ③ Shallow breathing.
   ④ Dysrhythmia.
   ⑤ Drowsy and disoriented.

7. Which one of these statements made by a new graduate indicates the charge nurse was effective when conducting an orientation program for the graduates regarding the pathophysiology behind acid-base balance?

   ① "Metabolic acidosis can occur from diuretic therapy due to the base excess."
   ② "Metabolic alkalosis can occur from a prolonged episode of diarrhea."
   ③ "Respiratory acidosis can occur from depression of the respiratory system from the use of opioids."
   ④ "Respiratory alkalosis can occur from hypoventilation due to post-operative pain."

8. Which one of these lab values might indicate a complication for a client with a nasogastric tube that has been set to low suction for 24 hours?

   ① pH–7.48; $PaCO_2$–35 mm Hg; HCO_3–28 mEq/L.
   ② pH–7.45; $PaCO_2$–36 mm Hg; HCO_3–25 mEq/L.
   ③ pH–7.33; $PaCO_2$–48 mm Hg; HCO_3–25 mEq/L.
   ④ pH–7.33; $PaCO_2$–36 mm Hg; HCO_3–21 mEq/L.

9. Which one of these nursing actions is the priority for a client who was admitted for vomiting 24 hours and presents with the ABG results pH–7.48; $PaCO_2$–45 mm Hg; HCO_3–29 mEq/L?

   ① The UAP weighs the client daily.
   ② The LPN irrigates the NG tube with tap water.
   ③ The RN administers sodium bicarbonate per protocol.
   ④ The RN administers oxygen via a rebreathing device per protocol.

10. Which one of these nursing actions is the priority for a client prior to the nurse performing an arterial blood gas on the client?

    ① Evaluate the Trousseau's Sign by using a sustained BP cuff and inflating it. Then evaluate for tingling (numbness) of the extremity.
    ② The nurse compresses ulnar and radial arteries simultaneously while instructing client to form a fist. Have client relax hand while releasing pressure on radial artery.
    ③ The nurse evaluates the reflex by using the reflex hammer.
    ④ Apply a tourniquet above the site where the nurse wants to draw the blood.

Answers and Rationales

1. What is the **priority of care** for a client who presents with the following **ABG report: pH–7.48; PaCO$_2$–33 mm Hg; HCO$_3$–23 mEq/L?**

   ① **CORRECT: This is correct since the client is experiencing respiratory alkalosis.**

   ② INCORRECT: The report is respiratory alkalosis.

   ③ INCORRECT: This report indicates respiratory alkalosis. This would be effective for respiratory acidosis.

   ④ INCORRECT: The problem is with hyper-ventilating; breathing needs to slow down.

The strategy is to begin with interpreting the ABG report. Always begin with the normal pH, which is 7.35–7.45; then drop the 7 and decimal point to get the value range for the PaCO$_2$ which is 35–45 mm Hg. Then you can divide the 45 by 2 and the range for the HCO$_3$ is 22–26 mEq/L.

In this question, the pH is high and the PaCO$_2$ is low, which means the client is breathing off too much CO$_2$. Remember the strategy "**ROME**." When the pH is opposite of the PaCO$_2$, then it is respiratory. The goal is to "**SLOW**" down the breathing and assist with rebreathing in order to hold on to more CO$_2$. *Refer to the assessments and interventions in the chart for Respiratory Alkalosis.* It is so easy! The assessments indicate the client is **HYPER**-ventilating and the care is to help client breathe "**SLOWER**." Now, we also have some more great news for you! Any time a client has a medical diagnosis that may result in hyperventilating, this concept of respiratory alkalosis will assist you in helping client return to homeostasis (acid-base balance). *Refer to Pathophysiology chart* to review specific medical conditions such as anxiety, apprehension, temperature, respiratory infection, etc. With any of these conditions, the nursing care will be the same. Of course, one of the different aspects of care will be for the nurse to determine the cause of the hyperventilation. For example, if it is

due to a fever, then this needs to be managed. (*Refer to Concept Thermoregulation for specifics.*) If it is due to anxiety, then assistance with coping needs to be initiated. (*Refer to Concept Coping for specifics.*)

Reduction of Risk: Monitor the results of the diagnostic testing (labs) and intervene as needed.

Reduction of Risk: Manage the care of a client with impaired ventilation/oxygenation.

2. What is the **priority of care** for a young female client in her 37th week of pregnancy who continues to **breathe at 32/minute** and is presenting with this **ABG report: pH–7.47; PaCO$_2$–32 mm Hg; HCO$_3$–24mEq/L?**

   ① INCORRECT: Administering the oxygen supplement per protocol will not fix the problem of hyperventilating and alkalosis.

   ② **CORRECT: This is correct since the client is experiencing respiratory alkalosis.**

   ③ INCORRECT: This report indicates respiratory *alkalosis*. This option would be effective for respiratory *acidosis*.

   ④ INCORRECT: The report is respiratory alkalosis.

The strategy is the same as in question 1. We know that "Repetition is the Mother of Learning"! We want you to learn to apply this concept across the continuum of nursing. This concept applies to OB clients, pediatric, psychiatric, medical/surgical clients, etc. Remember, "**HYPER**" will assist you with the assessments and "**SLOWER**" will assist you with the nursing interventions.

Reduction of Risk: Monitor the results of the diagnostic testing (labs) and intervene as needed.

Reduction of Risk: Manage the care of a client with impaired ventilation/oxygenation.

3. What is the **priority of care** for a client who had a thoracotomy 12 hours ago and is on 40% humidified oxygen with the following **ABG results: PaO_2–90%; pH–7.30; $PaCO_2$–48 mm Hg; HCO_3–26mEq?**

    ① **CORRECT: Position in high-Fowler's and encourage coughing and deep breathing. The client is experiencing respiratory acidosis from decreased ventilation. This may be from discomfort from the surgical procedure. Increasing the quality of ventilation by mobilizing any secretions and expanding the alveoli by these actions may resolve the problem.**

    ② INCORRECT: This does not address this situation.

    ③ INCORRECT: Notifying the healthcare provider about the report and expecting an order to increase oxygen percentage are not priorities.

    ④ INCORRECT: Administering an anti-anxiety agent and assisting the client with a rebreathing device to increase oxygen levels would create more problems with respiratory acidosis, since the client may slow down breathing and retain additional CO_2.

The strategy is to begin by interpreting the ABGs. Refer to rationale in question 1 regarding this process. There are also several strategies in this chapter to assist in simplifying and making this memorable for future use. After you conclude the results indicate respiratory acidosis, then it is time to organize the nursing care. "HYPO" will assist you in organizing the nursing assessments for respiratory acidosis. Remember, clients who **hypo**ventilate tend to hold on to CO_2. The goal is for the nursing care to assist in getting them to "BREATHE". The nursing care is organized around "BREATHE" to assist you with recall. Once again, the great news is that the assessments and interventions apply to any medical condition that causes clients to hypoventilate, such as pain, opioid usage, head injuries, COPD, etc. (*Refer to Pathophysiology Chart at the beginning of this chapter for more specifics regarding actual medical conditions.*) Initially if the problem is from hypoventilation, the nurse needs to correct the cause. While eventually the HCP may order oxygen, this would not be the priority over repositioning as described in option 1.

Of course, as a student, it is important to start at the very beginning with a noninvasive action if you have this as an option. The nurse would reposition anyway prior to administering oxygen to facilitate optimum utilization of the oxygen.

Do you notice any similar interventions with this concept and the concept on Oxygenation? While there are some differences in the mnemonic "BREATHE," we advise you focus on the similar interventions to assist you in making this easy and memorable!

Reduction of Risk: Monitor the results of the diagnostic testing (labs) and intervene as needed.

Reduction of Risk: Manage the care of a client with impaired ventilation/oxygenation.

4. Which one of these **clinical findings** would the nurse **document and report, indicating a problem** with a client who has **Guillain–Barré** and who developed a **respiratory infection** 48 hours ago?

    ① INCORRECT: This ABG is within normal limits and does not reflect this client.

    ② INCORRECT: This ABG reflects respiratory alkalosis and does not reflect this client.

    ③ INCORRECT: This ABG reflects metabolic alkalosis and does not reflect this client.

    ④ **CORRECT: This ABG represents respiratory acidosis which reflects this client.**

The strategy is to begin with the stem of the question. The chest wall excursion can be affected by Guillain-Barré and especially if there is another complication with a respiratory infection. The client will not be able to expire the CO_2 due to a decrease in the ability to breathe deeply. Once you have identified the medical condition, then match this up with the appropriate ABG values.

Physiological Adaptation: Recognize changes in a client condition and intervene as needed.

Reduction of Risk: Manage the care of a client with impaired ventilation/oxygenation.

5. What **clinical finding** is a **priority to report** to the healthcare provider for a client who has been **presenting with diarrhea for the last 48 hours** from an unknown etiology?

   ① CORRECT: Metabolic acidosis reflects this client.

   ② INCORRECT: Metabolic alkalosis does not reflect this client.

   ③ INCORRECT: Trousseau's sign would indicate a complication with hypocalcemia or low magnesium.

   ④ INCORRECT: Shallow breathing would indicate a complication with metabolic alkalosis.

The strategy is to link the clinical finding with pathophysiology. Prolonged diarrhea will result in a loss of bicarbonates. An easy way to remember this is to think about bicarbonates come out of the **bottom**! If base comes out of the bottom, the result is acidosis. *Refer to the "Referee who is calling the shots."* When fluid comes from the waist and up, acid is lost. The result is metabolic alkalosis. Also note that the pH and HCO_3 are both low. The strategy "**ROME**" can also assist you with determining what the blood gases are. Options 2 and 4 reflect metabolic alkalosis, so if you did not know the answer you could cluster these together and know that they could not be correct.

Physiological Adaptation: Manage the care of the client with a fluid and electrolyte imbalance.

6. Which of these **assessment findings** are important to monitor for a post-op client who is presenting with a **pH–7.32; $PaCO_2$–35 mm Hg; HCO_3–21mEq/L**? Select all that apply.

   ① INCORRECT: The BP would be decreased.

   ② CORRECT: Abdominal cramping, diarrhea, and muscle weakness can occur with metabolic acidosis.

   ③ INCORRECT: Breathing would be deep and rapid.

④ CORRECT: Dysrhythmia is a result of metabolic acidosis due to the alteration in the potassium level.

⑤ CORRECT: Drowsiness and disorientation can occur with metabolic acidosis.

The strategy is to link the system-specific assessments with the concept of metabolic acidosis. *Refer to "The Ds" to assist you in organizing this information.*

Physiological Adaptation: Manage the care of the client with a fluid and electrolyte imbalance.

Reduction of Risk Potential: Perform focused assessment.

7. Which one of these statements made by a new graduate indicates the charge nurse was effective when conducting an orientation program for the graduates regarding the **pathophysiology behind acid-base balance?**

   ① INCORRECT: It should read base loss.

   ② INCORRECT: It should read metabolic acidosis would be from diarrhea. Emesis would result in metabolic alkalosis.

   ③ CORRECT: "Respiratory acidosis can occur from depression of the respiratory system from the use of opioids." This would result in an increase in CO_2.

   ④ INCORRECT: This can occur from hyperventilation.

The strategy is to link this concept to the pathophysiology. When you understand this, it will be memorable. We recommend you apply this to your clients you care for in the hospital, so you can reinforce this newly learned information.

Physiological Adaptation: Identify the pathophysiology related to an acute or chronic condition.

8.   Which one of these lab values might **indicate a complication for a client with a nasogastric tube that has been set to low suction for 24 hours?**

① **CORRECT: Metabolic alkalosis may be a result of the suction or vomiting.**

② INCORRECT: This is a normal ABG and is not the result of a complication.

③ INCORRECT: The complication would not be respiratory acidosis.

④ INCORRECT: The complication would not be metabolic acidosis.

The strategy is to *refer to the "Referee who is calling the shots."* When any fluid comes out from above the waist, the loss is acid leading to metabolic alkalosis.

Physiological Adaptation: Manage the care of the client with a fluid and electrolyte imbalance.

Reduction of Risk Potential: Recognize complications; monitor results of diagnostic testing (labs).

9.   Which one of these **nursing actions** is the **priority** for a client who was admitted for **vomiting** 24 hours and presents with the **ABG results pH–7.48; pCO$_2$–45 mm Hg; HCO$_3$–29 mEq/L?**

① **CORRECT: Weight loss is an excellent evaluation of fluid loss or gain.**

② INCORRECT: Irrigating the NG tube with tap water would result in a further alteration in fluid and electrolytes.

③ INCORRECT: The client is already in metabolic alkalosis; no need for additional bicarbonate.

④ INCORRECT: There is not an indication that the client is experiencing respiratory alkalosis. This is not typically a complication from vomiting.

The strategy is to link the symptoms with the pathophysiology. **"WEIGHT"** will assist you in organizing the priority nursing interventions for a client presenting with metabolic alkalosis. Not only will this assist you in organizing the care, the mnemonic itself tells you one of the priority nursing actions; WEIGHT is one of the priority assessments to monitor fluid status.

Physiological Adaptation: Manage the care of the client with a fluid and electrolyte imbalance.

10.   Which one of these **nursing actions** is the **priority** for a client **prior to** the nurse **performing an arterial blood gas** on the client?

① INCORRECT: This test is used to evaluate for a low calcium and/or magnesium level.

② **CORRECT: The Allen's Test is done prior to an arterial puncture to verify patent radial and ulnar circulation. The nurse would then evaluate hand to turn pink quickly, indicating patency of radial artery. The process is then repeated for the ulnar artery.**

③ INCORRECT: Evaluating reflexes by using the reflex hammer is too vague as to location and does not address the question.

④ INCORRECT: Applying a tourniquet above the site where the nurse wants to draw the blood would obstruct the flow of blood in the artery.

The strategy is to recognize the need to evaluate for patent radial and ulnar circulation prior to the procedure.

Reduction of Risk Potential: Perform a focused assessment.

Decision-Making Analysis Form

Use this tool to help identify why you missed any questions. As you enter the question numbers in the chart, you will begin to see patterns of why you answered incorrectly. This information will then guide you toward what you need to focus on in your continued studies. Ultimately, this analytical exercise will help you become more successful in answering questions!!!

Questions to ask:

1. Did I have the knowledge to answer the question? If not, what information do I need to review?

2. Did I know what the question was asking? Did I misread it or did I miss keywords in the stem of the question?

3. Did I misread or miss keywords in the distractors that would have helped me choose the correct answer?

4. Did I follow my gut reaction or did I allow myself to rationalize and then choose the wrong answer?

	Lack of Knowledge (Concepts, Systems, Pathophysiology, Medications, Procedures, etc.)	Missed Keywords or Misread the Stem of the Question	Missed Keywords or Misread the Distractors	Changed My Answer (Second-guessed myself, i.e., my first answer was correct.)
Put the # of each question you missed in the column that best explains why you think you answered it incorrectly.				

If you changed an answer because you talked yourself out of the correct answer, or you second-guessed yourself, this is an **EASY FIX: QUIT changing your answers**!!! Typically, the first time you read a question, you are about 95% right! The second time you read a question, you start talking yourself into changing the answer. The third time you read a question, you do not have a clue—and you are probably thinking "Who in the heck wrote this question?"

On the other hand, if you read a question too quickly and when you reread it you realize you missed some key information that would impact your decision (i.e., assessments, lab reports, medications, etc.), then it is appropriate to change your answer. When in doubt, go with the safe route: your first thought! Go with your gut instinct!

As you gain confidence in answering questions regarding specific nursing concepts, you will be able to successfully progress to answering higher-level questions about prioritization. Please refer to the *Prioritization Guidelines* in this book for a structure to assist you with this process.

You CAN do this!

"Life is either a daring adventure or it is nothing."

HELEN KELLER

References for Chapter 7

Daniels, R. & Nicoll, L. (2012). *Contemporary medical-surgical nursing*, (2nd ed.). Clifton Park, NY: Delmar Cengage Learning.

Eliopoulos, C. (2014). *Gerontological nursing* (8th ed.), Philadelphia: Lippincott Williams & Wilkins.

Giddens, G. F. (2013). *Concepts for nursing practice*. St. Louis, MO: Mosby, an imprint of Elsevier.

Hogan, M. A. (2014). *Pathophysiology: Reviews and rationales* (3rd ed.) Boston, MA: Pearson.

Ignatavicius, D. D. and Workman, M. L. (2010). *Medical-surgical nursing: Patient-centered collaborative care* (6th ed.). Philadelphia: Elsevier/Saunders.

LeMone, P., Burke, K. M., and Bauldoff, G. (2011). *Medical-surgical nursing: Critical thinking in patient care* (5th ed.). Upper Saddle Road, NJ: Pearson/Prentice Hall.

Lewis, S., Dirksen, S., Heitkemper, M., Bucher, L., and Camera, I. (2011). *Medical surgical nursing: Assessment and management of clinical problem*s (8th ed.). St. Louis: Mosby.

Manning, L. and Rayfield, S. (2014). *Nursing made insanely easy* (7th ed.). Duluth, GA: I CAN Publishing, Inc.

National Council of State Boards of Nursing, INC. (NCSBN) 2012. *Research brief: 2011 RN practice analysis: linking the NCLEX RN® examination to practice.* Retrieved from https://www.ncsbn.org/index.htm

North Carolina Concept Based Learning Editorial Board (2011). *Nursing a concept based approach to learning*, Upper Saddle Road, NJ: Pearson/Prentice Hall.

Porth, C. (2011). *Essentials of pathophysiology* (3d ed.). Philadelphia, PA: Lippincott Williams ad Wilkins.

Porth, C. M. and Grossman, S. (2013). *Pathophysiology: Concepts of altered health states* (9th ed.). Philadelphia, PA: Lippincott Williams & Wilkins.

Rose, B. D., (2011). *Clinical physiology for acid-base and electrolyte disorders* (6th ed.). New York: McGraw-Hill.

Taber's cyclopedic medical dictionary (2005). Philadelphia, PA: F. A. Davis.

CHAPTER 8

Respiratory System: Linking Concepts to Pathophysiology of Diseases
Concept Oxygenation

A Snapshot of Oxygenation

Oxygenation is transport of oxygenated blood through the circulatory system to the cells and the return of oxygenated blood and carbon dioxide from the cells (Giddens, 2013). Oxygenation is impacted by ventilation, transport and perfusion. Ventilation is the exchange of oxygen that enters the lungs and is expelled as carbon dioxide from the lungs. Ventilation can be impaired by any disorder that affects the nasopharynx and lungs, (i.e., COPD, edema of the sinuses, etc.). Transport involves the ability of hemoglobin to deliver oxygen to the cells for metabolism and back to the alveoli to eliminate the carbon dioxide produced by cellular metabolism. Anemia from any cause, (iron deficiency anemia, anemia resulting from chemotherapy, etc.), impairs the transport (Refer to anemia in this chapter). Perfusion is the transport of oxygen by the blood to the cells, tissues and organs. Impairment of perfusion can result from decreased cardiac output, thrombi, and/or constriction of the blood vessels or from bleeding (Refer to Concept Perfusion Cardiac/Peripheral for specifics). Respiratory acidosis can result from decreased perfusion if there is a decreased ability to transport carbon dioxide to be eliminated (Refer to Concept Acid/Base for specifics). When oxygen does not reach the cells, ischemia or death of the tissue can result without intervention (Osborn, Wraa, Watson, & Holleran, 2104). Terms to know include:

Ischemia: insufficient oxygenated blood flow to the tissues that may result in cell injury or death.

Hypoxia: insufficient oxygen reaches the cells.

Anoxia: no oxygen reaches the cells.

Hypoxemia: decreased oxygen in the arterial blood.

Terms to know for changes in breath sounds as a result of altered oxygenation:

Breath sounds: Normal should be clear and equal bilaterally. (Need to know the normal first!)

Adventitious sounds: Sounds that should not be heard. These are abnormal/extra breath sounds.

Crackles: Auscultated during inspiration and do not clear with cough; occurs when fluid is in airway (previously known as *rales*); sounds are not continuous (may hear early with pneumonia, cardiac failure, and atelectasis).

Wheezes: May be auscultated during inspiration and/or expiration. The sounds are from air moving through narrowed passages; sound is continuous and music-like (heard with asthma, bronchitis, and/or chronic emphysema).

Pleural friction rib: Auscultated typically on inspiration over inflammation or the pleural area; many times is described as a grating sound (heard with pleuritis and presents with pain when breathing).

Stridor: Sounds like a crowing sound. This is high pitched and is heard with croup and/or acute epiglottitis.

Orthopnea: Client presents with difficult breathing unless sitting erect or standing. Results from an increase in pulmonary venous and capillary pressure in the lungs when client is lying supine, and is relieved when client sits upright.

Diminished breath sounds: Breath sounds that sound distant due to "trapped air" (emphysema, COPD).

Absent: No breath sounds are heard on the side of a collapsed lung (pneumothorax).

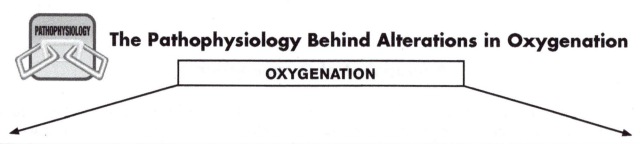

The Pathophysiology Behind Alterations in Oxygenation

Obstruction	Infection	Collapsed Lung	Pulmonary Artery Obstruction	Failure	Transport	Perfusion
• Asthma • COPD (Emphysema Bronchitis) • Cystic Fibrosis	**Upper Respiratory Tract:** • Croup • Epiglottitis • Tonsillitis **Lower Respiratory Tract:** • Pneumonia • Tuberculosis • Severe Acute Respiratory Syndrome (SARS)	• Pneumo-thorax • Hemothorax • Tension pneumo-thorax	• Pulmonary Emboli	• Acute Respiratory Failure (ARF) • Acute Respiratory Distress Syndrome (ARDS)	**Anemia Issues:** • Aplastic • Folic Acid Deficiency • Iron Deficiency • Hemolytic • Pernicious • Thalassemia • Sickle Cell Anemia	*Refer to Concept Perfusion and Shock Chapter* • Aneurysm • Heart Failure • Peripheral Artery Disease • Shock

System-Specific Assessments for Oxygenation

Dyspnea, orthopnea, and nocturnal.

Yes, early signs: ($\uparrow$ T, $\uparrow$ RR, $\uparrow$ HR, $\uparrow$ BP), restlessness; skin and mucous membranes pale; late signs: VS $\downarrow$, cyanosis, $\downarrow$ LOC, lethargy, lightheadedness. *(Geriatric clients: acute confusion is early sign.)*.

Secretions altered, productive cough (color, consistency, tenacity and odor, pink-tinged sputum = pulmonary edema, signs of infection (i.e., $\uparrow$ temp, $\uparrow$ WBC, etc.).

Precipitating factors: infection, immobility, allergens, stress, trauma, post-op complications, pleurisy.

Note characteristics of the cough (i.e., dry, moist, productive), alleviating or aggravating factors, discomfort with breathing; symptoms with cough such a fever or shortness of breath.

Evaluate SaO$_2$ < 95% on arterial blood gases (ABGs), pulse oximetry < 92%.

Adventitious breath sounds (wheezes, crackles, atelectasis after post-op); immobility; arrhythmias; use of accessory muscles, asymmetrical chest expansion; activity intolerance.

Linking Pathophysiology to System-Specific Assessments for Altered Oxygenation

Pathophysiology	System-Specific Assessments "DYSPNEA"
Dyspnea may occur as a result of narrowed airways from bronchoconstriction (i.e., asthma) or obstruction (i.e., chronic bronchitis, cystic fibrosis); poor gas exchange in the alveoli, (i.e., pneumonia, pulmonary edema); impaired nerve function or inadequate muscle to assist with air movement into the lungs, (i.e., cervical spinal cord injury). Altered oxygen transport, such as with anemia, can result in dyspnea due to insufficient blood cells carrying oxygen. Altered perfusion as a result of a reduction in cardiac output, such as in a myocardial infarction, can result in dyspnea due to hypoxia. Orthopnea refers to an abnormal condition during which a client must sit or stand to breathe. Clients with COPD may prefer to sleep while leaning forward over a table.	**D**yspnea, orthopnea and nocturnal–assess.
Yes, vital signs will be elevated due to a physiological response to compensate for the decrease in oxygenation. Temperature may be increased due to an infection. The change in the respiratory rate is due to the increase work to breathe. If client is using pursed-lip breathing on exhalation, it is to assist in keeping airways open longer. Tachycardia may occur due to anxiety from not being able to breathe or from anemia. The pale skin and mucous membranes can be from anemia or hypoxemia. A late sign of hypoxemia is cyanosis. As the hypoxia increases, there can be a decrease in the perfusion of blood to the brain, resulting in a decrease in the LOC. *Geriatric clients will typically present with an acute confusion due to the lack of oxygen.*	**Y**es, early signs: ($\uparrow$ T, $\uparrow$ RR, $\uparrow$ HR, $\uparrow$ BP); restlessness; skin & mucous membranes pale; late signs: VS $\downarrow$, cyanosis, $\downarrow$ level of consciousness (LOC), lethargy, lightheadedness. (*Geriatric clients: acute confusion is early sign.*)
Secretions can change from clear to yellow in color, which may indicate an infection. Pink-tinged secretions that are thin and frothy are seen in pulmonary edema. These secretions are thin because it is combined with water. If the hydrostatic pressure is very high, small capillaries break and sputum becomes pink tinged.	**S**ecretions altered, productive cough (color, consistency, tenacity and odor). Pulmonary edema: pink-tinged, frothy sputum. Signs of infection (i.e., $\uparrow$ temp, $\uparrow$ WBC, yellow secretions).
Precipitating factors must be determined in order to develop an appropriate plan of action. For example if hypoxia is from a post-op respiratory infection, the priority of care is T, C, and DB; if it is from stress, the care is to assist with healthy coping mechanisms.	**P**recipitating factors: infection, immobility, allergens, stress, trauma, post-op complications, pleurisy.
Noting characteristics of the cough will assist in plan of care. The cough is a defensive attempt to expectorate secretions or extra fluid in the lungs.	**N**ote characteristics of the cough (i.e., dry, moist, productive), alleviating or aggravating factors, discomfort with breathing; symptoms with cough such a fever or shortness of breath).
Evaluate SaO$_2$ pulse oximetry readings are typically less than the defined limits due to the decrease in the oxygen available for perfusion. ABGs may reveal a respiratory acidosis due to hypoventilation, an increase in carbon dioxide (i.e., COPD). If client is hyperventilating, outcome would be respiratory alkalosis (i.e., anxiety). (*Refer to Concept Acid Base Balance chapter for specifics.*)	**E**valuate SaO$_2$ < 95% on arterial blood gases (ABGs), pulse oximetry < 92%.
Adventitious breath sounds may occur from the mucus or secretions in the bronchi.	**A**dventitious breath sounds (wheezes, crackles, atelectasis after post-op); immobility; arrhythmias; use of accessory muscles, asymmetrical chest expansion; activity intolerance.

Linking Pathophysiology to System-Specific Assessments for Altered Oxygenation

The chart below illustrates different clinical situations that require ongoing assessment of altered oxygenation. As nurses, we want to be proactive and intervene early to minimize the potential for complications. Below you will find links to oxygenation, pathophysiology and the nursing care.

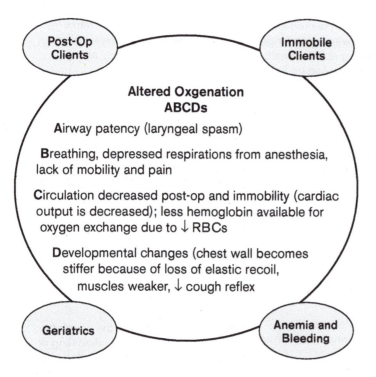

Post-Op Clients

Immobile Clients

Altered Oxgenation ABCDs

Airway patency (laryngeal spasm)

Breathing, depressed respirations from anesthesia, lack of mobility and pain

Circulation decreased post-op and immobility (cardiac output is decreased); less hemoglobin available for oxygen exchange due to ↓ RBCs

Developmental changes (chest wall becomes stiffer because of loss of elastic recoil, muscles weaker, ↓ cough reflex

Geriatrics

Anemia and Bleeding

The **ABCDs** will assist you in linking the pathophysiology with clients in various clinical situations. For example, with the post-op client immediately after surgery, there is a risk for an obstructed airway due to a laryngeal spasm post-extubation. In addition, there is a risk for depressed respirations from the anesthesia and the immobilization of the client. Both of which result in decreased circulation. The outcome is **Altered Oxygenation**.

The pathophysiology related to anemia and bleeding is the result of the decreased hemoglobin, which carries the oxygenated blood throughout the body. Again the outcome is the **Altered Oxygenation**.

As adults age, there are physiological changes that occur and the outcome is **Altered Oxygenation**. The early sign of altered oxygenation with the geriatric client is acute confusion.

Now, notice the similarity in the **Oxygenation** pathophysiology chart with the clinical conditions reviewed on the left. The one commonality is **Altered Oxygenation**.

As you look at the concept of oxygenation, how can you organize the early versus late assessments of "**DYPSNEA**"?

Refer to the **INSANELY EASY TIP** on the next page for the answer!

INSANELY EASY TIP for Learning
Priority System-Specific Assessments!!

System-Specific Assessments
Early and Late Signs of HYPOXIA

Early "STRESS"	Late "CRASH"

Symptoms of restlessness (acute confusion with Geriatric client) **T**achycardia (↑ HR) **R**espirations are increased (↑ RR) **E**levated blood pressure (↑ BP) **S**kin and mucous membranes pale **S**ounds in lungs–adventitious	**C**onfusion and stupor **R**espirations decreased (↓ RR) **A**rrhythmias **S**kin and mucous membranes cyanotic **H**eart rate (↓ HR), hypotension (↓ BP)

These early and late signs of hypoxia apply to ANY disease in the Respiratory System related to the concept of Altered Oxygenation (i.e., asthma, COPD, tonsillitis, pneumonia, etc.). They also apply to ANY clinical situation that results in alteration of oxygenation (i.e., post-operative, pain, immobile, anxious, shock, etc.).

When answering questions or providing client care, remember to organize the assessments based on EARLY versus LATE signs!

See how EASY this is! You CAN do this with just a few assessments!
Now, you can answer MANY questions and feel confident
with your PRIORITY assessments!

Alterations in Oxygenation

Common Labs/Diagnostic Tests/Therapeutic Procedures/Surgeries

Labs, Diagnostic Tests, and Procedures

Labs	Diagnostics Tests/Procedures
• ABG Analysis (Refer to Acid Base Concept for values) • CBC • Electrolytes • Sputum cultures • PT, PTT, INR **Cystic Fibrosis specific labs:** • Sweat chloride test • Stool analysis • Serum blood glucose for hyperglycemia	• Pulmonary function tests • Chest X-ray (Abdominal x-ray for meconium ileus with Cystic Fibrosis) • Pulse Oximetry • Chest Physiotherapy • Chest Tubes • Hemodynamic monitoring • Bronchoscopy • Thoracentesis

Alteration in Oxygenation
Common Medications for Oxygenation

Medications for Oxygenation	
Anticholinergics • Aclidinium Bromide (Tudorza, Pressair) • Ipratropium (Atrovent) • Tiotropium (Spiriva) **Beta 2 Agonists—Short Acting** • Albuterol (Proventil) • Bitolterol (Tornalate) • Levalbuterol (Xopenex) • Pirbuterol (Maxair) • Metaproterenol (Alupent) **Beta 2 Agonists—Long Acting** • Arformoterol Tartrate (Brovana) • Formoterol (Foradil) • Indacaterol Maleate (Arcapta) • Salmeterol (Serevent) **Erythropoietin** • Epoetin Alfa (Epogen, Procrit) **Phosphodiesterase 4 Inhibitors (PDE4)** • Roflumilast (Daliresp)	**Combination: (Beta 2 Agonist + Anticholinergic** • Albuterol & Ipratropium (Combivent) • Umeclidinium & Vilanterol Inhalation Powder (Anoro, Ellipta) **Combination: (Beta 2 Agonist + Corticosteroid)** • Fluticasone & Salmeterol (Advair) • Fluticasone Furoate & Vilanterol Inhalation Powder (Breo, Ellipta) • Mometasone Furoate & Formoterol (Dulera) • Budesonide & Formoterol (Symbicort) **Leukotriene Inhibitors** • Montelukast (Singulair) • Zafirlukast (Accolate) • Zileuton (Zyflo) **Mast Cell Stabilizers** • Cromolyn Sodium (Intal) • Nedocromil (Tilade)

First-Do Priority Interventions
"BREATHE"

B   Breath sounds, SaO_2, vital signs, DYSPNEA assess and monitor; O_2 as needed, assess for arrhythmias; lightheadedness.

R   Reposition to facilitate ventilation and perfusion, (i.e., HOB ↑ , up in chair, ambulate, particularly after surgery).

E   Evaluate airway status; prepare for oxygen supplement, (i.e., ambu bag); initiate EMERGENCY management as needed, (i.e., CPR, mechanical ventilation).

A   Assess and document ABG values, sputum color, consistency and amount, good oral care every 2 hours.

T   The airway needs to be suctioned PRN to maintain patency. Chest physiotherapy & postural drainage per protocol, bronchodilators and hand held nebulizers as prescribed.

H   Hand washing, wear appropriate PPE, apply infection control standards (*i.e., room placement, assignment, etc.*); cultures, (*before antibiotics, etc.*).

E   Encourage deep breathing and coughing, incentive spirometer, evaluate outcome of medications.

Educate/emotional support, encourage fluids based on clinical presentation.

Linking Pathophysiology to First-Do Priority Interventions for Altered Oxygenation

Pathophysiology	First-Do Priority Interventions "BREATHE"
Breath sounds need to be assessed due to the potential alteration in air exchange from secretions, adventitious sounds from fluid and/or secretions; absent sounds due to a pneumothorax; or distant from COPD. Due to altered oxygenation, the client may experience some lightheadedness when upright. Oxygen supplement will assist with the hypoxia.	Breath sounds, SaO_2, vital signs, DYSPNEA assess and monitor; O_2 as needed, assess for arrhythmias; lightheadedness.
Reposition client sitting up due to the impaired gas exchange to assist with lung expansion. Clients with acute or chronic impaired oxygenation breathe more easily in high Fowler's position or semi-Fowler's position. These positions will facilitate the movement of the diaphragm away from the lungs which will decrease the workload of breathing.	Reposition to facilitate ventilation and perfusion, (i.e., HOB ↑, up in chair, ambulate, particularly after surgery).
Evaluation of the airway status is an ongoing priority of care for clients with alteration in oxygenation in order to know how to further intervene. In addition to the assessment, it is imperative to evaluate the functioning of the emergency equipment to assure it is working effectively in case the client needs assistance with mechanical ventilation. Clients may require intubation with either an endotracheal tube or tracheostomy tube. Humidified oxygen is delivered to the trachea and bronchi. If breathing support is needed, then the ventilator will control the RR and volume.	Evaluate airway status; prepare for oxygen supplement, (i.e., ambu bag); initiate EMERGENCY management as needed, (i.e., CPR , mechanical ventilation).
Assess and document ABG values. ABGs may reveal a respiratory acidosis due to hypoventilation, an increase in carbon dioxide (i.e., COPD). If client is hyperventilating, outcome would be respiratory alkalosis (i.e., anxiety). (Refer to Concept Acid Base Balance chapter for specifics.) The color of the secretions will change from clear to yellow in color indicating an infection. The thin, pink-tinged secretions (because it is combined with water) are frothy and are seen with pulmonary edema. If the hydrostatic pressure is very high, small capillaries break and sputum becomes pink tinged. Oral care will minimize sores and dryness.	Assess and document ABG values, sputum color, consistency and amount, good oral care every 2 hours.
The airway needs ongoing suctioning to remove the secretions in order to optimize airway patency. Chest physiotherapy and postural drainage are performed to loosen and move secretions into the large airways where they can be expectorated. Postural drainage uses gravity and different positions to remove secretions after they are loosened from specific lung segments.	The airway needs to be suctioned PRN to maintain patency. Chest physiotherapy and postural drainage per protocol, bronchodilators and hand held nebulizers as prescribed.
Hand washing is a major nursing activity to prevent respiratory tract infections. If client does have a respiratory tract infection, then the PPE used will be based on the organism the client has (Refer to Concept Infection Control chapter for specifics). If there is an order for any type of cultures and to start antibiotics, obtain CULTURES 1st and then start the ANTIBIOTICS. Doorknobs and countertops should be cleaned to prevent transmission of infections.	Hand washing, wear appropriate PPE, apply infection control standards (i.e., room placement, assignment, etc.); cultures, (before antibiotics, etc.).
Encourage deep breathing and coughing for clients (i.e., immobilized, pneumonia, COPD, etc.) will increase lung expansion and facilitate oxygen exchange. Fluids, based on medical condition, will liquefy secretions. Educate regarding coughing or sneezing into a tissue will decrease the particles dispersed into the air. Health Promotion is always important for compliance!	Encourage deep breathing and coughing, incentive spirometer, evaluate outcome of medications. Educate/emotional support, encourage fluids based on clinical presentation.

SAFETY Summary: Concept Oxygenation

System-Specific Assessment "DYSPNEA"	First-Do Priority Interventions "BREATHE"	Evaluation of Expected Outcomes "No DYSPNEA"
Dyspnea, orthopnea & nocturnal **Y**es, early signs: ($\uparrow$ T, $\uparrow$ RR, $\uparrow$ HR, $\uparrow$ BP); restlessness; skin & mucous membranes pale; late signs: vital signs $\downarrow$, cyanosis, $\downarrow$ level of consciousness (LOC), lethargy, lightheadedness. (*Geriatric clients: acute confusion is early sign.*) **S**ecretions altered, productive cough (color, consistency, tenacity and odor). Pulmonary edema: pink-tinged, frothy sputum. Signs of infection (i.e., $\uparrow$ temp, $\uparrow$ WBC, yellow secretion, etc.). **P**recipitating factors: infection, immobility, allergens, stress, trauma, post op complications, pleurisy. **N**ote characteristics of the cough (i.e., dry, moist, productive), alleviating or aggravating factors, discomfort with breathing; symptoms with cough such a fever or shortness of breath). **E**valuate SaO$_2$ < 95% on arterial blood gases (ABGs), pulse oximetry < 92%. **A**dventitious breath sounds (wheezes, crackles, atelectasis after post-op); immobility; arrhythmias; use of accessory muscles, asymmetrical chest expansion; activity intolerance.	**B**reath sounds, SaO$_2$, vital signs, DYSPNEA assess & monitor; O$_2$ as needed, assess for arrhythmias; lightheadedness. **R**eposition to facilitate ventilation & perfusion, (i.e., HOB $\uparrow$, up in chair, ambulate, particularly after surgery). **E**valuate airway status; prepare for oxygen supplement, (i.e. ambu bag); initiate EMERGENCY management as needed, (i.e., CPR, mechanical ventilation). **A**ssess and document ABG values, sputum color, consistency & amount, good oral care every 2 hours. **T**he airway needs to be suctioned PRN to maintain patency. Chest physiotherapy & postural drainage per protocol, bronchodilators & hand held nebulizers as prescribed. **H**and washing, wear appropriate PPE, apply infection control standards (i.e., room placement, assignment, etc.); obtain cultures before antibiotics. **E**ncourage deep breathing & coughing, incentive spirometer, evaluate outcome of medications. **E**ducate/emotional support, encourage fluids based on clinical presentation.	**D**yspnea, orthopnea & nocturnal NONE **Y**es, vital signs Normal, No restlessness, color pink; no lightheadedness **S**ecretions, sputum color clear **P**recipitating factors NONE **NO** cough **E**valuation of SaO$_2$ > 95% on arterial blood gases (ABGs), O$_2$ sat > 92% **A**dventitious breath sounds, NONE; NO arrhythmias; NO use of accessory muscles; symmetrical chest expansion **NO** activity intolerance

Geriatric Client Will Present with
"ACUTE CONFUSION" as an Early Sign of Hypoxia!!!

Physiological Affects of Aging On Respiratory System "WEAKER"	Acute Confusion!	Priority First-Do Interventions "MO$_2$VE"
Weaker elastic recoil of the lungs during expiration because of less elastic collagen and elastin; expiration requires the active use of accessory muscles. **E**ffect of changes with aging results in a reduction in vital capacity and an increase in the residual volume = exchange of air is less and more air and secretions remain in the lungs. **A**lveoli are less elastic and fibrous tissue is developed. **K(C)**ontain fewer functional capillaries. **E**vidence of reduction in body fluid and fluid intake by drier mucous membranes, resulting in the development of mucous plugs and infection. **R**educed pain sensations can cause signs of respiratory infection to go unnoticed. **R**elaxed sphincters and slower gastric motility contribute to the risk of aspiration.		**M**ove the clients: assist to ambulate, sit, turn, ROM, etc.; immobility is a major threat to pulmonary health. **O**$_2$ Oxygen: O$_2$ sat, cough, deep breathe & incentive spirometry, etc. **V**ital signs, evaluate trends for altered oxygenation & intervene; very concerned with oral hygiene: prevent infections since these can lead to respiratory infections. This can also result in a decrease in appetite and cause generally poor health status. **E**liminate pain, if clients are in pain, they won't deep breath or move! **E**nvironment: conscious effort to minimize exposure to air pollution in environment. • Install and maintain air filters in heating and air conditioning. • Open windows to air out rooms. • Damp-dusting furnishings. • Vacuum regularly.

Pathophysiology: Obstructions
Chronic Obstructive Pulmonary Disease (COPD)

This section will focus ONLY on the exceptions of the system-specific assessments of "DYSPNEA" and the interventions of "BREATHE" in the plan of care for all clients with all diseases with alterations in oxygenation.

Chronic Obstructive Pulmonary Disease COPD encompasses two diseases, emphysema and bronchitis. COPD is due to the decrease in the elasticity of the lungs. This results in obstructed airflow out of the lung that impedes respirations.

Emphysema results in the alveolar wall destruction resulting in over extension of the air spaces. The air spaces become obstructed. Enzymes then destroy the connective tissue of the lungs (they lose their elasticity), and the lungs can no longer empty normally. The ability to expel the CO_2 is decreased and hypoxia becomes the driving force for the client to breathe.

Chronic bronchitis is the inflammation of the bronchi that causes increased mucous production. This increase in mucus production results in a chronic cough which leads to scarring of the bronchial lining. Asthma is intermittent obstruction. It can also result in increased mucus production and/ or the inflammation of the bronchi, all of which traps the air, and the client may experience difficulty with the expiratory phase of respiration (Black & Hawk, 2009).

	FIRST-DO	PRIORITY	INTERVENTIONS	
System-Specific Assessments	**Diet**	**Equipment**	**Plans/Interventions**	**Health Promotion**
Refer to "**DYSPNEA**" assessments and: • Assess for distant breath sounds • Note: barrel shaped chest • Clubbing of the fingers and toes	• Helpful to eat frequent smaller meals to conserve oxygen. • Soft, high-calorie foods	• O_2: only ↑ O_2 to 2–4 L/nasal cannula–or up to 40% Venturi mask or per HCP orders • Metered dose inhaler for bronchodilator administration or hand-held nebulizer • ECG monitoring	Refer to "**BREATHE**" Interventions and: • HOB ↑ or leaning over night stand to help open the airway for breathing • Use pursed lip breathing • May need systemic bronchodilator as prescribed	Teach client/family: • How to purse lip breathe. • How to pace activities with rest. • Importance of receiving recommended immunizations (i.e., influenza and pneumovax).

Exceptions and Additions by Diseases

Pathophysiology: Obstructions
Asthma

Asthma is an intermittent, obstruction that results in a reversible airway problem. It is a chronic inflammatory process that causes increased production of mucus secretions causing mucosal edema. This inflammation and increased constriction of the bronchi and the bronchioles of the airway, traps the air. This causes bronchospasms. Asthma can also be a result from emotional factors that can cause attacks in children. Exercise can initially improve the respiratory status, but later can lead to a significant decline. Asthmatic symptoms may be worse in cold, dry air and are better in warm, moist air (LeMone, Burke, & Bauldoff, 2011).

Potential Complication: Status Asthmaticus: This can be life threatening. Clients present with extreme wheezing, labored breathing, accessory muscle use, tightness in chest worsens, and distended neck veins are visible. This can result in a cardiac and/or respiratory arrest. In many situations, the client may be unresponsive to treatment.

	FIRST-DO	PRIORITY	INTERVENTIONS	
SYSTEM-SPECIFIC ASSESSMENTS	**DIET**	**EQUIPMENT**	**PLANS/INTERVENTIONS**	**HEALTH PROMOTION**
Refer to "**DYSPNEA**" assessments and "**TRAPS**": **T**achycardia, tachypnea **T**ightness in chest **R**estless **A**ssess wheezing **A**ccessory muscles are used **P**roduction of mucus **P**rologned expiration **S**aO$_2$ low	• Helpful to eat frequent, smaller meals to conserve oxygen • Soft, high-calorie foods	• O$_2$: Supplemental O$_2$ to maintain SaO$_2$ at 90% per HCP orders • Metered dose inhaler for bronchodilator administration or hand-held nebulizer • ECG monitoring **Status Asthmaticus:** • Emergency intubation. Oxygen, bronchodilators, epinephrine, and systemic steroid therapy. IV fluids for hydration during this episode.	Refer to "**BREATHE**" Interventions and: • Inhaled steroids and anti-inflammatory drugs to decrease edema. • May need systemic bronchodilator as prescribed. • If taking steroids, assess for decrease in immunity function. • Assess for hyperglycemia. • Monitor weight due to risk for fluid retention and weight gain.	Teach client/family: • How to purse lip breathe. • How to pace activities with rest. • Importance of receiving recommended immunizations (i.e., influenza and pneumovax). • Review importance of good mouth care and monitor for cold sores. • Review importance of drinking plenty of fluids. • If taking prednisone, take with food. • Review importance of using meds to prevent asthma, not for the time of onset of an attack. • Review respiratory hygiene to prevent respiratory infections.

Pathophysiology: Obstructions
Cystic Fibrosis

Cystic Fibrosis is a dysfunction of the exocrine glands that causes the glands to produce thick, tenacious mucus. It is a genetically transmitted as an autosomal recessive trait. Major organs affected are the lungs, pancreas, small intestine, and liver. Abnormally thick mucus results in mechanical obstruction of organs, which alters their functions. Sweat and salivary glands excrete excessive electrolytes, specifically sodium chloride (Porth & Grossman, 2013).

First-Do Priority Interventions	Health Promotion
S teatorrhea **S** weat test **I** leus-meconium **C** onstant hunger **K** vitamins **E** nzyme replacement **R** eduction of fat is out! **K** eep calories up **I** nfection **D** rink plenty of fluids	Teach client/family: • Medication regimen • Infection control precautions • Initial influenza vaccine at six months of age

©2014 I CAN Publishing®, Inc.

Exceptions and Additions by Diseases

Pathophysiology: Obstructions
Epiglottitis/Croup

While these two diagnoses are seen in the younger child due to the narrowed airway, we have included these to assist you in recognizing altered oxygenation from upper respiratory infections and obstructions. While "**DYSPNEA**" does apply to all clients with altered oxygenation, there are very specific assessments for these medical conditions. Remember, with upper respiratory obstruction, the problem is getting air into the client.

Epiglottitis is caused by Haemophilus influenza type B and/or group A Streptococcus on the epiglottis. The epiglottis is a leaf-shaped structure immediately posterior to the base of the tongue and lies above the larynx. Epiglottitis is characterized by edema and rapid inflammation, which leads to an enlarged epiglottis that can obstruct the upper airway.

Croup is an acute laryngotracheobronchitis (LTB) and is an inflammation of the larynx and trachea, most commonly seen in children less than five years of age. The most frequent causes are viral agents (influenza and para influenza virus, respiratory, synchytial virus). A croupy cough/stridor on inspiration that sounds like a horn, is the result of narrowed airway and is the most common clinical finding.

	FIRST-DO		PRIORITY	INTERVENTIONS
SYSTEM-SPECIFIC ASSESSMENTS	**DIET**	**EQUIPMENT**	**PLANS/INTERVENTIONS**	**HEALTH PROMOTION**
Refer to "**DYSPNEA**" assessments and: • Support the "**STRIDOR**": Epiglottitis **S**ore throat, swallowing difficulty ("seal bark" cough is classic sign of LTB) **T**emperature (low-grade for LTB, but > 102°F for epiglottitis) **R**apid, abrupt onset; retractions (suprasternal and substernal) **I**nspiratory stridor **D**rooling; characteristic position: sit with neck hyperextended (sniffing position and see "O") **O**pen mouth and tripod position **R**estless (anxiety) • Support the 4 "**D**s": EMERGENCY! **D**eep "barking" cough **D**ysphonia **D**rooling **D**ysphagia distress	• Limit milk intake	• Eliminate the use of tongue depressor • Do not do a throat culture if epiglottitis is suspected • Tents or hoods for O_2 and humidity (cool mist)	Refer to "**BREATHE**" Interventions and: • Keep upright in high-Fowler's position: never position in a supine position • Never do an oral pharyngeal airway assessment **SAFETY** **Insanely Easy Safety Review Tip!** **No oral pharyngeal airway assessments! Do NOT place in supine position!**	Teach client/family: • The importance of administering the Haemophilus Influenza immunization for child. • Conserve energy by anticipating child's needs to decrease crying.

Exceptions and Additions by Diseases

Other Respiratory Diseases With the Pathophysiology of Infection

Tonsillitis is an inflammation and infection of the palatine tonsils. It is most common in children but is often more severe in adults. Due to the frequency of young children presenting with inflamed tonsils, we have included tonsillitis as a medical condition present with upper respiratory inflammation. Stridor is not a classic assessment finding for tonsillitis. The classic finding usually is a very sore throat, but it can pose a potential threat of airway obstruction, particularly in children.

Physiology: Infection
Mycobacterium Tuberculosis (TB)

Tuberculosis (TB) is a reportable communicable disease. The primary infection is caused by the Mycobacterium tuberculosis, which is transmitted via the airborne route (*Refer to Concept Infection Control*). The body encases the TB bacillus with collagen and other cells, which typically appear as a Ghontubercule on the chest x-ray. The primary site or tubercle may progress to degeneration that can erode into the bronchial tree. The TB organisms are active and are present in the sputum as a result of the dead white blood cells, cheese-like mass of tubercule bacilli, and necrotic lung tissue. This material liquefies in time and may drain into the tracheal bronchial tree resulting in the spread of the disease by a cough. The area may never erode but may calcify and remain dormant following the primary infection. The tubercule, however, may contain living organisms that may be reactivated several years later. The majority of the people will harbor the primary infection, the TB bacilli, in a tubercule in the lungs and may not exhibit any symptoms of an active infection. Clients who are immunocompromised may unfortunately experience opportunistic infections (Daniels & Nicoll, 2012).

	FIRST-DO PRIORITY INTERVENTIONS			
System-Specific Assessments	**Diet**	**Equipment**	**Plans/Interventions**	**Health Promotion**
Refer to "**DYSPNEA**" assessments and: • Night sweats • ↑ Temperature • Hemoptysis • TB tests to confirm: acid-fast bacilli smear & culture • Note: Bacillus Calmette-Guerin (BCG) vaccine within 10 yrs, may have false postive Mantoux test. • Evaluate Mantoux test, chest x-ray to confirm false positive • Use QuantiFERON-TB Gold to determine if TB active or latent	• ↑ Protein, iron, vitamin • Avoid tyramine & histamine containing foods	• Prevent transmission (i.e., hand hygiene, application of PPE), with infection control prevention • Use airborne precautions until 3 consecutive sputum cultures are negative • Need of airborne infection isolation room (AIIR) negative pressure • Refer to Concept Infection Control for specifics	Refer to "**BREATHE**" Interventions and: • Prevent transmission, use airborne precaution until 3 consecutive sputum cultures are negative (*Refer to Concept Infection Control for specifics*) • **Report TB to CDC** • Ethambutol may cause vision changes, assess & report • Administer TB meds as prescribed	Teach client/family: • How to manage prescribed TB medications and importance of taking as prescribed. • Infection control precautions. • The importance of screening family members for TB. • Referrals to: social work, home health.

Exceptions and Additions by Diseases

Respiratory Diseases With the Pathophysiology of Infection
Pneumonia/Severe Acute Respiratory Syndrome (SARS)

Pneumonia is an acute inflammatory process that produces excess fluid in the lungs. The inflammatory process in the lung parenchyma results in edema and exudate that fill small airways and alveoli. The alveolar sacs become so filled with fluid that that the exchange of oxygen and carbon dioxide is greatly reduced. The fluid in the sacs becomes consolidated and is increasingly hard to expectorate. The most common causes are viral: (influenza, para influenza, respiratory syncytial virus (RSV) (seen primarily in infants and children), and bacteria: Streptococcus pneumonia, mycoplasma pneumonia and Staphyloccuss aureus, (the most common). If the client is immunocompromised, it is more likely that a fungal may be the cause of the pneumonia.

Severe Acute Respiratory Syndrome (SARS) is a severe acute respiratory syndrome. (SARS) is a result of the mutated coronavirus that can also cause the common cold. This virus can invade the pulmonary tissue, which can lead to an inflammatory response that can progress to respiratory failure. Need to follow airborne infection precautions.

	FIRST-DO	PRIORITY	INTERVENTIONS	
SYSTEM-SPECIFIC ASSESSMENTS	**DIET**	**EQUIPMENT**	**PLANS/ INTERVENTIONS**	**HEALTH PROMOTION**
Refer to "**DYSPNEA**" Assessments	• Diet as tolerated. • Smaller, more frequent meals may be better tolerated	• O_2 and humidity (cool mist) • PCA Pump for pain management	Refer to "**BREATHE**" Interventions	Teach client/family: • Pacing activity after discharge • Take all of antibiotics as prescribed • Report increase in sputum production, increased temp

Insanely Easy Tip for Assessing Acute Respiratory Infections!

Infection (pulmonary)

Need to assess response to activity tolerance (trend VS changes)

Fever, monitor (not a reliable assessment in the elderly client)

Elevated WBCs, exertion causes dyspnea and shortness of breath (SOB), may occur without exertion

Cough, productive, crackles (pneumonia) and wheezing

Tachypnea (↑ RR) and Tachycardia (↑ HR)

Increase mucus production (change in color, viscosity, quantity, odor)

O$_2$ sat decreased

Note restlessness, alteration in LOC

Exceptions and Additions by Diseases

Pathophysiology: Collapsed Lung
Pneumothorax/Hemothorax/Tension

Pneumothorax is the presence of air or gas in the pleural space resulting in a collapsed lung or atelectasis of that portion of the lung. This may occur as a result of trauma, thoracentesis, infection, or in older clients may occur from decreased lung elasticity and thickening alveoli. A spontaneous pneumothorax (a collapse lung) may occur with no trauma but occurs when a small bleb on the lung ruptures causing air to enter into the pleural space. The result is **ABSENT** breath sounds on the affected side.

Hemothorax is an accumulation of blood in the pleural space that can result in the collapsed lung if the bleeding is not stopped. Again the result is **ABSENT** breath sounds on the affected side.

Tension Pneumothorax is a complication that can occur when air enters the pleural space with inspiration and is not able to leave on expiration. This trapped air may result in pressure on the lung and heart. This increase in pressure may result in compression on the blood vessels limiting the venous return, resulting in a decreased cardiac output. This is a medical emergency and if not treated immediately, death may be the result.

SYSTEM-SPECIFIC ASSESSMENTS	FIRST-DO PRIORITY INTERVENTIONS			
	DIET	EQUIPMENT	PLANS/INTERVENTIONS	HEALTH PROMOTION
Refer to "**DYSPNEA**" assessments and: • Absent breath sounds (on affected side) • Breath sounds & chest wall expansion are asymmetrical • Sudden onset of persistent chest pain (pain on affected side with breathing) **Tension Pneumothorax:** • Mediastinum shifts away from affected side (causes decrease venous return)	• Diet as tolerated	• Support chest tube management • O_2 and humidity (cool mist) • PCA Pump for pain management	Refer to "**BREATHE**" Interventions and: • Position client to evacuate air or fluid • Document amount and color of drainage • Trend chest tube drainage per protocol	Teach client/family: • Pacing activity after discharge

---

Learning Priority System-Specific Assessments Made Easy!!!

Pneumothorax/Hemothorax/Tension
"THORAX"

Trach deviation to unaffected side (tension)

Hyper-resonance on percussion (pneumothorax); dull percussion (hemothorax)

O$_2$ sat. ↓; observe lips for paleness–cyanosis

Respiratory rate, & HR ↑, assess color of secretions, dyspnea; use of accessory muscles, pleuritic pain

Asymmetrical chest movement, appearance, anxious

X out breath sounds on affected side

Exceptions and Additions by Diseases

Water-Sealed Chest Drainage

• Chest tubes can be water-sealed or dry sealed. The picture below illustrates a water-sealed system. • Chest tubes are used to remove air or fluid from the pleural cavity from a pneumothorax or hemothorax. • The system is a one-way valve system that uses atmospheric pressure to keep air from entering the pleural cavity and allows air and fluid to drain.	**Important Facts in the Maintenance of Water-Sealed Chest Drainage:** • Equipment for drainage keep below the chest tube site, drains with gravity. • Evaluate all connections to make sure they are taped and secured. • Evaluate the drainage for amount, color; mark on collection chamber per protocol. • Eliminate "milking" or stripping of chest tube; leads to increased pleural pressure. • Eliminate clamping of chest tubes except to assess for leak in the system per protocol (Manning & Rayfield, 2014).

W ater seals—adding sterile fluid to chamber 2 cm.

A ir leak assessed by fast and continuous bubbling in this chamber!

T idaling is expected in water seal chamber.

E limination of tidaling water seal—lung re-expanded

R emember not to strip or milk tubing routinely

Suction control—The suction needs to have an order regarding the amount.

D rainage characteristics

R eview hourly and mark level on the collection chamber

A ssess output in comparison to previous hour

I dentify if there has been a trend with an increase or decrease in output

N ote when the chamber is half full

Exceptions and Additions by Diseases

Pathophysiology: Pulmonary Artery Obstruction
Pulmonary Emboli

Pulmonary Emboli occurs as a result of an obstruction of the pulmonary artery, caused by a substance such as a solid (blood clot or thrombus, bone marrow, fat), gas (air) or liquid (amniotic fluid) or sepsis. These substances enter the venous circulation forming a blockage in the pulmonary vasculature. The size of the embolus will have an impact on the severity of this complication. The most common cause of pulmonary emboli are from thrombi in the deep veins of the legs.

	FIRST-DO PRIORITY INTERVENTIONS			
SYSTEM-SPECIFIC ASSESSMENTS	**DIET**	**EQUIPMENT**	**PLANS/INTERVENTIONS**	**HEALTH PROMOTION**
Refer to "**DYSPNEA**" Assessments and Sudden Onset of The **8 "Ps"**: Pain Pleurisy Pleural Effusion Petechiae Pulse & Respirations ↑ (heart murmurs: S_3–S_4) Pressure (blood) ↓ Pulmonary sounds: adventitious (crackles) and congested Pulse Oximeter–O_2 sat ↓	• If on anti-coagulants, i.e., warfarin (Coumadin), decrease green leafy vegetables	• O_2 and humidity (cool mist), (mechanical ventilation may be needed) • Hemodynamic monitoring • IVs, central lines	Refer to "**BREATHE**" Interventions and: • Report sudden increase in respiratory rate, feeling of distress, and/or anxiety.	Teach client/family: • Medications, i.e., warfarin (Coumadin) • Importance of monitoring PT, INR • Report signs of bleeding

Exceptions and Additions by Diseases

Pathophysiology: Failure
Respiratory Failure (ARDS, ARF)

Acute Respiratory Distress Syndrome (ARDS) is a sudden and progressive respiratory system failure. It develops because of ischemia in the alveolar capillary membrane, which causes massive inflammation leading to increase permeability of the alveolar membrane. This increase in permeability allows fluid to leak into the interstitial spaces. In addition, the alveolar has a reduction in surfactant that weakens the aveoli causing collapse or filling of fluid, which leads to a worsening of the edema. It can result from trauma to the lungs, blunt trauma or inhalation of noxious fumes or fluid, anaphylaxis, acute pancreatitis or from pneumonia or sepsis.

Acute Respiratory Failure (ARF) is an inability of the body to sustain respiratory drive. The body is not oxygenating due to inadequate ventilation. The respiratory drive is maintained by the central nervous system directing the nerves and the muscles of respiration. Other causes of ventilatory failure can result from mechanical abnormalities of lungs or chest wall or impaired muscle function. Oxygen failure can result from a lack of perfusion to the pulmonary/capillary bed such as a pulmonary embolism. When the respiratory system fails, it leads to the development of respiratory acidosis due to the increasing CO_2 levels. The client almost always requires ventilator support (Lewis, Dirksen, Heitkemper, Bucher & Camera, 2011).

System-Specific Assessments	FIRST-DO PRIORITY INTERVENTIONS			
	Diet	Equipment	Plans/ Interventions	Health Promotion
Refer to "**DYSPNEA**" Assessments and: • Respirations progress from rapid to shallow to PROFOUND RESPIRATORY DISTRESS!	• Diet per protocol	• Mechanical ventilation • Hemo-dynamic monitoring • IVs, central lines • ECG monitor	Refer to "**BREATHE**" Interventions and: • Follow protocol for mechanical ventilator support	Teach client/family: • Ventilator management and how to communicate with client. • How to manage disease after discharge.

Exceptions and Additions by Diseases

Pathophysiology: Failure
Respiratory Failure (ARDS, ARF)

Ventilator Care

An Insanely Easy Way To Remember Ventilator Care

"VENTS"

View (monitor) ABGs, airway, and respiratory status.

Elevate HOB 30 degrees (equipment at beside: ambu bag, O_2, suction).

Note & document ventilator settings hourly: rate, FiO_2, tidal volume, mode of ventilation, or use of PEEP or CPAP, peak inspiratory pressure.

Notice gastrointestinal complications, (i.e., stress ulcer); nutritional needs.

Take note of settings (document) & alarms:
Low = Leak; volume (low pressure) alarms indicate low exhaled volume from cuff leak, disconnection, or tube displacement.
High = Dry; high pressure alarms indicate excess secretions, biting on tube, kinks, coughing, etc. Apnea: alarms = vent doesn't detect spontaneous respirations.

Suction tracheal tube: note color, amount, odor of secretions; position to promote mobility of secretions. Self-protection if needed; soft wrist restraints per HCP order.

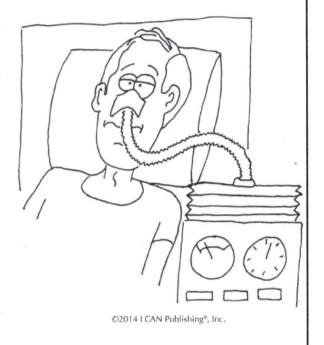

©2014 I CAN Publishing®, Inc.

Insanely Easy Way to Remember Ventilator Alarms!!!!
"LOW" = LEAK
"HIGH" = DRY

NEVER TURN OFF ALARMS on the VENTILATOR!!!!

Exceptions and Additions by Diseases

Pathophysiology: Transport
Anemia

Anemia is defined as an abnormally low number of circulating red blood cells (RBCs), low hemoglobin levels, or both (Porth, 2011). Anemia can be categorized in three ways: decreased production of red blood cells (RBCs), increased loss of RBCs, or premature destruction of RBCs (Giddens, 2013). Vitamin B_{12}, folate, and/or iron are necessary to form RBCs, so when these nutrients are low, the red blood cell production is also decreased. A reduction in the amount of erythropoietin, which normally stimulates the bone marrow to produce red blood cells, is another cause of anemia. This reduction in erythropoietin is a common result of chronic renal failure. Another form of anemia is Thalassemia, an autosomal-recessive genetic disorder that results in inadequate normal hemoglobin production.

SYSTEM-SPECIFIC ASSESSMENTS "TIRED"	FIRST-DO PRIORITY INTERVENTIONS			
	DIET	EQUIPMENT	PLANS/INTERVENTIONS "REST"	HEALTH PROMOTION
Tachycardia, tachypnea **I**ncrease in headache & shortness of breath **R**educed BP leads to postural hypotension; reduced color = pallor; in the corners of the mouth **E**valuate for beefy red tongue; fatigue; weakness, weight loss **D**yspnea on exertion; dizzy	• Refer to Concept Nutrition for specifics	• Blood pressure cuff	**R**est, encourage pacing of activities to avoid fatigue **E**ncourage diet high in iron **S**upplemental iron **T**rend Hgb and Hct results and clinical assessments	Teach client/family: • Foods high in iron for iron deficiency anemia (*Refer to Concept Nutrition for specifics*) • Safe administration of iron • Expected side effects from iron supplement

Exceptions and Additions by Diseases

Pathophysiology: Transport
Sickle Cell Anemia

Sickle cell anemia is a genetically based autosomal recessive condition. In affected clients, at least 40% of the hemoglobin is hemaglobin S (HbS), a mutated form of hemoglobin A. Hemoglobin S shrinks and causes the red blood cells (RBCs) to become stiff and form a sickle (C-Shape) that is sticky. This increases the blood viscosity and occludes small blood vessels. The increased blood viscosity leads to ischemia in the tissues and organs resulting in eventual necrosis due to capillary stasis and thrombosis. The sickle cells are trapped by the spleen, which further decreases the circulating RBCs and causes hypoxia. The damage to the red cell membrane causes a decrease in the life span of the sickle cells from the normal 120-day life span to 7–14 days. There are four clinical presentations clients with sickle cell may exhibit: **vaso-occlusive crisis** (long chain of stacked sickled cells occlude small venous and arterial blood vessels, decrease oxygenation and cause severe pain); **sequestration crisis** (sickled cells overwhelm the spleen, decrease the blood volume, blood pressure and causes deoxygenation); **aplastic crisis** (large amounts of destroyed blood cells place a huge demand on the bone marrow to replenish available circulating erythrocytes into the blood causing a complete shutdown of the bone marrow); and **hyperhemolytic crisis** (a massive increase in RBC destruction). Without treatment, sickle cell anemia can lead to multiple organ damage (Osborn, Wraa, Watson, & Holleran, 2014).

	FIRST-DO	PRIORITY	INTERVENTIONS	
SYSTEM-SPECIFIC ASSESSMENTS "TIRED"	**DIET**	**EQUIPMENT**	**PLANS/INTERVENTIONS "HOPS"**	**HEALTH PROMOTION**

Trend vital signs: ↑ RR, ↑ HR, Temp, ↓ BP; assess capillary refill, strength of pulses
 	
Inspirations & breath sounds, assess for adventitious lung sounds, shallow respirations. ↓ SaO$_2$ sat, assess CBC
 	
Renal function assess, BUN, Creatinine, bilirubin, urine output
 	
Evaluate skin/tissues for early signs of ulcers in peripheral tissues, signs of infection. Evaluate LOC (signs ↓ intracranial perfusion or bleeding)
 	
Describe & assess quality, location & duration of pain (scale 1–10); what exacerbates pain or makes it better?
	• Offer small meals (help avoid distention, nausea, vomiting)
	
	• Healthy diet of fruits, vegetables, grains, low sodium, low fat
		• Blood pressure cuff
		
		• PCA pump for narcotics for pain during crisis
			Hydration & electrolytes maintain balance: Encourage fluids
			  • Administer hypotonic fluids as prescribed (hypotonic ↓ tendency of RBCs to crystalize into sickle shape & promote dilution of occluded vessels)
			  • Monitor I & O; assess for fluid deficit from ↑ temp, vomiting & diarrhea (i.e., ↑ HR, ↑ RR)
			Oxygen: prevent acidosis, ↓ sickling, help with fatigue & pain
			  • O$_2$ as needed if SaO$_2$ sats < 80%/ or as prescribed
			  • Avoid O$_2$ therapy if not needed (suppresses bone marrow production of RBCs)
			  • Assess RR, breath sounds, monitor ABGs
			  • Encourage incentive spirometer every hour
			  • Pace activity with rest (↓ workload & oxygen demands)
			Pain assess (abdomen, joints) & medicate as prescribed
			  Prevent infections: good handwashing, appropriate PPE
			Support parents by encouraging genetic counseling
				Teach client/family:
				• Avoid activities that increase oxygen demands (i.e., air travel, high attitudes, strenuous exercise, etc.)
				• Need adequate fluids, (8 glasses of fluid/day, more with activity)
				• Pace activity with rest, avoid activity if movement causes pain; get adequate sleep
				• Monitor for signs of infection, (i.e., sores, ulcers, ↑ temp, cough, etc.); use good handwashing, avoid crowds
				• Referral for genetic counseling

Summary for Linking Pathophysiology to Interventions for Altered Oxygenation

The MO₂VE!

(sung to the tune of "If You're Happy And You Know It")

To get the best oxygenation you need to walk! (clap clap)

If you can't walk, then you sit in the chair, (clap clap)

If can't sit in the chair, then you do range of motion

If you can't do that, then you need to TURN! (clap clap)

As you have discovered and learned, with the **Oxygenation** concept, the assessment and interventions are applicable to all of the respiratory disorders described in this chapter. The respiratory disorders with exceptions or additions to the nursing assessments "**DYSPNEA**" or the interventions "**BREATHE**" have been outlined individually.

Now the questions are the following:

- "How do we apply this to clients who are post-op for an appendectomy, hysterectomy, etc.; an OB client following a caesarean section; or an immobilized client following a spinal cord injury?"

- "How do we prioritize the plan of care for a client who is bleeding after a trauma from a car accident or bleeding following surgery for hip replacement or for a client who has anemia?"

- "What is the priority of care for a hospitalized geriatric client who has a fractured hip, or admitted for any procedure?"

"**BREATHE**" outlines the priority interventions for a variety of clients with respiratory disorders. To prioritize the care, select interventions based on the clinical findings. In these situations, there are four priority actions. It is easy to plan care when you base their needs on the pathophysiology. ONE word will do it: the clients need to "**MO₂VE**"!!!!!

Move the clients: assist to ambulate, sit, turn, ROM, etc.

Oxygen: O₂ sat, cough, deep breathe and incentive spirometer, etc.

Vital signs, monitor, evaluate trends for altered oxygenation and intervene.

Eliminate pain. If clients are in pain, they don't want to deep breathe or move!

Clinical Decision-Making Exercises

1. Which of these clinical assessment findings would indicate a client is experiencing early signs of hypoxia? *Select all that apply.*
    ① Bradycardia.
    ② Cyanosis.
    ③ Restlessness.
    ④ Tachycardia.
    ⑤ Tachypnea.

2. What early symptom would an older adult present with when experiencing hypoxia?
    ① Confusion.
    ② Congested cough.
    ③ Temperature–102.4° F.
    ④ WBC–18,000 mm³.

3. Which of these nursing actions require the charge nurse to intervene with a LPN who is providing care for the child who is drooling, presenting with a deep "barking" cough?
    ① Discusses with the mom the rationale for not allowing child to drink milk.
    ② Maintains child in Fowler's position during the A.M. care.
    ③ Obtains a throat culture as ordered.
    ④ Encourages parents to hold child in the upright position.

4. Which of these statements made by a client with cystic fibrosis indicates an understanding of the pathophysiology?
    ① "Cystic fibrosis is an autosomal-recessive disorder resulting in excessive mucous production with chronic obstructive lung disease."
    ② "Cystic fibrosis is an autosomal-recessive disorder resulting in an inflammation of alveoli and bronchioles."
    ③ "Cystic fibrosis is an autosomal-recessive disorder resulting in an entrance of air into pleural cavity."
    ④ "Cystic fibrosis is an autosomal-recessive disorder resulting in complication with upper airway obstruction."

5. Which interventions would be most important to include in the plan of care for a client with pneumonia? *Select all that apply.*
    ① Place client in negative pressure room.
    ② Assist client in using a bedside commode.
    ③ Limit oral fluids.
    ④ Teach client to cough and deep breathe.
    ⑤ Evaluate effectiveness of the use of an incentive spirometer.

6. Which of these clinical findings indicate an expected outcome after the client has been suctioned?
    ① The HR is 100 bpm, RR–28/min.
    ② The client has a productive cough.
    ③ The breath sounds are clear and equal bilaterally.
    ④ The O_2 sat is 93%.

7. Which position would be most effective for a client who is in respiratory distress?
    ① Lithotomy position.
    ② Low-Fowler's position.
    ③ High-Fowler's position.
    ④ Sim's position.

8. Which of these clients with COPD should be assessed initially following the shift report?
    ① A client with clubbing of the fingers.
    ② A client presenting with distant breath sounds.
    ③ A client expectorating thin white secretions.
    ④ A client presenting with a HR–110 bpm, RR–28/min., and O_2 sat of 90%.

9. Which clinical assessment findings would the nurse document for a client with Tuberculosis? *Select all that apply.*
    ① Distant breath sounds.
    ② Excessive drooling.
    ③ Hemoptysis.
    ④ Night sweats.
    ⑤ Weight gain.

10. Which of these clients would be a priority for the nurse to assess immediately following shift report?
    ① A client with COPD who is presenting with distant breath sounds.
    ② A client with TB who is complaining of night sweats.
    ③ A post-op client presents with sudden onset of pleuritic pain and acute dyspnea.
    ④ A client with pneumonia with a T–100.4 F, HR–90 with a cough.

Answers and Rationales

1. Which of these clinical assessment findings would indicate a client is experiencing **early signs of hypoxia**? Select all that apply.
   ① INCORRECT: Bradycardia is a late sign of hypoxia.
   ② INCORRECT: Cyanosis is a late sign of hypoxia.
   ③ **CORRECT: Restlessness is an early sign of hypoxia.**
   ④ **CORRECT: Tachycardia is an early sign of hypoxia.**
   ⑤ **CORRECT: Tachypnea is an early sign of hypoxia.**

The strategy is to refer to "**STRESS**" for an easy way to organize assessments early assessments for signs of hypoxia. The great news is that these assessment findings apply to any client who is experiencing hypoxia! The early signs of hypoxia include:

Symptoms of restlessness (acute confusion with geriatric client)

Tachycardia (↑ HR)

Respirations are increased (↑ RR)

Elevated blood pressure (↑ BP)

Skin and mucous membranes pale

Sounds in lungs, adventitious

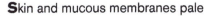

Physiological Adaptation: Assess client and respond to change in vital signs.

2. What early symptom would an **older adult** present with when **experiencing hypoxia**?
   ① **CORRECT: Confusion is an early sign of hypoxia for the elderly client.**
   ② INCORRECT: Cough is depressed in the elderly client.

   ③ INCORRECT: Elders do not present with the early sign of a temperature.
   ④ INCORRECT: Increased WBC–18,000 mm³ is not the earliest sign.

The strategy for answering this question is to know the earliest symptom for an elderly client with hypoxia, F & E imbalance, and/or UTI is confusion.
Health Promotion: Provide care and education for adults over 85 years.

3. Which of these nursing actions require the charge nurse to **intervene** with a LPN who is providing care for the **child who is drooling, presenting with a deep "barking" cough**?
   ① INCORRECT: There is no need for the charge nurse to intervene when nurse discusses with the mom the rationale for not allowing child to drink milk.
   ② INCORRECT: Acceptable practice; no need to intervene when maintaining child in Fowler's position during the A.M. care.
   ③ **CORRECT: Signs indicate epiglottitis. Never obtain a throat culture or inspect airway due to risk of causing a laryngospasm. Nurse needs to intervene to stop action!**
   ④ INCORRECT: No need to intervene when parents are encouraged to hold child upright.

The strategy for answering this question is to recognize that for a child with epiglottitis, no oral throat cultures or airway inspection should be performed due to the risk of a laryngeal spasm.
Management of Care: Recognize limitations of self/others and intervene.

4. Which of these statements made by a client with **cystic fibrosis** indicates an **understanding of the pathophysiology?**
   ① **CORRECT: "Cystic fibrosis is an autosomal-recessive disorder resulting in excessive mucous production with obstructive lung disease." This is the result of the pathophysiology that occurs with clients who have cystic fibrosis.**
   ② INCORRECT: "Cystic fibrosis is an autosomal-recessive disorder resulting in an inflammation of alveoli and bronchioles is pneumonia."
   ③ INCORRECT: "Cystic fibrosis is an autosomal-recessive disorder resulting in an entrance of air into pleural cavity would be a pneumothorax."
   ④ INCORRECT: "Cystic fibrosis is an autosomal-recessive disorder resulting in a complication with upper airway obstruction would be croup/epiglottitis."

The strategy is to remember, the excessive thick, tenacious mucus leads to obstruction that occurs in clients who have cystic fibrosis. The outcome from this finding will be altered oxygenation.

Physiological Adaptation: Identify pathophysiology related to an acute or chronic condition.

5. Which **interventions** would be most important to include in the plan of care for a **client with pneumonia?** Select all that apply.
   ① INCORRECT: Place client in negative pressure room would be if a client had tuberculosis.
   ② **CORRECT: Assist client in using a bedside commode is important to keep moving.**
   ③ INCORRECT: Limit oral fluids is incorrect since fluids will help liquefy the secretions.
   ④ **CORRECT: Teach client to cough and deep breathe to assist in removing secretions.**
   ⑤ **CORRECT: Evaluate effectiveness of the client performing the incentive spirometer to help expand the lungs.**

The strategy is to recognize the importance to keep a client with pneumonia on the "MO$_2$VE". The secretions in the lungs need to be expectorated and movement will assist in removing the secretions. Option 2 will assist with expanding the lungs. Option 4 with assist in the removal of the secretions. Option 5 will assist in keeping the lungs expanded. Each of these should be included in the plan of care for any client who has a respiratory infection, such as pneumonia. *Refer to the "MO$_2$VE" song to remember the importance of client movement.*

Physiological Adaptation: Provide pulmonary hygiene (i.e., incentive spirometry).

6. Which of these clinical findings indicate an **expected outcome** after the client has been **suctioned?**
   ① INCORRECT: The HR is 100 bpm, RR–28/min still indicates hypoxia.
   ② INCORRECT: A productive cough is not the clinical finding to evaluate suctioning.
   ③ **CORRECT: Breath sounds clear and equal bilaterally are the desired outcome!**
   ④ INCORRECT: The O$_2$ sat of 93% is not WDL. (Defined limit is >95%).

The strategy for this question is to recognize the desired outcome from this procedure is to improve the air exchange by removing secretions. The way to evaluate is by assessing the quality of the breath sounds. Whenever a client is suctioned, no matter what the medical condition is, the desired outcome should be an improvement in the breath sounds with bilateral, equal sounds and expansion.

Physiological Adaptation: Perform suctioning (i.e., oral, nasopharyngeal, endotracheal, tracheal).

7. Which **position** would be most effective for a client who is in **respiratory distress?**

   ① INCORRECT: Lithotomy position is used for a vaginal exam; will not facilitate lung expansion (This would indeed lead to respiratory distress!!)

   ② INCORRECT: Low-Fowler's position is not optimal for lung expansion.

   ③ **CORRECT: High-Fowler's position will assist in maximizing air exchange by optimal lung expansion.**

   ④ INCORRECT: Sim's position is side lying used for rectal exam, enema, etc. (This will not help with breathing! It will take your breath away!)

The strategy for this question is to have an understanding that the higher up a client is seated, the more the lungs can expand. Refer to the "MO_2VE" song.

Reduction of Risk: Manage the care of a client with impaired ventilation or oxygen.

8. Which of these clients with **COPD** should be **assessed initially** following the shift report?

   ① INCORRECT: Clubbing of the fingers is an expected finding for client with COPD.

   ② INCORRECT: Distant breath sounds are an expected finding.

   ③ INCORRECT: The expectoration of thin white secretions is an expected finding.

   ④ **CORRECT: A client presenting with a HR–110 bpm, RR–28/min., and O_2 sat of 90% is a priority due to signs of hypoxia.**

The strategy to answering this question is to know the "expected versus unexpected" assessment findings for hypoxia. This applies to any of the medical conditions included in the concept of oxygenation.

Management of Care: Prioritize delivery of client care.

9. Which **clinical assessment findings** would the nurse document for a client with **tuberculosis?** Select all that apply.

   ① INCORRECT: Distant breath sounds would be if a client had COPD.

   ② INCORRECT: Excessive drooling would be if a child had epiglottitis.

   ③ **CORRECT: Hemoptysis is a finding for tuberculosis (TB).**

   ④ **CORRECT: Night sweats is a finding for tuberculosis (TB).**

   ⑤ INCORRECT: Weight loss is the problem; not weight gain.

The strategy for answering this question is to know the TB assessments include night sweats, hemoptysis, and weight loss. The assessments for altered oxygenation "DYSPNEA" apply with TB as well.

Reduction of Risk Potential: Recognize trends and changes in client condition.

10. Which of these **clients would be a priority** for the nurse to assess **immediately** following shift report?

   ① INCORRECT: A client presenting with COPD who is presenting with distant breath sounds is a chronic and expected finding.

   ② INCORRECT: A client with TB who is complaining of night sweats is a concern, but not the priority over option 3 who is presenting with an emergency.

   ③ **CORRECT: A post-op client who presents with sudden onset of pleuritic pain and acute dyspnea is the priority due to the risk for death. (*Refer to 8Ps: Pulmonary Emboli.*)**

   ④ INCORRECT: A client with pneumonia with a T–100.4 F, HR–90 with a cough is a concern, but not the priority over option 3.

The strategy is to focus on the word "immediate" in the stem of the question. This indicates an emergency. If you did not know this answer, comparing and contrasting each option would assist you in selecting the correct answer. Option 1 is presenting with expected findings. Option 2 is a concern, but not compared to the emergency in option 3. Option 4 is not in acute distress.

Management of Care: Prioritize delivery of client care.

Decision-Making Analysis Form

Use this tool to help identify why you missed any questions. As you enter the question numbers in the chart, you will begin to see patterns of why you answered incorrectly. This information will then guide you toward what you need to focus on in your continued studies. Ultimately, this analytical exercise will help you become more successful in answering questions!!!

Questions to ask:

1. Did I have the knowledge to answer the question? If not, what information do I need to review?

2. Did I know what the question was asking? Did I misread it or did I miss keywords in the stem of the question?

3. Did I misread or miss keywords in the distractors that would have helped me choose the correct answer?

4. Did I follow my gut reaction or did I allow myself to rationalize and then choose the wrong answer?

	Lack of Knowledge (Concepts, Systems, Pathophysiology, Medications, Procedures, etc.)	Missed Keywords or Misread the Stem of the Question	Missed Keywords or Misread the Distractors	Changed My Answer (Second-guessed myself, i.e., my first answer was correct.)
Put the # of each question you missed in the column that best explains why you think you answered it incorrectly.				

If you changed an answer because you talked yourself out of the correct answer, or you second-guessed yourself, this is an **EASY FIX: QUIT changing your answers**!!! Typically, the first time you read a question, you are about 95% right! The second time you read a question, you start talking yourself into changing the answer. The third time you read a question, you do not have a clue—and you are probably thinking "Who in the heck wrote this question?"

On the other hand, if you read a question too quickly and when you reread it you realize you missed some key information that would impact your decision (i.e., assessments, lab reports, medications, etc.), then it is appropriate to change your answer. When in doubt, go with the safe route: your first thought! Go with your gut instinct!

As you gain confidence in answering questions regarding specific nursing concepts, you will be able to successfully progress to answering higher-level questions about prioritization. Please refer to the *Prioritization Guidelines* in this book for a structure to assist you with this process.

You CAN do this!

> *"To know even one life has breathed easier because you have lived. This is to have succeeded."*
>
> RALPH WALDO EMERSON

References for Chapter 8

Black, J M. and Hawks, J. H. (2009). *Medical surgical nursing: Clinical management for positive outcomes* (8th ed.). Philadelphia: Elsevier/Saunders.

Braine, M. (2009). *The role of the hypothalamus, part 1: The regulation of temperature and hunger*, Br J Neurosci Nurs, 66-72.

Daniels, R. & Nicoll, L. (2012). *Contemporary medical-surgical nursing*, (2nd ed.). Clifton Park, NY: Delmar Cengage Learning.

Eliopoulos, C. (2014). *Gerontological nursing* (8th ed.), Philadelphia: Lippincott Williams & Wilkins.

Giddens, G. F. (2013). *Concepts for nursing practice*. St. Louis, MO: Mosby, an imprint of Elsevier.

Hogan, M. A. (2014). *Pathophysiology, reviews and rationales*, (3rd Edition) Boston, MA: Pearson.

Ignatavicius, D. D. and Workman, M. L. (2010). *Medical-Surgical nursing: Patient-Centered collaborative care* (7th ed.). Philadelphia: Elsevier/Saunders.

Jenson, H. B. and Stanton, B. F., eds. (2011). *Nelson textbook of pediatrics*. (19th ed.). Philadelphia, Pa: Saunders/Elsevier.

LeMone, P. Burke, K. M. and Bauldoff, G. (2011). *Medical-surgical nursing: Critical thinking in patient care* (5th edition). Upper Saddle Road, NJ: Pearson/Prentice Hall.

Lewis, S., Dirksen, S., Heitkemper, M., Bucher, L., and Camera, I. (2011). *Medical surgical nursing: Assessment and management of clinical problems* (8th ed.). St. Louis: Mosby.

Manning, L. and Rayfield, S. (2014). *Nursing made insanely easy* (7th ed). Duluth, GA: I CAN Publishing, Inc.

Manning, L. and Rayfield, S. (2013). *Pharmacology made insanely easy* (4th ed.). Duluth, GA: I CAN Publishing, Inc.

McCance K, & Huether, S. (2013). *Pathophysiology* (7th ed.). St. Louis: Mosby/Elsevier.

National Council of State Boards of Nursing, INC. (NCSBN) 2012. *Research brief: 2011 RN practice analysis: linking the NCLEX RN® examination to practice*. Retrieved from https://www.ncsbn.org/index.htm

Nettina, S. L. (2013). *Lippincott manual of nursing practice* (10th ed.). Philadelphia, PA: Walters Kluwer Health/Lippincott Williams & Wilkins.

North Carolina Concept Based Learning Editorial Board. (2011). *Nursing a concept based approach to learning*. Upper Saddle Road, NJ: Pearson/Prentice Hall.

Osborn, K. S., Wraa, C. E., Watson, A. S., and Holleran, R. S. (2014). *Medical surgical nursing: preparation for practice* (2nd ed.). Upper Saddle Road, NJ: Pearson.

Pagana, K. D. and Pagana, T. J. (2014). *Mosby's manual of laboratory and diagnostic tests* (5th ed.). St. Louis, MO: Mosby, an imprint of Elsevier.

Porth, C. (2011). *Essentials of pathophysiology* (3rd edition). Philadelphia, PA: Lippincott Williams ad Wilkins.

Porth, C. M. and Grossman, S. (2013). *Pathophysiology, Concepts of altered health states* (9th edition). Philadelphia, PA: Lippincott Williams & Wilkins.

Potter, P. A., Perry, A. G., Stockert, P., and Hall, A. (2013). *Fundamentals of nursing* (8th ed). St. Louis, MO: Pearson/Prentice Hall.

Smeltzer, S. C., Bare, B. G., Hinkle, J. L., and Cheever, K. H. (2010). *Brunner & Suddarth's Textbook of medical-surgical nursing* (12th ed.). Philadelphia: Lippincott Williams & Wilkins.

Wagner, K. D. and Hardin-Pierce, M. C. (2014). *High-Acuity nursing* (6th ed.). Boston: Pearson.

NOTES

CHAPTER 9

Cardiovascular System Linking Concepts to Pathophysiology of Diseases
Concept Perfusion Cardiac/Peripheral

A Snapshot of Perfusion

Perfusion is generated by cardiac output. The heart pumps blood though arteries and capillaries, to all organs and tissues, delivering oxygen, nutrients, and removing cellular waste. The health of the cardiovascular system is essential for perfusion. Perfusion ranges from optimal perfusion to no perfusion resulting in the death of the tissue (Giddens, 2013, p. 148). There are two categories of perfusion: **central** and **local tissue** perfusion.

Cardiac perfusion is generated by cardiac output and involves both the electrical and mechanical functions. The output begins when the heart is stimulated by an electrical impulse that begins in the sinoatrial (SA) node. We will discuss this in more detail later in this chapter (*Refer to Cardiac Arrhythmia for specifics*). The mechanical function moves the blood through the heart and into the peripheral vascular system to supply blood to all of the tissues and organs in the body.

Tissue perfusion is the volume of blood that flows from the heart to the tissues. With each contraction of the heart, the force creates pressure, known as *capillary hydrostatic pressure*, which propels the blood through the capillaries to deliver oxygen and nutrients to the cells.

Terms to Know

Cardiac output is the volume of blood pumped from the left ventricle each minute (4–6 L/min).

Cardiac Output = Stroke Volume x Heart Rate

Stroke Volume is the amount of blood ejected from the left ventricle with each heartbeat.

Preload is the volume of blood returning to the heart that creates a stretch, or tension, of the myocardial fibers at the end of diastole.

Afterload is the pressure the heart must pump against.

Contractility is the strength of the contraction without respect to the preload.

When the ventricles contract, it is called **systole**. This creates pressure that closes the mitral and tricuspid valves so blood does not flow back into the atria. This same pressure then opens the aortic and pulmonic valves. The blood in the left ventricle goes to the aorta and the blood in the right ventricle is ejected into the pulmonary arteries. **Diastole** begins when the ventricles fill with blood. **Blood pressure** is maintained by the constriction or dilation of the arteries, capillaries, and veins (*Refer to Hypertension in this chapter for specifics*). Any disruption or reduction in perfusion can have consequences to the other systems of the body. When impaired perfusion is significant enough to reduce blood supply to the tissues, shock will occur (Porth, 2011). *Refer to concept Shock for specifics.*

Adequate perfusion to all of the body's systems, organs, tissues, and cells is essential. In addition to the concept of perfusion, you will see how important the concepts of oxygenation, fluid and electrolytes, pain, and health promotion are in the care of your client. When you finish this chapter, you will have the knowledge to make the appropriate assessments and will be able to make sound clinical decisions about the priority care your client needs. The cardiovascular system is indeed complex, but you can master this content!!! We now will show you how to make it **SIMPLEX** (**SIM**plify the com**PLEX**)!!!

Let's get started!

(Altered perfusion from volume loss and vasodilation will be discussed in the chapter on Shock.)

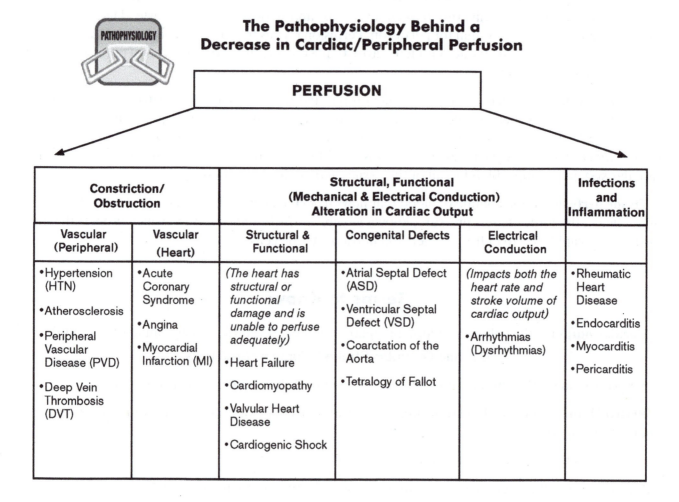

The Pathophysiology Behind a Decrease in Cardiac/Peripheral Perfusion

PERFUSION

Constriction/ Obstruction		Structural, Functional (Mechanical & Electrical Conduction) Alteration in Cardiac Output			Infections and Inflammation
Vascular (Peripheral)	Vascular (Heart)	Structural & Functional	Congenital Defects	Electrical Conduction	
•Hypertension (HTN) •Atherosclerosis •Peripheral Vascular Disease (PVD) •Deep Vein Thrombosis (DVT)	•Acute Coronary Syndrome •Angina •Myocardial Infarction (MI)	*(The heart has structural or functional damage and is unable to perfuse adequately)* •Heart Failure •Cardiomyopathy •Valvular Heart Disease •Cardiogenic Shock	•Atrial Septal Defect (ASD) •Ventricular Septal Defect (VSD) •Coarctation of the Aorta •Tetralogy of Fallot	*(Impacts both the heart rate and stroke volume of cardiac output)* •Arrhythmias (Dysrhythmias)	•Rheumatic Heart Disease •Endocarditis •Myocarditis •Pericarditis

Cardiac/Peripheral Perfusion

Associated Concepts
"HEART" Concepts

Cardiac and Peripheral Vascular Diseases	Health Promotion	Evaluate Perfusion	Assess Fluid & Electrolyte Balance	Respiratory Support Oxygenation	Treat Pain
Hypertension	X	X	X	X	"Silent Killer"
Peripheral Vascular Disease	X	X	X	X	X
Myocardial Infarction	X	X	X	X	X
Heart Failure	X	X	X	X	X
Infectious Heart Disease	X	X	X	X	X
Valvular Heart Disease	X	X	X	X	X

System-Specific Assessments for Cardiac and Peripheral Perfusion
Risk Factors

A risk factor assessment for cardiac and peripheral perfusion disorders is an important step for cardiac health promotion. Clients cannot change their genetic makeup or their family, but they can be aware of their risk factors. A critical role of nursing is to help guide clients to make lifestyle choices so they can change their modifiable risk factors to help prevent heart disease, hypertension, stroke, and peripheral vascular disease. These risk factors also contribute to diabetes and renal disease (Osborn, Wraa, Watson, and Holleran, 2014). The importance of working in partnership with the healthcare team to help your client achieve a healthy lifestyle is a gift that keeps on giving!

Non-Modifiable Risk Factors *(Cannot be changed)*	**Modifiable Risk Factors** *(Can be changed with lifestyle modifications)*
• Family History • Age • Gender • Genetics • Ethnicity (American Heart Association, 2012)	• Nicotine/Alcohol/Drug use • Hypertension • Hyperlipidemia • Sedentary lifestyle • Stress • Obesity • Diabetes • Metabolic Syndrome (*see below*)
Metabolic Syndrome A group of risk factors that raises the risk for heart disease and other health problems like diabetes and stroke.	**Five Risk Factors for Metabolic Syndrome** *(Three of the Five Risk Factors Confirm Metabolic Syndrome)* 1. ↑ Waistline > 102 cm (M); > 88 cm (F) 2. ↑ BP > 130/85 (or on meds to treat it) 3. ↑ Triglyceride level > 150 mg/dl (or on meds to treat it) 4. ↑ Fasting Blood Sugar > 110 mg/dl (or on meds to treat it) 5. ↓ HDL cholesterol level < 50 mg/dl (or on meds to treat it)

System-Specific Assessments for Cardiac and Peripheral Perfusion

A powerful question to ask all clients when you are beginning the initial assessment is: "What has changed in the last few days for you to need health care?" The answers can be revealing about the state of the client's health and provide a focus for your assessment. The client's history will guide the questions you ask and the assessments you make. As you review the many different disorders, diseases, and conditions that result from decreased cardiac and peripheral perfusion, you will find there are many similarities in the assessments. Instead of trying to remember all of the assessments for each of the diseases and disorders, we have used the word **"PUMPS"** to help organize and make it *INSANELY EASY* to learn the priority system-specific assessments for cardiac/peripheral perfusion.

P   Pulses: assess bilaterally and compare, peripheral and jugular vein distention (JVD), capillary refill > 3 seconds, auscultate heart sounds (presence of S_3 or S_4), heart rate, rhythm, (pulse ↓ or ↑ with arrhythmias), and BP. Assess for ↓ level of consciousness (LOC), syncope.

U   Urine output (> 30 mL/hour), I & O, and daily weights. Compare, contrast, and trend all.

M   Moist lung sounds (adventitious), ↑ respirations, check O_2 sat, assess for peripheral edema (compare R & L extremities).

P   Pain characteristics will vary (*see angina, MI, and PVD in this chapter for specifics*). Assess to see if pain increases with activity.

S   Skin color pale, cool extremities, ↑ temperature (i.e., infections of the heart or heart valves disorders).

Cardiac Sounds (Normal)	
S₁–"LUBB" Auscultate L of Sternum 4th or 5th Intercostal Space Tricuspid/Mitral Sites **(Apex of Heart)**	**S₂–"DUBB"** Auscultate R (Aortic site) and L (Pulmonic site) of Sternum 2nd and Left 3rd Intercostal Space **(Base of Heart)**

Cardiac Sounds (Abnormal)

INSANELY EASY TIP!

Link the syllables in *Heart Failure* and *Hypertension* to the heart sounds!!!!

S₃–"Heart – fail – ure" *(You might hear an S₃ with Heart Failure)* Auscultate L MCL, 5th Intercostal Space, Lying on L side	**S₄ – "Hy –per – ten – sion"** *(You might hear an S₄ with Hypertension)* Auscultate L MCL, 5th Intercostal Space, Lying on L side

"All Pigs Eat Too Much"

INSANELY EASY TIP to remember the heart sounds!

All – **A**ortic

Pigs – **P**ulmonic

Eat – **E**rb's Point

Too – **T**ricuspid

Much – **M**itral

Author Unknown

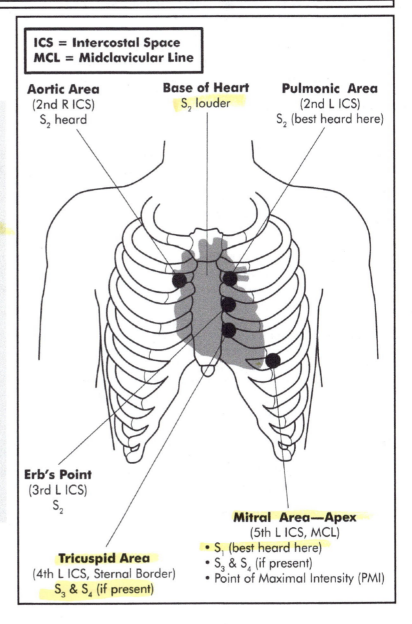

ICS = Intercostal Space
MCL = Midclavicular Line

Aortic Area
(2nd R ICS)
S₂ heard

Base of Heart
S₂ louder

Pulmonic Area
(2nd L ICS)
S₂ (best heard here)

Erb's Point
(3rd L ICS)
S₂

Tricuspid Area
(4th L ICS, Sternal Border)
S₃ & S₄ (if present)

Mitral Area—Apex
(5th L ICS, MCL)
• S₁ (best heard here)
• S₃ & S₄ (if present)
• Point of Maximal Intensity (PMI)

Linking Pathophysiology to System-Specific Assessments for Cardiac and Peripheral Perfusion

Pathophysiology	System-Specific Assessments
Pulses: The heart sounds, S_1 and S_2 indicate that the heart is pumping and the cardiac conduction system is working. S_3 and S_4 are abnormal heart sounds but may be present if the client has heart failure or hypertension (*refer to heart sounds on previous page for specifics*). Palpable peripheral pulses indicate the body and the extremities are receiving adequate perfusion. A client that is alert and responsive indicates there is perfusion to the brain.	**P**ulses (peripheral and JVD) assess bilaterally and compare, capillary refill $>$ 3 seconds, auscultate heart sounds (presence of S_3 or S_4), heart rate, rhythm, (pulse $\downarrow$ or $\uparrow$ with arrhythmias), and BP. Assess for $\downarrow$ level of consciousness (LOC), syncope.
Urine output $>$ 30 mL/hour is an indication that the kidneys are being perfused. The kidneys are affected early with decreased perfusion. If there is a decrease urine output and the body is retaining fluid, the excess fluid requires the heart to pump harder (*Refer to concept Fluid & Electrolytes for specifics*).	**U**rine output ($>$ 30 mL/hour), I & O, and daily weights. Compare, contrast, and trend all.
Moist lung sounds (adventitious) and edema. A client with heart failure or PVD may have edema or adventitious lung sounds present because the pumping action of the heart is not adequate to either return blood to the heart or pump blood to the body. This in combination with excess fluid leads to decreased oxygenation.	**M**oist lung sounds (adventitious), $\uparrow$ RR, check O_2 sat; edema (compare R & L extremities).
Pain: Chest pain is caused by inadequate oxygen to the heart muscle. Decreased perfusion = decreased oxygenation = chest pain (*Refer to angina and chest pain in this chapter*). Chest pain could indicate there is an increased workload demand on the heart. This could result from activity, medications, and/or increased heart rate. That in turn causes ischemia (chest pain) from inadequate perfusion. If there is decreased perfusion to the extremities with peripheral artery disease (PAD), the client experiences intermittent claudication, which is also pain from ischemia (*Refer to PAD in this chapter for specifics*).	**P**ain will vary (*refer to angina, MI, PVD for specifics*). Assess to see if pain increases with activity.
Skin Color: Pale skin and cool temperature may indicate a decrease in perfusion. Temperature elevations may occur with infections of the heart (*refer to Infections in this chapter*) or valve disease (*refer to Valve disorders in this chapter for specifics*).	**S**kin Color: pale, cool extremities, $\uparrow$ temp (for infections of the heart or heart valves disorders).

Alteration with Cardiac/Peripheral Perfusion

Common Lab/Diagnostic Tests/Therapeutic Procedures/Surgery

There are many lab and diagnostic tests and procedures used with cardiac/peripheral assessment and diagnosis. What is important for you to know is what the lab test or procedure is for, and what your responsibilities are in helping your client prepare prior to, during, and/or after the test or procedure. In addition to monitoring and trending, reporting the lab/test results to the healthcare provider is essential for timely quality care (Pagana & Pagana, 2014).

Labs	Diagnostics Tests/Procedures	Therapeutic Procedures/Surgery
• Electrolytes	• Electrocardiogram (ECG)	*The goal is to restore blood supply:*
• CBC	• Echocardiogram	• Intracoronary Stents
• PTT, PT, INR	• Chest X-ray	• Percutaneous Transluminal Coronary Angioplasty (PTCA)
• Platelets	• Stress Test	
• Liver Function Tests	• Cardiac Catheterization	• Laser ablation
• BUN and Creatinine	• Thallium Scan	• Coronary Artery Bypass Graft (CABG)
• Lipid Panel	• Positron Emission Tomography (PET)	
• Total Cholesterol Levels		• Intra-aortic Balloon Pump
• Low Density Lipoprotein (LDL) (Bad cholesterol)	• Magnetic Resonance Imaging (MRI)	• Temporary and Permanent Pacemakers
• High Density Lipoprotein (HDL) (Good cholesterol)	• Transesophageal Echocardiography (TEE)	• Left Ventricular Assist Device (LVAD)
• Glucose	• Hemodynamic Monitoring	• Automatic Implanted Cardiac Defibrillator (AICD)
• C-Reactive Protein	• Central Venous Pressure (CVP)	
• Homocysteine Level	• Pulmonary Artery Catheter (Swan–Ganz)	
• Urinalysis	*Refer to chapter on Shock for hemodynamic monitoring.*	
Cardiac Enzymes		
• Myoglobin		
• Troponin I & T		
• CK-MB		
Hypertension		
• Aldosterone		
• Renin Assay		
• Serum Corticoids (to rule out Cushing's Disease)		

Alteration with Cardiac/Peripheral Perfusion

Medications for Cardiac/Peripheral Perfusion

The following medications are some of many that are used for clients with cardiac/peripheral perfusion alterations (Manning & Rayfield, 2013). We recommend you review and learn these more-commonly prescribed medications (refer to the book *Pharmacology Made Insanely Easy* for specifics).

Common Cardiac and Peripheral Medications		Medications for Cardiac Dysrhythmias
Antihypertensives • Ace Inhibitors • Angiotensin 2 receptor blockers (ARB) • Beta-Adrenergic Blockers • Calcium Channel Blockers • Central Alpha 2 Agonists	**Anticoagulants** • Warfarin (Coumadin) • Heparin Sodium (Heparin) • Fondaparinu (Arixtra) • Enoxaparin (Lovenox) • Dabigatran (Pradaxa)	**Antidysrhythmics** • Adenosine (Adenocard) • Amiodarone (Cardarone) • Lidocaine • Procainamide (Pronestyl) • Propafenone (Rythmol)
HF Medications • Digitalis (Digoxin) • Natrecor (Nesirtide)	**Antiplatelets** • Aspirin • Aspirin & extended-release dipyridamole (Aggrenox) • Glycoprotein IIB/IIA Inhibitors • Clopidogrel (Plavix)	**Cholinergic Blockers** • Atropine (Isopto Atropine) (used for bradycardia)
Diuretics • Loop • Thiazides • Potassium Sparing	**Thrombolytic Agents** • Alteplase (Activase, tPA) • Streptokinase (Streptase)	**Adrenergics** • Epinephrine (Adrenaline) • Dobutamine (Dobutex) • Dopamine (Dopamine HCl)
Antianginal • Nitroglycerin	**Vasodilators** • Nitrates • Human B-Type Natriuretic Peptides (hBNP)	
Antilipemic • HMG CoA Inhibitors (Statins)	**Vasodilators (emergencies)** • Nitroprusside (Nipride)	
Hemorrheologic Agent • Pentoxifylline (Trental)		

First-Do Priority Interventions
"PERFUSE"

As you care for clients with cardiac and peripheral perfusion disorders, you will note there are many similarities in the interventions. We refer to these as *"Get A Lot of Bang for Your Buck"* interventions! The interventions are used with different clients with different disease processes that all have alterations in cardiac and/or peripheral perfusion. Priority interventions help achieve the desired outcome to maintain and/or improve perfusion.

P Position: HOB ↑. NOTE: if BP decreases, lower HOB to semi-Fowler's or supine position (*Refer to PVD for specifics on positioning*). Give supplement O_2 as needed. Avoid restrictive clothes, cold, and nicotine.

E Evaluate VS, pulses, edema (compare R & L extremities), lung sounds, ECG, CVP, and hemodynamic monitoring.

Evaluate surgical incision site: bleeding, skin temp, circulation, color, and healing.

R Report urine output < 30 mL/hour or trending ↓.

F Fluids: monitor amount; maintain patent IV line.
Note: ↓ fluids if heart failure or cardiogenic shock.

U Use **"CLUSTER"** to manage energy conservation (*Refer to Activity Tolerance in this chapter for specifics*).

S Support stockings or intermittent-compression devices (except for DVT on affected leg).

E Encourage ambulation/ROM to increase perfusion and circulation (except if there is chest pain, an infection of the heart, severe heart failure, or cardiomyopathy that requires rest).

Linking Pathophysiology to Interventions for Cardiac/Peripheral Perfusion "PERFUSE"

Pathophysiology	First-Do Priority Interventions
Position: A decrease in perfusion = decrease in oxygenation to the organs and tissues. Positioning client in an upright position helps facilitate the expansion of the lungs for adequate oxygenation (*refer to concept Oxygenation for specifics*). If the client's BP has decreased, semi-Fowler's to supine position will increase perfusion. Remember with decreased perfusion, you want to position the client to avoid constriction of blood flow and promote oxygenation. Cold and nicotine both cause vasoconstriction.	**P**osition HOB ↑. NOTE: if BP decreases, lower HOB to semi-Fowler's or supine position (*Refer to PVD for specifics on positioning*). Give supplement O_2 as needed. Avoid restrictive clothes, cold, and nicotine.
Evaluate: Assessments can change quickly (i.e., pulmonary edema, myocardial infarction, and arrhythmias). Comparing, contrasting, and trending assessments will indicate if there is decreased cardiac and peripheral perfusion or if the client is not adequately oxygenating. The evaluation of the healing of an incision site with clients who have had surgical procedures (i.e., coronary bypass surgery, valve replacements, pacemaker insertions, etc.) will indicate if there is adequate perfusion to the wound. Decreased perfusion to the incision site can delay wound healing.	**E**valuate VS, pulses, edema (compare R & L extremities), lung sounds, ECG, CVP, and hemodynamic monitoring. Evaluate surgical incision site: bleeding, skin temp, circulation, color, signs of infection, and healing.
Report Urine Output: The hourly urine output is an indication of the perfusion of the kidneys. A heart with failure or damage to the muscle or valves is unable to adequately perfuse vital organs. The kidneys are one of the first organs to be affected by decreased perfusion and are a significant clinical finding to indicate there is decreased perfusion to the body and organs.	**R**eport urine output < 30 mL/hr or trending ↓. Daily weights and compare.
Fluids are necessary for perfusion, but must be monitored closely, particularly when the decrease in perfusion is due to decreased pump action or failure. If there is excess fluid in the circulatory system, this causes an increased workload on the heart to pump the additional fluid. Diuretics are commonly used to reduce the volume the heart has to pump.	**F**luids: monitor amount, maintain patent IV line. (Note: ↓ fluids if HF or Cardiogenic Shock.)
Use "**CLUSTER**" (*Refer to Activity Tolerance later in this chapter*) to manage energy conservation with clients that have pump failure, infections, and/or inflammation of the heart. Prioritizing activities and pacing them with rest helps avoid an increased workload on the heart that results in decreased perfusion and inadequate oxygenation that can also lead to pain from ischemia.	**U**se "**CLUSTER**" to manage energy conservation (*Refer to Activity Tolerance in this chapter*).
Support stockings or intermittent-compression devices help increase the return of blood to the heart when the heart is unable to adequately perfuse or if there is peripheral constriction or blockages that prevent adequate return of blood to the heart.	**S**upport stockings or intermittent-compression devices (except for DVT on affected leg).
Encourage ambulation/ROM is important to help increase perfusion and circulation. Monitoring the client's response to the activity (i.e., VS, report of pain, O_2 sat, etc.) will help determine if the client is able to tolerate the activity.	**E**ncourage ambulation/ROM ↑ perfusion/ circulation (except if there is chest pain, an infection of the heart, severe heart failure, or cardiomyopathy that requires rest).

SAFETY Summary: Concept Cardiac/Peripheral Perfusion

System-Specific Assessment "PUMPS"	First-Do Priority Interventions "PERFUSE"	Evaluation of Expected Outcomes "PUMPS"
Pulses (peripheral & JVD) assess bilaterally & compare, capillary refill > 3 seconds, auscultate heart sounds (note presence of S_3 or S_4), heart rate, rhythm (pulse ↓ or ↑ with arrhythmias), & BP. Assess for ↓ level of consciousness (LOC), syncope. **U**rine output, (> 30 mL/hour), evaluate daily weights and compare. **M**oist lung sounds (adventitious) ↑ Resp, edema (compare R & L extremities). **P**ain will vary (*Refer to Angina, MI, PVD for specifics*). Assess to see if pain increases with activity. **S**kin color pale, cool extremities, ↑ temp (for infections of the heart or heart valves disorders).	**P**osition HOB ↑. NOTE: if BP decreases, lower HOB to semi-Fowler's or supine position (*Refer to PVD for specifics on positioning*). Give supplement O_2 as needed. Avoid restrictive clothes, cold, and nicotine. **E**valuate VS and pulses (compare R & L), edema (compare R & L), lung sounds, ECG, CVP & hemodynamic monitoring. Evaluate surgical incision site for bleeding, circulation, skin temp, color, signs of infection, and healing. **R**eport urine output < 30 mL/hour or trending ↓, daily weights and compare. **F**luids: monitor amount, maintain patent IV line. Note: ↓ fluids if heart failure or cardiogenic shock. **U**se "**CLUSTER**" to manage energy conservation (*Refer to Activity Tolerance in this chapter for specifics*). **S**upport stockings or intermittent-compression devices (except for DVT on affected leg). **E**ncourage ambulation/ROM to increase perfusion and circulation (except if there is chest pain, an infection of the heart, severe heart failure, or cardiomyopathy that requires rest).	**P**ulses and BP WDL for client **U**rine > 30 mL/hour **M**oist lung sounds resolved, no edema; respiratory rate WDL **P**ain, none or managed **S**kin warm and dry, color WDL for client

Exceptions and Additions by Diseases

Pathophysiology: Constriction/Obstruction
Hypertension

Hypertension (HTN) is sustained blood pressure taken at three different times that is equal to or greater than 140 systolic and 90 or greater diastolic. Hypertension leads to increased *afterload*, which requires the heart to work harder to pump against the pressure.

Hypertension is Staged Accordingly:

Pre-hypertension: Systolic 120–139 mm Hg/Diastolic 80–89 mm Hg

Stage 1: Systolic 140–159 mm Hg/Diastolic 90–99 mm Hg

Stage 2: Systolic = or > 160 mm Hg/Diastolic = or > 100 mmHg

There are two types of hypertension: **Primary hypertension** is caused by peripheral vascular resistance and **secondary hypertension** involves multiple systems, including the kidneys (Wagner and Hardin-Pierce, 2014).

Blood Pressure is Controlled By:

Arterial baroreceptors: Regulate vasodilation = (BP ↓) or constriction = (BP ↑) that is influenced by the peripheral vascular resistance and cardiac output.

Kidneys: Regulation of body fluid volume by excreting or retaining fluid based on the systemic fluid volume changes.

Renin-Angiotensin System: The release of renin causes a reduced blood supply to the kidneys. The ↓ BP results in angiotensin I combining with renin that is then converted to angiotensin II, (a potent vasoconstrictor). Angiotensin II is combined with aldosterone, which leads to the reabsorption of Na^+ and H_2O. This results in increased blood pressure.

Vascular auto regulation is influenced by the viscosity of the blood; the thicker the blood, the more resistance there is in the blood flow (Black & Hawk, 2009).

System-Specific Assessments
"BLOOD PRESSURE"

B BLOOD pressure: test 3 different times to diagnose; test for orthostatic hypotension, have client lay/sit and compare to standing, (confirm orthostatic hypotension if ↓ 20 mm Hg systolic or ↓ 10 mm Hg diastolic BP); record and report.

P Postural changes, make slowly to prevent syncope, fainting, falling.

R Retinal and visual changes, report.

E Evaluate risk factors and family history.

S Sodium (Na^+) and potassium (K^+), monitor.

S Should report headaches, particularly headaches when awakening in A.M.; often no symptoms. Known as the "Silent Killer."

U Urine evaluate, nocturia, monitor for ↑ BUN & Creatinine (may indicate renal involvement).

R Report blood sugar ↑, triglycerides ↑.

E Evaluate if taking any over-the-counter medications, avoid if possible.

Exceptions and Additions by Diseases

Pathophysiology: Constriction/Obstruction

Hypertension

PATHOPHYSIOLOGY

FIRST-DO PRIORITY INTERVENTIONS

System-Specific Assessments "BLOOD PRESSURE"	Diet	Equipment	Plans/Interventions	Health Promotion
BLOOD pressure: test 3 different times to diagnose; test for orthostatic hypotension, have client lay/sit and compare to standing, (confirm orthostatic hypotension if ↓ 20 mm Hg systolic or ↓ 10 mm Hg diastolic BP); record and report.	• Na⁺ intake ≤ than 2–6 gms/day	• Use appropriate size BP cuff for accurate measurements (2/3 size of the upper arm)	• Check BP lying down, sitting, and standing on three different days; record and report.	Teach client/family: • Hypertension can be asymptomatic— known as "SILENT KILLER."
Postural changes, make slowly to prevent syncope, fainting, falling.	• BMI = or < than 24.9	• Keep BP log	• Rise slowly in A.M. to prevent risk for falls.	• Report diplopia with retinal and visual changes.
Retinal and visual changes, report.	• Healthy Heart Diet (i.e., low Na⁺, fat and cholesterol)		• Sit at the side of the bed prior to ambulating.	• Report headaches in A.M., particularly in the occipital area.
Evaluate risk factors and family history.	• For specifics, refer to concept on Nutrition		• Educate about medications, symptoms to report.	• Keep log of BP.
Sodium (Na⁺) and potassium (K⁺), monitor.				• Lifestyle modifications (i.e., stop smoking, weight loss, exercise, etc.).
Should report headaches, particularly when awakening in A.M.; often no symptoms. Known as the *"Silent Killer."*				
Urine evaluate, nocturia, monitor for ↑ BUN & Creatinine (may indicate renal involvement).				
Report blood sugar ↑, triglycerides ↑.				
Evaluate if taking any over-the-counter medications, avoid if possible.				

INSANELY EASY TIP!

Remember **"HTN"** for Client Teaching!

H Have to take BP medications even if the BP is within normal range. **Don't stop taking medications suddenly.**

T Teach to **monitor BP every day** and keep a log. Note if any syncope or other adverse side effects occur.

N Need to **make lifestyle changes.**

Remember...

PREVENT FALLS!

Watch for Sudden Symptoms of ↓ BP When Rising!

SAFETY

Exceptions and Additions by Diseases

Pathophysiology: Constriction/Obstruction
Hypertension

Trend Potential Complication: Hypertensive Crisis

System-Specific Assessments	First-Do Priority Interventions "NOW MEDS"
Goal Decrease Blood Pressure Within 1 Hour	
• ↑ BP Systolic > 180, Diastolic > 110	**N**otify Healthcare Provider STAT
• ↑ Severe Headache	**O**xygen as needed, obtain IV Access
• ↑ Blurred Vision	**W**atch and Monitor
• ↑ Shortness of breath	• ECG • Monitor BP before and after meds/protocol • Neuro status, LOC
• ↑ Anxiety	**MEDS** Per Order
• ↑ Angina	• Nitroprusside (Nipride) • Nicardipine (Cardene)
• Epistaxis	• Labetalol (Normodyne)

This is a medical emergency and requires your vigilance while the hypertensive crisis is managed. The client will be at **Risk for Falls** with the administration of the BP meds as the blood pressure may drop rapidly, causing orthostatic hypotension. Trending the blood pressure as the medications are given will help keep the client safe and resolve the crisis.

Remember the crisis is due to the rapidly changing blood pressure.
Compare, Contrast and Trend the Blood Pressure!!!!

Exceptions and Additions by Diseases

Pathophysiology: Constriction/Obstruction
Peripheral Vascular Disease

Peripheral Vascular Disease occurs when there is interference with the blood flow to and from the heart and the extremities.

Peripheral Arterial Disease is a progressive narrowing and degeneration of arteries predominately in neck, abdomen, and legs and mainly affects the smaller vessels. The primary etiology is atherosclerosis.

Peripheral Venous Disease is a disease of the veins that results with inadequate blood flow from the extremities. It is often caused by what is referred to as Virchow's Triad: venous stasis, endothelial injury and hypercoagulability (Hogan, 2014).

INSANELY EASY TIP!
The "Ps" will help you remember the distinct differences between the arterial and peripheral vascular assessments.

System-Specific Assessments: The "Ps"

Peripheral Artery Disease	Peripheral Venous Disease
Pain–Sharp, sudden (Intermittent Claudication: pain occurs same point every time client walks)	**P**ain–Dull, heavy, and achy
Pallor–Pale and shiny, loss of hair growth	**P**allor–Brown, brawny, edema
Peripheral Temp–Cool	**P**eripheral Temp–Warm
Peripheral Circulation–No edema, capillary refill > 3 seconds	**P**eripheral Circulation–Lower leg edema
Pulses–Weak to no pulse	**P**ulses–Pulses present (may be difficult to palpate due to edema)

INSANELY EASY TIP!

Arterial has an **A.** Want to get blood **Away** from the heart!
Venous blood is **Blue**, the opposite. Get blood **Back** to heart!

Exceptions and Additions by Diseases

Pathophysiology: Constriction/Obstruction
Peripheral Vascular Disease
First-Do Priority Interventions

INSANELY EASY TIP!
Let Good Ole **"PAP"** make it easy to remember positions to use for clients with peripheral vascular disease:

Position

Ambulate

Prevent Pain

Peripheral Artery Disease	Peripheral Venous Disease
Position: Legs ↓ (dangling) when resting: (↑ arterial blood flow to extremity)	**P**osition: Legs ↑ when resting, 4 to 5 x/day for 20 minutes. (↑ venous blood return to heart)
Ambulate: Until pain starts, then rest until pain stops; gradually ↑ length and time of ambulation as tolerated	**A**mbulate: Encourage walking to increase circulation
Prevent Pain: Administer pain medications as prescribed	**P**revent Pain: Administer pain medications for dull, achy pain as prescribed

Avoid restrictive position (i.e., crossed or bent legs), restrictive clothes, cold, and nicotine.
Never apply direct heat to affected extremity.

Pathophysiology: Constriction/Obstruction
Peripheral Vascular Disease
Trend Potential Complication: Arterial and Venous Ulcers

Arterial Ulcers	Venous Ulcers
Appearance: regular borders, round	**Appearance**: irregular shape
Location: deep between toes or on feet	**Location**: ankles, lower leg
Pain: burning/throbbing	**Pain**: when leg is dependent, dull, heavy, and achy
Color: pale, gray or yellowish	**Color**: beefy red/ granulation
Drainage: little to none	**Drainage**: exudative wounds

"HEAL" those Ulcers!!!
Priority Interventions

H Healthy diet: High protein, zinc, vitamin A & C, increase calories as needed. Intake: 2,000 to 3,000 mL/fluid per day unless contraindicated.

E Evaluate skin and/or ulcers/wounds every shift/protocol. Provide wound care as prescribed; document depth, size, color, and drainage.

Equipment: May need vacuum-assisted wound closure system, wound and dressing material. Keep skin dry, use egg crate or other protectors, apply bed cradle to avoid pressure.

A Activity to increase circulation; avoid ambulation with open ulcers on bottom of feet until healed. If unable to ambulate or sit in chair, do ROM, change position frequently.

L List with client a plan to avoid ulcer development: (i.e., inspect skin daily, improve diet, activity, pain management, stop smoking, etc.). Instruct how to do wound care and dressing changes.

PREVENTION is the best approach to avoid ulcers!!
(Refer to concept Tissue/Skin Integrity for specifics.)

Exceptions and Additions by Diseases

Pathophysiology: Constriction/Obstruction
Deep Vein Thrombophlebitis/Thrombosis (DVT)

Trend a Potential Complication: DVT

Deep Vein Thrombophlebitis/Thrombosis (DVT) is an inflammation of the vein where a clot can form. When a clot forms, it can break away as an emboli and travel to different parts of the body, most commonly the lungs. DVTs are common but they are preventable. **Prevention is the key**, particularly with clients with circulatory problems and who are immobile!

FIRST-DO PRIORITY INTERVENTIONS

SYSTEM-SPECIFIC ASSESSMENTS "DVT"	DIET	EQUIPMENT	PLANS/INTERVENTIONS "REST"	HEALTH PROMOTION
Diameter of calf and thighs; compare bilaterally for swelling **V**ein tenderness and redness, note **T**emperature ↑ (also at site of clot, warm to touch)	• If taking warfarin (Coumadin), avoid green leafy vegetables • For specifics, refer to concept on Nutrition	• Support stocking or intermittent-compression devices (not on affected leg)	**R**est (bed rest: can use bedside commode as prescribed). **E**levate legs 6–8 inches at night, avoid constriction at the knee. **S**upport stockings and/or intermittent-compression devices on unaffected leg ONLY. Warm compresses to affected leg. **T**reat with anticoagulant therapy (i.e., Lovenox, Heparin, Coumadin). Refer to *Pharmacology Made Insanely Easy* for specifics. May need to prepare for inferior vena cava interruption surgery (filter trap for emboli) or removal of clot by thrombolysis, etc.	Teach client/family: • If taking warfarin (Coumadin), need monthly PT and INR blood tests. • Safety concerns to prevent injury particularly if on anticoagulants, (i.e., use electric razor only, soft toothbrush, etc.). • Report signs of bleeding, (i.e., nose, stools, abdominal distention, etc.).

INSANELY EASY TIP!

To prevent DVTs, clients need to MOVE and drink **FLUIDS** to keep **BLOOD MOVING!!!**

(Refer to MOVE in Concept Oxygenation for specifics)

Pathophysiology: Constriction/Obstruction
Angina
System-Specific Assessments: Angina

System-Specific Assessments "PRN"	First-Do Priority Interventions If "ANGINA" Occurs
Precipitated by exertion or rest	**A**ctivity STOP
Relief with nitroglycerin, pain < 15 min	**N**itroglycerin, 1tab SL every 5 min x 3
No other associated symptoms	**G**ive O_2 2–4 L/Nasal Cannula (NC)
	Instruct what symptoms to report to HCP
	Need for testing, Holter monitor, stress test
	Avoid smoking, high-fat diet, moderate activity with rest when pain is gone

Many clients who have never had a MI, or who will never have a MI, may experience angina. Angina indicates there is decreased perfusion to the heart tissue. Angina is a frightening experience; so it is imperative that you know how to recognize the symptoms and are proficient at prioritizing care. Equally important, is to teach your clients what to do when they have angina. Often the terms *angina* and *chest pain* are used interchangeably, which can be confusing. If you think about angina and chest pain on a continuum, it will help you understand the differences.

If angina has progressed along the continuum and is no longer relieved with rest or nitroglcyerin, there is a greater risk for an impending MI. Use the **"PQRST"** of pain assessment to determine the extent of the angina. The pain assessment, analyzing the labs (cardiac enzymes), and reviewing the ECG with the healthcare provider will assist the healthcare team to make the diagnosis. Most clients will also undergo a cardiac catheterization. This procedure allows for visualization of the arteries to determine if there are blockages or narrowing of the arteries of the heart. Treatment is often done during the cardiac catheterization to include angioplasty or stent placement (American Heart Association, 2012).

INSANELY EASY TIP!

If Angina is **relieved with REST** or **NITRO**, the client needs to be referred for follow-up care. The goal is to intervene before there is cardiac-tissue death.

If the angina is NOT relieved, the client/family should call 911 and have an ambulance take them to the emergency room!!

Exceptions and Additions by Diseases

Pathophysiology: Constriction/Obstruction
Acute Myocardial Infarction

Coronary Heart Disease (CHD) is the leading cause of morbidity and mortality in the United States. It is caused by partial or total thrombotic occlusion of the coronary arteries. **Coronary atherosclerosis** is the most common cause of CHD. It is the process of plaque buildup of cholesterol, lipids and cellular debris within the intimal layer of large arteries. Initially the heart is able to compensate as the myocardial cells develop collateral circulation.

Acute Coronary Syndrome (ACS) is the continuum from angina to a myocardial infarction (MI). The symptoms are due to the imbalance of myocardial oxygen supply and tissue demand. When there is not enough oxygen to meet the demands, the client experiences angina/chest pain. ACS is a term used to describe the spectrum of acute coronary disease including, unstable angina (UA), and acute ST segment elevation (STEMI) myocardial infarction (Porth & Grossman, 2013).

The Three Types of Angina

- **Stable:** (exertional) occurs with activity, exercise or emotional stress. Stable angina usually can be relieved by rest or nitroglycerin (Nitrostat).

- **Unstable:** (pre-infarction) occurs with exercise or emotional stress but increases in severity and duration over time.

- **Variant angina** (Prinzmetal's angina) is due to coronary artery spasm, often occurring during rest.

When the angina is no longer relieved with rest or nitroglycerin and lasts longer than 15 minutes, it can be a distinguishing factor in differentiating angina from chest pain in a client who may be experiencing an MI.

Ischemia: Lack of oxygen to tissues. It is reversible if the blood supply and oxygen are restored.

Injury: Tissue damage begins to occur when the blood and oxygen supply is not restored, leading to tissue necrosis.

Infarct: Tissue death is permanent damage.

The goal of nursing care for a client with a possible myocardial infarction is to intervene before there is tissue damage or death.

We do not expect you to be expert cardiac nurses at this point in your nursing development. (We bet you say, "Thank goodness!") However, this information will help you understand, assess and care for your clients with cardiac perfusion alterations. Even if you do not know about the specific disease, you will be able to provide **PRIORITY** care based on understanding the concept of perfusion!

Pathophysiology: Constriction/Obstruction
Acute Myocardial Infarction

Labs, Diagnostic Tests, and Therapeutic Procedures

Labs	Diagnostics Tests	Therapeutic Procedures

Serial Cardiac Enzymes
 	
(Injury or death of cardiac tissue causes cardiac enzymes to be released into the bloodstream. They are specific indicators if an MI has occurred).
 	
• Myoglobin (earliest marker but levels ↓ after 24 hours)
 	
Any ↑ in Troponin I or T indicates cardiac damage
• Troponin I: ↑ 2–4 hr; ↓ 7–10 days x 3 specimens, 6–8 hrs. apart
• Troponin T: ↑ 2–4 hr; ↓ 14–21 days x 3 specimens, 6–8 hrs. apart
 	
• CK-MB (creatinine kinase): ↑ 3–6 hr; ↓ 24–48 hours
• Electrolytes
• Total cholesterol levels, LDL & HDL
• Cholesterol levels
• C-Reactive protein
• Homocysteine level
	• Electrocardiogram (ECG)
	  Angina (ST ↓ = ischemia that can be reversed)
	  MI (ST ↑ = injury) (Note: there are non-ST ↑ MIs)
	  Q Wave = necrosis (tissue death, not reversible) Note: there are non-Q Wave myocardial infarction (NQMI).
	• Stress Test
	• Thallium Scan
	• Cardiac Catheterization
	• Positron Emission Tomography (PET)
	• Magnetic Resonance Imaging (MRI)
	• Transesophageal Echocardiography (TEE)
	• Echocardiogram
		Goal is to restore blood supply.
		• Intracoronary stents
		• Percutaneous Transluminal Coronary Angioplasty (PTCA)
		• Percutaneous Transluminal
		• Coronary Angioplasty (PTCA)
		• Laser Ablation
		• Coronary artery bypass graft (CABG)
		• Intra-Aortic Balloon Pump
		
		(Pagana & Pagana, 2014)

Troponin levels are the gold standard lab test for an MI (because they only go up with cardiac-tissue injury or death). Client history, troponin levels, ECG, and cardiac catheterization help confirm if the client has had an MI.

Exceptions and Additions by Diseases

Pathophysiology: Constriction/Obstruction
Acute Myocardial Infarction

Diagnostic Procedure: Cardiac Catheterization

Cardiac Catheterization determines the amount of blood flow in the coronary arteries. Many clients will immediately undergo a cardiac catheterization for diagnosis and/or treatment if an MI is suspected. It is done using a long, thin, flexible catheter that is inserted in the artery (i.e., femoral, brachial, radial, etc.) and is threaded through the coronary vessels. Dye allows visualization of arterial blockages or restriction of the blood flow in the coronary vessels of the heart. A catheter with a balloon tip may be used to perform an **angioplasty**. During an angioplasty, the balloon is inflated to compress the plaque against the artery wall to restore blood flow. Angioplasty can be combined with the permanent **stent** (a small, wire-mesh tube) that helps keep the artery open. Stents are coated with drugs to help prevent scar tissue from growing into the artery. The client will need antiplatelet medications for a period of time following the placement of a stent (Nettina, 2013).

Pre-Procedure "ACT NOW"	Post-Procedure "AFTER"
Assess for all allergies (i.e., shellfish, iodine, anesthetic agents; and any prior experience with sedation). **A**ssess ID of client. **C**onsent required. **T**each and answer questions about the procedure and post-procedure care. **N**PO prior to procedure/protocol. **O**bserve and assess baseline VS, pulses bilaterally to establish baseline. **W**atch for complications of decreased renal function: BUN and Creatinine to determine if kidneys can excrete contrast dye. Elderly have decreased glomerular filtration rate (GFR). **Notify HCP if client is taking metformin (Glucophage). Hold Metformin prior to test (due to lactic acidosis) as prescribed.**	**A**ssess VS frequently per protocol; assess site of insertion for bleeding, hematoma, monitor pulses, note color and temp of extremities distal to insertion site; compare and contrast to baseline assessment. **F**irst position supine with leg straight if catheter was inserted through the femoral artery, maintain bed rest per protocol. **T**rend clinical findings, (i.e., VS, I & O, peripheral pulses, etc.); give pain meds as needed, anticoagulants or antiplatelet medication as prescribed. **E**ncourage PO fluids and give IV fluids as ordered to flush dye. Evaluate BUN and Creatinine post-procedure. **R**emember discharge instructions per protocol. • Avoid strenuous exercise for prescribed period. • Report bleeding from site, chest pain, SOB, color, temp changes in extremity. • Restrict lifting as prescribed. • If stent placed, anticoagulation or antiplatelet therapy per protocol.

POST-CARDIAC CATHETERIZATION PRIORITY CARE: "PEE"

PUSH FLUIDS to FLUSH DYE FROM KIDNEYS!!

EVALUATE RENAL FUNCTION.

EVALUATE FOR BLEEDING AND CIRCULATION and intervene as needed!

Pathophysiology: Constriction/Obstruction
Acute Myocardial Infarction

System-Specific Assessments:
Comparison Of Angina And Chest Pain With Myocardial Infarction

ANGINA/CHEST PAIN	DESCRIPTION OF PAIN	ANGINA	MYOCARDIAL INFARCTION
Precipitating factors	Exercise, emotion, eating, exposure to cold or heat. Angina is severe if pain occurs at rest.	X	X
Quality	Pressure, squeezing, heaviness, smothering, burning, severe pain; pain increases with activity.	X	X
Region and radiation of pain	More localized.	X	
Pain radiates to other areas	May radiate across the chest, down the arms, substernal/retrosternal, through to the back, up to the neck and jaw, and upper abdomen.		X
Severity/Intensity: How severe is the pain based on age-appropriate pain scale?	Can range in severity (i.e., fatigue, flu-like, indigestion, heaviness, or like an elephant sitting on chest, etc.)	Severity varies by individual.	Often described as more intense and severe
Associated symptoms	Associated Symptoms with Pain: • Apprehension • Diaphoresis, cold, clammy skin • Dyspnea, orthopnea • Nausea and vomiting • Syncope, arrhythmias, palpitations		X
Timing and response to treatment	**Symptoms last < 15 minutes** Relief with rest and nitroglycerin (NTG)–one every 5 min x 3	X	
	Symptoms last > 15–30 minutes Not relieved with rest or nitroglycerin (NTG) Requires morphine for pain relief (monitor closely)		X

NOTE: Some clients are asymptomatic with an MI (often referred to as a "Silent MI"). See the following page for atypical symptoms presented by women and the elderly.

Exceptions and Additions by Diseases

Pathophysiology: Constriction/Obstruction
Acute Myocardial Infarction

Cardiac System-Specific Assessments For the Elderly

AGE-RELATED CHANGES

- Atypical symptoms due to ↓ neuro transmitters in the elderly.
- May NOT have ST segment elevation

Risks:
- Physically inactive
- Other chronic diseases

Physiological Changes
Thickening & loss of elasticity in:
- Blood vessels
- Heart muscle
- SA node = slower conduction to AV node
- Lung Tissue

(Wagner & Hardin-Pierce, 2014)

CLINICAL PICTURE FOR WOMEN

Women often have atypical symptoms and will minimize the significance of their symptoms.

Generalized Symptoms include (also applies to elderly):
- Fatigue
- SOB
- GI discomfort
- Heartburn

Important to Remember during Cardiac Assessment History:
Elderly and Women GENERALIZE and MINIMIZE symptoms.
This requires you to ask appropriate questions during the assessment!

Exceptions and Additions by Diseases

Acute Myocardial Infarction

System-Specific Assessments: Assessing the ECG for Signs of Ischemic or Necrotic Changes

The **electrocardiogram (ECG)** is a priority diagnostic assessment in clients admitted with angina or chest pain to rule out myocardial infarction (MI). It is not expected that you are able to read an ECG and interpret the findings; however there are some assessments you can make. One is looking at the ST segment. In the middle rhythm strip, you see a normal ST segment, (it will be flat). The rhythm strip on the left shows an ST segment that is depressed, below the baseline, indicating ischemic changes. This can be reversed if there is early intervention. With rest, the workload on the heart is decreased and oxygen administration can help reverse the ischemic changes. Remember, *ischemia* is a lack of oxygen to the heart tissue and it causes the pain. The rhythm strip on the right shows the ST segment is elevated above the baseline, indicating tissue damage and eventual tissue death. Again, with appropriate interventions, the damage can be contained to prevent further tissue death (see next page for interventions for MI). Heart tissue that is dead cannot pump. The larger the area of tissue death, the greater the decrease in cardiac output and perfusion is to the body.

You will hear the term "**STEMI**" MI which means the client with a MI is showing ST segment elevation on the ECG strip. Remember, elderly clients often do not have ST elevation with a MI and clients who have had a mild MI, may not present with ST elevation.

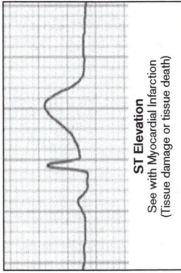

ST Elevation
See with Myocardial Infarction
(Tissue damage or tissue death)

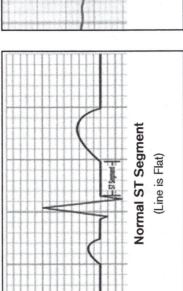

Normal ST Segment
(Line is Flat)

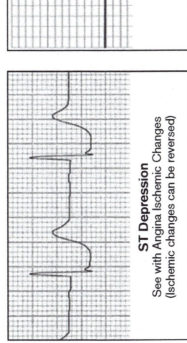

ST Depression
See with Angina Ischemic Changes
(Ischemic changes can be reversed)

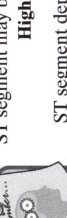

INSANELY EASY TIP!

ST segment may be **high** if the client had an **MI**.

High rhymes with MI!

ST segment depression occurs with angina.

Learn one and you have the other!

Exceptions and Additions by Diseases

Pathophysiology: Constriction/Obstruction
Acute Myocardial Infarction

Care of the Myocardial Infarction Client

SYSTEM-SPECIFIC ASSESSMENTS "CHEST"	TREATMENT GIVEN IN THE ORDER OF "OANM"	FIRST-DO PRIORITY INTERVENTIONS "HEART CARE"
Chest pain severe, heavy; may radiate; and is unrelieved with rest or nitroglycerin tabs. **H**ave associated symptoms, (i.e., ↑ RR, dyspnea, ↑ HR & palpitations; pale, cool, clammy skin; anxiety, fear; N & V; syncope, ↓ LOC, etc.) **E**nzyme (cardiac) elevations **S**T ↑, ECG changes **T**rend VS, urine output, I & O, O_2 sat, and hemodynamic monitoring, etc. **Geri Alert:** Elderly and women may not have typical symptoms; often the complaint is fatigue and/or abdominal discomfort. Elderly may not have ST segment elevation.	**O**xygen administration (based on ABGs and/or O_2 sat) in acute care settings to ↑ amount of circulating oxygen for heart. **A**spirin to help break up platelets (client may have taken at home). (Faster action from the ASA by chewing the tablet). **N**itrates: vasodilation is essential to increase blood flow and help relieve pain. (Nitroglycerin tabs may be taken SL 5 minutes apart or until relief up to 3 tabs). If no relief, morphine may be used). **M**orphine given for pain if nitrates do not work or if client is very anxious. Also has some vasodilating properties. **(Caution: can cause respiratory depression, monitor closely.)** This protocol may vary based on the needs of individual client, (i.e., O_2 sat level, if they took nitroglycerin tabs SL or aspirin at home or on the way to the hospital). The priority remains: **OANM!**	**H**eart sounds monitor, note development of S_3 or S_4, hourly urine & VS until stable or per protocol. Have IV access. **E**CG. Place on cardiac monitor, document rhythm strips/protocol. Notify HCP of cardiac arrhythmias *(Refer to arrhythmias in this chapter for specifics).* **A**ssess peripheral pulses, capillary refill, and color. **A**ssess for fluid volume overload (i.e., I & O, daily weights. edema, JVD). **A**nalyze lab results, cardiac enzymes, electrolytes, ABGs, renal and liver function. **R**espiratory status assess, breath sounds, RR, O_2 sat, ABGs, administer O_2 as prescribed. **T**reatment: Prepare client for any diagnostic procedure or surgery, i.e., cardiac catheterization, CABG, etc. *(Refer to cardiac catheterization and CABG in this chapter for specifics).* **C**PR, encourage all family members to learn. **A**ctivity pace with rest to decrease O_2 demands on the heart and conserve energy **R**ehabilitation (cardiac); begin per protocol. **E**ducate about medications, how to take, side effects, what signs and symptoms to report, etc.

(American Heart Association, 2012)

Remember **"PUMPS"** and **"PERFUSE"** as part of your assessment and interventions!

Exceptions and Additions by Diseases

Pathopysiology: Constriction/Obstruction   Acute Myocardial Infarction

System-Specific Assessments "CHEST"	Diet	Equipment	FIRST-DO PRIORITY INTERVENTIONS — Plans/Interventions "HEART CARE"	Health Promotion
Chest pain severe, heavy, may radiate, and is unrelieved with rest or nitroglycerin tabs. **H**ave associated symptoms, (i.e., ↑RR, dyspnea, ↑HR & palpitations; pale, cool, clammy skin; anxiety, fear; N & V; syncope, ↓LOC, etc.) **E**nzyme (cardiac) elevated **S**T↑, ECG changes **T**rend VS, urine output, I & O, O_2 sat, and hemodynamic monitoring, etc.	• Low fat, low cholesterol, low sodium • Heart Healthy Diet (*Refer to concept Nutrition for specifics*)	• ECG monitoring • Oxygen therapy • Hemodynamic monitoring equipment • IV pumps	**H**eart sounds monitor, note development of S_3 or S_4; hourly urine & VS until stable or per protocol. Have IV access. **E**CG. Place on cardiac monitor, document rhythm strips/protocol. Notify HCP if cardiac arrhythmias (*Refer to arrhythmias in this chapter for specifics*). **A**ssess peripheral pulses, capillary refill, and color. **A**ssess for fluid volume overload (i.e., I & O, daily weights. edema, JVD). **A**nalyze lab results, cardiac enzymes, electrolytes, ABGs, renal and liver function. **R**espiratory status assess, breath sounds, RR, O_2 sat, ABGs, administer O_2 as prescribed. **T**reatment: Prepare client for any diagnostic procedure or surgery, i.e., cardiac catheterization, CABG, etc. (*Refer to cardiac catheterization and CABG in this chapter for specifics*). **C**PR, encourage all family members to learn. **A**ctivity pace with rest to decrease O_2 demands on the heart and conserve energy **R**ehabilitation (cardiac); begin per protocol. **E**ducate about medications, how to take, side effects, what signs and symptoms to report, etc.	Teach client/family: • Occupational and physical therapy to learn how to perform ADLs. • Diet • Medications • Refer to Cardiac Rehab • Symptoms to report to HCP, WT gain > 2lbs/day, chest pain • Lifestyle modifications and reduction of modifiable risk factors (i.e., smoking-cessation classes, weight loss, etc.) • Refer family for CPR training

Remember **"PUMPS"** and **"PERFUSE"** as part of your assessment and interventions!

Exceptions and Additions by Diseases

Pathophysiology: Constriction/Obstruction
Acute Myocardial Infarction

Coronary Artery Bypass Graft (CABG)

Coronary Artery Bypass Graft (CABG) restores vascularization of myocardium. The surgery involves using a vein (saphenous vein) or artery (mammary artery) to bypass the obstruction of one or more coronary vessels. The client is placed on a cardiopulmonary bypass machine while the client's body temperature is lowered to decrease the rate of metabolism and demand for oxygen. On completion of the surgery, the client is re-warmed, pacemaker wires inserted if needed, and grafts are observed for patency and leakage as the cardiopulmonary bypass machine is removed (Osborn, Wraa, Watson & Holleran, 2014).

Caring for a post-op CABG client involves multiple system care with constant ongoing assessments. Even with the complexity of the surgery, remember your basic post-op care.

INSANELY EASY TIP!
Remember the priority is **"POST-OP CARE"**

Patency of airway; lung sounds; O_2 sat; provide needed ventilator care; encourage cough, deep breathing, and incentive spirometer

Observe for bleeding, monitor CBC, clotting factors (platelets, INR, PT, and PTT)

Skin color, lips and mucous membranes note; evaluate surgical wound for healing and note any redness, swelling, drainage

Trend vital signs, signs of infections, and increase in temp or WBCs

Output of chest tube and drains; monitor, evaluate and trend I & O and drainage

Pain (N & V), patent catheters, assess and manage

Cardiac monitor; monitor level of consciousness

Anesthesia response (i.e., patent airway, breath sounds, LOC, etc.), administer medications as prescribed

Renal function, urine output < 30 mL/hr., evaluate BUN and Creatinine

Electrolytes and fluids monitor closely
Encourage movement, ambulation

Remember the post-op CABG client needs to **"MO$_2$VE"**!
(Refer to concept Oxygenation for specifics.)

Pathophysiology: Structural, Functional (Mechanical & Electrical Conduction)

Heart Failure

Heart failure occurs when the heart muscle is unable to pump effectively to meet the body's metabolic needs. The inadequate pumping action results in decreased cardiac output, decreased tissue perfusion, pulmonary and systemic congestion, and myocardial hypertrophy. There are two dysfunctions that contribute to heart failure: diastolic dysfunction and systolic dysfunctions (Ignatavicius & Workman, 2010).

Diastolic dysfunction is when the heart has to pump against extreme pressure (afterload), similar to what occurs with hypertension. This in turn decreases the preload and leads to decreased stroke volume. **Systolic dysfunction** is when the ventricles of the heart are damaged, similar to what occurs with a MI, and no longer contract effectively. This causes decreased stroke volume that leads to increase preload. The ventricle becomes distended and the result is decreased cardiac output. (You may want to review the terms from the beginning of the chapter.)

Heart failure can be **acute or chronic** and may occur on the **right or left side** of the heart. A combination of both right and left heart failure is common. **Acute heart failure** may present as pulmonary edema or cardiogenic shock (*refer to information later in this chapter*). **Chronic heart failure** may be the result of myocardial infarction, cardiogenic shock, kidney failure, valve disorders, or undesirable effects of corticosteroids. Heart failure can be managed with a therapeutic regime consisting of medications and lifestyle changes, i.e., diet, exercise, avoiding smoking, routine follow-up, etc. (Ignatavicius & Workman, 2010).

Cardiomyopathy is severe heart disease that can lead to heart failure. The client experiences symptoms very similar to heart failure that result in a significant impact to the client's ability to perform activities of daily living. The cause of cardiomyopathy may be genetic or acquired. There are three categories: dilated, hypertrophic and restrictive. Hypertrophic cardiomyopathy is often associated with sudden death. The clinical findings and the treatment of cardiomyopathy are managed with medications and activity restrictions. Occasionally the client requires an implantable cardioverter-defibrillator, pacemaker or heart transplant (Wagner & Hardin-Pierce, 2014).

Heart failure is one of the most frequent diagnoses for readmission to the hospital. Providing the client with care instructions is a required standard of care and an important part of health promotion. Some of the written instructions and/or educational materials that need to be reviewed with clients prior to discharge include:

- A follow-up visit or contact within 48 to 72 hours of discharge
- Activity level
- Diet
- Follow-up appointment
- Discharge medications
- Weight monitoring
- What to do if symptoms worsen

Cardiac health promotion is an essential part of what nurses to do. Client teaching is now linked to reimbursement for the hospital, so …

Remember to TEACH, Evaluate (teach back), and Document Your Teaching!!

As nurses say … Not Documented, Not Done!!

Exceptions and Additions by Diseases

Pathophysiology: Structural, Functional (Mechanical and Electrical Conduction)

Heart Failure: System-Specific Assessments

Left-Sided Heart Failure "DYSPNEA"		Right-Sided Heart Failure In addition to "EDEMA," everything is UP!
Dyspnea, orthopnea, and nocturnal.		**E**nlarged liver
Yes, vital signs. *Early signs:* ↑RR, ↑HR, ↑ BP, restless, skin and mucous membranes pale. (Geri clients: acute confusion is early sign). *Late signs:* VS ↓, cyanosis, ↓ level of consciousness, lethargy.	Left sided Heart failure = **Lungs** **D**yspnea **Y**ellow secretions (SS—infection) **S** tridor, ↓SaO₂ **P**ulmonary crackles, pulse ↑ **N**asal flaring, grunting, retracting **E** levation in the RR **A** ctivity intolerance **Right sided Heart failure = Rest of body** **E** nlarged liver (hepatomegaly) **D** istended neck veins (not infants) **E** nlarged spleen **M** ost edema in LE **A** scites, anorexia ©2014 I CAN Publishing®, Inc.	**D**istended neck veins, JVD (jugular vein distention)
Secretions altered, productive cough (i.e., color, consistency, tenacity and odor); pink-tinged, frothy sputum = pulmonary edema. (*Refer to pulmonary edema for specifics.*) Signs of infection (i.e., ↑ temp, ↑ WBC, etc.).		**E**nlarged spleen
		Most edema in lower extremities
Precipitating factors: infection, immobility, allergens, stress, trauma, post-op complications, and pleurisy.		**A**scites, ↑ weight > 2 lbs./24 hr.
Note characteristics of the cough (dry, moist); discomfort with breathing.		*EDEMA will result in the following:* ↑ HR, peripheral pulses (may be bounding) ↑ Blood pressure ↑ RR (due to the ascites increasing pressure on the diaphragm) ↑ Confusion
Evaluate SaO₂ < 95% with arterial blood gases (ABGs), pulse oximetry < 92%.		
Adventitious breath sounds (wheezes, crackles), atelectasis after post-op, immobility), arrhythmias (late), use of accessory muscles, asymmetrical chest expansion, activity intolerance		

CONCEPTS

Refer to concept Oxygenation assessments for specifics.

CONCEPTS

Refer to concept Fluid Balance assessments for specifics.

Exceptions and Additions by Diseases

Pathophysiology: Structural, Functional (Mechanical and Electrical Conduction)

Heart Failure

SYSTEM-SPECIFIC ASSESSMENTS	FIRST-DO PRIORITY INTERVENTIONS				HEALTH PROMOTION
	DIET	EQUIPMENT	PLANS/INTERVENTIONS	PLANS/INTERVENTIONS	
See *"DYSPNEA" and "EDEMA" on previous page.*	• Low fat • Low cholesterol • Low sodium • Heart Healthy Diet • Refer to concept Nutrition	• ECG monitoring • Oxygen therapy • Hemo-dynamic monitoring equipment • IV pumps	**LEFT-SIDED HEART FAILURE "BREATHE"** **B**reath sounds, (adventitious), SaO2, O2 sat, vital signs, and **"DYSPNEA"**, monitor; O2 as needed; assess for arrhythmias. **R**eposition to facilitate ventilation and perfusion (i.e, HOB ↑, up in chair, ambulate, particularly after surgery). **E**valuate airway status; prepare for O2 supplement (i.e., ambu bag); initiate EMERGENCY management as needed. **A**ssess & document ABG values, sputum color, consistency & amount, good oral care q 2 hours. **T**he airway needs to be suctioned PRN to maintain patency. Chest physiotherapy & postural drainage per protocol, use bronchodilators, handheld nebulizers as prescribed. **H**and-washing, wear appropriate PPE, apply infection control standards as appropriate. **E**ncourage deep breathing and coughing, incentive spirometer. Evaluate outcome of meds. Educate/emotional support.	**RIGHT-SIDED HEART FAILURE "RESTRICT"** **R**educe IV flow rate. **E**valuate **"EDEMA"**, measure abdominal girth (compare & contrast). **S**emi-Fowler's position, position to promote perfusion (i.e., HOB ↑ except with ↓ BP, legs ↑, but not above heart level. **T**reat with diuretics as prescribed. **R**educe fluid and sodium intake as prescribed. **I** & O and daily weights, trend daily weights, weight gain > 2 lbs./day report to HCP. **C**irculation, color, temp. **C**heck for fluid volume ↑ (i.e., edema in extremities, JVD, etc.). **T**urn and re-position at least every 2 hours.	Teach client/family: • Diet • Medications • Refer to Cardiac Rehab • Symptoms to report to HCP: WT gain > 2 lbs./day, chest pain • Lifestyle modifications (i.e., smoking cessation classes, weight loss, etc.) • Refer family for CPR training

The assessments and interventions represent **Oxygenation** for L Heart Failure and **Fluid Balance Excess** for R Heart Failure.

CONCEPTS

Exceptions and Additions by Diseases

Pathophysiology: Structural, Functional
(Mechanical and Electrical Conduction)
Activity Tolerance—Important Aspect of Care for Cardiac Clients

Activity tolerance is not a separate concept but rather a critical part of care for several concepts. Client teaching about activity tolerance is a priority any time the client may have decreased **perfusion** (i.e., heart failure, PVD, etc.), decreased **oxygenation** (i.e., COPD, asthma, etc.), or **pain** (i.e., from injury, surgery, etc.). When a client is unable to perform the activities of daily living because of shortness of breath, pain, orthostatic hypotension, etc., it impacts the client's quality of life.

It is difficult for clients to learn how to pace their activities. Clients are accustomed to doing what they want, when they want. Think about it ... what if you had to prioritize taking a shower or eating breakfast or making your bed? The result of any of these activities may cause shortness of breath or pain requiring rest. That is the reality for clients with decreased perfusion, decreased oxygenation, or pain—or all of them. These clients must prioritize and pace their daily activities with rest. As a nurse, it is a priority to assist your client with this process. The chart below will guide you in your assessments and interventions to help clients learn how to manage their activities of daily living.

Activity Tolerance

System-Specific Assessments "ACTIVE"	First-Do Priority Interventions "CLUSTER"
These are the steps to determine if a client has activity intolerance: *(The client's subjective input is also important)*	**C**alm when providing care; cluster care, pace activities with rest periods. Do NOT over stimulate.
Assess VS, pain level, and O_2 sat prior to activity	**L**ook for clinical findings that $\uparrow O_2$ requirements (i.e., fever, overexertion, etc.) and intervene appropriately.
Conduct activity	
Trend VS, pain, O_2 sat during and 3 minutes after activity; report and document tolerance to activity.**(If client's VS, O_2 sat, and/or pain level do not return to baseline within 3 minutes, this is evidence that the client has activity intolerance.)**	**U**pright position when eating.
	Support client and family emotionally.
Intervene and stop if client not tolerating activity	**T**each how to prioritize activities.
Vary activity with rest based on client's clinical assessment	**E**valuate activity tolerance by assessing HR, RR, BP, color changes, O_2 saturation, and pain level before and 3 minutes after activity. Document and report activity tolerance assessment. Monitor the trends and revise plan as needed and/or notify HCP.
Educate how to prioritize and pace activities with rest	**R**est periods with activities, review appropriate exercise.

Exceptions and Additions by Diseases

Pathphysiology: Structural, Functional (Mechanical and Electrical Conduction)
Trend Potential Complication: Pulmonary Edema

Pulmonary edema is fluid in the alveoli of the lungs primarily resulting from heart failure. This is caused by increased pressure in the pulmonary blood vessels. The point is: there is fluid in the lungs! The client is literally drowning and requires immediate intervention.

 Your goal as a nurse is to recognize the signs and symptoms of **pulmonary edema** and intervene early. It helps if you have a "**DOG MAD**" to help!

System-Specific Assessments	First-Do Priority Interventions	
Onset of symptoms may be rapid	**DOG MAD**	This is an EMERGENCY! Notify rapid response and healthcare provider.
• ↑ Anxiety (early sign) • ↑ RR (RESPIRATORY DISTRESS, ↓ O₂ sat) • ↑ pulse, palpitations • ↑ adventitious lung sounds (crackles & audible wheezing) • ↑ cough with frothy, pink-tinged sputum (classic sign)	**D**o ↑ HOB **O**xygen **G**ive diuretics **M**orphine **A**fterload decrease **D**ecrease preload ©2014 I CAN Publishing®, Inc. 	**D**o ↑ HOB **O**xygen: ↑ oxygen to tissues, evaluate ABGs *(refer to concept Acid Base for specifics)*. **G**ive Diuretics: ↓ fluid overload by ↑ urine output. Monitor for ↓ K⁺ level (risk for Digoxin {DIG} toxicity). Daily weights, I & O. **M**orphine: ↓ preload to ↓ workload; helps with anxiety, monitor for ↓ respirations. **A**fterload decrease: Ace Inhibitors, Beta Blockers, Nitroprusside (can also decrease preload). **D**ecrease preload: nitroglycerin, morphine, furosemide (Lasix), ↓ heart rate.

INSANELY EASY TIP!
"DOG MAD"

Exceptions and Additions by Diseases

Pathophysiology: Structural, Functional (Mechanical and Electrical Conduction)
Congenital Heart Defects

Many students dread reviewing all of the pediatric congenital cardiac defects. In order to simplify this, we want you to know the following:

1. How do you remember if the cardiac heart defect is a *cyanotic* or *acyanotic* defect?

2. Which way does the blood shunt?

3. Which side of the heart has the most pressure in the cyanotic or acyanotic defects?

INSANELY EASY TIP to Simplify Volumes of Information!
Twelve minutes or less and you will have this down!

1. Remember all of the **Ts** are cyanotic and there are only four: **Tetralogy of Fallot, Truncus Arteriosus, Transposition of the Great Vessel, Tricuspid Atresia.** The other letters are acyanotic defects.

2. Remember, **"CPR"** for cyanotic heart defects. Typically, we do not do CPR with infants, unless they have a respiratory problem. **CPR is only a mnemonic to help you organize which defect has greater pressure in the heart and the side for shunting.** Remember that in the acyanotic heart defects, there is Always Some Loss = **ASL** of blood (this is simply a memory tool to assist you in recalling this information). Think about it. If the infant has a **VSD** = Ventricular Septal Defect, there is a loss of blood from the shunting. If the infant has coarctation of the aorta, there is adequate perfusion in the upper extremities (proximal) to the coarctation, but decreased perfusion in the lower extremities (distal) to the coarctation. In the chart below, notice that in the cyanotic defects (they all begin with a **T**) **the pulmonic pressure is greater than the systemic.** See how easy this is with this memory tool? There is also a right-to-left **shunt.** In the **acyanotic heart defects, it is exactly the opposite.** Remember, if you get one down, the other is the opposite. Thus, in the acyanotic heart defects there is a greater pressure in the **systemic in contrast to the pulmonic pressure.** There is also a **left-to-right shunt.**

3. Review acyanotic heart defects: **Systemic pressure is greater than pulmonic pressure and there is a left-to-right shunt. "ALWAYS SOME LOSS."** Cyanotic heart defects: **Pulmonic pressure is greater than systemic and there is right-to-left shunt = "CPR."**

System-Specific Assessments

ACYANOTIC ALWAYS SOME LOSS "ASL"		CYANOTIC (Ts) "CPR"	
ACYANOTIC (always)	**C**YANOTIC (Ts)	**A**CYANOTIC (always)	**C**YANOTIC (Ts)
Systemic (some) →	**P**ulmonic pressure	**S**ystemic (some) ←	**P**ulmonic pressure
Left (*shunt*) (loss) →	**R**ight (*shunt*)	**L**eft (*shunt*) (loss) ←	**R**ight (*shunt*)

Exceptions and Additions by Diseases

Pathophysiology: Structural, Functional (Mechanical and Electrical Conduction)

Valvular Heart Disease

Valvular heart disease is an abnormality or dysfunction that interferes with unidirectional blood flow and results from damage of one or more of the heart's four valves (tricuspid, pulmonic, mitral, and aortic). Valvular heart disease can be congenital or acquired. The valves on the left side of the heart are more likely to be affected because of the high pressure. When there is *stenosis* of the valve, the opening is narrowed and it impedes the flow of the blood forward. Valve insufficiency results in the valve not closing properly and regurgitation or backward flow of the blood occurs. Stenosis or insufficiency can occur in any of the four valves. **Valve replacement surgery** may be required when the valve is no longer functional due to increased stenosis or insufficiency. There are two common types of valve replacements: Mechanical and tissue (usually from animals such as pigs). See the table below for the advantages and disadvantages of each.

Valve Replacement	Advantages	Disadvantages
Mechanical	Last for lifetime	Required to take anticoagulants for life due to risk for clots
Tissue	Does not require anticoagulants	Last 10 to 20 years, then replacement needed

		FIRST-DO	PRIORITY	INTERVENTIONS	
SYSTEM-SPECIFIC ASSESSMENTS	**DIET**	**EQUIPMENT**	**PLANS/INTERVENTIONS**	**HEALTH PROMOTION**	
Common for all valve disorders: • Murmur • Dyspnea • Fatigue **Left-Sided Valves' Dysfunction (mitral and aortic)** ↑ Pulmonary artery pressure ↑ Ventricular hypertrophy = ↓ Cardiac Output **Right-Sided Valves' Dysfunction (tricuspid and pulmonic)** ↑ Right atria pressure ↑ Peripheral edema, JVD, hepatomegaly = ↑ **Fluid in body** In the elderly, heart valves become more fibrotic and thicken; results in hypertension and stress on the mitral valve.	• Low fat • Low cholesterol • Low sodium • Heart Healthy Diet • *Refer to concept Nutrition*	• ECG monitoring • Oxygen therapy with humidity • Hemo-dynamic monitoring equipment • IV pumps	• Prepare for possible valve replacement or repair. • Follow post-op care similar to CABG. • REST during active disease process, then pace activity with rest	Teach client/family: • After heart valve repair or replacement, client will require prophylactic antibiotics prior to dental work, surgery/invasive procedures • Diet • Medications (anticoagulants) for mechanical valve replacements, required to take for life • Need to monitor weight daily • Symptoms to report to HCP: weight gain > 2 lbs./day, chest pain • Refer family for CPR training	

Exceptions and Additions by Diseases

Pathophysiology: Structural, Functional (Mechanical & Electrical Conduction)
Trend Potential Complication: Cardiogenic Shock

Cardiogenic Shock is related to pump failure (inability of the heart to pump to meet the oxygenation needs of the client). It is most often due to extensive cardiac-tissue damage from a myocardial infarction. The result is significant reduction in the cardiac output that eventually leads to multiple system organ failure because of the inadequate perfusion of blood and oxygen. Cardiogenic shock has a high mortality rate (Wagner & Hardin-Pierce, 2014 and Nettina, 2013).

Be alert for EARLY Signs with clients who have had a massive MI and/or post CABG.

System-Specific Assessments	First-Do Priority Interventions "STAT"
Early Signs • Restless, anxious • ↑ Respirations • ↑ Heart Rate >100 • BP may be within client's normal range in early stages **Late Changes** • ↓ BP < 90 mm systolic or (30 mm < systolic baseline) • ↓ urine < 30 mL/hr. for at least 2 hours. • ↓ peripheral pulses, weak and thready • ↓ LOC • Adventitious lung sounds (monitor lungs for pulmonary edema—pink-tinged, frothy sputum) • Cool, clammy skin	**S**tart O_2 or increase as needed (may need intubation). **T**rends and changes; notify HCP of early signs: restlessness, anxiety changes, trends in vital signs. **A**nalyze rhythm, heart rate, BP, and RR. **A**dminister meds per order/protocol (i.e., diuretics, morphine, nitroglycerin, vasopressors, etc.). **T**rend fluid volume status to prevent fluid overload (a heart that is failing cannot adequately pump). *Client may require a balloon pump or bypass surgery.* *Recognize those early signs? They are the early signs of hypoxemia!!* *You knew that! (Refer to concept Oxygenation and concept Shock for specifics.)*

Exceptions and Additions by Diseases

Pathophysiology: Structural, Functional (Mechanical and Electrical Conduction)
Cardiac Monitoring

Because many nurses are on units where clients are undergoing continuous cardiac monitoring, it is important to have an understanding of lead placement. The electrocardiogram (ECG) is a picture of the heart's electrical activity. Lead wires are attached to electrodes placed on the client's chest (*see diagram below*). The lead sends, by remote receiver, the electrical activity of the heart so it can be visualized on a heart monitor. The monitor may be at the bedside or in a different location with a monitoring technician who continually observes the monitor for cardiac dysthymias (telemetry) (Ellis, 2012). The following pictures illustrate several commonly used lead placements for continuous monitoring. When you are on a unit with continuous telemetry monitoring it is important that you know which lead (Lead I, II, III, or MCL1) is being used for monitoring and document accordingly.

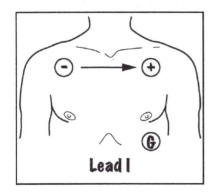

Lead I

The electrodes are placed on the client based on what lead is being used to monitor the heart. The plus sign indicates the electrode is in a positive position and the negative sign indicates the electrode is in a negative position and the G stands for the ground lead electrode. The electrodes send an electrical picture of the direction of the cardiac impulse that you see on the ECG strip, which is why you sometimes see the complexes going up and sometimes you see the complexes going down. The reason is simply the direction the impulse is coming toward or going away from the electrode (Ellis, 2012).

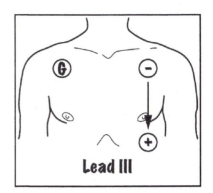

Lead III

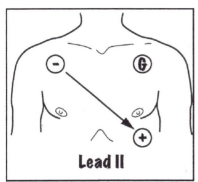

Lead II

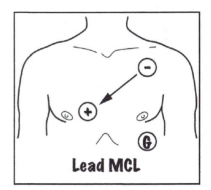

Lead MCL

If the client is being monitored, the standard of care is the rhythms strips are analyzed and documented at least once per shift or more often per unit protocol. As a nurse, you need to know how to correctly place the electrodes on the client and how to attach the leads according to the unit protocol. **This is a priority because you might have to put electrodes and leads on in an EMERGENCY!** *(In clinical, if there is an opportunity, ask the staff if you can place the electrodes on the client and connect the leads. Great opportunity for practice!)*

Exceptions and Additions by Diseases

Pathophysiology: Structural, Functional (Mechanical and Electrical Conduction)
Cardiac Normal Conduction System

Cardiac rhythm begins with a normal electrical stimulation of the heart. The electrical stimulation comes from the depolarization and repolarization process, which produces a rhythmic contraction of the myocardium, known as a heartbeat. The repolarization returns the cell back to a negative resting state (referred to as *polarized*). The SA node, known as the pacemaker of the heart, is comprised mostly of positively charged electrical potassium (K^+) ions (intracellular) with stronger electrical positive sodium (Na^+) on the outside of the cell (extracellular) (Ellis, 2012).

How the Normal Conduction Process Begins:

1. Electrical charge occurs within the SA node when Na^+ ions enter the cells and K^+ ions (a small amount) leak out of the cells.

2. Cells are now positively charged = depolarization.

3. Electrical impulse travels from SA node, cell to cell = R & L atria contraction.

4. Impulse travels to AV node.

5. AV node sends impulse through the bundle of His (both the right & left branches) through the Purkinje fibers = R & L ventricular contraction.

6. Cells recover, K^+ returns to cell, and Na^+ moves out = repolarization.

Cardiac Cells Have Unique Features:

- **Automaticity**: Ability to create an impulse outside of stimulation.

- **Conductivity**: Ability to pass the impulse along to other cells.

- **Excitability**: Ability to respond to a stimulus with depolarization.

- **Contractility**: Ability to contract.

What this means is other cardiac cells can become the pacemaker if the SA node fails. Failure in any part of the conduction system will result in a variation in the conduction. The other cells in the AV node and the ventricles have different rates. The SA node rate is 60–100 bpm, but the AV node (40–60 bpm) and the ventricles (20–40 bpm) are slower. If the ventricles become the pacemaker, then this is a PROBLEM!

We are now going to analyze some strips to determine if the conduction system is operating correctly.

Pathophysiology: Structural, Functional
(Mechanical and Electrical Conduction)
Cardiac Normal Conduction System

Below is a diagram of normal distinct waveforms that each beat creates on an electrocardiograph. This is the first step to analyzing cardiac arrhythmias.

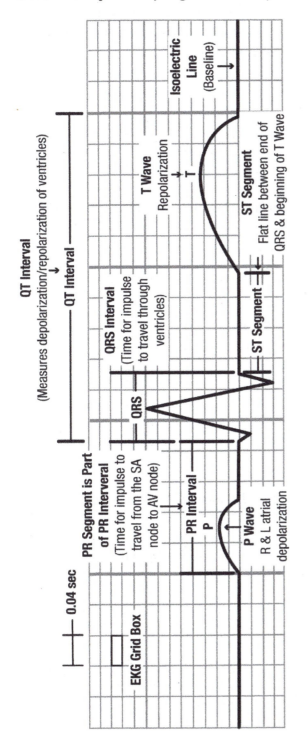

P Wave — R & L Atrial depolarization			QRS Wave — R & L Ventricular Depolarization		T Wave — R & L Ventricular Repolarization		
SA Node Pacemaker	AV Node	PR Segment	Bundle of His	Purkinje Network Fibers	ST Segment	T Wave	Isoelectric Line (Baseline)
		Flat line between P wave & QRS			Flat line between end of QRS & beginning of T wave		
• No electrical activity	• Location: R atria (link to ventricles from atria)		• Location: between R & L ventricles	• Network of fibers to carry impulses directly to ventricles	• No electrical activity	• **Ventricular repolarization**	• No electrical activity
• Location: R atria	• Transmit electrical impulse to Bundle of His		• Send electrical impulse down the R & L bundles, to Purkinje Fibers	• Initiates **R & L ventricular contraction**			
• **Depolarized = Contraction of R & L atria**							

Pathophysiology: Structural, Functional (Mechanical and Electrical Conduction)

Cardiac Rhythms: Determining the Heart Rate and Rhythm

A **rhythm strip** (typically a six-second strip) is a printout of the heart's electrical activity so the nurse can analyze the rhythm. The **six-second strip** that you see below is an example of what is printed when a client is being monitored. The lines you see on the ECG paper mark three seconds of the six-second strip. In this example, there are two three-second marks = a six-second strip. The assessment of the strip is done every shift per protocol or PRN if the client is experiencing an arrhythmia.

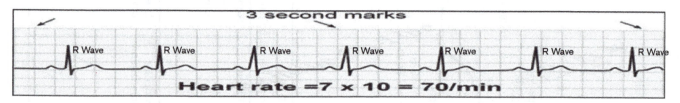

The Steps to Analyze a Six-Second Strip:

Step 1: Analyze the strip to determine the heart rate. Here is a **quick method** to determine the approximate heart rate:

- Count the # of R waves (R is part of QRS complex) in a six-second strip.

- Multiply the # of R waves by 10. (There are 10 {6 seconds} in a minute) 10 x 6 seconds = 60 seconds = 1 minute) = heart rate per minute (bpm).

- In the above example, there are 7 R waves in the 6-second strip. Multiply 7 x 10 = heart rate of approximately 70 bpm.

Step 2: Determine if the heart rate is (based on an adult client):

- **Sinus rhythm** (rate 60–100 bpm)

- **Bradycardia** (< 60 bpm)

- **Tachycardia** (> 100 bpm)

Step 3: Look to see if the rhythm is regular. Are the R waves equal distances apart or are they irregular? (In the above example, the rhythm is regular.)

Step 4: Determine if the waveforms described in the first diagram are present in this strip:
- **Is there a P wave?** (Yes, there is a P wave before every QRS.)

- **Is there a QRS complex?** (Yes, there is a QRS complex following the P wave.)

- **Is there a T wave?** (Yes, there is a T wave after every QRS.)

Step 5: Analyze the findings. In the above example: Heart rate = 70, rhythm regular, all waveforms present = Sinus rhythm. If there are any missing waveforms, or the heart rate is not 60–100 bpm, then there is some type of an arrhythmia. (More to come later in this chapter about analyzing arrhythmias!)

Let's Practice What You Have Learned!

1. Where does the electrical impulse originate?

2. What does the P wave represent?

3. What does the QRS complex represent?

4. What does the T wave represent?

5. What is the normal heart rate range for sinus rhythm?

6. What is the normal heart rate range for sinus bradycardia?

7. What is the normal heart rate range for sinus tachycardia?

8. What is the length of a typical rhythm strip used for analysis?

Let's try a six-second strip analysis!

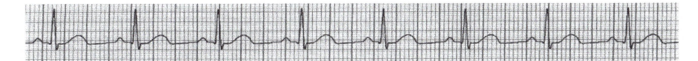

9. Using the quick method, what is the heart rate in the strip above?

10. Are all of the waveforms present? (Is there a P wave before every QRS followed by a T wave?)

11. Is the rhythm regular or irregular?

12. What is the interpretation for this strip?

Check your answers below.

Great Job! That was easy! Let's Move On!

Pathophysiology: Structural, Functional (Mechanical and Electrical Conduction)
Cardiac Rhythms: Analyzing the Conduction System

Let's look at the length of time it takes for the stimulation (impulse) to travel through the conduction system. A delay in any of the intervals represents a block in the conduction system. Here are some simple facts to get you started as we look at the conduction times on this strip. **Note:** All of the following strips are to be considered six-second strips.

In a rhythm strip:
  Each little box = 0.04 seconds of time
  Each large square is comprised of 5 little boxes
  Each large square = 0. 20 seconds

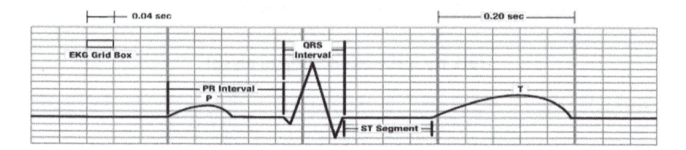

Determining the Times For The Electrical Conduction Path

Determining the PR Interval *(represents time from SA node to AV node).*
The normal range of time for the PR Interval is 0.12 to 0.20 seconds.

Step 1: Count the number of little boxes between the beginning of the P wave to the beginning of the QRS. (In the example, there are 4¼ little boxes between the beginning of the P wave and the beginning of the QRS.)

Step 2: There are 4¼ little boxes (4.25). Multiply 4.25 x 0.04 sec (time of each little box). **4.25 x 0.04 sec = 0.17 seconds** (this is within the normal PR interval range of 0.12–0.20 seconds).

Determining the QRS Interval *(represents time from AV node to bundle of His or R & L, to Purkinje fibers).*
The normal range of time is 0.06 to 0.12 seconds.

Step 1: Count the number of little boxes between the beginning of the QRS and the end of the QRS.

Step 2: There are 2¼ little boxes (2.25). Multiply by 0.04 sec = **2.25 x 0.04 = 0.09 seconds** (within normal for the QRS Interval of 0.06–0.12 seconds).

Note: An instrument called calipers is used to obtain the most accurate results when reading strips and counting the little boxes. In these examples, we have estimated. Do not worry if you do not have calipers because **to be successful in answering questions on NCLEX®, what is important to know is the normal range for the PR and QRS intervals.** Now that you have practiced measuring the intervals, it is easy to see that any increase in the interval beyond the normal range is an increase in the time it takes the electrical impulse to travel through the conduction system. Just like on a highway, anything can block or delay the travel time. A delay in the intervals is referred to as a block. There are many different types of blocks, some are asymptomatic, and others require immediate intervention. As the blocks increase in time, or there are disconnects between the P waves and the QRS, the blocks have a greater potential to cause complications. Clients become symptomatic when the heart rate increases or decreases and results in a decrease in perfusion. We will discuss blocks later in this chapter.

Pathophysiology: Structural, Functional (Mechanical and Electrical Conduction)
Analyzing Cardiac Rhythms: Sinus Rhythms

After you have completed the steps to determine the heart rate and rhythm, and have calculated the PR and QRS intervals, you are ready to analyze the strip to determine the type of cardiac rhythm your client has.

Normal Sinus Rhythm is what we have been using in our examples. It is when the heart rate is normal (60–100 bpm) and the rhythm is regular. In addition, there is a P wave before each QRS, a T wave following the QRS, and the intervals (PR and QRS) are within the normal range. This indicates there is a normal conduction pattern. Sinus Rhythm is actually the only normal rhythm.

Normal Sinus Rhythm

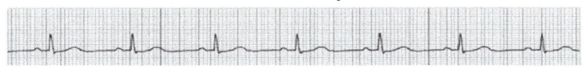

HEART RATE	RHYTHM REGULARITY	P WAVE	PR INTERVAL	QRS INTERVAL
60–100 bpm	Regular	Before each QRS	0.12 to 0.20 seconds	0.06 to 0.12 seconds

Sinus Arrhythmia is still considered sinus because there is a P wave before every QRS complex and the conduction intervals are within normal range. The only difference between this strip and the sinus rhythm strip above is the rhythm is irregular. Usually sinus arrhythmia has no clinical symptoms and does not require treatment. All of us have some irregularity in our heart rhythm at times. As a nurse, your responsibility is to document the rhythym.

Sinus Arrhythmia

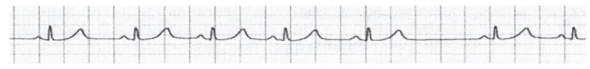

HEART RATE	RHYTHM REGULARITY	P WAVE	PR INTERVAL	QRS INTERVAL
Usually 60–100 bpm	Irregular	Before each QRS	0.12 to 0.20 seconds	0.06 to 0.12 seconds

Cardiac Arrhythmias, also known as *dysrhythmias*, are alterations in the normal electrical stimulation of the heart. There are many causes for cardiac arrhythmias; they can be benign or have lethal consequences. A unique fact about cardiac muscle cells is that they can act (fire an impulse) without stimulation. This is referred to as automaticity. Ectopic pacemakers can take over as the main pacemaker or cause irregular or premature beats. An arrhythmia can be as simple as the heart rate being too slow or too fast.

The remaining strips we will discuss are considered arrhythmias. Let's begin with sinus bradycardia.

Exceptions and Additions by Diseases

Pathophysiology: Structural, Functional (Mechanical and Electrical Conduction)
Cardiac Arrhythmias (Dysrhythmias) Sinus: Bradycardia and Tachycardia

Sinus Bradycardia is sinus because there is a P wave before every QRS complex and the conduction intervals are within normal range. **The only difference between this strip and the normal sinus rhythm strip is that the rate is < 60 bpm.** It can possibly indicate sinus node conduction alteration requiring medications to increase the heart rate if the client becomes symptomatic. Symptoms occur when the rate decreases to a point where there is decreased cardiac output resulting in decreased perfusion.

Sinus Bradycardia

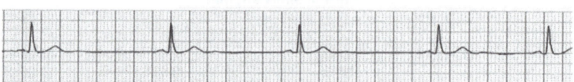

HEART RATE	RHYTHM REGULARITY	P WAVE	PR INTERVAL	QRS INTERVAL
Bradycardia < 60 bpm	Regular to slightly irregular	Before each QRS	0.12 to 0.20 seconds	0.06 to 0.12 seconds

Sinus Tachycardia is sinus because there is a P wave before every QRS complex and the conduction intervals are within normal range. The only difference between this strip and the normal sinus rhythm strip is the rate is > 100 bpm. The heart rate increases when there is a need for increased cardiac output in response to (i.e., hypovolemia, respiratory distress, fever, pain, medications, etc.). Always treat the underlying cause. Clients with sinus tachycardia are at a higher risk for coronary artery disease (CAD) because of the increased myocardial oxygen demand and the resulting decreased diastolic filling.

Sinus Tachycardia

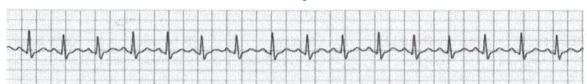

HEART RATE	RHYTHM REGULARITY	P WAVE	PR INTERVAL	QRS INTERVAL
Tachycardia > 100 bpm	Regular	Before each QRS	0.12 to 0.20 seconds	0.06 to 0.12 seconds

Safety is a priority with both of these arrhythmias.
A heart rate too slow or too fast can cause decreased perfusion.
Decreased perfusion can lead to syncope and a risk for falls.
Implement Fall Protocols!!!

Pathophysiology: Structural, Functional (Mechanical and Electrical Conduction)

Arrhythmias (Dysrhythmias) Atrial: Atrial Flutter and Atrial Fibrillation

Atrial Arrhythmias still have a P wave, but it is different than the P wave that comes from the SA node. One of the other atrial cells has taken over as the pacemaker. Atrial rhythms can have a very high heart rate resulting in decreased perfusion.

Atrial Flutter has P waves that can appear saw-toothed (see the image below) and may also be referred to as "flutter waves." When you analyze the ECG strip, you may actually see a ratio of 2:1 (2 P waves for every 1 QRS) or a 3:1, (3 P waves for every 1 QRS). This atrial block may also be variable and cause atrial flutter to appear as a regular or irregular rhythm.

Atrial Flutter

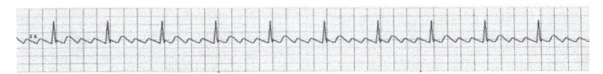

HEART RATE	RHYTHM REGULARITY	P WAVE	PR INTERVAL	QRS INTERVAL
Atrial Rate (P waves) 240–400 pm Ventricular Rate (QRS) slow to rapid	Regular	More P waves than QRS waves	Not applicable	0.06 to 0.12 seconds

Atrial Fibrillation is a disorganized, very rapid, irregular atrial rhythm resulting in an increased or decreased ventricular rate. As you look at the strip below, P waves are hard to distinguish because they are firing so quickly. This is referred to as *fibrillation*. However, not all of the P waves are conducting to the AV node to stimulate the ventricles to contract. There are more P waves than QRS complexes and the rate is very irregular. When the rate is < 100 bpm, it is called *controlled atrial fibrillation*. If the rate is > 100 bpm, it is *uncontrolled atrial fibrillation*. If the client cannot be converted to a sinus rhythm through cardioversion or medications, the goal is to keep the heart rate < 100 bpm.

Atrial Fibrillation

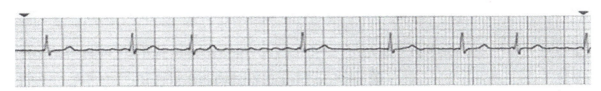

HEART RATE	RHYTHM REGULARITY	P WAVE	PR INTERVAL	QRS INTERVAL
Atrial Rate (P waves) 350–600 pm Ventricular Rate (QRS) slow to rapid	Irregular	Fibrillation (fine to course) (more P waves than QRS waves)	Not applicable	0.06 to 0.12 seconds (it may be < 0.06 seconds when the HR is very rapid)

Pathophysiology: Structural, Functional
(Mechanical and Electrical Conduction)
Arrhythmias (Dysrhythmias) Atrial: Atrial Flutter and Atrial Fibrillation

Atrial Flutter/Fibrillation

System-Specific Assessments "ATRIA"	First-Do Priority Interventions
Asymptomatic: client may be asymptomatic and the arrhythmia is found on a routine healthcare visit **T**rend HR: may vary in rate and is irregular; ↓ BP, SOB and ↓ O_2 sat if perfusion is inadequate. **R**eport syncope, particularly when rising out of bed **I**ncidents of chest pain **A**ltered LOC **Clients become symptomatic (often with activity) as a result of lack of perfusion to carry oxygenated blood to the body.**	**Clients are treated when symptomatic or if HR > 100** • O_2 supplement as needed • Falls precautions • Medications to decrease heart rate (i.e., calcium channel blockers, beta blockers, Digoxin); Adenosine for heart rate > 150 bpm • Anticoagulants to prevent clots; client teaching about safety, monitoring PT levels, diet, etc. (refer to *Pharmacology Made Insanely Easy* for specifics) • Prepare client for possible cardioversion (refer to chart comparing cardioversion and defibrillation in this chapter) **Goal** • If atrial fibrillation does not convert to sinus rhythm, keep the heart rate < 100 bpm with medications

Potential Complications from Chronic Atrial Fibrillation
Risk for blood clots and stroke.
(Clots form as the blood pools in the atrium because of the fibrillation)

Clients require anticoagulants as long as they remain in atrial fibrillation!!!

Risk for falls from decreased or increased heart rates.
Implement Fall Protocols!!!

Pathophysiology: Structural, Functional (Mechanical and Electrical Conduction)
Cardiac Arrhythmias (Dysrhythmias): Heart Blocks

Heart Blocks: There are several types of heart blocks that can occur along the electrical conduction path between the atria and the ventricles. A first-degree AV heart block is a delay in conduction time through the AV node (PR interval is > 0.20 seconds) and requires no treatment. It would only be documented. Second-degree AV heart blocks occur when some of the impulses are blocked at the AV node and only some of the P waves are followed by a QRS. Some blocks can be treated with medications and others require interventions, like a pacemaker (LeMone, Burke, and Bauldoff, 2011).

There are several different types of second-degree AV heart blocks, but we are not going to discuss all of them in this book. **The most important point we want you to remember about AV heart blocks is there is a block somewhere in the conduction system, which causes a delay in the conduction time.** Treatment is required when the heart rate decreases to the point there is decreased perfusion and clients become symptomatic.

Third-degree AV heart blocks (complete heart block) require immediate intervention with an insertion of a pacemaker. We want you to be able to recognize a third-degree AV heart block on a rhythm strip. A third-degree heart block cannot sustain adequate perfusion. All impulses are blocked at the AV node and secondary or tertiary pacemakers respond. The result is no connection between the P wave and the QRS. Clients become symptomatic when the heart rate decreases to the point of inadequate perfusion. When you analyze the strip below, see how the P waves have their own rhythm and the QRS has its own rhythm and they are definitely not dancing together; in fact, they are divorced!

Third-Degree AV Heart Block (Complete Heart Block)

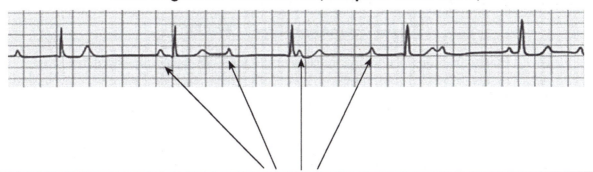

HEART RATE	RHYTHM REGULARITY	P WAVE	PR INTERVAL	QRS INTERVAL
Atrial: faster than ventricular	Usually regular in rhythm but can be irregular	Uniform, but more P waves than QRS waves)	No consistent interval	May be narrow < 0.06 seconds or wide > 0.12 seconds

Exceptions and Additions by Diseases

Pathophysiology: Structural, Functional
(Mechanical and Electrical Conduction)
Cardiac Arrhythmias (Dysrhythmias): Third-Degree or Complete Heart Block

Procedure: Pacemakers

Pacemakers can be temporary or permanent. They consist of a generator and electrodes that are attached to the myocardial muscle. Temporary pacemakers use an external battery pack; whereas permanent pacemakers have an internal pacing unit. Pacemakers can be single-chamber that only pace the SA or AV node, or dual chambers that pace both the SA and AV nodes (*see Pacemaker strip on next page*). Pacemakers are indicated for clients with symptomatic bradycardia, third-degree (complete heart block), or atrial or ventricular tachydysrhythmias (Black & Hawk, 2009).

Pacemaker Settings:

- **Fixed-rate Pacemaker (VOO):** fires at preset rate regardless of client's heart rate
- **Ventricular Demand Pacemaker (VVI):** paces the ventricle with both pacing and sensing capabilities, (i.e., if pacemaker is set at 65 and client's HR is 75, it will not fire; if client's HR is 60, the pacemaker will fire.)
- **DDD Pacemaker:** Most common; senses and paces the atrium and ventricle separately. It is rate responsive, (i.e., if there are more P waves, than QRS complexes, the pacemaker provides a paced QRS to match or if the P wave is too slow, it provides a paced P wave (Ellis, 2012).

Types of Pacemakers:

- **External (Transcutaneous) Pacing:** used in emergencies.
- **Epicardial (Transthoracic) Pacing:** used after open-heart surgery; lead wires are inserted through the thoracic musculature to the heart for pacing.
- **Endocardial (Transvenous) Pacing:** a pacing electrode is threaded through a large central vein to the right ventricle for direct contact with the endocardium.

Post-Pacemaker Care: "PACER"

P Pulse; monitor HR and BP, teach client to take HR every day and notify HCP if the pulse is < 5 bpm below the set rate on pacemaker. **P**ain meds as needed.

A Assess insertion site for redness, drainage, swelling, hematoma.

C Control and minimize shoulder movement initially; may need a sling. **C**lient instructed to have no heavy lifting for two months.

E Evaluate rhythm strip for pacemaker spike (based on type of pacemaker).

R Record insertion time, model #, settings, rhythm strip, client's response. Recommend client wear medical alert bracelet and carry pacemaker ID card. Inform healthcare providers prior to undergoing any diagnostic tests (i.e., MRI, etc.).

Use gloves when handling wires of temporary pacemakers. For temporary pacemakers, keep spare pacemaker, batteries, and cables at bedside.

Pathophysiology: Structural, Functional (Mechanical and Electrical Conduction)

Cardiac Dysrhythmias: Heart Blocks (Third-Degree and Complete) Pacemaker Rhythym Strips

Single-Chamber Pacemaker (pacing the SA node). Note: there are no P waves, just the pacemaker spike.

Pacing Spike Before P Wave

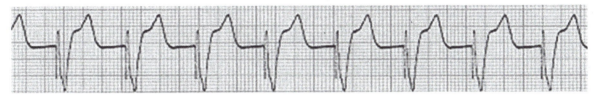

Failure to Capture (pacemaker failure) Note: there are pacer spikes without a P Wave or a QRS.

Pacing Spikes With No Capture

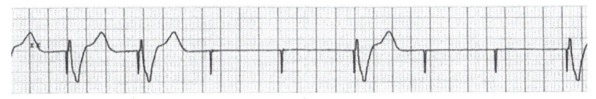

Nursing Responsibilities for Pacemaker Malfunction

Failure to Capture: Pacing spikes without QRS ⟶ Notify HCP: may need to ↑ voltage delivered

Failure to Sense: Pacing spikes at intervals different than programmed ⟶ Notify HCP: ↓ amplitude that pacemaker recognizes as electrical activity

Discharge on T wave: Life-threatening ventricular arrhythmia ⟶ Notify HCP: requires repositioning of lead wires

(Ellis, 2012)

> Remember, your nursing responsibility is to recognize malfunctions and notify the HCP! It is all about **SAFETY**!

Implement Fall Protocols!!!

Client may experience syncope with decreased perfusion (↓ HR & ↓ BP).

Report equipment failure to healthcare provider immediately!!

Exceptions and Additions by Diseases

Pathophysiology: Structural, Functional (Mechanical and Electrical Conduction)
Cardiac Arrhythmias (Dysrhythmias): Ventricular Rhythms (Premature Ventricular Contractions)

Ventricular rhythms originate in the ventricles and not with the SA node. Therefore, you do not see a P wave. Ventricular rhythms are life-threatening arrhythmias and require immediate intervention. The QRS complexes are often wide and bizarre in appearance.

Premature ventricular beats, known as PVCs, originate in the ventricles. The significance to you is that they can become deadly when they occur frequently or if they land on the T wave during repolarization when the heart is vulnerable to arrhythmias. PVCs require close monitoring and may require treatment. In the six-second strip below, there are four PVCs; multiply that by ten (there are 10 {6 seconds in a minute}) and you have approximately 40 PVCs per minute! This requires immediate intervention. Sometimes PVCs can look different. This is referred to as multi-focal PVCs (PVCs originate from different ventricular pacer cells) (Ellis, 2012).

Premature Ventricular Beats (PVCs)

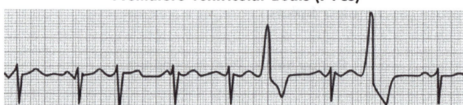

HEART RATE	RHYTHM REGULARITY	P WAVE	PR INTERVAL	QRS INTERVAL
Dependent on underlying rhythm (in example above, rate = 60 bpm)	Single ectopic beat comes early	No P waves	Not measurable	Wide and bizarre > 0.12 seconds

System-Specific Assessments	First-Do Priority Interventions Note PVCs can be due to hypoxemia. Give O$_2$
Occasional PVCs (occur in healthy individuals) ——→	No treatment, but monitor closely.
PVCs with a slow bradycardia rhythm ——→	Give atropine: The increase in the heart rate will help terminate the PVCs needed to maintain circulation.
Frequent PVCs or PVCs that discharge on T wave: Life-threatening ventricular arrhythmia ——→	Identify cause and treat (i.e., O$_2$ sat decrease, myocardial injury, stress, caffeine, hyper or hypokalemia, etc.). Administer Amiodarone or Lidocaine per protocol. Some clients may be started on Beta Blockers for treatment.

Potential Complication! If PVCs become more frequent or occur on the T wave (when the heart is repolarizing and vulnerable) there is ↑ risk for Ventricular Tachycardia or Ventricular Fibrillation or Cardiac Arrest. **Treat per Protocol!!!**

Pathophysiology: Structural, Functional (Mechanical and Electrical Conduction)

Cardiac Arrhythmias Dysrhythmias: Ventricular Tachycardia

Ventricular Tachycardia (VT) is a lethal rhythm. Ventricular tachycardia is considered present when there are three or more PVCs in a row and the rate is > 100 bpm. Your client may be conscious and may be able to tolerate the ventricular tachycardia for a short time if there is some perfusion occurring. This will not last and eventually the client will lose consciousness with the decrease in perfusion. Once the client becomes unconscious and no longer has a pulse, the client requires immediate intervention.

Ventricular Tachycardia (VT)

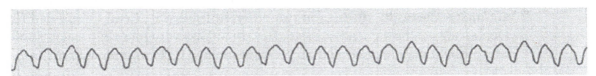

Heart Rate	Rhythm Regularity	P Wave	PR Interval	QRS Interval
150–250 bpm	Usually regular	No P waves	Not measurable	Wide > 0.12 seconds

System-Specific Assessments	First-Do Priority Interventions
• Note rhythm strip or ECG. • Check responsiveness. • **Check for palpable pulse** (ventricular tachycardia may have a pulse initially). • Check respirations (anticipate respiratory arrest will follow). • Check BP (most likely absent or not audible). May have seizures. • Not all ventricular tachycardia is pulseless.	**Call rapid response team per hospital protocol!** **For Ventricular Tachycardia with a pulse:** • Treat clients with medications (i.e., Amiodarone, Lidocaine, or Procainamide). **For Pulseless Ventricular Tachycardia, immediately implement:** • Begin CPR until the defibrillator is connected to the client. (Minimize interruptions in chest compressions.) • Rapidly defibrillate: initially begin with 120 joules with a biphasic machine and increase in a step approach until you reach 200 joules. • Follow ACLS protocol for medications.

Must establish pulselessness by checking carotid or femoral pulse prior to beginning ACLS protocol.

Exceptions and Additions by Diseases

Pathophysiology: Structural, Functional (Mechanical and Electrical Conduction)
Cardiac Arrhythmias (Dysrhythmias): Asystole

Asystole/ventricular standstill, also known as *cardiac standstill*, is when there is no electrical activity, no conduction of impulses, and no pulse. This results in no perfusion to the cells or tissues of the body and is usually the result of significant hypoxia or body-system failure. This is often a terminal rhythm and CPR must begin immediately (Ellis, 2012).

When you see this rhythm, it is always a priority to check to see if the leads on the client are intact. **Check the rhythm in two different leads** (i.e., Lead I and Lead II, etc.). Depending where the lead is located, it could be a very fine ventricular fibrillation, which would require defibrillation versus beginning CPR with no defibrillation.

You need to have a rhythm to defibrillate!
(No defibrillation with asystole)

Asystole (Ventricular Standstill)

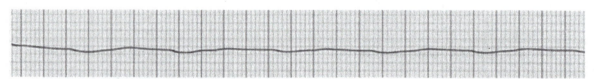

Heart Rate	Rhythm Regularity	P Wave	PR Interval	QRS Interval
Absent	Absent	No P waves	Absent	Absent

System-Specific Assessments	First-Do Priority Interventions
• **Check rhythm in two leads** (i.e., Lead I and Lead II, etc.) to R/O possibility of fine Ventricular Fibrillation • No palpable pulse • No BP • Unconscious	**Treat immediately. Call rapid response team per hospital protocol.** • Begin CPR • Give O_2 per protocol/ABG results/O_2 sat • Follow ACLS protocol for medications • Prepare to defibrillate if a rhythm is re-established. There must be a heart rhythm for defibrillation to be effective.

Pathophysiology: Structural, Functional (Mechanical and Electrical Conduction) Cardiac Arrhythmias (Dysrhythmias): Assessments of ECG for Signs of Ischemia or Tissue Death

The ECG strips below were discussed earlier in the chapter with respect to the clinical assessment findings that indicate cardiac ischemia or cardiac tissue death. Now that you are more familiar with looking at ECG strips, the changes in the ST segment should be more obvious to you. Again, we emphasize that as a beginning nurse, you will not know everything about interpreting ECG strips. However, you now understand it is a priority to know what the ST segments elevations or depressions mean. Look how much you have learned!

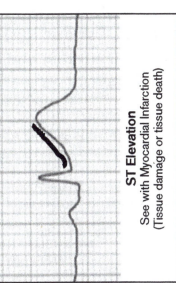

ST Elevation
See with Myocardial Infarction
(Tissue damage or tissue death)

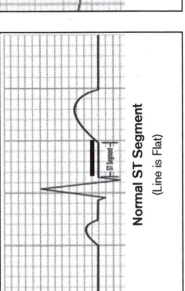

Normal ST Segment
(Line is Flat)

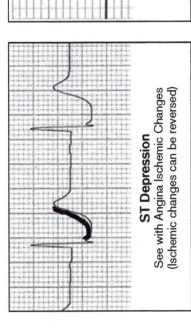

ST Depression
See with Angina Ischemic Changes
(Ischemic changes can be reversed)

Assessing For T Wave Changes (Possible Indication of Elevated or Decreased Potassium Levels)

Assessing the ECG strip for signs of high or low potassium levels is another important clinical assessment if your client is being monitored. The elevations and depressions in the T wave may be the first thing you observe with a client with alterations in his or her potassium level. You would then confirm with a lab test. (*Refer to concepts Nutrition and Potassium for specifics.*)

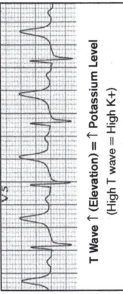

T Wave ↑ (Elevation) = ↑ Potassium Level
(High T wave = High K+)

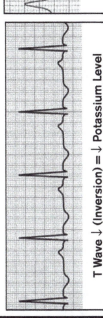

T Wave ↓ (Inversion) = ↓ Potassium Level
(Low T wave = Low K+) *Initially, T Wave might be flat.*

INSANELY EASY TIP!
PotaTOES, TomaTOES,
AvocadTOES,
BananaTOES, and
OrangeTOES
are High in K+.

Remember the TOEs!!

Exceptions and Additions by Diseases

Pathophysiology: Structural, Functional (Mechanical and Electrical Conduction)
Cardiac Arrhythmias (Dysrhythmias): Cardioversion and Defibrillation

Cardioversion is an elective procedure. The client receives a counter shock to the heart that is synchronized with the QRS complex. It is used with atrial arrhythmias (uncontrolled atrial fibrillation), supraventricular tachycardia, and ventricular tachycardia with a pulse. A low voltage (50-100 Joules) is used.

Defibrillation is an unsynchronized shock to the heart that stops all electrical activity of the heart allowing the SA node to take over and reestablish a rhythm that will provide adequate perfusion. It is used with ventricular fibrillation or pulseless ventricular tachycardia.

Defibrillate or cardiovert? That is the question! When it comes to defibrillation and cardioversion, it can be confusing. **Below are some basic facts that will help you become a cardiac whiz!**

Elect to Cardiovert: Get in Sync!!! "CARDIOVERT"	Defibrillate: Do or DIE!!! "DEFIBRILLATE"
Conscious client, sedate and medicate for pain	**D**efibrillate only on an unconscious client
Anticoagulation prior to cardioversion	**E**mergency–Call a Code
Requires shock to be synchronized, use low joules	**F**ibrillation ventricular or pulseless ventricular tachycardia
Done only by HCP	**IV** needed for drugs according to ACLS protocol
IV will be needed	**B**egin CPR and continue in between defibrillations
Oxygen before and after, NOT during	**R**espiratory, support with oxygen
Vital signs and rhythm evaluate throughout	**I**ncrease joules as needed (defibrillate x 3 only at max joules)
Elective procedure, need consent	**L**ocate crash cart
Rhythms for cardioversion include atrial fibrillation	**L**earn to correctly place paddles/electrode pads
Tell everyone to clear prior to shock; use conduction medium to prevent burns	**A**lways use conduction medium to prevent burns
	Tell everyone to clear prior to shock
	Evaluate vital signs, rhythm, and response to meds

PUSH THAT BUTTON BEFORE YOU SHOCK!

DON'T PUSH THAT BUTTON WHEN YOU DEFIBRILLATE!!!

Be **SAFE** for Both Cardioversion and Defibrillation

Skin protect from burns with conduction medium

Always place paddles/electrode pads correctly

Find crash cart to have at bedside

Everyone clear prior to shock

SAFETY

Are you ready to see how much you know about cardiac arrhythmias?

You are going to be surprised!!! Answer these questions about the strip below:

1. Are there P waves?

2. Is there a QRS?

3. Is there a T wave?

4. What is the rate?

5. What is the rhythm?

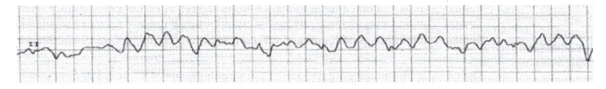

6. When do you use cardioversion?

7. What action should you take with the arrhythmia below?

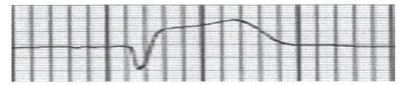

8. What is your interpretation of this ST segment below?

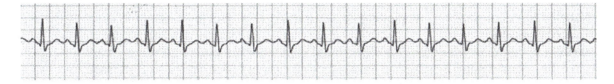

9. What should you keep at the bedside for safety with a client with a temporary pacemaker?

Answers:

1. Yes 2. Yes 3. Yes 4. 160 bpm 5. Sinus tachycardia
6. Atrial fibrillation 7. Defibrillate 8. ST elevation, may be
indicative of an MI 9. Spare pacemaker, batteries, cables

We bet you answered them all correctly!!!

Can you believe how much you have learned?

Excellent! Let's finish this chapter!

Exceptions and Additions by Diseases

Pathophysiology: Infections and Inflammation
Rheumatic Heart Disease, Endocarditis, Myocarditis, Pericarditis

Rheumatic Heart Disease is a condition when there is systemic inflammation with valvular deformity that follows an acute or repeated episode of rheumatic fever (Beta-hemolytic streptococcus). *Carditis* is the most destructive result from rheumatic fever and it occurs in about 50% of the clients. *Pericarditis* may also occur.

Pericarditis is fluid accumulation within the pericardial sac that compresses the heart. It can be acute or chronic. It often occurs after a respiratory infection, but may also occur after a myocardial injury, rheumatic fever, systemic lupus erythematous, or rheumatoid arthritis, etc.

Endocarditis (also known as *infective endocarditis*) is an inflammation of the lining of the heart and involves the endothelial lining of the heart, commonly in the mitral valve. The most common cause is the organism Staphylococcus Aureus.

Myocarditis is the inflammation of the myocardial wall and may extend to the pericardium, resulting in pericarditis. The most common cause is a viral infection caused by Coxsackie B Enterovirus. It can also be the result of an immunologic response due to radiation, chemical poisons, drugs, or burns. It causes diffuse swelling and damage to the myocardial cells that leads to a weakening of the heart muscle that results in decreased contractibility. Without intervention, myocarditis can progress to cardiomyopathy and heart failure (LeMone, Burke, and Bauldoff, 2011).

System-Specific Assessments (Comparison Chart for Infective/Inflammatory Disorders

SYSTEM-SPECIFIC ASSESSMENTS	MURMUR	FEVER	DYSPNEA	TACHYCARDIA	PERICARDIA FRICTION RUB	PAIN
Rheumatic Heart Disease (a complication of Rheumatic Fever)	X	X	X (from heart failure)	X	X	X (chest pain)
Pericarditis	X	X	X	X	X	X (Pain sudden and sharp. **To distinguish pain from chest pain, have client lean forward to see if the pain is relieved.**)
Endocarditis (characteristic micro embolization occurring throughout body, i.e., petechiae	X (present later in disease process)	X	X	X		X (muscle aches)
Myocarditis	X	X	X	X	X (rare)	X (stabbing pain)

INSANELY EASY TIP to remember the assessments
of 4 Infective/Inflammatory Heart Diseases!

The **EXCEPTIONS** (there are only two). The rest are the SAME.
Endocarditis doesn't have pericardia friction rub.
Pericarditis pain is relieved by sitting and leaning forward!!!

Pathophysiology: Infections and Inflammation
Rheumatic Heart Disease, Endocartitis, Myocarditis, Pericarditis

	FIRST-DO PRIORITY INTERVENTIONS			
SYSTEM-SPECIFIC ASSESSMENTS	**DIET**	**EQUIPMENT**	**PLANS/INTERVENTIONS "REST"**	**HEALTH PROMOTION**
See System-Specific Comparison Chart on previous page.	• Low Fat • Low Cholesterol • Low Sodium • Heart Healthy Diet • Refer to concept Nutrition for specifics	• ECG monitoring • Oxygen therapy with cool mist • Hemodynamic monitoring equipment • IV pumps	**R**est: Strict bed rest during the active disease process (↓ cardiac workload). **E**valuate VS, lung and cardiac sounds, emotional support. **S**epsis: Manage infection (i.e., monitor ↑ WBCs, ↑ temp, administer antibiotics). **S**upport pain management. **T**each client symptoms of heart failure to report to the HCP.	Teach client/family about: • Diet • Medications • Need to monitor weight daily • Report signs of infection, ↑ temp, and signs of heart failure • Symptoms to report to HCP: WT gain > 2 lbs./day, chest pain • Refer family for CPR training

Remember infections and inflammation of the heart require **REST** to decrease the workload of the heart while it heals. "**REST** to **RECOVER**"

Trend Potential Complication:

Cardiac Tamponade can result from fluid accumulation in the pericardial sac that results in a life-threatening emergency (Wagner & Hardin-Pierce, 2014).

System-Specific Assessments	First-Do Priority Interventions
• Sudden onset of pulsus paradoxus: > 10 mm Hg ↓ in systolic BP during inspiration. • Tachycardia. • Diminished heart sounds. • Narrowed pulse pressure < 30 mm Hg: Pulse pressure is the difference between diastolic & systolic BP. Normal pulse pressure = 30–40 mm Hg. Narrowed pulse pressure is < 30 mm Hg.	• Contact healthcare provider immediately. • Give pain or anti-anxiety medications as ordered. • Prepare for pericardiocentesis or pericardial window if needed to remove fluid.

Clinical Decision-Making Exercises

1. Which one of these clinical assessment findings should the nurse document and report for a client who has a diagnosis of right-sided heart failure indicating a complication with cardiac perfusion?

   ① Peripheral edema, ascites, jugular vein distention (JVD).

   ② Weight gain, crackles in lower bilateral bases of the lung fields, JVD.

   ③ Periorbital edema, moist cough, ascites.

   ④ Frothy, pink-tinged sputum; RR–30; anxious in appearance.

2. Which nursing plan of action indicates the LPN understands how to appropriately care for a client with peripheral artery disease?

   ① Measures the diameter of the calf of the leg and compares to unaffected leg.

   ② Positions the affected leg above the level of the heart.

   ③ Applies compression stockings after client gets out of bed.

   ④ Assists client to dangle legs off the side of the bed.

3. Which one of these physical assessment findings should the nurse document in the chart for a client who has chronic peripheral arterial disease (PAD)?

   ① Peripheral edema in bilateral ankles.

   ② The calf of the right leg is larger than the calf of the left leg.

   ③ When the legs are dependent, the color is rubor and pale when elevated.

   ④ Walking increases circulation and helps relieve the client's pain.

4. Based on the Standards of Practice for a client with an acute myocardial infarction, which plans would be appropriate for this client? *Select all that apply.*

   ① Bed rest.

   ② Supplemental oxygen.

   ③ Soft diet.

   ④ Continuous cardiac monitoring for an elevated ST segment and/or arrythmias.

   ⑤ Evaluate the serum amylase level.

5. Which one of these orders for a client who is in cardiogenic shock should the nurse question?

   ① Give morphine IV as ordered.

   ② Monitor and document client's level of consciousness.

   ③ Monitor urine output hourly.

   ④ Start IV of normal saline at 150 mL/hour.

6. Which one of these actions by the unlicensed assistive personnel (UAP) caring for a client with infective endocarditis requires immediate intervention from the nurse?

   ① The UAP reminds the client to take rest periods throughout the day.

   ② The UAP helps the client with his/her activities of daily living.

   ③ The UAP encourages frequent ambulation in the hall during the day.

   ④ The UAP reports to the nurse the client's HR has increased from 68 bpm to 88 bpm.

7. Which one of these nursing actions, included in the quality assurance program for heart failure clients, is most appropriate to delegate to the unlicensed assistive personnel?

① Assess breath sounds and check for edema daily.

② Check charts to make certain clients are receiving Carvedilol (Coreg) as ordered.

③ Encourage client to drink fluids hourly.

④ Weigh all clients as ordered.

8. Based on the rhythm strip below, what should be the first action of the nurse?

① Defibrillate with 200 joules.

② Give atropine.

③ Assess strip in two different leads.

④ Prepare for cardioversion.

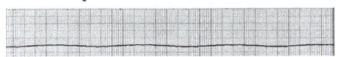

9. Based on the strip below, which of the following orders should be the priority for the nurse to implement?

① Teach client to avoid eating green leafy vegetables.

② Start potassium as prescribed.

③ Instruct client to avoid potatoes and bananas in his/her diet.

④ Discontinue IV of normal saline with 20 mEq/L of potassium.

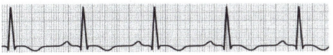

10. Based on the strip below, for a client with a fixed-rate pacemaker, what is the priority nursing action?

① Continue to monitor and document rhythm strips.

② Notify the healthcare provider.

③ Check the O_2 sat and reposition the probe.

④ Reassure the client that these symptoms are normal with a fixed-rate pacemaker.

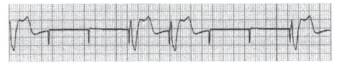

Answers and Rationales

1. Which one of these **clinical assessment findings** should the nurse document and report for a client who has a diagnosis of **right-sided heart failure indicating a complication with cardiac perfusion**?

    ① **CORRECT: Peripheral edema, ascites, jugular vein distention (JVD) are signs of right-sided heart failure.**

    ② INCORRECT: Weight gain, crackles in lower bilateral bases of the lung fields, JVD. This represents both left-sided heart failure and right-sided heart failure.

    ③ INCORRECT: Periorbital edema, moist cough, ascites. This represents both left-sided heart failure and right-sided heart failure.

    ④ INCORRECT: Frothy, pink-tinged sputum, R–30, anxious in appearance. This represents left-sided heart failure.

The strategy is to remember the pathophysiology with altered cardiac perfusion, such as with right-sided and left-sided heart failure. With right-sided heart failure, the pumping action of the heart cannot adequately return the circulating fluid volume, which results in fluid accumulating in the body. With left-sided heart failure, the blood cannot be adequately perfused to the body and backs into the lungs causing impaired respirations. *Insanely Easy Tip:* **Right = Rest of body. Left = Lungs.**

Instead of memorizing every cardiac disease, the bottom line is that if the client is experiencing any complication with the "**PUMP**," there will most likely be a complication with the "**PERFUSION.**" This is true in peripheral vascular disease as well. The concept is that the pump is not able to "**PERFUSE**" and the result is altered peripheral perfusion. **Insanely Easy Tip:** Anytime there is **decreased perfusion**, regardless of the disease, there can be **pain** (remember ischemia, intermittent claudification), **pale** (no blood = pale color), **pulmonary** (less perfusion = less oxygen), and **pee** (kidneys hate being left out of the perfusion so they decrease the urine output). By now, you are seeing the similarities. **It is easier to remember the concept of perfusion than multiple disease processes.**

Reduction of Risk Potential: Perform system-specific assessment.

Physiological Adaptation: Identify pathophysiology related to an acute or chronic condition and manage the care of a client with alteration in tissue perfusion (i.e., cardiac, peripheral).

2. Which nursing **plan of action** indicates the LPN understands how to appropriately care for a client with **peripheral artery disease?**

    ① INCORRECT: Measure the diameter of the calf of the leg and compare to unaffected leg. This would be done when evaluating for a DVT.

    ② INCORRECT: Position the affected leg above the level of the heart. This would not be affective for peripheral artery disease because the circulation of the blood is having difficulty getting to the extremities. This would be appropriate for peripheral venous disease.

    ③ INCORRECT: Apply compression stockings after client gets out of bed. Compression stockings are worn to help with circulation when the client is on bed rest, not when ambulating.

    ④ **CORRECT: Assist client to dangle legs off the side of the bed. This position helps the blood circulate to the extremities.**

The strategy is to understand the pathophysiology of peripheral vascular disease. The conclusion you can make is that anytime there is an alteration in cardiac perfusion you want to position the client to assist with circulation. In peripheral artery disease, the circulating blood is not adequately **perfusing** from the heart to the extremities. Positioning the client with his legs dangling helps blood circulate to the lower extremities. In peripheral venous disease, the challenge is getting the circulating blood back to the heart; therefore elevation of the legs would facilitate perfusion. Of course, you have to ask if the heart can handle the extra blood from the extremities. Would you want to elevate the legs above the level of the heart if the client was in cardiogenic shock? Of course not!

What a great connect! You are on the road to linking the concept of altered cardiac perfusion with your nursing care! It takes time, but you first need to learn the information, transfer it to your long-term memory, and then apply this to both test questions and clinical experiences. Remember, one step at a time!

Insanely Easy Tip: Arteries carry blood **Away** from the heart and Veins (**Blue** blood) carry blood **Back** to the heart

Basic Care and Comfort: Promote circulation by positioning.

Physiological Adaptation: Manage the care of a client with alteration in tissue perfusion (i.e., cardiac, peripheral).

3. Which one of these **physical assessment findings** should the nurse document in the chart for a client who has **chronic peripheral arterial disease (PAD)**?

① INCORRECT: Peripheral edema in bilateral ankles. This reflects peripheral venous disease.

② INCORRECT: The calf of the right leg is larger than the calf of the left leg. This reflects peripheral venous disease and may be from a DVT.

③ **CORRECT: When the legs are dependent, the color is rubor and pale when elevated. This reflects PAD.**

④ INCORRECT: Walking increases circulation and helps relieve the client's pain. This reflects peripheral venous disease.

The strategy is to understand the pathophysiology of peripheral vascular disease (PVD). In peripheral artery disease (PAD), the circulating blood is not adequately **perfusing** from the heart to the extremities. Positioning clients with their legs dangling helps the blood circulate to the lower extremities. Consequently, if the legs are elevated, their color will be pale. The strategy is similar to question number 2.

In peripheral venous disease, the challenge is to get the circulating blood back to the heart; therefore peripheral edema may be present in bilateral ankles. If there is a DVT from the PVD, there will be an enlarged calf. Ambulation is great for increasing circulation and minimizing the stasis of the blood due to the PVD. In PAD, however, the client needs to **REST** until that pain stops, since the pain is from lack of blood supply (perfusion) to the extremity.

Insanely Easy Tip: Remember the "**Ps**" with **PAD**: **Pain** is sharp and sudden (intermittent claudification. **Pallor** is pale and extremity may be shiny with loss of hair growth. **Peripheral** temperature may be cool due to decreased perfusion.

Remember the "**Ps**" with **PVD**: **Pain** is dull, heavy, and achy. **Pallor** is brown, brawny. **Peripheral** temperature may be warm. Edema is also evident.

You now have strategies for questions and clinical situations regarding cardiac/peripheral perfusion for both arterial and venous insufficiency. Now, let's review another type of client who may experience these complications. For example, what if the client experiences a cardiac catheterization? What are the priority assessments following this procedure that are similar to this concept? Since a cardiac catheterization is performed by using a long, thin, flexible catheter that is inserted into the artery (i.e., femoral, brachial, radial, etc.), and during the procedure a balloon is inflated to compress the plaque against the artery wall to restore blood flow, then the concern following this procedure would be **arterial perfusion**. The assessments would be **similar** in that the nurse should asses the **pulse, color, and temperature of the affected extremity distal to the insertion site to evaluate for alterations in perfusion from the procedure.**

What about PVD? As we know, the concept is the pooling of blood in the extremities from altered cardiac perfusion. Who would experience this? Clients might not have PVD, but they have the stasis of blood in extremities due to immobility. It is just a different cause! What about clients on bed rest (immobility), post-op for any procedures, clients with spinal cord injuries who are paralyzed, geriatric clients, etc.?

Insanely Easy Tip: **Keep client MOVING!** If this is impossible due to paralysis or necessary post-op restrictions, then apply compression stockings or sequential compression devices to optimize perfusion of the blood.

Concepts can be so much easier than memorizing 50 diseases!!!

Basic Care and Comfort: Promote circulation by positioning.

Physiological Adaptation: Manage the care of a client with alteration in tissue perfusion (i.e., cardiac, peripheral).

4. Based on the **Standards of Practice** for a client with an **acute myocardial infarction,** which plans would be appropriate for this client? *Select all that apply.*

    ① **CORRECT: Bed rest. This decreases the need for oxygen and decreases the workload demand on the heart during the acute phase of a client who has recently had an MI. Increase in activity progresses gradually.**

    ② **CORRECT: Supplemental oxygen. Due to the injured heart muscle, there is an impaired ability to pump oxygenated blood. The supplemental oxygen helps get more oxygen to the red blood cells.**

    ③ INCORRECT: Soft diet. The appropriate diet for client with a cardiac problem is a "Heart Healthy Diet," (low sodium, low fat, low cholesterol).

    ④ **CORRECT: Continuous cardiac monitoring for an elevated ST segment and/or arrythmias. Clients with heart tissue damage are more prone to dysrhythmias during the acute phase due to the decreased oxygen supply to the heart. Clients need continuous cardiac monitoring for potentially fatal dysrhythmias.**

    ⑤ INCORRECT: Drawing serum amylase. This test is for pancreatitis, not for heart disease.

The strategy is to understand what is happening during an acute myocardial injury and/or tissue death to the heart muscle. The heart is unable to manage the workload to provide adequate cardiac output (**perfusion**) to meet the body's needs. The goal of nursing care is to help decrease the workload of the heart by bed rest and oxygen, and to monitor for potential deadly arrhythmias that require immediate nursing intervention.

The link here is that even if you did not remember exactly what the nursing care is for this client, you understand the concept of Cardiac/Peripheral Perfusion and you know the importance of implementing the nursing care necessary to protect the pump that is having trouble with perfusion. Remember, if clients have PAD and they experience pain during activity from intermittent claudification, then all activity should STOP to allow the blood to flow to the extremity. With a myocardial infarction, the pain is due to ischemia but it is from a lack of blood flow in the heart! **REST** is the buzzword for both of these clinical presentations. Options 1 and 2 will assist in decreasing the oxygen requirements

and allow the heart to rest. Supplemental oxygen is a great support to a heart that is experiencing ischemia and helps minimize further damage.

Insanely Easy Tip for Option 4 is to remember the ST segment might be high if the client had an MI. "**High** rhymes with **MI!** ST segment depression occurs with angina. Learn one, you have got the other!

Management of Care: Provide client care consistent with the Standards of Practice.

Physiological Adaptation: Manage care with alteration in tissue perfusion (cardiac).

5. Which one of these orders for a client who is in cardiogenic shock should the nurse question??

    ① INCORRECT: Give morphine IV as ordered This order is appropriate as it helps relieve pain, calm anxiety, and has vasodilating properties that help increase the blood supply to the heart.

    ② INCORRECT: Monitor and document client's level of consciousness. This assessment is important in helping you determine what state of shock your client is in.

    ③ INCORRECT: Monitor urine output hourly. This is an appropriate intervention to help the nurse determine the fluid balance of the client on an hourly basis and to detect early trends of decreasing urine output indicating decreasing perfusion to the kidneys and progression of the stage of shock.

    ④ **CORRECT: Start IV of normal saline at 150mL/hour. Need to question because cardiogenic shock is a result of the inability of the heart to adequately pump. Increased fluid volume would be increase the workload on a heart already compromised.**

The strategy is to to know the pathophysiology of cardiogenic shock. With cardiogenic shock, it is contraindicated to increase fluids to a client because the heart has a decreased capacity to pump adequately to maintain cardiac output. Therefore, you would question an order to increase fluid volume because that will result in additional workload for the heart, and the heart cannot handle added volume without adverse effects.

Physiological Adaptation: Manage care with alteration in tissue perfusion (cardiac).

Management of Care: Verify appropriateness and/or accuracy of a treatment order.

6. Which one of these actions by the **unlicensed assistive personnel (UAP)** caring for a **client with infective endocarditis requires immediate intervention from the nurse?**

   ① INCORRECT: The UAP uses a soft toothbrush during oral hygiene. This action is correct to prevent injury to the gums in the mouth, which can lead to infections of the heart.

   ② INCORRECT: The UAP helps the client with his/her activities of daily living. This is correct because clients with endocarditis need rest to decrease the workload of the heart.

   ③ **CORRECT: The UAP encourages frequent ambulation in the hall during the day. This action requires immediate intervention because a client with infective endocarditis needs rest to allow the heart to heal.**

   ④ INCORRECT: The UAP reports to the nurse the client's HR has increased from 68 bpm to 88 bpm.

The strategy is to know that with inflammatory and infectious diseases of the heart, **rest** is required for recovery. Rest decreases the workload of the heart and the demand for oxygen during the acute phase of the infective endocarditis.

Now does this sound familiar—**REST**?! Where have you heard this within this concept? Refer to questions 3 and 4. Both peripheral artery disease and a myocardial infarction need REST! Here we are again, with a different disease, but one that can also result in an alteration of cardiac perfusion. We hope you are seeing the trend. Bottom line is whether the perfusion alteration is from a MI, PAD, heart failure or an infection or inflammation of the heart, conserving oxygen is the priority! REST is an important aspect of care.

We realize this chapter includes a lot of information; however, the majority of the assessments are about focusing on "**PUMPS**" and the nursing interventions are to facilitate "**PERFUSION**"!

Remember the *Insanely Easy Tip* about Activity Tolerance? It is a critical aspect of care with clients who have cardiac disease! "**CLUSTER**" was the **Priority Intervention** for the client's care to conserve oxygen!

Management of Care: Supervise care provided by others.

Reduction of Risk Potential: Use precautions to prevent injury and/or complications associated with a diagnosis.

Physiological Adaptation: Manage care with alteration in tissue perfusion (cardiac).

7. Which one of these **nursing actions,** included in the **quality assurance program for heart failure clients,** is most appropriate to **delegate to the unlicensed assistive personnel?**

   ① INCORRECT: Assess breath sounds and check for edema daily. UAPs cannot assess.

   ② INCORRECT: Check charts to make certain clients are receiving Carvedilol (Coreg) as ordered. UAPs cannot give medications and this non-selective beta blocker would be contraindicated in clients with heart failure.

   ③ INCORRECT: Encourage client to drink fluids hourly. This extra fluid may put too much demand on the heart muscle. It would be important to manage the fluids based on the protocol for the individual client and the degree of cardiac failure.

   ④ **CORRECT: Weigh all clients as ordered. UAPs can weigh clients, which is an appropriate intervention in caring for clients with altered perfusion from heart failure.**

The strategy is to know the nursing interventions that are **PRIORITY** and the standard of care for cardiac perfusion for clients with a diagnosis of heart failure. We have been reviewing the importance of REST with several of these questions; however, as we link the rationale for REST it would make sense that if there is a problem with the "**PUMP**" on the right side of the heart and the blood is not being perfused and is remaining in the extremities, there may be an increase in the client's weight. If there was a problem with the left side of the heart, then the fluid would remain in the lungs, resulting in adventitious lung sounds, SOB, and the potential complication of pulmonary edema.

Monitoring the client's fluid balance, which directly impacts the workload of the heart, is a **PRIORITY**. The nurse would be required to trend daily weights for increase in weight > 2 lbs./day. The increase in weight would indicate an increase in the fluid volume the heart would have to pump. However, it is within the scope of practice for the UAP to take the daily weights, and report and record the findings.

You might be saying to yourself, "I know NOTHING about DELEGATION!" On the NCLEX® you will need to know about the scope of practice and safe delegation; however, you did NOT need knowledge about scope of practice for this question because it focused on the standard of care for this concept/disease. For example, even if the delegation was correct for Option 1, the assessment was not frequent enough. Yes, UAPs do NOT assess, but we realize your goal at this moment is to learn the concept of perfusion. (If you need a good reference for these management concepts for the NCLEX®, we recommend reading *Nursing Made Insanely Easy*. The management concepts are simplified, fun, and designed for NCLEX®, success! Refer to reference list at the end of this chapter.)

Option 2 is inappropriate because this medication is contraindicated for clients with heart failure. (Refer to *Pharmacology Made Insanely Easy* in the reference list at the end of the chapter). Yes, UAPs do NOT administer meds, but even with this information, the med should not be given to this client, because it may slow the heart rate down. While UAPs can encourage clients to take fluids, this would be contraindicated for a client with heart failure.

Weight is a great answer for any client who has an alteration in perfusion, whether it is from dehydration (i.e., GI clients with nausea and vomiting), or when there is a concern with fluid overload.

Remember the image of the lung and ankle with edema for an *Insanely Easy Tip* to memorize this information.

Management of Care: Provide care with the legal scope of practice and participate in quality assurance program.

Physiological Adaptation: Manage the care of a client with a fluid imbalance.

Physiological Adaptation: Manage care with alteration in tissue perfusion (cardiac).

8. Based on the rhythm strip below, what should be the first action of the nurse?

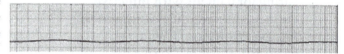

① INCORRECT: Defibrillate with 200 joules. There is no rhythm or electrical activity, which must be present for defibrillation to be effective.

② INCORRECT: Give atropine. This is done for bradycardia dysrhythmias. This would be ineffective with asystole.

③ **CORRECT: Assess strip in two different leads. This must be done to distinguish fine ventricular fibrillation from asystole. Ventricular fibrillation would require defibrillation and not CPR, which would be done for this rhythm of asystole.**

④ INCORRECT: Prepare for cardioversion. Cardioversion is done for atrial fibrillation or a very fast atrial or ventricular rhythm but not for asystole.

The strategy is to be able to recognize this rhythm strip as a life-threatening arrhythmia and take appropriate action. It is a **PRIORITY** with suspected asystole to check the rhythm in a second lead to be sure it is asystole and not fine ventricular fibrillation, which would require defibrillation as compared to asystole, where CPR is the priority.

Reduction of Risk Potential: Manage the care of the client on telemetry.

9. Based on the strip below, which of the following orders should be the priority for the nurse to implement?

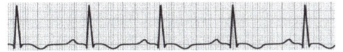

① INCORRECT: Teach client to avoid eating green leafy vegetables. This is not applicable as green leafy vegetables are high in vitamin K.

② **CORRECT: Start potassium as prescribed. The depressed T waves are most likely due to a decreased potassium level that needs to be replaced before additional cardiac arrhythmias occur.**

③ INCORRECT: Instruct client to avoid potatoes and bananas in their diet. This is incorrect as these foods are high in potassium and would be correct to have in the client's diet. (Remember the pota**TOES** and banana**TOES**)!

④ INCORRECT: Discontinue IV of normal saline with 20 mEq/L of potassium. The client needs potassium, so you would not want to stop the infusion of potassium without an alternate source of potassium.

The strategy is to recognize that the inverted T waves most likely are a sign of hypokalemia. Decreased potassium levels in any client increase the potential for cardiac arrhythmias, but it is of particular concern with clients who have cardiac disease. How the potassium is given may vary based on the potassium level, other clinical findings, and the degree of cardiac involvement. It is a **PRIORITY** for the nurse to recognize the inverted T wave as a sign of hypokalemia, check the potassium level, and notify the healthcare provider so additional K$^+$ may be added. *Refer to concept Nutrition for specifics on foods high and low in K$^+$.*

Physiological Adaptation: Manage the client with electrolyte imbalance.

10. Based on the strip below, for a client with a fixed-rate pacemaker, what is the priority nursing action?

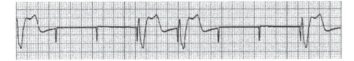

① INCORRECT: Continue to monitor and document rhythm strips. This requires intervention because there are pacer spikes without capture on a fixed-rate pacemaker.

② **CORRECT: Notify the healthcare provider because there is a malfunction of the pacemaker. It is a fixed rate and every pacer spike should result in a QRS (contraction of the ventricles). In this ECG strip, there are pacer spikes without QRS complexes.**

③ INCORRECT: Check the O$_2$ sat and reposition the probe. This would not result in the rhythm pictured.

④ INCORRECT: Document the client as asymptomatic. You may document the client is asymptomatic but this strip still requires intervention because the pacemaker is not functioning normally.

The strategy is to know what kind of pacemaker the client has. If it is a fixed-rate pacemaker as indicated, there should be a pacer spike before every QRS. The rhythm pictured above is a failure to capture that requires intervention by the nurse to notify the healthcare provider to assess the pacemaker function. The result of a malfunctioning pacemaker is decreased perfusion!

Reduction of Risk Potential: Manage the care of the client on telemetry. Evaluate response to procedures and treatments.

Decision-Making Analysis Form

Use this tool to help identify why you missed any questions. As you enter the question numbers in the chart, you will begin to see patterns of why you answered incorrectly. This information will then guide you toward what you need to focus on in your continued studies. Ultimately, this analytical exercise will help you become more successful in answering questions!!!

Questions to ask:

1. Did I have the knowledge to answer the question? If not, what information do I need to review?
2. Did I know what the question was asking? Did I misread it or did I miss keywords in the stem of the question?
3. Did I misread or miss keywords in the distractors that would have helped me choose the correct answer?
4. Did I follow my gut reaction or did I allow myself to rationalize and then choose the wrong answer?

	Lack of Knowledge (Concepts, Systems, Pathophysiology, Medications, Procedures, etc.)	Missed Keywords or Misread the Stem of the Question	Missed Keywords or Misread the Distractors	Changed My Answer (Second-guessed myself, i.e., my first answer was correct.)
Put the # of each question you missed in the column that best explains why you think you answered it incorrectly.				

If you changed an answer because you talked yourself out of the correct answer, or you second-guessed yourself, this is an **EASY FIX: QUIT changing your answers**!!! Typically, the first time you read a question, you are about 95% right! The second time you read a question, you start talking yourself into changing the answer. The third time you read a question, you do not have a clue—and you are probably thinking "Who in the heck wrote this question?"

On the other hand, if you read a question too quickly and when you reread it you realize you missed some key information that would impact your decision (i.e., assessments, lab reports, medications, etc.), then it is appropriate to change your answer. When in doubt, go with the safe route: your first thought! Go with your gut instinct!

As you gain confidence in answering questions regarding specific nursing concepts, you will be able to successfully progress to answering higher-level questions about prioritization. Please refer to the *Prioritization Guidelines* in this book for a structure to assist you with this process.

You CAN do this!

> *"We are what we repeatedly do. Excellence, therefore, is not an act but a habit."*
>
> ARISTOTLE

References for Chapter 9

Agency for Healthcare Research and Quality (2012). Retrieved from http://psnet.ahrq.gov/primer.aspx?primerID=4

American Heart Association (2012). Understand your risk of heart attack. Retrieved from http://www.heart.org/HEARTORG/Conditions/HeartAttack/UnderstandYourRiskofHeartAttack/Understand-Your-Risk-of-Heart-Attack_UCM_002040_Article.jsp

American Heart Association. (2014). Retrieved from http://www.heart.org/HEARTORG/Conditions/Conditions_UCM_001087_SubHomePage.jsp

Black, J M. and Hawks, J. H. (2009). *Medical surgical nursing: Clinical management for positive outcomes (8th ed.).* Philadelphia: Elsevier/Saunders.

Daniels, R. & Nicoll, L. (2012). *Contemporary medical-surgical nursing,* (2nd ed.). Clifton Park, NY: Delmar Cengage Learning.

Ellis, K. M. (2012). *EKG: Plain and simple* (3rd ed.). Upper Saddle Road, NJ: Pearson.

Eliopoulos, C. (2014). *Gerontological nursing* (8th ed.), Philadelphia: Lippincott Williams & Wilkins.

Giddens, G. F. (2013). *Concepts for nursing practice.* St. Louis, MO: Mosby, an imprint of Elsevier.

Hogan, M. A. (2014). *Pathophysiology: Reviews and rationales* (3rd ed.) Boston, MA: Pearson.

Ignatavicius, D. D. and Workman, M. L. (2010). *Medical-surgical nursing: Patient-centered collaborative care* (6th ed.). Philadelphia: Elsevier/Saunders.

LeMone, P., Burke, K. M., and Bauldoff, G. (2011). *Medical-surgical nursing: Critical thinking in patient care* (5th ed.). Upper Saddle Road, NJ: Pearson/Prentice Hall.

Lewis, S., Dirksen, S., Heitkemper, M., Bucher, L., and Camera, I. (2011). *Medical surgical nursing: Assessment and management of clinical problems* (8th ed.). St. Louis: Mosby.

Manning, L. and Rayfield, S. (2014). *Nursing made insanely easy* (7th ed.). Duluth, GA: I CAN Publishing, Inc.

Manning, L. and Rayfield, S. (2013). *Pharmacology made insanely easy* (4th ed.). Duluth, GA: I CAN Publishing, Inc.

National Council of State Boards of Nursing, INC. (NCSBN) 2012. *Research brief: 2011 RN practice analysis: linking the NCLEX RN® examination to practice.* Retrieved from https://www.ncsbn.org/index.htm

National Institutes for Health (2011). *What is metabolic syndrome?* Retrieved from http://www.nhlbi.nih.gov/health/health-topics/topics/ms/

Nettina, S. L. (2013). *Lippincott manual of nursing practice* (10th ed.). Philadelphia, PA: Walters Kluwer Health/Lippincott Williams & Wilkins.

North Carolina Concept Based Learning Editorial Board (2011). *Nursing a concept based approach to learning,* Upper Saddle Road, NJ: Pearson/Prentice Hall.

Osborn, K. S., Wraa, C. E., Watson, A. S., and Holleran, R. S. (2014). *Medical surgical nursing: Preparation for practice* (2nd ed.). Upper Saddle Road, NJ: Pearson.

Pagana, K. D. and Pagana, T. J. (2014). *Mosby's manual of laboratory and diagnostic tests* (5th ed.). St. Louis, MO: Mosby, an imprint of Elsevier.

Porth, C. (2011). *Essentials of pathophysiology* (3d ed.). Philadelphia, PA: Lippincott Williams ad Wilkins.

Porth, C. M. and Grossman, S. (2013). *Pathophysiology: Concepts of altered health states* (9th ed.). Philadelphia, PA: Lippincott Williams & Wilkins.

Potter, P. A., Perry, A. G., Stockert, P., and Hall, A. (2013). *Fundamentals of nursing* (8th ed.). St. Louis, MO: Pearson/Prentice Hall.

Smeltzer, S. C., Bare, B. G., Hinkle, J. L., and Cheever, K. H. (2010). *Brunner & Suddarth's Textbook of medical-surgical nursing* (12th ed.). Philadelphia: Lippincott Williams & Wilkins.

Wagner, K. D. and Hardin-Pierce, M. C. (2014). *High-Acuity nursing* (6th ed.). Boston: Pearson.

NOTES

CHAPTER 10

Linking Multiple Systems to Pathophysiology of Diseases
Concept Perfusion/Shock

A Snapshot of Impaired Central Perfusion

Impairment of central perfusion occurs in medical conditions that decrease cardiac output or result in shock. Cardiac output is decreased when the myocardium has inadequate perfusion, the heart does not receive effective impulse conduction or the heart valves are not functioning appropriately. These can all result in SHOCK! Shock is the inability of central perfusion to supply blood to peripheral tissues leading to organ failure. Any condition that compromises the delivery of oxygen to organs and tissues can result in shock. Shock can progress rapidly and be a life-threatening process. The client's outcome can be improved by early detection followed by a rapid response.

Older adult clients can die quickly due to the reduced compensatory mechanisms causing them to progress rapidly through the stages of shock. Baroreceptor response to catecholamine secretions is decreased, so it may not improve cardiac contractibility or cause vasoconstriction as in the younger adult. This prolonged decrease in the ability to compensate, leads to a sustained low cardiac output and blood pressure.

Shock is defined by the pathophysiological causes.

> **Cardiogenic Shock:** Heart or pump failure.
>
> **Hypovolemic Shock:** A decrease in the intravascular volume of 10 to 15% or more.
>
> **Obstructive Shock:** Mechanical blockage in the heart or great vessels.
>
> **Distributive Shock:** Wide spread vasodilation and increased capillary permeability. There are three kinds of shock in this category: anaphylactic, neurogenic, or septic.

Cardiac output (CO) is defined as the amount of blood pumped in 1 minute. It is the Heart Rate multiplied by the Stroke volume. Normal range: 4 to 8 L/min with an average of 6 L/min.

Stroke Volume is defined as each contraction ejecting a volume of 70 mL into the arterial system. Stroke volume has a major influence on cardiac output and is determined by the preload, afterload, and the contractile state of the heart. (*Refer to Concept Cardio/Peripheral Perfusion for additional definitions.*)

Central Venous Pressure (CVP) evaluates the pressure within the right atrium or within the large veins in the thoracic cavity. A normal CVP may range from 2-6 mm Hg.

Chapter 10 **Multiple Systems: Perfusion/Shock**

Mean Arterial Pressure (MAP) represents the average pressure during the cardiac cycle.

Pulmonary Artery Pressure (Swan-Ganz) is evaluated during systole and diastole, which reflects the right and left ventricular pressures; and pulmonary wedge pressure (PCWP), which is an indirect indicator of the left ventricular pressure and cardiac output (CO), reflecting the heart's output in liters per minute, cardiac index (CI), systemic vascular resistance (SVR), pulmonary vascular resistances (PVR), and various stroke volumes.

Easy definition is the **Pulmonary Artery Wedge Pressure (PAWP)** is a direct reflection of the pressure in the left cardiac chambers and reflects left ventricular end diastolic pressure. An upward trend indicates elevation in pressures and/or fluid, where a decrease in trend indicates dehydration or severe vasodilation. Normal range is 4–12 mm Hg.

 The Bottom Line is that shock results in the failure to maintain adequate perfusion to vital organs! Shock is dynamic! The client is in constant change, either progressively improving or deteriorating.

The Pathophysiology Behind Impaired Central Perfusion

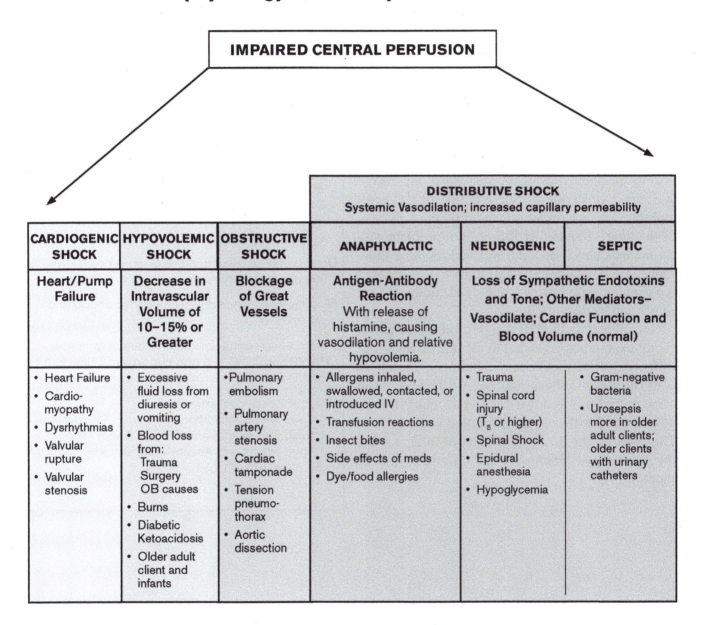

IMPAIRED CENTRAL PERFUSION

CARDIOGENIC SHOCK	HYPOVOLEMIC SHOCK	OBSTRUCTIVE SHOCK	DISTRIBUTIVE SHOCK Systemic Vasodilation; increased capillary permeability		
			ANAPHYLACTIC	**NEUROGENIC**	**SEPTIC**
Heart/Pump Failure	Decrease in Intravascular Volume of 10–15% or Greater	Blockage of Great Vessels	Antigen-Antibody Reaction With release of histamine, causing vasodilation and relative hypovolemia.	Loss of Sympathetic Endotoxins and Tone; Other Mediators– Vasodilate; Cardiac Function and Blood Volume (normal)	
• Heart Failure • Cardio-myopathy • Dysrhythmias • Valvular rupture • Valvular stenosis	• Excessive fluid loss from diuresis or vomiting • Blood loss from: Trauma Surgery OB causes • Burns • Diabetic Ketoacidosis • Older adult client and infants	• Pulmonary embolism • Pulmonary artery stenosis • Cardiac tamponade • Tension pneumo-thorax • Aortic dissection	• Allergens inhaled, swallowed, contacted, or introduced IV • Transfusion reactions • Insect bites • Side effects of meds • Dye/food allergies	• Trauma • Spinal cord injury (T$_5$ or higher) • Spinal Shock • Epidural anesthesia • Hypoglycemia	• Gram-negative bacteria • Urosepsis more in older adult clients; older clients with urinary catheters

Priority – System-Specific Assessments Made EASY!
Concept: Impaired Central Perfusion (Shock)

A key to safe care is to recognize the early trends in the clinical findings the client is presenting with that indicate a change in the perfusion. Let us begin by saying that in order to simplify these system specific assessments, remember the PAWP is a direct reflection on the left side of the heart and the CVP is a direct reflection on the right side of the heart. Remember if there is a problem with cardiogenic shock or fluid overload, both of these values will be increased. In contrast to this, if there is a problem with hypovolemic shock, both of these values will be decreased.

Note, that both the HR and RR will increase with clients experiencing shock. The BP and urine output will trend down in shock. If, however, the client is in cardiogenic shock, the BP will increase. The urine output trends down due to the compensatory mechanism for the shock (alteration in perfusion). The chart on the next page will assist in organizing the comparison findings of the different types of shock.

System-Specific Assessments: "PUMPS"

Pulses weak, RR trending up to > 40 / min., BP (initial stage remains normal; ↑ to compensate, then drops to < 50 to 60 mm Hg as shock progresses. ↓ LOC, syncope (Pulse ↑ and progresses to > 140 / min.) Assess heart sounds (S_3, S_4); capillary refill increased. (*Refer to the chapter, Cardiovascular System: Concept Cardio/Peripheral Perfusion for reivew of S_3 and S_4.*) Assess breath sounds.

   **Pulses weak, thready–Hypovolemic Shock.

Urine output (monitor trending down in hourly output). Always compare to previous assessment.

Mucous membranes dry (Hypovolemic Shock) and pale in color.

Pump is decreasing so ↓ cardiac output; pressure.
   PAWP and (CVP) – ↓ with Hypovolemic Shock.
   PAWP and (CVP) – ↑ with Cardiogenic Shock.

Skin color pale, cool extremities.
   **Fever with Septic Shock
   **Rash with Anaphylactic/ Septic Shock
   **Angioedema with Anaphylactic Shock
   Seizures with all types of shock.

	Comparison of the Clinical Findings and Plan of Care Between the Different Types of Shock			
Types of Shock	**Hemodynamic Changes**	**Clinical Findings**	**Critical Complications**	**Plan of Care**
Cardiogenic Shock	Crackles; ↑ CVP, PAWP	Cardiac enzymes: Troponin; ECG changes (associated with MI and dysrhythmias)	Dysrhythmias, MI, heart failure; risk for fluid overload	Oxygen as prescribed, monitor ECG, monitor for ↑ CVP, PAWP. Meds to ↑ cardiac output.
Hypovolemic Shock	↓ CVP	↓ Hgb and Hct– hemorrhage ↑ Hct–dehydration	Lactic acidosis; Multi-Organ Dysfunction Syndrome (MODS)	Oxygen as prescribed; volume replacement due to blood loss; volume expander; monitor for ↓ CVP, PAWP.
Obstructive Shock	↑ CVP	ECG changes (associated with MI and dysrhythmias)	Pulmonary embolism; tension pneumothorax	Medical treatment to relieve obstruction; Monitor for ↑ CVP.
Distributive Shock: Anaphylactic	↓ CVP	Flushed with fever; rash	Airway obstruction; angioedema	Oxygen as prescribed; maintain airway; support laryngeal edema; epinephrine/ Benadryl IV.
Neurogenic	↓ HR, BP, CVP	Flushed with fever	Evaluate for fluid overload	Bradycardia may require atropine; administer vasoconstrictor medications.
Septic	Flushed with fever; rash; seizures with all types; ↓ CVP	Blood cultures– blood, urine, wound; Coagulation tests– PT, INR, aPTT	Disseminated Intravascular Coagulation (DIC)	Oxygen as prescribed; evaluate origin of infection; IV fluids, volume expanders; cardiotonics.

As you review the chart on this page, note the only time the **CVP increases is if there is a problem with the heart** as there is in **cardiogenic shock or an obstruction.** Clients with shock as a result of **hypovolemia or vasodilation as in anaphylactic, neurogenic, and/or septic will present with a decrease in the CVP reading.**

Now, let's move on and review the trends of the physiological changes that can occur with clients in shock.

Priority System-Specific Assessments Made EASY!
TREND PROGRESSION OF THE PHYSIOLOGICAL CHANGES IN SHOCK

Assessment	Early	Compensatory	Progressive	Refractory: WAY TOO LATE
Level of consciousness	Anxious	More restless	LOC ↓	Obtunded
Heart Rate/bpm	<100 (may WDL)	Trending up > 100 bpm	Continuing > 120 bpm	> 140 bpm
Blood Pressure	Normal	Trending to slight ↑	< 70–90 mm Hg	< 50–80 mm Hg
Respirations/min	Normal	Trending to 20–30/ min	Continuing > 30–40/min	> 40/min
Urine Output	≥ 30 mL / hr	Trending < 20–30 mL/hr	Continuing < 5–30 mL/hr	Negligible
Skin	Cool, pink, dry	Cold, pale, dry moist	Cold, pale, moist	Cold, mottled, cyanosis, dry

Notice, all of these values decrease with the exception of the HR and RR! The magic number is "**4**"! HR > 140 bpm; RR > 40/min. Now if you are a student who does like mnemonics, refer to the next page to assist you in organizing these in a different format.

Priority System-Specific Assessments Made EASY!					
HYPOVOLEMIC SHOCK: Early vs. Late Assessments! Keep Client ALIVE!					
"SHOCK"	**S**kin Color (Tissue Perfusion)	**H**eart Rate, RR, MAP (Cardiac Perfusion)	**O**utputs (Urine) (Elimination)	**C**ognition	**K** (c)omplications
Early Assessments	Cool, pale, and dry	HR, RR Normal or ↑; MAP– Normal or ↓ MAP 5–10 mm Hg	≥ 30 mL/hr	Anxious	Compensate
Late Assessments	Cold, pale, and moist	HR & RR ↑ and (HR ↑ and weak) (RR ↑ and shallow) MAP < 90 mm Hg systolic; ↓ MAP > 20 mm Hg	< 0.05 mL/Kg/hr	LOC ↓	Multiple Organ Dysfunction Syndrome (MODS

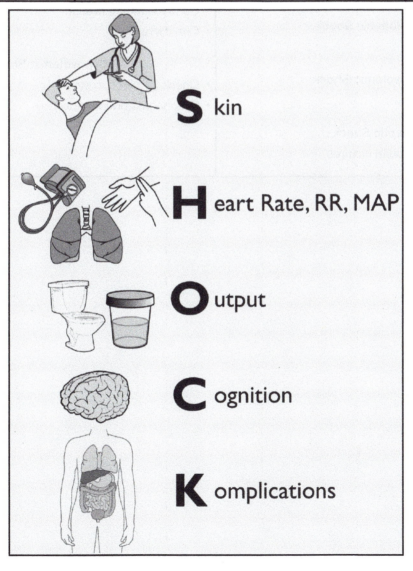

SAFETY: System-Specific Assessments

Labs Procedures and Diagnostic Tests

Labs	Diagnostics Tests
All Types of Shock	**Cardiogenic Shock**
• CBC with diff • PT, PTT, INR, platelets	• ECG
• BUN/Creat • Urinalysis	• Cardiac echocardiogram
• Electrolytes • ABGs	• Computerized Tomography (CT)
	• Cardiac Catheterization
Cardiogenic Shock	• Chest x-ray
• Cardiac Enzymes	
	Hypovolemic Shock
Hypovolemic Shock	• Check for blood in stool
• Type and Crossmatch	• Esophagastroduodenoscopy
Septic Shock	
• Blood, urine, and wound cultures	

Medication / Fluids Comparison for Different Kinds of Shock		
Shock	**Medications**	**IV Fluids**
Cardiogenic	Treat dysrhythmia; decrease afterload with ionotropic drugs. Medications to increase CO.	
Hypovolemic	Vasopressors if fluid resuscitation not effective. (i.e., dopamine).	0.9% NS or Lactated Ringers. May need colloids (albumin, Hespan, blood and blood products)
Obstructive	Treatment more about releasing obstruction.	
Distributive: **Anaphylactic**	Epinephrine & Benadryl, IV.	
Neurogenic	Vasoconstrictor meds. Bradycardia may be treated with atropine.	IV fluids, volume expanders
Septic	Cultures prior to antibiotics; administer antibitoics within one hour of order. Vasopressors: Norepinephrine (Levophed) or dopamine ↓ vasodilation. Corticosteroids. Heparin, Clotting factors, Platelets, Plasma. Vasopressin (Anti-diuretic hormone). Consider Xigris (activated protein C) if high risk of death.	
All Types of Shock	Proton pump inhibitors (prevent stress ulcers). Prilosec, Nexium; Heparin, low molecular weight (prevent DVT).	

First-Do Priority Interventions "PERFUSE"

Begin by identifying the cause of the shock! An easy approach to the care for these clients is to always remember the **ABC**s:

Airway (respiratory support)

Bleeding (maintain fluid volume)

Circulation (position to increase blood volume to vital organs; (*be careful if problem is cardiogenic shock!*)

Document trends in VS, CVP, PAWP, breath sounds

Ensure venous access with 14 to 16 gauge peripheral line or central line. Educate client and family. Emotional support.

Fluids DECREASE if Cardiogenic Shock.

GI support: assess bowel sounds, distention; NG tube as prescribed.

Hemodynamic monitoring: Monitor, document and provide safe care.

I & O monitor; monitor trending down and trending up in response to nursing care such as after infusing blood or volume expanders.

Remember hemodynamics: **CVP** is an index of the **right side's ability to handle venous return.** An increase in the **CVP** may indicate **hypervolemia or poor contractility** of the cardiac muscle. **A decrease in the CVP** may indicate **hypovolemia or vasodilation.**

The **PAWP is a reflection of the left cardiac chambers** and reflects left ventricular end diastolic pressure. An upward trend is indicative of **increase in pressures and/or fluid in contrast to a decrease in the trend indicates dehydration or severe vasodilation.**

Position for Hypovolemic Shock by lowering the head to supine or 10 degrees, ↑ legs to increase blood volume to vital organs. High Fowler's position to decrease further venous return to the left ventricle if Cardiogenic shock exists.
  Perfusion of tissue and/or circulation maintained by controlling bleeding; maintaining fluid volume by blood and/or blood products; IV fluids; volume expanders (colloid solutions); and monitor I&O.

Evaluate underlying cause! VS (BP and pulses); signs of bleeding; weight, ECG, CVP & other hemodynamic lines in place.
  Evaluate incision site for bleeding, circulation, skin temp, color; LOC; evaluate bowel sounds and distention; maintain NPO as prescribed; frequent oral hygiene; possible NG tube if client has a paralytic ileus and/or visceral ischemia.
  Ensure venous access: 2 large-bore (14 to 16 gauge) peripheral lines or central line for IV medications and fluid resuscitation.

Respiratory function maintained. Review pulse oximetry, ABGs, breath sounds; orientation, LOC.
  Report urine output < 30 mL / hr or trending ↓ ; Monitor BUN/ Creatinine; maintain rest in bed.

Fluids (↓ Fluids if HF or Cardiogenic Shock) Refer to chart on Comparison of Fluids for Shock. Monitor neurogenic and cardiogenic shock for fluid overload!

Use oxygen supplement as prescribed (PRIORITY)! Maintain airway.

SAFETY! Equipment at bedside: nonrebreather mask, bag, valve mask, suctioning equipment. Ventilator if necessary, pulse oximeter. Keep client warm, no chilling. Prevent falling/injuries. Seizure precautions.

Educate, prepare for and evaluate ongoing hemodynamic monitoring. Monitor cerebrovascular pressure; cardiac output, pulse pressure, pulmonary artery pressures; LOC; eliminate sensory overload caused by environment.
  Emotional support for client and family. Keep family informed of client's condition.

Priorities for Hemodynamic Monitoring

CATHETERS	USE	NORMAL VALUE/ COMPLICATIONS
Central venous pressure (CVP) *Measures **Right Atrial Pressure** or larger vein in thoracic cavity.*	• Infuse fluids • Obtain venous blood samples	1–8 mm Hg (With an **average of 6 mm Hg**) ↑ = hypervolemia or poor contractility ↓ = hypovolemia, vasodilation
Pulmonary artery pressure (PAP) (located in pulmonary artery) PAS PAD	***Not used for fluid infusion Measures the pressure in the **left cardiac** chambers and reflects ventricular end diastolic pressure. (Systolic/Diastolic= PAS/PAD)	15–26 mm Hg (Average of 20) 5–15 mm Hg (**Average of 12**)
Pulmonary artery wedge pressure (PAWP)	When not in use, leave balloon **deflated and in locked position** (always aspirate the same amount of air out that was put in to wedge the catheter).	4–12 mm Hg (**Average of 6–12**) ↑ = hypervolemia, pressure ↓ = hypovolemia, vasodilation
Cardiac output (CO)	Reading on cardiac output	4–6 L/min (**Average 6**)
Mixed venous oxygen saturation (SvO$_2$)	Balance between oxygen supply and demand	60-80%
Arterial lines	Continuous information about changes in BP and use for arterial blood samples	Monitor wave form
CONCLUSION = INSANELY EASY TIP for REMEMBERING THESE VALUES! **6–12** *(With exception of PAS)*	Values: Great news ... Do you see the trend in the values? CVP average **6** PAWP average **6–12** CO **6** The KEY is to know that nurses review **trends and ranges**. This will help you recall the average is between **6–12**.	Both lines: **Risk for infection** or air **emboli**. The **balloon** for the wedge should **be deflated** to prevent pulmonary infarction. With the pulmonary artery line, ventricular dysrhythmias may occur particularly during the insertion.

SAFETY Summary: Concept of Impaired Central Perfusion

System-Specific Assessment "PUMPS"	First-Do Priority Interventions "PERFUSE"	Evaluate Outcomes "PUMPS"
Pulses weak, RR trending up to > 40/min.; BP (initial stage remains normal, ↑ to compensate, then drops to < 50 to 60 mm Hg as shock progresses. ↓LOC, syncope (Pulse ↑ and progresses to > 140/min. Assess heart sounds (S_3, S_4); capillary refill increased. Assess breath sounds. Hypovolemic shock. **Pulses weak, thready **U**rine output (monitor hourly trends) **M**ucous membranes dry (Hypovolemic Shock) & pale **P**ump is decreasing so ↓ cardiac output; pressure **P**AWP and (CVP) – ↓ with Hypovolemic Shock **P**AWP and (CVP) – ↑ with Cardiogenic Shock **S**kin color pale, cool extremities **Fever with SEPTIC SHOCK **Rash with Anaphylactic/ Septic Shock **Angioedema with Anaphylactic Shock **S**eizures with all types of shock.	**P**osition for Hypovolemic Shock by lowering the head to supine or 10 degrees, ↑ legs to increase blood volume to vital organs. High Fowler's position to decrease further venous return to the left ventricle if Cardiogenic shock exists. **P**erfusion of tissue and/or circulation maintained by controlling bleeding; maintaining fluid volume by blood and/or blood products; IV fluids; volume expanders (colloid solutions); and monitor I & O. **E**valuate underlying cause! VS (esp. BP and pulses); signs of bleeding; Weight, ECG, CVP & other hemodynamic lines in place. **E**valuate incision site for bleeding, circulation, skin temp, color; LOC; Evaluate bowel sounds and distention; maintain NPO as prescribed; Frequent oral hygiene; Possible NG tube if has a paralytic ileus and/or visceral ischemia. **E**nsure venous access: 2 large-bore (14 to 16 gauge) peripheral lines or central line for IV medications and fluid resuscitation. **R**espiratory function maintained. Review pulse oximetry, ABGs, breath sounds, and orientation, LOC. **R**eport urine output < 30 mL/hr or trending ↓ ; Monitor BUN/ Creatinine; maintain rest in bed. **F**luids (↓ Fluids if CHF or Cardiogenic Shock)** Refer to chart on Comparison of Fluids for Shock. Monitor neurogenic and cardiogenic shock for fluid overload! **U**se oxygen supplement as prescribed (PRIORITY)! Maintain airway. **S**AFETY! Equipment at bedside: (nonrebreather mask, bag, valve mask, suctioning equipment, Ventilator if necessary, pulse oximeter. Keep client warm, no chilling. Prevent falling/injuries. Seizure precautions. **E**ducate, prepare for and evaluate ongoing hemodynamic monitoring. Monitor Cerebrovascular pressure; Cardiac output, Pulse pressure, Pulmonary artery pressures; LOC; eliminate sensory overload caused by environment. **E**motional support for client and family. Ongoing inform family of condition of client.	**P**ulse–BP WDL for client **U**rine WDL, No edema, crackles **M**ucous membranes WDL **P**ump WDL for client (CVP 2-6 mm Hg) **S**kin warm & dry, color WDL for client. No seizures, Safety is maintained with equipment, environment. etc. This equates to SAFE client care!

INSANELY EASY TIP!

Another strategy to assist you in remembering the priority interventions for hypovolemic shock is to review the mnemonic below. Shock is a decrease in venous return! Cardiogenic shock, however, is a complication from heart failure or pump failure. "**SHOCK**" will assist you in reviewing the priority plan of care for hypovolemic shock.

Help Stamp Out Shock

S   **SOLUTIONS** add volume and will increase venous return. Increase the rate. A combination of fluids, blood and plasma expanders (dextran, plasma and albumin) are commonly used. Watch for I.V.s with meds in them. We wouldn't want to turn up the I.V. rate of Pitocin!

H   **HEMODYNAMICS** are a way to measure potential shock and evaluate interventions. CVP–(normal is a lucky 6) low CVP means DVR, (decreased venous return) or fluid deficit. Elevated CVP means fluid overload as seen in cardiogenic shock. Low BP reading is one parameter that spells trouble.

Monitor it every few minutes. As meds are given to increase the BP, it may come up quickly.

O   **OXYGEN** will saturate those red blood cells and decrease tissue starvation.

C   **CHECK** the skin which is often cold and clammy.

K   **KICK** up the feet and legs! There's a lot of blood volume in the legs. Elevate them and let gravity help increase venous return. Don't put the head down. Trendelenburg position may increase cranial pressure, ocular pressure and pressure on the diaphragm.

SAFETY Summary: Concept of Impaired Central Perfusion

The image below will help you remember the pathophysiology of shock. The number 1 shows the arm being cut off. This will result in hypovolemic shock if immediate intervention is not taken. The blood coming out of the injury certainly is not returning to the heart. **The result: Decreased Venous Return!** The number 3 represents sweat. This guy could also experience hypovolemic shock if he was to sweat out his volume. **The result: Decreased Venous Return!** The number 2 is by his spinal cord which could also be damaged from a gunshot wound or fall. In this situation, the nerves have been cut. There is less venous constriction due to absent nerve stimulation. If life got complicated for this fellow and he developed a severe infection resulting in septic shock, then the blood vessels will dilate due to the gram negative organisms. **The result: Decreased Venous Return!** The exception to the decrease in venous return is with Cardiogenic shock since the pathophysiology is from heart or pump failure.

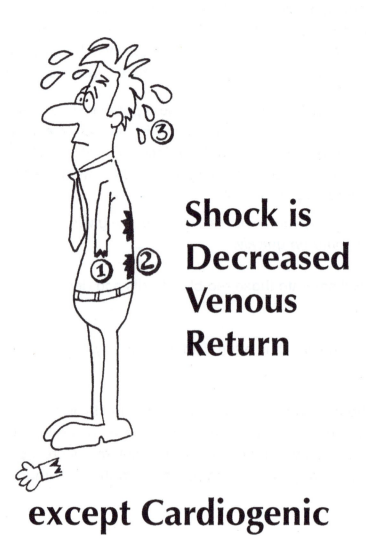

Shock is Decreased Venous Return

except Cardiogenic

Clinical Decision-Making Exercises

1. Which of these statements made by the charge nurse who is conducting an orientation program on the pathophysiology of cardiogenic shock indicates an appropriate understanding of this shock?

   ① "Cardiogenic shock occurs due to a mechanical blockage in the heart."

   ② "Cardiogenic shock occurs due to a pump or heart failure."

   ③ "Cardiogenic shock occurs due to a decrease in the intravascular volume."

   ④ "Cardiogenic shock occurs due to a widespread vasodilation and increased capillary permeability."

2. Which of these clinical findings would be a priority to report for a client who is experiencing cardiogenic shock?

   ① CVP–6 mm Hg.

   ② PAWP–6 mm Hg.

   ③ Cardiac Output–6L/min.

   ④ Crackles in bilateral lung fields.

3. Which of these clinical assessment findings would alert the nurse to intervene due to complications from bleeding following a GI surgery? *Select all that apply.*

   ① CVP of 2 mm Hg.

   ② Urine output from 60 mL/hr to 38 mL/hr.

   ③ BP–140/95.

   ④ PAWP–15 mm Hg.

   ⑤ HR from 80 bpm to 120 bpm in 1 hour.

4. Which of these plans would be a priority for a client who is bleeding following a GI surgery and presenting with a BP of 96/58?

   ① Administer Benadryl to assist with the rash.

   ② Elevate the head of the bed.

   ③ Decrease fluid intake to prevent overload.

   ④ Position the client flat with legs elevated.

5. Which of these clinical assessment findings would indicate a therapeutic response from dopamine for a client who is in hypovolemic shock? *Select all that apply.*

   ① Peripheral pulses remain difficult to palpate.

   ② Urine output increased from 45 mL/hr to 60 mL/hr.

   ③ BP from 140/90 to 98/64 in 2 hours.

   ④ CVP from 2 mm Hg to 6 mm Hg.

   ⑤ Increase in state of alertness.

6. What is the priority of care for a client who is experiencing septic shock from urosepsis?

   ① Administer antibiotic therapy as prescribed.

   ② Administer Benadryl as prescribed.

   ③ Monitor for an increase in the CVP value.

   ④ Assess for a bounding pulse.

7.   Which of these clients should the nurse assess immediately after shift report?

① A client with a CVP reading of 5 mm Hg.

② A client who was in hypovolemic shock, and now has a CVP of 6 mm Hg, BP–130/80.

③ A client who was stung by a bee and is in the ER with wheezing.

④ A client is in shock with a BP–120/78, restless, HR–92 bpm.

8.   Which of these new orders should the nurse question?

① Administer 1 unit of blood as prescribed for a client in hypovolemic shock.

② Administer Epinephrine IV as prescribed for a client experiencing anaphylactic shock.

③ Administer antibiotics for a client in septic shock.

④ Administer 2 units of blood as prescribed for a client in cardiogenic shock.

9.   Which of these nursing actions by the UAP would require the charge nurse to intervene for a client who is in hypovolemic shock?

① The UAP elevates the head of the bed during the bath.

② The UAP encourages fluid as prescribed.

③ The UAP performs frequent oral care.

④ The UAP monitors the urine output and reports an output change of 60 mL/hr to 40 mL/hr in one hour.

10. Which of these clinical assessment findings would be important to monitor and report for a client in hypovolemic shock? *Select all that apply.*

① BP–150/80.

② Heart Rate–130 bpm (weak).

③ CVP–6 mm Hg.

④ Respiratory Rate–40/min.

⑤ Pulse–bounding.

Answers and Rationales

1. Which of these **statements made by the charge nurse** who is conducting an **orientation program** on the pathophysiology of **cardiogenic shock** indicates an appropriate **understanding** of this **shock?**

   ① INCORRECT: "Cardiogenic shock occurs due to a mechanical blockage in the heart." (Obstructive shock)

   ② **CORRECT: "Cardiogenic shock occurs due to a pump or heart failure." True.**

   ③ INCORRECT: "Cardiogenic shock occurs due to a decrease in the intravascular volume." (Hypovolemic shock)

   ④ INCORRECT: "Cardiogenic shock occurs due to a widespread vasodilation and increased capillary permeability." (Distributive shock)

The strategy is to review the Pathophysiology Chart to assist you in organizing the different categories of shock.

Physiological Adaptation: Identify the pathophysiology related to an acute or chronic condition.

2. Which of these **clinical findings** would be a **priority to report for a client who is experiencing cardiogenic shock?**

   ① INCORRECT: CVP 6 mm Hg. The CVP would be elevated in cardiogenic shock.

   ② INCORRECT: PAWP 6 mm Hg This would be elevated in cardiogenic shock.

   ③ INCORRECT: Cardiac Output 6L/min This would be decreased in cardiogenic shock.

   ④ **CORRECT: Crackles in bilateral lung fields. Fluid may be in the lungs due to the pump failure.**

The strategy is to review the Comparison of Clinical Findings and Plan of Care Between the Different Types of Shock. The easy approach for remembering this information is that the cardiac pump is no longer effective and fluid can accumulate in the cardiopulmonary system, resulting in crackles (adventitious breath sounds.) Options 1 and 2 would be elevated in cardiogenic shock. Six is a great number (half a dozen) and is within the defined range for the CVP. Multiply 6x2 and this will assist you in remembering the PAWP value (12). This is within the defined range. The cardiac output would be low in cardiogenic shock. (Normal range is 4-6L/min.) *See how easy this is! You are a genius! Just remember the number 6 and you have these values all covered!*

Reduction of Risk Potential: Recognize signs and symptoms of complication and intervene as needed.

3. Which of these **clinical assessment findings** would alert the nurse to intervene due to complications from **bleeding following a GI surgery**? Select all that apply.

① **CORRECT: CVP of 2 mm Hg. This is decreased due to bleeding.**

② **CORRECT: Urine output from 60 mL/ hr to 38 mL/hr. The trend is down due to bleeding.**

③ INCORRECT: BP–140/95. The BP would not be high if there was a complication from bleeding.

④ INCORRECT: PAWP–15 mm Hg. The PAWP would not be high; it would be low.

⑤ **CORRECT: HR from 80 bpm to 120 bpm in 1 hour. This is a sign of bleeding.**

The strategy is to identify that if a client is bleeding, then the potential complication may be hypovolemic shock. "**PUMPS**" will assist you in organizing the system specific findings for shock. Now, the great news is that these assessments apply to any client who is experiencing hypovolemic shock (*Refer to Pathophysiology Chart for specific medical conditions.*) Another insanely easy tip is that the number to keep in your long-term memory for CVP & PAWP is 6!

Reduction of Risk Potential: Recognize signs and symptoms of complications and intervene appropriately when providing care.

Reduction of Risk Potential: Assess client and respond to changes in vital signs.

Reduction of Risk Potential: Recognize trends and changes in client condition and intervene as needed.

4. Which of these **plans would be a priority** for a client who is bleeding **following a GI surgery** and presenting with a **BP of 96/58**?

① INCORRECT: Administer Benadryl to assist with the rash. This would be for an allergic reaction.

② INCORRECT: Elevate the head of the bed. This would result in further decrease in the BP.

③ INCORRECT: Decrease fluid intake to prevent overload. This client would need more fluids.

④ **CORRECT: Position the client flat with legs elevated. This will assist in perfusing the vital organs.**

The strategy is to consider the nursing care that is organized in the mnemonic "**PERFUSE**". Also, review the rationale for specific care. If the head of the bed was elevated for this client, the BP would continue to drop. (option 2). Option 4 will increase the blood flow to the vital organs which is the priority for a client progressing to hypovolemic shock. Remember, **lower the HOB for a low BP**.

Reduction of Risk Potential: Recognize signs and symptoms of complications and intervene appropriately when providing care.

Reduction of Risk Potential: Assess client and respond to changes in vital signs.

Basic Care and Comfort: Implement measures to promote circulation.

5. Which of these **clinical assessment findings** would indicate a **therapeutic response from dopamine for a client who is in hypovolemic shock**? Select all that apply.

① INCORRECT: Peripheral pulses remain difficult to palpate. BP remains low.

② **CORRECT: Urine output increased from 45 mL/hr to 60 mL/hr. Therapeutic response.**

③ INCORRECT: BP from 140/90 to 98/64 in 2 hours. BP has decreased versus increased.

④ **CORRECT: CVP from 2 mm Hg to 6 mm Hg. Therapeutic response.**

⑤ **CORRECT: : Increase in state of alertness. Therapeutic response.**

The strategy (*Refer to the book, Pharmaoclogy Made Insanely Easy, for more specifics.*). The therapeutic effects of dopamine hydrochloride are due to its positive inotropic effect on the myocardium, increasing the cardiac output and improving circulation to the renal vascular bed. Therefore, the nurse would observe for an increase in hourly urine output, increase in blood pressure, an increase in CVP, and increase in the state of alertness from the client. Options 1 and 3 do not indicate that the effect has been therapeutic. These symptoms indicate hypovolemia has continued. (*Refer to Expected outcomes for "PUMPS" for more specifics.*)

Pharmacological and Parenteral Therapies: Evaluate client response to medication (i.e., therapeutic effects, side effects, adverse reactions).

6. What is the **priority of care** for a client who is experiencing **septic shock** from urosepsis?

   ① **CORRECT: Administer antibiotic therapy as prescribed. This is the priority for client.**

   ② INCORRECT: Administer Benadryl as prescribed. There is no allergic reaction.

   ③ INCORRECT: Monitor for an increase in the CVP value. The CVP would decrease.

   ④ INCORRECT: Assess for a bounding pulse. This bounding pulse would be present in a client with cardiogenic shock.

The strategy is to understand the priority of care is to eradicate the organism that is causing the urosepsis. The bacteria's endotoxins and mediators need to be eliminated in order to decrease the vasodilation effect.

Physiological Adaptation: Medical Emergencies.

Management of Care: Prioritize delivery of care.

7. Which of these clients should the **nurse assess immediately after shift report?**

   ① INCORRECT: A client with a CVP reading of 5 mm Hg. This is a normal value.

   ② INCORRECT: A client who was in hypovolemic shock, and now has a CVP of 6 mm Hg, BP–130/80. This is trending up and is not a priority.

   ③ **CORRECT: A client who was stung by a bee and is in the ER with wheezing. This client may be experiencing an anaphylactic reaction. Airway is the priority!**

   ④ INCORRECT: A client is in shock with a BP–120/78, restless, HR–92 bpm. This is a concern due to the restlessness and HR, but in comparison to option 3 it is not a priority. The BP has not decreased. The client in option 3; however, may progress to a respiratory arrest based on the clinical assessments.

The strategy is using the airway-breathing-circulation (ABC) guidelines for establishing priorities. (*Refer to Concept Priorities for specifics.*) It is also using the guideline that the nurse should prioritize by using "*early versus late*". Option 4 includes early signs of shock and option 3 is an acute risk for an airway obstruction.

Physiological Adaptation: Medical Emergencies.

Reduction of Risk Potential: Recognize signs and symptoms of complication and intervene appropriately when providing care.

Management of Care: Prioritize delivery of care.

8. Which of these **new orders** should the **nurse question?**

   ① INCORRECT: Administer 1 unit of blood as prescribed for a client in hypovolemic shock. There is no need to question this order. This would be appropriate for this client.

   ② INCORRECT: Administer Epinephrine IV as prescribed for a client experiencing anaphylactic shock. There is no need to question this order. This would be appropriate for this client.

   ③ INCORRECT: Administer antibiotics for a client in septic shock. There is no need to question this order. This would be appropriate for this client.

   ④ **CORRECT: Administer 2 units of blood as prescribed for a client in cardiogenic shock. This must be questioned. Cardiogenic shock is a result of heart or pump failure. The heart will not be able to handle this volume.**

The strategy is to link the pathophysiology of the different types of shock with the orders. The key words in the stem of the question is "new order is priority to question." This indicates if the order was implemented, then this would not be consistent for client safety.

Management of Care: Verify appropriateness and/or accuracy of medication order.

9. Which of these **nursing actions by the UAP** would require the **charge nurse to intervene** for a client who is in **hypovolemic shock?**

    ① **CORRECT: The UAP elevates the head of the bed during the bath. This will result in the BP decreasing more than it already is from the hypovolemic shock. There needs to be an intervention since the UAP is providing care that is not consistent with the standard of care for this type of shock.**

    ② INCORRECT: The UAP encourages fluid as prescribed. Standard of practice; no intervention necessary.

    ③ INCORRECT: The UAP performs frequent oral care. Standard of practice; no intervention necessary.

    ④ INCORRECT:The UAP monitors the urine output and reports an output change of 60 mL/hr to 40 mL/hr in one hour. Standard of practice; no intervention necessary.

The strategy is to link the nursing care with the pathophysiology that is occurring with the hypovolemic shock. If there is a loss in volume, there will be less blood to pump and can result in a low blood pressure. Elevating the head of the bed will cause BP to decrease even more.

Management of Care: Report (Recognize) unsafe care of healthcare personnel and intervene as appropriate (i.e., improper care).

10. Which of these **clinical assessment findings** would be important to monitor and report for a client in **hypovolemic shock?** Select all that apply.

    ① INCORRECT: BP–150/80. BP would be low if there was a problem with hypovolemia.

    ② **CORRECT: Heart Rate–130 bpm (weak). This is correct. HR is compensating from loss of blood.**

    ③ INCORRECT: CVP–6 mm Hg. This is within defined limits. No need to report. CVP would be decreased if there was a complication from hypovolemia.

    ④ **CORRECT: Respiratory Rate–40/ min. Tachypnea indicates shock is progressing.**

    ⑤ INCORRECT: Pulse–bounding. This would be a symptom of distributive shock.

The strategy is to organize the system specific assessment findings around the types of shock. Note, BP and CVP are not low as would be the case if there was low volume. If the heart does not have a lot of volume to pump, then it would make sense the blood pressure would decrease. This is the reason the HR and RR are elevated, so they can attempt to compensate for the blood loss. The pulse may be bounding in distributive shock.

Physiological Adaptation: Assess client and respond to changes in vital signs.

Physiological Adaptation: Recognize signs and symptoms of complications and intervene appropriately when providing care.

You have just mastered another concept!!

Decision-Making Analysis Form

Use this tool to help identify why you missed any questions. As you enter the question numbers in the chart, you will begin to see patterns of why you answered incorrectly. This information will then guide you toward what you need to focus on in your continued studies. Ultimately, this analytical exercise will help you become more successful in answering questions!!!

Questions to ask:

1. Did I have the knowledge to answer the question? If not, what information do I need to review?

2. Did I know what the question was asking? Did I misread it or did I miss keywords in the stem of the question?

3. Did I misread or miss keywords in the distractors that would have helped me choose the correct answer?

4. Did I follow my gut reaction or did I allow myself to rationalize and then choose the wrong answer?

	Lack of Knowledge (Concepts, Systems, Pathophysiology, Medications, Procedures, etc.)	Missed Keywords or Misread the Stem of the Question	Missed Keywords or Misread the Distractors	Changed My Answer (Second-guessed myself, i.e., my first answer was correct.)
Put the # of each question you missed in the column that best explains why you think you answered it incorrectly.				

If you changed an answer because you talked yourself out of the correct answer, or you second-guessed yourself, this is an **EASY FIX: QUIT changing your answers**!!! Typically, the first time you read a question, you are about 95% right! The second time you read a question, you start talking yourself into changing the answer. The third time you read a question, you do not have a clue—and you are probably thinking "Who in the heck wrote this question?"

On the other hand, if you read a question too quickly and when you reread it you realize you missed some key information that would impact your decision (i.e., assessments, lab reports, medications, etc.), then it is appropriate to change your answer. When in doubt, go with the safe route: your first thought! Go with your gut instinct!

As you gain confidence in answering questions regarding specific nursing concepts, you will be able to successfully progress to answering higher-level questions about prioritization. Please refer to the *Prioritization Guidelines* in this book for a structure to assist you with this process.

You CAN do this!

> *"Strength does not come from physical capacity. It comes from an indomitable will."*
>
> GANDHI

References for Chapter 10

Black, J M. and Hawks, J. H. (2009). *Medical surgical nursing: Clinical management for positive outcomes* (8th ed.). Philadelphia: Elsevier/Saunders.

Daniels, R. & Nicoll, L. (2012). *Contemporary medical-surgical nursing*, (2nd ed.). Clifton Park, NY: Delmar Cengage Learning.

Ellis, K. M. (2012). *EKG: Plain and simple* (3rd ed.). Upper Saddle Road, NJ: Pearson.

Eliopoulos, C. (2014). *Gerontological nursing* (8th ed.), Philadelphia: Lippincott Williams & Wilkins.

Giddens, G. F. (2013). *Concepts for nursing practice*. St. Louis, MO: Mosby, an imprint of Elsevier.

Hogan, M. A. (2014). *Pathophysiology, reviews and rationales*, (3rd Edition) Boston, MA: Pearson.

Ignatavicius, D. D. and Workman, M. L. (2010). *Medical-Surgical nursing: Patient-Centered collaborative care* (7th ed.). Philadelphia: Elsevier/Saunders.

LeMone, P. Burke, K. M. and Bauldoff, G. (2011). *Medical-surgical nursing: Critical thinking in patient care* (5th edition). Upper Saddle Road, NJ: Pearson/Prentice Hall.

Lewis, S., Dirksen, S., Heitkemper, M., Bucher, L., and Camera, I. (2011). *Medical surgical nursing: Assessment and management of clinical problems* (8th ed.). St. Louis: Mosby.

Manning, L. and Rayfield, S. (2014). *Nursing made insanely easy* (7th ed). Duluth, GA: I CAN Publishing, Inc.

Manning, L. and Rayfield, S. (2013). *Pharmacology made insanely easy* (4th ed.). Duluth, GA: I CAN Publishing, Inc.

National Council of State Boards of Nursing, INC. (NCSBN) 2012. *Research brief: 2011 RN practice analysis: linking the NCLEX RN® examination to practice*. Retrieved from https://www.ncsbn.org/index.htm

Nettina, S. L. (2013). *Lippincott manual of nursing practice* (10th ed.). Philadelphia, PA: Walters Kluwer Health/Lippincott Williams & Wilkins.

North Carolina Concept Based Learning Editorial Board. (2011). *Nursing a concept based approach to learning*. Upper Saddle Road, NJ: Pearson/Prentice Hall.

Osborn, K. S., Wraa, C. E., Watson, A. S., and Holleran, R. S. (2014). *Medical surgical nursing: preparation for practice* (2nd ed.). Upper Saddle Road, NJ: Pearson.

Porth, C. (2011). *Essentials of pathophysiology* (3rd edition). Philadelphia, PA: Lippincott Williams ad Wilkins.

Porth, C. M. and Grossman, S. (2013). *Pathophysiology, Concepts of altered health states* (9th edition). Philadelphia, PA: Lippincott Williams & Wilkins.

Potter, P. A., Perry, A. G., Stockert, P., and Hall, A. (2013). *Fundamentals of nursing* (8th ed). St. Louis, MO: Pearson/Prentice Hall.

CHAPTER 11

Neurological System
Linking Concepts to Pathophysiology of Diseases
Concept Intracranial Regulation

A Snapshot of Intracranial Regulation

Regulation is a term that refers to maintaining balance. *Intracranial regulation* (ICR) refers to promoting an environment that is conducive to optimal functioning of the brain by maintaining balance. Anything that affects the contents of the cranium and impacts the regulation of optimal functioning of the brain is included in this concept. ICR is defined as mechanisms or conditions that impact intracranial processing and function (Giddens, 2013).

Problems with *perfusion*, *neurotransmission*, and *pathology* are three categories that describe ICR dysfunction.

Perfusion delivers oxygen and nutrients by the ongoing supply of blood. The perfusion pressure can be affected by an internal blockage of a vessel, severe hypotension, or the loss of vessel integrity from damage to or excessive pressure on a vessel and can have a negative impact on the intracerebral perfusion. The outcome(s) of the disruption of the perfusion depend on what part of the brain is affected and the period of time it took for perfusion to be restored.

Normal neurotransmission requires functioning neurons, nerves, and neurotransmitters. These neurotransmitters can be either excitatory or inhibitory. Seizures are one example of an alteration in neuronal activity. Seizures can manifest as a disruption in the motor control, sensory perception, behavior, and/or autonomic function (Giddens, 2013).

Pathology of the brain can present as several medical conditions such as inflammatory conditions, brain tumors, and degenerative diseases. Alzheimer's disease is a degenerative process that results in changes primarily in the gray matter from a loss of neurons. The basal ganglia is damaged in clients with Parkinson's disease. The exact degenerative process varies with each of these diseases; however, the result is the same—*disruption of cerebral regulation and function*. Several of the most common inflammatory conditions of the brain are abscesses, inflammatory conditions, and meningitis. Once again, just like the degenerative diseases, the etiology varies with each of the inflammatory conditions, but the result is the same: a disruption in cerebral regulation and function.

Physiological Consequences of Impaired Intracranial Regulation

Increased Intracranial Pressure (IICP): Normal is 5–15 mm Hg. The outcome of increased intracranial pressure is impaired perfusion.

Measurement of Cerebral Perfusion Pressure (CPP): Subtract ICP from the mean arterial pressure (MAP). CPP should be between 60 and 70 mm Hg in clients with IICP to avoid ischemia. For example: *The mean arterial pressure is 80 and the ICP is 15; to determine the CPP, set up your formula to read:*

80 MAP–15 ICP = 65 CPP, which is within the normal range of 60–70 mm Hg

Cerebral Edema is an increase in brain size which negatively affects cerebral perfusion. This can result in hypoxia to the brain.

Glasgow Coma Scale (GCS) is a scale used to evaluate the client's level of consciousness and monitor the outcomes and progress from treatment. The GCS evaluates motor, eye opening, and verbal ability. GCS is beneficial in evaluating changes in the level of consciousness for clients with encephalitis, head injuries, etc. Some complications from neurological injuries can occur quickly and mandate immediate intervention and treatment.

PATHOPHYSIOLOGY The Pathophysiology Behind Intracranial Regulation

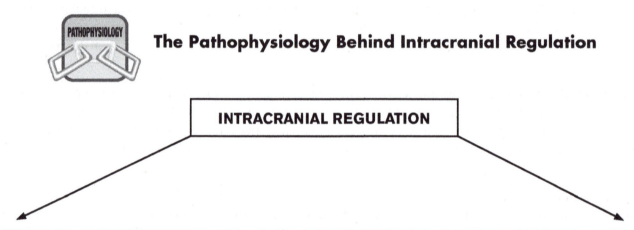

INTRACRANIAL REGULATION

Perfusion			Neurological Transmission	Pathology		
Ischemic Stroke	Hemorrhagic Stroke	Head Injury		Brain Neoplasm	Degenerative	Inflammation
Embolic Thrombotic	Subarachnoid bleed Intracranial bleed Aneurysm that has ruptured	Head trauma from traumatic injury Epidural (extradural) bleed (a bleed resulting in a hematoma forming between the dura and the skull Subarachnoid bleed (a bleed resulting in a hematoma forming between the dura and arachnoid space) Spinal cord injury secondary from head or neck trauma	Epilepsy Seizure Myasthenia Gravis Guillain-Barré Syndrome	Benign brain tumor Malignant brain tumor	Dementia Alzheimer's Disease Amyotrophic Lateral Sclerosis (ALS) Multiple Sclerosis Parkinson's Disease	Viral/Bacterial Meningitis Encephalitis Brain abscess

System-Specific Assessments: "HEADS"

As you review the many diseases that can alter intracranial regulation, resulting in increased intracranial pressure, you will note there are many similar system-specific assessments.

The bottom line is there is something going on in the **"HEADS"** of clients that should not be present, such as a bleed; skull fracture from a head injury; a growth, such as a tumor; or extra fluid (cerebral edema). **HEADS** will assist you in organizing the common assessment findings. Nurses do not diagnose; however, nurses must feel confident about what to assess and what these specific assessments are.

In order to simplify this further, the **early signs and symptoms for IICP**, for both the infant/child and adult; a review of the **assessment of the pupils**; the **Glasgow Coma Scale**; and the **Cranial Nerves** are outlined on the following pages. A discussion of complications follows; a review of the comparison of the vital signs for clients in shock versus those experiencing increased intracranial pressure (IICP); and the ominous late sign of increasd ICP, the Cushing's Triad, which can be an indication of impending herniation. The last complication to be reviewed is the Syndrome of Inappropriate Antidiuretic Hormone (SIADH) and/or Diabetes Insipidus (DI).

H   Headache is severe

E   Evidence of a CSF leak from nose or ears; VS (Refer to Cushing's Triad); cranial nerves II, III, IV, and/or VI

Eyes for PERRLA (Pupils Equal Round, Reactive to Light, and Accommodation is present)

Evidence of vomiting not preceded by nausea; may be projectile

A   Airway status PRIORITY! O$_2$ sat, swallowing/gag reflex

Alteration in RR (i.e., Cheyne-Stokes respirations)

Alteration in fluid and electrolytes (urine/blood: Na$^+$ and osmolality)

D   Deterioration in IICP—early vs. late; Glasgow Coma Scale

S   Seizures
Sensory and motor function impaired
Speech changes

Neurological Changes That Occur in the Older Adult Client
Signs of Cognitive Impairment

In the older adult, assess the mental status and orientation prior to continuing the assessment of the neurological function.

S **S**ignificant memory loss; suspicious and/or agitated?

H **H**as awareness of person, place, time, situation?

O **O**bjects (short-term memory). Can client identify three or four common objects; then ask to recall in five minutes. Lack of judgment?

R **R**esponsiveness to time frame; ADLs; able to recall the president's name?

T **T**he sensory deficits (i.e., hearing and vision) that client is not aware of?

Older clients may **"MOANE"** a lot when they are confused. **MOANE** will assist you in organizing the causes of confusion in older adult clients.

M Metabolic changes: urinary tract infections, fluid and electrolyte imbalances, hyper/hypoglycemia

O Output (cardiac): dysrhythmia, congestive heart failure, myocardial infarction

A Acidosis (respiratory)/hypoxia: shallow breathing, infection, pneumonia

N Neurologic: cerebral edema, infections, vascular insufficiency

E Environmental: hypothermia, hyperthermia, different surroundings

Priority System-Specific Assessments Made Easy!

Early and Late Signs of INCREASED INTRACRANIAL PRESSURE

Infant/Child Early ("PIES")	Adult Early (LOC Changes)
Projectile vomiting; poor feeding	Restless
Increased high-pitch cry; headache	Irritable
Enlarged (bulging) fontanels	Lethargic
Separation of the suture lines (enlarged head circumference)	
Late (Note all are ↓) ↓ LOC ↓ Reflexes ↓ PERRLA ↓ Ventilation (Hypoventilation)	Late (Note all are ↓) ↓ LOC ↓ Reflexes ↓ PERRLA ↓ Ventilation (Hypoventilation)

PRIORITIES

These early and late signs of IICP apply **to any of the neurological diseases that are reviewed in the concepts that alter intracranial regulation and may result in cerebral edema.** You do NOT have to remember every neurological disease. Just remember: *the infant's head is getting round like "PIES" early on and the adult is getting more **lethargic** when there is any **increased pressure in the head**.* These early findings are not good signs and need intervention to prevent from progressing to late signs that could result in herniation.

System-Specific Assessments: PERRLA

Pupils Equal Reactive to Light
Moving All Extremities to command

Pupillary response should be round pupils, midline, equal in size, and brisk reaction equally to bright light and should accommodate to distance.

Abnormal findings include some of these pupillary changes. If there is a lesion in the brain, then there will be ipsilateral pupillary changes. (*These changes mean that they occur on the same side as the cerebral lesion.*) Contralateral pupillary changes can occur; however, this *means that the change is on the side opposite of the cerebral lesion.* Sluggish or no pupillary response to light and poor or absent accommodation indicates an intracranial change such as edema or a bleed.

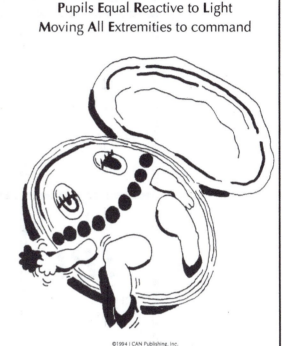

©1994 I CAN Publishing, Inc.

Glasgow Coma Scale is a tool to assist in evaluating the level of consciousness and monitor the trends and outcomes from treatment:

I'm running!

© 1994 I CAN Publishing, Inc.

System-Specific Assessments: Glasgow Coma Scale

Glasgow Coma Scale (GCS): The best GCS score is 15. Less than 8 is associated with a severe head injury and coma. A score of 9 to 12 indicates a moderate head injury. Greater than 13 reflects a minor head trauma.

Eye opening—Range from 4 to 1

Verbal—Range from 5 to 1

Motor—Range from 6 to 1

1. MOTOR
2. VERBAL
3. EYES OPEN

System-Specific Assessments: Cranial Nerves

1 God gave us one nose (olfactory)	**2** God gave us two eyes (optic)	**3,4,6** Makes my eyes do tricks! (oculomotor, trochlear, abducens)
5 **TRI** Rhymes with Tri (for Trigeminal)	**7** Can fit nicely across your face to help you remember the Facial Cranial nerves	**8** Fits nicely in your ear to assist you to remember the acoustic
9, 10 Is under the chin. (glossopharyngeal, vagus)	**11** Put a 1 on each shoulder and then shrug. The 1s should not fall off (spinal accessory)	**12** For tongue movement (hypoglossal)

©2008 I CAN Publishing, Inc.

Many students find it difficult to remember all 12 of the cranial nerves. This strategy has been developed to simplify the ability to easily remember them. On the chart above, notice there is only one nose (*olfactory*), which represents the first cranial nerve. God gave us two eyes (*optic*), which is the second cranial nerve. You can remember this cranial nerve by recalling "optic vision." Cranial nerves 3, 4, and 6 make your eyes do tricks (*oculomotor*, *trochlear*, and *abducens*). The fifth cranial nerve is recalled by remembering 5 rhymes with tri (*trigeminal*).

The seventh cranial nerve is recalled by visualizing placing the number 7 across your face with the top of the 7 going across your forehead and the bottom part going down over your face. To remember the eighth cranial nerve, think of the number 8 (*acoustic*) fitting nicely in your ear. When you evaluate cranial nerves 9 and 10, this assessment is under your chin (*glossopharyngeal* and *vagus*). Notice these two nerves have a "g" in their spelling, and one of the assessments for these nerves is to check the gag reflex. As you progress to the 11th cranial nerve (*spinal accessory*), visualize the number 1 on each shoulder which should remain in place as clients shrug their shoulders. For the 12th cranial nerve (*hypoglossal*), visualize a client sticking his tongue out from side to side and saying, "The end!"

System-Specific Assessments: Cranial Nerve V

Notice that if **Cranial Nerve V (trigeminal)** is disturbed, there is a brief paroxysmal pain and spasm of the face. This disorder affects the sensory branches of the trigeminal nerve. Facial twitching and grimacing are characteristic. The pain is excruciating! This is a unilateral sensory disturbance and results in *Trigeminal Neuralgia*, also known as *tic douloureux*. If you only remember one assessment for this condition it is **"PAIN"** that is described as severe, stabbing, and shocklike. The pain is initiated by the cutaneous stimulation of the affected nerve area. Activities such as chewing; washing the face; brushing teeth; or extremes of temperature, either on the face or in food, can initiate the pain. Remember, **lukewarm** food is the client's preference since hot food is very painful. Food that can be easily chewed is important to include in the plan. Protein and calories in the diet should be included.

TRIGEMINAL NEURALGIA

Pain is excruciating

Avoid hot or cold

Increase protein and calories

Nerve, cranial V

Eye care

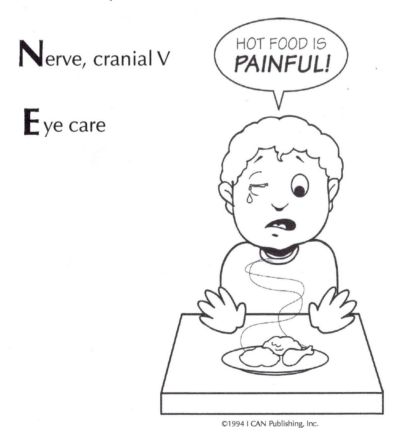

HOT FOOD IS *PAINFUL!*

System-Specific Assessments: Cranial Nerve VII

If **Cranial Nerve VII (facial)** is affected, there is a disruption of the motor branches on one side of the face, which results in muscle weakness or flaccidity on the affected side. This transient cranial nerve disorder is called *Bell's Palsy*. The client will present with inability to close eyelid on affected side. Drooping of the mouth and decrease in taste sensation may also occur. The major goals with this condition are to maintain a positive image and prevent complications. **"IMAGE"** will assist you in organizing the nursing interventions.

I   Image should be supported by explaining that the condition is self-limiting with minimal, if any, residual effects. Client may require counseling.

M   Methycellulose eye drops during day. Ophthalmic ointment and eye patches may be required at night.

A   Antivirals, moist heat may relieve pain, if present; and corticosteroids should be started immediately after symptoms occur.

G   Give meticulous oral hygiene.

E   Evaluate ability to eat.

BELL'S PALSY

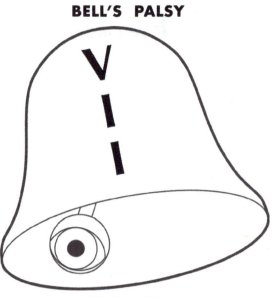

System-Specific Assessments: Complications

Note: These complications can occur anytime there is a condition that results in IICP.

The chart below will assist you in organizing the Vital Signs of Shock and IICP! The great news (as you can see in the chart) is that the signs are exactly opposite for each—with *one exception*: both can cause a loss of consciousness.

	VITAL SIGNS FOR SHOCK VS. IICP	
Shock	**Vs.**	**IICP**
↓	BP	↑
↑	Pulse	↓
↑	Resp	↓
↓	Temp	↑
↓	Pulse Press	↑
↓	LOC	↓

System-Specific Assessments: Complications

Note: These complications can occur anytime there is a condition that results in IICP.

Cushing's Triad is a late clinical finding that is characterized by an increase in the systolic blood pressure with a **widened pulse pressure** and **bradycardia**. Remember, the pulse pressure is the difference between the systolic and diastolic readings. These are late responses and indicate severe IICP with failure of autoregulation. The **respiratory patterns** progress from **Cheyne-Stokes respiration, to central neurogenic hyperventilation, to apneustic breathing (a sustained respiratory inspiratory effort), and irregular breathing as ICP increases**. If the client is on mechanical ventilation, the respiratory pattern will not be noticed. Typically, when the hypothalamus is affected by intracranial pressure, there is also a complication with hyperthermia. Note, this is not part of the Cushing's Triad.

CUSHING'S TRIAD is an ominous late sign of increased ICP and an indication of impending herniation.

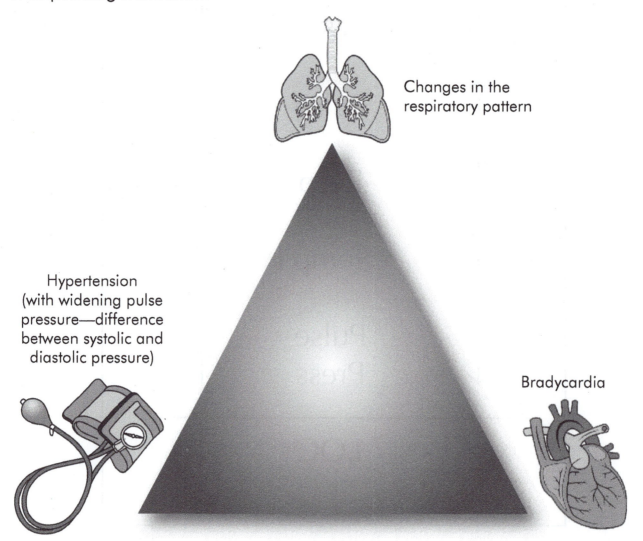

Changes in the respiratory pattern

Hypertension (with widening pulse pressure—difference between systolic and diastolic pressure)

Bradycardia

System-Specific Assessments: Complications

For specifics, refer to Endocrine System (Pituitary)

You may be wondering why we are reviewing the pituitary with the concept Intracranial Regulation. Unfortunately, Syndrome of Inappropriate Antidiuretic Hormone (SIADH) can occur if the hypothalamus has been damaged or there is an increase in the cerebral edema from a neurological medical condition. This is a medical condition that occurs when the hypothalamus has been damaged and can no longer regulate the release of the antidiuretic hormone (ADH).

As a result of this pathophysiology, fluid is retained due to the overproduction of vasopressin (the antidiuretic hormone) from the posterior pituitary gland. This can occur as a result of a malignant tumor, head injury, trauma, etc.

Treatment of SIADH includes restriction of fluid, administration of oral demeclocycline (Declomycin), and treatment of hyponatremia. The client may present with disorientation, vomiting, and/or a headache. If not treated, SIADH may result in a seizure and/or coma.

Diabetes Insipidus (DI) is a condition where large amounts of urine are excreted as a result of a deficiency of ADH from the posterior pituitary gland. This occurs when the hypothalamus has been damaged and can no longer regulate the release of ADH. This can occur as a result of a malignant tumor, head injury, trauma, pituitary gland tumor, or surgery around the pituitary gland, etc. Treatment of DI consists of fluid replacement, careful attention to laboratory values, and replacement of essential nutrients.

Labs for SIADH:

↓ Urine output ↑ Specific gravity **(CONCENTRATED)**

↑ Urine osmolality; ↑ Urine sodium

↓ Serum osmolality ↓ Serum sodium **(DILUTE)**

Labs for DI:

↑ Urine output ↓ Specific gravity **(DILUTE)**

↓ Urine osmolality; ↓ Urine sodium

↑ Serum osmolality; ↑ Serum sodium **(CONCENTRATED)**

System-Specific Diagnostic Tests and Procedures

Diagnostic Tests	Procedures
Serum Osmolality	Cerebral Angiogram
Serum Sodium	Cerebral Computed Tomography (CT) scan
Urine Osmolality	Electroencephalography (EEG)
Urine Sodium	Glasgow Coma Scale (GCS)
Specific Gravity	Intracranial pressure (ICP) monitoring
	Lumbar puncture (spinal tap)–Cerebrospinal analysis
	Magnetic resonance imaging (MRI) scan
	Positron emission tomography (PET)

Pathophysiology: Intracranial Regulation

Medications

The following medications represent some of the drugs prescribed for clients with medical conditions involving intracranial regulation.

Common Medications Most Frequently Used for Alterations with Intracranial Regulation	
Anticonvulsant Agents • Phenytoin (Dilantin) • Gabapentin (Neurontin) • Valproic acid (Depakote) • Carbamazepine (Tegretol) • Lamotrigine (Lamictal) **Cholinergic Agents** • Neostigmine (Prostigmin) • Pyridostigminde (Mestinon) • Edrophonium (Tensilon) **Anticholinergic Agents** • Benztropine mesylate (Cogentin) • Trihexyphenidyl h (Artane) • Procyclidine (Kemadrin)	**Osmotic Diuretic** • Mannitol (Osmitrol)) **Adrenocortical Hormones** • Dexamethasone (Decadron) **Dopaminergics** • Levodopa (L-DOPA, Larodopa) • Carbidopa/levodopa (Sinemet) • Amantadine (Symmetrel) **Dopamine Agonists** • Pramipexole (Mirapex) • Ropinirole (Reqpuip) • Bromocriptine (Parlodel)

First-Do Priority Interventions

"PERFUSE"

As you review the many medical diseases that can result in increased intracranial pressure, you will realize that many of the interventions are similar. **"PERFUSE"** will assist you in organizing these nursing actions.

Encourage client NOT to **"COUGH,"** since it will result in increased intracranial pressure. Any time there is pathology that can cause an increase in intracranial pressure resulting in an alteration of intracranial regulation, **"COUGH"** can be a problem. Each of the following actions may result in increased intracranial pressure, so advise client NOT to **"COUGH"** with the exception of controlling temperature:

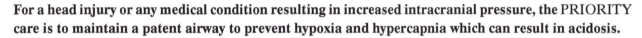

- **C** Cough; control temperature (fever can ↑ ICP)
- **O** Oral tracheal/endotracheal suctioning
- **U** Use force when blowing nose
- **G** Get neck/hip to an extreme flexion/extension position
- **H** Hypercapnia creates vasodilation

For a head injury or any medical condition resulting in increased intracranial pressure, the PRIORITY **care is to maintain a patent airway to prevent hypoxia and hypercapnia which can result in acidosis.**

Intracranial Pressure (ICP): Normal is 5–15 mm Hg. The outcome of increased intracranial pressure is impaired perfusion. **Measurement of Cerebral Perfusion Pressure (CPP):** Subtract ICP from the mean arterial pressure (MAP). CPP should be between 60 and 70 mm Hg in clients with IICP to avoid ischemia.

Position: elevate HOB 30°, head in midline neutral position to promote venous drainage.

Evaluate airway patency; monitor oxygen levels, administer oxygen as needed; monitor O_2 sat (administer O_2 as prescribed); "HEADS;" lung sounds; vital signs; I & O; IICP; PERRLA; GCS (LOC); fluid and electrolytes (Na^+) per protocol.

Remember to avoid neck, hip/knee flexion or extension; logroll with repositioning; assist with ADLs.

Feedings: assess swallowing function first.

Use correct body alignment to promote cerebral blood flow (perfusion); avoid use of restrictive clothes, cold, and nicotine.

Safety–seizure precautions; stimulation ↓; no sedatives or narcotics; restrict fluids; control temp; discuss importance for client not to **"COUGH"** so ICP will not ↑. *(Refer to Linking Pathophysiology to Interventions for Decreasing ICP on page 260.)* Hyper-oxygenate with 100% oxygen prior to and following suctioning. Maintain bed rest; skin integrity *(Refer to concept Immobility)*.

Evaluate ICP–goal to maintain at 5 to 15 mm Hg; maintain CPP between 60 and 70 mm Hg. Eliminate risk of constipation.

Linking Pathophysiology to
Interventions for Decreasing Intracranial Pressure

Pathophysiology	Interventions
Position HOB: Intracranial venous system consists of canals and sinuses. Unlike the peripheral venous system, there are no valves. Interventions promoting venous outflow from the head decrease cerebral volume, helping to lower ICP.	**P**osition HOB 30°; align neck and head midline with body (to prevent compression of jugular vein).
Evaluate airway: Endotracheal suctioning stimulates coughing, which can ↑ ICP. Only suction when needed. Poor ventilation will precipitate respiratory acidosis or an ↑ in the $PaCO_2$. Carbon dioxide has a vasodilating effect on the cerebral arteries, which increases cerebrovascular blood flow and ICP. **E**valuate pupils for PERRLA. Cranial nerves II, III, IV, and VI may be affected by a lesion and/or cerebral edema. **E**valuate drainage from nose with Dextrostix; if glucose is present, it is indicative of a cerebrospinal leak (CSF); spinal fluid dries with a yellow halo around edges of drainage. **E**valuate urine osmolality, and urine Na$^+$ and serum osmolality and serum Na$^+$. Refer to complications of Syndrome of Inappropriate Antidiuretic Hormone (SIADH) or Diabetes Insipidus (DI).	**E**valuate airway patency; monitor oxygen levels; administer oxygen as needed; monitor lung sounds ("HEADS"); vital signs; I & O; IICP–goal to maintain at 5 to 15 mm Hg; maintain CPP between 60 and 70 mm Hg; GCS (LOC). **E**valuate pupils for PERRLA. **E**valuate drainage of fluid from nose, ears, and mouth. If CSF occurs, then elevate HOB and assess for the development of signs such as nuchal rigidity indicating a problem with meningitis. (*Refer to p. 285 for specifics.*) **E**valuate urine osmolality, and urine Na$^+$ and serum osmolality and serum Na$^+$. Refer to complications of Syndrome of Inappropriate Antidiuretic Hormone (SIADH) or Diabetes Insipidus (DI).
Remember to promote venous outflow from the head to decrease cerebral volume and assist in lowering ICP.	**R**emember to avoid neck, hip/knee flexion or extension. Logroll with repositioning.
Feedings are important in order to facilitate appropriate nutrition to assist with healing. Swallowing function should be assessed prior to initiating any enteral feeding.	**F**eedings: assess swallowing function first.
Use position to decrease ICP. Restrictive clothes, cold and nicotine can ↑ ICP. ↓ fluid to ↓ cerebral edema.	**U**se correct body alignment to promote cerebral blood flow (perfusion); avoid use of restrictive clothes, cold, and nicotine. Monitor I & O.
Safety: Sedatives can mask neurological changes and/or cause respiratory depression. Temperature increase can IICP. Coughing, suctioning, blowing nose, straining, etc., can IICP.	**S**afety: seizure precautions. Stimulation ↓. No sedatives or narcotics. Restrict fluids. Control temp; avoid coughing. When suctioning, hyper-oxygenate with 100% oxygen prior to and after suctioning. Suction only as needed. A 1 mm Hg change in $PaCO_2$ is a 3% change in cerebral blood flow.

Evaluate ICP. If > 15 mm Hg, the outcome could be impaired cerebral perfusion.
   Elimination: Constipation can raise ICP by increasing intra-abdominal pressure because of straining when defecating.
	Evaluate ICP to maintain at 5 to 15 mm Hg.
	
	   Eliminate constipation with use of stool softeners and laxatives.

SAFETY Summary: Concept Intracranial Regulation

System-Specific Assessments "HEADS"	First-Do Priority Interventions "PERFUSE"	Evaluation of Expected Outcomes
Headache is severe. **E**vidence of a CSF leak from nose or ears; **VS** *(refer to Cushing's Triad)*; neurological checks; cranial nerves II, III, IV, and/or VI. Assess eyes for **PERRLA** (**P**upils **E**qual **R**ound and **R**eactive to **L**ight and **A**ccommodation is present.) Evidence of vomiting not preceded by nausea; may be projectile. **A**irway status PRIORITY! O₂ sat, swallowing/gag reflex. **A**lteration in RR (i.e., Cheyne-Stokes respirations). **A**lteration in F & E (Urine/blood: Na⁺ & osmolality); I & O. **D**eterioration in (IICP-early vs. late-**Glasgow Coma Scale**); dilated, pinpoint, or asymmetric pupils. **S**eizures; Sensory and motor function impaired; Speech changes.	**P**osition: elevate HOB 30°, head in midline neutral position to promote venous drainage. **E**valuate airway patency, monitor oxygen levels, administer oxygen as needed, monitor O₂ sat (administer O₂ as prescribed), lung sounds ("**HEADS**"); vital signs; I & O; IICP, GCS (LOC); fluid and electrolytes (Na⁺); CSF leak; **PERRLA**, cranial nerves. **R**emember to avoid neck, hip/knee flexion or extension. Logroll with repositioning; assist with ADLs. **F**eedings: assess swallowing function first. **U**se correct body alignment to promote cerebral blood flow (perfusion); avoid use of restrictive clothes, cold, and nicotine. **S**afety—seizure precautions; stimulation ↓; no sedatives or narcotics. Restrict fluids. Control temp. Discuss importance for client not to "**COUGH**", so ICP will not ↑. *(Refer to Linking Pathophysiology to Interventions for Decreasing ICP.)* When suctioning, hyper-oxygenate with 100% oxygen prior to and after suctioning. Maintain bed rest; skin integrity. *(Refer to concept Immobility.)* **E**valuate ICP–goal to maintain at 5 to 15 mm Hg; maintain CPP between 60 and 70 mm Hg	**H**eadache is not present. **E**vidence of no CSF leak; **VS** WDL; **cranial nerves** have no deviation from the norm *(swallowing/gag reflexes intact)*. **PERRLA**; no vomiting. **A**irway patent with O₂ sats in normal range for client as prescribed by HCP; lung sounds are clear and equal bilaterally; VS WDL; I & O are specific to guidelines as outlined by HCP; ICP maintained at 5–15 mm Hg; serum and urine osmolality and sodium remain WDL. I & O WDL for client. **D**eterioration in GCS not present. GCS within range as ordered by HCP. **S**eizures absent; Sensory and motor function within norm for client. Speaking with no changes from norm.

Exceptions and Additions by Diseases

Pathophysiology: Perfusion
Cerebrovascular Accidents (Strokes)

Cerebrovascular Accidents (CVA, Brain Attack, or Stroke): A CVA is the disruption of the supply of blood to a specific area in the brain. This is secondary to ischemia, brain attack, hemorrhage, and embolism. This may result in tissue necrosis and sudden loss of brain function. It is the leading cause of adult disability in the United States. Atherosclerosis, resulting in cerebrovascular disease, many times precedes the development of a stroke.

FIRST-DO PRIORITY INTERVENTIONS

System-Specific Assessments "FAST"	Diet	Equipment	Plans/Interventions	Health Promotion
Face–smile or stick out tongue. **Arms**–raise together and observe for weakness or inability. **Speak**–ask to speak name and address; assess for slurring. **Time** is BRAIN! If any of the first three are deficient, call 911!!	• Thickening in liquid to prevent aspiration. • Place food on the unaffected side of the mouth. • Teach client to swallow with neck flexed. • Swallow studies.	• Communication board if language is affected. • Assistive devices for lifting and/or ambulation. Home safety (i.e., bars in bathtub area, by toilet, and no throw rugs, etc.) • Suction available to use in case of aspiration. • Ambu bag. • Oxygen.	• Transfer techniques. • Support with aphasia. • Risk prevention such as falls, fatigue, and fever (signs of infection). • Assess gag reflex.	• Refer to occupational therapy for assistance in activities of daily living (ADLs). • Physical therapy for tertiary prevention program. • Speech therapy. • Counseling for coping with a chronic disease. • Safety risk assessment prior to discharge.

INSANELY EASY TIP!   Summary of "CVAs"

C   Communication skills (speech therapy); counseling

d **V**   **V**Ts–Prevention through sequential stockings, etc. *(Refer to concept Cardiac Peripheral Perfusion.)*

A   Airway management; prevent aspiration–give thickened fluids initially

S   Safety Risk for falls; physical and occupational therapy

Functions of the Left and Right Brain Hemispheres

The graphic below will assist you in reviewing the functions of both the left and right cerebral hemispheres. Notice that if the left cerebral hemisphere is affected, then the right side of the body is affected.

Left Cerebral Hemisphere "MALL"

M athematic skills

A nayltical Thinking

L anguage

L inear Thinking

Stroke on left side affects **RIGHT** side of the body

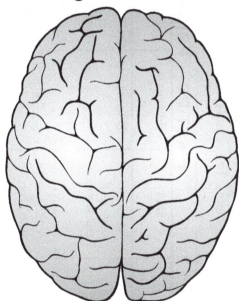

Right Cerebral Hemisphere "PAVE"

Stroke on right side affects **LEFT** side of the body

P roprioception; poor impulse control/judgement; perception of depth loss

A wareness of spatial

V isual changes such as hemianopsia

E xistence of left side of body is lost— left hemiplegia/hemiparesis

Exceptions and Additions by Diseases

Pathophysiology: Perfusion
Head Injury With IICP

Head Injury is an open or penetrating trauma that compromises the integrity of the skull. A head injury may also be closed or a blunt trauma where the skull integrity is maintained. Many times, skull fractures occur with head injuries. If there is a decrease in the blood supply to the brain tissue or a direct impact from the trauma, there may be damage to the tissue. With the glucose levels in the brain being affected negatively, this may result in alteration in the ability for the neurological synapses to occur. Injuries to the brain may be associated with a hemorrhage such as an epidural, intracerebral, or subdural bleed; or a cerebrospinal fluid leakage. Any brain injury, tumor, or fluid may contribute to the risk for cerebral edema. IICP, cerebral hypoxia, and brain herniation are also complications that may occur from a head injury. The exceptions will ONLY FOCUS on when there is an actual IICP from the head injury. The nursing assessment for general IICP focuses on any change in the contents of the cranium. We are using the same mnemonic for ICP, but now there is a problem due to the actual IICP. You will see similarities with the assessments.

			FIRST-DO PRIORITY INTERVENTIONS	
SYSTEM-SPECIFIC ASSESSMENTS "HEADS"	DIET	EQUIPMENT	PLANS/INTERVENTIONS "BRAINS"	HEALTH PROMOTION
Headache is severe	• Enteral feedings if unable to eat.	• Side rails up	**B**ed (Head) ↑ at least 30°	• Physical therapy
Evidence of a CSF leak from nose or ears (fluid tests positive for glucose)		• Padded side rails	**R**estful, calm environment	• Occupational therapy
Alteration in RR (i.e., Cheyne-Stokes respirations), monitor for respiratory acidosis (↑ $PaCO_2$)	• Assess swallow reflex once able to take oral feedings.	• Suction	**A**sess Na^+ level and I & O; posturing; PERRLA; VS (monitor for respiratory acidosis, ↑ $PaCO_2$); O_2 sat, ICP; NC; VS/ characteristics of headache	• Recreational and/or speech therapists
Alteration in F & E (Na^+) and osmolarity due to risk for diabetes insipidus/SIADH		• Airway	**I**mmobility (*Refer to concept Mobility*)	• Social services
Deterioration in LOC; dilated, pinpoint, or asymmetrical pupils; deterioration of motor function, posturing (decerebrate, decorticate, or flaccidity); (Refer to Cushing's Triad)		• Ambu bag	**N**ote if there is CSF fluid leak. If present, keep bed elevated and monitor for meningitis (nuchal rigidity). Report to HCP. (*Refer to Meningitis in the Exceptions and Additions by Disease in this chapter.*) Note if there is any posturing such as decorticate/ decerebrate.	• Rehabilitation facilities
Seizures			**S**eizure precautions	

Exceptions and Additions by Diseases

Pathophysiology: Perfusion
Spinal Cord Injury

A **spinal cord injury (SCI)** is damage to the spinal cord that is inside the spinal column. Most SCIs result in the loss of sensory and motor function along with the loss of elimination control. *Quadriplegia* is defined by a paralysis/paresis of all four extremities and the trunk and is a result of the cervical region injury. At the level of C4 or higher, this injury presents a risk for altered spontaneous ventilation. *Paraplegia/paresis* is defined by a paralysis of the lower extremities below T1. Trauma is the major cause of SCIs. Due to swelling, typically the client will be entubated if T_6 or above.

FIRST-DO PRIORITY INTERVENTIONS

SYSTEM-SPECIFIC ASSESSMENTS "PARALYZED"	DIET	EQUIPMENT	PLANS/INTERVENTIONS "SPINAL CORD"	HEALTH PROMOTION
Pressure (blood) is ↓ more when sitting	• First 48 hours, assess gastrointestinal function frequently; decrease in function may require the use of a nasogastric tube to decrease distention.	• Traction	**S**kin integrity, sensation	• Occupational and physical therapy to learn how to perform ADLs.
Ability to feel, touch, discriminate between sharp and dull and hot and cold is absent	• Increase protein and calories in diet; may need to decrease calcium.	• Splints	**P**sychological support	• Reestablish mobility using either braces, crutches, or electric or manual wheelchairs.
Respirations shallow	• Increase roughage in diet to optimize bowel function.	• Braces	**I**mmobility	• Recreational therapy to assist with diversion.
Absent deep-tendon reflexes		• Casts	**N**utrition, fluid and electrolytes	• Social services to assist with financial resources, home-care needs, and adaptations necessary for the home prior to discharge.
Lack of muscle tone (flaccidity)			**A**ltered tissue perfusion	• SCI support group can assist in adapting emotionally to body image and lifestyle changes.
Yes, can have dependent edema			**L**oss of bowel and bladder function (may need manual stimulation)	• Bowel and bladder training.
Zero reflexive and autonomic function below level of the injury is caused by neurogenic shock for several days to weeks			**C**ardiaovascular stability; complications: autonomic dysreflexia, orthostatic hypotension, neurogenic shock	
Evaluate skin breakdown, respiratory system, and/or infection			**O**utput and intake; trend with urine and bowel	
Decreased/lack of temperature regulation: hypo/hyperthermia			**R**espiratory function/support	
			Determine and monitor neurological status	

First-Do Priority Interventions (Perfusion): Spinal Cord Injury

S   Skin integrity, sensation: reposition every two hours (hourly when in wheelchair). Pressure-relief devices should be used both in the wheelchair and bed. Sexual Function: review with client about alterations in sexual function and alternative strategies.

P   Psychological support: accept periods of depression. Healthcare provider may prescribe an H_2 histamine antagonist to prevent the development of ulcers. Encourage independence whenever possible. Encourage family involvement. Emphasize client's potential. Initiate open dialogue regarding sexual function. Assist with community resources. Assist in setting realistic short-term goals.

I   Immobility: teach to use a wheelchair. Encourage active range-of-motion (ROM) exercises when possible and assist with passive ROM as necessary. Different braces will allow client to regain some function through mobility if client has sustained an incomplete injury. The use of a wheelchair will also assist client with functional mobility. (*Refer to concept Mobility.*)

N   Nutrition, fluid and electrolytes: refer to Diet under **"First-Do Priority Interventions"** on the **Physiology: Perfusion Spinal Cord Injury** chart. Prevent complications of nausea and vomiting. Evaluate bowel sounds and ability to tolerate oral fluids. Evaluate ongoing for a paralytic ileus.

A   Altered tissue perfusion: Three complications can result in altered tissue perfusion. Nerurogenic shock, orthostatic hypotension, and autonomic dysreflexia. Neurogenic shock will be discussed here. The other two will be discussed later in the mnemonic and chapter. Neurogenic shock is a common response of the spinal cord following an injury. Symptoms include hypotension, bradycardia, flaccid paralysis, loss of reflex activity below level of injury. Dependent edema can result from an increased venous capacity from the loss of peripheral vasomotor tone. Symptoms may be treated with atropine or vasopressors. *Managing hypothermia, preventing cardiovascular compomrise and instability, and preventing complications with DVTs are important to include in the plan of care for clients with neurogenic shock. The DVTs are associated with neurogenic shock due to venous pooling that happens due to venous vasodilation. Thermoregulation may occur due to loss of vasomotor tone in blood vessels that normally dilate and constrict to maintain body temperature.* Anticoagulants may be prescribed to prevent the development of a deep-vein thrombosis (DVT). Compression stockings or sequential compression devices can prevent complications of venous stasis.

L   Loss of bowel and bladder function: *See Bowel and Bladder Retraining.*

C **C**ardiaovascular stability: Monitor vital signs and evaluate changes. Hypothermia, hypoxia, and vagal stimulation precipitate neurogenic shock. Assess muscle strength and deep-tendon reflexes as resolution of shock occurs. Orthostatic hypotension is another complication that can occur with these clients. This can occur when clients change position due to the interruption in functioning of the autonomic nervous system. Along with this comes the pooling of blood in the lower extremities when in the upright position. The client's position should be changed slowly, and when placing in a wheelchair it should be reclined. The client should wear thigh-high elastic hose or sequential compression stockings to assist in facilitating venous return.

O **O**utput and intake: client may be NPO for several days. Fluid balance and nutritional support are necessary. If required, TPN may be administered per protocol. Adequate fluid intake is necessary. Fluid will help in preventing urinary calculi and bladder infections, and assist in maintaining soft stools.

R **R**espiratory function/support: the priority is to monitor the respiratory status. Lesions at or above the phrenic nerve or swelling from a lesion immediately below C4 can affect involuntary respirations. Assess for equal breath sounds and chest movement and presence of dyspnea. Suction client as needed and provide the client with oxygen. Assist with intubation and mechanical ventilation as needed. Client may need the nurse to apply abdominal pressure to assist in coughing. Review the importance of using the incentive spirometer, and the need to cough and deep breathe regularly. Change position within limits of SCI. Assess for complications of pneumonia, atelectasis, and pulmonary emboli.

D **D**etermine and monitor neurological status: assess client's ability to move all extremities; strength. Do a sensory examination, including pain and touch. Review presence of deep-tendon reflexes. Evaluate neurological assessment: Glasgow Coma Scale, PERRLA, vital signs, and cranial nerves for any complications.

Intracranial Regulation, Oxygenation, Perfusion/Shock, Tissue/Skin, Mobility, Elimination, Fluid and Electrolytes, Nutrition, and Coping

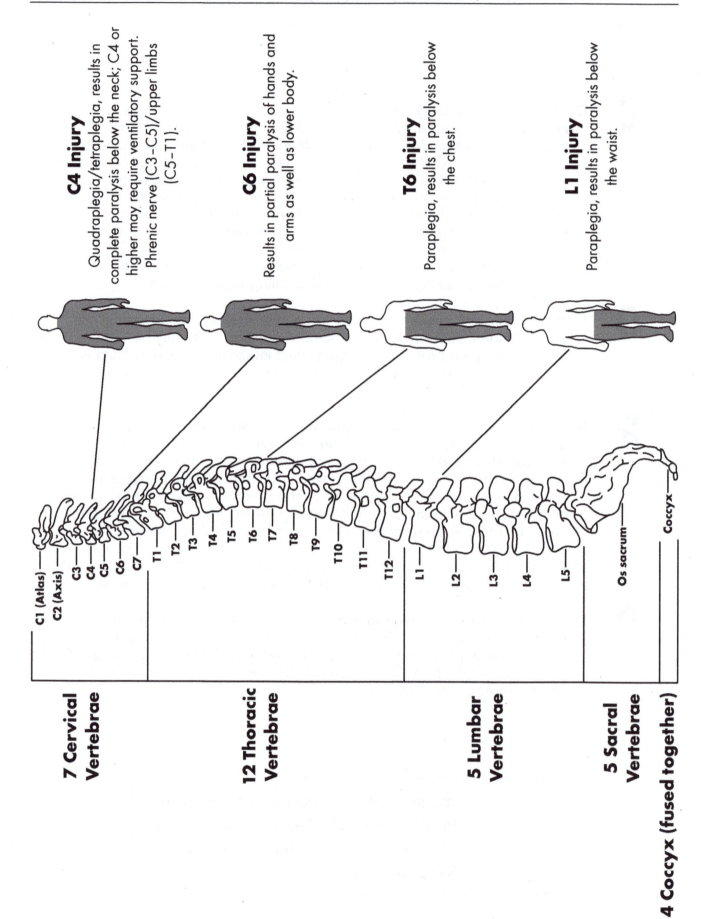

C4 Injury

Quadraplegia/tetraplegia, results in complete paralysis below the neck; C4 or higher may require ventilatory support. Phrenic nerve (C3–C5)/upper limbs (C5–T1).

C6 Injury

Results in partial paralysis of hands and arms as well as lower body.

T6 Injury

Paraplegia, results in paralysis below the chest.

L1 Injury

Paraplegia, results in paralysis below the waist.

C1 (Atlas)
C2 (Axis)
C3
C4
C5
C6
C7
T1
T2
T3
T4
T5
T6
T7
T8
T9
T10
T11
T12
L1
L2
L3
L4
L5
Os sacrum
Coccyx

7 Cervical Vertebrae

12 Thoracic Vertebrae

5 Lumbar Vertebrae

5 Sacral Vertebrae

4 Coccyx (fused together)

Bowel and Bladder Retraining for Clients With Spinal Cord Injuries

T Teach urinary elimination methods (Credé method prior to bladder elimination, intermittent catheterization to client/caregiver.) Monitor temperature.

R Routine schedule is imperative for both bladder and bowel programs.

A After meals (30 minutes); consistent/routine teach bowel retraining.

I Increase fluid and fiber intake for bowel retraining in addition to rectal stimulation; stool softeners; use of Valsalva maneuver; massage abdomen along large intestine. Induce defecation by digital stimulation, suppository, or as a last plan, enema. Monitor I & O. Encourage fluids to prevent UTI. Monitor for signs of infection. Infection control measures!

N Note the importance of monitoring I & O carefully to prevent complications with autonomic dysreflexia! *(Refer to Autonomic Dysreflexia.)*

On the NCLEX® you may be asked to assess and manage a client with alteration in elimination; initiate a toileting schedule. Clients with SCI may need bladder and bowel retraining based on level of injury.

Autonomic Dysreflexia Assessments and Plan

While the nurse is assessing the cause for this condition, the head of the bed should be elevated and BP should be assessed. The neck CANNOT be manipulated, so the entire bed will need to be placed in a reverse Trendelenberg in order to assist with decreasing the blood pressure. This will maintain the head in alignment. These clients are typically on beds that allow this position. This condition occurs due to the stimulation of the sympathetic nervous system. In addition, there is an inadequate compensatory response by the parasympathetic nervous system. Clients who have lesions below T6 do not experience dysreflexia since the parasympathetic nervous system is able to neutralize the sympathetic response. A stimulus that is triggered in the lower part of the body can cause the sympathetic stimulation.

Sympathetic STIMULATION of the nervous system can result in sudden severe headache, extreme hypertension, pallor below the level of the spinal lesion, blurred vision, nausea, and diaphoresis. Stimulation of the parasympathetic nervous system can cause bradycardia, flushing above the lesion (flushed face and neck), along with nasal stuffiness.

The cause needs to be determined and treated. Assess for the stimuli: full (distended) bladder from kinked or blocked urinary catheter, urinary calculi, or retention; fecal impaction; funny feeling with the skin (i.e., tight clothing or cold draft on lower part of the body). If autonomic dysreflexia does occur, elevate the HOB, check BP for hypertension, HR for bradycardia, and remove any tight clothes or stockings. Administer nitrates or hydralazine.

Teaching is necessary for client to understand the importance of regular fluid intake and to increase the frequency of intermittent catheterization. It is also important to explain the actions client should take if he/she experiences autonomic dysreflexia.

AUTONOMIC DYSREFLEXIA (Injuries at T$_6$ or Higher)

Causes
1. **F**ull bladder
2. **F**ecal impaction
3. **F**unny feeling with the skin

Assessments
1. Flushing and Diaphoresis
2. Headache
3. Hypertension
4. Bradycardia

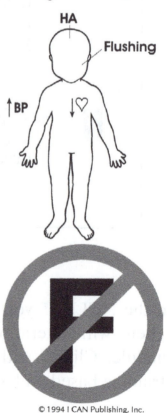

© 1994 I CAN Publishing, Inc.

Exceptions and Additions by Diseases

Pathophysiology: Neurological Transmission Seizures

Seizures: A seizure is the interruption of normal electrical discharge of the neurons within the brain. This can result in alterations in the level of consciousness and/or changes in the sensory and motor skills.

Epilepsy is used to define a syndrome characterized by chronic, recurring, abnormal brain electrical activity that causes seizures.

SYSTEM-SPECIFIC ASSESSMENTS "CAESAR"	DIET	EQUIPMENT	PLANS/INTERVENTIONS	HEALTH PROMOTION
		FIRST-DO	PRIORITY INTERVENTIONS	
Consciousness level	• NPO following a seizure	• Oxygen	• Position on side following a seizure. (See *Priority Interventions: "PROTECTS" from injury due to seizures on the next page.*)	• Educate client to identify triggers resulting in a seizure; avoid alcohol.
Affected body part(s)–where seizure started and the progression		• Entubation equipment		• Review aura to assist with a plan for safety.
Eyes for pupil response		• Suction, airway		• Educate client regarding safe medication administration. May not stop abruptly.
Salivation is altered				• Consult with counselor to assist in coping.
Alteration in skin color and urination (incontinence)				• Consult with social service if needs financial support with meds.
Reduced muscle tone				• If seizure affects employment, refer to social agencies for vocational review and evaluation.
				• If seizure affects a school-age child, then this should be reported to the disability office, so an intervention can be done to assist with an Individualized Education Program (IEP).
				• Review importance of wearing medical alert bracelet or having an identification card.
				• Safety Risk Assessment prior to discharge.

Summary for Seizure Interventions: Reduce "HARM" An Insanely Easy Tip!

Harm protection; remove unsafe objects.

Airway patency (suction, ambu bag, mask, airway equipment, etc.).

Restraining is INAPPROPRIATE. Record and observe event.

Mouth should NEVER have anything placed in it during a seizure.

Monitor compliance with taking anticonvulsant medications. Teach danger of stopping abruptly.

Priority Interventions: "PROTECTS" From Injury Due to Seizures

SAFETY is always a concern with any client. The great news is that while we are reviewing these seizure precautions for clients with intracranial regulatory problems, such as a head injury, brain tumor, and intracranial bleed, these precautions also apply to any client who is at a high risk for seizures. The question is, who are these clients?

1. Syndrome of Inappropriate Antidiuretic Hormone (SIADH)
2. Diabetes Insipidus (DI)
3. Hypo/Hypernatemia
4. Pregnancy-Induced Hypertension (OB client)
5. Epilepsy
6. Febrile seizures for an infant
7. Heat Stroke
8. Infection resulting in sepsis with hyerthemia

If you have not studied these medical diagnoses, we will refer you to these interventions to assist in continuing to make the links to this care. *Remember, it takes repeating information over and over (approximately eight times) to be able to move the information into your long-term memory!* As a client advocate, our priority goals are to always **"PROTECT"** clients from injury and to promote SAFETY!

P Protect privacy and protect from injury (support head if on floor) and reposition furniture for client safety. Protect from falls.

R Review respiratory status. Restrictive clothing should be loosened. Restraints are not used. Remain with client who is having a seizure. Do not force anything into mouth or open jaw during a seizure. Do not use padded tongue blades.

O Oral pharyngeal airway; maintain patency.

T Turn on side to ↓ risk of aspiration after the seizure.

E Equipment available, such as suction, ambu bag, airway, and padded side rails (bed low position). Educate client regarding aura (sensation prior to seizure) to assist with a plan to provide safety. Review post-ictal (the period immediately following the seizure), so client understands what is to be expected (lethargy, weakness, etc.) following a seizure.

C Check VS, NC, injuries, reorient post seizure.

T The onset and duration of seizure, assessments of client prior to, during, and after the seizure *(i.e., LOC, color, activity, location of where it started, progression, etc.)* should be documented. Reorient client after the seizure.

S Suction oral secretions. Seizure precautions include bed in lowest position and padding side rails to prevent injury; equipment at bedside.

Exceptions and Additions by Diseases

Pathophysiology: Neurological Transmission
Myasthenia Gravis

Myasthenia Gravis is a progressive neuromuscular disease. This can be from a decrease in the acetylcholine level at the receptor sites in the neuromuscular junction. This can result in a disturbance in the transmission of the nerve impulses resulting in skeletal muscle weakness. Myasthenia gravis literally means **"grave muscle weakness."** Muscle weakness can improve with rest and worsen with increased activity.

		FIRST-DO PRIORITY INTERVENTIONS		
SYSTEM-SPECIFIC ASSESSMENTS "WEAK"	**DIET**	**EQUIPMENT**	**PLANS/INTERVENTIONS "WEAK"**	**HEALTH PROMOTION**
Weakness of diaphragm, **RESPIRATORY**, and intercostal muscles. Assess the progress of the descending muscle weakness.	• Small, frequent, high-calorie meals and schedule at time when medications are peaking.	• Oxygen • Endotracheal intubation equipment	**W**atch status—**RESPIRATORY** system. Assess the progress of the descending muscle weakness.	• Educate client to take meds at the same time each day and with food.
Eyes—assess to determine if client is unable to close.	• Use thickener in liquids as necessary.	• Suctioning equipment	**E**yes—May need to patch or tape eyes shut at night to prevent damage to the cornea. Keep meds at specified times which is usually 4 times per day. Lubricate with eye drops during the day and ointment at night if unable to close eyes completely.	• Eat within 45 minutes of taking the meds to strengthen chewing and reduce the risk for aspiration.
Assess swallowing reflex.		• Bag valve mask	**A**ssess swallowing.	• Consult physical therapy for medical equipment if needed.
Keep complications away and monitor for **RESPIRATORY COMPROMISE and FAILURE!!!!!** (*See next page for comparison of Myasthenic Crisis and Cholinergic Crisis.*)		• Assistive devices	**K**eep complications away; adapt energy conservation measures; allow for rest periods. Monitor for RESPIRATORY COMPROMISE and FAILURE.	• Consult with occupational therapy for assistive devices if needed for ADLs. • Support communication and swallowing by consulting with speech and language therapist. • Perform a comprehensive home-risk assessment

INSANELY EASY TIP! Remember "Mind to Ground" for the direction of the progression (descending) of the muscle weakness! This is easy since Myasthenia Gravis starts with an "**M** and **G**" as well.

CHOLINERGIC CRISIS (Overmedicated)

T witching of the muscles progressing to point of respiratory muscle weakness (mechanical ventilator)

W atch for cholinergic findings such as hypersecretions (nausea, diarrhea, respiratory secretions) and hypermotility (abdominal cramps)

I ncrease in the (anticholinesterase)— more cholinergic findings)

T ensilon has NO POSITIVE effects on signs and can actually worsen findings

C linical findings decrease with anticholinergic medication, such as atropine

H ypotension

Atropine may be administered!

MYASTHENIC CRISIS (Undermedicated)

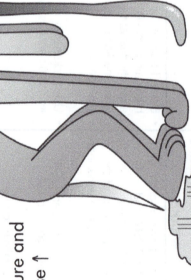

R espiratory muscle weakness (may require mechanical ventilator)

E valuate for Myasthenic findings (weakness, incontinence, fatigue; absent cough/swallow reflex)

S ymptoms decrease temporarily with administration of Tensilon

P ressure and pulse ↑

Neostigmine may be administered!

BOTTOM LINE: If you only remember one piece of information from this page, remember the priority assessment is to assess the RESPIRATORY system for depression! Safety is always the priority, and we start with BREATHING!!

Pathophysiology: Neurological Transmission
Guillain-Barré Syndrome (GBS)

Guillain-Barré Syndrome is an acute, rapidly progressing motor neuropathy involving the nerve roots in the spinal cord and medulla. This inflammatory, demyelinating disorder can result in edema, and compression of the nerve roots leading to a rapidly ascending paralysis. Motor and sensory impairment may occur.

FIRST-DO   PRIORITY   INTERVENTIONS

System-Specific Assessments "WEAK"	Diet	Equipment	Plans/Interventions "WEAK"	Health Promotion
Weakness of diaphragm, RESPIRATORY, and intercostal muscles. Assess airway. Assess the progression of the ascending muscle weakness.	• Small, frequent, high-calorie meals and schedule at time when medications are peaking.	• Oxygen • Endotracheal intubation equipment	**W**atch status—RESPIRATORY system. Assess the progression of the ascending muscle weakness.	• Provide both family and client psychological support.
Evaluate bowel sounds, I & O, ECG, and blood pressure.	• Use thickener in liquids as necessary.	• Suctioning equipment	**E**valuate for involvement of the autonomic nervous system: • Paralytic ileus • Orthostatic hypotension • Urinary retention • Cardiac dysrhythmias • Hypertension	• Provide both family and client information about disease and care.
Assess swallowing reflex and difficulty talking. (CN VII).		• Bag valve mask		• Prevent complications with depression by active listening and support with a counselor.
Keep complications away and monitor for hypoxia if respiratory muscles become involved. Monitor changes in the respiratory assessment. Respiratory support by assisting with mechanical ventilation. Suction and airway equipment at the bedside.	• NPO if swallowing and coughing reflexes are involved.	• Assistive devices	**A**ssess cough and swallow reflexes frequently. Remain with client when eating; have suction equipment available.	• Provide simple explanations of procedures.
Assess risk factor: cause is frequently a history of an acute illness.			**K**eep complications away and monitor for hypoxia if respiratory muscles become involved. To prevent complications of depression provide simple explanations of procedures. Explain that complete recovery is anticipated. Provide support psychologically during assisted ventilation. Support family with knowledge of disease.	• Explain that complete recovery is anticipated. • Provide support during assisted ventilation. • Support family with knowledge of disease.

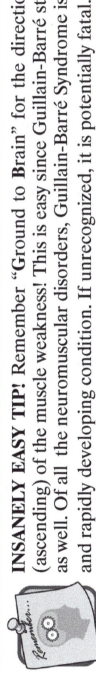

INSANELY EASY TIP! Remember "**Ground to Brain**" for the direction of the progression (ascending) of the muscle weakness! This is easy since Guillain-Barré starts with a "**G and B**" as well. Of all the neuromuscular disorders, Guillain-Barré Syndrome is the most progressive and rapidly developing condition. If unrecognized, it is potentially fatal.

Exceptions and Additions by Diseases

Pathophysiology: Brain Neoplasm

Brain tumors can occur in any part of the brain, and can be classified based on the origin of the tissue or cell. The various types of brain tumors include the benign meningiomas (meninges), malignant gliomas (neuroglia cells), acoustic neuromas (acoustic cranial nerve), and pituitary adenomas. **Supratentorial** tumors occur in the cerebral hemispheres. **Infratentorial** tumors are below the tentorium and include tumors in the cerebellum and brain stem. Brain tumors can apply pressure to the brain tissue surrounding the tumor. Regardless of the type or site of the brain tumor, increased intracranial pressure (ICP), cerebral edema, and other neurological deficits may occur.

System-Specific Assessments "HEADS"	Diet	Equipment	Plans/Interventions "BRAINS"	Health Promotion
		FIRST-DO PRIORITY INTERVENTIONS		
Headache is most severe in AM; affected by position	• NPO progressing to clear liquids.	• Pen light to evaluate pupils	**B**ed (Head) elevated to semi to low-Fowler's for client who had supratentorial surgery; if had infratentorial surgery, then bed should be flat and position on either side; avoid positioning in supine. Maintain head and neck in midline. Never in Trendelenburg. Avoid sudden movements.	• Answer any questions regarding pre- and post-op care for a client with a craniotomy.
Emesis with or without nausea; progressively becoming projectile. Edema of the optic disc (papilledema)		• Suction	**R**estful, calm environment; reduce edema around medulla by keeping NPO for 24 hours and ↓ vomiting following a craniotomy. Regulate fluids by offering clear liquids after awake and swallow and gag reflex return. Closely monitor I & O (SIADH: DI). *(Refer to Endocrine System: Posterior Pituitary gland for specifics.)*	• Initiate support from support groups.
Evidence of a CSF leak from nose or ears (fluid tests positive for glucose)		• Ambu bag	**A**ssess Na⁺ level and I & O; posturing; PERRLA; VS (monitor for respiratory acidosis, ↑PaCO₂); O₂ sat; ICP; NC (Glasgow Coma Scale); VS/characteristics of headache; cranial nerve assessments; carefully evaluate LOC; increasing lethargy or irritability may be indicative of IICP. Avoid "COUGH."	• Refer to social services for ongoing support with resources.
Alteration in F & E (Na⁺) and osmolarity due to risk for diabetes insipidus (SIADH); I & O			**I**mmobility *(refer to concept Mobility)*	
Deterioration in LOC; Glasgow Coma Scale, neurological checks: dilated, pinpoint or asymmetric pupils *(refer to Cushing's Triad)*; dizziness and vertigo			**N**ote if there is a CSF fluid leak, keep bed in semi-Fowler's and monitor for meningitis (nuchal rigidity). Report to HCP. *(See Meningitis in the Exceptions and Additions by Disease in this chapter.)* Note temperature changes: when the hypothalamus is involved there may be complications with the temperature regulation and/or the respiratory system.	• Refer to physical and speech therapy.
Seizures: focal or generalized. Sensory disturbances: language, visual, coordination			**S**eizure precautions *(refer to Priority Interventions: "PROTECTS" from Injury due to Seizures).* Support pain with appropriate pain relief. Avoid narcotic analgesics. Acetaminophen is frequently used.	• Refer to occupational therapy.

Pathophysiology: Brain Neoplasm (Craniotomy)

Craniotomy is a surgical opening in the skull to perform a complete or partial resection of the brain tumor.

FIRST-DO   PRIORITY   INTERVENTIONS

SYSTEM-SPECIFIC ASSESSMENTS "NEURO"	DIET	EQUIPMENT	PLANS/INTERVENTIONS AFTER A CRANIOTOMY "POST-OP CARE"	HEALTH PROMOTION
Neurological Status: Glasgow Coma Scale (LOC) **E**valuate the vital signs; evaluate pain **U**nderstand the pain level so this can be treated adequately **R**emember, the HOB should be elevated 30° and placed in a neutral position. Risks are seizures and post-op bleeding **O**mit straining from a bowel movement	• NPO initially.	• Pen light to evaluate pupils • Suction • Ambu bag • Airway	**P**rocedure—Explain to client and family the procedure (HCP) and answer questions that are within the scope of practice. **O**utcomes and questions should be written to make certain all are answered. **S**upport client and family and encourage significant other to be present. **T**he Living Will and Durable Power for Healthcare Decisions should be completed. **O**mit aspirin for at least 72 hours prior to the procedure. **P**rovider of care needs to know if taking any complementary or alternative meds. **C**heck vital signs per protocol. **A**dequate treatment of pain. **R**isks: Post-op bleeding and seizures. **E**levate HOB 30° and place client in a neutral position.	• Answer any questions regarding pre- and post-op care for a client with a craniotomy. • Initiate support from support groups. • Refer to social services for ongoing support with resources. • Refer to physical and speech therapy. • Refer to occupational therapy.

Exceptions and Additions by Diseases

Pathophysiology: Degenerative Alzheimer's Disease (Dementia)

Alzheimer's is a nonreversible type of dementia that progressively develops over many years. Alzheimer's is characterized by memory loss, problems with judgment, and changes in personality.

Dementia is defined as multiple cognitive deficits that impair memory and can affect language, motor skills, and/or abstract thinking. Seventy-five percent of dementia is Alzheimer's disease.

FIRST-DO   PRIORITY   INTERVENTIONS

SYSTEM-SPECIFIC ASSESSMENTS	DIET	EQUIPMENT	PLANS/INTERVENTIONS "MEMORY"	HEALTH PROMOTION

Refer to stages on the next page.	• Check swallow reflex prior to any po nutrition.	• Install door locks that cannot be opened easily; alarms on doors.
		
		• Keep a lock on water heater and the thermostat, and keep water temperature down to a safe level.
		
		• Good lighting on stairs.
		
		• Handrails on stairs. Mark edges of steps with colored tape.
		
		• Mattress on the floor.
		
		• Secure electrical cords to baseboards.
		
		• Handrails in the bathroom, bedside, and tub. Shower mat in bathtub.
			Memory–assess cognition
			Environment structured
			Memory trained
			Overstimulation is out; ↓ it
			Routine schedules
			Yes, safety is important: **"The Six Fs"**
			
			   Fall prevention
			   Fatigue support
			   Function optimally
			   Family support
			   Free environment from clutter
			   Facilitate communication
				• Fall prevention
				
				• Social services
				
				• Occupational therapy
				
				• Home health for safety
				
				• Support groups for family members and client
				
				• Perform a comprehensive home-risk assessment

Seven Stages of Alzheimer's Disease

Alzheimer's Stages	Clinical Findings
Stage 1: No impairment	No memory issues
Stage 2: Very mild cognitive decline	Forgetful of everyday objects (eyeglasses, wallet, etc.); don't know friends
Stage 3: Mild cognitive decline	May be measurable in a detailed medical exam or clinical testing (i.e., difficulty in remembering names/words. Difficulty in social situations.)
Stage 4: Moderate cognitive decline	Limited memory of recent occasions, current events; difficulty paying bills and managing money.
Stage 5: Moderately severe cognitive decline	Inability to recall important details such as telephone number, address, etc. Memory of SELF and FAMILY remains intact. Needs help with ADLs. Disoriented as to place/time.
Stage 6: Severe cognitive decline	Memory continues to worsen. Loss of awareness of recent events. May recall own name, but not personal history. May experience significant personality changes such as delusions, hallucinations, etc. Wanders. Requires assistance with ADLs. Sleep/wake cycle is disrupted. Episodes of renal and urinary incontinence are increased.
Stage 7: Very severe cognitive decline	Unable to respond to environment, speak, and control movement. Speech is unrecognizable; urinary incontinence; impaired swallowing and unable to eat without assistance; ataxia.

(Alzheimer's Association National Office, 2013)

The ultimate priorities of care for clients with Alzheimer's and any form of dementia are to maintain SAFETY throughout each stage and to promote INDEPENDENCE as long as possible!

Exceptions and Additions by Diseases

Pathophysiology: Degenerative Multiple Sclerosis

Multiple sclerosis is an an autoimmune disorder that develops plaques that damage the white matter of the central nervous system (CNS). The damage to the myelin sheath can cause an interference with the transmission of impulses between the CNS and the body.

SYSTEM-SPECIFIC ASSESSMENTS "THE SIX MS"	FIRST-DO PRIORITY INTERVENTIONS			
	DIET	EQUIPMENT	ACTIVITY/POSITION, PROCEDURE	HEALTH PROMOTION
Mobility is altered (risk for falls) **M**ovements (involuntary) **M**uscle weakness in arms, legs, speaking **M**ood (depression) **M**onitor respiratory/renal function (i.e., assess for respiratory/UTI infection) **M**onitor cough reflex	• Check swallow reflex prior to any PO nutrition. • Provide food that is easy to chew.	• Assistive devices as needed.	Assist to function **INDEPENDENTLY** as long as possible **"The Seven Fs"** • **F**all prevention • **F**atigue support • **F**unction optimally • **F**amily Support • **F**ree environment from clutter • **F**acilitate communication • **F**ever (monitor and manage) due to being prone to infection	• Fall prevention • Occupational therapy • Home health • Support groups for family members and client • Perform a comprehensive home-risk assessment

Priority System-Specific Assessments for Multiple Sclerosis The "Ds"

Diplopia

Dysphagia

Dysarthria (slurred and nasal speech)

Decrease in hearing acuity

Decrease in muscle tone (spasticity)

Decrease in muscle strength–weak (ataxia)

Decrease in bowel function (constipation)

Decrease in bladder function (areflexia, urgency, nocturia)

Decrease in cognition (loss of memory, judgment is impaired)

Decrease in chewing

Decrease in respiratory system strength

Decrease in ability to exert for prolonged periods of time

First-Do Priority Interventions:
"SAVE" Client From Long-Term Complications of MS

S Support due to MS being a debilitating condition. Review sources of support (friends, family, spiritual figures, support groups).

Speech patterns (fatigue when talking); support with periods of rest. Facilitate effective communication (dysarthria) by using a communication board.

Swallowing—Monitor for aspiration and provide food that is easy to chew; evaluate cough and swallowing reflexes; observe client when taking fluids.

Skin integrity—Monitor and prevent pressure areas and complications with immobility *(refer to concept Tissue and Skin Integrity and concept Mobility)*.

Safe home and hospital environments should be maintained by ↓ injury (i.e., walk with assistive devices, wide base of support, skin precautions).

A Activity tolerance—conserve energy by clustering care and planning for periods of rest.

Adequate respiratory function—Prevent respiratory tract infection. Prevent aspiration (i.e., sit up with meals); evaluate cough reflex.

V Visual acuity—apply alternating eye patches to treat diplopia. Teach scanning techniques.

E Encourage fluids and additional measures to decrease risk of the development of a urinary tract infection. Assist with bladder elimination (intermittent self-catheterization, bladder pacemaker, Credé maneuver {apply manual pressure on abdomen over the bladder to expel urine}).

Home-Care Management

S Safety measures due to decreased sensation (i.e., wear protective clothing in winter, evaluate temperature of bathwater, avoid heating pads and constrictive clothing).

E Encourage physical therapy to maintain muscle function and decrease spasticity. Encourage family to assist with self-care needs.

L Learn meds and undesirable effects; learn measures to maintain voiding; may need to learn self-catheterization.

F Frequent relapses are associated with an increase in physiological and psychological stress.

Exceptions and Additions by Diseases

Pathophysiology: Degenerative
Parkinson's Disease

Parkinson's Disease is a progressive neurological disorder that affects motor function and is debilitating. Four symptoms are characterized by this disease: bradykinesia (slow movement), muscle rigidity, a postural instability, and tremors. Due to the overstimulation of the basal ganglia by acetylcholine, the four symptoms occur. The acetylcholine and dopamine that are secreted in the body produce inhibitory and excitatory effects on the muscles. The decreased dopamine production is a result of the overstimulation of the basal ganglia by acetylcholine due to the degeneration of the sustantia nigra. The acetylcholine dominates, resulting in making it difficult to control smooth muscles. The treatment of Parkinson's is to increase the dopamine or decrease the acetylcholinine in the client's brain.

FIRST-DO   PRIORITY   INTERVENTIONS

System-Specific Assessments "The S's"	Diet	Equipment	Plans/Interventions "MOBILE"	Health Promotion
Stooped posturing	• Check swallow reflex prior to any PO nutrition.	• Electric razors	**M**obile as long as possible	• Fall prevention
Slow, shuffling, and propulsive gait		• Safe environment—no throw rugs, have effective lighting, etc.	**O**ral pharyngeal assess for swallowing prior to starting dietary intake	• Occupational therapy
Swallowing and chewing difficulty	• Smaller, more frequent meals.	• Suction equipment nearby due to risk for aspiration	**"BRAT"** Clinical findings: **B**radykinesia, **R**igidity, **A**kinesia, and **T**remors *(Focus on fall precautions)*	• Speech therapy
Swing in moods	• Add commercial thickener to thicken food.			• Dietary support
Shows progressive impairment with ADLs			**I**nteraction (communication); assist to function independently as long as possible	• Home health
Slow, monotonous speech				• Support groups for family members and client
Shows a mask-like expression			**L**OC—cognitive and mental state	• Perform a comprehensive home-risk assessment
Symptoms (autonomic)—orthostatic hypotension, flushing, diaphoresis			**E**valuate for aspiration, pneumonia, and memory deficits	

PATHOPHYSIOLOGY

Pathophysiology: Degenerative
Amyotrophic Lateral Sclerosis

Amyotrophic Lateral Sclerosis (ALS) is a degenerative neurological disorder of the upper and lower motor neurons that is a rapidly progressive and typically fatal disease. ALS can result in the deterioration and death of the motor neurons. Progressive paralysis and wasting of the muscles can eventually result in respiratory paralysis and death. Cognition is not typically affected. The cause can be genetic. At this time, there is no cure. Death usually occurs from respiratory failure within two to five years of the initial clinical findings.

FIRST-DO PRIORITY INTERVENTIONS

SYSTEM-SPECIFIC ASSESSMENTS "THE Ds"	DIET	EQUIPMENT	PLANS/INTERVENTIONS "ABCs"	HEALTH PROMOTION
Decrease in muscle strength **D**ecrease in muscles (atrophy) **D**ysphagia **D**ysarthria **D**eep-tendon reflexes: hyperreflexia *Note: pneumonia can be caused by respiratory weakness and paralysis leading to ineffective airway exchange. Assess respiratory system routinely and administer antibiotics as prescribed.*	• Meet nutritional needs for calories, fiber, and fluids. • When no longer able to swallow, provide enteral nutrition as prescribed.	• Ventilator assistance later in disease progression as needed.	**A**irway, ABGs, administer O₂, suction prn **A**ssess establishment of advanced directives **B**reathe, turn, cough q 2 hrs **C**ommunication—facilitate (board/therapist) Depression/coping—assess Ensure safety with oral intake; assess swallowing reflex. Energy conserving measures Fluids, thicken Give enteral nutrition as prescribed when no longer able to swallow Head of bed 45° Incentive spirometry/chest physiotherapy; intermittent positive-pressure ventilation as needed	• Initiate referral to the dietician. • Initiate referral to social service. • Initiate referral to physical therapy. • Initiate referral to psychologist. • Initiate referral to occupational therapy. • Review extended care in the home or long-term care facility. • Consider a referral for a speech therapist for speech and swallowing issues. • During terminal phase, consider hospice for support. • Spiritual support.

Concept Similarities for Degenerative Disorders

	SYSTEM-SPECIFIC ASSESSMENTS FOR CONCEPTS			
Degenerative Disorders	**Safety/ Mobility** Risk for Falls	**Communication** Unrecognizable Speech	**Oxygenation/ Nutrition** Depressed Swallowing/ Gag Reflex	**Infection Control** Risk for Pneumonia
Later Stages of Alzheimer's Disease	X	X	X	X
Multiple Sclerosis	X	X	X	X
Parkinson's Disease	X	X	X	X
Amyotrophic Lateral Sclerosis (ALS)	X	X	X	X

The priority goal for the nursing care is to assist client to remain INDEPENDENT as long as possible!

Pathophysiology: Inflammation
Meningitis

Meningitis is an acute viral or bacterial infection that causes inflammation of the meninges—the membranes that protect the brain and the spinal cord. Several organisms can result in meningitis. *Viral* or *aseptic meningitis* is the most common and typically does not need treatment. Fungal meningitis is very rare; however, it is common in clients with AIDS. *Bacterial*, or *septic meningitis*, is less common, but is a more severe and highly communicable disease with a high mortality rate. The quicker care is initiated the better the outcome for the client.

Kernig's Sign: When client attempts to extend the leg after thigh is flexed and there is pain or resistance at the knee and the hamstring muscles, this is diagnostic of the Kernig's sign.

Brudzinski's Sign: When the neck is flexed, there is reflex flexion of the hips.

System-Specific Assessments "NECKS"	Diet	First-Do Equipment	Priority Plans/Interventions "MENINGES"	Interventions Health Promotion
Nuchal rigidity **E**levated fever, HR (signs of shock), excruciating headache, eyes–photophobia **C**hills, cranial nerves involved **K**ernig's or Brudzinski's sign positive **S**eizures	• Young children will have a change in feeding and experience nausea and vomiting. • Limit fluids due to cerebral edema.	• Personal protective equipment: mask, gloves.	**M**onitor "NECK". **E**nvironmental stimuli ↓. **N**onopoid analgesics for HA to avoid masking LOC. **I**solation precautions per protocol until antibiotics have been administered for 24 hours or as ordered. Implement fever-reduction measures. **N**ote to report meningococcal infections to public health department. **G**ive antibiotics for appropriate organism as prescribed by HCP. **E**ducate client, family, and staff about infection-control practice, droplet precautions. **S**afety, such as seizure precautions. Support before, during, and after a spinal tap.	• Infection-control principles per protocol *(refer to concept Infection Control)*. • Report per protocol to CDC. • Haemophilus influenza type b (Hib) vaccine–infants should receive this for bacterial meningitis. • Pneumococcal polysaccharide vaccine (PPSV)–vaccinate adults who are immunocompromised, have a chronic disease, who smoke cigarettes, reside in an extended-living care facility. Follow CDC guidelines for revaccination. • Meningococcal vaccine (MCV4) (Neisseria meningitides)–adolescents should receive the vaccine on schedule and prior to living in a residential setting in college.

INTERDISCIPLINARY TEAM FOR ALL CLIENTS WITH "ALTERATION IN THE INTRACRANIAL REGULATION"

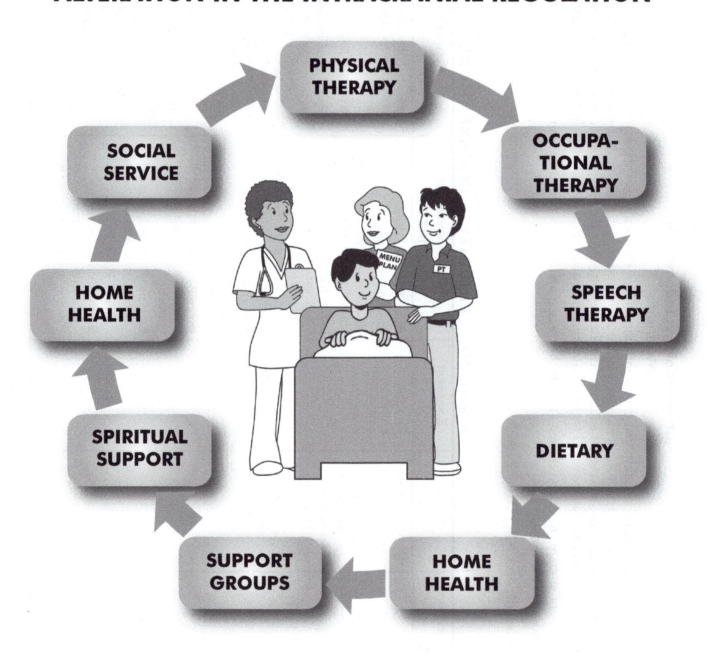

Clinical Decision-Making Exercises

1. During the evaluation, which assessment indicates an early sign of increased intracranial pressure for a client newly diagnosed with a cerebral vascular accident (CVA)?

   ① An alteration in the ability to answer questions and respond to verbal stimuli.

   ② Client has consensual response of pupils.

   ③ Decorticate posturing.

   ④ Heart Rate–50 bpm, BP–190/60.

2. Which nursing interventions are appropriate to help decrease the development of increased intracranial pressure for a client with a head injury? *Select all that apply.*

   ① Assessment of client's neurological status.

   ② Maintain head in midline neutral position with HOB elevated to 30°.

   ③ Keep client's room quiet and dark.

   ④ Position client with HOB 20°.

   ⑤ Administration of acetaminophen (Tylenol) for a temperature of 100.1°F.

3. What would be the priority nursing intervention for a young adult with the diagnosis of a closed-head injury following an accident who is being admitted to the Neuro Unit? Client is alert, oriented, but lethargic and has clear liquid draining from the nose.

   ① Apply a packing in the nose to prevent further drainage.

   ② Reposition from side to side.

   ③ Maintain the head of the bed elevated.

   ④ Encourage client to blow nose to remove secretions.

4. The nurse is conducting a physical assessment of a client with a neurological complication. What is the appropriate instruction to give the client to assess the function of the client's cranial nerve XI?

   ① "Follow my fingers with your eyes."

   ② "Stick out your tongue."

   ③ "Shrug your shoulders."

   ④ "Smile."

5. Which one of these plans indicates safe care for a client who has dysphagia?

   ① Provide a clear-liquid diet.

   ② Place food on the affected side of the mouth to minimize aspiration.

   ③ Provide thickened liquids.

   ④ Teach client to hyper-extend neck to swallow.

6. When admitting a client with Amyotrophic Lateral Sclerosis (ALS) who has difficulty communicating, the nurse is attempting to obtain an initial assessment. Which question by the nurse is most appropriate when addressing the client?

   ① "Do you ever have any difficulty breathing or swallowing?"

   ② "Please describe which ADLs you are having difficulty completing?"

   ③ "Please explain how long you have been experiencing these symptoms and when they first began."

   ④ "Can you describe the sensations you are having in your chest?"

7. What is the best room assignment for a client with increased intracranial pressure?

    ① A room near the busy nurses' station in order to assure close observation.

    ② A room with another client that is mobile and active to assist in preventing social isolation.

    ③ A room with a client that is in for observation due to seizure activity.

    ④ A room that is quiet with a decrease in environmental stimulation.

8. Which one of these documentations in the client's chart indicates an understanding of the nursing care priority for a client diagnosed with amyotrophic lateral sclerosis (ALS)?

    ① Client discussed concerns and feelings regarding the challenges with having a chronic disease.

    ② Reviewed with client the importance of having a plan for the future when cognition is affected by the disease.

    ③ Client turning, coughing, and deep breathing every 2 hours along with incentive spirometry and chest physiotherapy.

    ④ Client repositioned in bed every 4 hours to prevent skin breakdown.

9. A client with a history of Myasthenia Gravis is presenting with a HR of 112 BPM, RR 24/min with accessory muscle use, anxiety and restlessness. Which of these would be appropriate immediate nursing interventions? *Select all that apply.*

    ① Elevate HOB.

    ② Administer Lasix 40 mg IV.

    ③ O_2 per MD order.

    ④ Teach client the importance of wearing a medical identification bracelet.

    ⑤ Apply a lubricating eye drop.

10. For a client with increased intracranial pressure (IICP), which of these nursing actions by the LPN would require intervention by the charge nurse?

    ① Encourages client to cough and suctions orally q 1-2 hours.

    ② Removes restrictive clothing.

    ③ Restricts fluids.

    ④ Maintains the HOB at 30°.

1. During the evaluation, **which assessment indicates an early sign of increased intracranial pressure for a client newly diagnosed with a cerebral vascular accident (CVA)?**

   ① **CORRECT: An alteration in the ability to answer questions and respond to verbal stimuli. Changes in the LOC are the earliest change with increased intracranial pressure.**

   ② INCORRECT: Client has consensual response of pupils. While pupillary equality is an important assessment, it is not the earliest sign.

   ③ INCORRECT: Decorticate posturing. This would occur later as the intracranial pressure increases.

   ④ INCORRECT: Heart Rate–50, BP–190/60. The vital signs are later changes.

The strategy is to organize the system-specific assessments between the early and the late signs. No matter what the cause of the increased intracranial pressure, the earliest sign of a change is a change in the LOC. The Glasgow Coma Scale is a tool that will assist with this assessment. The key for safe care is to be able to recognize early changes to prevent the progression to later complications.

Physiological Adaptation: Perform focused assessment

2. Which nursing interventions are appropriate to help **decrease** the **development of increased intracranial pressure** for a client with a head injury? *Select all that apply.*

   ① INCORRECT: Assessment of client's neurological status. This will do nothing to prevent IICP.

   ② **CORRECT: Maintain head in midline neutral position with HOB 30°. This will help promote venous drainage and ↓ cerebral volume.**

   ③ **CORRECT: Keep client's room quiet and dark. Decrease in stimulation will decrease an increase in the ICP.**

   ④ INCORRECT: Position client with HOB 20°. This will not decrease the development of IICP.

   ⑤ **CORRECT: Administration of acetaminophen (Tylenol) for a temperature of 100.1°F. A temperature will cause IICP.**

The strategy for answering this question is to organize the nursing care around the mnemonic **PERFUSE. HEADS** will assist you in organizing the assessments for any client that is at risk for IICP. This will apply to any client with a head injury, brain tumor, etc. (Refer to Pathophysiology Chart for specifics.)

Physiological Adaptation: Manage the care of a client with alteration in cerebral perfusion

3. What would be the **priority nursing intervention** for a young adult who is being admitted to the Neuro Unit with the diagnosis of a **closed-head injury** following an accident? Client is alert, oriented, but lethargic and has **clear liquid draining from nose.**

   ① INCORRECT: Apply packing in the nose to prevent further drainage. This is not necessary.

   ② INCORRECT: Reposition from side to side. The HOB should be elevated.

   ③ **CORRECT: Maintain the head of the bed elevated.**

   ④ INCORRECT: Encourage client to blow nose to remove secretions. This will cause IICP.

The strategy is to remember to prevent further pressure in the head. Elevating the HOB will help promote venous drainage and ↓ cerebral volume. "PERFUSE" will assist you in organizing the nursing care for clients who are at risk for IICP. Once there is a CSF leak, then it is important for the nurse to assess ongoing for meningitis, since there is an opening for bacteria due to the cerebral spinal fluid leak.

Physiological Adaptation: Manage the care of a client with alteration in cerebral perfusion.

4. The nurse is conducting a **physical assessment** of a client with a neurological complication. What is the appropriate instruction to give the client to assess the **function of the client's cranial nerve XI**?

    ① INCORRECT: "Follow my fingers with your eyes." This evaluates cranial nerves 3, 4, and 6.

    ② INCORRECT: "Stick out your tongue." This evaluates cranial nerve number 12.

    ③ **CORRECT: "Shrug your shoulders." This is how to evaluate cranial nerve number XI (spinal accessory).**

    ④ INCORRECT: "Smile." This would involve the facial nerve (number 7).

The strategy is to refer to the cranial nerve chart. There is a strategy for each of these to assist in remembering. For cranial nerve XI, imagine the numeral 1 on each of your shoulders and as you shrug your shoulders the 1 should stay in place on each shoulder and not fall off.

Physiological Adaptation: Perform focused assessment.

5. Which one of these plans indicates **safe care for a client who has dysphagia**?

    ① INCORRECT: Provide a clear-liquid diet. This can cause aspiration.

    ② INCORRECT: Place food on the affected side of the mouth to minimize aspiration. It should be on unaffected side.

    ③ **CORRECT: Provide thickened liquids to prevent aspiration.**

    ④ INCORRECT: Teach client to hyper-extend neck to swallow. The neck should be flexed.

The strategy is to prevent aspiration for any client, especially if there is a complication with dysphagia. Thickened liquids will decrease the risk for aspiration.

Basic Care and Comfort: Manage the client's nutritional intake.

6. When admitting a client with **Amyotrophic Lateral Sclerosis (ALS)** who has **difficulty communicating**, the nurse is attempting to obtain an initial assessment. Which question by the nurse is **most appropriate** when addressing the client?

    ① **CORRECT: "Do you ever have any difficulty breathing or swallowing?" The priority is airway and respiratory system.**

    ② INCORRECT: "Please describe which ADLs you are having difficulty completing." Not a priority.

    ③ INCORRECT: "Please explain how long you have been experiencing these symptoms and when they first began." Not a priority.

    ④ INCORRECT: "Can you describe the sensations you are having in your chest?" Not a priority.

The strategy is to use the priority principle of the **"ABCs"**, since these clients can get into problems with pneumonia resulting in difficulty breathing or swallowing. This principle of the **"ABCs"** will assist in answering questions about prioritizing with many clients. While the other options need to be addressed, they are not the priority. Refer to concept Priority for specific principles for answering questions.

Physiological Adaptation: Perform focused assessment.

7. What is the **best room assignment** for a client with **increased intracranial pressure**?

    ① INCORRECT: A room near the busy nurses' station will be too much stimulation.

    ② INCORRECT: A room with another client that is mobile and active to assist in preventing social isolation will be too much stimulation.

    ③ INCORRECT: A room with a client that is in for observation due to seizure activity will be too much stimulation.

    ④ **CORRECT: A room that is quiet with a decrease in the environmental stimulation will be effective in decreasing IICP.**

The strategy for this question is to remember that with any client who has IICP the goal is to decrease the environmental stimuli to prevent complications.

Safety and Infection Control: Room assignments.

Physiological Adaptation: Manage the care of a client with alteration in cerebral perfusion.

8. Which one of these **documentations** in the client's chart indicates an understanding of the **nursing care priority for a client diagnosed with amyotrophic lateral sclerosis** (ALS)?

   ① INCORRECT: Client discussed concerns and feelings regarding the challenges with having a chronic disease. While this is important, it is not the priority.

   ② INCORRECT: Reviewed with client the importance of having a plan for the future when cognition is affected by the disease. While this is important, it is not the priority.

   ③ **CORRECT: Client turning, coughing, and deep breathing every 2 hours along with incentive spirometry and chest physiotherapy. This is the priority to prevent pneumonia.**

   ④ INCORRECT: Client repositioned in bed every 4 hours to prevent skin breakdown. Not frequent enough.

The strategy is to use the "**ABCs**" to assist in prioritizing. Pneumonia can be caused by respiratory weakness and paralysis leading to ineffective airway exchange. Assess respiratory system routinely and assist with turning, coughing, and deep breathing every 2 hours along with the incentive spirometry and chest physiotherapy.

Physiological Adaptation: Provide pulmonary hygiene (i.e., chest physiotherapy, incentive spirometry).

9. A client with a history of **Myasthenia Gravis** is presenting with a **HR of 112 bpm, RR 24/min with accessory muscle use, anxiety and restlessness**. Which of these would be **appropriate immediate nursing interventions?** *Select all that apply.*

   ① **CORRECT: Elevate HOB. This will assist with lung expansion.**

   ② INCORRECT: Administer Lasix 40 mg IV. There is no indication of fluid overload.

   ③ **CORRECT: O₂ per MD order. This addresses the clinical symptoms of hypoxia.**

   ④ INCORRECT: Teaching client the importance of wearing a medical identification bracelet is not an immediate need.

   ⑤ INCORRECT: Applying a lubricating eyedrop is not an immediate need.

The strategy is to focus on the immediate concern with hypoxia and then to address these in the options. The principle for answering this is using the guidelines for the "**ABCs**." The basic need for oxygen (airway) is indeed the priority as it is with many of the degenerative disorders in addition to many other medical conditions.

Reduction of Risk Potential: Recognize signs and symptoms of complications and intervene appropriately when providing care.

10. For a client with **increased intracranial pressure (IICP)**, which of these **nursing actions by the LPN** would require intervention by the charge nurse?

    ① **CORRECT: Encourages client to cough and be suctioned orally q 1-2 hours. This will require intervention due to this being unsafe and not within the standard of practice for a client with IICP. Coughing and suctioning will cause further IICP.**

    ② INCORRECT: Removes restrictive clothing. This is included in the standard of care and does not require intervention.

    ③ INCORRECT: Restricts fluids. This is included in the standard of care and does not require intervention.

    ④ INCORRECT: Maintains the HOB at 30°. This is included in the standard of care and does not require intervention.

The strategy for any client with IICP is to encourage client NOT to "COUGH," since these will result in increased intracranial pressure any time there is pathology that can result in an increase in the intracranial pressure, with the exception of controlling temperature.

Cough; control temperature (fever can ↑ ICP)

Oral tracheal/endotracheal suctioning

Use force when blowing nose

Get neck/hip to an extreme flexion/extension position

Hypercarbia creates vasodilation;
HOB elevated 30°

Management of Care: Recognize unsafe care of healthcare personnel and intervene as appropriate, i.e., improper care.

Physiological Adaptation: Manage the care of a client with alteration in cerebral perfusion.

Decision-Making Analysis Form

Use this tool to help identify why you missed any questions. As you enter the question numbers in the chart, you will begin to see patterns of why you answered incorrectly. This information will then guide you toward what you need to focus on in your continued studies. Ultimately, this analytical exercise will help you become more successful in answering questions!!!

Questions to ask:

1. Did I have the knowledge to answer the question? If not, what information do I need to review?
2. Did I know what the question was asking? Did I misread it or did I miss keywords in the stem of the question?
3. Did I misread or miss keywords in the distractors that would have helped me choose the correct answer?
4. Did I follow my gut reaction or did I allow myself to rationalize and then choose the wrong answer?

	Lack of Knowledge (Concepts, Systems, Pathophysiology, Medications, Procedures, etc.)	Missed Keywords or Misread the Stem of the Question	Missed Keywords or Misread the Distractors	Changed My Answer (Second-guessed myself, i.e., my first answer was correct.)
Put the # of each question you missed in the column that best explains why you think you answered it incorrectly.				

If you changed an answer because you talked yourself out of the correct answer, or you second-guessed yourself, this is an **EASY FIX: QUIT changing your answers**!!! Typically, the first time you read a question, you are about 95% right! The second time you read a question, you start talking yourself into changing the answer. The third time you read a question, you do not have a clue—and you are probably thinking "Who in the heck wrote this question?"

On the other hand, if you read a question too quickly and when you reread it you realize you missed some key information that would impact your decision (i.e., assessments, lab reports, medications, etc.), then it is appropriate to change your answer. When in doubt, go with the safe route: your first thought! Go with your gut instinct!

As you gain confidence in answering questions regarding specific nursing concepts, you will be able to successfully progress to answering higher-level questions about prioritization. Please refer to the *Prioritization Guidelines* in this book for a structure to assist you with this process.

You CAN do this!

> *"Failure will never overtake me if my determination to succeed is strong enough."*
> OG MANDINO

References for Chapter 11

Alzheimer's Association National Office. (2013). Stages of alzheimer's. Retrieved from www.alz.org/alzheimers_disease_ stages_of _alzheimers.asp

Berman, A. J., and Snyder S. (2012). *Fundamentals of nursing: concepts, process, and practice* (9th ed). Upper Saddle River, NJ: Prentice-Hall.

Brain Trauma Foundation (2003). *Guidelines for acute medical management of severe traumatic brain injury of infants, children and adolescents.* Retrieved Dec 27, 2010, at www.braintrauma.org/pdf/protected/guidelins_pediatric.pdf.

Daniels, R. & Nicoll, L. (2012). *Contemporary medical-surgical nursing,* (2nd ed.). Clifton Park, NY: Delmar Cengage Learning.

Eliopoulos, C. (2014). *Gerontological nursing* (8th ed), Philadelphia: Lippincott Williams & Wilkins.

Giddens, G. F. (2013). *Concepts for nursing practice.* St. Louis, MO: Mosby, an imprint of Elsevier.

Hogan, M. A. (2014). *Pathophysiology, reviews and rationales,* (3rd Edition) Boston, MA: Pearson.

Ignatavicius, D. D. and Workman, M. L. (2010). *Medical-Surgical nursing: Patient-Centered collaborative care* (6th ed.). Philadelphia: Elsevier/Saunders.

LeMone, P. Burke, K. M. and Bauldoff, G. (2011). *Medical-surgical nursing: Critical thinking in patient care* (5th edition). Upper Saddle Road, NJ: Pearson/Prentice Hall.

Lewis, S., Dirksen, S., Heitkemper, M., Bucher, L., and Camera, I. (2011). *Medical surgical nursing: Assessment and management of clinical problems* (8th ed.). St. Louis, MO: Mosby.

Manning, L. and Rayfield, S. (2014) *Nursing made insanely easy* (7th ed). Duluth, GA: I CAN Publishing, Inc.

National Council of State Boards of Nursing, INC. (NCSBN) 2012. *Research brief: 2011 RN practice analysis: linking the NCLEX RN® examination to practice.* Retrieved from https://www.ncsbn.org/index.htm

North Carolina Concept Based Learning Editorial Board. (2011). *Nursing a concept based approach to learning.* Upper Saddle Road, NJ: Pearson/Prentice Hall.

Phan N., Hemphill JC: *Management of acute severe traumatic brain injury.* Retrieved on Nov 27, 2010, at www.uptodate.com/ online/content/topic.do?topicKey=medneuro/4782.

Porth, C. (2011). *Essentials of pathophysiology* (3d edition). Philadelphia, PA: Lippincott Williams ad Wilkins.

Porth, C. M. and Grossman, S. (2013). *Pathophysiology, concepts of altered health states* (9th edition). Philadelphia, PA.

Potter, P. A., Perry, A. G., Stockert, P., & Hall, A. (2013). *Fundamentals of nursing* (8th ed). St. Louis, MO: Mosby.

Smith E. R., Amin-Hanjani S. Evaluation and management of elevated intracranial pressure in adults. Retrieved Nov 27, 2010, at www.uptodate.com/online/content/topic.do?topicKey=cc_neuro/4543.

NOTES

CHAPTER 12

Gastrointestinal/Biliary System
Linking Concepts to Pathophysiology of Diseases
Concept Metabolism

A Snapshot of Metabolism

The gastrointestinal (GI) system is one long tube from the mouth to the anus—or we can refer to it "**From the Mouth Headed South**"! The GI/Biliary system cannot be studied in isolation as "it functions in a fascinating relationship of various organs and biochemical systems working synergistically to provide nutrition to every cell in the body while assisting the body to rid itself of solid and semisolid waste" (Daniels & Nicoll, 2012, p. 1294). It is comprised of the mouth, pharynx, esophagus, stomach, and small and large intestines. Accessory digestive organs that are part of the biliary system include the gall bladder, pancreas, and the liver (the liver will be covered in chapter 13). The major concept of the two systems is metabolism and the key function is digestion (LeMone, Burke, & Bauldoff, 2011).

Metabolism is intricately linked with other concepts, most significantly with fluid and electrolytes, acid-base balance, infection, nutrition, and pain. The causes of the disorders/diseases may be from other systems, but the result directly affects the GI/Biliary system, which can make the signs and symptoms complex (Daniels & Nicoll, 2012). Due to the common clinical findings of vomiting, diarrhea, and bleeding, there will be an alteration in the fluid and electrolyte balance, resulting in fluid volume deficit. If the fluid volume deficit is due to bleeding, the result may be hypovolemia and/or anemia. The fluid volume deficit may then result in metabolic acidosis (diarrhea) or metabolic alkalosis (vomiting). Infections are the cause of many disorders of the GI/Biliary

FROM THE MOUTH HEADED SOUTH!

system and may lead to potential complications (i.e., gastritis, viruses, peritonitis, appendicitis, etc.). Many of the different diseases or conditions in the GI/Biliary system affect one or more of the following physicological processes needed for adequate nutrition: oral intake, digestion, absorption, elimination, and/or cellular metabolism and can result in nutritional deficiencies. The concept of pain is often what forces clients to seek medical attention and the pain can vary in intensity, location, and type. (*Refer to the concepts of fluid and electrolytes, acid-base, infection, nutrition, and pain.*) Because this chapter will require your best assessment skills, we are going to share *Insanely Easy Tips* throughout to help you master this content with confidence!

The Pathophysiology Behind Alterations In Metabolism in the Gastrointestinal/Biliary System

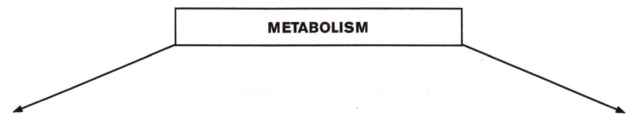

Anatomical & Functional Changes				Infection	Inflammation	Obstruction
Weakened/ Incompetent Lower Esophageal Sphincter (LES)	Erosion in the Mucosa Lining of the GI tract	Motility	Weakness in Muscles in Wall of the GI Tract	Hyper-motility Resulting in Vomiting & Diarrhea	Inflammation	Obstruction
• Gastro-esophageal Reflux Disease (GERD)	• Gastric and Peptic Ulcers (H. pylori) (gastritis, peptic ulcer disease)	• Irritable Bowel Syndrome (IBS) • Hirsch-sprung's disease	• Hernia (Hiatal)	**Diarrhea** *Etiology from:* **Bacteria** • Salmonella • Escherichia coli • Clostridium difficile • Vancomycin-resistant Enterococcus **Virus** • Rotavirus **Parasites** • Giardia (giardiasis) **Medications** • Antibiotics • Magnesium-based antacids	**Inflammatory Bowel Disease (IBD) Acute** • Appendicitis • Peritonitis • Gastroenteritis **Inflammatory Bowel Diseases (IBD) Chronic** • Ulcerative Colitis • Crohn's Disease • Diverticulitis **Biliary System Diseases** • Pancreatitis • Cholecystitis	• Cholelithiasis (Gall stones) • Intestinal Obstructions • Mechanical • Neurogenic • Vascular • Colon Cancer & Tumors • Colostomy • Ileostomy **Pediatrics:** • Pyloric Stenosis

Gastrointestinal/Biliary Metabolism
Associated Concepts: "FAINT"

An **INSANELY EASY WAY** to remember important interconnected concepts with GI/Biliary disorders!

Gastrointestinal/Biliary Concepts
Clients may "FAINT"

from Fluid or Acid-base imbalance, Infection, Nutrition, or The pain

GASTROINTESTINAL AND BILIARY DISEASES	FLUID & ELECTROLYTE BALANCE	ACID-BASE BALANCE	INFECTION	NUTRITION BALANCE	THE PAIN
Gastroesophageal Reflux Disease (GERD)				X	X
Gastric and Peptic Ulcers	X		X	X	X
Irritable bowel syndrome (IBS)	X	X		X	X
Hirschsprung's disease	X	X		X	
Hernia (Hiatal)				X	X
Diarrhea	X	X	X	X	X
Inflammatory Bowel Disease (IBD) Acute Appendicitis Peritonitis Gastroenteritis	X	X	X	X	X
Inflammatory Bowel Diseases (IBD) Chronic Ulcerative colitis Crohn's disease Diverticulitis	X	X	X	X	X
Pancreatitis	X	X	X	X	X
Cholelithiasis (Gall stones) Cholecystitis	X	X	X	X	X
Intestinal Obstructions Mechanical Neurogenic Vascular	X	X	X	X	X
Colon Cancer, Tumors Colostomy/Ileostomy	X	X	X	X	X
Pediatrics: Pyloric stenosis	X	X	X	X	X

System-Specific Assessments for Gastrointestinal/Biliary Metabolism

The many similarities in the assessments of the GI/Biliary system and metabolism may be confusing, but the chart on the previous page can help you simplify and focus the assessment. Essentially you are assessing for five concepts when you assess for the concept of GI/Biliary metabolism. Remember "**FAINT**": fluid and electrolyte balance, acid-base balance, infection, nutrition, and the pain affect metabolism. Most likely a client experiencing vomiting, diarrhea, bleeding, pain, or unexplained weight loss will seek healthcare. If you focus on the assessments of these concepts, you and the healthcare team will be able to determine the cause and treat the client accordingly. The mnemonic "**ABDOMEN**" will make it INSANELY EASY to prioritize assessments!

A Assess for pain level "**PQRST**."
Participating factors, when pain occurs
Quality, rebound tenderness, retraction
Region & radiation of pain to other areas, associated symptoms
Severity of pain using pain scale
Timing & response to treatment; what makes it better or worse
(i.e., before or after meals, position, etc.)

B Breath sounds (auscultate for equality and for adventitious lung sounds).
Bowel sounds assess (normal 5–30 sounds/minute); note if absent, decreased or high pitched; note when last bowel movement occurred.

D Distention of abdomen, measure and document, compare and contrast, signs of bleeding ($\uparrow$ HR, RR), emesis, stools; auscultate breath sounds (prevent atelectasis from client not taking deep breaths due to distention or pain).

O Observe for temperature changes and $\uparrow$ WBCs; signs of infection; note color, odor, amount, consistency of drainage from incisions; condition of skin, redness or swelling at drainage tubes insertion site.

M Monitor fluid intake, output, electrolytes, daily weight; vital signs: compare, contrast, and trend.

E Evaluate labs: liver function tests, amylase, Hgb, Hct, cholesterol, triglycerides, electrolytes, glucose, etc.

N Nutritional status assess: history of weight loss or gain, appetite; labs: pre-albumin, albumin, iron, calcium, and electrolytes.

System-Specific Assessments for Metabolism

Pathophysiology	System-Specific Assessmemts
Assessment of pain can help guide the nurse where to begin. It is often what brings the client to seek medical attention. "PQRST" pain assessment and the client's story and history of what they have been experiencing will provide valuable information.	**A**ssess pain level "**PQRST.**"
Breath sounds may be diminished. Client will not take deep breaths due to anesthesia & pain meds effects, abdominal distention and/or pain. Bowel sounds: result of movement of air & fluid in intestines. Normal BS are heard 5–30 times/min. Hyperactive BS = loud, gurgling rushed sounds; hypoactive BS = soft, low, widely separated sounds, 1–2 occurring in 2 minutes; absent sounds = sounds are not heard for 3–5 minutes of auscultating in each quadrant. When BS absent, note when last bowel movement was and if there is distention; could indicate a bowel obstruction. Loud, growling sounds or hyperactive sound may indicate ↑ intestinal motility, i.e., diarrhea. Hyperactive BS are above obstructions and minimal to no BS below an obstruction.	**B**reath sounds, (auscultate for equality and for adventitious lung sounds). Bowel sounds assess (normal 5–30 sounds /minute); note if absent, decreased or high-pitched; note when last bowel movement occurred.
Distention of of the abdomen may indicate accumulation of fluid, feces, flatus or a protrusion (indicate a hernia). Wavelike movement indicates peristalsis and may occur with an intestinal obstruction. A pulsating mass needs to be reported immediately. Inspect for signs of bleeding: (i.e., guaiac check of stools and emesis) & abdominal distention. Changes in vital signs (↑ HR, RR), level of pain, labs and diagnostic procedures may indicate bleeding or fluid loss.	**D**istention of abdomen, measure and document, compare and contrast, signs of bleeding (↑ HR, RR), emesis, stools; auscultate breath sounds (prevent atelectasis from client not taking deep breaths due to distention or pain).
Observe for signs of infection. If WBCs, temp are ↑, may indicate a possible infection or the client is fighting off an infection. Note history of nausea and vomiting or travel outside of the country, (i.e., risk for parasite or virus). Infections can occur from many sources, (i.e., parasites, viruses, drains and tubes, rupture or erosion of stomach or intestinal lining leaking abdominal contents in the peritoneal cavity, etc.).	**O**bserve for temperature changes and ↑ WBCs; signs of infection: note color, odor, amount, consistency of drainage from incisions; condition of skin; redness or swelling at drainage tubes insertion site.
Monitor to to prevent dehydration, fluid volume excess and/or to prevent hypovolemic shock. If the client is NPO for a procedure or an obstruction, may need to maintain fluid balance with IV fluids as prescribed.	**M**onitor fluid intake, output, electrolytes, daily weight; vital signs: compare, contrast and trend.
Evaluate labs and procedures results and notify the healthcare provider about the results in a timely manner so the appropriate care can be provided.	**E**valuate labs: liver function tests, amylase, Hgb, Hct, cholesterol, triglycerides, electrolytes, glucose, etc.
Nutritional deficits in NPO clients begin within 4–5 days; nutrition balance may be maintained with total parental nutrition (TPN), or tube feedings. If the albumin ↓, third spacing may occur in interstitial spaces; albumin/protein replacement will be needed. If the client is hypovolemic from loss of fluids (i.e., emesis, diarrhea, or bleeding), there will be ↓ fluid volume = ↓ perfusion = heart works harder to pump. Bone loss & fractures may result from ↓ Ca⁺⁺ levels. If client is anemic from loss of blood, there is ↓ oxygen carrying capacity and the heart works harder. Vomiting and diarrhea can cause metabolic alkalosis or acidosis.	**N**utritional status assess: history of weight loss or gain, appetite; labs: pre-albumin, albumin, iron, calcium, and electrolytes.

Gastrointestinal/Biliary Metabolism
Common Lab/Diagnostic Tests/Therapeutic Procedures/Surgery

There are many labs and diagnostic tests and procedures used with gastrointestinal/biliary assessment and diagnosis. What is important for you, as a nurse, is to know what the lab, test, or procedure is for and what your responsibilities are in helping your client prepare prior to, during, and/or after the test or procedure. In addition to monitoring and trending, reporting the lab/test results to the healthcare provider is essential for timely quality care.

Labs	Diagnostics Tests/Procedures	Therapeutic Procedures/Surgery
• Electrolytes • CBC • PTT, PT, INR • Platelets • Liver function tests • BUN and Creatinine • Lipid Panel • Cholesterol Level • Glucose • Serum albumin • Prealbumin • H. pylori antigen test **Gall Bladder & Pancreas** • ↑ Amylase & Lipase (2–3x normal) (if pancreas involved) • ↑ Bilirubin: total, direct, indirect (if common bile duct blocked) • ↑ Clotting times: PT, PTT, INR prolonged (risk of bleeding) • ↑ Glucose (↓ insulin production if loss of function of the islets of Langerhans) • ↑ Liver enzymes (AST, ALP, ALT, & LDH) (associated with liver involvement or blockage of the common bile duct) • ↑ WBCs (inflammation) • Urine amylase • ↓ Albumin (edema, 3rd spacing) • ↓ Calcium and Magnesium (due to fat necrosis with pancreatitis). • ↓ Protein levels (edema, 3rd spacing)	**Gastrointestinal** • Abdominal X-rays • Barium Swallow or Upper GI series • Gastric Analysis • Gastric Emptying Study • Esophagogastroduodenoscopy • Gastroscopy • Biopsy Specimens • Abdominal Ultrasound • Magnetic Resonance Imaging (MRI) • Barium Enema • Colonoscopy • Guaiac Fecal Occult Blood Test • Small Bowel Series • Stool Specimen and Culture **Gastrointestinal** • Gallbladder Scans • Cholangiography • Computed Tomography (CT) • Endoscopic Retrograde Cholangiopancreatography (ENCP) • Magnetic Resonance Cholangiopancreatography (MRCP)	• Nissen Fundoplication Surgery • Gastrectomy • Gastroduodenostomy (Billroth I) • Gastrojejunostomy (Billroth II) • Pylorplasty • Appendectomy • Laparoscopic Cholecystectomy • Cholecystectomy • Bowel Resection • Colectomy • Colostomy & Ileostomy Surgery • Pancreatoduodenectomy (Whipple Procedure) *(Pagana & Pagana, 2014)*

Alteration with Gastrointestinal/Biliary Metabolism Medications

The following medications are some of the many that are used for clients with gastrointestinal/biliary alterations (Manning & Rayfield, 2013). We recommend you review and learn these more-commonly prescribed medications (refer to the book *Pharmacology Made Insanely Easy* for specifics).

Common Medications for Gastrointestinal/Biliary

Antiulcer Agents
- Antacids
- Histamine2 Blockers
- Anticholinergics
- Proton Pump Inhibitors
- Pepsin Inhibitor
- Prostaglandin E Analog (Cyto)

Mucosal Protectant
Sucralfate (Carafate)

Gastrointestinal Disorders
- Anti-Emetic Agents
- Laxatives: Simulant/Emollient
- Bulk Forming Agents
- Laxatives: Lactulose
- Antidiarrheal

Prokinetic Agents
- Metoclopramide (Reglan)
- Octreotide (Sandostatin)

Antiprotozoal Agent
Metronidazole (Flagyl)

Antibiotics for Ulcers
- Metronidazole (Flagyl)
- Amoxicillin (Amoxil)
- Clarithromycin (Biaxin)
- Tetracycline

Antibiotics
- Macrolides
- Penicillins
- Sulfonamides
- Vancomycin Hydrochloride
- Carbapenems

Irritable Bowel Syndrome
- Alosteron (Lotronex)
- Lubiprostone (Amitiza)
- Sulfasalazine (Azulfidine)

Inflammatory Bowel Disease
- Anticholinergics
- Antimicrobials
- Corticosteroids

First-Do Priority Interventions

"GASTRO"

Priority interventions for the client with alterations in metabolism resulting from diseases of the GI/Biliary system are based on the assessment findings. You will primarily compare, contrast, and trend assessment findings that revolve around **Fluid** and electrolyte balance, **Acid-base** balance, **Infection**, **Nutrition** and/or **The** pain. Sound familiar? You bet! Once again, remembering "**FAINT**" will assist in determining the priority interventions no matter what the underlying disease process is.

"**GASTRO**" is an INSANELY EASY WAY to remember the priority interventions!

G   GI function: note amount of output (i.e., emesis, diarrhea, bleeding, drainage from tubes, etc.). Record amount, color, smell; monitor if vomiting or massive output from NG tube for metabolic alkalosis, and ↓ Na$^+$, K$^+$, Ca^{++}; monitor if diarrhea: for metabolic acidosis and ↓ Na$^+$, K$^+$, Ca^{++}; test emesis and stools for blood (i.e., guaiac stools).

A   Assess "**PQRST**", relief of pain, note if relieved with (i.e., food), pain medications/order (note: pain medication may be withheld until a DX is made because pain meds can mask symptoms and hinder the diagnostic process). Provide comfort with position; use diversion activity until pain medication may be given.

S   Sustain and/or enhance nutrition; may need oral supplements, vitamins, feeding tubes, TPN, etc.

T   Teach about medications, diet, and available vaccinations (i.e., flu, rotavirus, etc.). Teach to "**MO$_2$VE**" (*refer to Oxygenation concept for specifics*), ambulation to promote oxygenation, aide in healing and peristalsis.

R   Review I & O, daily weights; lab and diagnostic procedure results; compare, contrast, and trend findings.

O   Observe, compare, and contrast vital signs, labs, abdominal girth for potential complications (i.e., bleeding, peritonitis, distention, infection, paralytic ileus, etc.) and bowel sounds. Report a change in or absent bowel sounds immediately as it may be a complication such as intestinal obstruction, peritonitis, or paralytic ileus.

First-Do Priority Interventions

Pathophysiology	First-Do Priority Interventions
GI function care will depend on what assessments have been made. If the client has nausea, vomiting, and/or diarrhea, the care will focus on maintaining fluid and electrolytes balance. The GI assessment is imperative to monitor and trend due to the risk of electrolyte imbalances and metabolic acidosis and alkalosis. (*Refer to Concept Acid Base for specifics.*)	**G**I function: note amount of output (i.e., emesis, diarrhea, bleeding, drainage from tubes, etc.). Record amount, color, smell; monitor if vomiting or massive output from NG tube for metabolic alkalosis, & $\downarrow$ Na^+, K^+, Ca^{++}; monitor if diarrhea: for metabolic acidosis & $\downarrow$ Na^+, K^+, Ca^{++}; test emesis & stools for blood (i.e., guaiac stools).
Assessment of pain, "PQRST" and relief is important to manage. A client that is in pain does not heal as quickly and they tend to not take deep breaths because of the pain. They also may not be unable to assume a position that will expand the diaphragm. Because of pain, the client may be reluctant to sit up or to ambulate, which also can lead to decrease oxygenation. The limited deep breathing can lead to atelectasis and put the client at risk for infection. This makes pain management very important in the care of the client to avoid potential complications. (*Refer to concepts Pain, Oxygenation, Fluid and Electrolytes for specifics.*)	**A**ssess "PQRST", relief of pain, note if relieved with (i.e., food), pain medications/order, (note: pain medication may be withheld until a DX is made because pain meds can mask symptoms & hinder the diagnostic process). Provide comfort with position; use diversion activity until pain medication may be given.
Sustain and/or enhance nutrition is essential for the GI/Biliary client. Although the client may be NPO, the nurse is often the advocate and leader with the healthcare team to ensure the client's nutritional needs are met. The client at a minimum needs IV fluids if NPO or is experiencing severe vomiting and diarrhea. Nutritional supplements (i.e., TPN, tube feedings, oral supplements, vitamins, albumin and protein, etc.) are needed for prolonged NPO status. It is important for the nurse to help coordinate with the interdisciplinary team, specifically a dietician to do a comprehensive nutritional assessment.	**S**ustain and/or enhance nutrition, may need oral supplements, vitamins, feeding tubes, TPN, etc.
Teach GI/Biliary clients about diets and medications (i.e., when meds should be taken; with, before or after meals, drug/drug interactions, and side effects to report, etc.). Medications, like antacids must be taken 1–3 hours after meals and cannot be taken within 1–2 hours of other medications. Also need to instruct about the need for activity to promote oxygenation, increase peristalsis, and help with pain management. Refer clients for vaccinations if needed.	**T**each about medications, diet, and available vaccinations (i.e., flu, rotavirus, etc.). Teach to "**MO$_2$VE**" (*refer to Oxygenation concept for specifics*), ambulation to promote oxygenation, aide in healing and peristalsis.
Review I & O; daily weights are critical with GI clients particularly with vomiting and diarrhea. Clients who have tubes, drains, ileostomies, procedures like paracentesis of the abdomen require measurement of amount of fluid, color, odor documented so adequate intake is given to replace the fluid lost so fluid balance is maintained.	**R**eview I & O, daily weights; lab and diagnostic procedure results, compare, contrast, and trend findings.
Observe, compare and contrast vital signs, lab values, daily weights, etc. Increased HR, RR or decrease in BP and/or Hct & Hgb may indicate bleeding or hypovolemia. Increased WBC may indicate an infection. Decreased albumin and protein may indicate nutritional deficits and/or potential for third spacing. Elevated liver enzymes could indicate involvement of the liver. (*Refer to Exception and Additions in this chapter.*) Trending abdominal girth and bowel sounds provide information about the intestinal tract function and recognition of potential complications.	**O**bserve, compare and contrast vital signs, labs, abdominal girth for potential complications (i.e., bleeding, peritonitis, distention, infection, paralytic ileus, etc.) and bowel sounds (report a change in or absent bowel sounds immediately as it may be a complication such as intestinal obstruction, peritonitis or paralytic ileus).

SAFETY Concept Gastrointestinal/Biliary Metabolism

System-Specific Assessment "ABDOMEN"	First-Do Priority Interventions "GASTRO"	Evaluate Outcomes "ABDOMEN" WDL
Assess for pain level, "PQRST" Participating factors, when it occurs Quality, rebound tenderness, retraction Region and radiation of pain to other areas, associated symptoms Severity of pain using pain scale Timing and response to treatment; what makes it better or worse (i.e., before or after meals, position, etc.).	**G**I function: note amount of output (i.e., emesis, diarrhea, bleeding, drainage from tubes, etc.). Record amount, color, smell; monitor if vomiting or massive output from NG tube for metabolic alkalosis, & ↓ Na^+, K^+, Ca^{++}; monitor if diarrhea: for metabolic acidosis and ↓ Na^+, K^+, Ca^{++}; test emesis and stools for blood (i.e., guaiac stools).	**A**ssess for pain, rebound tenderness, retraction–NONE or pain is managed.
Breath sounds, (auscultate for equality and for adventitious lung sounds).	**A**ssess "PQRST", relief of pain, note if relieved with (i.e., food), pain medications/order, (note: pain medication may be withheld until a DX is made because pain meds can mask symptoms and hinder the diagnostic process). Provide comfort with position; use diversion activity until pain medication may be given.	**B**owel sounds assess, absent or high pitched–WDL
Bowel sounds assess (normal 5–30 sounds/ minute); note if absent, decreased or high pitched; note when last bowel movement occurred.	**S**ustain and/or enhance nutrition, may need oral supplements, vitamins, feeding tubes, TPN, etc.	**D**istention of abdomen, measure and document: WDL
Distention of abdomen, measure & document, compare & contrast, signs of bleeding (↑HR, RR), emesis, stools; auscultate breath sounds (prevent atelectasis).	**T**each about medications, diet, & available vaccinations (i.e., flu, rotavirus, etc.). Teach to "MO₂VE" (refer to Oxygenation concept for specifics), ambulation to promote oxygenation, aide in healing & peristalsis.	**O**bserve for temperature changes and ↑WBCs; signs of infection: No infection, NO bleeding, No respiratory distress.
Observe for temperature changes & ↑WBCs; signs of infection; note color, odor, amount, consistency of drainage from incisions; condition of skin; redness or swelling at drainage tubes insertion site.	**R**eview I & O, daily weights; lab & diagnostic procedure results, compare, contrast, and trend findings.	**M**onitor fluid intake, output, urine and stools, electrolytes, daily weight, VS: Vital signs, fluid balance, weight, stools WDL for client.
Monitor fluid intake, output, electrolytes, daily weight; VS: compare, contrast & trend.	**O**bserve, compare & contrast vital signs, labs, abdominal girth for potential complications (i.e., bleeding, peritonitis, distention, infection, paralytic ileus, etc.) and bowel sounds (report a change in or absent bowel sounds immediately as it may be a complication such as intestinal obstruction, peritonitis or paralytic ileus.	**E**valuate labs: Labs WDL for client.
Evaluate labs: liver function tests, amylase, Hgb, Hct, cholesterol, triglycerides, electrolytes, glucose, etc.		**N**utritional status WDL for client.
Nutritional status assess: history of weight loss or gain, appetite; labs: pre-albumin, albumin, iron, calcium, and electrolytes.	*Refer to the associated concepts "FAINT" for specifics.*	

Pathophysiology: Anatomical & Functional Changes (Weakened/ Incompetent Lower Esophageal Sphincter (LES) Gastroesophageal Reflux Disease (GERD)

Gastroesophageal Reflux Disease (GERD) is a backward flow of stomach contents into the esophagus. It is the result of relaxation of the lower esophageal sphincter (LES). The lowered LES pressures delays gastric emptying. The delayed gastric emptying leads to the reflux. The reflux most often consists of hydrochloric acid or gastric and duodenal contents containing bile acid and pancreatic juice. This can lead to inflammation of the esophagus and can cause erosion.

PATHOPHYSIOLOGY

Exceptions and Additions by Diseases

An Insanely Easy Way to Remember Priority Interventions for GERD "REFLUX"

R egurgitation & esophageal spasms prevent

E levate head of bed

F ood—small meals, sit up 30–60 min after meals

L ifestyle must be modified

U se of Prilosec, Prevacid, Nexium, Reglan, antacids, H$_2$ histamine antagonists

X out foods that ↓LES pressure & ↑ acid production

SYSTEM-SPECIFIC ASSESSMENTS "BURPS"	FIRST-DO	PRIORITY	INTERVENTIONS	
	DIET	EQUIPMENT	PLANS/ INTERVENTIONS	HEALTH PROMOTION
Burping & flatus is increased, dyspepsia occurs after eating certain foods, or fluid.	• 4–6 small meals per day (avoid large meals.)	• Blocks to elevate head of bed.	• Position upright, at night HOB ↑6–8 inches with blocks; avoid positions that increase LES pressure, (i.e., bending, straining, lying down, constriction at waist, etc.).	Teach client/ family: • Health Promotion (i.e., get exercise, stop smoking, no alcohol, weight reduction, etc.).
Upright position relieves pain, bending, straining or lying down increases pain.	• Do not eat within 4 hours of bedtime.			
Regurgitation may cause throat irritation.	• Avoid foods & meds that ↓LES pressure & ↑ acid production (i.e., fatty fried, caffeinated and carbonated beverages, peppermint, spicy food, tomatoes, alcohol, citrus fruits, etc.). Keep diary of foods and medication that contribute to GERD.		• Monitor for complications of aspiration, pneumonia, broncho-spasm.	• Avoid constrictive clothing around waist.
Recurrent heartburn can mimic heart attack.				• How to take medications.
Pain location, characteristics, severity; use PQRST.				• Avoid meds that ↓LES pressure (i.e., calcium channel blockers, valium, anti-cholinergics, etc.).
Pain occurs after eating; may last up to 2 hrs.				
Symptoms occurring 4–5 times per week indicative of GERD.	• *Refer to concept on Nutrition for specifics.*			

Exceptions and Additions by Diseases

Pathophysiology: Anatomical & Functional Changes (Erosion In The Mucosa Lining Of The GI Tract)
Peptic Ulcer Disease (PUD)

Peptic Ulcer Disease (PUD) is a result of the erosion that involves the mucosal lining of the esophagus, stomach or duodenum. The ulcer develops when the mucosal barrier is unable to protect the mucosa from the hydrochloric acid and pepsin, digestive juices. The etiology can be from excess gastric acid, decreased mucous production that protects the mucosa cells, increased delivery of acid or infection by the bacteria Heliocobactor pylori, known as H. pylori. The ulcers can be superficial or deep lesions that penetrate through the muscles and into the blood vessels causing hemorrhage. It can lead to perforation of the wall of the stomach or intestines if not treated. The major risk factor is use of aspirin and NSAIDS (Nonsteroidal Anti-Inflammatory). NSAIDS interrupt prostaglandin synthesis which is necessary for maintaining the gastric mucosal barrier. Smoking is also a significant risk factor. Often gastric ulcers are chronic, and duodenal ulcers may have periods of remission and exacerbation (Osborn, Wraa, Watson, & Holleran, 2014).

System-Specific Assessments "ULCER"	First-Do Priority Interventions			
	Diet	Equipment	Plans/Interventions	Health Promotion
Upper epigastric pain (i.e., gnawing, burning, or hunger-like pain).	• 4–6 small meals per day	• Saline lavage and NG tube if indicated for bleeding	• Remain upright after eating is best.	Teach client/family:
Look for signs of bleeding, emesis (hematemesis), bloody stools (melena), vital sign changes, perforation or obstructions.	• Do not eat within 4 hours of bedtime	• Gastric samples for H.pylori testing	• Monitor vital signs for bleeding (↑HR, ↑RR, color, late signs BP↓, ↓ urine output).	• Health Promotion (i.e., avoid use of aspirin, NSAIDS, smoking); need adequate rest, etc.
Complaint of pain most often when stomach is empty or at night.	• Limit caffeine and alcohol at night	• Stool samples of occult blood	• Assess abdomen for distension, firmness, bowel sounds.	• How to take medications, timing of medications: antacids 1–3 hours after meals. Schedule to give 1 hour apart from other medications.
Eating, antacids often relieves the pain.	• Limit milk to 1 glass/ meal (milk ↑ acid production)			• Report any bleeding or tarry stools.
Radiating pain through abdomen— may indicate perforation imminent; board-like abdomen—perforation occurring.	• Keep diary of foods eaten			• Avoid medications (i.e., aspirin, NSAIDS, corticosteroids, etc.) that can cause bleeding.
	• Refer to concept on Nutrition for specifics			

Common symptoms experienced by the elderly with PUD: Remember **"ABC"**

Anorexia, weight loss, and vomiting
Bleeding, anemia (from use of NSAIDS)
Chest pain

Pathophysiology: Anatomical & Functional Changes
(Erosion In The Mucosa Lining Of The GI Tract)
Peptic Ulcer Disease (PUD)

Trend Potential Complications: Obstruction, Bleeding and Perforation

Gastric outlet obstruction (or pyloric obstruction) results from edema, inflammation and scarring of the pylorus. **Bleeding** occurs from erosion of a small or large vessel(s). Small vessels result in a slow insidious loss of blood and the client may have occult blood in the stool. The large vessels may result in hemorrhage and a potential for shock. The client may present with bloody or coffee ground emesis and have melena (dark tarry stools). **Perforation** occurs when the ulcer erodes through the mucosal wall that causes gastroduodenal contents containing acid pepsin, bile and pancreatic juice to enter the abdominal cavity causing an inflammatory process and peritonitis. The more common and serious complications are bleeding and perforation (Lewis, Dirksen, Heitkemper, Bucher & Camera, 2011).

SAFETY   **There are two major potential complications that, as a nurse, you want to monitor for with Peptic Ulcer Disease:**   **PRIORITIES**

.Bleeding and Perforation PRIORITY Assessments

RECOGNIZING BLEEDING	**RECOGNIZING PERFORATION**
You may not actually see the bleeding with ulcers, but you will be able to recognize the trends:	Assessing the abdomen is essential to detect changes in the firmness or distention of the abdomen.
Early signs of fluid volume deficit:	**Epigastric pain radiating across the abdomen:**
HR ↑, RR ↑, color ↓	**A rigid, board like abdomen**
Late signs BP ↓ , urine output ↓	**Absence of bowel sounds**
Report ASAP to the HCP	**Report ASAP to the HCP**

Vigilant comparing, contrasting and trending assessments will help you detect early any potential complications!!!

 **CONCEPTS**   Refer to concepts on Perfusion (shock) and Fluid Balance.

Exceptions and Additions by Diseases

Pathophysiology: Anatomical and Functional Changes
(Erosion In The Mucosa Lining Of The GI Tract)
Gastrointestinal/Biliary Surgery

Surgery	Nursing Care "POST-OP CARE"
Gastrectomy: removal of all or part of stomach	**P**atency of airway, lung sounds, O_2 sat, encourage cough and deep breathing and incentive spirometer
	Observe for bleeding, monitor CBC, clotting factors
Gastroduodenostomy (Billroth I): lower portion of stomach removed, remaining portion attached to duodenum	**S**kin color, lips & mucous membranes note, evaluate surgical wound for healing, note any redness, swelling, drainage
	Trend VS, signs of infections, ↑ Temp or WBCs, bowel sounds, note if present, absent, hypo or hyperactive
Gastrojejunostomy (Billroth II): lower portion of stomach is removed, remaining part attached to the jejunum	**O**utput (I & O), nausea, vomiting, diarrhea, J tube, NG tube, T tube, monitor, evaluate & trend output and drainage
	Pain; patent catheters, assess
Pyloroplasty: opening between stomach and small intestine enlarged to increase gastric emptying	**C**ardiac monitor for arrhythmias; monitor level of consciousness (LOC)
	Anesthesia response; administer medications as prescribed
	Renal function, BUN & Creatinine evaluate for renal function
	Encourage movement, ambulation **E**lectrolyte & fluids monitor closely

---

INSANELY EASY TIP to Prevent Post-Op Complications!
Clients with big abdominal incisions do not want to take deep breaths so ... have your clients "**MO₂VE**" Post-Operatively!!

Move the clients: assist to ambulate, sit, turn, ROM, etc. (With GI, "**MO₂VE**" helps with motility).

O₂xygen: O_2 sat, cough, deep breathe and incentive spirometer, etc. (Abdominal incisions hurt, clients will not take deep breaths.)

Vital signs, evaluate trends for altered oxygenation and intervene, trend bowel sounds, (absence, hypo, or hyperactive).

Eliminate pain, if clients are in pain, they don't want to deep breathe or move!

The MO₂VE!

(sung to the tune of "If You're Happy And You Know It")

To get the best oxygenation you need to walk! (clap clap)
If you can't walk, then you sit in the chair, (clap clap)
If can't sit in the chair, then you do range of motion
If you can't do that, then you need to TURN! (clap clap)

Pathophysiology: Anatomical and Functional Changes
(Erosion In The Mucosa Lining Of The GI Tract)
Trend Potential Complication of GI Surgery: Dumping Syndrome

Dumping syndrome: A group of symptoms that occur after eating due to a shift of fluid to the abdomen due to rapid gastric emptying or from a high carbohydrate intake. The sudden influx of hypertonic fluid causes the small intestine to pull fluid from the extracellular space to convert the hypertonic fluid to isotonic fluid. The fluid shift causes a decrease in the circulating volume resulting in syncope, palpitation, and dizziness. Clients undergoing Billroth I, II, or bariatric surgery are at a greater risk because the stomach is unable to control the amount and rate of the chime that enters the small intestine following a meal.

System-Specific Assessments	First-Do Priority Interventions "DUMPIN"
Early Symptoms (≤ 30 min p meals) • Vertigo • Diaphoresis • Tachycardia • Palpitations • Nausea & vomiting **Late Symptoms (≥ 60 min p meals)** • Cramping • Dizziness & Diaphoresis • Confusion	**D**iet: high-protein, high-residue, low/moderate carbohydrates; avoid sugars (milk, sweets, fruit, fruit juice, honey, syrup, etc.). **U**rge small, frequent meals. **M**edications–antispasmodic: bentyl (Dicyclomine); slow absorption of carbohydrates; acarbose (Prandase). **P**osition/teach client to remain supine for 30 minutes after meals or when vasomotor symptoms occur. **I**nstruct client to monitor for signs and symptoms of hypoglycemia. (Remember: "*Cold and clammy, I need some candy.*") **N**o fluids within 1 hour before or after meals.

DUMPING SYNDROME

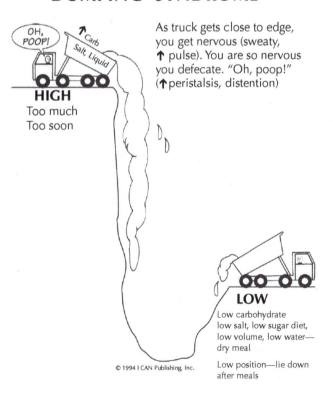

As truck gets close to edge, you get nervous (sweaty, ↑ pulse). You are so nervous you defecate. "Oh, poop!" (↑peristalsis, distention)

OH, POOP!

↑ Carb
Salt, Liquid

HIGH
Too much
Too soon

LOW
Low carbohydrate low salt, low sugar diet, low volume, low water— dry meal

Low position—lie down after meals

© 1994 I CAN Publishing, Inc.

Pathophysiology: Anatomical and Functional Changes (Motility) Irritable Bowel Syndrome (IBS)

Irritable Bowel Syndrome (IBS) is a functional disorder of motility in the intestine. There are three possible components that are involved: GI motility, visceral hypersensitivity, and neurotransmitter imbalance. Motility can be altered by diet and emotional state. The intestinal hypersensitivity is the result of exaggerated response to varied stimuli (i.e., stress, food, hormonal changes, etc.). Studies have shown clients with IBS experience pain differenlty in the colon than clients without IBS (Black & Hawk, 2009).

INSANELY EASY TIP to remember!

Clients with Irritable Bowel Syndrome need
NO "**STRESS**"!!

Stools vary from loose, diarrhea, and constipation.
Teach to avoid foods that are irritating (gas-forming, caffeine, alcohol).
Record food intake and bowel patterns to refine diet and prevent exacerbations.
Encourage high-fiber diet.
Stress reduction and exercise.
Symtpoms to report: rectal bleeding, weight loss.

Pathophysiology: Anatomical and Functional Changes (Motility) Hirschsprung's Disease

Hirschsprung's disease (*congenital megacolon*) is a blockage of the large intestine due to improper muscle movement in the bowel. It is a congenital condition. Nerves in between the muscle layers that trigger contractions are missing from a part of the bowel. Areas without such nerves cannot push material through the intestine, which causes a blockage. The intestinal contents build up which leads to intestinal blockage and abdominal distention. The client may require a temporary colostomy.

INSANELY EASY TIP to remember!

With Hirschsprung's Disease,
there is NO "**POO**"!!

Poor feeding, low to no weight gain, vomiting.
Output; NO POO (meconium) after birth and/or first POO within 24–48 hours after birth.
Output may include explosive stools, older child is constipated.

Pathophysiology: Weakness In Muscles In The Wall Of The GI Tract

Hernias

Hernias are an abnormal protrusion of an organ tissue or part of an organ through the structure that normally contains it. Hernias may be acquired or congenital and are classified by their location (i.e., inguinal, umbilical incisional, or ventral hernias). Complications of hernias are minimal if they are reducible. If the contents cannot be returned to the abdominal cavity, it is referred to as an *incarcerated hernia* and the risk of complications like obstruction of the bowel where the hernia is located is increased. Another complication is a *strangulation hernia* where the blood supply to the bowel and tissues in the hernia sac are diminished and necrosis of the tissue can occur.

Hiatal hernia is the protrusion of part of the stomach into the thoracic cavity through a weakness in the esophageal hiatus muscles in the diaphragm. Most clients are asymptomatic and the incidence increases with age. Symptoms of the hiatal hernia and the nursing care are similar to clients who have gastroesophageal reflux disease (GERD). When medical treatment is not effective, a surgery called *Nissen fundoplication* may be done (Smeltzer, Bare, Hinkle & Cheever, 2010).

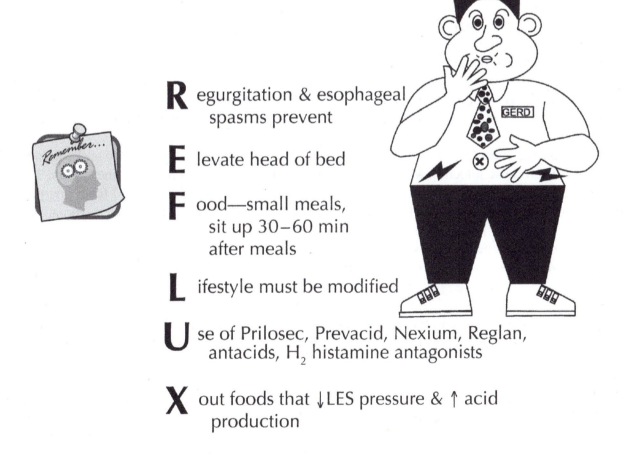

R egurgitation & esophageal spasms prevent

E levate head of bed

F ood—small meals, sit up 30–60 min after meals

L ifestyle must be modified

U se of Prilosec, Prevacid, Nexium, Reglan, antacids, H_2 histamine antagonists

X out foods that ↓LES pressure & ↑ acid production

Exceptions and Additions by Diseases

Pathophysiology: Infections—Hypermotility Resulting in Vomiting and Diarrhea
(Bacteria, Viruses, and Parasites)

Diarrhea is frequent liquid stools caused by a variety of disorders. The most common etiologies are from bacteria, viruses, parasites, and medications.

Bacteria

Helicobacter pylori (H. pylori) infection often infects the stomach during childhood. It is a common cause of peptic ulcers and it is present in about half the people in the world. Most individuals do not get sick from it and it is often detected when individuals develop signs and symptoms of a peptic ulcer. It can be treated with antibiotics.

Salmonella is one of the most common causes of food poisoning that usually results from incorrect preparation of food, such as chicken, turkey and eggs. It can also be transmitted in the water, handling of pets, particularly reptiles, weakened immune system and antibiotic use. Individuals experience chills, **vomiting and diarrhea** with pain and fever in severe cases.

Escherichia coli (E. coli) usually does not cause any harm and lives in the intestine of people and animals. There are a few strains, (i.e., E. coli O157:H7), that can cause **severe abdominal cramps, bloody diarrhea and vomiting**. Exposure to E. coli is from contaminated water or food, particularly raw vegetables and undercooked ground beef. Most infected individuals recover in 7 days, but young children and older adults can develop a form of kidney failure called hemolytic uremic syndrome (HUS) that can be life threatening.

Clostridium difficile (C. difficile or C. diff) most commonly affects older adults in hospitals or long term care after antibiotic use, however, recently infections are more frequent, difficult to treat and are occurring in healthy young adults. The symptoms can range from **mild (diarrhea for 2–3 days) to severe with (10–15 episodes of diarrhea per day)** with fever, dehydration and can result in life-threatening inflammation of the colon. It has become increasingly difficult to treat with resistance to antibiotic therapy.

Vancomycin-resistant Enterococcus normally lives in the intestines and on the skin and does not cause symptoms. It can cause infection when the individual is ill or has a weakened immune system. The most common sites include the intestines, the urinary tract, and in wounds. It is spread from one person to another through casual contact or through contaminated objects. Most often, VRE is spread from the hands of a healthcare provider. It has become resistant to antibiotics, most specifically Vancomycin. The symptoms vary depending on the site of the infection (i.e., burning on urination with a urinary tract infection or **diarrhea**, fever with infection in the intestines).

Viruses

Rotavirus may cause **severe watery diarrhea** with associated vomiting and abdominal pain. It is a major cause of diarrhea across the world but in the U.S. a rotavirus vaccine has been available since 2006.

Parasites

Giardia (giardiasis) is a microscopic parasite that's found worldwide. It is waterborne and can be found in streams and lakes as well as municipal water supplies, swimming pools and spas. It is particularly prevalent in areas with poor sanitation. It can also be transmitted through food and person-to-person contact. It causes abdominal cramping, **nausea and watery diarrhea**.

Exceptions and Additions by Diseases

Pathophysiology: Infections—Hyper-motility Resulting in Vomiting and Diarrhea (Bacteria, Viruses, and Parasites)

SYSTEM-SPECIFIC ASSESSMENTS	FIRST-DO PRIORITY INTERVENTIONS			
	DIET	EQUIPMENT	PLANS	HEALTH PROMOTION
Common Symptoms Vomiting (Metabolic Alkalosis) & Diarrhea (Metabolic Acidosis) & Fever = Fluid & Electrolyte Deficit *(Refer to concept Fluid and Electrolytes for specifics)*	• Diet will vary based on infection • NPO for bowel rest • Will need IV FLUIDS! • Usually begin with clear liquids, then 4–6 small meals/day • Need supplemental fluids • TPN • Refer to concept on Nutrition for specifics	• Saline lavage and NG tube if indicated for GI bleeding • IV pumps • Have bedside commode available for diarrhea	• Strict I & O, daily weights • Monitor fluid & electrolytes • HOB ↑ to prevent aspiration • Stool cultures • Blood cultures • Stool specimens • Good hand-washing	Teach client/family: • Good hand-washing • Take all antibiotics as prescribed • Report any side effects of medications • Importance of fluid intake • Get Rotovirus vaccine

---

IMPORTANT POINTS TO REMEMBER!

DON'T GIVE ANTIDIARRHEAL MEDICATIONS if there is a suspected infection (diarrhea is the way the organisms leave the body)!

SAFETY: Falls Precautions
Keep that commode handy!
We don't want clients falling while rushing to the bathroom
and/or from syncope due to decrease BP due to fluid loss!

Remember, the elderly will have an ↑ risk for fluid volume deficit and falls.

Exceptions and Additions by Diseases

Pathophysiology: Inflammation
Inflammatory Bowel Disease (IBD)

Inflammatory Bowel Disease (IBD) can be both acute and chronic. It affects segments and structures throughout the gastrointestinal tract.

Acute Inflammatory Bowel Disease (IBD) includes:

Gastroenteritis is an inflammation of the stomach and intestinal tract that primarily affects the small bowel. Bacteria, viruses or parasites can cause tissue damage and inflammation that disrupt the intestinal flora. The damage is caused by the release of endotoxins that stimulate the mucosa lining of the intestines to have greater secretions of water and electrolytes into the intestines. The excess sodium and protein rich fluid exceed the bowel's ability to reabsorb the fluid resulting in diarrhea.

Appendicitis is an inflammation of the vermiform appendix. When the appendix becomes obstructed, it causes an increase in the intraluminal pressure that can lead to thrombosis, edema and bacterial into the lumina. This can lead to necrosis of the bowel wall. **If perforation occurs, it can lead to peritonitis.**

Peritonitis is an inflammation of the peritoneal membrane. Peritonitis causes severe systemic responses to include alterations in circulation and fluid shifts that lead to fluid volume and electrolytes imbalances. The resulting inflammatory process diverts blood away from the bowel to address the infection. The decrease in blood supply decreases peristalsis and the result is similar to that of a bowel obstruction. The inflammatory process causes increased abdominal pressure that pushes up on the diaphragm, making it difficult to breathe. This can lead to decreased oxygenation and atelectasis, which may result in an increased risk of pulmonary infections.

INSANELY EASY TIP to Remember
Acute Inflammatory Bowel Diseases Assessments!

Use **"GAP"** to remember the differences.
The rest of the assessments are the same!!
(Refer to the chart on the next page and you will see!!)

Gastroenteritis: large amounts of diarrhea (metabolic acidosis) and hyperactive bowel sounds.

Appendicitis: pain at the McBurney's Point.

Peritonitis: rigid, board-like abdomen.

Pathophysiology: Inflammation
Inflammatory Bowel Disease (IBD)

Comparison of System-Specific Assessments
Revolving Around the Concepts "FAINT"

System-Specific Assessments	Gastroenteritis	Appendicitis	Peritonitis
Fluid & Electrolytes	X	X	X
Diarrhea	X **May have up to 10 or more watery stools per day in severe cases.**	X	
Nausea and Vomiting	X	X	X
Acid Base	Metabolic Acidosis (Diarrhea)	Metabolic Acidosis (Diarrhea) and/or **Metabolic Alkalosis** (Vomiting)	Metabolic Alkalosis (Vomiting)
Infection and **I**nflammation	X	X	X
Nutrition (May need nutritional support particularly during acute episodes)	X Liquids during acute episodes (i.e., broth, non-sugar drinks, etc.). IV fluids if unable to tolerate fluids, ease back into solid foods.	X Supplemental IV fluids as prescribed during acute episode followed by diet as prescribed.	X Bowel rest with IV fluids, enteral feeding or TPN may be needed.
The Pain	X Generalized pain and cramping; bowel sounds hyperactive.	X Begins with dull pain progressing to acute pain that comes in waves, localized in the RLQ, **McBurney's Point** (halfway between the anterior superior iliac crest and umbilicus); decreased bowel sounds; rebound tenderness in RLQ (Rovsing's sign).	X Diffuse pain or localized at site of involvement; may present with a **distended, board-like abdomen** with diminished or absent bowel sounds.
Tissue/Skin Integrity	X Frequent diarrhea with irritation to skin.	X Diarrhea with irritation to skin.	

(Refer to Concepts: Fluid and Electrolyte Balance, Acid Base, Nutrition, Infection Control, Pain and Tissue/Skin Integrity for specifics.)

Exceptions and Additions by Diseases

Pathophysiology: Inflammation
Chronic Inflammatory Bowel Disease (IBD)

Crohn's Disease (Regional Enteritis) consists of inflammatory lesions that can occur anywhere from the mouth to the anus. The most common area is the small intestine. The lesions involve all layers of the intestinal walls that include long ulcers with short areas of strictures. This causes the bowel wall to thicken and the resulting scar tissue interferes with the movement of chime and malabsorption of nutrients can result. The disease can have exacerbations and remissions.

Ulcerative Colitis consists of edema and inflammation of the rectum that progresses from the sigmoid colon and expands the length of colon. It usually begins in the rectum and moves upward through the large intestine in a continuous pattern from the distal to the proximal colon. It involves the mucosa and submucosa and can cause bowel obstruction as the intestinal wall thickens. Other complications include malabsorption of nutrients, fluid and electrolyte imbalances (Porth & Grossman, 2013). The most severe complication with a high mortality rate is toxic megacolon (a severe swelling and enlargement in the colon resulting in decreased blood flow leading to ischemia and tissue death in the bowel). Perforation of the colon may result.

Diverticular Disease refers to two disorders: diverticulosis and diverticulitis.

Diverticulosis is a non-inflammatory process. Abnormal saclike out-pouching of the intestinal wall called *diverticula*, occur from the high pressure required to move fecal material through the intestines. The high pressure causes the formation of the diverticula in natural weak areas in the intestinal wall where arteries penetrate the intestinal mucosal wall. The client is often asymptomatic. Irritation and inflammation occur when the diverticula do not drain, resulting in diverticulitis. Care of the client is aimed at preventing diverticulitis by encouraging a high-residue (fiber) diet (Daniels & Nicoll, 2012).

Diverticulitis occurs when the diverticula do not drain, resulting in inflammation and irritation. The episodes may be acute or chronic. The result of chronic diverticulitis is scarring and narrowing of the bowel. The trapped, hard, stone-like pieces of feces (fecalith) or food (i.e., small seeds) and/or bacteria can lead to bleeding and infection. Complications of ischemia and perforation or obstruction of the bowel can occur from the increased intraluminal pressure. The priority of care is to prevent exacerbation of the disease. Clear liquid or low-residue (fiber) diets are recommended during acute episodes (Daniels & Nicoll, 2012).

Goal is **PREVENTION!**
Health Promotion/Prevention Instructions Include:
• Diet: high-residue (fiber)
• Recognition of early symptoms of diverticulitis

Nursing Care for Inflammatory Bowel Disease (IBD)

Revolves around the Concepts "FAINT"

Does this sound familiar?

Concepts	Crohn's Disease	Ulcerative Colitis	Diverticulitis
Fluid & Electrolytes	X	X	X
Diarrhea	X Number of episodes of diarrhea vary, may have episodes of constipation.	X Diarrhea: 10–20 episodes/day during severe episodes, blood may be present in stools.	X Bowel changes, constipation or diarrhea, may have rectal bleeding; stools may narrow over time.
Nausea and Vomiting			X
Acid Base	**Metabolic Acidosis** (Diarrhea)	**Metabolic Acidosis** (Diarrhea)	**Metabolic Acidosis** (Diarrhea) and/or **Metabolic Alkalosis** (Vomiting)
Infection and **I**nflammation	X	X	X
Nutrition (May need nutritional support particularly during bowel rest)	X Because pain may result from eating, clients may ↓ intake to prevent pain = ↓ weight; may have malabsorption of nutrients.	X Limit dairy if lactose intolerant, limit residue (fiber) in diet if problematic.	X During acute episodes, bowel rest is needed and TPN will be required.
The Pain	X Diffuse abdominal pain depending on involvement of the GI tract, commonly in right lower quadrant (RLQ); pain may be relieved with defecation; a RLQ mass may be palpable (Daniels & Nicoll, 2012).	X Abdominal pain generally in left lower quadrant (LLQ).	X Abdominal pain/tenderness, intermittent becoming steady in the left lower quadrant (LLQ); a LLQ mass may be palpable due to inflammatory response (LeMone, Burke, & Bauldorf, 2011).
Tissue/Skin Integrity	X Frequent diarrhea with irritation to skin.	X Frequent diarrhea with irritation to skin.	X May have irritation during episodes of diarrhea.

(Refer to Concepts: Fluid and Electrolyte Balance, Acid Base, Nutrition, Infection Control, Pain and Tissue/Skin Integrity for specifics.)

Trend for Potential Complications of Bowel
OBSTRUCTION and/or PERFORATION

(Refer to bowel obstruction and PERFORATION in this chapter.)

Exceptions and Additions by Diseases

Pathophysiology: Inflammation: Inflammatory Bowel Disease (IBD)

FIRST-DO PRIORITY INTERVENTIONS

System-Specific Assessments	Diet	Equipment	Plans/Interventions "CRAMPS"	Health Promotion
See chart on previous page for assessments.	• High in protein. • High calories. • Low-residue diet during acute diverticulitis; when stable, gradually ↑ residue. • Diverticulosis: high-residue & avoid seeds (i.e., popcorn, sunflower, etc.) with diverticular disease to prevent diverticulitis. • Frequent, smaller meals. • Multi-vitamin. • Maintain log of foods eaten; note if symptoms occurred & how long after eating. • Refer to concept Nutrition for specifics.	• Central lines and TPN when indicated during bowel rest.	**C**ontrol diarrhea: Note quality, quantity, consistency and number of stools per day. **R**eplace fluids: need adequate fluids to prevent dehydration during severe episodes of diarrhea; output measure & record. **A**ntimicrobials and anti-cholinergics may be given. **M**aintain nutritional needs, ↑ protein, calories, vitamins; may need TPN during acute phase. **P**rotect skin after stools, cleanse with soap & water & apply moisture protective barrier. **P**ain control. **S**upport emotionally/coping; stress management classes. An Insanely Easy Way to Remember the Priority Nursing Care for IBS: **C** ontrol diarrhea **R** eplace fluids **A** ntimicrobials anticholinergics may be given **M** aintain nutritional needs **P** rotect skin pain control **S** upport emotionally/coping	Teach client/family: • Health Promotion (i.e., no smoking, alcohol intake, etc.) • Stress reduction. • Healthy diet (see column on diet). • Avoid NSAID use (may cause exacerbation of symptoms). • Do not use antibiotics unless they have been prescribed by HCP. • Need for regular exercise. • Symptoms to report: signs of bowel perforation (fever, severe abdomen pain).

Exceptions and Additions by Diseases

Pathophysiology: Inflammation Cholecystitis

Cholecystitis is an inflammation of the gallbladder. Most clients who have cholecystitis have **Cholelithiasis** (gallstones). The gallstone formation involves several factors: bile becomes saturated with cholesterol and forms solid crystals and then the crystals come together to form stones. Most stones are formed in the gallbladder but they may form in the common ducts or in the hepatic ducts of the liver. If the stone(s) obstructs the cystic duct of the gallbladder, the client experiences acute cholecystitis. The inflamed gallbladder wall becomes edematous and is thickened. It may have areas of gangrene and necrosis. If the stone(s) lodge in the common duct, inflammation of the bile duct and pancreatitis can occur. Cholecystitis may be acute or chronic (Osborn, Wraa, Watson & Holleran, 2014).

FIRST-DO PRIORITY INTERVENTIONS

SYSTEM-SPECIFIC ASSESSMENTS "PAIN"	DIET	EQUIPMENT	PLANS/INTERVENTIONS	HEALTH PROMOTION
Pain upper right quadrant (RUQ) with Murphy's sign (pain with deep inspiration with palpation under the right sub-costal margin), diaphoresis, rebound tenderness **Assess** vital signs, WBC, note any jaundice (rare), assess lung sounds (pain causes shallow respirations), O₂ sat **Inspect** for clay-colored stools and dark urine **Nausea** and vomiting, anorexia often after eating high fat foods caused by biliary colic	• NPO initially during acute stage • May need TPN during acute stage Progress diet as ordered: • Bland • Low in fat • Small frequent meals • Vitamin supplements (fat soluble) • Bile salts if needed • Refer to concept on Nutrition for specifics	• NG tube if indicated during acute episode • Central lines for fluids	• Pain management: hydromorphine (Dilaudid) or Morphine as prescribed • Bile acid may be given to dissolve bile stones (caution with clients with liver disease) • Antiemetic • Antibiotics **Procedures:** • May need extracorporeal shock wave (lithotripsy) to break up stones • Cholecystectomy to remove stones; if cholecystectomy needed, give post-op care. (*Refer to POST-OP CARE earlier in the chapter*)	Teach client/family: • Health Promotion (i.e., adequate rest, stress reduction, no smoking, etc.) • Report signs of bowel perforation (severe pain, fever) • Diet teaching

Elderly may not present with pain or fever.

Don't give Meperidine (Demerol) as it may cause seizures in older clients.

Exceptions and Additions by Diseases

Pathophysiology: Inflammation
Pancreatitis

Pancreatitis is an inflammation of the pancreas that results in the auto-digestion of the pancreas by its enzymes. When the enzymes phospholipase A, lipase, and elastase are activated before they get to the intestines and leak into the pancreatic tissue, tissue damage begins. This breakdown of the tissue and cell membranes results in edema (lack of pancreatic enzymes lead to lack of absorption of proteins, decrease albumin), vascular damage, hemorrhage, and necrosis. The fibrous changes can cause a loss of function of the islets of Langerhans resulting in diabetes mellitus or elevated blood sugars. It is thought it might be triggered by the reflux of bile from the duodenum into the pancreatic duct or pancreatic duct obstruction by gallstones. Most cases are mild, but when it continues the pancreatic parenchyma is destroyed. Pancreatitis may be acute or chronic (Porth & Grossman, 2013).

FIRST-DO   PRIORITY   INTERVENTIONS

System-Specific Assessments "PAINFUL"	Diet	Equipment	Plans	Health Promotion
Pain begins suddenly mid-epigastric area radiating to back or left flank or left shoulder. Worse when lying or after eating. No relief with vomiting. **A**ssess vital signs, ↑ serum glucose, WBC; note any jaundice color, assess lung sounds (pain causes shallow respirations: monitor O₂ sat). **I**nspect for clay-colored stools. **N**ausea and vomiting, anorexia, may have weight loss. **F**lank with ecchymosis (Turner's Sign). **U**mbilical (periumbilical) discoloration bluish (Cullen's sign). **L**ook for fluid volume imbalance, daily weights, edema, 3rd spacing. **L**isten for bowel sounds, risk for paralytic ileus.	• Initially will be NPO until pain stops and bowel sounds are present (may take to 3–7 days), will need TPN. • Progress to clear liquids & advance to low fat as prescribed. • Small, frequent meals. • Vitamin supplements (fat soluble). • Refer to concept on Nutrition for specifics.	• NG tube if indicated during acute episode for decompression • Central lines	**Treat pain:** • Pain management: hydromorphine (Dilaudid) or Morphine per order **Other Medications needed:** • Pancreatic enzyme replacement • Antiemetic • H₂ blockers • Anticholinergics • Insulin if needed per order for elevated blood sugar • May need IV albumin for 3rd spacing **Position of comfort:** • Initially need rest • HOB ↑ 45 degrees (semi-Fowler's) or side lying with knees flexed • Risk for disseminated intravascular coagulation (DIC)	Teach client/family: • Health Promotion (i.e., adequate rest, stress reduction, no smoking, no alcohol, etc.) • Report signs of bowel perforation (severe pain, fever, board like abdomen, no bowel sounds or stools) • Diet teaching

Exceptions and Additions by Diseases

Pathophysiology: Obstructions
Intestinal Bowel Obstruction

Intestinal obstruction: This is a partial or complete blockage of forward movement of the intestinal contents. Almost 90% of the bowel obstructions occur in the small intestines. The cause is a narrowing of the lumen of the intestines. The bowel normally secretes 6–8 L of electrolyte rich fluid daily, which is mostly absorbed by the body. When an obstruction occurs, it causes distention and a temporary increase in the peristalsis. Some of the fluid is removed with vomiting. This causes a severe reduction in the circulating fluid volume leading to an elevated hematocrit and hemoglobin that can lead to vascular occlusions. As the obstruction continues, the bowel becomes flaccid, retaining more fluid that increases the intraluminal pressure that then decreases the venous return. This causes vessels to become fragile, raises the cell permeability and allows fluid to escape into the peritoneal cavity. The resulting release of endotoxins can lead to endotoxic shock and death. There are several factors that can lead to the problem.

Mechanical factors include:
- Adhesions, hernias, cancer.
- Volvulus (a twisting of the bowel) is more common in the elderly.
- Intussusception (a telescoping of the bowel into an adjacent section of the bowel that lies distal to it) is more common in infants 10–15 months of age.

Neurogenic factor:
- Paralytic ileus (a lack of peristaltic activity) that can often occur after abdominal surgery, pancreatitis, or prolonged immobility, etc.

Vascular factors:
- Occur anytime there is a decrease or interrupted blood supply to the large or small bowel from a blocked artery, partial or complete.

Colonrectal cancer is cancer of either the colon or rectum that can be spread through blood or the lymphatic system. The tumors affect the color, size and amount of stool elimination depending on the location of the tumors. Tumors in the descending colon result in stools that are often dark reddish-brown, but tumors and lesions of the ascending and transverse colon result in obstruction of the stool. The stools can become ribbon like that contain bright red blood and mucous. Most colonrectal cancers develop from adenomatous polyps. This type of cancer grows slowly but once it becomes malignant, it invades the bowel wall. The tumors can then cause necrosis and ulcerations of the bowel wall and blood supply. The malignant tumors spread to nearby organs and blood borne metastasis can spread to the liver and may also involve the lungs, kidneys and bones. The treatment is usually surgery and removal of the tumors but radiation and chemotherapy may be used in conjunction with the surgery or alone with inoperable tumors.

Pyloric Stenosis: Pyloric stenosis is a narrowing of the pylorus, the opening from the stomach into the small intestine. Food passes from the stomach into the first part of the small intestine through a valve called the pylorus. In pyloric stenosis, the muscles of the pylorus are thickened, preventing the stomach from emptying into the small intestine. The cause of the thickening is unknown, although genetic factors may play a role and it occurs more often in boys than in girls, and is rare in children older than 6 months. The care is very similar to care for bowel obstructions (Jenson & Stanton, 2011).

Exceptions and Additions by Diseases

Pathophysiology: Obstructions
Intestinal Bowel Obstruction

System-Specific Assessments "BLOCK"	Diet	FIRST-DO PRIORITY INTERVENTIONS — Equipment	Plans/Interventions "RELIEF"	Health Promotion
Bowel sounds check. High-pitch or absent may indicate blockage.	• Will be NPO with nasogastric (NG) or Nasointestinal tube (NI) until bowel sounds are present & blockage resolved.	• Nasogastric tube (NG): (tube into stomach) to decompress stomach and to remove gastric contents and fluid.	**R**elieve obstruction and pressure (close monitoring to prevent perforation due to pressure).	Teach client/family: • Health Promotion (i.e., adequate rest, stress reduction, no smoking, no alcohol, etc.)
Look for fluid-volume imbalance, visible peristalsis abdominal distention (measure, compare, contrast, document); may have projectile vomiting.	• Will need TPN.	**If there is a mechanical obstruction, use:**	**E**valuate NG or NI tube: note amount, color, odor every 8 hours or per protocol, check to see that tube is secure; irrigate tube per protocol; provide oral care.	• Report signs of bowel perforation (severe pain, fever, board like abdomen, no bowel sounds or stools).
Observe quantity, consistency of stools, measure and document.	• Then advance diet as tolerated.	• Nasointestinal tube (NI) tube: (long tube inserted in through the nose to intestines with a weighted tip to move tube to the point of obstruction for decompression & removal of contents & fluid).	**L**ook at skin integrity of nostril of insertion and provide skin care.	• Teach colostomy care if applicable.
Check vital signs, labs (↑WBC, ↓H & H, ↓ potassium).	• Small, frequent meals at first best.	• Central lines may be needed.	**I**ntake and Output: manage fluid balance, strict I & O, daily weights, compare, contrast, and trend.	
Keep strict monitoring of I & O, note NG tube output, color; amount of emesis, daily weights.	• Refer to concept Nutrition for specifics.	• Colostomy or Ileostomy supplies if surgery done.	**E**valuate and provide pain management: hydromorphine (Dilaudid) or Morphine per order.	
Pyloric Stenosis: Projectile vomiting, belching, constant hunger. Babies have failure to thrive, see wavelike motion of the stomach prior to vomiting.			**F**ollow up after surgery if needed: may require temporary or permanent colostomy/ileostomy depending on location and extent of obstruction. Pyloraplasty or surgery may be needed to fix the pyloric valve for pyloric stenosis. (*Refer to POST-OP CARE earlier in chapter*).	

Pathophysiology: Obstructions
Intestinal Bowel Obstruction
Trend Potential Complication: Perforation of the Bowel

Intestinal obstructions, if not relieved, will lead to increasing pressure and the risk of perforation. Your nursing care should include constant monitoring of the abdominal girth. Compare, contrast, and trend the output from the NG or NI tube to assess early increasing abdominal pressure that could lead to perforation. If perforation occurs, intervene immediately and notify the healthcare provider. Use "**PERFORATE**" to guide your priority interventions with a client who is at risk of perforation.

P Pain in chest or abdominal (often sudden onset epigastric pain that radiates to back or right shoulder.
Provider immediately notified.

E Emergency surgery required, prepare.

R Record and trend VS , (↑ HR, ↑ RR, ↑ Temp) ↑ pain, ↑ abdominal girth, ↑ WBC; document assessment.

F Fluid replacement as ordered.

O Obtain and insert nasogastric (NG) or nasointestinal (NI) tube as ordered.

R Record and monitor I & O, compare, contrast, and trend findings.

A Abdominal distention, rigidity, board like abdomen, rebound tenderness.
Abdominal X-ray Stat; Do NOT give any contrast material until perforation is ruled out.

T Trend changes in abdominal distention, bowel sounds.

E Evaluate drainage from surgical drains, amount, color, odor, and document.

Exceptions and Additions by Diseases

Pathophysiology: Obstructions
Bowel Diversions: Colostomy and Ileostomy

Colostomy: can be located in any part of colon (ascending, transverse, sigmoid).	**Ileostomy:** is located in the small intestine, the ileum.
A part of the colon (large intestine) is surgically cut and attached to the hole (stoma) through the abdominal wall creating a route for stools to be removed from the body.	It bypasses the large intestine.
	A part of the ilium (small intestine) is surgically cut and attached to the hole (stoma) through the abdominal wall creating a route for stools to be removed from the body.
The more colon that remains, the more formed and normal the stool appears.	The stool content is more liquid in consistency and the shorter bowel decreases the absorption of nutrients.
Colostomies high in the colon produce more liquid stools that are difficult to regulate and require the client to continually wear an ostomy appliance.	The client is not able to regulate their bowels and must continually wear an ostomy appliance.

Priority Concepts:
  Fluid volume & electrolyte balance
  Tissue/Skin Integrity
  Health Promotion
	Priority Concepts:
	  Fluid Volume and Electrolyte Balance
	  Tissue/Skin Integrity (ileostomy contents highly irritating)
	  Health Promotion

The higher the ostomy is in the digestive process, the stools will be more liquid in consistency with less control of elimination.
Note: Ileostomy has a higher risk for fluid volume and electrolyte loss.

Connie may be able to regulate her stools with regular irrigations and not have to wear an ostomy appliance.	Iris will always need to wear an ostomy appliance because her stool is liquid and it cannot be regulated. Instructing how to cleanse the skin and how to avoid embarrassing odors will be very important.

Pathophysiology: Obstructions
Bowel Diversions: Colostomy and Ileostomy
Use the "ABCD & E" for Colostomy/Ileostomy Care

A Assess stoma; color, protrusion, and condition of skin around it.

B Bowel function, measure stool amount, consistency, color, and odor.

C Clean stoma and surrounding skin with warm water and soap; rinse with water and pat dry.
Cut circle in appliance 1/8 to 1/4 inch > stoma, fill in irregular stoma borders with skin paste, secure and hang ostomy appliance in dependent position.

D Diet recommendations: low-residue diet first few weeks, high-residue diet later to help form stools. Avoid/limit gas, odor-producing foods (i.e., broccoli, cauliflower), or any food such as seeds, corn, etc. that are indigestible fibers. (*Refer to concept Nutrition for specifics.*)

E Emotional support; use of therapeutic communication and health promotion client teaching to assist client to do self-care. (*Refer to concept Health Promotion for specifics.*) Refer client to ostomy support group for assistance and guidance for activities of daily living, supplies, and support.

Stoma on a colostomy or ileostomy is an artificial opening that has no nerves.

A stoma that is gray, blue, or purple is NOT healthy.

A stoma should be PINK and MOIST!!

Exceptions and Additions by Diseases

Pathophysiology: Obstructions
Management of Tubes

INSANELY EASY TIP!!

For all tubes & drains Going In and Out of the Body!
(i.e., Jackson Pratt drain tube, T tube, Nasogastric (NG), Nasointestinal (NI) tube, etc.)

PRIORITIES for "TUBE" Management

Tube: know what is the purpose

U need to trend drainage color, odor, and amount

Be sure tube is patent and in the correct position

Electrolytes & fluid balance, manage

Trend and Manage Fluid & Electrolyte Balance!

Remember the Gastrointestinal/Biliary concepts linked to the concept of Metabolism.

These concepts will guide your assessments and priority interventions—
no matter what the disease process is!!!

Clients may "**FAINT**"

From **F**luid or **A**cid-Base **I**mbalance, **I**nfection, **N**utrition, or **T**he Pain

Isn't This Insanely Easy? You are now a GI/Biliary Genius!!!!

Clinical Decision-Making Exercises

1. Which of the nursing actions is appropriate for the nurse to delegate to the UAP for a client who is one-day post-operative following a cholecystectomy?

    ① Empty the T-tube drainage bag and report the amount of drainage noted.

    ② Instruct the client to avoid broccoli, fried chicken, and cheese.

    ③ Obtain vital signs and monitor for changes.

    ④ Assist the client to ambulate in the hall.

2. Upon auscultation of a client's bowel sounds, the nurse notes soft gurgling sounds occurring 5–30 times per minute. Which of these indicate an appropriate conclusion from the assessment?

    ① Excessive intestinal motility.

    ② Normal sounds.

    ③ Rapid gastric emptying.

    ④ Reduced intestinal peristalsis.

3. When caring for a client with peptic ulcer disease, which assessment finding is the highest priority for the nurse to report to the healthcare provider?

    ① Board-like abdomen with shoulder pain radiating to the back.

    ② Burning sensation 2 hours after eating.

    ③ Coffee-ground emesis.

    ④ Nausea and vomiting.

4. Which of these assessment findings is a priority to report for a client with an ileostomy?

    ① Urine specific gravity 1.028.

    ② Heart rate was 78 BPM is now 86 BPM.

    ③ Urine output from 75 mL/hour to 40 mL/hour.

    ④ Weight from 150 lbs. to 144 lbs. in 4 weeks.

5. Which of these physiological changes may happen with a client with Crohn's disease following an excess number of liquid stools?

    ① Low-pitched bowel sounds.

    ② Metabolic acidosis.

    ③ Metabolic alkalosis.

    ④ Pain in the epigastric area of the abdomen.

6. What clinical findings would be most important to report to the provider of care for a client who is admitted with the diagnosis of peptic ulcer disease?

    ① HR–80 BPM and increased to 110 BPM, BP–138/88 decreased to 110/70.

    ② HR–72 BPM and increased to 80 BPM, RR–18/min and increased to 22/min.

    ③ HR–90 BPM and increased to 105 BPM, urine output was 65 mL/hr is now 50mL/hr.

    ④ HR–65 BPM, RR 20/min decreased to 18/min, and BP 138/88 increased to 142/90.

7. Which of these clinical findings would be most important to include in the documentation and report to the healthcare provider after assessing a client with diverticulitis? *Select all that apply.*

   ① Temperature 102.2 1°F.

   ② Client reports pain is relieved after eating.

   ③ Client reports having chills.

   ④ Client reports pain at level 7 on a scale of 1-10 in left lower abdominal quadrant.

   ⑤ Client reports dyspepsia after eating.

8. Which nursing intervention would be the priority for a client who is presenting with vomiting secondary to cholecystitis?

   ① Assess vital signs every 8 hours.

   ② Daily weight.

   ③ Incentive spirometer–daily.

   ④ Report a urine specific gravity that is 1.003.

9. Which of these nursing actions by the UAP for a client with gastro esophageal reflux disease (GERD) would require intervention by the charge nurse?

   ① Gives client a peppermint for his dry mouth.

   ② Leaves the HOB elevated after the A.M. care.

   ③ Immediately picks up an object off the floor that client dropped.

   ④ Encourages client to drink fluids between meals.

10. Which one of these discharge-teaching plans indicates the nurse understands the diet for client recovering from an episode of diverticulitis?

    ① Reviews the importance of eating a diet high in residue to prevent problems with constipation.

    ② Reviews the importance of eating a diet high in protein to assist in healing.

    ③ Reviews the importance of decreasing sodium in the diet.

    ④ Limits the intake of chocolate due to contributing to the relaxation of the lower esophageal sphincter (LES).

Answers and Rationales

1. Which of the **nursing actions is appropriate** for the nurse to **delegate to the UAP** for a client who is **one-day post-operative following a cholecystectomy?**

    ① INCORRECT: Empty the T-tube drainage bag and report the amount of drainage noted. This would be done by the nurse because of the assessment needed about the drainage.

    ② INCORRECT: Instruct the client to avoid broccoli, fried chicken, and cheese. UAPs can not do client teaching but even if you did not know that, this would not be an appropriate instruction for a client one day post-op cholecystectomy. The diet would be clear liquids progressing to a low fat diet as tolerated.

    ③ INCORRECT: Obtain vital signs and monitor for changes. Although taking vital signs may be done by the UAP, the UAP would not monitor for changes. That is the role of the RN to monitor trends in vital signs in order to intervene as needed.

    ④ **CORRECT: Assist the client to ambulate in the hall. This is an appropriate action post operatively to promote deep breathing and prevent potential complications (i.e., deep vein thrombosis, atelectasis, etc.)**

The strategy is to know basic post-op care. The priorities post-operatively with any surgery are to get the client moving! Moving is very important to prevent post-operative complications like atelectasis and deep vein thrombosis. Clients with abdominal incisions do not like to take deep breaths because of the pain from the incision. This increases the risk for atelectasis and potential infections. Ambulation requires an upright position and helps clients to open their airway. Prior to deep breathing and ambulation, remember to administer pain medication to help the client take deep breaths and move without pain.

The link here is that even if you did not remember exactly what the nursing care is for this client, you understand **POST-OP CARE** and that it applies to any kind of surgery (i.e., cholecystectomy, thoracic, appendectomy, Billroth I or II, etc.). You know the importance of implementing the nursing care to promote perfusion, oxygenation and help avoid potential complications.

An Insanely Easy Tip is to remember "**POST-OP CARE**" and to get your clients to "**MO$_2$VE**"! (*Refer to description in this chapter.*)

Reduction of Risk: Provide postoperative care; implement measures to promote circulation.

2. Upon auscultation of a client's **bowel sounds,** the nurse notes soft **gurgling sounds occurring 5–30 times a minute.** Which of these indicate an appropriate conclusion from the assessment?

    ① INCORRECT: Excessive intestinal motility. The sounds would be heard more frequently than 5–30 times a minute.

    ② **CORRECT: Normal sounds. Normal bowel sounds are heard 5–30 times a minute.**

    ③ INCORRECT: Rapid gastric emptying. This would be heard more frequently than 5–30 times a minute.

    ④ INCORRECT: Reduced intestinal peristalsis. This would be heard less frequently than 5–30 times a minute.

The strategy is to know normal system-specific assessment, so you will know when to intervene. Comparing, contrasting, and trending assessment findings are a priority for everything you do in nursing. Bowel sounds heard less than 5 a minute could indicate the effects of anesthesia, impending obstruction, or paralytic ileus following surgery. Hyperactive bowel sounds may be present with diarrhea or irritable bowel syndrome. Absent bowel sounds may indicate an obstruction. Often you will hear hyperactive bowel sounds above the obstruction. These assessments would need to be reported to the healthcare provider

Physiological Adaptation: Perform focused assessment; assess and respond to changes in vital signs or clinical findings.

3. When caring for a client with peptic ulcer disease, which assessment finding is the **highest priority for the nurse to report to the healthcare provider?**

① **CORRECT: Board-like abdomen with shoulder pain radiating to the back. This indicates a complication with perforation.**

② INCORRECT: Burning sensation 2 hours after eating. This may indicate an ulcer which is a concern, but not the priority over option a. Option 1 is a medical emergency. Option 2 is a clinical finding with ulcers.

③ INCORRECT: Coffee-ground emesis. This is a concern due to old blood (bright red would indicate a hemorrhage), but Option 1 is still priority due to the immediate complications a perforation can cause.

④ INCORRECT: Nausea and vomiting. This is a concern, but there is no indication that the client is bleeding.

The strategy to answer this question is to know that radiating pain to the back may indicate perforation imminent along with a board like abdomen, which is a medical emergency. Distention of abdomen may indicate accumulation of fluid such as blood from the perforation. The key to answering this question is to compare and contrast the options and ask yourself, "**Which finding can cause the highest risk to the client?**"

Reduction of Risk Potential: Recognize signs and symptoms of complications and intervene appropriately when providing care.

4. Which of these **assessment findings** is a **priority to report** for a client with an **ileostomy?**

① INCORRECT: Urine specific gravity 1.003. This indicates urine is dilute which would not be a complication from an ileostomy.

② INCORRECT: Heart rate was 78 BPM is now 86 BPM. This is not a significant increase.

③ **CORRECT: Urine output from 75 mL/ hour to 40 mL/hour. This is a trend down.**

④ INCORRECT: Weight from 150 lbs. to 147 lbs. in 4 weeks. This is not a significant decrease over the course of 4 weeks.

The strategy to answer this question is to know many of these GI diseases can lead to the complication of fluid deficit from the diarrhea or in this case liquid stools due to the location of the ileostomy. Think Diarrhea = risk for fluid deficit. Isn't that easy! You do NOT have to remember every GI disorder that has diarrhea or loose stools. As a nurse, you may not know the actual disease, but you will be able to recognize the trends in the changes in the vital signs, the client's color, the abdominal assessment (abdomen–soft, hard, distended, etc.), and the stools. Remember HR ↑, RR ↑, color ↓, later on BP ↓, urine output ↓ = fluid deficit. The key is to assess the trends early, intervene, and not wait until the client is in late signs of shock due to hypovolemia with no early intervention. (*Refer to concept Fluid and Electrolytes for specifics.*)

Physiological Adaptation: Manage the care of the client with a fluid and electrolyte imbalance; Intervene with a client who has an alteration in bowel elimination.

5. Which of these **physiological changes** may happen with a client with **Crohn's disease following an excess number of liquid stools?**

① INCORRECT: Low-pitched bowel sounds. These clients will have high-pitched bowel sounds because of the hypermobility of the bowels that occurs with diarrhea.

② **CORRECT: Metabolic acidosis. Bicarbonate is lost in the stools resulting in acidosis.**

③ INCORRECT: Metabolic alkalosis. Bicarbonate is lost in the stools, so this is not a true statement.

④ INCORRECT: Pain in the epigastric area of the abdomen. Pain in the right and left lower quadrants occurs with Crohn's disease. Epigastric pain is more indicative of peptic ulcer disease.

The strategy for answering this question is to link pathophysiology with the clinical findings that occur with Crohn's disease. Prolonged diarrhea results in metabolic acidosis (metabolic acidosis = pH < 7.35 and HCO_3 < 22). (*Refer to Concept on Acid Base for specifics*). Pathophysiology is a great link for making your life easier. Just think that **Base comes out of the Bottom with diarrhea**. If base is lost, then the client can develop metabolic acidosis. Ulcerative colitis and Crohn's disease both present with pain in the right and left quadrants but not in the epigastric area, which is more indicative of peptic ulcer disease.

Physiological Adaptation: Identify pathophysiology related to an acute or chronic condition.

6. What clinical findings would be most important to **report to the provider of care** for a client who is admitted with the **diagnosis of peptic ulcer disease?**

   ① **CORRECT: HR–80 BPM and increased to 110 BPM, BP–138/88 decreased to 110/70.**

   ② INCORRECT: HR–72 BPM and increased to 80 BPM, RR–18 and increased to 22. Not significant.

   ③ INCORRECT: HR–90 BPM and increased to 105 BPM, urine output was 65 mL/h is now 50mL/h.

   ④ INCORRECT: HR–65 BPM, RR 20 decreased to 18, and BP 138/88 increased to 142/90. Not significant.

The strategy to answer this question is to link what you know about the clinical findings and potential complications of peptic ulcer disease to the given clinical findings. You want to think about complications, because the stem of the question is asking you what would be important to report and you then want to think about the most significant complications that can occur with peptic ulcer disease is bleeding and perforation. As you review the distractors in the question, you are looking for signs of bleeding, emesis (hematemesis), bloody stools (melena), vital sign changes perforation or obstructions with clients who have peptic ulcer disease. The vital signs in Option 1 are trending significantly which may indicate the client is bleeding. Other options are not as significant. These assessment findings can be applied to any of the GI diagnoses that may have a potential complication of bleeding.

Insanely Easy Tip is to remember the signs of fluid volume deficit, everything is decreased!

↓ **Vascular volume = ↑ HR**

↓ **Blood Pressure**

Reduction of Risk Potential: Recognize trends and changes in vital signs and client condition and intervene appropriately.

7. Which of these clinical findings would be most important to **include in the documentation and report to the healthcare provider** after assessing a client with **diverticulitis?** *Select all that apply:*

   ① **CORRECT: Temperature 102.2 F indicates an inflammation/infection process may be occurring.**

   ② INCORRECT: Client reports pain is relieved after eating. This would be more common with an ulcer.

   ③ **CORRECT: Client reports having chills. This may indicate an infection is occurring.**

   ④ **CORRECT: Client reports pain at level 7 on a scale of 1–10 in the left lower abdominal quadrant. Indicates a problem with diverticulitis.**

   ⑤ INCORRECT: Client reports dyspepsia after eating. This may indicate a complication with GERD.

The strategy to answer this question is to link the pathophysiology of the diverticulitis with inflammation and infection. Then no matter what the disease process is, you know that "temperature and pain" are linked to inflammation and infection. If the client has any acute, chronic, infections (bacteria, viruses, parasites), these all will present with some type of pain and temperature. The key is that you may not recognize the medical diagnosis; however, you recognize that it is an infection and if there is a temperature this can lead to fluid-volume deficit along with electrolyte imbalance. The pain described in the other distractors would not be indicative of diverticulitis, as it is the only chronic inflammatory bowel disease that presents with LLQ pain, but the other signs of infection are the same with any of these medical conditions.

Management of Care: Document care.

Reduction of Risk Potential: Recognize signs and symptoms of complications and intervene appropriately.

8. Which **nursing intervention would be the priority** for a client who is presenting with **vomiting secondary to cholecystitis?**

   ① INCORRECT: Assess vital signs every 8 hours. The VS should be assessed more frequently than 8 hours.

   ② CORRECT: Daily weight. This client could present with dehydration from the vomiting which could be monitored with a daily weight.

   ③ INCORRECT: Incentive spirometer–daily. The focus should be on vomiting since this is the focus in the question. If it were appropriate for question, the time frame is incorrect, since it should be performed frequently as prescribed (i.e., every 1–2 hours).

   ④ INCORRECT: Report a urine specific gravity that is 1.003. This would indicate urine is diluted which would not be true of fluid-volume deficit.

The strategy to answer this question is again to link the pathophysiology of what occurs with vomiting to the priority interventions for the concept of Fluid-Volume Deficit. Any of the GI diseases that may cause vomiting and/or diarrhea could result in a potential complication of fluid-volume deficit. One of the most accurate assessments for this concept is to monitor the daily weight. The priority intervention of daily weights can cover a lot of diagnoses with the potential for fluid-volume deficit! Remember daily weight is a great assessment to monitor deficit of fluid (*refer to concept Fluid and Electrolytes for specifics*).

Basic Care: Monitor client's hydration status.

9. Which of these **nursing actions by the UAP** for a client with gastro esophageal reflux **disease (GERD)** would **require intervention** by the charge nurse?

   ① **CORRECT: Gives client a peppermint for his dry mouth. This will lower the LES causing reflux.**

   ② INCORRECT: Leaves the HOB elevated after the A.M. care. Correct action; no need to intervene.

   ③ INCORRECT: Immediately picks up an object off the floor that client dropped. Clients should avoid positions that increase LES pressure (i.e., bending, straining, lying down). Correct action; no need for intervention.

   ④ INCORRECT: Encourages client to drink fluids between meals. Correct action. No action needed.

The strategy is to again link pathophysiology of GERD with the potential causes that can lower the lower esophageal sphincter (LES) and cause reflux. Colas, alcohol, benzodiazepines, channel blockers, chocolate, peppermint, and narcotics lower the relaxation of the lower esophageal sphincter (LES) that will contribute to the reflux of gastric acid and pepsin into the esophagus. A key to good nursing care is to understand the link with the pathophysiology and foods that result in a ↓ LES pressure. It is important to also intervene if another healthcare team member is providing unsafe care. This information is important for the health promotion of clients and would be a priority to include in client teaching prior to discharge. This knowledge can help clients manage their disease and avoid further admissions to the healthcare setting.

Management of Care: Supervise and recognize limitation of self and others, seek assistance or corrective action.

Health Promotion and Maintenance: Provide client and family with information about condition/illness or outcomes.

10. Which one of these **discharge-teaching plans** indicates the nurse **understands** the diet for client recovering from an episode of **diverticulitis?**

   ① **CORRECT: Reviews the importance of eating a diet high in residue to prevent problems with constipation. Since, constipation increases the problem with diverticula, increasing residue is recommended.**

   ② INCORRECT: Reviews the importance of eating a diet high in protein to assist in healing. Not necessary for this medical diagnoses.

   ③ INCORRECT: Review the importance of decreasing sodium in the diet. This would be appropriate for a client with a cardiac complication, but not for diverticulosis.

   ④ INCORRECT: Limit the intake of chocolate due to contributing to the relaxation of the lower esophageal sphincter (LES). This would be important for a client with GERD.

The strategy to answer this question is to understand the priority of care with diverticulosis by linking it to the pathophysiology of diverticulosis and diverticulitis. The goal of care is to prevent clients with diverticulosis from developing diverticulitis. The diverticula of diverticulosis are caused from the high pressure needed to move fecal material. Constipation only increases this pressure and causes the diverticula not to drain resulting in irritation and inflammation. Trapped feces and food in the diverticula can cause bleeding and infection. A diet high in residue helps prevent constipation that can trap food particles in the diverticula. The other options given do not apply to diverticulosis. The goal of nursing and healthcare is to prevent possible potential complications and to help the client manage their disease at home.

Basic Care: Intervene with a client who has an alteration in nutritional intake.

Reduction of Risk Potential: Provide client and family with information about condition.

Decision-Making Analysis Form

Use this tool to help identify why you missed any questions. As you enter the question numbers in the chart, you will begin to see patterns of why you answered incorrectly. This information will then guide you toward what you need to focus on in your continued studies. Ultimately, this analytical exercise will help you become more successful in answering questions!!!

Questions to ask:

1. Did I have the knowledge to answer the question? If not, what information do I need to review?
2. Did I know what the question was asking? Did I misread it or did I miss keywords in the stem of the question?
3. Did I misread or miss keywords in the distractors that would have helped me choose the correct answer?
4. Did I follow my gut reaction or did I allow myself to rationalize and then choose the wrong answer?

	Lack of Knowledge (Concepts, Systems, Pathophysiology, Medications, Procedures, etc.)	Missed Keywords or Misread the Stem of the Question	Missed Keywords or Misread the Distractors	Changed My Answer (Second-guessed myself, i.e., my first answer was correct.)
Put the # of each question you missed in the column that best explains why you think you answered it incorrectly.				

If you changed an answer because you talked yourself out of the correct answer, or you second-guessed yourself, this is an **EASY FIX: QUIT changing your answers**!!! Typically, the first time you read a question, you are about 95% right! The second time you read a question, you start talking yourself into changing the answer. The third time you read a question, you do not have a clue—and you are probably thinking "Who in the heck wrote this question?"

On the other hand, if you read a question too quickly and when you reread it you realize you missed some key information that would impact your decision (i.e., assessments, lab reports, medications, etc.), then it is appropriate to change your answer. When in doubt, go with the safe route: your first thought! Go with your gut instinct!

As you gain confidence in answering questions regarding specific nursing concepts, you will be able to successfully progress to answering higher-level questions about prioritization. Please refer to the *Prioritization Guidelines* in this book for a structure to assist you with this process.

You CAN do this!

> *"Success is liking yourself, liking what you do, and liking how you do it."*
>
> MAYA ANGELOU

References for Chapter 12

Agency for Healthcare Research and Quality (2012). Retrieved from http://psnet.ahrq.gov/primer.aspx?primerID=4

American Cancer Society (2011). Retrieved from http://www.cancer.org/treatment/treatmentsandsideeffects/physicalsideeffects/ostomies/ileostomyguide/ileostomy-problems

Black, J M. and Hawks, J. H. (2009). *Medical surgical nursing: Clinical management for positive outcomes* (8th ed.). Philadelphia: Elsevier/Saunders.

Daniels, R. & Nicoll, L. (2012). *Contemporary medical-surgical nursing,* (2nd ed.). Clifton Park, NY: Delmar Cengage Learning.

Eliopoulos, C. (2014). *Gerontological nursing* (8th ed.), Philadelphia: Lippincott Williams & Wilkins.

Giddens, G. F. (2013). *Concepts for Nursing Practice.* St. Louis, MO: Mosby, an imprint of Elsevier.

Hogan, M. A. (2014). *Pathophysiology, reviews and rationales,* (3rd Edition) Boston, MA: Pearson.

Ignatavicius, D. D. and Workman, M. L. (2010). *Medical-Surgical nursing: Patient-Centered collaborative care* (7th ed.). Philadelphia: Elsevier/Saunders.

Jenson, H. B. and Stanton, B. F., eds. (2011). *Nelson textbook of pediatrics.* (19th ed.). Philadelphia, Pa: Saunders/Elsevier.

LeMone, P. Burke, K. M. and Bauldoff, G. (2011). *Medical-surgical nursing: Critical thinking in patient care* (5th edition). Upper Saddle Road, NJ: Pearson/Prentice Hall.

Lewis, S., Dirksen, S., Heitkemper, M., Bucher, L., and Camera, I. (2011). *Medical surgical nursing: Assessment and management of clinical problems* (8th ed.). St. Louis: Mosby.

Manning, L. and Rayfield, S. (2014). *Nursing made insanely easy* (7th ed). Duluth, GA: I CAN Publishing, Inc.

Manning, L. and Rayfield, S. (2013). *Pharmacology made insanely easy* (4th ed.). Duluth, GA: I CAN Publishing, Inc.

National Centers for Disease Control & Prevention (2014). Retrieved from http://www.cdc.gov/rotavirus/index.html?s_cid=cs_281

National Council of State Boards of Nursing, INC. (NCSBN) 2012. *Research brief: 2011 RN practice analysis: linking the NCLEX RN® examination to practice.* Retrieved from https://www.ncsbn.org/index.htm

National Library of Medicine & National Institutes of Health (2013). Retrieved from http://www.nlm.nih.gov/medlineplus/ency/article/001140.htm

Nettina, S. L. (2013). *Lippincott manual of nursing practice* (10th ed.). Philadelphia, PA: Walters Kluwer Health/Lippincott Williams & Wilkins.

North Carolina Concept Based Learning Editorial Board. (2011). *Nursing a concept based approach to learning.* Upper Saddle Road, NJ: Pearson/Prentice Hall.

Osborn, K. S., Wraa, C. E., Watson, A. S., and Holleran, R. S. (2014). *Medical surgical nursing: preparation for practice* (2nd ed.). Upper Saddle Road, NJ: Pearson.

Pagana, K. D. and Pagana, T. J. (2014). *Mosby's manual of laboratory and diagnostic tests* (5th ed.). St. Louis, MO: Mosby, an imprint of Elsevier.

Porth, C. (2011). *Essentials of pathophysiology* (3rd edition). Philadelphia, PA: Lippincott Williams ad Wilkins.

Porth, C. M. and Grossman, S. (2013). *Pathophysiology, Concepts of altered health states* (9th edition). Philadelphia, PA: Lippincott Williams & Wilkins.

Potter, P. A., Perry, A. G., Stockert, P., and Hall, A. (2013). *Fundamentals of nursing* (8th ed). St. Louis, MO: Pearson/Prentice Hall.

Smeltzer, S. C., Bare, B. G., Hinkle, J. L., and Cheever, K. H. (2010). *Brunner & Suddarth's Textbook of medical-surgical nursing* (12th ed.). Philadelphia: Lippincott Williams & Wilkins.

Wagner, K. D. and Hardin-Pierce, M. C. (2014). *High-Acuity nursing* (6th ed.). Boston: Pearson.

NOTES

CHAPTER 13

Hepatic System
Linking Concepts to Pathophysiology of Diseases
Concept Liver Metabolism

A Snapshot of Liver Metabolism

The liver plays an important role in many of the body's essential physiological functions. It is the great METABOLIZER! It is the detoxification center for medications, hormones, drugs, poisons, and body waste products. The liver is involved with digestion and the metabolism of proteins, carbohydrates and fats. It also is involved in the synthesis of many substances to include clotting factors, cholesterol and it stores substances like vitamins and minerals. The blood supply to the liver is provided by the hepatic artery carrying oxygen-rich blood and the portal vein carrying oxygen-poor blood but rich in nutrients (Daniels & Nicoll, 2012). The good news is the diseased liver has an amazing ability to regenerate itself and only needs about 10–20% functioning ability to maintain life.

The chart on the next page will visually give you a picture of the pathophysiology of the liver and some of its most important functions. Although the main concept of the liver is metabolism, there are many interconnected concepts that are a part of the liver metabolism. They include: pain, fluid balance, nutrition, perfusion, infection, tissue and skin integrity, oxygenation, and cognition. WOW! Some sources report that the liver has over 500 functions, but not to worry! In this chapter we are going to focus on the most important functions! Take some time to process the chart on the next page and then we will help you pull it all together as you proceed through this chapter. There will be *Insanely Easy Tips* to help you along the way!

The Pathophysiology Behind An Alteration In Liver Metabolism

METABOLISM

Pain	Fluid Balance	Nutrition	Perfusion	Infection	Tissue/Skin Integrity	Oxygenation	Metabolism
Inflammatory Process	**Ascites** (↓ Metabolism of plasma proteins i.e., albumin = ↓ colloid osmotic pressure) **Edema** (↓ Metabolism & excretion of ADH and aldosterone = ↑ ADH and ↑ aldosterone levels)	**Protein** (↓ Metabolism, synthesis and storage of plasma proteins and amino acids) **Carbohydrate** (↓ Metabolism of carbohydrates and storage of glycogen and ability to convert glucose to glycogen (glycogenesis)) **Fat** (↓ Metabolism and synthesis of fats from proteins and carbohydrates; ↓ synthesis of phospholipids transported as lipoproteins (important for cellular function) **Cholesterol** (↓ Synthesis and excretion, necessary component of bile salts for digestion) **Fat Soluble Vitamins and Minerals** ↓ Storage of Vitamins A, D, E, K; B12, copper and iron)	**Bleeding—↑ Clotting time** (↓ Metabolism and synthesis of plasma proteins (i.e., clotting factors, Fibrinogen I and prothrombin II, Factor V, VII, VIII, IX, X, Vit E and K) **Anemia, Thrombocytopenia** due to ↑ portal vein pressure that blocks blood flow from the spleen = splenomegaly = ↓ RBCs, WBCs, and platelets **Esophageal varices** (↓ Metabolism and ↓ excretion of ADH and aldosterone = ↑ ADH and ↑ aldosterone levels = kidneys retain fluid and blood supply in liver; shunted to portal veins = ↑ portal hypertension)	**Leukopenia** (↓ WBC due to ↑ portal vein pressure blocks blood flow from the spleen = splenomegaly = ↓ WBCs) **Depressed Immunity** (↓ Metabolism of plasma proteins and ↓ albumin levels lead to depression in cell mediated immune response) **Decrease filtering of blood of bacteria** (↓ in the function of Kupffer cells with liver damage)	**Jaundice** (↓ Metabolism of bile salts (essential for fat and fat-soluble vitamins digestion and absorption. Blocked bile ducts, cause ↑ bile in liver and ↓ excretion of bilirubin = jaundice due to ↑ bilirubin levels in blood.) **Edema** (↓ Metabolism and ↓ excretion of ADH and aldosterone = ↑ ADH and ↑ aldosterone levels = kidneys retain fluid and blood supply in liver) **Petechiae** (↓ Platelets) Palmar erythema, Spider angiomas **Pruritus**	**Oxygenation** (↓ due to pressure on diaphragm from ascites, respiratory acidosis) **Anemia** (Predisposition for hemorrhage due to ↓ blood coagulation due to deficiency of blood coagulation factors synthesized by hepatocytes, and/or thrombocytopenia)	**Encephalopathy** (↓ due to no metabolism of harmful toxins, like ammonia, a by-product of protein digestion. Because portal blood flow is ↓ or is bypassing the liver and ammonia is not converted to urea and excreted by kidneys, ammonia levels ↑ leading to decrease in cognitive functioning and level of consciousness) **Drug toxicity** (↓ Detoxification by liver of medications) ↓ Steroid metabolism, and excretion = (i.e., ↑ estrogen, progesterone and testosterone; *some of the drugs where pharmokinectics are impacted by ↓ liver function)* **Decreased Energy** ↓ Metabolism and anemia

Pathophysiology: Liver Metabolism

Common Labs, Diagnostic Tests, and Therapeutic Procedures

Labs	Diagnostics Tests/Procedures
↑ AST, ↑ ALT (most specific for damage to liver tissue)	**Liver biopsy:** MOST DEFINITIVE TEST (identifies the degree of tissue damage)
↑ ALP (Alkaline phosphatase)	**X-Ray:** Identifies ascites, hepatomegaly, enlarged spleen
↑ Bilirubin: total, direct, indirect	**Esophagogastroduodenoscopy (EGD):** detect presence of esophageal varices
↑ PT, PTT, INR (prolonged clotting time)	**Transjugular Intrahepatic Portosystemic Shunt (TIPS):** treat complications of portal hypertension
↑ Albumin	**Paracentesis:** Done to remove excess fluid for pain relief with ascites and to check fluid for infection. An albumin concentration count can be done to confirm presence of portal hypertension.
↓ HcT, Hgb, ↓ WBC	**Computed Tomography (CT)** of head
↓ Platelets	**Magnetic Resonance Imaging (MRI):** Can detect disease, tumors and blockages in the liver
↓ Protein levels	**Electroencephalogram (EEG):** Detects abnormalities in the brain like encephalopathy
Serologic markers: Identifying presence of hepatitis virus	
Hepatitis antibody serum testing related to the strain of hepatitis	

INSANELY EASY TIP to remember the Liver Enzymes!

The "**ABCs**"

Alcoholism (↑ AST, ↑ ALT)

Biliary obstruction "plugged" (↑ ALP)

Cirrhosis (↑ AST, ↑ ALT)

Pathophysiology: Liver Metabolism

Medications

The following medications represent some of the many used for clients with metabolism alterations in the hepatic systemt. We recommend you review and learn these more-commonly prescribed medications (refer to the book *Pharmacology Made Insanely Easy* for specifics).

Common Medications for Hepatic System Disorders

Antibiotics

Dosages of antibiotics may have to be adjusted based on the degree of liver damage

Drugs to Prevent Itching
- Antihistamines hydroxyzine (Atarax)
- Diphenhydramine (Benadryl)
- Questran

Hepatitis
- Ribavirin
- Lamivudine
- Interferon

Vitamins
- Vitamin A, D, E, K

Ascites (Diuretics)
- Bumetanide (Bumexs)
- Furosemide (Lasix)
- Spironolactone (Aldactone)

Encephalopathy
- Lactulose
- Neomycin

Promote Bile Flow
- Ursodeoxycholic Acid
- Urso (Actigal)

Drugs That Can Cause Hepatotoxicity

- Verify orders when drugs that are hepatotoxic are ordered for clients with liver disease.
- Monitor closely liver functions tests.
- Notify the HCP of adverse effects and abnormal lab values.
- Instruct the client what signs and symptoms to report to their healthcare provider.

ACE inhibitors

Acetaminophen

Alcohol

Iron overdose

Erythromycins

Estrogens

Fluconazole (Diflucan)

Isoniazid (INH)

Itraconazole (Sporanox)

Ketoconazole (Nizoral)

Nonsteroidal anti-inflammatory drugs (NSAIDs)

Phenothiazines

Phenytoin (Dilantin)

Rifampin (Rifadin)

Sulfamethooxazole and trimethoprin (Bactrin, Septra)

Sulfonamides

Pathophysiology: Liver Metabolism

Linking Pathophysiology to Plan of Care with Alteration in Metabolism from Liver Disease

Pathophysiology	Plan of Care"METABOLIZE"
Malnutrition: ↓ metabolism results in ↓ synthesis and storage of plasma proteins and amino acids; ↓ metabolism of carbohydrates and storage of glycogen and ability to convert glucose to glycogen (glycogenesis); ↓ metabolism & synthesis of fats from proteins & carbohydrates; ↓ synthesis of phospholipids transported as lipoproteins for cellular function; ↓ synthesis & excretion necessary component of bile salts for digestion; and ↓ storage of Vitamins A, D, E, K; B12, copper & iron.	**M**alnutrition–(*Refer to Nutrition chart in this chapter on diet for liver.*) Consult dietician to analyze and develop diet plan. Monitor weight, basal metabolism, and labs: Ca^{++}, iron, albumin, protein, etc. for trends of potential complications (i.e., loss of colloid osmotic pressure, etc.)
Energy decreased due to ↓ metabolism and nutrition; anemia due to ↓ RBC production by spleen due to ↑ portal vein pressure blocking blood flow to spleen = ↓ O_2 carrying capacity to tissues = ↓ SaO_2, ↑ RR, fatigue and ↓ energy. Evaluate pain: due to inflammatory process of liver disease or from pressure on organs or nerves by tumors.	**E**nergy decreased, assess tolerance for activity and pace activity with rest. Ensure client gets adequate sleep and nutrition for healing. Evaluate pain level frequently; provide pain med as prescribed & offer alternatives methods of relief. Evaluate if pain med is effective. (*Refer to concept Pain*)
Tissue/Skin Integrity may be impaired from ascites & edema causing pressure points due to ↓ colloidal osmotic pressure, and ↑ ADH levels & ↑ aldosterone levels. Jaundice develops when the liver cannot manage the broken down blood cells due to ↓ metabolism of bile salts (needed for fat & fat-soluble vitamins digestion & absorption), and there is ↓ excretion of bilirubin in the urine.	**T**issue/Skin Integrity: observe skin for non-blanchable areas and pressure points q 4 hrs. or/protocol. Turn or reposition q 2 hrs. Use pressure-alternating mattress, assess wounds for healing (granulation tissue), note color, odor and amount of drainage. Ensure dietary needs are met; ↑ fluids as prescribed. Assess for pruritus, meds as prescribed for relief.
Ascites & Anasarca develops due to ↓ metabolism of plasma proteins & albumin resulting in ↓ colloid osmotic pressure, (fluid leaks into the interstitial spaces). If ascites severe = ↓ ability of client to expand the diaphragm; RR becoming rapid & shallow. Edema due to ↑ ADH and ↑ aldosterone cause kidneys to retain fluid. (*Refer to concept Renal Perfusion.*)	**A**scites & Anasarca: Change position; avoid friction when moving; measure & document abdominal girth daily. Prepare for paracentesis if needed; if done, document amount, color, & VS post procedure. Assess for edema: amount & location. Monitor daily weights, I & O; and skin for breakdown.
Bleeding is due to ↑ in time to clot due to ↓ metabolism & synthesis of plasma proteins (i.e., clotting factors: fibrinogen I and prothrombin II, Factor V, VII, VIII, IX, X, and vitamins E & K. Anemia and thrombocytopenia may develop. Esophageal varices develop due to enlarged blood vessels in lower esophagus due to blocked blood flow in the liver = ↑ pressure in portal system as result of ↑ ADH & ↑ aldosterone. Kidneys retain fluid, shunting the blood supply in liver to portal veins. Smaller blood vessels, not designed for ↑ volume of blood, leak/rupture resulting in bleeding. (*Refer to concept Perfusion, Cardiac/Peripheral for specifics.*)	**B**leeding: Assess for ↑ HR, RR or ↓ BP; lab work (i.e., clotting factors, platelets, Hgb, Hct); for signs of bleeding; Observe emesis and stools for blood, note abdominal distention, measure abdomen girth for bleeding. Provide soft toothbrush; ↓ roughage/ irritating food to avoid damage to intestinal & esophageal mucosa; prevent irritation and bleeding.
Oxygenation ↓ due to pressure on diaphragm from ascites, respiratory acidosis. Clients may have anemia due to ↓ RBC production by the spleen because of ↑ portal-vein pressure that blocks blood flow to the spleen = ↓ O_2 carrying capacity to the tissues = ↓ SaO_2, ↑ RR , fatigue/activity intolerance. (*Refer to concept Oxygenation for specifics.*)	**O**xygenation: HOB to Semi-fowler's ↓ pressure of abdomen on diaphragm (ascites), monitor RR, SaO_2, assess lungs for adventitious breath sounds, note shallow breaths and encourage deep breathing, use incentive spirometer every 1–2 hrs. as prescribed.
Labs: for impact of ↓ liver metabolism, (i.e. clotting factors, CBC, albumin and protein levels, BUN & Creatinine, ↑ AST, ↑ ALT. ALP ↑ (Alkaline phosphatase) may indicate biliary obstruction and ↑ AST, ↑ ALT may indicate damage from cirrhosis.	**L**abs: (see lab chart in this chapter) for labs to monitor and report to healthcare team so appropriate care may be provided and complications prevented.
Infection: Risk due to leukopenia (↓ WBC) due to ↑ portal vein pressure blocks blood flow from the spleen = splenomegaly = ↓ WBCs; have depressed immunity due to ↓ metabolism of plasma proteins & ↓ albumin levels; leads to depression in cell mediated immune response & ↓ filtering of bacteria from blood due to ↓ function of Kupffer cells with liver damage.	**I**nfection: monitor for ↑ Temp, WBCs, administer antibiotics as prescribed; use appropriate personal protective equipment (PPE). (*Refer to concept Infection Control for specifics.*)
ZZZs Encephalopathy results when ammonia, produced by protein digestion, is not metabolized by the liver into urea and excreted by the kidneys due to ↓ portal blood flow that bypasses liver. The ↑ ammonia levels, lead to damage of the nervous system & ↓ cognitive functioning and level of consciousness.	**Z**ZZs Encephalopathy: Early signs: change in personality; sleep patterns, breath musty, sweet odor, ↓ cognition & LOC, ↑ confusion, poor concentration and judgment. Late: early signs more severe, unconsciousness to coma. Monitor ammonia levels; (lactulose to ↓ levels).
Excrete & rid of toxins: Drug toxicity can occur due to ↓ detoxification by liver of medications, (i.e., ↓ steroid metabolism, & excretion leads to (i.e., ↑ estrogen, progesterone & testosterone).	**E**xcrete & rid of toxins, drugs, poisons, etc. Collaborate with HCP to ↓ administration of drugs metabolized by liver; monitor side effects and renal function.

Pathophysiology: Liver Metabolism

Evaluation of Expected Outcomes

The METABOLIZER is Working When Expected Outcomes are Met!

Malnutrition: Nutrition status adequate to maintain energy and prevent protein catabolism

Edema and Anasarca: Decrease/no edema and anasarca

Evaluate pain: No pain or pain controlled with medication or alternative methods of relief

Tissue/Skin Integrity: Skin and tissue intact, no decubitus ulcers, wounds healing

Ascites: No ascites, or decreased ascites

Bleeding: No bleeding; Hct, Hgb, and platelets WDL

Oxygenation: RR, SaO$_2$ WDL; lung sounds clear to auscultation

Labs: WDL for client

Infection: No signs of infection

ZZZs: No decrease in LOC, ammonia levels WDL

Excrete and rid of toxins: No adverse side of effects from medications or toxins

---

Can you name all of the concepts that are interconnected with the Hepatic System and at least one priority intervention? Give it a try. We bet you can do it!

1. Intervention:	2. Intervention:	3. Intervention:	4. Intervention:
5. Intervention:	6. Intervention:	7. Intervention:	8. Intervention:

You may have thought of different interventions, but listed are a few of the priority interventions for each concept:

1. **Pain:** Administer pain med as prescribed; monitor medications for liver toxicity
2. **Fluid Balance:** I & O; daily weights & trend
3. **Nutrition:** Consult with dietician to meet nutritional needs; monitor labs of prealbumin and albumin
4. **Perfusion:** Monitor for signs of bleeding (i.e., ↑ HR & RR, abdominal distention); monitor PTT, PT, platelets; provide soft toothbrush to prevent bleeding of the gums
5. **Infection:** Observe for signs of infection (i.e., ↑ WBC, temp); use appropriate PPE for hepatitis (standard precautions & contact)
6. **Tissue/Skin Integrity:** Turn every two hours; monitor skin for areas that do not blanch, particularly pressure points
7. **Oxygen:** Incentive spirometer every 1–2 hours while awake; HOB in semi to Fowler's position; monitor CBC for anemia
8. **Metabolism:** Provide rest while in acute stages of disease; work with HCP to question medications that are hepatotoxic; monitor ammonia level for elevation

Pathophysiology: Liver Metabolism
Concept: Nutrition

Nutrition: The liver has a major impact on the metabolism of nutrients. Liver damage can cause decrease metabolism of carbohydrates, fat, and protein. The decrease in the metabolism of glucose affects the client's ability to maintain normal blood glucose levels, which is necessary for energy to the body. As the liver cells become damaged, the decrease in the fat metabolism decreases the blood levels of cholesterol. Cholesterol is necessary component of bile salts that aid in digestion and it is required for the production of hormones (cortisone, adrenaline, estrogen and testosterone and Vitamin D). The decrease metabolism of protein results in hypoalbuminemia necessary to maintain colloid osmotic pressure. When the liver cannot adequately store amino acids, the client may experience generalized edema such as with anasarca. In addition, a damaged liver cannot adequately store fat-soluble vitamins, B12, iron and copper. They are needed in the formation and synthesis of hemoglobin, necessary for blood clotting, energy for the body, cell growth and organ protection. Malnutrition can lead to further liver damage resulting in a destructive cycle (Hogan, Gingrich, Wilcutts, & Deleon, 2007).

The result of so many nutritional deficits is the client may require nutritional supplements to include vitamins and minerals, to meet nutritional needs. Small meals, 4–6 times per day are often better tolerated and help ensure the client gets the necessary calories to prevent further nutritional deficits. The dietician is an important interdisciplinary team member to consult to assess and analyze the nutritional needs of the client to prevent further malnutrition and the resulting complications. The next chart illustrates the many nutritional needs of a client with liver disease.

Pathophysiology: Liver Metabolism
Concept: Nutrition

PATHOPHYSIOLOGY

NUTRITIONAL NEEDS FOR THE CLIENT WITH LIVER DISEASE

Protein *Plant protein tolerated best.* **"PROTEIN"**	Carbohydrates *Need to maintain blood sugar.* **"CARB"**	Fat *Need for energy, absorption of nutrients.* **"FATS"**	Vitamin A *Need for vision & cell growth in vital organs.* **"O & G"**	Vitamin D *Need for bone health.* **"BONES"**	Vitamin E *Need for platelet aggregation & immune function.*	Vitamin K *Need for clotting.* **"LEAF"**	Vitamin B12 (Cobalamin) *Need for formation of RBCs & nerve function.* **"FISH"**	Iron & Copper *Need for synthesis of hemoglobin; prevent anemia.* **"IRON"**
Peanut butter Remember all beans Offer cottage cheese, yogurt, (soy milk, best for liver disease) Tuna, tofu; try grains Eggs, encourage vegetable for liver disease (i.e., peas, avocados) Include chicken, turkey Nuts and seeds (pistachios, almonds, sesame seeds, etc.) **Alert:** If jaundiced or ↑ ammonia level, ↓ protein to none as pre-scribed.	Cereal, Oatmeal Apples, strawberries, blueberries Real Whole grains Beans, nuts and seeds	Fat: Olive oil, sunflower oil Avocados, all nuts Tuna, try peanut butter Salmon, soy milk Fat amount for liver disease varies to maintain nutrition **Alert: Restrict with jaundice.**	Orange veggies and fruit (sweet potato, carrots, cantaloupe) Green veggies (spinach, broccoli)	Beef Organ meat, calf liver Need cheese Egg yolks Salmon, can tuna in water Soy milk, yogurt, fortified with vitamin D	Wheat germ (best) Nuts (almonds and hazelnuts) Sunflower: seeds and oil	Leafy green vegetables (spinach and Brussels spouts) Eggs Asparagus Fiber: beans & soybeans	Fish, smoked salmon, tuna Include dairy milk, soy, cheese, eggs Should eat meat, liver High-fortified cereals **Alert:** If jaundiced or ↑ ammonia level, ↓ protein to none as prescribed.	Include fish, chicken, eggs & green leafy vegetables Raisins, sunflower seeds and legumes are good Organ meats like liver and other red meats Need Vitamin C to help absorb iron in diet

Pathophysiology: Liver Metabolism
Concept: Nutrition

We bet that when you looked at the diet chart on the previous page, you said, "No way can I remember all of the different foods and the vitamins and minerals the client needs!"

You know what? We were overwhelmed too! So, below is an

INSANELY EASY TIP
to remember the dietary needs for liver disease!

"GO NUTSO"!

"NUTSO" has all the foods that will help meet his nutritional needs.

G reen leafy vegetables: include avocados

O range fruits & vegetables (other fruits are good too)

N uts, seeds (sunflower & sesame) & peanut butter, too

U need to eat beans a lot

T una, salmon

S unflower & olive oils, soy milk

O atmeal, whole grains

Pathophysiology: Liver Metabolism
Hepatitis

Hepatitis is an inflammation of the liver that is caused by viruses, toxins, or chemicals (drugs). Viral hepatitis is one of the most common blood-borne infections in the U.S. The pathophysiology of all types of hepatitis is similar. Hepatocytes undergo pathologic changes and are damaged in two ways: through direct action of the virus or through cell-mediated response to the virus. Inflammation of the liver with necrosis occurs and results in decrease liver function. The degree of loss of function is related to the level of hepatocellular damage. The most common types are:

Hepatitis A (HAV) is due to the ingestion of contaminated food or water. It is transmitted through close personal contact via the fecal-oral route. Clients at risk are children and adults in day care centers or long-term living facilities.

Hepatitis B (HBV) can be an acute or chronic infection that is transmitted through blood. Risk factors include unprotected sex, contact with infected blood, contaminated needles (i.e., drug users) and infants born to infected mothers.

Hepatitis C (HCV) is transmitted through the blood. It has the same risk factors as hepatitis B.

Hepatitis D (delta agent) is a co-infection with hepatitis B (HBV). The risk factors are clients with injectable drug abuse or clients who have received clotting factor concentrates.

Hepatitis E (HEV) is transmitted via the fecal oral route and comes from contaminated food or water. It mostly affects pregnant women in developing countries.

Acute hepatitis can lead to: chronic hepatitis (i.e., HBV, HCV, HDV), cirrhosis of the liver and fulminant hepatitis. Cirrhosis and fulminant hepatitis both can lead to increased necrosis and inability of liver cells to regenerate. This results in hepatic encephalopathy and eventually irreversible liver failure and death.

Pathophysiology: Liver Metabolism
Hepatitis

	FIRST-DO PRIORITY INTERVENTIONS			
SYSTEM-SPECIFIC ASSESSMENTS "JAUNDICE"	**DIET**	**EQUIPMENT**	**PLANS/INTERVENTIONS "PREVENT"**	**HEALTH PROMOTION**

Jaundice (icteric phase), pruritus
 	
Assess VS, low-grade temp
 	
Urine: dark color
 	
Nausea/vomiting, anorexia, nutritional needs assess
 	
Decrease energy, fatigue
 	
Inspect stools, may be clay colored
 	
Inspect labs: monitor ALT, AST, ALP for liver damage; CBC, clotting factors, platelets for potential bleeding
 	
Complain of RUQ abdominal pain, tenderness and/or muscle/joint pain
 	
Edema, ascites, hepatomegaly, splenomegaly, assess weight, I & O
	• ↑ Carb
	• ↑ Calorie (goal is 2500–3000 calories/day
	• May need vitamin supplements (B complex, folic acid)
	• ↓ Fat (moderate level)
	• ↓ Protein (moderate to low to none with progression of liver damage)
	• Small frequent meals
	• Refer to concept on Nutrition for specifics
	
	REMEMBER: GO NUTSO!
		• Central lines
		• TPN when nutritionally indicated
			Private room, or client with same infection (Hepatitis).
			
			Require contact precautions with Hepatitis B & C, blood, GI secretions, use needleless system for delivery of medication & parenteral solutions. (*Refer to Concept Infection Control for specifics.*)
			
			Report cases of hepatitis to health department.
			Refer high risk clients for vaccinations.
			
			Evaluate liver function (only necessary medications to avoid further liver damage).
			
			Very necessary to REST to promote hepatic healing.
			
			Educate client & family on measures to prevent transmission of hepatitis.
			
			Necessary to avoid sexual intercourse until hepatitis antibody test is negative.
			
			Teach about diet, ↑ carb, ↑ calorie ↓ fat (moderate level), ↓ protein (moderate to low to none with progression of liver damage), small frequent meals. Lifestyle Changes: no alcohol, smoking, liver toxic medications (NSAIDS, Tylenol, etc.).
				• Report cases of hepatitis to health department.
				• Vaccinations for high-risk individuals.
				Teach client/family about:
				• Lifestyle Changes:
				  • No alcohol
				  • No smoking
				  • No liver toxic medications (i.e. NSAIDS, Tylenol, etc.)
				• Contact precautions and how disease is transmitted.
				• Instruct to never to donate blood, body organs or tissue.

ELDERLY CONCERNS:

Hepatitis may be more severe in the elderly client!

Exceptions and Additions by Diseases

Pathophysiology: Liver Metabolism
Hepatitis Immunizations

INSANELY EASY TIP about Hepatitis Immunizations!

Vaccinations Available	Hepatitis A	Hepatitis B	Hepatitis C	Hepatitis D	Hepatitis E
Note: Children who have not been vaccinated as infants need to complete the series by twelve years of age.	**X (2 doses)** • 1 year of age • 1½ year *Recommended for childcare workers.*	**X (3 doses)** • 12 hours of age • 1-2 months • 6-18 months *Recommended for all children and healthcare providers.*	None	None	None

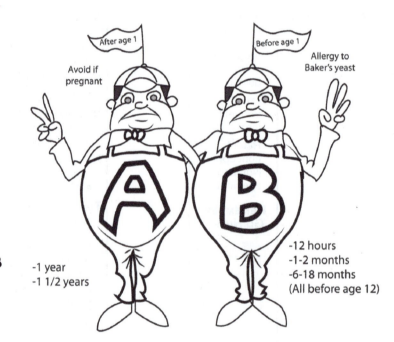

Hepatitis A and B

"Tweedle A and Tweedle B,

A takes 2 and B takes 3

A's after 1 and B's before 1"

Pathophysiology: Liver Metabolism
Hepatitis Infection Control
Transmission of Hepatitis

Transmitted	Hepatitis A	Hepatitis B	Hepatitis C	Hepatitis D	Hepatitis E
Anal (Fecal) and oral (**E**at)	X				X
Blood & **B**ody and **C**ontaminated needles		X	X	X (co-exists with B)	

INSANELY EASY TIP on Transmission!

Hepatitis **A and E** =

Anal (fecal)

Eat (oral) contaminated food and water

Hepatitis **B and C** =

Blood & **B**ody and **C**ontaminated needles

Infection Control

Personal Protective Equipment is the Same for
all the types of Hepatitis
= Standard + Contact

See what YOU KNOW about HEPATITIS!!! GENIUS!!!!

Exceptions and Additions by Diseases

Pathophysiology: Liver Metabolism
Cirrhosis of the Liver

Cirrhosis of the liver is the scarring of liver tissue, which interferes with normal liver function. It is the final stage in the progression of liver disease to include hepatitis. The liver becomes cirrhotic and is nodular in consistency with bands of fibrosis (scar tissue). There are four types of cirrhosis, alcoholic (consumption of a pint or more of alcohol per day), biliary (obstruction of the bile duct and can be a result of heart failure), post hepatic (from chronic hepatitis B or C) and cardiac secondary to the end stage of heart failure. The most common cause of cirrhosis in the U.S. is alcoholism. There is severe inflammation and significant destruction of the hepatocytes. This alters the flow of vascular and lymphatic systems and results in bile stasis causing jaundice. Portal vein hypertension (increased pressure in portal vein caused by obstruction or congestion) develops from the increased capillary pressure. The increase in portal hypertension causes collateral blood vessels to develop in the stomach, rectum and the esophagus. The vessels become distended and cause **varices**. These varices can easily rupture and bleed, particularly in the esophagus where the varices become irritated by food and alcohol. The portal hypertension also causes stasis of the blood in the spleen leading to splenomegaly with an increased breakdown of white blood cells, (leukopenia), red blood cells (anemia) and platelets (thrombocytopenia). This results in the client becoming more susceptible to infections. The damaged liver also results in decreased production of albumin, which results in decreased colloidal osmotic pressure. Fluid then leaves the blood vessels and enters the abdomen (third spacing) and leads to **ascites**.

Hepatic encephalopathy results because the damaged liver can no longer clear protein metabolic wastes. Therefore ammonia is not converted to urea and eliminated through the kidneys. The increase ammonia levels accumulate in the bloodstream and cross the blood-brain barrier into the brain tissue leading to the hepatic encephalopathy (Osborn, Wraa, Watson, & Holleran, 2014).

Pathophysiology: Liver Metabolism

Cirrhosis of the Liver
System-Specific Assessments: "ASCITES"

The system-specific assessments for cirrhosis of the liver can be **INSANELY EASY!** Just think of what you assess for and remember "**ASCITES.**"

A   Airway assess because of ascites, bleeding, hematemesis, melena

Asterixis (clients hands appear to "flap" due to release of the dorsiflexion of the wrists)

S   Splenomegaly swelling, peripheral edema

C   Complain of abdominal pain, weight loss

Confusion/personality changes, changes in LOC with increase ammonia levels

I   Inspect lab work (bilirubin, serum protein, albumin, CBC, PT, PTT, INR, ammonia; ↑ ammonia levels indicate liver is unable to break down protein metabolic waste products, (ammonia to urea) to be excreted by kidneys

T   Trend other signs and symptoms: fetor hepaticus (liver breath), caput medusae (enlarged tortuous, visible blood vessels that radiate from umbilicus).

E   Evaluate liver enzymes for elevation

S   Skin: pruritus, jaundice, petechiae, palmar erythema, spider angiomas, ecchymosis, edema and ascites

Exceptions and Additions by Diseases

Pathophysiology: Liver Metabolism
Cirrhosis of the Liver

	FIRST-DO PRIORITY INTERVENTIONS			
SYSTEM-SPECIFIC ASSESSMENTS "ASCITES"	DIET	EQUIPMENT	PLANS/INTERVENTIONS "METABOLIZE"	HEALTH PROMOTION

Airway assess because of ascites, bleeding, hematemesis, melena **A**sterixis (clients hands appear to "flap" due to release of the dorsiflexion of the wrists) **S**plenomegaly swelling, peripheral edema **C**omplain of abdominal pain, weight loss **C**onfusion/ personality changes & LOC with increase ammonia levels **I**nspect lab work: bilirubin, serum protein, albumin, CBC, PT, PTT, INR, ammonia levels **T**rend other signs & symptoms: fetor hepaticus (liver breath), caput medusae (enlarged tortuous, visible blood vessels that radiate from umbilicus) **E**valuate liver enzymes for elevation **S**kin: Pruritus, jaundice, petechiae, palmar erythema, spider angiomas, ecchymosis, edema and ascites	• ↑ Carb
	• ↑ Calorie (goal is 2500–3000 calories/day)
	• May need vitamin supplements (B complex, folic acid)
	• ↓ Fat (moderate level)
	• ↓ Protein (moderate to low to none with progression of liver damage)
	• Small frequent meals
	• TPN when nutritionally indicated
	• Refer to concept on Nutrition for specifics
		• Central lines
		• Sengston Blakemore tube or other esophageal tamponade tube for compression with esophageal varices
		• Equipment safety for Sengston Blakemore: have scissors at bedside if develop respiratory distress. NPO, nothing down the tube
			Malnutrition: *See chart in this chapter for diet.*
			Edema: compare & contrast, location, amount of edema, daily weights.
			  Evaluate pain: frequently & provide both pain medications & alternative methods of relief.
			Tissue/Skin Integrity: Turn client q 2 hours, use pressure alternating mattress, asses wounds for healing, avoid friction when moving, observe skin for pressure points and non-blanchable areas, medicate as prescribe to relieve pruritus.
			Ascites and anasarca: Change position, measure and document abdominal girth daily.
			Bleeding: Assess emesis, stools for blood, note abdominal distention, provide soft toothbrush for dental care and avoid roughage in diet to avoid damage to intestinal and esophageal mucosa. Administer non-selective beta blockers, vasopressors, vitamin K for bleeding as prescribed.
			Oxygenation: HOB to Semi-fowler's to reduce pressure of abdomen on diaphragm, monitor RR, SaO$_2$, lung sounds.
			Labs: *See chart in this chapter for labs.*
			Infection: monitor WBCs, temp; administer antibiotics as ordered; use appropriate PPE.
			ZZZs Sleepiness, personality changes, LOC for possible ↑ in ammonia level: will need Lactulose to ↓ levels (refer to *Pharmacology Made Easy*).
			Excrete and rid of toxins, drugs, poisons, etc. Collaborate with the HCP when administering drugs metabolized by the liver, minimize if possible. Monitor for adverse side effects; monitor renal function.
				Teach client/family about:
				• Lifestyle changes:
				  • No alcohol
				  • No smoking
				  • No liver toxic medications (i.e., NSAIDS, Tylenol, etc.)
				• Position in a semi-Fowler's with ascites for comfort and ease of breathing.
				• Signs and symptoms of potential complication of encephalopathy to report.
				• Report weight gain > 2 lbs/day.
				• Use soft toothbrush and avoid roughage in diet to prevent bleeding in the esophagus and intestines.

Pathophysiology: Liver Metabolism
Cirrhosis of the Liver
Procedure: Paracentesis

Pre-Procedure "ACT NOW"	During and Post-Procedure
Assess allergies, identification of client. **C**onsent (informed) required. **T**each, give explanation of paracentesis; assure client's questions are answered. **N**eed to void or insert Foley prior to procedure as prescribed, sedation if needed. **O**bserve and monitor for vital signs prior to procedure. **W**eight, take prior to procedure, measure abdominal girth.	• Record weight, abdominal girth before and after procedure. • Close monitoring of vital signs during procedure and then every 2–4 hours per protocol post-procedure. • Label and send specimen of fluid to lab as prescribed. • Maintain pressure at insertion site for several minutes after & apply dressing to site as prescribed. • Document color, consistency, and amount of fluid removed; condition of insertion site, evidence of leakage. • Position the client for comfort following the procedure. • I & O every 4 hours or per protocol. • Give albumin, IVs, diuretics as prescribed. • Monitor for signs and symptoms of hypovolemia (i.e., ↑ HR, RR), change LOC if large volumes of fluid are removed. • Monitor signs and symptoms of infection (WBCs, ↑ temperature, redness at insertion site (Nattina, 2013).

Pathophysiology: Liver Metabolism
Cirrhosis of the Liver
Trend Potential Complications: Esophageal Varices

MEDICAL EMERGENCY when Esophageal Varices Ruptured!!!
Fluid-Volume Deficit: Hypovolemia from Bleeding

SYSTEM-SPECIFIC ASSESSMENTS "THE Ds"	FIRST-DO PRIORITY INTERVENTIONS "FLUIDS"
Decrease in vascular volume = tachycardia **D**rop in postural blood pressure leading to syncope **D**ecrease too much in BP can lead to shock **D**ecrease weight (sudden loss) **D**ry mucous membranes **D**ecrease in neck vein size (flat) **D**ecrease in urine output (oliguria) **D**ecrease in skin turgor (not valid assessment for elderly client)	**F**luid (blood) replacement, administer meds to help stop bleeding: give non-selective beta blockers, vasopressors, vit K per order **L**evel of consciousness, (safety) report to HCP **U**rine < 30 mL/hour, report trends **I** & O **D**ocument daily weight, vital signs **S**afety: may need an esophagogastric balloon tamponade (i.e., Sengstaken-Blakemore tube or Minnesota tube); have scissors at bedside for emergency removal of tube.

LINK the **Concept of Fluid Balance** with **Fluid Loss:**
Bleeding from Esophageal Varices.

See, you knew the **PRIORITY** Care for **Fluid-Volume Deficit!**

See how *Insanely Easy* that was!!

Exceptions and Additions by Diseases

Pathophysiology: Liver Metabolism
Cirrhosis of the Liver
Trend Potential Complication: Equipment Malfunction

Indication for Esophagogastric balloon tamponade: A client with known portal hypertension or prior variceal hemorrhage that has severe upper GI bleeding that will not clear with gastric lavage and pharmacologic therapy.

Esophagogastric Balloon Tamponade: Equipment and Procedure Priorities

If your client presents with the following system-specific assessments then there is:

"DISTRESS"
A Medical Emergency With A Esophagogastric Balloon Tamponade Equipment

Dyspnea, use of accessory muscles

Increase respiratory rate, noisy respirations, choking

Sat O$_2$ decreased, ABGs decreased

Tachycardia

Restless, anxious,

Evaluate lung sounds (may be absent), asymmetrical chest movement

Scissors needed to cut gastric balloon port of tube
Support client

Priority of Care–Oxygenation and Safety

Notify the Healthcare Provider or Rapid Response Immediately!

**EMERGENCY Equipment Failure: Keep scissors at bedside
to cut the gastric balloon port of tube to allow air to escape!!!**

**Oxygenation ↓ due to airway obstruction (dislodgement of tube and
the esophageal balloon into the oropharynx).**

Your Priority Thinking in this Situation, Saved the Client's Life!!

Pathophysiology: Liver Metabolism
Cirrhosis of the Liver
Trend Potential Complications: Hepatic Encephalopathy

Hepatic Encephalopathy: The liver is responsible for changing toxic substances that are either made by the body or taken into the body (such as medicines) and make them harmless. When the liver is damaged, these toxins build up in the bloodstream. Ammonia, which is produced by the body when proteins are digested, is one of the harmful substances that is metabolized by the liver and converted to urea to be excreted by the kidneys. Hepatic encephalopathy results because the damaged liver can no longer clear protein metabolic wastes. Therefore ammonia is not converted to urea and eliminated through the kidneys. The increase in ammonia levels accumulate in the bloodstream and cross the blood-brain barrier into the brain tissue leading to the hepatic encephalopathy. Hepatic encephalopathy may occur suddenly in people who previously had no liver problems when damage occurs to the liver. More often, the condition is seen in people with chronic liver disease.

SYSTEM-SPECIFIC ASSESSMENTS "AMMONIA"	FIRST-DO PRIORITY INTERVENTIONS
Ammonia blood levels increase (Early) **M**usty or sweet odor to breath (Early) **M**ental fogginess, changes in thinking, mild confusion, mood changes (Early) **O**rientation decreases, drowsiness, confusion can progress to coma (Late) **N**eed assistance, sluggish movement, poor judgment (Late) **I**nappropriate behavior or severe personality changes (Late) **A**gitation, excitement, abnormal movement of hands, Asterixis (Late)	• Can be a medical emergency if symptoms have progressed from mild to severe to a coma state. • Observe and monitor client for possible causes (i.e., GI bleed, electrolyte imbalance, often potassium). • Decrease protein in diet to ↓ ammonia productions but may need nutritional support (i.e., TPN, tube feedings) due to malnutrition risk. • Lactulose administer to inhibit diffusion of ammonia from colon into the blood stream (*Refer to Pharmacology Made Easy*). • Other drugs that may be given include neomycin and Rifaximin, an antibiotic. • Avoid medications toxic to the liver. • Life support if the person is in a coma. May have cerebral edema.

Clinical Decision-Making Exercises

1. Which one of these lab values would be a priority to report to the healthcare provider with a client with cirrhosis of the liver?

    ① Elevated ammonia level.

    ② Elevated ALT and AST levels.

    ③ Elevated bilirubin level.

    ④ Decreased albumin level.

2. What information should be included in the discharge teaching plan of care for a client who has hepatitis B? *Select all that apply.*

    ① Hepatitis B can be spread by ingestion of contaminated food or water.

    ② Hepatitis B can be spread by drug abuse and sexual contact.

    ③ Clients who have hepatitis B are at risk for contracting hepatitis D.

    ④ Standard precautions only are needed in caring for clients with Hepatitis B.

    ⑤ Vaccination will lower the client's risk of contracting hepatitis C.

3. Which of these clinical assessment findings would be a priority to report to the healthcare provider for a client admitted with cirrhosis and portal hypertension?

    ① HR 100 BPM is now 122 BPM.

    ② Urine output was 88mL/hour is now 68mL/hour.

    ③ Jaundice and peripheral pulses +1.

    ④ Respirations were 23/minute and now are 17/minute.

4. What is an appropriate plan of care for a client admitted with hepatitis C? *Select all that apply.*

    ① Encourage intake of oatmeal, whole grains, strawberries, and apples.

    ② Instruct the client to avoid alcohol.

    ③ Instruct client that after 3 months they may donate blood.

    ④ Encourage periods of rest initially followed by gradual increase in activity.

    ⑤ Place in a room with another client who has an infection.

    ⑥ Administer acetaminophen (Tylenol) for mild discomfort.

5. Which of these clinical findings would be a priority to report for a client with cirrhosis of the liver?

    ① A decrease in the ammonia level.

    ② An abdominal girth of 55 cm that was 72 cm.

    ③ Client is having flapping tremors of the wrist and fingers.

    ④ Hgb is 12g/dL and Hct is 38%.

6. What is the priority action for a client with ascites of the abdomen from cirrhosis of the liver has these clinical findings: O_2 Saturation of 92%, respiratory rate of 24/minute that was 18/minute, and is complaining of shortness of breath?

    ① Notify the healthcare provider immediately.

    ② Place the client in high Fowler's position.

    ③ Assess the lung sounds.

    ④ Take the client's vital signs.

7. What is the priority intervention for a client with a Blakemore Sangston tube in place and is presenting with a heart rate of 110 bpm, RR–28/min, noisy respirations, dyspnea, and choking?

    ① Reposition the tube.

    ② Place the client in semi-Fowler's position.

    ③ Suction the oral airway.

    ④ Get the scissors from the bedside to cut the balloon port of tube.

8. Which of these prescribed orders should the nurse question with a client who has a history of liver disease and is being discharged from the hospital?

    ① Discharge with a referral to home health.

    ② Teach client to begin slowly increasing activity with scheduled rest periods.

    ③ Discharge with a prescription for Advil (Ibuprofen) for mild discomfort.

    ④ Discharge with instructions to notify the healthcare provider for any signs of bleeding.

9. What personal protective equipment is required when providing care for a client with a new diagnosis of hepatitis B? *Select all that apply.*

    ① Gloves when handling body fluids.

    ② Gown and gloves when changing the bed after an episode of diarrhea.

    ③ Mask when entering the room.

    ④ Goggles when entering the room.

    ⑤ N 95 mask on the client when leaving the room.

10. Which of these interventions would be important to implement in preventing potential complications for an elderly client with cirrhosis of the liver?

    ① Instruct the client to increase the intake of protein in their diet.

    ② Place the client on an alternating pressure air mattress.

    ③ Ambulate the client in the hall every 4 hours while awake.

    ④ Instruct the client to use a firm toothbrush with vigorous motion when brushing their teeth.

Answers and Rationales

1. Which one of these **lab values** would be a **priority to report** to the healthcare provider with a client with **cirrhosis of the liver?**

    ① **CORRECT: Elevated ammonia level is an indication that the liver is failing in breaking down protein waste products. The ammonia is not being converted to urea to be excreted by the kidneys. The client will need Lactulose to bring the ammonia level down.**

    ② INCORRECT: Elevated ALT and AST levels. Levels would already be elevated because of the cirrhosis.

    ③ INCORRECT: Elevated bilirubin level. Levels would already be elevated.

    ④ INCORRECT: Decreased albumin level. Important to monitor because it is the cause of ascites, but the increase ammonia levels would be a priority.

The strategy to answer this question is to know the pathophysiology of liver failure and that increasing ammonia levels indicate the liver is no longer able to break down protein waste products into urea and the ammonia has crossed the blood brain barrier. As a nurse you would want to identify the **early** signs of hepatic encephalopathy (i.e., change in sleep patterns; breath with musty, sweet odor; changes in thinking; mild confusion; forgetfulness; poor concentration and judgment; and personality or mood changes) and intervene before the client progresses to loss of consciousness or coma. Monitoring the client's ammonia level and reporting it to the HCP are priority interventions.

Reduction of Risk Potential: Recognize signs and symptoms of complications and intervene appropriately.

Physiological Adaptation: Identify pathophysiology related to an acute or chronic condition

2. What **information** should be included in the **discharge** teaching plan of care for a client who has **hepatitis B?** Select all that apply.

    ① INCORRECT: Hepatitis B can be spread by ingestion of contaminated food or water. Hepatitis A & E are spread by contaminated food or water, not B

    ② **CORRECT: Hepatitis B can be spread by drug abuse and sexual contact. This is how it is spread.**

    ③ **CORRECT: Clients who have hepatitis B are at risk for contracting hepatitis D. True, Hepatitis D can be a co-infection with Hepatitis B.**

    ④ INCORRECT: Standard precautions only are needed in caring for clients with hepatitis B. Standard precautions plus contact precautions are appropriate for clients with hepatitis B.

    ⑤ INCORRECT: Vaccination will lower the client's risk of contracting hepatitis C. There is no vaccination for Hepatitis C. Health Promotion through client education on how to prevent Hepatitis C is the best method. The instruction should include avoiding IV drug abuse and unprotected sex.

The strategy for answering this question is to be knowledgeable about the different types of hepatitis and how they are transmitted. It is important in discharge planning to include the infection control precautions and health promotion activities at home. You just made a good link to the concept of infection control! (*Refer to Concept Infection Control for specifics.*)

Safety and Infections Control: Apply principles of infection control

Health Promotion and Maintenance: Provide information about health maintenance recommendations (immunizations, etc.)

3. Which of these **clinical assessment findings** would be a **priority** to report to the healthcare provider for a client admitted with **cirrhosis and portal hypertension?**

① CORRECT: HR 100 BPM is now 122 BPM. This could indicate a sign of bleeding. There is an increased risk of bleeding due to the increased portal hypertension, which causes collateral blood vessels to develop in the stomach, rectum and the esophagus. The vessels become distended and cause varices that can easily rupture and bleed. The increase in the heart rate is an early sign of fluid volume deficit due to bleeding as the heart tries to compensate for the decrease circulatory volume.

② INCORRECT: Urine output was 88mL/hr. is now 68mL/hr. This would be important to continue to monitor but not the priority.

③ INCORRECT: Jaundice and peripheral pulses +1. These are clinical findings seen with a client with cirrhosis. Although the pulses are +1, they are palpable indicating there is circulation.

④ INCORRECT: Respirations were 23/min and now are 17/min. This would be important to continue to monitor, but it is not the priority over option 1.

The strategy to answer this question is to know the pathophysiology of cirrhosis and the impact portal hypertension has on the body. Knowing that there is an increased risk of bleeding, you were able to connect the trending of the increased heart rate as an early sign of potential complication of hypovolemia due to bleeding as a result of the pathophysiology of cirrhosis with portal hypertension. The great nurse that you are allowed you to be able to pick up on early signs (increased heart rate) that result from the heart having to work harder to pump the reduced volume of blood to provide adequate perfusion. You used your prioritization strategy of trending for potential complications knowing this client was at risk. In this question you pulled together multiple concepts of fluid balance, perfusion, and oxygenation. Great job!

Reduction of Risk: Assess and respond to changes in client vital signs.

Reduction of Risk Potential: Recognize signs and symptoms of complications and intervene appropriately.

4. What is an **appropriate plan** of care for a client admitted with **hepatitis C?** Select all that apply.

① CORRECT: Encourage intake of oatmeal, whole grains, strawberries, and apples. These foods are a great choice to increase the carbohydrate in the diet, which would be recommended for a client with hepatitis.

② CORRECT: Instruct the client to avoid alcohol. The diseased liver is unable to metabolize potential toxins like alcohol.

③ INCORRECT: Instruct client they may donate blood after 3 months. This is not true; the client with a history of hepatitis should never give blood.

④ CORRECT: Encourage periods of rest initially followed by gradual increase in activity. Rest is important during the acute stages of the disease so the metabolic demands on the liver are decreased and there is time for healing. As the client improves, they can increase their activity, but pace it with rest periods.

⑤ INCORRECT: The client can be placed in a room with another client who has an infection. This is not correct. The client can be placed in a room with another client who requires the same infection control precautions.

⑥ INCORRECT: Use acetaminophen (Tylenol) for mild discomfort. This is not correct because Tylenol is hepatotoxic.

The strategy for answering this question is to link the care of the client with the pathophysiology of hepatitis C. The care included knowing the recommended diet, avoiding hepatotoxic alcohol and Tylenol and understanding the importance for rest with clients who have any liver disease. Decreasing the metabolic demands on the body through rest, allows the liver to heal. Look at how much you knew regarding the care for a client with hepatitis! Congratulations on your ability to begin connecting the pathophysiology to the important aspects of care!

Physiological Adaptation: Evaluate the effectiveness of the treatment with acute/chronic diagnosis.

Physiological Adaptation: Identify the pathophysiology related to acute or chronic conditions

Basic Care and Comfort: Manage client's nutritional intake.

5. Which of these **clinical findings** would be a **priority to report** for a client with **cirrhosis** of the liver?

① INCORRECT: A decrease in the ammonia level. It would be important to report an increase in the ammonia level, not a decrease. A decrease would be a desired outcome.

② INCORRECT: An abdominal girth of 55 cm that was 72 cm. The decrease in the amount of ascites is important to document and is a desired outcome, but is not the priority to report..

③ **CORRECT: Client is having flapping tremors of the wrist and fingers. This clinical finding (Asterixis) indicates a potential complication of hepatic encephalopathy. Along with this clinical finding it would be important to note the ammonia level and to anticipate the need for Lactulose to be give.**

④ INCORRECT: Hgb is 12g/dL and Hct is 38%. These levels are within normal range.

The strategy for answering this question is to understand the pathophysiology of cirrhosis of the liver and to recognize and intervene early with clinical findings that indicate a potential complication such as hepatic encephalopathy. You connected the pathophysiology of the encephalopathy that results when ammonia, produced by proteins digestion, is not metabolized by the liver into urea and excreted by the kidneys to the clinical findings of this potential complication. Your quick and accurate assessment is reported to the healthcare provider ensures the client receives timely care to prevent further decline in the client's condition.

Reduction of Risk Potential: Recognize signs and symptoms of complications/intervene appropriately.

6. What is the **priority action** for a client with **ascites of the abdomen** from cirrhosis of the liver has these clinical findings: **O_2 saturation of 92%, respiratory rate of 24/minute that was 18/minute, and is complaining of shortness of breath?**

① INCORRECT: Notify the healthcare provider immediately. Before notifying the healthcare provider, there are interventions you can do as a nurse to immediately improve the client's status.

② **CORRECT: Place the client in semi to high Fowler's position. This is important to do with any client experiencing respiratory distress unless the position is contraindicated (i.e., client with low BP, neuro client with increased intracranial pressure). The position helps open the airway and allow the lungs to fully expand. The pressure of the fluid from the ascites is increasing the intra-abdominal pressure and limiting the client's ability to fully expand their lungs.**

③ INCORRECT: Assess the lung sounds. This is an important assessment, but it would not be the priority to do with a client experiencing respiratory distress.

④ INCORRECT: Take the client's vital signs. This is also an important assessment, but it would not be the priority to do with a client experiencing respiratory distress.

The strategy to answer this question is to connect the concept of oxygenation with the impact of ascites on the respiratory system. In this question it was important to connect the fluid from the ascites has the potential to push up on the diaphragm, limiting the ability of the client to breathe deeply. You connected the concept of oxygenation (*Refer to Concept Oxygenation for specifics*) and the priority care for a client in respiratory distress to a client with ascites from liver disease! The great news is that this question could have been written about a client with pneumonia, bronchitis, or any medical condition that contributes to hypoxia and the answer would be the same! Great Connect!!!

Reduction of Risk Potential: Recognize signs and symptoms of complications/intervene appropriately.

7. What is the **priority intervention** for a client with a **Blakemore Sangston tube** in place and is presenting with a **heart rate of 110 bpm, RR–28/min, noisy respirations, dyspnea, and choking**?

   ① INCORRECT: Reposition the tube. This is not the correct intervention for the client's current status.

   ② INCORRECT: Place the client in high Fowler's position. Although the client is experiencing respiratory distress, it is not due to the position of the client but due to the tube becoming dislodged from its correct position.

   ③ INCORRECT: Suction the oral airway. This would not help the client's situation.

   ④ **CORRECT: Get the scissors from the bedside to cut the balloon port of tube. This is the correct intervention based on the client's clinical picture. The client has airway obstruction from dislodgment of tube & the esophageal balloon migrating into the oropharynx. You have to be prepared to cut the tube so the client can breathe.**

The strategy to answer this question is to be knowledgeable about the equipment being used with your clients and to know the potential complications. With the Blakemore Sangston tube it is important to keep the scissors at the bedside so you are ready for this kind of emergency. Notice the similarities between the clinical presentations for both client in questions #6 and #7. They are both hypoxic; however, question #7 has an added piece of information including the tube. This was a hint to you that an immediate intervention may have a focus on the cause of the clinical findings. Your preparedness and quick clinical decision-making saved the client's life. Wow, aren't you glad you were prepared?

Safety and Infection Control: Assure appropriate and safe use of equipment in performing client care.

Reduction of Risk Potential: Recognize signs and symptoms of complications and intervene appropriately.

8. Which of these **prescribed orders** should the **nurse question** with a client who has a history of **liver disease** and is being **discharged from the hospital**?

   ① INCORRECT: Discharge with a referral to home health. This would not need to be questioned, as it would be an appropriate referral for a client with liver disease being discharged.

   ② INCORRECT: Teach client to begin slowly increasing activity with scheduled rest periods. This would not be questioned because a client with liver disease needs to slowly progress activity with adequate rest periods while the liver is healing.

   ③ **CORRECT: Discharge with a prescription for Advil (Ibuprofen) for mild discomfort. This is correct, you would want to question if there was another mild pain reliever that could be ordered that did not have hepatotoxic properties of Advil (Ibuprofen) because of the client's liver disease.**

   ④ INCORRECT: Discharge with instructions to notify the healthcare provider for any signs of bleeding. This would be a correct discharge instruction for a client with liver disease.

The strategy to answer this question is you had to link the information you knew about the pathophysiology of liver disease with a client being discharged. This required linking of the appropriate care for a client with liver disease with the potential hepatotoxic properties of drugs, specifically Advil (Ibuprofen). You then connected that knowledge to the need to manage the care of your client and question an order that could potentially cause further damage to an already diseased liver. You demonstrated great nursing leadership and you were an advocate for your client.

Management of Care: Verify appropriateness and/ or accuracy of a treatment order.

9. What **personal protective equipment** is required when providing care for a client with a new diagnosis of **hepatitis B**? Select all that apply.

    ① CORRECT: Gloves when handling body fluids. This is standard precaution for any client.

    ② CORRECT: Gown and gloves when changing the client's bed after an episode of diarrhea. This is standard precaution for any client.

    ③ INCORRECT: : Mask when entering the room. This would not be required for hepatitis B or as part of standard precautions.

    ④ INCORRECT: Goggles when entering the room. This would not be required for hepatitis B or as part of standard precautions. Goggles would be worn if there were a danger of body fluids splashing.

    ⑤ CORRECT: Gloves worn when entering the room. This is required for contact precautions needed for clients with Hepatitis B as it is transmitted by blood and body fluids that can remain on surfaces in the room.

The strategy for answering this question is to be knowledgeable about Infection Control Standards with respect to the required personal protective equipment needed for Hepatitis. You then link the information you know about standard and contact precautions to the care of the client with hepatitis B. This would apply to clients with any type of hepatitis or any disease requiring contact precautions. (*Refer to Concept Infection control for specifics.*)

Safety and Infection Control: Apply principles of infection control

10. Which of these interventions would be important to implement in **preventing potential complications** for an **elderly client with cirrhosis of the liver?**

    ① INCORRECT: Instruct the client to increase the intake of protein in their diet. This is contraindicated in a client with liver disease with jaundice. Protein intake should be moderate to low.

    ② CORRECT: Place the client on an alternating pressure air mattress. This is correct; an alternating pressure air mattress can prevent pressure points that can lead to loss of skin integrity. There are several factors that make this client at risk for skin breakdown. The client is elderly and their skin has less elasticity and is thin and fragile. Also, a client with liver disease often has nutritional deficiencies that can lead to skin breakdown. The client has ascites and pitting edema and the weight of the fluid can cause pressure points that can lead to skin breakdown.

    ③ INCORRECT: Ambulate the client in the hall every 4 hours while awake. This would not be correct, as clients with liver disease need rest with minimal activity while the liver is healing.

    ④ INCORRECT: Instruct the client to use a firm toothbrush with vigorous motion with brushing their teeth. This would not be correct, as you would want to have the client use a soft toothbrush to prevent bleeding of the gums due to decreased clotting factors, and the potential for esophageal varices.

The strategy to answer this question is to link the pathophysiology of liver disease with the risk for potential bleeding and the resulting ascites and edema from decreased metabolism of protein and albumin leading to a decrease in the colloidal osmotic pressure. With the elderly, precautions related to maintaining skin integrity are an important part of nursing care. Look how much you know about the hepatic system and how many connections you have made in providing quality care for your client! Excellent!!!!

Physiological Integrity: Use measures to maintain skin integrity.

Decision-Making Analysis Form

Use this tool to help identify why you missed any questions. As you enter the question numbers in the chart, you will begin to see patterns of why you answered incorrectly. This information will then guide you toward what you need to focus on in your continued studies. Ultimately, this analytical exercise will help you become more successful in answering questions!!!

Questions to ask:

1. Did I have the knowledge to answer the question? If not, what information do I need to review?

2. Did I know what the question was asking? Did I misread it or did I miss keywords in the stem of the question?

3. Did I misread or miss keywords in the distractors that would have helped me choose the correct answer?

4. Did I follow my gut reaction or did I allow myself to rationalize and then choose the wrong answer?

	Lack of Knowledge *(Concepts, Systems, Pathophysiology, Medications, Procedures, etc.)*	Missed Keywords or Misread the Stem of the Question	Missed Keywords or Misread the Distractors	Changed My Answer *(Second-guessed myself, i.e., my first answer was correct.)*
Put the # of each question you missed in the column that best explains why you think you answered it incorrectly.				

If you changed an answer because you talked yourself out of the correct answer, or you second-guessed yourself, this is an **EASY FIX: QUIT changing your answers**!!! Typically, the first time you read a question, you are about 95% right! The second time you read a question, you start talking yourself into changing the answer. The third time you read a question, you do not have a clue—and you are probably thinking "Who in the heck wrote this question?"

On the other hand, if you read a question too quickly and when you reread it you realize you missed some key information that would impact your decision (i.e., assessments, lab reports, medications, etc.), then it is appropriate to change your answer. When in doubt, go with the safe route: your first thought! Go with your gut instinct!

As you gain confidence in answering questions regarding specific nursing concepts, you will be able to successfully progress to answering higher-level questions about prioritization. Please refer to the *Prioritization Guidelines* in this book for a structure to assist you with this process.

You CAN do this!

> *"What the mind can conceive and believe, and the heart desire, you can achieve."*
>
> NORMAN VINCENT PEALE

References for Chapter 13

Black, J M. and Hawks, J. H. (2009). *Medical surgical nursing: Clinical management for positive outcomes (8th ed.).* Philadelphia: Elsevier/Saunders.

Centers for Disease Control (2010. When someone close to you has chronic hepatitis B. Retrieved from http://www.cdc.gov/ hepatitis/HBV/PDFs/HepBWhenSomeoneClose-BW.pdf

Daniels, R. & Nicoll, L. (2012). *Contemporary medical-surgical nursing,* (2nd ed.). Clifton Park, NY: Delmar Cengage Learning.

Ellis, K. M. (2012). *EKG: Plain and simple* (3rd ed.). Upper Saddle Road, NJ: Pearson.

Eliopoulos, C. (2014). *Gerontological nursing* (8th ed.), Philadelphia: Lippincott Williams & Wilkins.

Giddens, G. F. (2013). *Concepts for nursing practice.* St. Louis, MO: Mosby, an imprint of Elsevier.

Hogan, M. A. (2014). *Pathophysiology: Reviews and rationales* (3rd ed.) Boston, MA: Pearson.

Hogan, M. A., Gingrich, M.M., Willcutts, K., and DeLeon, E. (2007). *Prentice hall reviews & rationales: Nutrition & diet therapy.* Upper Saddle Road, NJ: Prentice Hall.

Ignatavicius, D. D. and Workman, M. L. (2010). *Medical-surgical nursing: Patient-centered collaborative care* (6th ed.). Philadelphia: Elsevier/Saunders.

LeMone, P., Burke, K. M., and Bauldoff, G. (2011). *Medical-surgical nursing: Critical thinking in patient care* (5th ed.). Upper Saddle Road, NJ: Pearson/Prentice Hall.

Lewis, S., Dirksen, S., Heitkemper, M., Bucher, L., and Camera, I. (2011). *Medical surgical nursing: Assessment and management of clinical problems* (8th ed.). St. Louis: Mosby.

Manning, L. and Rayfield, S. (2014). *Nursing made insanely easy* (7th ed.). Duluth, GA: I CAN Publishing, Inc.

Manning, L. and Rayfield, S. (2013). *Pharmacology made insanely easy* (4th ed.). Duluth, GA: I CAN Publishing, Inc.

National Council of State Boards of Nursing, INC. (NCSBN) 2012. *Research brief: 2011 RN practice analysis: linking the NCLEX RN₍ₐ₎ examination to practice.* Retrieved from https://www.ncsbn.org/index.htm

National Institutes of Health, Office of Dietary Supplements. Dietary Fact Sheets. Retrieved from http://ods.od.nih.gov/ factsheets/list-all/

Nettina, S. L. (2013). *Lippincott manual of nursing practice* (10th ed.). Philadelphia, PA: Walters Kluwer Health/Lippincott Williams & Wilkins.

North Carolina Concept Based Learning Editorial Board (2011). *Nursing a concept based approach to learning,* Upper Saddle Road, NJ: Pearson/Prentice Hall.

Osborn, K. S., Wraa, C. E., Watson, A. S., and Holleran, R. S. (2014). *Medical surgical nursing: Preparation for practice* (2nd ed.). Upper Saddle Road, NJ: Pearson.

Pagana, K. D. and Pagana, T. J. (2014). *Mosby's manual of laboratory and diagnostic tests* (5th ed.). St. Louis, MO: Mosby, an imprint of Elsevier.

Porth, C. (2011). *Essentials of pathophysiology* (3d ed.). Philadelphia, PA: Lippincott Williams ad Wilkins.

Porth, C. M. and Grossman, S. (2013). *Pathophysiology: Concepts of altered health states* (9th ed.). Philadelphia, PA: Lippincott Williams & Wilkins.

Potter, P. A., Perry, A. G., Stockert, P., and Hall, A. (2013). *Fundamentals of nursing* (8th ed.). St. Louis, MO: Pearson/Prentice Hall.

Smeltzer, S. C., Bare, B. G., Hinkle, J. L., and Cheever, K. H. (2010). *Brunner & Suddarth's Textbook of medical-surgical nursing* (12th ed.). Philadelphia: Lippincott Williams & Wilkins.

Wagner, K. D. and Hardin-Pierce, M. C. (2014). *High-Acuity nursing* (6th ed.). Boston: Pearson.

CHAPTER 14

Linking Concepts to Pathophysiology of the Endocrine System
Metabolism Pituitary, Thyroid, and Adrenal

A Snapshot of Metabolism

The endocrine system plays a major role with metabolism in the body that helps regulate homeostasis and equilibrium among the cells, tissues, organs and systems. It regulates functions such as, growth, fluid and electrolyte balance and energy production. It is mainly controlled by the pituitary gland (known as the "master gland), which controls most other hormones through communication with the hypothalamus. Other glands include the thyroid and parathyroid glands, adrenal glands and the pancreas (*Refer to Chapter 15, Diabetes Mellitus for specifics*). The hormones released by the endocrine system are chemical messengers that are transported throughout the body and help regulate the body's responses.

Pituitary Gland: The pituitary gland is often called the "master gland" because the hormones secreted by this gland regulate most of the endocrine functions. The gland has two parts, the anterior pituitary and the posterior pituitary. This content will focus primarily on the posterior pituitary. The posterior gland is primarily made of nervous tissue and its function is to store and release antidiuretic hormone (ADH). The purpose of ADH, also known as vasopressin, is to control serum osmolality and water balance. It does that by decreasing urine production, and by reabsorbing water back into the circulatory system. The thyroid-stimulating hormone (TSH) is produced by the pituitary gland. It stimulates the thyroid gland in response to varying levels of T_3 and T_4 to increase or decrease the levels in the blood. There are two primary pituitary disorders involving the secretion of ADH: diabetes Insipidus (DI) and Syndrome of Inappropriate Antidiuretic Hormone (SIADH) (Porth & Grossman, 2013).

Thyroid Gland: The thyroid gland maintains the metabolic rate and tissue growth in the body. It also regulates iodine metabolism. The thyroid gland produces three hormones: triiodothyronine (T_3) (regulates cellular metabolism), thyroxine (T_4) (responsible for cellular metabolism), and throcalcitonin (calcitonin) that regulates serum calcium levels by decreasing the amount of calcium absorbed by the bones and reabsorption into the kidneys whenever serum calcium levels are elevated. The secretion of T3 and T_4 is regulated by the anterior pituitary gland by the release of thyroid stimulating hormone (TSH). The hormones are responsible for stimulating growth, increasing the metabolic rate, heart rate and glucose. Iodine is essential to the synthesis and proper functioning of T_3 and T_4 (Porth & Grossman, 2013).

Adrenal Gland: The adrenal glands are located above each kidney and are composed of adrenal medulla (the inner layer) and adrenal cortex (the outer layer). The adrenal medulla secretes catecholamines (i.e., epinephrine, norepinephrine and dopamine) and the adrenal cortex produces mineralocorticoids (aldosterone), glucocorticoids (cortisol), androgens and estrogens. Epinephrine and norepinephrine increase the body's metabolic rate and are responsible for the "fight or flight" response. In addition they increase insulin levels. The glucocorticoids (cortisol) assist the body in its response to stress, suppressing inflammation and increasing the serum glucose level as antagonist to the increase insulin response. Glucocorticoids play an essential role in the metabolism of carbohydrates, fat, protein and enhance protein synthesis and breakdown in addition to decreasing pain (Porth & Grossman, 2013).

The Pathophysiology Behind Alterations in Metabolism

METABOLISM: ENDOCRINE SYSTEM

Posterior Pituitary "MASTER GLAND"		Thyroid		Adrenal	
Diabetes Insipidus (DI)	Syndrome of inappropriate antidiuretic hormone (SIADH) Pituitary tumor	Hyperthyroidism (Graves Disease)	Hypothyroidism (Myxedema)	Cushing's Disease	Addison's Disease
↓ Antidiuretic Hormone (ADH) = Excess fluid excretion–Polyuria Serum Electrolytes (↑ concentrated) • ↑ Na$^+$ • ↑ Osmolality Urine Electrolytes (diluted) • ↓ Na$^+$ • ↓ Osmolality • ↓ Specific Gravity	↑ Antidiuretic Hormone (ADH) = Excessive water retention Serum Electrolytes ↓ (diluted) • ↓ NA$^+$ • ↓ Osmolality Urine Electrolytes ↑ (Concentrated) • ↑ Na$^+$ • ↑ Osmolality • ↑ Specific Gravity	↑ Triiodothyronine (T3) ↑ Thyroxine (T4) ↓ Thyroid Simulating Hormone (TSH) = **Hypermetabolic State** • ↑ O$_2$ consumption by tissue • ↑ Metabolism of protein, lipids, carbohydrates, and vitamins • ↑ of Thyroid gland size–respiratory problems • ↑HR, RR, BP	↓ Triiodothyronine (T3) ↓ Thyroxine (T4) ↑ Thyroid Simulating Hormone (TSH) = **Hypometabolic State** • ↓ O$_2$ Consumption • ↑ fluid volume (Interstitial fluids around face) • ↓ HR, RR, BP	↑ **ACTH or Over Secretion of the Adrenal Cortex** **Mineralocorticoids:** • ↑ Aldosterone = ↑ Na$^+$ absorption = ↑ Na$^+$ level • ↑ K$^+$ excretion = ↓ K$^+$ level ↑ **Glucocorticoids Cortisol =** ↑ Serum glucose	↓ **ACTH or Insufficiency of Adrenal Cortex** **Mineralocorticoids:** • ↓ Aldosterone = ↓ Na$^+$ absorption = ↓ Na$^+$ level • ↑ K$^+$ absorption = ↑ K$^+$ level ↓ **Glucocorticoids Cortisol =** ↓ serum glucose • ↑ Melanin Stimulating Hormone = ↑ pigmentation • ↓ Androgens

PATHOPHYSIOLOGY

Alterations with Metabolism

Common Labs/Diagnostic Tests/Therapeutic Procedures/Surgeries

Labs, Diagnostic Tests, and Procedures

Labs	Diagnostics Tests/Procedures	Therapeutic Procedures/Surgery
Thyroid • Thyroid-simulating hormone (TSH) • Triiodothyronine (T$_3$) • Thyroxine (T$_4$) **Pituitary** • Osmolality Serum (Range: 285 to 295 mOsml/kg) • Osmolality Urine **Critical Values** • Overhydration < 100 mOsm/kg of H$_2$O; Dehydration > 800 mOsm/kg of H$_2$O • Urine Specific Gravity 1.003-1.030 g/mL • BUN: 8–25 mg/dL **Adrenal** • CTH (cosyntropin) stimulation test	**Thyroid Scan** (Identify nodules or growths in thyroid gland). May be done with Radioiodine (^{123}I or ^{131}I) Uptake • Assess if client had radiographic contrast agents within 4 weeks or oral contraceptives (may cause false elevations) • Assess intake of iodine containing medications, thyroid medications and foods high in iodine prior to the test • *This test is contraindicated in pregnancy* **Electrocardiogram (ECG)**	• Thyroidectomy (Partial or Complete) (Pagana. & Pagana 2014).

Alteration with Metabolism
Medications for Endocrine Metabolism

The following medications represent some of the many used for clients with metabolism alterations in the endocrine system. We recommend you review and learn these very commonly prescribed medications. (*Refer to the Pharmacology Made Insanely Easy Book for specifics*).

Common Medications for Endocrine

Thyroid	Pituitary	Adrenal
• Levothyroxine T4 (Levothroid, Synthroid, Eltroxin, Levoxyl) **Antithyroids** • Methimazole (Tapazole) • Propylthiouracil (PTU) • Strong iodine solution (Lugol's Solution) • Radioactive iodine (^{131}I)	• Somatropin (Genotropin, Nutropin) • Vasopressin (Pitressin Synthetic) • Desmopressin (DDAVP, Stimate)	• Corticosteroids

Pathophysiology: Posterior Pituitary Gland

Diabetes Insipidus and Syndrome of Inappropriate Antidiuretic Hormone

Diabetes Insipidus (DI), known as *central diabetes insipidus*, is caused from antidiuretic hormone (ADH) (vasopressin) insufficiency that leads to excess fluid excretion. It usually results from damage to the hypothalamus or pituitary gland, (i.e., head injury, neurosurgery, pituitary tumors, or brain infections, etc.). Normally the hypothalamus detects dehydration and signals the pituitary gland to reabsorb water, but because of the ADH insufficiency, large amounts of urine are excreted. Cell membrane permeability to water is decreased and the result is the excretion of large amounts of hypotonic fluid, up to 12 liters per day. Nephrogenic diabetes insipidus is rare and is caused by the kidneys failing to respond to the ADH (i.e., kidney disease, hypercalcemia, effects of certain medications, etc.). Diabetes insipidus is often an acute episode, but may become chronic requiring lifelong treatment (Wagner & Hardin-Pierce, 2014).

Syndrome of Inappropriate Antidiuretic Hormone (SIADH) is the result of excessive antidiuretic hormone (ADH) (vasopressin). The body cannot excrete water with resulting dilutional serum hyponatremia and hypo-osmolality. The continued release of ADH causes the water retention from the renal tubules and leads to extracellular fluid volume increase.

Note: Low serum concentration does not necessarily mean that the total body sodium is less than normal. In reality, numerous clients may experience hyponatremia as a result of an excess of total body fluid (which may occur with heart failure or cirrhosis of the liver). Clients with significant hyperlipidemia or hypoproteinemia may present with serum sodium that is lower than it actually is (pseudohyponatremia) (Metheny, 2012). *Syndrome of Inappropriate Antidiuretic Hormone Secretion* (SIADH) produces a special kind of hyponatremia that results in an excessive amount of water retention. Medical conditions may result in the complication of SIADH from either the release of too much antidiuretic hormone or the renal response to the hormone being intensified (Metheny, 2012). This release of the antidiuretic hormone (ADH) is termed inappropriate, since in typical situations a low serum sodium level would depress the ADH activity.

The Pathophysiology Behind Metabolism with the Posterior Pituitary Gland

POSTERIOR PITUITARY GLAND
CONCEPT FLUID & ELECTROLYTES—THE "F & E"

Fluid Balance		Electrolytes Balance	
SIADH	**Diabetes Insipidus**	**SIADH**	**Diabetes Insipidus**
Hypervolemia ↑ Extracellular Fluid Volume Excess	Hypovolemia ↓ Extracellular Fluid Volume Deficit	Serum Hyponatremia ↓ Na⁺ < 135 mEq/L	Serum Hypernatremia ↑ Na⁺ > 145 mEq/L
↑ Antidiuretic Hormone (ADH) = Fluid retention	↓ Antidiuretic Hormone (ADH) = Excessive water excretion (Polyuria)	**Serum Electrolytes** **(diluted)** ↓ Na⁺ ↓ Osmolality **Urine Electrolytes** **(concentrated)** ↑ Na⁺ ↑ Osmolality ↑ Specific Gravity	**Serum Electrolytes** **(concentrated)** ↑ Na⁺ ↑ Osmolality **Urine Electrolytes** **(diluted)** ↓ NA⁺ ↓ Osmolality ↓ Specific Gravity

INSANELY EASY TIP!

Remember, the Labs are the Opposite of Each Other.
You Know One, you Know the Other!!

Diabetes Insipidus Labs	SIADH Labs
Serum Concentrated ↓ ADH ↑ NA⁺ ↑ Osmolality	**Serum Dilute** ↑ ADH ↓ NA⁺ ↓ Osmolality
Urine Dilute ↓ NA⁺ ↓ Osmolality ↓ Specific Gravity	**Urine Concentrated** ↑ NA⁺ ↑ Osmolality ↑ Specific Gravity

Pathophysiology: Posterior Pituitary Gland

Comparison of System-Specific Assessments for Diabetes Insipidus and Syndrome of Inappropriate Antidiuretic Hormone

Diabetes Insipidus System-Specific Assessments Fluid Volume Deficit due ↓ ADH	SIADH System-Specific Assessments Fluid Volume Overload due to ↑ ADH
Assessments are about Fluid Volume Deficit (*Refer to Concept Fluid Volume for specifics*) • Polyuria: abrupt onset of ↑ urine output = 5-20L/day • Polydipsia: excessive thirst • Nocturia • ↓ Weight from fluid loss • Dehydration: (i.e., ↑ HR, ↓ BP, muscle weakness, syncope, constipation)	Assessments are about Fluid Volume Excess (*Refer to Concept Fluid Volume for specifics*) **Early Changes** • Headache • Anorexia, weakness • Muscle cramps • ↑ Weight (not edema because water, not sodium is retained) **Late Changes** (*due to hyponatremia from excess fluid volume*) • Changes in personality, hostility • Deep tendon reflexes ↓ • Risk for seizures • Nausea, vomiting, diarrhea **Need to intervene quickly to prevent the client from progressing to Respiratory Distress & Coma**
FIDO HAS DIABETES INSIPIDUS  ©1994 Adapted from Creative Educators	SOGGY SID HAS SIADH 

Pathophysiology: Posterior Pituitary Gland
First-Do Priority Interventions:
Comparison of Interventions with Diabetes Insipidus and SIADH

Diabetes Insipidus Fluid Volume Deficit due ↓ ADH	Concepts: Fluid & Electrolytes	SIADH Fluid Volume Overload due to ↑ ADH
• Regular diet • Avoid foods and drinks that have a diuretic effect, (i.e. caffeine). • Add bulk, fiber and juices to prevent constipation.	**Diet** *(Refer to Concept on Nutrition for specifics)*	• Eat yogurt to help prevent oral yeast infections in the mouth. • Avoid high salt content foods that cause fluids to be retained.
• IV pump for administering Vasopressin • Fall alarms may be needed because of orthostatic hypotension	**Equipment**	• IV pumps • Seizure equipment (i.e. suction, airway)
Fluid Volume Deficit • ↑ Fluids to replace loss. Signs of fluid deficit, ↑ HR, ↑ RR • Daily weights, I & O, compare, contrast & trend • Monitor vital signs • SAFETY: Risk for falls due to hypovolemia, ensure safe route to bathroom, lights, and place bedside commode near by if needed. **Serum Hypernatremia (Concentrated)** • SAFETY: Seizure precautions • Monitor for signs of increased serum Na$^+$ & give appropriate care *(Refer to Concept Fluid Deficit & Sodium in this chapter for specifics)* **CONCEPTS** • Encourage to communicate feelings, fears.	**Plans/ Interventions**	**Fluid Volume Excess** • ↓ Fluids to 500–1000ml/day • Daily weights, I & O, compare, contrast & trend • Monitor for adventitious lung sounds, ↑ BP • Monitor cardiovascular status, ↓ vital signs • Pace activity with rest to ↓ myocardial oxygen demands **Serum Hyponatremia (Dilutional)** • SAFETY: Seizure precautions • Monitor for signs of decreased serum Na$^+$ & give appropriate care *(Refer to Concept Fluid Excess & Sodium in this chapter for specifics)* **CONCEPTS** • Encourage to communicate feelings, fears.
Teach: • Take daily weight and compare, report weight loss > 2 lbs./day. • Drink fluids to match output as prescribed. • Provide skin and mouth care. • Apply lotions without alcohol to cracked skin.	**Health Promotion**	**Teach:** • Take daily weight and compare, report weight gain > 2 lbs./day. • Fluid restriction as prescribed. • Avoid high salt content foods or additives to prevent retention of fluids. • Report any altered mental status or SOB.

Posterior Pituitary Gland: Concepts for Diabetes Insipidus
Concept Fluid Volume Deficit

System-Specific Assessments "The Ds"	First-Do Priority Interventions "FLUIDS"	Evaluation of Expected Outcomes "The Ds"
Decrease in weight **D**ry mucous membranes = ↑ thirst **D**ecrease in BP **D**ecrease fluid to pump so pulse ↑ **D**ecreased skin turgor **D**ecreased specific gravity **Labs** • ↑ BUN, serum osmolality, Na⁺, Hct NOTE: Clients with Diabetes Insipidus have large amounts (4–20 L/day) of urine output = fluid volume deficit due to ↓ antidiuretic hormone.	**F**luid replacement required **L**evel of consciousness, (safety) report to HCP **U**rine (note clients with DI have large amounts of urine (4–20 L/day) output. **I** & O monitor, compare, contrast & trend **D**ocument daily weight monitor for trends, vital signs **S**afety: Have suction equipment available 　**S**afety: Medication administration of Vasopressin **Replace output with intake to include electrolytes with Diabetes Insipidus per protocol!!** **Often caused from head injury– monitor neuro status** *(Refer to Concept Fluid & Electrolytes for specifics)*	**D**ecrease in weight; weight within 2 lbs of client normal **D**ecreased urine output; urine output WDL **D**ry mucous membranes = ↑ thirst, Membranes moist, ↓ thirst **D**ecrease in BP; BP WDL **D**ecrease fluid to pump so pulse ↑ Pulse WDL **D**ecreased skin turgor; skin turgor improved **D**ecreased specific gravity WDL **Labs** • BUN, serum osmolality, Na, Hct WDL **Discharge Teach:** • Drink fluids, monitor urine output • Daily weight, report gain or loss > 2 lbs/day

---

INSANELY EASY TIP!

Fluid Volume Deficit with Diabetes Insipidus is due to

↓ ADH = ↑ Urine Output = ↑ Serum Na⁺ (concentrated)

Does this sound familiar?

It's all about the Fluid & Electrolytes!!!!!

Posterior Pituitary Gland: Concepts for Diabetes Insipidus
Concept Hypernatremia

System-Specific Assessments	First-Do Priority Interventions "FLUIDS"	Evaluation of Expected Outcomes "DRIED"
FLUID DEFICIT is the cause of ↑ Na⁺ (Hemoconcentration) • ↑ Dryness of mucous membranes • ↑ Concentration in urine due to decrease urine output; • ↑ Deep muscle reflexes • ↑ Red, flushed skin • ↑ Restless (irritable) progressing to confusion • ↑ Serum Na⁺ > 145 mEq/L • ↑ Temperature; I & O • ↑ Thirst (may be ↓ in elderly!) • ↑ Risk for seizures • ↑ HR • Decreased weight; decreased blood pressure; decreased CVP Note: **all of the arrows are going** ↑ except the BP, CVP, weight, and urine output	Note: that the hypernatremia is **from excessive fluid loss from the lack of antidiuretic hormone that occurs in Diabetes Insipidus.** Many times sodium does need to be restricted when the sodium is high however with Diabetes Insipidus the sodium is high (serum concentration) because the client is dry.	**D**ry mucous membranes: membranes (moist), Urine output WDL for client. **D**eep muscle reflexes WDL for client **R**ed, flushed skin not present; restless (irritable), progresses to confusion; alert/oriented **R**eview lab: Serum Na⁺ 135–145 mEq/L WDL **I**ncreased temperature (afebrile). **I** & O WDL; No increase in urine concentration; No increase in thirst, No seizures. **E**levated HR; HR WDL for client. **D**ecreased weight (within normal range for client); decreased CVP WDL (normal:1–8 mm Hg)

INSANELY EASY TIP for Diabetes Insipidus!
There is Fluid Volume Deficit due to:
↓ ADH = ↑ Urine output = ↑ Serum Na⁺ (concentrated)
Remember
The serum Na⁺ is HIGH
Because the Client is DRY!

Remember, the Labs are the Opposite of Each Other. You Know One, you Know the Other!!

Diabetes Insipidus Labs	SIADH Labs
↑ Serum Values	↓ Serum Values
↓ Urine Values	↑ Urine Values

Posterior Pituitary Gland: Syndrome of Inappropriate Antidiuretic Hormone (SIADH) Concepts
Concept Fluid Volume Excess–SIADH

POTENTIAL WATER INTOXICATION from ↑ ADH Concept Fluid Volume Excess–SIADH		
System-Specific Assessments	**First-Do Priority Interventions "RESTRICT"**	**Evaluation of Expected Outcomes**
• ↑ BP • ↑ Respirations & ↑ dyspnea, orthopnea • ↑ crackles in lungs • ↑ Pulse (may be normal) but bounding • ↑ confusion, LOC • ↑ weight > 2lbs/24 hr **Note: No edema because water retained, not sodium with SIADH** *Refer to Concept Fluid & Electrolytes for specifics*	**R**educe IV flow rate **E**valuate breath sounds & ABGs, VS, LABS **S**emi to high Fowler's position **T**reat with oxygen & diuretics as ordered **R**educe fluid, sodium intake as prescribed **I** & O and daily weight, compare, contrast and trend **C**irculation, color, LOC **T**urn & position at least every 2 hours **May have to give 200–300 ml of hypertonic IV fluids. Monitor for fluid overload!**	• No dyspnea, orthopnea, • Lungs clear, no wheezing, rhonchi • No cough or pink-tinged frothy sputum • Weight within 2 lbs of client normal • Lab values normal

INSANELY EASY TIP!
There is Fluid Volume Excess due to:

↑ ADH = ↑ Fluid Volume = ↓ Serum Na⁺ (diluted)

It is all about Fluid and Electrolyte Balance!

Posterior Pituitary Gland: Syndrome of Inappropriate Antidiuretic Hormone (SIADH) Concepts

Concept Serum Hyponatremia

SAFETY		
Concept Serum Hyponatremia SIADH / Sodium 135-145 mEq/L		
System-Specific Assessments	**First-Do Priority Interventions "SODIUM"**	**Evaluation of Expected Outcomes**
Dilutional Hyponatremia (Water excess) "HIGH Fluid Retention" • ↓ Serum Na⁺ < 135 mEq/L • ↓ Impaired cerebral function • ↓ LOC; risk for seizures • ↓ Muscle strength • ↓ Deep Muscle Reflexes (DTR) • ↑ Blood Pressure • ↑ Urine output • ↑ Weight *Refer to Concept Fluid & Electrolytes–Fluid Balance and Sodium for specifics*	**S**eizure precautions **O**ccurs in Addison disease, diabetic acidosis & renal disease; clients who are NPO; SIADH; perspiring, vomiting, diarrhea; burns or excessive administration of D_5W **D**aily weight; Diet foods high in Na⁺ (i.e., milk, condiments, cheese, etc.) as prescribed if needed **I**f retaining fluids, restrict fluids **U**nderstand the cause: give IV fluids as directed **M**onitor vital signs (temp, HR, BP); I & O; weight is one of the best indicators of fluid status; skin turgor; and neurological assessments (pupils, LOC); safety (fall precautions; change positions slowly)	• Serum Na⁺ 135-145 mEq/L • Impaired cerebral function improved • LOC normal for client; no seizures • Muscle strength WDL • Deep Muscle Reflexes (DTR) WDL • Blood Pressure WDL • Urine output WDL • Weight WDL

INSANELY EASY TIP for Hyponatremia with SIADH!

↑ ADH = Fluid Retention = ↓ Serum Na⁺ (dilutional)

The serum Na⁺ is LOW
Because the client is WET!!

(Sorry, it does not rhyme, but you get the picture!)

An Insanely Easy Way to Remember Diabetes Insipidus and SIADH!!!
WARNING – You might start singing this song during a test!!!!
S-I-A-D-H (Syndrome of Inappropriate Antidiuretic Hormone)
Lyrics © (Sing to tune: BINGO) by Darlene A. Franklin, RN MSN

Chorus
S-I-A-D-H, S-I-A-D-H,   S-I-A-D-H,
This hormone stops the Pee Pee.

Verse 1
Brain tumors, trauma, and bad bugs
A complication might be—
S-I-A-D-H, S-I-A-D-H,   S-I-A-D-H,
This hormone stops the Pee Pee.

Verse 2
Low output, sodium; gained weight
And high specific gravity
S-I-A-D-H, S-I-A-D-H,   S-I-A-D-H,
This hormone stops the Pee Pee.

Verse 3
 But, Diabetes Insipidus
The opposite you'll see
Pee, Pee…Give IVs…
Pee Pee…Give IVs…
Pee, Pee…Give IVs…
Vas-o-pressin they need!

Verse 4
High output, sodium; pounds lost,
And low specific gravity
Pee, Pee…Give IVs.....
Pee Pee…Give IVs…
Pee, Pee…Give IVs…
Vas-o-pressin they need!

SOGGY SID HAS SIADH

SALT

FIDO HAS DIABETES INSIPIDUS

H2O

©1994 Adapted from Creative Educators

Pathophysiology: Hyperthyroidism and Hypothyroidism

Hyperthyroidism is caused by an excessive release of TSH by the pituitary gland. When there is a decrease in the circulating hormones T3 and T4, the thyroid-stimulating hormone (TSH) is released by the anterior pituitary to stimulate the thyroid into producing more T3 and T4. This leads to hypermetabolic state, which increases the oxygen demand of the tissues. This in turns leads to increase metabolism of lipids, protein, carbohydrates and vitamins and causes a slow deterioration of the thyroid function. Graves disease is a common cause of hyperthyroidism. *Goiter* describes the enlargement of the thyroid gland as it attempts to compensate for the decrease of thyroid hormones. Clients may require a thyroidectomy (total or partial) to manage the disease (Daniels & Nicoll, 2012). A total thyroidectomy will require life long thyroid replacement therapy. Another choice of treatment would be radioactive iodine that may be used to destroy the thyroid cells to decrease production of the thyroid hormones. Iodine (necessary for the synthesis of thyroid hormones) deficiency can result from taking the anti-thyroid drugs or a decrease in iodine intake

Thyroid storm is a life-threatening crisis that results from an extreme hypermetabolic state. This results in hyperthermia (102–106 degrees), tachycardia and seizures.

Hypothyroidism results in hypometabolic state in the body due to decrease amounts of circulating thyroid hormones, T3 and T4. The decrease levels of T3 and T4 stimulate the anterior pituitary to release TSH to stimulate the thyroid to produce more T3 and T4. In hypothyroidism TSH is high because the cells are not getting the T3 and T4 they need. The signal to the pituitary is to release more TSH. The manifestations may develop slowly over time. Myxedema occurs when hypothyroidism is not treated. Proteins accumulate in the interstitial spaces causing an increase of fluid in the space. The fluid (mucinous edema) is often located in the facial area (periorbital edema).

Myxedema coma is rare, but life threatening. It results from a very severe hypometabolic state with cardiovascular collapse, hypotension, hypoglycemia, hypoventilation, coma and death if left untreated.

Physiology Thyroid Gland
Concept Metabolism

THYROID GLAND HYPERTHYROIDISM & HYPOTHYROIDISM			
Nutrition		**Energy**	
Hyperthyroidism	**Hypothyroidism**	**Hyperthyroidism**	**Hypothyroidism**
Hypermetabolic State	**Hypometabolic State**	**Hypermetabolic State**	**Hypometabolic State**
↑ Metabolism = Weight loss	↓ Metabolism = Weight gain	↑ O₂ consumption by tissue	↓ O₂ Consumption
• ↓ Protein	• Constipation	• ↑ HR	• ↓ HR
• ↓ Lipids	• Hair loss	• ↑ RR	• ↓ RR
• ↓ Carbohydrates	• Dry Skin	• ↑ BP	• ↓ BP
• ↓ Vitamins		• Emotional labile	• ↓ Energy
• Diarrhea		• Feel hot	• Fatigue
			• Feel cold

Pathophysiology: Thyroid Gland
System-Specific Assessments Comparison for Hyperthyroidism and Hypothyroidism

Making them Insanely Easy!!!

Hyperthyroidism (Graves Disease) Everything is Increased (except weight) INCREASED	Hypothyroidism (Myexedema) Everything is Decreased (except weight) DECREASED
• ↑ Heart Rate, may hear S3 heart sound • ↑ Peristalsis (Diarrhea) • ↑ Basal Metabolism Rate = ↓ Weight (despite ↑ appetite) • ↑ Insomnia • ↑ Intolerance to heat (they feel HOT) • ↑ Reflexes • ↑ Emotional lability **Appearance:** Goiter, exophthalmos, thin hair, flushed moist skin	• ↓ Heart Rate (late finding) • ↓ Peristalsis (Constipation) • ↓ Basal Metabolism Rate = ↑ Weight (despite no calorie ↑) • ↓ Energy (fatigue, lethargic) • ↓ Tolerance to cold (they feel COLD) • ↓ Reflexes • ↓ Energy, lethargic **Appearance:** Goiter, periorbital edema, hair loss, course dry skin

GO GETTER GERTRUDE

MORBID MATILDA

Pathophysiology: Thyroid Gland
First-Do Priority Interventions:
Comparison of Interventions with Hyper and Hypothyroidism

Hyperthyroidism (Graves Disease)		Hypothyroidism (Myxedema)
Hyperthyroidism = ↑ dietary intake • ↑ Calories & ↑ vitamin supplements • ↑ Small meals, finger foods • AVOID iodine-rich foods (i.e., cod, iodized salt, milk, etc.); causes decreased stimulation of thyroid hormones • Refer to Concept on Nutrition for specifics	**Diet**	Hypothyroidism = ↓ dietary intake • ↓ Calories • ↓ Fat • ↑ Residue (fiber & fluids) • ↑ Fruits & vegetables (healthy low calorie foods) • Include iodine in the diet (i.e. iodized salt, milk, cod, etc.)
• Keep room temperature cool or to comfort level	**Equipment**	• Keep room temperature warm, extra blankets • No external heating devices like electric blankets
• Monitor cardiovascular status: ↑ HR, RR, & ↑ BP with widened pulse pressure • Pace activity with rest to ↓ energy use • ↑ HOB to ↓ eye pressure • Monitor mental stability • Promote a calm environment • Prepare for possible thyroidectomy	**Plans/Interventions**	• Monitor cardiovascular status: ↓ HR, RR, BP • Encourage communicating feelings, fears. • Skin care, turn every 2 hours • Encourage exercise as tolerated (i.e., walking, up in chair, etc.)

Teach:
• How to provide eye protection & lubrication
• Daily weights to help ensure no additional weight loss
• Client and family to be alert to changes in behavior
• Taking anti-thyroid medications, beta blockers, iodine solutions (Refer to *Pharmacology Made Insanely Easy*)
• May use Radioactive Iodine Therapy (contraindicated in pregnancy or with nursing mothers)
	Health Promotion	**Teach:**
		• Importance of diet and exercise
		• Need to take life time medication of Levothyroxine sodium (Synthroid)
		  • Take 1–2 hours before breakfast
		  • Monitor closely when starting
		  • Monitor elderly closely who have coronary disease for increase heart rate
		  • Refer to *Pharmacology Made Insanely Easy*
		• No Alcohol
		• Use caution with CNS depressants

Elderly Alert With Hyperthyroidism

Monitor the older adult and/or the elderly client closely presenting with a **NEW development of atrial fibrillation!** The atrial fibrillation may be a result of a new diagnosis of hyperthyroidism.

Any client with hyperthyroidism who **has a history and is currently being managed for heart failure and/or atrial fibrillation** needs to be monitored for **tachycardia and altered perfusion.**

Pathophysiology: Thyroid Gland
First-Do Priority Interventions:
Radioactive Iodine Therapy for Hyperthyroidism

First-Do Priority Interventions for Radioactive Iodine Therapy

"SAFE"

Stay away from small children 2–4 days after treatment

Avoid using same toilet or toothbrush as others for 2 weeks; use disposable eating utensils

Flush toilet 3 times, flush washing machine 1x after use before washing other clothes

Eliminate use of laxative 2–3 days after treatment to get rid of stool contaminated with radiation

G iven for Hyperthyroidism and Thyroid cancer

O ffspring may be harmed by treatment- Do not give if pregnant or breastfeeding

odine (Radioactive Iodine) destroys thyroid cells

©2013 I CAN Publishing®, Inc.

T hyroid function studies are an indication for taking this med (to visualize iodine uptake)

E ncourage client to increase fluid intake and to void frequently; eliminate coughing and expectorating

R adiation sickness may occur- intense nausea, vomiting, hematemesis, and epistaxis

Pathophysiology: Thyroid Gland
Surgical Procedure: Thyroidectomy for Hyperthyroidism

Priority Care for Thyroidectomy

Pre-Op "ACT NOW"	POST-OP THYROIDECTOMY	Post-Op "BOW TIE"

Allergies assess
 	
Consent signed
 	
Teach client:
• Importance of taking propylthiouracil (PTU) 4–6 weeks prior to surgery: (helps prevent thyroid storm)
• Important to take Iodine 10–14 days prior to surgery: ($\downarrow$ gland size, & $\downarrow$ bleeding)
 	
NPO prior to surgery per orders
 	
Observe client & notify healthcare provider if client fails to comply with pre-op med regime listed above
 	
Watch cardiac status, ECG, vital signs
	B leeding
	   Beware Thyroid Storm
	
	O pen airway
	
	W hisper
	
	T rach set
	
	I ncision
	
	E mergency
	
	©1994 I CAN Publishing, Inc.
		Bleeding: Assess incision site & behind neck
		
		Open airway: Check for symptoms of respiratory distress; position semi-Fowlers (avoid tension on the suture line)
		
		Whisper Assess for laryngeal nerve damage (ask to speak when awake from surgery)
		
		Trach set at bedside for 24 hours (airway obstruction from bleeding or edema)
		  Equipment: Have suction equipment at bedside
		
		Incision: Monitor for symptoms of bleeding
		
		Emergency–Monitor for symptoms of $\downarrow$ calcium if parathyroid gland is damaged or removed (see next page for explanation)
		• Chvostek's sign
		• Trousseau's sign
		• Tingling of fingers & toes
		• Have **Calcium Gluconate available**
		
		(Refer to Concept Hypocalcemia)

The BOW TIE will help you remember the "ABCs" post-thyroidectomy:

Airway: check for swelling, vocal cord damage

Bleeding: check around and behind incision

Calcium: check for $\downarrow$ Ca$^+$(if parathyroid gland is injured)

Pathophysiology: Thyroid Gland
Trend Potential Complication of Thyroidectomy
Hypocalcemia

Parathyroid Glands are embedded in the thyroid gland but they have nothing to do with the function of the thyroid gland. Parathyroid actually means near the thyroid. The potential complication occurs if the parathyroid gland is injured or accidently removed during a thyroidectomy. The parathyroid gland function is to secrete parathyroid hormone (PTH). The PTH increases calcium absorption by the kidneys and therefore increases calcium levels and decreases phosphorus (phosphate) levels through excretion. If the parathyroid gland is injured or removed, the client may develop hypocalcemia. **Assessing for decreased calcium (hypocalcemia) is a priority assessment following a thyroidectomy.** (*Refer to the Concept Calcium for specifics*).

SAFETY		
Concept Hypocalcemia / Serum Calcium < 9 mg/dL		
System-Specific Assessments "TWITCH"	**First-Do Priority Interventions "SAFE"**	**Evaluation of Expected Outcomes NO "TWITCH"**
Trousseau's Sign (hand finger spasms)	**S**eizure precautions; environmental stimuli decrease	**T**rousseau's Sign (hand finger spasms); NO trousseau's sign
Watch for dysrhythmias (↓ pulse, ↑ ST segment, prolonged QT interval on ECG)	**A**dminister calcium supplements; phosphate binders because of ↑ phosphorus (Refer to connection below). Use stool softeners since Amphogel can lead to constipation. Teach client how to prevent constipation.	**W**atch for dysrhythmias (↑ pulse, ↑ ST segment, prolonged QT interval–ECG); NO dysrhythmias
Increase in anorexia, nausea, vomiting; ↓ LOC		**I**ncrease in anorexia, nausea, vomiting; ↓ LOC; No nausea, vomiting or ↓ LOC
Tetany, twitching, seizures	**F**oods high in calcium (i.e. dairy, green); educate	**T**etany, twitching, seizures; NONE
Chvostek's sign (facial twitching)		**C**hvostek's sign is not present
Hypotension, hyperactive deep tendon reflexes (DTR)	**E**mergency equipment on standby; evaluate for bone disorder (osteomalacia); careful with bones	**H**ypotension, hyperactive DTR; No hypotension or hyperactive DTR

Remember the Connection between Calcium and Phosphorus:

If one is UP the other is DOWN!!!

↓ Ca⁺⁺ then ↑ Phosphorus

↑ Ca⁺⁺ then ↓ Phosphorus

Pathophysiology: Thyroid Gland
Trend Potential Complication
Hyperthyroidism: Thyroid Storm

Thyroid Storm is life-threatening emergency with a high mortality rate. It is an extreme state of hyperthyroidism resulting from a large amount of thyroid hormone being released into the blood stream, which results in very rapid increase in the metabolic rate. It can happen following a thyroidectomy or from an infection, trauma, and diabetic ketoacidosis or digitalis toxicity.

System-Specific Assessments	First-Do Priority Interventions
• ↑ Temperature (102°–106°)	• Oxygenation– Maintain airway, O₂ if needed
• ↑ Heart Rate	• Cardiac monitor
• ↑ Blood Pressure	• Reduce temperature, only use acetaminophen (salicylate ↑ thyroxine level)
• ↑ Respirations	• Administer IV fluids to prevent vascular collapse
• ↑ Blood glucose	• Administer Insulin as prescribed (only in small amounts only as blood sugar is a response to hypermetabolic state)
• ↑ Risk for seizures (from high temp), chest pain, dyspnea	• Administer glucocorticoids as prescribed to prevent shock
	• Administer propylthiouracil (PTU) to prevent release of thyroid hormone

An **Insanely Easy Way** to Remember About a Thyroid Storm:
All System-Specific Assessments are **Increased** because of the **Hypermetabolism!!!**

Pathophysiology: Thyroid Gland
Trend Potential Complication
Hyperthyroidism: Myxedema Coma

Myxedema Coma is life-threatening emergency. It is a generalized hypometabolic state resulting from an extreme or prolonged hypothyroidism. It occurs when a client suddenly stops taking their medication or if hypothyroidism goes untreated. It can also result from infection, heart failure or stroke.

System-Specific Assessments	First-Do Priority Interventions
• ↓ Respirations significantly	• Oxygenation (hypoxia)–maintain airway, monitor ABGs for metabolic acidosis
• ↓ Heart Rate	• Cardiac monitor (potential cardiac compromise)
• ↓ Blood Pressure	• IV fluids to ↑ circulation
• ↓ Cardiac output (cardiovascular collapse)	• Temp ↓, warm client w/blankets
• ↓ Blood glucose	• Administer glucose as needed
• ↓ Temperature	• Administer IV Synthroid per order
• ↓ Sodium	• Administer corticosteroids as ordered
• ↓ LOC (Stupor to coma), cerebral hypoxia	

An **Insanely Easy Way** to Remember Myxedema Coma:

All System-Specific Assessments are **Decreased** due to **Hypometabolism!!!**

Pathophysiology: Adrenal Gland
Cushing's Disease and Addison's Disease

Cushing's Disease is a result of excess secretion of glucocorticoid (cortisol and adrenocorticotropic hormone) from the adrenal cortex. It can also result from taking too much corticosteroid medications like prednisone for clients who have asthma or rheumatoid arthritis. The result of the increase in cortisol is a persistent increase in blood glucose levels hyperglycemia known as "steroid diabetes". Osteoporosis can develop because the protein matrix and calcium that make up the bone are affected by excess cortisol. It decreases calcium absorption from the intestines and increases calcium excretion by the kidneys. It can be so severe that it can result in bone fractures along with the protein wasting that causes muscle weakness. Additional results include hypokalemia, and increase sodium with resulting water retention leading to hypertension. This becomes a risk for the client to develop heart failure and stroke. The appearance of the client changes with the abnormal fat distribution and the edema with truncal obesity known as the "buffalo" hump. Infection becomes an increased risk and with the suppression of the inflammatory response, clients are not symptomatic. Mental changes can occur to include memory loss and poor cognition and depression (Osborn, Wraa, Watson & Holleran, 2014).

Addison's Disease is a chronic adrenocortical insufficiency because of the idiopathic destruction of the adrenal glands and often has other immune disorders associated with it. Insufficient hormonal secretions of mineralocorticoids and glucocorticoids results in decrease production of cortisone resulting in a decrease in blood glucose levels (hypoglycemia). The decrease in aldosterone production causes a decrease in sodium absorption and increased sodium excretion resulting in increased water excretion. The client then experiences hypovolemia and hypotension. In addition the potassium is retained (moves in the opposite direction of the sodium) causing hyperkalemia and the risk for cardiac arrhythmias. Also with Addison's, there is reduced removal of calcium by the kidneys and there is increase calcium released into the blood circulation. This is from the resulting hypovolemia from adrenal insufficiency that reduces the amount of calcium filtered by the kidneys. Calcium may also be increased because of removal of calcium from the bones (Daniels & Nicoll, 2012).

Pathophysiology: Adrenal Gland
The Pathophysiology Behind Metabolism with the Adrenal Gland

ADRENAL GLAND: CONCEPT FLUID, ELECTROLYTES, AND GLUCOSE

↑ ACTH or Over Secretion of the Adrenal Cortex Cushing Disease				↓ ACTH or Insufficiency of Adrenal Cortex Addison's Disease			
Sodium	Potassium	Glucose	Calcium	Sodium	Potassium	Glucose	Calcium
Hypernatremia ↑ Na > 145mEq/L Mineralocorticoids: ↑ Aldosterone = ↑ NA+ absorption = ↑ NA+ level	Hypokalemia ↓ K < 3.5 mEq/L Mineralocorticoids: ↑ Aldosterone = ↑ NA+ absorption = K moves opposite NA+ = ↓ K level	Glucose > 120 mg/dL ↑ Glucocorticoids: (Cortisol) = ↑ Blood Sugar	Hypocalcemia ↓ Ca++ < 9 mEq/L Calcium leaves bones & is excreted in urine = ↓ Ca	Hyponatremia ↓ Na < 135mEq/L Mineralocorticoids: ↓ Aldosterone = ↓ NA+ absorption = ↓ NA+ level	Hyperkalemia ↑ K > 5 mEq/L Mineralocorticoids: ↑ Aldosterone = ↑ NA+ absorption = K moves opposite NA+ = retained K = ↑ K level	Glucose < 70 mg/dL ↓ Glucocorticoids: (Cortisol) = ↓ Blood Sugar	Hypercalcemia ↑ Ca++ > 10.5 mEq/L Reduced removal of calcium by the kidneys and increase Ca++ into the blood circulation

Are you overwhelmed with all of those lab values above?

Are you saying, "There is NO WAY I am going to remember that"?

Well, we were too! So here it is!

An Insanely Easy Way to Remember Labs for the Adrenal Glands:

Remember the Phrase **"SOME PEOPLE GET COLD"** (*Check out the next page!*)

Let's examine how it works ...

Pathophysiology: Adrenal Gland
System-Specific Assessments Adrenal Glands Labs

Remember the saying, "Some People Get Cold"? Now put the labs with it:

Some = (Na^+) People = (K^+) Get = (Glucose) Cold = (Ca^{++})

Start with either Cushing's Disease or Addison's, then the other disease is just the opposite!

HINT: **CU**shing has **U** in it for **UP** so start with Na^+ **UP**

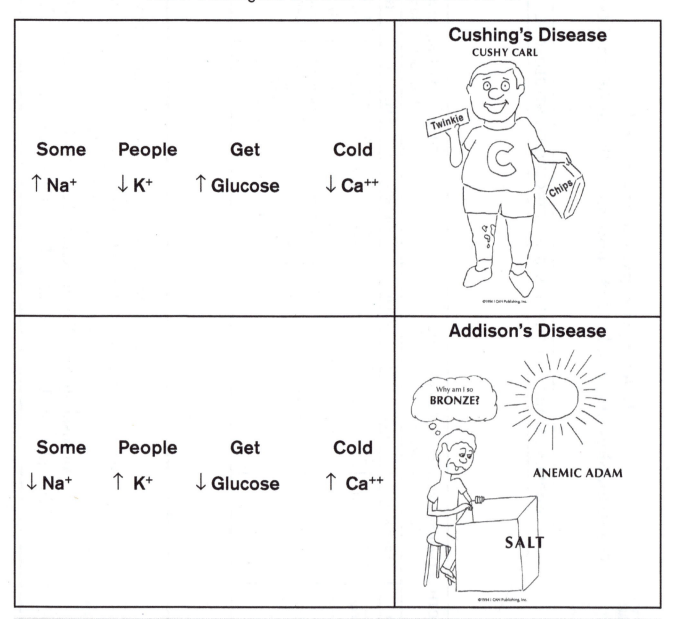

Some	People	Get	Cold
↑ Na^+	↓ K^+	↑ Glucose	↓ Ca^{++}

Cushing's Disease
CUSHY CARL
Twinkie
Chips

Some	People	Get	Cold
↓ Na^+	↑ K^+	↓ Glucose	↑ Ca^{++}

Addison's Disease
Why am I so BRONZE?
ANEMIC ADAM
SALT

Wasn't that an **Insanely Easy Way** to Remember your labs
for Cushing's and Addison's!!!!!
You've Got it NOW! BRILLIANT !!!!!!

Pathophysiology: Thyroid Gland
Cushing's Disease and Addison's Disease
System-Specific Assessments Comparison Chart

Cushing's Disease "CUSHY" Carl Concepts: Altered Fluid & Electrolytes & Glucose Metabolism	Addison's Disease Anemic "ADAM" Concepts: Altered Fluid & Electrolytes & Glucose Metabolism
Changes in fat distribution: (i.e., moon face, truncal obesity, & buffalo hump), retaining fluid ($\uparrow$ Na$^+$)	**A**drenal Crisis develops rapidly
m**U**uscle wasting	**D**evelop chronic symptoms of fatigue and weakness
Signs of bruising and petechiae (fragile blood vessels)	**A**lways need lifelong glucocorticoid therapy **A**norexia, nausea, vomiting, diarrhea
High emotional irritability/depression	**M**elanocyte stimulating hormone levels $\uparrow$ = hyperpigmentation
You have to monitor Labs:	**M**onitor Labs:
• $\uparrow$ NA$^+$ = $\uparrow$ BP (sodium and water retention)	• $\downarrow$ NA$^+$ = $\downarrow$ BP, water excretion, dehydration, dizziness, risk for falls
• $\downarrow$ K$^+$ = Cramps, cardiac arrhythmias, $\downarrow$ (inverted) T wave	• $\uparrow$ K$^+$ = Cardiac arrhythmias, $\uparrow$ (peaked) T waves
(Refer to Concept Cardiac/Peripheral Perfusion for specifics)	*(Refer to Concept Cardiac/Peripheral Perfusion for specifics)*
• $\uparrow$ Glucose = Hyperglycemia (i.e., "Hot & Dry, My Sugar is High") poor healing, risk for infection	• $\downarrow$ Glucose = Hypoglycemia, (i.e., "Cold & Clammy, I Need Some Candy") weakness, fatigue
• $\downarrow$ Ca^{++} = Risk for fractures (osteoporosis) (Ca^{++} leaves bones & excreted in urine)	• $\uparrow$ Ca^{++} = joint pain, constipation
CUSHY CARL	**ANEMIC ADAM**

Pathophysiology: Adrenal Gland
Cushing's Disease and Addison's Disease
First-Do Priority Interventions Comparison Chart:

Cushing's Disease Concepts: Altered Fluid & Electrolytes & Glucose Metabolism		Addison's Disease Concepts: Altered Fluid & Electrolytes & Glucose Metabolism
• Low sodium diet • Low fat diet • Increase potassium intake as prescribed • May need to follow diabetic food guidelines if blood sugar is ↑	**Diet** *(Refer to Concept Nutrition for specifics)*	• ↑ Calories, supplemental glucose if needed • Decrease potassium intake as prescribed • Increase sodium intake as prescribed
• Cardiac monitor if needed	**Equipment**	• Cardiac monitor if needed
• Monitor cardiovascular status, vital signs, monitor for ↑ BP particularly if client has hypertension (↑ Na^+ & H_2O can ↑ BP) ***Remember wherever Na^+ goes there goes H_2O!*** • Monitor labs: Na^+ K^+, & Ca^{++} • Monitor for fluid overload due to ↑ Na^+ (i.e., lung sounds, edema, JVD, etc.) • Monitor for signs of infection • Skin care, turn q 2hrs, encourage to move • Monitor blood glucose for signs of hyperglycemia ***"Hot & dry, my sugar is high"***	**Plans/ Interventions**	• Monitor cardiovascular status, vital signs • Monitor labs: Na^+ K^+, & Ca^{++} • Monitor for signs of GI bleed • Encourage to communicate feelings, fears • Skin care, turn q 2hrs, encourage to move • Monitor blood glucose for signs of hypoglycemia ***"Cold and clammy, I need some candy"***
Teach: • How to take daily weights and compare • How to prevent fractures and skin trauma • How to prevent infections, signs and symptoms to report • Use caution if driving or using heavy machinery	**Health Promotion**	**Teach:** • Pace activity with rest, report severe fatigue • Importance of diet and exercise • Need to take medication as ordered • No alcohol and avoid caffeine

Insanely Easy Tip!

Nursing care for Cushing's Disease and Addison's Disease revolves around the Concepts of Electrolytes (Na$^+$, K$^+$, & Ca^{++}) & Glucose Metabolism

Let's review some important points.

Cushing's Disease				Addison's Disease			
Some	People	Get	Cold	Some	People	Get	Cold
↑ Na$^+$	↓ K$^+$	↑ Glucose	↓ Ca^{++}	↓ Na$^+$	↑ K$^+$	↓ Glucose	↑ Ca^{++}
Cushing Disease: increased sodium due to increased aldosterone level ↑ Aldosterone levels = ↑ Absorption of ↑ H$_2$O & ↑ Na$^+$ ↑ NA$^+$ absorption = K$^+$ moves opposite NA$^+$ = ↓ K$^+$				**Addison's Disease has decreased sodium due to decreased aldosterone level.** ↓ Aldosterone levels = ↓ Absorption of ↓ H$_2$O & ↓ Na$^+$ ↓ NA$^+$ absorption = K$^+$ moves opposite NA$^+$ = ↑ K$^+$			
Cushing Disease increased Cortisol (due to disease/excess intake of corticosteroid) causes increased blood sugars ↑ Cortisol = ↑ Glucose (Serum) = "Hot and Dry ... My Sugar is High"				**Addison's Disease Glucocorticoids (Cortisol): decreased causes decreased blood sugar** ↓ Glucocorticoids (Cortisol) = ↓ Glucose (Serum) = "Cold and Clammy, I need some Candy"			
Cushing Disease: Calcium leaves bones and is excreted in urine ↓ Ca^{++} = Brittle Bones = Risk for Fractures, Falls				**Addison's Disease: Reduced removal of calcium by the kidneys and increase Ca^{++} in blood circulation** ↑ Ca^{++} = Need for Fluids & Fiber (Prevent Stones & Constipation) Monitor for Cardiac Dysrhythmias!			

YOU GOT THIS!!! LET'S FACE IT...
YOU ARE AN ENDOCRINE GENIUS!!!!!

Clinical Decision-Making Exercises

1. Which assessment finding would be most important to report in a client who is one day post-thryroidectomy?

    ① Calcium level was 8. 5mEq/L and is now 10mEq/L.

    ② Absence of Chvostek's sign.

    ③ A 1 cm size amount of bloody drainage on the dressing.

    ④ Presence of Trousseau's sign.

2. Which of statement made by the client with a diagnosis of hypothyroidism indicates a need for additional teaching?

    ① "I will add an Ensure supplement every day to my diet."

    ② "I will increase the amount of iodine in my diet."

    ③ "I will consume more leafy green vegetable with my meals."

    ④ "I will be sure to use iodized salt when seasoning meals."

3. While assessing a client with Cushing's disease, which clinical assessment finding should be reported to the physician immediately?

    ① Dependent edema of +1 in ankles and calves.

    ② Weight gain of 1 lb. since the previous day.

    ③ Spiked T waves on the ECG monitor.

    ④ Respiratory crackles in bilateral lower lung fields.

4. What would be the priority of care for a client with Grave's disease who is presenting with these changes 2 hours later: a HR that was 78 bpm and is now 115 bpm, a temperature change from 98.9° F and is now 102.5° F, serum glucose was 89 mg/dL and is now 158 mg/dL?

    ① Give aspirin 600 mg PO stat.

    ② Place the client in a supine position.

    ③ Place client on a cardiac monitor.

    ④ Administer glucagon (GlucaGen) IV per order.

5. Which of these interventions would be appropriate for a nurse caring for a client with SIADH?

    ① Have suction equipment and an airway at the bedside

    ② Give the client a soda to drink as requested.

    ③ Encourage the client to increase their fluid intake.

    ④ Monitor the client's weight once a week.

6. Which of these nursing actions by the new nurse with a client with Diabetes Insipidus requires immediate intervention by the charge nurse?

    ① Weighs client daily.

    ② Provides meticulous skin care.

    ③ Limits oral fluid intake.

    ④ Uses alcohol-free skin care products.

7. Which of these system-specific assessments with a client with a diagnosis of Addison's disease should be reported to the healthcare provider?

① Calcium level 9.7mEq/L

② Potassium level 6.5 mEq/L

③ Serum sodium 139 mEq/L.

④ Serum glucose 180 mg/dL.

8. What would be the highest priority of care for a client diagnosed with syndrome of inappropriate anti-diuretic hormone (SIADH)?

① Teach the client to report large amounts of urine output.

② Instruct the UAP to encourage continued hydration in the client.

③ Report a weight gain of 2.5 pounds in 24 hours.

③ Monitor for signs and symptoms of hypovolemia.

9. What should be included in the discharge-teaching plan for a client with Cushing's disease? *Select all that apply.*

① Monitor BP twice a week and keep a log to share with your healthcare provider.

② Avoid potatoes, bananas and cantaloupes in your diet.

③ Use salt instead of salt substitute with your meals.

④ Report to your healthcare provider if you are feeling hot, dry, flushed in the face.

⑤ Do a complete home assessment to identify potential hazards for falls.

10. The nurse observes the following rhythm strip of a client with Cushing's disease. Which of the following interventions is most appropriate?

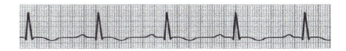

① Obtain an order for hypertonic fluids

② Obtain an order to increase the sodium intake in the diet.

③ Contact the HCP and hold the potassium supplement.

④ Contact the HCP and obtain an order for a potassium supplement.

Answers and Rationales

1. Which **assessment finding** would be **most important to report** in a client who is one day **post-thryroidectomy?**

    ① INCORRECT: Calcium level was 8. 5 mEq/L and is now 10 mEq/L. The calcium level is within normal range and post thyroidectomy you would be concerned with low calcium levels.

    ② INCORRECT: Absence of Chvostek's sign. This clinical finding does not indicate elevated calcium levels.

    ③ INCORRECT: A 1 cm size amount of bloody drainage on the dressing. This would be an expected finding.

    ④ **CORRECT: Presence of Trousseau's sign. This is a clinical finding that indicates a decreased calcium level, which is a risk post thyroidectomy due to injury or accidental removal of the parathyroid gland. It may be necessary to give calcium gluconate.**

The strategy for answering this question: Linking the information you know about the risks post thyroidectomy to the clinical findings of decreased calcium levels. You were able to apply the concept of hypocalcaemia to the clinical findings you assessed post thyroidectomy... Wasn't that Easy!!!

Reduction of Risk: Recognize signs and symptoms of complications/intervene appropriately.

2. Which of **statement** made by the client with a diagnosis of **hypothyroidism** indicates a **need for additional teaching?**

    ① **CORRECT: "I will add an Ensure supplement every day to my diet." A client with hypothyroidism does not need additional calories because of the decrease in metabolism. They need to decrease their calorie intake.**

    ② INCORRECT: "I will increase the amount of iodine in my diet." This is correct for hypothyroidism.

    ③ INCORRECT: "I will consume more vegetables with my meals." This is correct because you want a healthy low calorie diet because of the decreased metabolism.

    ④ INCORRECT: "I will be sure to use iodized salt when seasoning meals." This is correct for hypothyroidism because they need the iodine.

The strategy for answering this question is linking the physiology of hypothyroidism with the concept of the diet. Clients with hypothyroidism need to reduce weight by eating a healthy low calorie diet. They also need iodine or foods rich in iodine such as codfish or milk to be included in their dietary plan of care.

Physiological Integrity: Intervene with client who has an alteration in nutritional intake.

3. While assessing a client with **Cushing's disease,** which clinical **assessment finding should be reported** to the physician **immediately?**

    ① INCORRECT: Dependent edema of +1 in ankles and calves. This is insignificant and with Cushing's Disease, clients do not have edema because the sodium is elevated due to the increase ADH.

    ② INCORRECT: Weight gain of 1 lb. since the previous day. Not significant for 24 hours.

    ③ INCORRECT: Spiked T waves on the ECG monitor. With Cushing's Disease, there is low potassium levels so the T wave would be inverted (*Refer to Concept Cardiac/ Peripheral Perfusion for specifics*).

    ④ **CORRECT: Respiratory crackles in bilateral lower lung fields. This would be**

a concern because with where sodium goes, so does water! The crackles in the lung would need to be reported because of the potential for respiratory distress.

The strategy for answering this question is to recognize the potential complications that can occur with increased sodium levels. Increased sodium leads to fluid volume excess. With fluid volume excess, monitoring the respiratory status is a priority. This requires the nurse to compare, contrast and trend the assessment findings with auscultating the lung sounds and assessing the respiratory rate in order to intervene early with a potential complication. Trending is an important part of prioritizing care (*Refer to Prioritizing Chapter for specifics*). Good job connecting the increased sodium level with an increase in fluid!

Reduction of Risk Potential: Recognize trends and changes in client condition and intervene as needed.

4. What would be the **priority of care for a client with Grave's disease** who is presenting with these changes 2 hours later: a **HR that was 78 bpm and is now 115 bpm**, a **temperature change from 98.9° F and is now 102.5° F, serum glucose was 89 mg/dL and is now 158 mg/dL?**

    ① INCORRECT: Give aspirin 600 mg PO stat. This is not correct, you only use acetaminophen because salicylate ↑ thyroxine level.

    ② INCORRECT: Place the client in a supine position. Incorrect, you need to elevate the head of the bed to help them with expanding the lungs and airway and additionally you may need to give the client some oxygen.

    ③ **CORRECT: Place client on a cardiac monitor. Correct, the clinical findings in the stem of the question indicates a thyroid storm. Placing the client on a cardiac monitor is a priority. Remember everything is elevated, the metabolism rate and that includes a very rapid heart rate.**

    ④ INCORRECT: Administer glucagon (GlucaGen) IV per order. This would not be appropriate; it is for low calcium level.

The strategy for answering this question is to recognize the clinical findings of a thyroid storm which is the result of extreme hypermetabolism and to intervene appropriately. The thyroid storm can occur suddenly and it is important to assess and recognize the clinical findings and intervene early to prevent potential complications. Linking the concepts of cardiac perfusion with a very rapid heart rate to the physiology of what occurs in a thyroid storm, you were able to select the right answer. Yes!!!

Reduction of Risk: Recognize signs and symptoms of complications and intervene appropriately.

Physiological Adaptation: Manage care with alteration in hemodynamics, tissue perfusion (cardiac).

5. Which of these **interventions** would be **appropriate** for a nurse caring for a client with **SIADH?**

    ① **CORRECT: Have suction equipment and an airway at the bedside. This is needed due to risk of seizures.**

    ② INCORRECT: Give the client a soda to drink as requested. Sodas contain large amounts of sodium, which would further increase the retention of fluids. The sodium is low due to being diluted.

    ③ INCORRECT: Encourage the client to increase their fluid intake. With SIADH, there would be fluid restrictions, not an increase.

    ④ INCORRECT: Monitor the client's weight once a week. This is incorrect because of the fluid volume excess with SIADH, it is important to monitor the weight daily and report weight gains of 2 lbs or greater/day.

The strategy for answering this question is linking the concepts of fluid volume excess with the physiology of increased ADH with SIADH. You know that because of the excess antidiuretic hormone, the client is holding on to fluids. The decreased serum sodium is diluted, but caution is needed with giving sodium to prevent retention of more fluids. Because of the decreased sodium, the client is at risk for seizures. Having the suction equipment and airway at the bedside is a priority. Good job...you have linked two concepts; you knew the clinical findings and appropriate inventions for the concept of electrolytes and fluid balance and applied them successfully based on the physiology of SIADH. In addition, you correctly used your prioritization strategy with safety that includes safe and appropriate use of equipment!!! Great job!

Safety and Infection Control: Facilitate appropriate and safe use of equipment

Reduction of Risks: Use precautions to prevent injury and/or complication associated with a diagnosis.

Physiological Adaptation: Manage the care of the client with a fluid and electrolyte imbalance.

6. Which of these **nursing actions** by the new nurse with a **client with Diabetes Insipidus** requires **immediate intervention** by the charge nurse?

① INCORRECT: Weighs client daily. This action is correct with Diabetes Insipidus because you need to monitor the fluid volume loss due to the large amounts of urine being excreted.

② INCORRECT: Provides meticulous skin care. This action is correct because of the potential dehydration with Diabetes Insipidus, good skin care is important to avoid skin breakdown.

③ **CORRECT: Limits oral fluid intake. This would need intervention because the client with Diabetes Insipidus is excreting large amounts of urine daily (4 – 20 L/day) due to the deficiency of the antidiuretic hormone. The need for fluid replacement is essential to avoid hypovolemia. The clients also experience polydipsia (excessive thirst) and need to increase fluids to replace output as prescribed.**

④ INCORRECT: Uses alcohol-free skin care products. This would be correct because alcohol is drying to the skin and clients with Diabetes Insipidus already have dry skin from the fluid loss.

The strategy to answer this question is to recognize when the care is inappropriate based on the physiology of the disease process and intervene to correct it. This is a professional responsibility of the nurse. You knew limiting oral fluids would not be appropriate with a client with Diabetes Insipidus with the large amount of urine excreted each day. You linked the concepts of fluid balance with the physiology of Diabetes Insipidus and applied to the care of the clients. You are really getting good at pulling it all together!!!

Physiological Adaptation: Manage the care of the client with a fluid and electrolyte imbalance.

Management of Care: Recognize limitations of self/others, seek assistance / corrective measures.

7. Which of these **system-specific assessments** with a client with a diagnosis of **Addison's disease** should be **reported to the healthcare provider?**

① INCORRECT: Calcium level 9.7 mEq/L. This is within the normal range for calcium and clients with Addison's Disease would have calcium levels that would be elevated.

② **CORRECT: Potassium level 6.5 mEq/L. This is correct. This is a dangerously high level for potassium that can lead to cardiac dysrhythmias. It requires immediate intervention to bring the potassium level down.**

③ INCORRECT: Serum sodium 139 mEq/L. This is within the normal range for sodium and clients with Addison's Disease would have sodium levels that would be decreased.

④ INCORRECT: Serum glucose 180 mg/dL. This level, although on the high side of normal would not take priority over the potassium level. A glucose of 180 mg/dL does not have the life threatening potential that a K^+ level of 6.5 mEq/L has.

The strategy to answer this question is to know your normal values of the electrolytes, to know the expected clinical findings for Addison's disease based on the physiology of the disease process and then to link it to the appropriate nursing care. You were able to do this because you have learned your values for your electrolytes and knew what the low and high values can mean. Bottom line, a potassium level that is high, whether it was from Addison's disease, or renal disease or from a client who is on a potassium sparing diuretic, requires immediate intervention because of the potential life threatening arrhythmias!!!! You correctly prioritized the care, trending potential complications with accurate assessment findings and you made an excellent clinical decision that may have saved the client's life! **GENIUS!!!!!**

Physiological Adaptation: Manage the care of the client with a fluid and electrolyte imbalance.

Reduction of Risk: Perform and/or evaluate diagnostic testing.

8. What would be the **highest priority of care** for a client diagnosed with **syndrome of inappropriate anti-diuretic hormone (SIADH)?**

   ① INCORRECT: Teach the client to report large amounts of urine output. A client with SIADH would not have large amounts of urine output because of the increased amounts of the antidiuretic hormone.

   ② INCORRECT: Instruct the UAP to encourage continued hydration in the client. The client would require fluid restriction because of the increased levels of antidiuretic hormones that is causing the kidneys to retain fluid.

   ③ **CORRECT: Report a weight gain of 2.5 pounds in 24 hours. This is important with SIADH because it indicates the client is holding on to fluid. Yes, it is a clinical finding for SIADH, but as the nurse, we need to stay on top of the fluid increase to prevent potential complications such as respiratory distress. Remember anytime a client is gaining over 2 lbs a day, indicates water retention.**

   ④ INCORRECT: Monitor for signs and symptoms of hypovolemia. This would not be true for a client with SIADH.

The strategy for this question is linking the physiology of SIADH with the increased sodium and water retention due to excess antidiuretic hormone with the clinical finding of a greater than 2 lb. weight gain in a day. The role of the nurse is to intervene early with reporting the weight gain, so that the appropriate treatment is implemented before the client has complications from the increased fluid (i.e., respiratory distress, increase fluid volume that causes an increase workload on the heart, etc.). Once again, you successfully linked the concepts of fluid balance, perfusion, and metabolism together with physiology and made a great clinical decision! You have also effectively used the prioritization strategy of trending for potential complications! Yes!!!

Physiological Integrity: Monitor client's hydration **status.**

Reduction of Risk: Recognize trends and changes in the client's condition and intervene appropriately.

9. What should be included in the **discharge-teaching plan** for a client with **Cushing's disease?** Select all that apply.

   ① **CORRECT: Monitor BP twice a week and keep a log to share with your healthcare provider. This is important because of the increased sodium and water, a client is at risk for increased blood pressure and it needs to be monitored.**

   ② INCORRECT: Avoid potatoes, bananas and cantaloupes in your diet. The client needs to include these foods in their diet because they are rich in potassium and with Cushing disease; there is a decreased potassium level.

   ③ INCORRECT: Use salt instead of salt substitute with your meals. Salt is not recommended for a client with Cushing because of their already elevated sodium level. A salt substitute would be ok because it has potassium in it and the potassium level is low with Cushing's Disease.

   ④ **CORRECT: Report to your healthcare provider if you are feeling hot, dry, flushed in the face. The client needs to know the signs of high blood sugar and when to report them. Hyperglycemia is a clinical finding with Cushing's Disease.**

   ⑤ **CORRECT: Do a complete home assessment to identify potential hazards for falls. This is important to do because although the calcium level is high, the calcium is being pulled from the bones. A client needs to be proactive to help prevent falls in the home and the potential for fractures.**

The strategy to answer this question is know the clinical findings associated with the physiology of Cushing's Disease. One of your primary roles is to teach the client and their family about their disease and to prepare them for when they go home. Health promotion begins with client teaching that helps clients learn how to care for themselves or their family members at home. Linking the clinical findings to important teaching points helps the client know what to report to the healthcare provider to prevent complications. This helps the client to take an active role in their care.

Health Promotion and Maintenance: Provide client and family with information about condition/illness or outcomes.

10. The nurse observes the following **rhythm strip of a client with Cushing's disease**. Which of the following **interventions is most appropriate?**

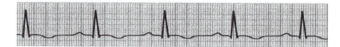

① INCORRECT: Obtain an order for hypertonic fluids. The strip does not represent a need for fluid and with Cushing disease, the sodium level is elevated contradicting the need to give hypertonic fluids.

② INCORRECT: Obtain an order to increase the sodium intake in the diet. The strip does not represent a need to increase the sodium intake with Cushing Disease because the sodium level is elevated. Sodium would be restricted.

③ INCORRECT: Contact the HCP and hold the potassium supplement. The strip with the depressed T waves, indicates the potassium level may be low and a supplement may be needed, it would not be held.

④ **CORRECT: Contact the HCP and obtain an order for a potassium supplement. The strip with the depressed T waves indicates that the potassium level is low. Linking that the low potassium levels found with Cushing Disease, there would be a need for a potassium supplement.**

The strategy for answering this question is linking what you know about low potassium levels with what you learned in the cardiac perfusion chapter. Link it with the fact that low potassium levels cause depressed T waves; link that with the physiology of Cushing Disease and the clinical finding of low K^+ levels and you have your answer. In this question you pulled together the concepts of electrolytes, with cardiac perfusion with metabolism!!! Concept link (*Refer to Concept Cardiac/Peripheral Perfusion and Concept Fluid and Electrolytes for specifics*). Excellent!

Reduction of Risk: Manage the care of a client on telemetry.

Decision-Making Analysis Form

Use this tool to help identify why you missed any questions. As you enter the question numbers in the chart, you will begin to see patterns of why you answered incorrectly. This information will then guide you toward what you need to focus on in your continued studies. Ultimately, this analytical exercise will help you become more successful in answering questions!!!

Questions to ask:

1. Did I have the knowledge to answer the question? If not, what information do I need to review?

2. Did I know what the question was asking? Did I misread it or did I miss keywords in the stem of the question?

3. Did I misread or miss keywords in the distractors that would have helped me choose the correct answer?

4. Did I follow my gut reaction or did I allow myself to rationalize and then choose the wrong answer?

	Lack of Knowledge (Concepts, Systems, Pathophysiology, Medications, Procedures, etc.)	Missed Keywords or Misread the Stem of the Question	Missed Keywords or Misread the Distractors	Changed My Answer (Second-guessed myself, i.e., my first answer was correct.)
Put the # of each question you missed in the column that best explains why you think you answered it incorrectly.				

If you changed an answer because you talked yourself out of the correct answer, or you second-guessed yourself, this is an **EASY FIX: QUIT changing your answers**!!! Typically, the first time you read a question, you are about 95% right! The second time you read a question, you start talking yourself into changing the answer. The third time you read a question, you do not have a clue—and you are probably thinking "Who in the heck wrote this question?"

On the other hand, if you read a question too quickly and when you reread it you realize you missed some key information that would impact your decision (i.e., assessments, lab reports, medications, etc.), then it is appropriate to change your answer. When in doubt, go with the safe route: your first thought! Go with your gut instinct!

As you gain confidence in answering questions regarding specific nursing concepts, you will be able to successfully progress to answering higher-level questions about prioritization. Please refer to the *Prioritization Guidelines* in this book for a structure to assist you with this process.

You CAN do this!

"The genius thing that we did was, we didn't give up!"

JAY-Z

References for Chapter 14

Black, J M. and Hawks, J. H. (2009). *Medical surgical nursing: Clinical management for positive outcomes (8th ed.)*. Philadelphia: Elsevier/Saunders.

Daniels, R. & Nicoll, L. (2012). *Contemporary medical-surgical nursing,* (2nd ed.). Clifton Park, NY: Delmar Cengage Learning.

Ellis, K.M. (2012). *EKG: Plain and simple* (3rd ed.). Upper Saddle Road, NJ: Pearson.

Eliopoulos, C. (2014). *Gerontological nursing* (8th ed.), Philadelphia: Lippincott Williams & Wilkins.

Giddens, G. F. (2013). *Concepts for nursing practice.* St. Louis, MO: Mosby, an imprint of Elsevier.

Hogan, M. A. (2014). *Pathophysiology: Reviews and rationales* (3rd ed.) Boston, MA: Pearson.

Ignatavicius, D. D. and Workman, M. L. (2010). *Medical-surgical nursing: Patient-centered collaborative care* (6th ed.). Philadelphia: Elsevier/Saunders.

LeMone, P., Burke, K. M., and Bauldoff, G. (2011). *Medical-surgical nursing: Critical thinking in patient care* (5th ed.). Upper Saddle Road, NJ: Pearson/Prentice Hall.

Lewis, S., Dirksen, S., Heitkemper, M., Bucher, L., and Camera, I. (2011). *Medical surgical nursing: Assessment and management of clinical problems* (8th ed.). St. Louis: Mosby.

Manning, L. and Rayfield, S. (2014). *Nursing made insanely easy* (7th ed.). Duluth, GA: I CAN Publishing, Inc.

Manning, L. and Rayfield, S. (2013). *Pharmacology made insanely easy* (4th ed.). Duluth, GA: I CAN Publishing, Inc.

Metheny, N.M. (2012). *Fluid and electrolyte balance: Nursing considerations* (5th ed.). Sudbury, MA: Jones and Barlett Learning.

National Council of State Boards of Nursing, INC. (NCSBN) 2012. *Research brief: 2011 RN practice analysis: linking the NCLEX RN® examination to practice.* Retrieved from https://www.ncsbn.org/index.htm

Nettina, S. L. (2013). *Lippincott manual of nursing practice* (10th ed.). Philadelphia, PA: Walters Kluwer Health/Lippincott Williams & Wilkins.

North Carolina Concept Based Learning Editorial Board (2011). *Nursing a concept based approach to learning,* Upper Saddle Road, NJ: Pearson/Prentice Hall.

Osborn, K. S., Wraa, C. E., Watson, A. S., and Holleran, R. S. (2014). *Medical surgical nursing: Preparation for practice* (2nd ed.). Upper Saddle Road, NJ: Pearson.

Pagana, K. D. and Pagana, T. J. (2014). *Mosby's manual of laboratory and diagnostic tests* (5th ed.). St. Louis, MO: Mosby, an imprint of Elsevier.

Porth, C. (2011). *Essentials of pathophysiology* (3d ed.). Philadelphia, PA: Lippincott Williams ad Wilkins.

Porth, C. M. and Grossman, S. (2013). *Pathophysiology: Concepts of altered health states* (9th ed.). Philadelphia, PA: Lippincott Williams & Wilkins.

Potter, P. A., Perry, A. G., Stockert, P., and Hall, A. (2013). *Fundamentals of nursing* (8th ed.). St. Louis, MO: Pearson/Prentice Hall.

Smeltzer, S. C., Bare, B. G., Hinkle, J. L., and Cheever, K. H. (2010). *Brunner & Suddarth's Textbook of medical-surgical nursing* (12th ed.). Philadelphia: Lippincott Williams & Wilkins.

Wagner, K. D. and Hardin-Pierce, M. C. (2014). *High-Acuity nursing* (6th ed.). Boston: Pearson.

CHAPTER 15

Endocrine System: Linking Concepts to Pathophysiology of Diabetes Mellitus

Concept Glucose Metabolism

A Snapshot of Glucose Metabolism

Glucose metabolism represents a very complex physiologic process by which glucose is utilitzed by the body. Glucose metabolism is influenced by multiple variables, but the ultimate end result on a cellular level is the use of glucose for energy or adenosine triphosphate (ATP) synthesis (Giddens, 2013).

Pancreas: Beta Cells, located in the islets of Langerhans in the pancreas, secrete the hormone insulin, which facilitates the movement of glucose across cell membranes into cells resulting in a decrease in the blood glucose levels. Insulin prevents excessive breakdown of glycogen in the liver and in muscle, facilitates the formation of lipid while inhibiting the breakdown of stored fats, and assists in moving amino acids into cells for protein synthesis. Insulin is necessary for optimizing normal carbohydrate metabolism and glucose utilization. When eating food, insulin levels begin to rise in minutes, peak in 30 to 60 minutes, and return to baseline in 2–3 hours.

Diabetes Mellitus (also referred to as *diabetes*) is a disorder of hyperglycemia resulting from defects in insulin secretion, insulin action, or both leading to abnormalities in carbohydrate, protein, and fat metabolism (American Diabetes Association, 2012). Diabetes Mellitus (DM) is a complex (*do not worry; we are going to simplify this, so it will not be so complex!*) multi-system disease characterized by the absence of, or a severe decrease in, the secretion or utilization of insulin. It is a destruction of alpha and beta cells of the pancreas. There is a dependency on insulin to prevent ketoacidosis and maintain life. Several types of diabetes will be reviewed in this chapter: type 1 diabetes mellitus (type I DM), type 2 diabetes mellitus (type 2 DM), and gestational diabetes.

Cells produce the hormone **glucagon** that stimulates the breakdown of glycogen in the liver, the formation of carbohydrates in the liver, and the breakdown of lipids in both the liver and adipose tissue. The primary function of **glucagon** is to decrease glucose oxidation and increase blood glucose levels. Through **glycogenolysis** (the breaking down of glycogen to increase blood glucose concentration to an optimal level) and **gluconeogenesis** (the formation of glucose from fats and proteins), glucagon prevents blood glucose from decreasing below a certain level when the body is fasting or between meals.

Delta Cells produce somatostatin, which is thought to be a neurotransmitter that inhibits the production of both glucagon and insulin.

Normal serum glucose levels range between 70–110 mg/dL (both preprandial and postprandial); this state is referred to as euglycemia.

Hyperglycemia is the term used to describe a state of elevated blood glucose levels, generally defined as greater than 126 mg/dL in the fasting state or greater than 200 mg/dL with an oral glucose tolerance test.

Ketoacidosis is an extreme increase in the hyperglycemic state. Metabolism of fat results in fatty acid production resulting in a conversion to ketone bodies. This increase in ketone bodies can lead to metabolic acidosis. This can be a complication of type 1 diabetes mellitus.

Hypoglycemia refers to a state of insufficient or low blood glucose levels, defined as less than 70 mg/dL generally from the use of exogenous insulin or one of the sulfonylurea agents.

Now that we have gotten through this mountain of definitions, we can move on to the fun part of simplifying these formal terms! There still are a few more terms that need to be defined such as specific laboratory and diagnostic tests, but we will review these as we get to the designated sections throughout the chapter. Let's begin with pathophysiology!

Endocrine System
The Pathophysiology Behind Alteration in Glucose Metabolism

Glucose Metabolism: Endocrine System–The Pancreas
SERUM GLUCOSE (Normal 70–110 mg/dL)

Hyperglycemia (Serum glucose > 126 mg/dL)	Hypoglycemia (Serum glucose < 70 mg/dL)
Absence of, or a decrease in, the secretion or utilization of insulin. (Serum glucose > 126 mg/dL)	Extracellular / intracellular processes from too much insulin or oral anti-diabetic agents. (Serum glucose < 70 mg/dL)
• Insulin resistance • Diabetes Mellitus, type 1 • Diabetes Mellitus, type 2 • Gestational Diabetes • Pancreatitis • Cushing's Disease/Syndrome	• Insulin treatment • Medical diagnoses with inadequate counter-regulatory hormones • Glycogen storage diseases • Starvation • Liver disease progressing to failure

Glucose Metabolism: Endocrine System
Common Labs/Diagnostic Tests/Procedures

Random Blood Glucose Test: A random blood glucose can be drawn any time of day with out regard to fasting. Elevated blood glucose levels may occur after meals, after stressful events, in samples drawn from an IV site, or if client does have diabetes mellitus.

Fasting Blood Glucose Test: Client does not ingest any caloric intake other than water for at least 8 hours prior to the test. The sample generally reflects glucose level from hepatic production. The diagnosis of diabetes mellitus is made when a client's fasting blood glucose level is greater than 126 mg/dL. The fasting blood glucose measurement provides the best information and is the preferred method of diagnosing diabetes mellitus.

Post-prandial Glucose Test: Serum glucose is measured 2 hours following a meal. This reflects the efficiency of the insulin-mediated glucose uptake by peripheral tissues. Normal glucose levels should return to fasting levels within 2 hours.

Oral Glucose Tolerance Test: A fasting blood glucose is drawn at the beginning of the test. Client then drinks an identified amount of glucose. Serum levels of glucose are drawn every 30 min (or designated intervals by HCP) for 2 hours. Monitor for hypoglycemia throughout the procedure.

Hemoglobin A$_{1c}$ (HbA$_{1C}$) or **Glycosylated hemoglobin:** Glucose normally attaches to the hemoglobin molecule on a red blood cell. Hemoglobin is the part of a red blood cell that carries oxygen to the cells and sometimes joins with the glucose in the blood stream. As a result, the higher the blood glucose levels, the higher the levels of glycosylated hemoglobin (HbA$_{1C}$) (Guyton, 2010). This value is an average blood glucose level measured over the previous 3 months. It is recorded as a percentage and is useful in evaluating long-term glycemic control.

Labs

Diagnostics (The criteria for diagnosis are two or more abnormal test results with two or more values outside the normal range.)

Labs	Diagnostics Tests/Procedures
• **Serum glucose:** 70–110 mg/dL (Fasting)	• **Oral glucose tolerance test–1 hour:** < 200 mg/dL; 2 hours < 140mg/dL (normal reading). • **Oral glucose Level:** > 200 mg/dL is diagnostic of diabetes mellitus.
• **Glycosylated hemoglobin (HbA$_{1c}$):** Nondiabetic 4–6% • **Good diabetic control:** < 6.5%, (2%–6.4%) • **Poor diabetic control:** > 7% • **Serum Potassium:** 3.5–5.0 mEq/L	• **Fasting blood glucose test:** 126 mg/dL; FBG > 126 mg/dL is diagnostic for diabetes mellitus. • **Two-hour postprandial blood sugar:** normal is 65–139 mg/dL. • A test > 180 mg/dL strongly suggests the diagnosis of diabetes mellitus, but must have other glucose testing for diagnosis confirmation.

The Pathophysiology Behind Alteration in Glucose Metabolism

CONCEPTS

Glucose Metabolism

Glucose Metabolism–Diabetes Mellitus Type 1 Multiple Concepts "LIFE":			COMPLICATIONS from poorly controlled Diabetes Electrolytes/Acidosis	
Loss of Fluids (Volume Deficit)	**Infection/ Integumentary**	**Food** (Malnutrition)	**Ketoacidosis/Metabolic Acidosis** (Most Serious Metabolic Disturbance)	**Loss of Electrolyte** (Imbalance)
• Hyperglycemia will cause an ↑ in the osmotic gradient.	• Impaired immune function due to an alteration in the immune system response that results in impairment of white cells for phagocytosis.	• Polyphagia (Tissue breakdown and wasting results in hunger).	• Ketones: An increase in mobilization of fat and protein as energy when glucose is unavailable.	• Hyperkalemia – As the pH of the blood decreases (acidosis), the accumulating H^+ ions move from the extracellular fluid to the intracellular.
• Water moves out of the cells into the circulating volume to ↓ the osmolarity.	• Persistent glycosuria predisposes to urinary tract infections.	• Weight loss (with Type 1 DM); glucose is not available to the cells; body begins to break down fat and protein stores for energy.	• Fat metabolism causes breakdown products called ketones to form.	• The movement of the hydrogen ions into the cells promotes the movement of potassium out of the cells into the extracellular fluid, which results in severe intracellular potassium depletion and elevated extracellular potassium levels.
• Due to the ↑ in the circulating volume; water is not reabsorbed from the renal tubules, resulting in a significant polyuria (↑ in urine output).	• Delayed wound healing. **Integumentary:**	• Fatigue and weight loss due to wasting of lean body mass.	• Ketones accumulate in the blood and are excreted through the kidneys and lungs.	• With this potassium leaving the intracellular space, transient hyperkalemia develops.
• As a result of the polyuria, the loss of fluids may result in dehydration. The thirst mechanism will assist in compensating for this fluid loss, so the outcome will be polydipsia.	• Lipodystrophy (hypertrophy of subcutaneous tissue) from using the same injection sites repeatedly.		• Ketones interfere with the body's acid-base balance by producing hydrogen ions. The pH can decrease and metabolic acidosis can develop. **Compensation:**	• This elevated serum potassium level can result in lethal dysrhythmias.
	• The tissues become hardened and may have an orange-peel appearance.		• Respiratory system increases rate and depth. • Acetone breath. Kussmaul's respirations.	

System-Specific Assessments for Glucose Metabolism (Diabetes Mellitus)

An Insanely EASY Tip to remember signs and symptoms of HYPERGLYCEMIA is to remember **"FLUSHED"**! Of course the **"3 Ps"** work as well! (polyuria, polydipsia, polyphagia) The pathophysiology chart describes the pathophysiology for these assessment findings. The assessment becomes your guide as it does with the other concepts we have discussed. It is important to remember the priority assessment findings in order to assist you in prioritizing nursing care. Later on in the chapter, we will review an easy way to remember the system specific assessments for hypoglycemia, but for now, let's focus on hyperglycemia.

Flushed skin and fruit-like breath odor (acetone)

Listless/lethargic

Unusual thirst, urine output increased, hunger (early)

Skin dry and warm

Hyperventilate (rapid breathing)

Elevated respirations and increased nause and vomiting (later findings)

Drowsiness, decrease in appetite (nausea/vomiting)

"Fido" is the diabetic dog, and is exhibiting all of the signs and symptoms of hyperglycemia. Since the cells are starving for the lack of sugar, Fido is dreaming of food. He has a huge appetite. His food bowl is empty because he is always trying to feed those starving cells (**POLYPHAGIA**). The sugar content in his blood is pulling fluid from the cells which makes him very thirsty (**POLYDIPSIA**). Since his kidneys are compensating by dumping extra fluid and sugar out into the street (**POLYURIA**), he has totally wet down the fire hydrant. Look at Fido's pants! They are way too big and do not fit any more. The sugar and fluid that he has taken in have not gone into his cells, since there is no insulin to assist in crossing over into the cells. As a result, poor Fido has LOST WEIGHT. *We will discuss the management of care as we proceed forward in this chapter. At this time, please take a minute to reflect over the pathophysiology for the clinical findings a client may present with who has a problem with glucose metabolism from diabetes mellitus.*

©1994 Adapted from Creative Educators

Linking Pathophysiology to the Plan of Care for Alteration in Glucose Metabolism from Diabetes Mellitus (Hyperglycemia)

Pathophysiology	Plan of Care for "LIFE"
Loss of Fluids (Volume Deficit): 1. Hyperglycemia will cause an ↑ in the osmotic gradient. 2. Water moves out of the cells into the circulating volume to ↓ the osmolarity. 3. Due to the ↑ in the circulating volume; water is not reabsorbed from the renal tubules, resulting in a significant **polyuria** (↑ in urine output). 4. As a result of the polyuria, the loss of fluids may result in dehydration. The thirst mechanism will assist in compensating for this fluid loss, so the outcome will be **polydipsia**. Protein catabolism and potassium loss may occur resulting in weakness.	**L**oss of Fluids (Volume Deficit): 1. Monitor Intake and Output and trend. Monitor weight and trend. 2. Monitor vital signs and trend. Monitor for tachypnea due to fluid loss. 3. Assess characteristics of lips and mucous membranes and skin turgor (poor assessment for the geriatric client).4. Monitor for postural hypotension and assess for syncope and weakness.5. Fall precautions. 6. Labs: *Monitor Serum glucose, BUN, Hct, Specific Gravity; HgbA1c,(note these will all be elevated if there is fluid deficit).*
Infection/Integumentary: Impaired immune function due to an alteration in the immune system response that results in impairment of white cells for phagocytosis. Persistent glycosuria predisposes to urinary tract infections and delayed wound healing. **I**ntegumentary: Lipodystrophy (hypertrophy of subcutaneous tissue) from using the same injection sites repeatedly. The tissues become hardened and may have an orange-peel appearance.	**I**nfection/Integumentary: 1. Monitor and trend temperature; assess for signs of an upper respiratory (URI) (i.e., congestion, cough, color of the secretions, etc.). 2. Monitor and assess for signs of an urinary tract infection (UTI) such as dysuria, frequency, increase in the white blood cells, etc. 3. Monitor and assess for signs of infection in a wound. 4. (Folds of the skin, feet, toes.) Teach proper foot care (*Refer to chart on Do's and Don'ts for Foot Care*). Teach to clean cuts with warm water and mild soap, dry gently followed with a dry dressing.
Food (Malnutrition): When glucose is not available to the cells, the body begins to break down fat and protein stores for energy. Wasting of lean body mass can result from this process. Tissue breakdown and wasting results in hunger (**polyphagia**). The result is *ketones* in the blood due to fatty acid breakdown which can also cause metabolic acidosis. Compensation is done by the Kussmaul respirations (increase in the rate and depth) and an acetone breath may occur due to metabolic acidosis (other findings may include acetone/fruity breath, headache, nausea, vomiting, decrease in the LOC, seizures.)	**I**ntegumentary: Assess Integumentary system for any skin redness, breakdown, etc. Monitor for lipodystrophy from insulin injections (Refer to insulin teaching for specifics). **F**ood (Malnutrition): 1. Assess and monitor trend with weight loss. 2. Assess and monitor for fatigue along with the weight loss. 3. Monitor serum glucose and teach client the skill for self-monitoring blood glucose proficiency. 4. Assess understanding of importance of eating at regular intervals with no alcohol intake. Assess understanding of how to regulate insulin to exercise and nutritional intake to avoid hypoglycemia. (*Refer to chart on Teaching Plan for Administration of Insulin*). Develop health promotion plan to teach management. 5. Monitor dietary practices (*Refer to Nutritional Guidelines for Diabetes*). Encourage frequent rest periods. 6. Evaluate for ketones in the blood and urine. Teach client how to monitor. 7. Assess and trend the RR and for acetone breath; nausea and vomiting; level of consciousness, seizures. 8. Assess for headache, decrease in the LOC, and/or seizures.
Electrolytes/Acidosis (Complications from poorly controlled diabetes): **Ketones** accumulate in the blood and are excreted through the kidneys and lungs. Ketones interfere with the body's acid-base balance by producing hydrogen ions. The pH will decrease and **metabolic acidosis** will develop. **Hyperkalemia**: As the pH of the blood decreases (acidosis), the accumulating H$^+$ ions move from the extracellular fluid to the intracellular. The movement of the hydrogen ions into the cells promotes the movement of potassium out of the cells into the extracellular fluid, which results in severe intracellular potassium depletion and elevated extracellular potassium levels. With potassium leaving the intracellular space, transient hyperkalemia develops. The change in the total body potassium can result in lethal dysrhythmias.	**E**lectrolytes/Acidosis: *Complications from poorly controlled diabetes.* Evaluate serum glucose for hyperglycemia; electrolytes (acidosis); serum potassium level; increase in the urine ketones and sugar levels. Assess client's understanding of diagnosis/treatment. Electrolytes: Monitor potassium level. Monitor for cardiac changes in the T wave from potassium changes (*Refer to Concept Potassium Balance chapter for specifics*).

Pathophysiology: Glucose Metabolism
Evaluation of Expected Outcomes
"LIFE" Works When Expected Outcomes are Met!

L Loss of fluid (Fluid Deficit) is not a problem. I & O, vital signs, weight are WDL for client. Lips and mucous membranes moist and skin turgor WDL for client (not a valid assessment for elderly clients). Labs WDL. No falls from syncope due to fluid deficit.

I Infection/Integumentary: No evidence of infection (afebrile, WBC within defined limits). Skin and tissue intact, no decubitus.

F Food (Malnutrition): Nutrition status is adequate to maintain energy. Eating a nutritious diet with a serum glucose level WDL. No complications with hyper/hypoglycemia. Weight WDL for client.

E Electrolytes/Acidosis: Serum glucose, HbA_{1c}, serum pH, serum potassium, urine and serum ketones WDL for client.

Pathophysiology for Long-Term Complications

Glucose Metabolism: (Diabetes Mellitus Type 1): Long-Term Chronic Complications with Multiple Concepts			
Macrovascular Complications: **Perfusion**	Microvascular Complications: **Sensory Perception**	Microvascular Complications: **Elimination**	Microvascular Complications: **Coping**
Glycoprotein cell wall deposits → small vessel disease → accelerated atherosclerosis • Coronary artery disease • Cerebrovascular disease • Increased LDL levels • Peripheral vascular disease • Infection	**Glycoprotein cell wall deposits** → small vessel disease → result with inadequate blood supply to the nerve tissue and high blood glucose levels can cause metabolic changes within the neurons. **Diabetic neuropathy:** (Sensorimotor neuropathy) Symmetrical loss of protective sensation • Numbness and tingling in the extremities • Peripheral neuropathy may cause general pain and tingling; may progress to painless neuropathy • Wasting of intrinsic muscles • Diabetic foot ulceration • Charcot changes in joint **Retinopathy** → loss of vision (secondary to chronic exposure of ocular lens and retina to hyperosmolar fluids).	**Autonomic neuropathy:** Gastroparesis (leading to constipation and blockage). This can also lead to urinary incontinence, decreased sweating, and orthostatic hypotension. Interferes with the ability to recognize episode of hypoglycemia. **Autonomic neuropathy:** Microangiopathy affects the glomerular capillaries, resulting in thickening and increased permeability of the glomerular basement membrane, progressing to nephropathy → End stage renal failure.	**Autonomic neuropathy** • Impotence

SAFETY Concept: Glucose Metabolism (Hyperglycemia)– Diabetes Mellitus

System-Specific Assessment Assess for Long-term Chronic Complications	First-Do Priority Interventions Health Promotion for Long-term Chronic Complications	Evaluation of Expected Outcomes
• Neuro (**Sensory Perception**): Cerebrovascular disease: visual changes, BP, numbness in distal extremities. "**FAST**": Facial drooping, **A**rm weakness, **S**peech changes, Time is BRAIN!	• Neuro: Hypertension: Teach client to report headaches (persistent and transient), numbness in distal extremities, vision changes. Signs of a CVA; "**FAST**": Face–(Face for drooping; **A**rms for weakness and/or ability to raise together; **S**peech for stating name, address – slurring? Time is BRAIN!) If any of the "**FAST**" are deficient or present, immediate intervention is imperative. These are PRIORITY assessments for a CVA!	• Participates in ongoing health promotion activities to prevent complications with cerebrovascular, cardiovascular disease.
• Vision (**Sensory Perception**)– Retinopathy: Loss of vision	• Encourage annual eye exams. Encourage management of glucose. Note: When a child is 10 years-old and has had diabetes for 3–5 years, an ophthalmologic exam should be done and involve the interdisciplinary team for support.	• Monitors vision as recommended per standard.
• Cardiac (**Perfusion**): Coronary artery disease: BP for elevations; monitor cholesterol (HDL, LDL, triglycerides) HbA$_{1c}$	• Monitor BP, fatigue chest pain; peripheral edema. Monitor cholesterol (HDL, LDL, and triglycerides). Encourage regular exercise. Diet: low-fat, high in fruits, vegetables, and whole grain. Teach client to report headaches, SOB, swelling of feet, infrequent urination. Monitor HbA$_{1c}$ every 3 months. Avoid tight-fitting clothing around legs due to risk for altered perfusion to lower extremities.	• Labs monitored for trends and remain WDL for client. No signs of headaches, SOB, swelling of the feet, or infrequent urination.
• GI Gastroparesis (**Elimination**): Assess for any constipation and/ or signs of obstruction such as vomiting	• Report any unusual changes in bowel movements, vomiting. NG tube may be prescribed if client is vomiting or comatose. Frequent oral care will be important due to risk of dehydration from vomiting and the tube. Assess and monitor bowel sounds.	• No complications with constipation or vomiting.
• Coping (**Impotence**)	• Refer to HCP for support and education to assist with family dynamics.	• Seeks support and copes successfully with the sexual dysfunction of impotence.
• Renal System (**Elimination**): Nephropathy can progress to end stage renal failure: assess I & O, creatinine clearance; Monitor blood pressure	• Encourage annual analysis of BUN and creatinine clearance. Monitor BP. • Review the importance of avoiding alcohol, soda, and NSAIDs. • Teach to consume 2–3 L of fluid daily from beverage sources and food. Drink an adequate amount of water. Report any decrease in urine output to HCP. Refer to Concept "Altered Renal Perfusion" if client progresses to failure and end stage renal disease.	• Creatinine clearance is monitored, BUN, I & O, and BP are monitored to prevent complications with renal failure.
• Sensorimotor neuropathy: (**Sensory Perception**): Numbness and tingling in the extremities; diabetic foot ulceration	• Monitor serum glucose levels; provide foot care. Teach client the importance and how to evaluate feet daily. Monitor for falls and prevent injury from heat, etc. Encourage annual exams by a podiatrist (*Refer to Do's and Don'ts for Foot Care in this chapter*).	• No falls or injuries. Normal serum glucose and ongoing foot care to prevent complications.

Glucose Metabolism: Diabetes Mellitus

Health Promotion Information to Include in the Educational Plan for The Do's and Don'ts of Foot Care

The DOs of Foot Care	The DON'Ts of Foot Care
• Inspect feet daily. Use mild soap and warm water and pat gently when drying.	• Use commercial remedies for removing calluses or corns.
• Perform nail care following a bath or shower.	• Wear open-toe or open-heel shoes.
• Use cotton or lamb's wool to separate overlapping toes.	• Wear plastic shoes for feet protection.
• Use a powder with cornstarch if feet get sweaty.	• Go barefoot.
• Wear socks made of wool or lamb that are clean and absorbent.	• Use heating pads or hot water bottles.
• Wear shoes that fit correctly and are leather. Wear slippers with soles.	• Stand or sit for prolonged periods of time or cross legs.
• Shake out shoes prior to putting on.	
• Follow health care setting protocol for nail care. Some allow the use of clippers for trimming straight across the toenails and then filing edges with an emery board or nail file. If clippers or scissors are contraindicated, the nails should be filed straight across.	
• Refer to Concept Tissue Integrity for specifics on diabetic foot ulcers.	

Glucose Metabolism (Diabetes Mellitus) for the Older Adult
PLAN FOR ADMINISTRATION OF INSULIN

"**CONFUSION**" is used periodically in this book to organize assessments and/or the plan of care for the older adult, since "CONFUSION" is a priority to consider when planning SAFE nursing care!

Consider mental status and abilty to handle injections due to manual dexterity.

Oriented and mentally able to make judgments on medications?

Note if client can acccess the injection sites.

Financially able to pay for the supplies?

Understands the risk of hypoglycemia unawareness (i.e., does not experience early signs of hypoglycemia related to age). The use of beta-adrenergic blockers also may mask the recognition of hypoglycemia.

Support system for the client.

Identify the client's attitude about needle and supplies.

Other medications? Polypharmacy?

Need to assess client's and/or family's ability to demonstrate serum glucose testing.

SAFETY Concept: Glucose Metabolism (Hyperglycemia)– Diabetes Mellitus

System-Specific Assessment	First-Do Priority Interventions Health Promotion for Nutrition	Evaluation of Expected Outcomes
• Assess and monitor trend with weight loss. • Assess and monitor for fatigue along with the weight loss. • Monitor serum glucose and teach client the skill for self-monitoring blood glucose proficiency. • Assess understanding of importance of eating at regular intervals with no alcohol intake. • Assess understanding of how to regulate insulin with exercise and nutritional intake to avoid hypoglycemia (*Refer to chart on Teaching Plan for Administration of Insulin*). • Monitor dietary practices.	**Nutritional Guidelines** **N**utrition should be planned to coordinate food intake with insulin activity, onset and peak. **U**se artificial sweetners. **T**he grams of carbohydrates consumed should be counted. **R**ecognize that **15 g of carbohydrates are equal to 1 carbohydrate exchange**. **I**ntervals should be regular for eating meals. **T**o help control cholesterol, include residue (fiber) in the diet to increase carbohydrate metabolism. **I**ncrease physical activity and restrict calories as appropriate to assist with weight loss (for obese clients). **O**rganize caloric intake, so that the fat content will be below 30%. **N**utrition (calories and food intake) should be similar daily. Refer to dietician and diabetes nurse educator. **Guidelines for Food Selections** **A**void canned fruits in heavy syrup, instead select food packed in water. **V**egetables, fresh fruit, whole-grain cereals, and breads should be included to provide residue (fiber) to prevent constipation. **O**ils and margarines that are liquid at room temperature are better than when solid. **I**ngredient that is the highest-content ingredient is listed first on the food label. **D**o select foods in which majority of calories do not come from a fat source.	• Nutrition status adequate to maintain energy. • Eating a nutritious diet with a serum glucose level WDL. • No complications with hyper/hypoglycemia. • Weight WDL for client.

SAFETY Concept: Glucose Metabolism (Hyperglycemia)– Diabetes Mellitus

System-Specific Assessment	First-Do Priority Interventions Teaching Plan for **INSULIN** Administration	Evaluation of Expected Outcomes
Always begin any teaching with assessing client's (family member/s) current knowledge level regarding the subject (in this situation it is diabetes and the plan for administering insulin). Part of this initial assessment should also include the socioeconomics, support system (family, spouse, etc.), and cultural parameters.	**I**nstruct how to do a Self-Monitoring of Blood Glucose (*Refer to SMBG guidelines on next page*). Always start by washing hands! **N**ever administer cold insulin; it increases discomfort at the site. **S**unlight, heat, and freezing are not allowed with insulin! **U**nrefrigerated, open 10 mL vial of insulin should be discarded after 30 days, regardless of amount used. Use ONLY insulin syringes to administer insulin. It is no longer recommended when performing an injection at home to use alcohol for cleansing the skin prior to the injection. **L**ower the risk for inconsistent concentration of insulin by rolling the vial between the palms of the hands. **I**nsulin pens should be discarded after 1 week of storage at room temperature. Regular cartridges, which do not contain preservatives, may be left unrefrigerated for up to 1 month. **N**ote that the abdomen (provides most rapid insulin absorption) is the main site for insulin subcutaneous injections. Rotate sites; these should be 1 inch apart. Note the expiration date on the bottle of insulin. When mixing insulin, draw up clear before cloudy! Aspirating is no longer recommended for self-injection. **Check dose with a second nurse prior to administering.** Demonstrate how to perform the steps to do a subcutaneous injection. **P**umps may be used for clients on rigorous diabetes therapy or blood sugar monitoring 4–6 times a day. **U**se of excessive carbohydrate ingested can be handled with a bolus of insulin from the pump. **M**akes it possible to deliver a continuous infusion of short-acting insulin over a 24-hour period, which provides a tight glucose control. **P**ump is operated by a battery. **S**ite of insertion is monitored for swelling and redness. Pump is refilled and reprogrammed when site is changed–q 2 to 3 days (per protocol).	**Immediate outcomes:** • Client will demonstrate the steps of how to administer insulin. • Client verbally gives a teach-back regarding safe administration. **Long-term outcomes:** • Nutrition status adequate to maintain energy. • Eating a nutritious diet with a serum glucose level WDL. • No complications with hyper/hypoglycemia. • Weight WDL for client.

SAFETY Concept: Glucose Metabolism (Hyperglycemia)–Diabetes Mellitus

System-Specific Assessment	First-Do Priority Interventions Instructions to Teach Priorities For Self-Monitoring of Blood Glucose (SMBG)	Evaluation of Expected Outcomes
Always begin any teaching with assessing client's (family member/s) current knowledge level regarding the subject (in this situation it is diabetes and the plan for administering insulin and general management). Part of this initial assessment should also include the socioeconomics, support system (family, spouse, etc.), and cultural parameters.	**S**elf-monitoring of blood glucose (SMBG). It is no longer recommended to use alcohol to cleanse the skin prior to injection at home. Should ALWAYS check the accuracy of the strips with the control solution provided. Review importance of keeping record of time, date, level of glucose, insulin dose, food intake, and other events that may alter glucose metabolism, such as stress, illness, other medications, etc. **M**ust teach guidelines for recording and responding to results. Teach how to handle supplies and equipment with return Demonstration (TEACH BACK). Teach when to do a SMBG: sick/under stress; starting a new med; when client thinks glucose is too high or too low; with ↑ or ↓ of weight; any change in med dose, diet, or level of physical exercise or activity. **B**lood needed is only 1 large drop. **G**etting blood: Use side of finger pad versus the center of the finger. If need to use forearm then different equipment will be required. Give and share instructions and discuss a plan for client with diabetes mellitus (*Refer to "DIET"*). **D**iet: Regularly scheduled meals. Understand the food groups and need for balanced nutrition. Provide written information about dietary needs. **I**nfection control, injury prevention: Report infections immediately to HCP. Insulin requirements may increase with infections. Decreased healing and slower in lower extremities. Avoid tight-fitting clothing around the legs due to risk for altered perfusion to lower extremities. Discuss safe foot care. **E**xercise: Establish an exercise program. Review how to adjust insulin and food intake to meet requirements of increase in activity. If client plays sports, do not use the dominant extremity for insulin injections that is used in the activity. **T**each about medication management (*Refer to the book, Pharmacology Made Insanely Easy*). **T**each signs and symptoms of hyper/hypoglycemia.	• Client will demonstrate how to perform self-monitoring of blood glucose (SMBG). • Client verbally gives a teach-back regarding safe management.

Common Medications for Glucose Metabolism

Teaching guidelines will be reviewed in the Health Promotion Section of this chapter. *Reference: Pharmacology Made Insanely Easy!*

Common Medications for Glucose Metabolism		
INSULINS:	**ORAL ANTIDIABETIC AGENTS:**	**ORAL ANTIDIABETIC AGENTS:** *(cont'd.)*

Rapid Acting
• Lispro insulin(Humalog)
• Aspart (Novolog)
• Glulisine (Apidra)
 	
Short Acting
• Regular
• Humulin R
• Novolin R
• Velosulin (for use in pumps)
 	
Intermediate Acting
• NPH
• Humulin N
• Novolin N
 	
Long Acting
• Lantus
• Levemin
 	
Combination
• NPH 70: Regular 30
• NPH 50: Regular 50
	Biguanide
	• Metformin (Glucophage)
	
	Sulfonylureas
	  First Generation
	  • acetohexamide (Dymelor)
	  • chlorpropamide (Diabinese)
	  • tolazamide (Tolinase)
	  • tolbutamide (Orinase)
	  Second Generation
	  • glimepiride (Amaryl)
	  • glipizide (Glucotrol)
	  • glyburide (Diabeta)
	
	Insulin Sensitizer
	• rosiglitazone (Avandia)
	• pioglitazone (Actos)
	
	Alpha-Glucosidase Inhibitors
	• acarbose (Precose)
	• miglitol (Glyset)
	
	Amylin Mimetics
	• pramlinitide (Symlin)
		Incretin Mimetics
		• exenatide (Byetta)
		
		Gliptins
		• sitagliptin (Januvia)
		
		Meglitinides
		• repaglinide (Gluconorm, Prandin)
		
		HYPERGLYCEMIC AGENT:
		
		• Glucagon (Glucagen
		
		(Manning and Rayfield, 2013)

Prototype Medication (Insulin)

The chart below will assist you in reviewing the onset, peaks, and durations of the commonly prescribed insulins. On a lighter note, the jingle at the bottom of the page will assist you in remembering assessments for "high versus low blood sugar."

CLASSIFI-CATION	GENERIC (TRADE NAME)	ONSET	PEAK	DURATION
Rapid-Acting	Lispro insulin (Humalog)	< 15 min.	0.5–1 1/2 hr.	3–4 hr.
Short-Acting	Regular insulin (Humulin R)	30 to 60 min.	2–3 hr.	5–7 hr.
Intermediate-Acting	NPH insulin (Humulin N)	1–2 hr.	4–12 hr.	18–24 hr.
Long-Acting	Insulin glargine (Lantus)	1–1 1/2 hr.	None	20–24 hr.
70% NPH and 30% Regular	Humulin 70/30	30 min.	2–4 hr	14–24 hr.
75% insulin lispro protamine and 25% insulin lispro	Humalog 75/25	15–30 min.	30 min.–2 1/2 hr.	16–20 hr.

Hypoglycemia
(sung to the tune of

"Row, Row, Row Your Boat")

Hot and dry
Your sugar's high.
Your insulin is what you need.

Cold and clammy
You need some candy,
And milk will help indeed.

Guidelines for "Sliding Scale" Insulin

Although administering insulin using the sliding scale has disadvantages, and there are now improved ways to better control glucose levels, it is still important to understand the sliding scale process. This section will define the term, review several principles of sliding scale therapy, and then how to adapt this in clinical practice.

The term *"sliding scale"* refers to the progressive increase in the pre-meal or nighttime insulin dose, based on pre-defined blood glucose ranges. **Sliding scale insulin regimens approximate daily insulin requirements.**

The general principles of sliding scale therapy are:

- There is a pre-set amount of carbohydrate to be eaten at each meal.

- The basal (background) insulin dose doesn't change. The same long-acting insulin dose is taken no matter what the serum glucose level.

- The serum glucose level before the meal or at bedtime is the basis for the bolus insulin.

- The serum glucose level before the meal is the basis for the pre-mixed insulin.

Disadvantages of the sliding scale regimen:

- There are no accommodation changes in the insulin needs in relation to stress, activity or snacks.

- Carbohydrates still must be counted.

- Since the high serum glucose correction and food bolus cannot be split, this regimen is less effective in covering a pre-meal high serum glucose.

Fixed Dose

With this method, a set amount of insulin is given at each meal, and the amount per meal can be the same or different. For example, someone may take 8 units at breakfast, 5 units at lunch and 7 units at dinner, or 8 units for all meals. The advantage of this method is primarily ease-of-use. The amount is the same regardless of the serum glucose readings or what the client eats. The negative side is the rigidity. When dietary intake (especially carbohydrate intake) varies widely, the blood glucose may well follow, and the client will end up with a pattern of erratic readings.

Application of the Sliding Scale Regimen

Sliding Scale

A sliding scale varies the dose of insulin based on serum glucose level. The higher the serum glucose the more insulin the client will take.

The sliding scale method is more precise than fixed dose insulin in that it takes account of the fact that client's serum glucose is not always in the normal range before meals. Sliding Scale requires a bit more "client investment" than fixed dose.

If a client wants more control over their serum glucose, is willing to do the requisite monitoring, and committed to a structured meal plan, then the method works well.

Note: Sliding scale insulin may be used with other clients who are nondiabetics and who have an elevated serum glucose due to (i.e., receiving TPN, severe illness, medication administration, etc.).

Refer below for an example.

A client has an order for 8 AM Lente (Humulin L) 10 units SubQ and is on a sliding scale insulin. The morning blood glucose level is 188mg/dL. The sliding scale orders are:

Serum glucose	Insulin order
< 170 mg/dL	No insulin
170-240 mg/dL	**5 units regular insulin SubQ**
241–300 mg/dL	10 units regular insulin SubQ
> 300 mg/dL	Notify provided of care for new prescription

How many units of insulin should the nurse administer?

Answer and Rationale: The answer is 15 units. There is an order for **10 units** to be administered, but the sliding scale requires for a serum glucose from 170–240 mg/dL to receive another **5 units** which would be added to the **10 units** to total **15 units**. A good way to remember this is to take what you have ordered and then add to the scale to get the total. (*Refer to question #8 in Clinical Decision Making Exercises at the end of the chapter for another example.*)

Insanely Easy Tip!
Think of the sliding scale insulin as a PRN medication. You give it when the serum glucose level is elevated per protocol.

Complications of Insulin Therapy

Hypoglycemia: *Refer to Health Promotion Plan for Comparing Plan of Care for Hypoglycemia and Hyperglycemia on page 420.*

Hormones that counteract the effectiveness of insulin: Cortisol, Epinephrine, and Glucagon.

Medications can also affect insulin and the serum glucose. "SUGAR" will assist you in remembering medications that can cause hyperglycemia. "SHAKES" will assist you in remembering medications that cause hypoglycemia. (p. 417)

Lipodystrophy: Teach client never to give cold insulin. Rotate injection sites.

Somogyi Effect: Hypoglycemia followed by rebound hyperglycemia. The pathophysiology is that the hypoglycemia leads to hormone secretion that is counter-regulatory and then the liver produces glucose. This increase in glucose level, along with insulin resistance secondary to increased hormone levels, is believed to contribute to this rebound hyperglycemia.

Most often occurs at night. The serum glucose increases between 2 and 4 AM and again at 7 AM. If early AM are < 50 to 60 mg/dL and the 7 AM are > 180 to 200 mg/dL, rebound hyperglycemia may have occurred. The dose of intermediate-acting insulin at supper time may need to be decreased, or the dose given at bedtime. May also be treated by increasing calories at bedtime to prevent this phenomenon.

An Insanely Easy Way to Remember Priorities with Somogyi Effect!

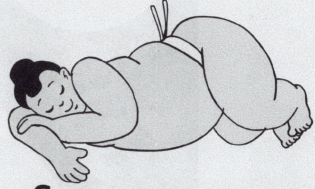

"SOMO" the wrestler is demonstrating when this effect occurs (asleep) and the time the serum glucose will decrease and increase! "SOMO" is also reviewing with you how to manage this effect.

Surge in glucose level most often occurs at night.

hyp**O**glycemia (2–4 AM) → hyperglycemia (7 AM)

Manage by decreasing bedtime dose or increasing calories at bedtime

c**O**rtisol, glucagon, epinephrine results in this rebound hyperglycemia

See how EASY this is!
Four statements do it!

©2014 I CAN Publishing®, Inc.

Complications of Insulin Therapy (cont'd.)

Dawn Phenomenon: An increase in the blood glucose level between 4 to 8 AM without the preceding nocturnal hypoglycemia. This phenomenon is an attempt to normalize pre-breakfast glucose levels often resulting in early-morning hypoglycemia. The release of growth hormone and cortisol causes this elevation in the blood glucose. This may be managed by adjusting insulin and increasing it for the overnight period.

As you see in the image below, during the night the blood glucose level got low, resulting in the nighttime release of growth hormone and cortisol. As a result of this rise in these hormones, the blood glucose elevates in the early AM (pre-dawn when the sun is rising!) Hormones that counteract insulin are cortisol, epinephrine, glucagon and growth hormone.

Medications That Can Result in Hyper/Hypoglycemia

There are many medications that affect serum glucose. Although the list can go on and on, we have simplified this by reviewing some of the priority medications that may cause the serum glucose to be elevated or decreased.

Examples of drugs that cause Hyperglycemia:

Salicylates, steroids (prednisone)

Using certain drugs to treat schizophrenia and psychosis

Glucagon

Albuterol (Ventolin)

Risperidone (Risperdal)

Examples of drugs that cause Hypoglycemia:

Sitgliptin (Januvia)

Hydrochlorothiazide + metoprolol (Lopressor HCT)

Alcohol, Aloe

Keep in mind any of the antidiabetic agents can result in hypoglycemia

Exenatide (Byetta)

Salicylate (Numerous trade names of aspirin formulations. Check labels.)

Glucose Metabolism (Diabetes Mellitus)

Health Promotion for "SICK DAY" Guidelines

This is such an important aspect in teaching clients with diabetes mellitus due to the risk of developing fluid and electrolyte imbalances which can result in metabolic acidosis and cardiac dysrhythmias.

"SICK DAY" Guidelines for Client with Diabetes Mellitus	
Sports drinks, soups, fruit drinks, fluids that replace electrolytes–increase intake of these drinks high in carbohydrate.	Call healthcare provider if any of these findings in "**VOMITING**" occur!
If unable to eat and have replaced 4–5 meals with liquids, then notify HCP.	**V**omiting occurs more than once or diarrhea occurs more than 5 hours or longer than 24 hours.
Check serum glucose q 3–4 hrs and urine ketones when voiding.	**O**rientation is decreased or client is getting more confused.
Keep someone with client and get plenty of rest.	**M**ust recognize symptoms of hyper and hypoglycemia!
Do not skip or omit insulin injections or oral medications unless directed by HCP.	**I**llness lasts longer than 2 days.
Always follow HCP instructions regarding blood glucose and insulin or oral hypoglycemic agents.	**T**emperature is > 38.9°C (102°F), does not respond to acetaminophen, or lasts > 12 hours.
Yes, client should get rest; do not over exert self and stay warm.	**I**ncrease in breathing.
	Not able to tolerate fluids.
	Glucose (blood) > 240 mg/dL.

"An ounce of prevention is worth a pound of cure!"

BENJAMIN FRANKLIN

System: Endocrine System

Linking Pathophysiology with Assessment Findings with Hypoglycemia

**Glucose Metabolism: Endocrine System–The Pancreas
HYPOGLYCEMIA (Serum Glucose < 70 mg/dL)**

Adrenergic (autonomic: ↑ epinephrine levels): Mild Reactions	Neuroglycopenic ↓ glucose to the brain (Decrease in cognitive functioning): Severe Reactions
Tremors, tachycardia	**C**onfusion, ↓ concentration → coma
Irritability, impaired vision	**O**rientation–↓ LOC
Restless	**M**ental illness
Excessive hunger	**A**pathy, lethargy–severe
Diaphoroesis **	**S**eizures

**Diaphoresis although is not mediated via adrenergic nerve endings, it is typically grouped with the adrenergic manifestations of hypoglycemia. Adrenergic reactions usually occur during rapid decreases in blood glucose levels. All of these clinical findings can also occur during other stressful or anxiety producing events.

Health Promotion Plan for Comparing Care for Hypoglycemia and Hyperglycemia

Hypoglycemia Management < 70 mg/dL "CARBOHYDRATE"	Hypoglycemia Management Due to Insulin	Hyperglycemia "FLUIDS"
Cause needs to be determined as to the reason for hypoglycemia to prevent in future. (i.e., skipping a meal, too much exercise without enough carbohydrates, alcohol intake, nausea and vomiting resulting in fluid and electrolyte imbalance, etc.). **A**ssess glucose levels and symptoms "TIRED"! **R**eview simple carbohydrates clients with DM should have available, (refer to examples under 1. in next row). **B**etween meal snacks at the peak action of insulin (refer to prototype insulin). **O**mit or limit simple carbohydrates between meal-snacks and increase complex carbohydrates and protein. **H**YDRATE **Y**es, HYDRATE **D**ehydration prevented with REHYDRATION! **R**ehydrate with 4 oz. sugar free, noncaffeinated liquid every 1/2 hr to prevent dehydration when sick. **A**ssess client's understanding of insulin DM management. **T**each client to recognize signs (TIRED). **E**valuate by having a "TEACH BACK" session.	**Always refer to guidelines provided by HCP.** • Treat signs of hypoglycemia with 15 to 20 grams of carbohydrates. Examples for immediate response: 4–6 oz. of fruit juice such as orange juice/ grape juice; 8 oz. milk (preferred if a client is experiencing a mild reaction). Lactose is immediately provided with the milk, as well as protein and fat for extended action. Glucose tablets per manufacturer's suggestion to equal 15 gm., 8–10 hard candies, or 1 tsp. of honey. • Reevaluate blood glucose in 15 min. • If blood glucose is still low, (< 70 mg/dL), give 15 to 20 gm. more of carbohydrates. • Reevaluate blood glucose in 15 min. • If blood glucose is within normal limits, take 7 g protein (if the next meal is more than an hour away) to minimize risk for rebound hypoglycemia. *Examples*: 2 tablespoons of peanut butter, 8 oz. milk; 1 string cheese (If simple carbohydrates are taken to increase blood glucose, client should plan on eating protein or complex carbohydrates to prevent rebound hypoglycemia.) • If client is unconscious or not able to swallow, glucagon can be administered subcutaneously, intramuscularly, or IV.	**F**luid intake of oral fluids. **L**evels > 250 mg/dl(blood glucose)– restrict exercise. **U**rine should be tested for ketones and reported if abnormal. **I**nsulin should be administered as prescribed. Identification wristband should be worn by the client at all times. **D**r., nurse practitioner, physician's assistant (HCP) should be notified if symptoms continue.  **Insanely Easy Tip!** This jingle will help you remember the skin temperature if a client is presenting with hyperglycemia! *"Hot and Dry; your sugar is high!"* Remember, if we you are "hot and dry", the **PRIORITY** would be some "**FLUID**" to drink. This will assist you in remembering the measures to take if a client is hyperglycemic.

Pathophysiology: Complications with Hyperglycemia

Diabetic Ketoacidosis (DKA) and
Hyperosmolar Hyperglycemic Nonketotic Syndrome (HHNS)

Diabetic Ketoacidosis is a complication of an extreme elevation in the hyperglycemic state. When the glucose is not available to the cells, the body begins to break down fat and protein stores for energy. The metabolism of fats results in fatty acid production, which are converted to ketone bodies. The result of this increase circulating of ketone bodies precipitates the development of metabolic acidosis that results from poorly controlled diabetes. Hyperkalemia, hypokalemia, or normal potassium value can occur depending on the amount of water loss; glucose and ketones in the urine will be elevated.

Type 2 Diabetes: System Specific Physiology: A combination of insulin resistance and inadequate inulin secretion to compensate. Client is not dependent on insulin, but there is a deficiency in the insulin due to an excessive need for insulin. Ketoacidosis is not typically a problem due to the limited insulin production. Hyperosmolar Hyperglycemic Nonketotic Syndrome (HHNS) is the complication that may occur in older adults with type 2 diabetes (*Refer to the Comparison Chart outlining the differences between the complications*).

Hyperosmolar Hyperglycemic Nonketotic Syndrome (HHNS) is a complication that occurs primarily in older adult clients with type 2 diabetes. The breakdown of fat for cellular function does not occur since insulin production is adequate. Severe hyperglycemia can still occur. Dehydration and a severe electrolyte imbalance may exist; however, there will be no acidotic state. This is characterized by hyperglycemia values greater than 600 mg/dL. Due to the insulin production, even though it is low there is no breakdown of fat and production of ketone bodies which consequently prevents the development of acidosis. HHNS can lead to profound dehydration (10–15% loss of body water), hyperosmolality (increased concentration) of plasma, and an elevated blood urea nitrogen level.

Comparisons of Complications of Type 1 and Type 2 Diabetes

Diabetic Ketoacidosis (DKA), Hyperosmolar Hyperglycemic Nonketotic Syndrome (HHNS), and Hypoglycemia

System-Specific Assessments	DKA (Hyperglycemia) *Type 1*	HHNS (Hyperglycemia) *Type 2*	Hypoglycemia
Neurological (Intracranial Regulation)	Confusion → coma	More severe	Difficulty concentrating, coordinating
Gastrointestinal (Elimination)	Abdominal pain, N/V, Anorexia, Diarrhea	Normal with no GI changes	Normal, may be hungry!
Skin temperature (Thermoregulation)	Warm, dry and flushed	Warm, dry and flushed	Cold and Clammy
CV (Perfusion): Heart Rate	Tachycardia, Weak	Tachycardia	Tachycardia
Respiratory system (Oxygenation): Respirations Breaths	Deep and rapid → Kussmaul Respirations Acetone breath: fruity	Tachypnea Normal	Shallow Normal
Renal System (Elimination): Urine Output	Increased	Increased	Normal

---

INSANELY EASY TIPS for prioritizing the differences between DKA, HHNS, and Hypoglycemia!

1. DKA is the only one that presents with GI complications. Hypoglycemia = Hungry!

2. DKA and HHNS have hot and dry skin. Hypoglycemia + Cold and Clammy!

3. DKA is only one with Kussmaul respirations and acetone breath!

4. Urine output is increased with DKA and HHNS and normal with Hypoglycemia!

See, you CAN do this!

Laboratory Values Comparisons of Complications of Type 1 and Type 2 Diabetes

Diabetic Ketoacidosis (DKA), Hyperosmolar Hyperglycemic Nonketotic Syndrome (HHNS), and Hypoglycemia

Laboratory Values	DKA (Hyperglycemia) *Type 1*	HHNS (Hyperglycemia) *Type 2*	Hypoglycemia
Glucose	↑	↑	↓
Sodium	↑ *hyper natremia*	↑	Normal
Potassium	(initially ↓) ↑	↓	Normal
Hematocrit	↑ *hyper volemia*	↑	Normal
Serum Osmolality	↑	↑	Normal
pH	↓	Normal	Normal
HCO₃	↓	Normal	Normal
PaCO₂	↑	Normal	Normal
BUN, Creatinine	↑	↑	Normal
Serum Ketones	↑	Normal	Normal
Urine Ketones	↑	Normal	Normal

Concept Linking DKA and HHNS to the Concept of Hypovolemia and Hypernatremia!

INSANELY EASY TIPS for prioritizing the differences between these labs!

1. Serum Glucose is **Elevated with both** DKA and HHNS! Low with Hypoglycemia! **Only lab value that is not normal with (Hypoglycemia.)** !

2. Serum **Potassium is High in DKA** due to trying to correct the acidosis; **Low in HHNS** due to diuresing!

3. Serum **Sodium is High for both DKA and HHNA** due to the water loss!

4. **pH is Low in DKA** due to the acidosis from ketones!

Linking DKA and HHNS to the Concept of Fluid and Electyrolytes: Hypovolemia and Hypernatremia

Do you see any similarities between lab reports in the chart on the previous page that can be linked to any previous concepts you have learned? Of course the answer we are looking for is DKA and HHNS, since labs are all normal in hypoglycemia with the exception of the serum glucose.

Do you agree with the facts that the labs for serum sodium indicate hypernatremia and hyperosmolality and hematocrit indicate hypovolemia? These concepts can be a priority for a client who is receiving furosemide (Lasix) or a client who is not drinking fluids and has been out in extremely hot weather. Geriatric clients may experience hypovolemia and hypernatremia due to not having a strong sense of being thirsty in addition to the physiological changes with their body fluid as they age. The point is that these concepts apply to more clients than just these clients with diabetes mellitus. Let's link these to the concept of hypovolemia.

The questions to ask yourself are would include the following:

1. What would I expect the **HR and BP** to be for a client with hypovolemia?

2. What would be the **PRIORITY SAFETY** issue for this client? (*Refer to Concept Fluid Balance for specifics.*)

3. What would be the **PRIORITY INTERVENTIONS**?

4. What change may occur with the **CARDIAC RHYTHM** for the client with **HHNS**?

How are you doing?
Does it make sense?
Stop and reflect over what you have just learned!!

Answers:
1. HR would increase and BP eventually would decrease (HR is working to compensate with less volume).
2. One PRIORITY SAFETY issue would be the risk for falls!
3. A few PRIORITY INTERVENTIONS would include fluid replacement, oral care, daily weights, monitor I & O, and watch the trends.
4. A flattend or inverted T wave due to hypokalemia.

Comparing Plan of Care for Complications of Type 1 and Type 2 Diabetes

DKA, HHNS, and Hypoglycemia!

Plan of Care	DKA *Type 1*	HHNS *Type 2*	Hypoglycemia
1. Rapid isotonic fluid (0.9% sodium chloride) replacement to optimize the perfusion of the vital organs.	X	X	
2. Follow with hypotonic fluid (0.45% sodium chloride) to continue to hydrate & replace losses.	X	X	
3. Administer Regular Insulin (Humulin R) 0.1 unit/kg as an IV bolus and then follow with a continuous IV infusion of Regular Insulin at 0.1 units/kg/hr.	X	X	
4. When serum glucose levels get to 250mg/dL, add glucose to IV fluids to decreased risk of cerebral edema that can be associated with significant changes in the serum osmolality.	X	X	
5. Do not decrease blood glucose faster than 100 mg/hr.	X	X	
6. Monitor serum glucose hourly.	X	X	
7. Monitor serum potassium levels. These may initially be high due to the compensatory exchange of H^+ for K^+ in renal tubules to correct acidosis. With insulin therapy; however, potassium will shift back into the cells. At this time the client must be now monitored for hypokalemia. Provide potassium replacement therapy in IV fluids, as lab values indicate. Monitor urine output to assure adequacy prior to starting IV potassium supplement.	X		
8. For severe acidosis (ph < 7.0), administer sodium bicarbonate slowly IV. Monitor potassium levels closely, since correcting acidosis too rapidly may result in hypokalemia.	X		
9. Potassium may be prescribed to manage hypokalemia (potassium levels are low from the osmotic diuresing).		X	
10. If client is alert and is able to swallow, give carbohydrate (15–20 gm) by mouth.			X
11. If a client presents with hypoglycemia, milk is preferred if experiencing a mild reaction. Lactose is immediately provided with the milk, as well as protein and fat for extended action.			X
12. If client is unconscious, administer glucagon.			X

INSANELY EASY Summary Tips
for **PRIORITIZING MANAGEMENT** of DKA, HHNS, and HYPOGLYCEMIA!!

First tip is if you need a way to remember the difference between the potassium changes in DKA and HHNS, just begin with the concept that metabolic acidosis is trying to compensate by exchanging H⁺ for K⁺ ions, resulting in **HYPERKALEMIA** in DKA.

HHNS is all about **DIURESING** and the **LOSS OF POTASSIUM**. With **P**ee (urine) there is a loss of **P**otassium! Remember, there is a small amount of insulin, so there is no breakdown of fat and production of ketone bodies that consequently prevents the development of acidosis. HHNS can lead to profound dehydration.

Both DKA and HHNS

1. The priority in both DKA and HHNS is to **HYDRATE** client with rapid amounts of isotonic fluid to maintain perfusion of the vital organs.
2. **REGULAR INSULIN (RAPID ACTING)** needs to be administered IV.
3. Do not decrease blood glucose **FASTER THAN 100 MG/HR**.
4. Monitor **GLUCOSE LEVELS** every hour.

Only DKA

1. Monitor for **HYPERKALEMIA** due to the acidosis.
2. Monitor the **PH FOR SEVERE ACIDOSIS**.

Only HHNS

1. Monitor for **HYPOKALEMIA** from diuresing.
2. Monitor urine output to assure safety. Remember when **STARTING IV POTASSIUM SUPPLEMENT**, it must be diluted and administered slowly! (NEVER administer potassium IVP or with a bolus! This can result in a death! *Not part of the plan!*)

Only HYPOGLYCEMIA

1. If client is alert and is able to swallow, **GIVE CARBOHYDRATE (15–20 GM) BY MOUTH**.
2. If a client presents **WITH HYPOGLYCEMIA, MILK IS PREFERRED** if experiencing a mild reaction. Lactose is immediately provided with the milk, as well a protein and fat for extended action.
3. If client is **UNCONSCIOUS OR NOT ABLE TO SWALLOW, GLUCAGON** can be administered subcutaneously, intramuscularly, or intravenously.

This is a lot of information! If you understand this page, you have mastered these complications in a very short period of time. Celebrate your success by taking a break! Remember, "Repetition is the mother of learning"! If you are like most of us, these complications will need reinforcement and practice!! Be kind to yourself. We know you CAN master this concept. As with all good things in life, it will take some time!

Exceptions and Additions by Diseases

Pathophysiology: Glucose Metabolism
Diabetes Mellitus (Type 2)

System Specific Pathophysiology: A combination of insulin resistance and inadequate insulin secretion to compensate. Client is not dependent on insulin, but there is a deficiency in the insulin due to an excessive need for insulin. Ketoacidosis is not typically a problem due to the limited insulin production. Hyperosmolar Hyperglycemic Nonketotic Syndrome (HHNS) is the complication that may occur in older adults with type 2 diabetes (*Refer to the Comparison Chart outlining the differences between the complications in this chapter*). Onset is usually around 35 years-old, but it may also occur at any age. Overweight or obese people require additional insulin. A strong family history may also be a cause if the client is not obese. These clients are usually controlled by an oral hypoglycemic and diet, but may require insulin during stressful times.

SYSTEM-SPECIFIC ASSESSMENTS "WEIGHT"	DIET	EQUIPMENT	PLANS/INTERVENTIONS	HEALTH PROMOTION
Weight gain (obese). **Eye sight** (vision disturbances). **Increase** onset typically after age 40 years; 45-50 years it peaks. **Gets** recurrent monilia or vaginal yeast infections. **Has** malaise and fatigue. **The** first 5–10 years the client is asymptomatic.	• Review importance for weight loss. • Avoid simple sugars. • Include a diet to meet nutritional needs and to maintain optimum glucose levels. • Decrease cholesterol level. • Meal plan: Carbohydrates should be a minimum of 130 g/day (preference is whole grains, fruits, vegetables, low fat milk). • Fiber intake should be 14 g/1000kcal; Foods should be selected with a low glycemic index. **Less than 7% of total calories should be saturated fats.** • Protein should be 15% to 20% of total calories. • Include omega-3 fatty acids in the diet.	• May need exercise equipment, exercise consistently not sporadic. (Same as with Diabetes (type 1) • SMBG equipment	• Review oral hypoglycemic agents for Diabetes (type 2). "WEIGHT" may also be incorporated into plan of care. Weight loss or assists with maintenance of normal weight. Evaluate eye sight as ordered. Exercise. Insulin needs are decreased due to the reduction in the blood glucose level routine exercise. Glucose blood levels have less extreme fluctuations. Hypertension is decreased.	• Oral antidiabetic agents; refer to reference below. Discuss signs and symptoms of hyper and hypoglycemia. RISK FACTORS: Obese Body weight > 20% from normal Ethnicity: African American and Latino Sedentary lifestyle Eats diets high in fat, sugar, and processed foods, fast food

FIRST-DO   PRIORITY   INTERVENTIONS

Exceptions and Additions by Diseases

Pathophysiology: Glucose Metabolism
Gestational Diabetes Mellitus (GDM)

While the focus for this book is not the maternity client, this medical condition is a significant component with this concept. This section will focus on the system specific assessments, "First Do Interventions", the expected outcomes for labor, and the priority assessments for the neonate following the delivery with a mother who has diabetes mellitus.

System Specific Pathophysiology involves the impaired tolerance to glucose with the initial onset or recognition throughout pregnancy. The ideal serum glucose range throughout pregnancy should be 70–110 mg/dL. A few weeks following delivery the symptoms of diabetes mellitus may subside. Within 5 years, however, 50% of women will develop symptoms of diabetes mellitus. Without effective management, gestational diabetes can cause increased risks to the fetus. These diagnostic procedures below are only the exceptions from the previous reviewed labs and diagnostic tests. Of course, all of the diabetic labs, procedures/ tests for complication, etc. would also be performed with the client who is diagnosed with gestational diabetes. Now, the concern we are adding in this section involves the evaluation of the fetus.

Diagnostic Tests/Procedures

- Biophysical profile to evaluate fetal well-being is done once or twice weekly starting around 28 to 34 weeks' gestation; this is based on the presence of BP and /or glucose control.

- Nonstress test to assess fetal well-being.

- Amniocentesis with alpha-fetoprotein at 15 to 20 weeks' gestation to evaluate for risk of neural tube defects.

- Continue to monitor the client's blood glucose; monitor fetus, and instruct client to document daily kick counts.

- Fetal echocardiograpy evaluated between 20 and 22 weeks; repeated at 34 weeks.

After delivery, the mother's neonate is high risk for hypoglycemia. The priority assessments that need immediate intervention with this neonate includes the "**JITTERS**":

Jitteriness

Increase high-pitched dry, lethargy

Twitching

The heel stick blood glucose level < 40 mg/dL in the newborn
    (< 25 mg/dL in the preterm newborn)

Eye rolling

Respirations irregular

Seizures. The priority intervention will be to provide frequent oral and/or gavage feedings or continuous parenteral nutrition early after birth to treat the hypoglycemia. If neonate is unable to orally feed, then an IV should be started and monitored.

Exceptions and Additions by Diseases

Pathophysiology: Glucose Metabolism
Gestational Diabetes Mellitus (GDM)

	FIRST-DO	PRIORITY	INTERVENTIONS	
SYSTEM-SPECIFIC ASSESSMENTS	**DIET**	**EQUIPMENT**	**PLANS/INTERVENTIONS**	**HEALTH PROMOTION**
• Hyperglycemia • Thirsty • Nausea • Abdominal pain • Frequent urination • Flushed dry skin • Fruity breath • Excess weight during pregnancy • Rapid pulse	• Well-balanced; avoid refined sugar; no skipping of meals.	• Teach client home blood glucose monitoring. • Refer to SMBG for specifics	• During the Intrapartum period, as long as the fetus is responding well and presents with appropriate oxygenation, then the pregnancy should progress to term with a normal vaginal delivery. • For pre-gestational diabetes, the blood glucose levels are managed with IV glucose and regular insulin. • GDM mothers may require rapid acting insulin IV; IV glucose is not administered to these clients. • Fetal monitoring is imperative throughout labor. During postpartum, the metabolic and endocrine changes will rapidly change after delivery. Insulin requirements will decrease significantly for the mother and will continue to be labile over the next 2 weeks. • GDM mother's glucose will return to normal following delivery. Pre-gestational diabetic mothers will need to go through a period of diabetic re-regulation.	• The importance of exercise as prescribed. • Educate mom how to evaluate fetal movement counts starting at 28 weeks' gestation. • Review the importance of reviewing the client's glucose. Reinforce about diet and exercise. • Review the anti-diabetic agents with the client.

An **INSANELY EASY Tip** to assist you in reviewing the expected outcomes for labor will be reviewed below in the mnemonic "**FETAL.**"

F etal and maternal well being—monitor ongoing

E xpect insulin requirements to increase during 2nd and 3rd trimester

T he medication of choice is insulin. There is limited use of glyburide (DiaBeta) at this time.

A nticipate a vaginal delivery

L ook for hypoglycemia during postpartum; insulin requirements will decrease

I WILL HAVE TO BE MONITORED FOR LOW BLOOD SUGAR AFTER DELIVERY...

...I CAN EXPECT TO HAVE A NORMAL VAGINAL DELIVERY IF I AM MONITORED!

Clinical Decision-Making Exercises

1. What lab value would best indicate the desired outcome for a client with type 2 diabetes mellitus?
    ① Fasting blood sugar of 127 mg/dL.
    ② HbA$_{1c}$ < 6%.
    ③ Serum glucose < 130 mg/dL.
    ④ HbA$_{1c}$ > 7%.

2. Which assessments indicative of hypoglycemia would be most important to report to the next shift for a client who received 6 units of regular insulin 3 hours ago?
    ① Kussmaul's respirations and diaphoresis.
    ② Anorexia and lethargy.
    ③ Diaphoresis and trembling.
    ④ Polydipsia and polyuria.

3. Which statement made by the nursing student indicates an understanding of the pathophysiology for a diabetic who has ketones in the urine?
    ① There is an increase in mobilization of fat and protein as energy when glucose is unavailable. Fat metabolism causes breakdown products called ketones to form.
    ② There is too much intake of fats and foods high in cholesterol.
    ③ There is too much insulin available that contributes to the development of ketones to form in the urine.
    ④ As the pH of the blood increases (alkalosis), the accumulating H$^+$ ions move from the intracellular fluid to the extracellular resulting in the development of ketones.

4. Which of these clinical findings need to be reported to the healthcare provider for a client who has a history of diabetes mellitus and is admitted to the hospital with an acute infection?
    ① Serum glucose of 170mg/dL and BUN of 15 mg/dL.
    ② pH–7.25, PCO$_2$–45 mm Hg, HCO$_3$–17 mEq/L.
    ③ K$^+$–3.9mEqL and Creatinine–0.8 mg/dL.
    ④ pH–7.39, PO$_2$–96%, HCO$_3$–23 mEq/L.

5. Which of these assessment findings should be reported to the healthcare provider for a client with type 2 diabetes?
    ① Excessive thirst and hunger.
    ② BP 148/92 and fatigue.
    ③ Alert and oriented.
    ④ BUN–24 mg/dL and urine specific gravity of > 1.030.

6. Which of these statements would indicate that the client understands their discharge teaching on diabetic foot care? *Select all that apply.*
    ① "I will use mild foot powder when my feet are sweaty."
    ② "I will check my feet daily for injuries and lacerations."
    ③ "I will only walk barefoot when I am at home."
    ④ "I should not apply external heat."
    ⑤ "I can wear open toe shoes as long as I am careful."

7. Which of these orders should be questioned for a client with a history of diabetes mellitus and presents to the ER with a BP of 90/60, pulse–108 bpm, serum glucose 620mg/dL?

   ① Administer IV fluids 0.9 NS at a rate of 150 mL/hour.

   ② Monitor BUN, creatinine and I and O.

   ③ Administer Regular insulin IV as prescribed.

   ④ Administer Lasix 40 mg IV as prescribed.

8. A client has an order for 8am Lente (Humulin L) 15 units SubQ and is on a sliding scale insulin. The morning blood glucose level is 278mg/dl. The sliding scale orders are:

Blood glucose	Insulin order
< 170 mg/dL	No insulin
170–240 mg/dL	5 units regular insulin SubQ
241–300 mg/dL	10 units regular insulin SubQ
> 300 mg/dL	Notify provided of care for new prescription

   Select the correct number marked on the syringe below for the amount of insulin you would administer.

   ① 2

   ② 1

   ③ 3

   ④ 4

   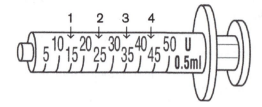

9. Which of these clients should be assessed immediately following shift report?

   ① A client with COPD who has an O_2 saturation reading of 90%.

   ② A client with diabetes mellitus with a HbA_{1c} > 7%.

   ③ A client with type 2 diabetes mellitus presenting with a urine output increase from 90 mL/hr to 200 mL/ and serum Na^+ 147 mEq/L.

   ④ The LPN reports that a client who is performing self-monitoring of blood glucose is using the side of the finger pad instead of the center of the finger.

10. What would be the priority of nursing care for a client presenting with a serum glucose of 48 mg/dL and is listless but arousable?

    ① Immediately notify the healthcare provider.

    ② Provide food high in protein.

    ③ Provide an 8 oz. glass of milk.

    ④ Reassess the glucose in 10 minutes.

1. What **lab value** would best indicate the desired outcome for a client with **type 2 diabetes mellitus?**

   ① INCORRECT: Fasting serum glucose of 127mg/dL: Fasting serum glucose test > 126 mg/dL is diagnostic for diabetes mellitus.

   ② **CORRECT: HbA$_{1c}$ < 6%. Good diabetic control < 6.5%, (2%–6.4%).**

   ③ INCORRECT: Serum glucose < 130 mg/dL. Serum glucose: 70–110 mg/dL (Fasting)

   ④ INCORRECT: HbA$_{1c}$ > 7%. Poor diabetic control is > 7%.

The strategy for answering this is to know that the HbA$_{1c}$ is the most accurate lab value in determining how client is being managed.

Reduction of Risk: Perform diagnostic testing (glucose monitoring).

2. Which assessments **indicative of hypoglycemia** would be most important to report to the next shift for a client who received **6 units of regular insulin 3 hours ago?**

   ① INCORRECT: Kussmaul's respirations and diaphoresis. This assessment would be from hyperglycemia due to compensating for metabolic acidosis from burning ketones for energy due to lack of inslulin.

   ② INCORRECT: Anorexia and lethargy. While we are concerned with lethargy, the client will be hungry. All of the information in the option must be correct.

   ③ **CORRECT: Diaphoresis and trembling. Remember "Hot and dry your blood sugar is high; cold and clammy you need some candy!" Regular insulin peaks in 3 hours, so it is a priority to assess for hypoglycemia. Signs of low blood sugar occur from adrenergic (autonomic: ↑ epinephrine levels).**

   ④ INCORRECT: Polydipsia and polyuria. These would be important for hyperglycemia, but the question is asking about a client who received regular insulin 3 hours ago indicating a concern with the peak time.

The strategy is to know the insulin and peak times which are outlined in *Pharmacology Made Insanely Easy!*

Pharmacological and Parenteral Therapies: Evaluate client response to medication

3. Which statement made by the nursing student indicates an **understanding of the pathophysiology for a diabetic who has ketones in the urine?**

   ① **CORRECT: There is an increase in mobilization of fat and protein as energy when glucose is unavailable. Fat metabolism causes breakdown products called ketones to form. Ketones accumulate in the blood and are excreted through the kidneys and lungs. Ketones interfere with the body's acid-base balance by producing hydrogen ions. The pH can decrease and metabolic acidosis can develop.**

   ② INCORRECT: There is too much intake of fats and foods high in cholesterol. This not the pathophysiology.

   ③ INCORRECT: There is too much insulin available that contributes to the development of ketones to form in the urine. The opposite would be true if it said there is not enough insulin.

   ④ INCORRECT: As the pH of the blood increases (alkalosis), the accumulating H⁺ ions move from the intracellular fluid to the extracellular resulting in the development of ketones. This is not accurate. As the pH of the blood decreases (acidosis), the the accumulating H⁺ ions move from the extracellular fluid to the intracellular. The movement of the hydrogen ions into the cells promotes the movement of potassium out of the cells into the extracellular fluid, which results in severe intracellular potassium depletion and elevated extracellular potassium levels.

The strategy is to know the pathophysiology of the clinical assessments, so you will be able to always link to this concept.

Physiological Adaptation: Identify the pathophysiology related to an acute or chronic condition (i.e., signs and symptoms).

4.   Which of these **clinical findings** need to be **reported to the healthcare provider** for a client who has a **history of diabetes mellitus** and is admitted to the hospital with an acute infection?

①   INCORRECT: Serum glucose of 170 mg/dL and BUN of 15 mg/dL. The BUN is within normal limits, so the client is not dehydrated. While the glucose is high, it is not the priority to report over option 2 which is an acute complication.

②   **CORRECT: pH–7.25, PCO$_2$–45 mm Hg, HCO$_3$–17 mEq/L. This interpretation is metabolic acidosis which would indicate ketoacidosis, a complication of DM. Fat metabolism causes breakdown products called ketones to form. Ketones accumulate in the blood and are excreted through the kidneys and lungs. Ketones interfere with the body's acid-base balance by producing hydrogen ions. The pH can decrease and metabolic acidosis can develop.**

③   INCORRECT: K$^+$–3.9mEqL and Creatinine–0.8 mg/dL. These are both within normal ranges. As the pH of the blood decreases (acidosis), the accumulating H$^+$ ions move from the extracellular fluid to the intracellular. The movement of the hydrogen ions into the cells promotes the movement of potassium out of the cells into the extracellular fluid, which results in severe intracellular potassium depletion and elevated extracellular potassium levels. With this potassium leaving the intracellular space, transient hyperkalemia develops.

④   INCORRECT: pH–7.39, PO$_2$–96%, HCO$_3$–23 mEq/L. These are within normal ranges.

The strategy is to understand the laboratory values in order to link to the medical condition. This concept of metabolic acidosis applies to any client who develops acidosis for any reason such as with diarrhea or aspirin overdose. The etiology (cause) may be different, but the outcomes are the same. Remember, in metabolic acidosis both the pH and the HCO$_3$ are low. An easy way to remember this information is outlined in the Acid Base chapter (*Refer to concept on Acid Base Balance for more specifics*).

Physiological Adaptation: Recognize signs and symptoms of complication and intervene appropriately.

5.   Which of these assessment findings should be **reported to the healthcare provider** for a client with **type 2 diabetes**?

①   INCORRECT: Excessive thirst after exercising. This is not a priority over option 4. Client needs to drink more fluids, but is not exhibiting any signs of dehydration.

②   INCORRECT: BP 148/92 and fatigue. Blood pressure is elevated which can lead to fatigue, but is not a priority over option 4.

③   INCORRECT: Alert and oriented. No need to report!

④   **CORRECT: BUN–24 mg/dL and urine specific gravity of > 1.030. These lab values are high indicating fluid loss. Hyperosmolar Hyperglycemic Nonketotic Syndrome (HHNS) could be a complication that is resulting in these values. Further assessment is necessary such as serum sodium, potassium, serum osmolality, hematocrit, urine output. All of these will be high except the potassium will be low.**

The strategy for this question is to recognize a potential complication from type 2 diabetes is Hyperosmolar Hyperglycemic Nonketotic Syndrome (HHNS). Refer to the chart in this chapter comparing the labs and assessments between DKA, HHNS, and Hypoglycemia. The key with HHNS is to monitor the I & O along with the labs to prevent hypovolemia, hypokalemia, and further complications with cardiac dysrhythmias.

Physiological Adaptation: Manage the care of a client with a fluid and electrolyte imbalance.

6. Which of these statements would indicate that the **client understands their discharge teaching on diabetic foot care?** Select all that apply.

    ① CORRECT: **"I will use mild foot powder when my feet are sweaty." Goal is to keep feet dry to prevent moisture that will allow the growth of micro-organisms that can lead to infection.**

    ② CORRECT: **"I will check my feet daily for injuries and lacerations." This is important to prevent infection from occurring.**

    ③ INCORRECT: "I will only walk barefoot when I am at home." This will lead to foot injury.

    ④ CORRECT: **"I should not apply external heat." No heating pads or hot water bottles should be applied to the extremities of a client with diabetes mellitus due to risk of being burnt from change in pain recognition from a peripheral neuropathy.**

    ⑤ INCORRECT: "I can wear open toe shoes as long as I am careful." Closed-toe shoes should be worn to prevent injury to soft tissue of the toes and feet.

The strategy for answering this question can be found in the chart on the Do's and Don'ts for Foot care. SAFETY is priority!

Reduction of Risk Potential: Potential for Complications of diagnostic tests/treatments/procedures.

7. Which of these orders should be **questioned** for a client with a **history of diabetes mellitus** and presents to the ER with a **BP of 90/60, pulse–108 bpm, serum glucose 620mg/dL?**

    ① INCORRECT: Administer IV fluids 0.9 NS at a rate of 150 mL/hour. There is no need to question this order, since client needs fluids.

    ② INCORRECT: Monitor BUN, creatinine and I and O. There is no need to question this order since renal function and I & O are crucial to assess to determine renal function and the comparison of fluid going in to fluid being excreted.

    ③ INCORRECT: Administer Regular insulin IV as prescribed. This would be

an appropriate order to manage the hyperglycemia.

    ④ CORRECT: **Administer furosemide (Lasix) 40 mg IV as prescribed. The VS indicate low volume and the serum glucose is extremely high. The last thing the client needs is to take a diuretic resulting in further fluid loss which can lead to hypovolemic shock.**

The strategy is to focus on the vital signs and the serum glucose value. Even if you had no idea what was taking place with the client, the priority would be to manage the fluid loss and correct the cause. The key is definitely never to administer a drug that will promote additional diuresing.

Pharmacological and Parenteral Therapies: Evaluate appropriateness and accuracy of medication order.

8. A client has an order for 8 AM Lente (Humulin L) 15 units SubQ and is on a sliding scale insulin. The morning blood glucose level is 278 mg/dL. The sliding scale orders are:

Blood glucose	Insulin order
< 170 mg/dL	No insulin
170–240 mg/dL	5 units regular insulin SubQ
241–300 mg/dL	10 units regular insulin SubQ
> 300 mg/dL	Notify provided of care for new prescription

Place the correct number marked on the syringe for the amount of insulin you would administer?

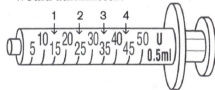

    ① CORRECT: **2– There is already an order to administer 15 units, and then add the additional amount that is included in the sliding scale. 15 + 10 = 25 units. For example, if the blood glucose had been 180 mg/dL, then you would have added 15 + 5 = 20 units.**

    ② INCORRECT: 1–If the blood glucose had been < 170 mg/dL then the answer would have been 15 units total due to no sliding scale amount.

③ INCORRECT: 3– This amount would be way too much and would break the standard of care based on the above order. This amount in the syringe (35 units) would indicate a medication error due to administering 20 extra units to the client that is not included in the order.

④ INCORRECT: 4– This amount would be way too much and would break the standard of care based on the above order for > 300 mg/dL.

The strategy is to take the amount ordered and add to the designated insulin order based on the glucose level.

Pharmacological and Parenteral Therapies: Titrate dosage of medication based on assessment and ordered parameters (i.e., giving insulin according to blood glucose levels).

9.   Which of these clients **should be assessed immediately** following shift report?

① INCORRECT: A client with COPD who has an O_2 saturation reading of 90%. Chronic disease with an O_2 saturation reading may be normal for client.

② INCORRECT: A client with diabetes mellitus with a HbA_{1c} > 7%. This client is not being managed effectively, but is in no acute distress that would mandate immediate assessment.

③ **CORRECT: A client with type 2 diabetes mellitus presenting with a urine output increase from 90 mL/hr to 200 mL/ hr in a 2 hour period with a serum Na^+ 147mEq/L. There is an extreme trending up of the urine output with an elevated sodium level which may indicate fluid loss. There needs to be further assessment and intervention to determine the serum glucose and vital signs. Serum potassium may be a concern due to the diuresing , so the level should be evaluated along with the ECG montitor to evaluate the T wave. If potassium is low, there is a risk for a inverted or flat T wave.**

④ INCORRECT: The LPN reports that a client who is performing self-monitoring of blood glucose is using the side of the finger pad instead of the center of the finger. This is appropriate practice to prevent injury to the fingers. No need for assessment.

The strategy is to compare and contrast the options to determine which client is in the most acute distress. Typically the selection will be "acute prior to chronic". The trend in the urine output was a strong clue that the nurse should intervene.

Management of Care: Prioritize delivery of care.

10.   What would be the **priority of nursing care** for a client presenting with a **serum glucose of 48 mg/dL** and is **listless but arousable**?

① INCORRECT: Immediately notify the healthcare provider. An intervention needs to be done first!

② INCORRECT: Provide food high in protein. Not the immediate action for hypoglycemia,

③ **CORRECT: Provide an 8 oz. glass of milk. Treat signs of hypoglycemia with 15 to 20 g carbohydrates. Examples: 4–6 oz of fruit juice such as orange juice/ grape juice; 8 oz milk; glucose tablets per manufacturer's suggestion to equal 15 gm, 8–10 hard candies, or 1 tsp. of honey.**

④ INCORRECT: Reassess the glucose in 10 minutes. An intervention is a priority to reassessing due to SAFETY. Brain needs blood sugar!

The strategy is to recognize the client is experiencing hypoglycemia, and this must be corrected NOW! The key is that since the client is arousable the treatment can be orally; however, if the client is nonarousable (unconscious) or not able to swallow, glucagon can be administered subcutaneously, intramuscularly, or intravenously.

Reduction of Risk Potential: Recognize signs and symptoms of complications and intervene appropriately when providing care.

Decision-Making Analysis Form

Use this tool to help identify why you missed any questions. As you enter the question numbers in the chart, you will begin to see patterns of why you answered incorrectly. This information will then guide you toward what you need to focus on in your continued studies. Ultimately, this analytical exercise will help you become more successful in answering questions!!!

Questions to ask:

1. Did I have the knowledge to answer the question? If not, what information do I need to review?
2. Did I know what the question was asking? Did I misread it or did I miss keywords in the stem of the question?
3. Did I misread or miss keywords in the distractors that would have helped me choose the correct answer?
4. Did I follow my gut reaction or did I allow myself to rationalize and then choose the wrong answer?

	Lack of Knowledge (Concepts, Systems, Pathophysiology, Medications, Procedures, etc.)	Missed Keywords or Misread the Stem of the Question	Missed Keywords or Misread the Distractors	Changed My Answer (Second-guessed myself, i.e., my first answer was correct.)
Put the # of each question you missed in the column that best explains why you think you answered it incorrectly.				

If you changed an answer because you talked yourself out of the correct answer, or you second-guessed yourself, this is an **EASY FIX: QUIT changing your answers**!!! Typically, the first time you read a question, you are about 95% right! The second time you read a question, you start talking yourself into changing the answer. The third time you read a question, you do not have a clue—and you are probably thinking "Who in the heck wrote this question?"

On the other hand, if you read a question too quickly and when you reread it you realize you missed some key information that would impact your decision (i.e., assessments, lab reports, medications, etc.), then it is appropriate to change your answer. When in doubt, go with the safe route: your first thought! Go with your gut instinct!

As you gain confidence in answering questions regarding specific nursing concepts, you will be able to successfully progress to answering higher-level questions about prioritization. Please refer to the *Prioritization Guidelines* in this book for a structure to assist you with this process.

You CAN do this!

"If nobody ever pushed and pulled us ... we'd all be perfect circles instead of stars."

AUTHOR UNKNOWN

References for Chapter 15

American Diabetes Association. (2012). *Standards of medical care in diabetes.* Retrieved from http://www.nlm.nih.gov/medlineplus/ency/article/003482.htm

Black, J M. and Hawks, J. H. (2009). *Medical surgical nursing: Clinical management for positive outcomes (8th ed.).* Philadelphia: Elsevier/Saunders.

Daniels, R. & Nicoll, L. (2012). *Contemporary medical-surgical nursing,* (2nd ed.). Clifton Park, NY: Delmar Cengage Learning.

Ellis, K. M. (2012). *EKG: Plain and simple* (3rd ed.). Upper Saddle Road, NJ: Pearson.

Eliopoulos, C. (2014). *Gerontological nursing* (8th ed.), Philadelphia: Lippincott Williams & Wilkins.

Giddens, G. F. (2013). *Concepts for nursing practice.* St. Louis, MO: Mosby, an imprint of Elsevier.

Guyton, A., & Hall, J. (2010), *Textbook of medical physiology* (12th edition). Philadelphia: Sanders.

Hogan, M. A. (2014). *Pathophysiology: Reviews and rationales* (3rd ed.) Boston, MA: Pearson.

Ignatavicius, D. D. and Workman, M. L. (2010). *Medical-surgical nursing: Patient-centered collaborative care* (6th ed.). Philadelphia: Elsevier/Saunders.

Institute for Safe Medication Practices. (2012). ISMP's List of High Alert Medications. National Medication Errors Reporting Program. Retrieved from http://www.ismp.org/tools/highalertmedications.pdf

LeMone, P., Burke, K. M., and Bauldoff, G. (2011). *Medical-surgical nursing: Critical thinking in patient care* (5th ed.). Upper Saddle Road, NJ: Pearson/Prentice Hall.

Lewis, S., Dirksen, S., Heitkemper, M., Bucher, L., and Camera, I. (2011). *Medical surgical nursing: Assessment and management of clinical problems* (8th ed.). St. Louis: Mosby.

Manning, L. and Rayfield, S. (2014). *Nursing made insanely easy* (7th ed.). Duluth, GA: I CAN Publishing, Inc.

Manning, L. and Rayfield, S. (2013). *Pharmacology made insanely easy* (4th ed.). Duluth, GA: I CAN Publishing, Inc.

National Council of State Boards of Nursing, INC. (NCSBN) 2012. *Research brief: 2011 RN practice analysis: linking the NCLEX RN® examination to practice.* Retrieved from https://www.ncsbn.org/index.htm

Nettina, S. L. (2013). *Lippincott manual of nursing practice* (10th ed.). Philadelphia, PA: Walters Kluwer Health/Lippincott Williams & Wilkins.

North Carolina Concept Based Learning Editorial Board (2011). *Nursing a concept based approach to learning,* Upper Saddle Road, NJ: Pearson/Prentice Hall.

Osborn, K. S., Wraa, C. E., Watson, A. S., and Holleran, R. S. (2014). *Medical surgical nursing: Preparation for practice* (2nd ed.). Upper Saddle Road, NJ: Pearson.

Pagana, K. D. and Pagana, T. J. (2014). *Mosby's manual of laboratory and diagnostic tests* (5th ed.). St. Louis, MO: Mosby, an imprint of Elsevier.

Porth, C. (2011). *Essentials of pathophysiology* (3d ed.). Philadelphia, PA: Lippincott Williams ad Wilkins.

Porth, C. M. and Grossman, S. (2013). *Pathophysiology: Concepts of altered health states* (9th ed.). Philadelphia, PA: Lippincott Williams & Wilkins.

Potter, P. A., Perry, A. G., Stockert, P., and Hall, A. (2013). *Fundamentals of nursing* (8th ed.). St. Louis, MO: Pearson/Prentice Hall.

Smeltzer, S. C., Bare, B. G., Hinkle, J. L., and Cheever, K. H. (2010). *Brunner & Suddarth's Textbook of medical-surgical nursing* (12th ed.). Philadelphia: Lippincott Williams & Wilkins.

Wagner, K. D. and Hardin-Pierce, M. C. (2014). *High-Acuity nursing* (6th ed.). Boston: Pearson.

CHAPTER 16

Genitourinary System
Linking Concepts to Pathophysiology of Diseases
Concept Elimination

A Snapshot of Elimination

Elimination is the excretion of waste products. Urinary elimination is when urine passes from the kidneys through the urinary tract through the urethra. Bowel elimination is the passage of stool through the intestinal tract. Elimination can be affected by numerous disease processes to include stroke, cardiovascular disease, impaired cognitive function or any neurological disorder. Alterations in elimination can be due socioeconomic issues, insufficient fiber in the diet, not drinking enough fluids and/or the lack of exercise. Surgery, anesthesia and medications and painful elimination can also lead to alterations in elimination. The urinary tract is sterile above the urethra and with normal function pathogens are washed out with the urine during voiding (LeMone, Burke, & Bauldoff, 2011). It consists of the bladder, ureters, and urethra. Some key terms are:

Dysuria: painful or difficult urination

Urgency: a compelling and sudden need to urinate

Nocturia: voiding two or more times a night

Hematuria: blood in urine

Adequate diet and fluids and maintenance of regular urinary and bowel elimination practices are essential for normal function (Giddens, 2013). Renal failure and bowel elimination processes are reviewed in chapter 12, the Gastrointestinal/Biliary Systems, and chapter 17, the Renal System.

The Pathophysiology Behind An Alteration In Elimination

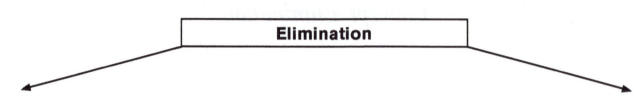

Control		Retention/Blockage		Infection	
Urinary	**Bowel**	**Urinary**	**Bowel**	**Urinary**	**Bowel**

• Urinary Incontinence
 	
• Enuresis (Bedwetting)
	• Fecal Incontinence
	
	• Diarrhea
	
	• Refer to Gastrointestinal/ Biliary System for specifics
		• Benign Prostatic Hypertrophy
		
		• Renal Calculi
			• Bowel Obstructions
			
			• Refer to Gastrointestinal/ Biliary System for specifics
				• Lower Urinary Tract
				  • Cystitis
				  • Urethritis
				  • Prostatitis
				
				• Upper Urinary Tract Pyelonephritis
					• Infections of Small or Large Bowel
					
					• Refer to Gastrointestinal/ Biliary System for specifics

---

Aging Changes in the Genitourinary System: Everything Decreases

↓ Kidneys size

↓ Glomerular filtration rate

↓ Renal blood flow

↓ Bladder size

↓ Ability to withhold urine

↓ Urethra thickness

↓ Muscles (thin & weaken) control of sphincters

↓ Urine output

Genitourinary System: Concept Elimination
Pathophysiology of the Interconnected Concepts with Genitourinary Disorders

Concepts	Pathophysiology	Plan of Care
Pain Relief Urinary tract infections Pyelonephritis Renal Calculi	Pain with urinary tract infections and pyelonephritis is due to the inflammation of the tissue from the bacteria. UTIs cause burning and itching. Flank pain with pyelonephritis is from inflammation of the kidneys. Kidney stones cause severe pain as they travel down the ureters.	•Assess Pain with "**PQRST**" •Give pain meds as prescribed; pain meds can ↑ constipation, administer with stool softeners & laxatives as needed (elderly particularly), encourage fluid intake •Note abdominal/flank tenderness or pain •Assess for firmness, hardness of abdomen, bladder distention or supra pubic fullness
Observe Fluid Balance: Urinary retention, Renal calculi Benign prostate hypertrophy (TURP with Continuous Bladder Irrigation)	Fluid volume deficit or dehydration can be a contributing factor with UTIs, kidney stones or BPH. The urine is more concentrated, or remains in the bladder where bacteria can grow. Adequate fluids & diet can help prevent kidney stones. Fluid overload can be due to: inability to void and retaining urine, renal calculi or the enlarged prostate blocking the urethra. If not resolved, may lead to renal failure. Unless contraindicated fluid intake should be encouraged.	**Dehydration (fluid loss):** VS–Early: ↑ HR & ↑ RR, (↓ LOC in elderly), Late: ↓ BP. **Encourage adequate fluid intake:** PO fluids 2500–3000 mL/day unless contraindicated (i.e., heart failure, renal disease, etc.). •IV fluids if needed or unable to take adequate PO fluids •May need electrolyte replacement. **Fluid volume overload:** ↑ HR & ↑ RR, ↑ BP, bounding pulses, •Document amount, color, smell, signs of bleeding in urine and stool. •I & O, daily weights (compare & contrast, trend). Remember a 1 Kg or 2.2 lbs weight gain is 1 Liter of fluid retained! •See TURP and Continuous Bladder Irrigation in this chapter for specifics. • Refer to chapter on Concept for Fluid Balance for specifics.
Treat INFECTION Urinary tract infections	Bacteria enter the bladder from the urethra and can travel through the bladder to the kidneys. Females, because of their anatomy, are at higher risk. Infections can cause renal calculi. Infections can occur with skin breakdown with urinary or bowel incontinence if the skin is not kept clean and dry. Good body hygiene helps to decrease the amount of bacteria on the skin or in the perineal area.	•↑ WBCs, CBC •↑ Temperature •↑ Adventitious lung sounds •Urine & Stool Cultures & Sensitivity •Instruct on how to take antibiotics if prescribed, need to take all of medication •Monitor for adverse effects or allergic reactions •Use appropriate personal protective equipment (PPE), when handling bodily fluids (urine, stool).
Tissue/Skin Integrity Urinary & Bowel Incontinence	Incontinence can lead to an increase in the moisture on the skin resulting in an increase for risk of organism growth. With a risk for alteration in the albumin due to a decreased nutritional intake, this can result in skin breakdown and complications with healing. In addition to these physiological changes, if the client does not move and continues with ongoing pressure with minimal relief, a compromise in circulation may also contribute to an alteration in skin/tissue integrity.	•Monitor for non-blanchable areas •Keep skin dry, protect skin when client is incontinent •Turn & reposition q 2 hrs. or more frequently if needed •Position to avoid pressure points, particularly if client is edematous •Ambulation, up in chair, ROM to promote circulation •Refer to the chapter Tissue/Skin Integrity for specifics
You Prevent Injury Urinary incontinence, urgency	Incontinent clients or clients with urgency are in a hurry to get to the bathroom and may fall. UTIs, particularly with the elderly, can lead to ↓ LOC. Pain medication given for UTI and renal calculi can cause drowsiness and syncope, and ↑ the risk for falls.	•Evaluate cognitive status for ability to get to bathroom •Evaluate mobility •Call light within reach for help to bathroom, bedside commode if needed •Need light in the bathroom •Refer to Concept Safety/Prevention of Injury for specifics
Support Nutrition Renal calculi (stones) UTI	Analysis of renal calculi can determine the composition of the stone, which guides the dietician to plan a diet to help client avoid foods that are high in the minerals comprising the stones. Adequate protein, calories and vitamins are essential for healing and to fight infections.	•Need adequate residue in diet (particularly with constipation or bowel retraining) •Renal calculi need specific diets based on analysis of kidney stones •Follow prescribed diet, supplements as needed •Evaluate nutritional status: protein albumin, pre-albumin, Hgb, Hct, calcium, iron • Refer to Nutrition Concept for specifics

INSANELY EASY TIP to remember
Expected Outcomes for the Associated Concepts
With Elimination!!

Just remember "POTTYS"!

Pain—The client's pain will be eliminated and/or controlled

Observe **Fluid Balance**—The client's fluid status will be balanced

Treat **Infection**—The client will be free from infection or be treated with appropriate antibiotic therapy

Tissue/**Skin Integrity**—The client's Skin and Tissue Integrity are maintained and/or are healing

You Prevent **Injury**—Client will be free from injury or falls

Support **Nutrition**—The client's nutritional status will be adequate to promote healing and/or changes made

Evaluation of Expected Outcomes requires clinical judgment to evaluate if the priority care has been effective. If it has not been effective, then you need to make a clinical decision about what you would do differently to achieve the outcomes. An interdisciplinary approach with client and family input is always the best way!

Pathophysiology: Elimination

Labs, Diagnostic Tests, and Procedures

Labs	Procedures/Diagnostic Tests
Urinalysis (UA) Suggestive of UTI: • ↑ WBCs > 10,000/ mm3 • ↑ Nitrites • Bloody, cloudy urine	**Cystoscopy (for complicated UTIs) with Voiding Cystourethrography (VCUG)** • Detects urethral or bladder injury • VCUG detects if urine refluxes into ureters (taken while voiding) • Dye is not nephrotoxic, it is absorbed into bloodstream
Urine Culture • Done if repeated infections, poor response to antibiotics, repeated infection in toilet-trained male	**Electromyography (EMG)** • Determines strength of pelvic muscles–Electrical Pelvic Stimulation **Ultrasound** **Urodynamic Testing** • Different tests visualization of the bladder • Pressure inside bladder • Rate and degree of bladder emptying and bladder pressure with certain activities
24-Hour Urine • Creatinine, BUN, Na+, Ca++, catecholamine, protein or for Creatinine clearance	**Magnetic Resonance Imaging (MRI)** **X-Ray of Kidney, Ureters, Bladder (KUB)** **Intravenous Pyelogram (IVP)**
BUN & Creatinine • ↑ could indicate renal damage	**Gallium Scan For Renal Calculi** **Extracorporeal Shock Wave Lithotripsy (ESWL):** may use to break up renal calcali
Blood Cultures	**Stenting** **Retrograde Ureteroscopy**
C-Reactive Protein	**Percutaneous Ureterolithotomy/Nephrolithotomy**
Erythrocyte Sedimentation Rate (ESR) • During acute or chronic inflammation	**Open Surgery** • Ureterolithotomy (into the ureter) • Pyelolithotomy (into the renal pelvis) • Nepholithotomy (into the kidney)
Prostate Specific Antigen (PSA) • Measures amount of protein produced by prostate gland in blood • ↑ in level (> 4 to 10ng/ ml) may indicate cancer	**Prostate Hypertrophy** **Digital Rectal Exam (DRE)** enlarged, smooth prostate **Transrectal Ultrasound (TRUS)** and needle biopsy to R/O prostate cancer **Surgical Procedures** **Transurethral Resection of Prostate (TURP)** • Resectoscope (similar to cystoscope) goes in through urethra • Trims excess prostatic tissue • Enlarges passageway of urethra thru prostate gland **Other Surgical Procedures Include:** • Transurethral Needle Ablation (TUNA) • Balloon Dilation of the Prostate • Transurethral Laser Incision (TULIP) • Transurethral Electrovaporization of the Prostate (TUVP) • Prostatic Stents • Uralift • Simple or Radical Prostatectomy

Pathophysiology: Elimination

Medications

The following medications represent some of the many used for clients with alterations in elimination in the genitourinary system. We recommend you review and learn these commonly prescribed medications. (*Refer to the Pharmacology Made Insanely Easy Book for specifics*).

Common Medications for Elimination

Antibiotics/Penicillins
- Amoxicillin (Amoxil)
- Amoxicillin/clavulanate potassium (Augmentin)

Cephalosporins
- Cephalexin (Suprax)
- Ceftazidime (Rocephin)
- Cephalexin (Keflex)
- Cefacroxil (Duricef)
- Cefuroxime (Ceftin)

- **Fluoroquinolones**
- Ciprofloxacin (Cipro)
- Levofloxacin (Levaquin)
- Ofloxacin (Floxacin)

Aminoglycosides
- Gentamycin (Garamycin)
- Amikacin (Kantrex)
- Tobramycin (Nebcin)

Macrolides

Sulfonamides

Urinary Analgesics
- Phyenazopyridine (Pyridium)
- Phyenazopyride (Urogesic)

Urinary Agents
- Bethanechol (Duvoid, Urabeth, Urecholine)
- Solifenacin (VESI care)

Muscarinic Antagonists
- Darifenacin (Enablex)
- Oxybutynin (Ditropan)

Drugs for Benign Prostate Hypertrophy (BPHs)
- Tamsulosin (Flomax)
- Tadalafil (CIALIS)
- Alfuzosin (Uroxatral)

Pathophysiology: Control
Urinary Incontinence/Retention

Urinary Incontinence is a loss of bladder control with a range of severity that can be caused by many things. There are numerous medications that affect elimination by decreasing the contractility of the urinary detrusor muscle or increasing the urinary sphincter resistance or causing retention or incontinence of urine (Black & Hawk, 2009).

One of the most common reasons for urinary incontinence is from a urinary tract infection that irritates the bladder, causing strong urges to urinate. Other types of incontinence include:

- **Stress**: Loss of small amounts of urine when coughing, laughing, usually related to weak pelvic muscles.

- **Urge**: Unable to stop flow to get to bathroom usually related to overactive detrusor muscle.

- **Overflow**: Urinary retention with losses of small amounts of urine because of an overextended bladder.

- **Reflex**: Involuntary loss of small amounts of urine often related to spinal cord alterations or injury.

- **Functional**: Impact of physical, cognitive or social impairment to make it to the bathroom.

- **Total incontinence**: Unpredictable, involuntary incontinence that does not normally respond to treatment.

Bedwetting is also known as nighttime incontinence or nocturnal enuresis. Generally, bed-wetting before age 6 or 7 is not a concern because the child may still be developing nighttime bladder control. Some of the causes could include: small bladder, inability to recognize a full bladder, hormone imbalance, stress, urinary tract infection, sleep apnea, diabetes, chronic constipation or a structural problem in the urinary tract or nervous system.

Exceptions and Additions by Diseases

Pathophysiology: Control
Urinary Incontinence/Retention

Safety	
Concept Health Promotion (Bladder Training)	
SYSTEM-SPECIFIC ASSESSMENTS **"ABCs"**	**FIRST-DO PRIORITY INTERVENTIONS** **"TRAIN" BLADDER**

Assess client's intake and output and usual voiding patterns:
  Urinary retention
  Frequency
  Urgency
  Nocturia
  Enuresis (bedwetting)
 	
Bladder distention/incontinence/spasms
 	
Coping: ↓ socialization/depression
 	
Remember to Provide Privacy!
	Teach urinary elimination methods (Crede's method– manual pressure on the bladder to void prior to bladder elimination), intermittent catheterization.
	
	Routine schedule is imperative for bladder training. Running water can help initiate voiding.
	  Restrict fluids prior to bedtime, avoid alcohol, & caffeine.
	
	After meals (30 min) CONSISTENT/ROUTINE for voiding.
	  Active practice of Kegal exercises (tightening of pelvic floor muscles).
	
	I & O monitor.
	
	Need to encourage fluids to prevent UTI. Drink juices (i.e., cranberry) to ↑ acidity of urine.
	  Need to monitor for infection, temp, WBC & implement appropriate PPE.
	
	Notify the Provider of Supra-pubic fullness and inability to void.

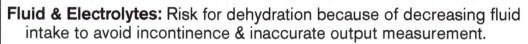

Priority Concepts for Urinary Control

Fluid & Electrolytes: Risk for dehydration because of decreasing fluid intake to avoid incontinence & inaccurate output measurement.

Tissue/Skin Integrity: Urine incontinence can lead to skin breakdown if client is not kept clean and dry.

Coping: Incontinence can be very embarrassing to the client; clients may decrease interaction with others; may lead to depression.

Injury/Safety: Incontinent clients are in a hurry to get to the bathroom and are at an increased risk for falls.

Refer to Concepts Fluid & Electrolytes, Tissue/Skin Integrity, and Coping for specifics.

**Decreased thirst mechanism increases the
risk of dehydration.**

Pathophysiology: Control
Bowel Incontinence/Constipation

Fecal Incontinence (bowel incontinence) is the inability to voluntarily control bowel movements. It can occur at specific times like after meals. It may range from partial incontinence to uncontrolled flatus. There are many other potential causes of bowel incontinence, including diarrhea, constipation, inflammatory bowel disease, nerve damage due to diabetes, spinal cord injury, or impaired cognition following a stroke or Alzheimer's disease. The incontinence is often the result of alteration in the nerve supply to the anal sphincter that can occur with neuromuscular diseases. It can also result from trauma, or inflammatory processes. Psychological factors like depression as well as physical factors can contribute to the incontinence.

Diarrhea is frequent loose bowel movements resulting from a variety of disorders. The goal is to treat the cause and to slow down the peristalsis. Elderly and the very young are at risk from dehydration without adequate fluid replacement. Protection of the skin is essential to avoid skin breakdown by using a protective barrier.

Constipation is having three or less bowel movements per week or difficulty in passing fecal material. It can result in straining while trying to have a bowel movement and a feeling of incomplete evacuation. Constipation is more common in older adults that can result from inadequate amounts of residue (fiber), fluid, activity (immobility can be a cause) or neurologic conditions like Parkinson's disease or stroke. Constipation is often a result of medications particularly opioids, antihistamines or antidepressants (Osborn, Wraa, Watson, & Holleran, 2014).

Exceptions and Additions by Diseases

Pathophysiology: Control
Bowel Incontinence/Constipation

Safety	
Concept Health Promotion (Bowel Training)	
SYSTEM-SPECIFIC ASSESSMENTS "ABCs"	**FIRST-DO PRIORITY INTERVENTIONS "TRAIN" BOWELS**
Assess client's usual bowel habits: 　Constipation 　Impaction 　Hard stools 　Feeling of rectal fullness 　Cramps 　Incontinence of stools **B**owel (abdomen distension, hypo or hyper active bowel sounds) **C**oping: ↓ Socialization/ Depression **Remember to Provide Privacy!**	**T**each Kegal exercise. Teach position for defecation: lean forward with pressure on abdomen with hands and bear down. Teach not to ignore urge to defecate. **R**outine schedule is imperative for bowel training. Begin with cathartic (Ducolax) for simulation of peristalsis for 2–3 weeks prior for bowel movements. **A**fter meals (30 min) CONSISTENT/ROUTINE of using toilet (drinking warm fluids before trying to have BM can help) **I**ncrease fluid (2500–3000 ml/day) unless contraindicated & residue (vegetables, fruit, whole grains) increase intake; rectal stimulation if needed; stool softeners; use of Valsalva maneuver; massage abdomen along large intestiner. **N**eed to encourage fluids to prevent constipation. 　**N**eed to monitor for infection, temp, WBC & implement appropriate PPE. **Notify the Provider of abdominal distention or if unable to have a bowel movement.**

Priority Concepts for Bowel Control

Fluid & Electrolytes: Risk for dehydration because of decreasing fluid intake to avoid bowel incontinence or fullness because of lack of bowel movement.

Tissue/Skin Integrity: Stool incontinence can lead to skin breakdown if effected area is not kept clean and dry.

Coping: Incontinence can be very embarrassing to the client; clients may decrease their interaction with others; may lead to depression.

Injury/Safety: Clients in a hurry to get to the bathroom are at risk for falling. The use of the Valsalva maneuver can lead to a loss of consciousness, resulting in a fall.

Refer to Concepts Fluid & Electrolytes, Tissue/Skin Integrity, Coping, Injury for specifics.

Increased use of laxatives can lead to poor regulation of bowels.

Pathophysiology: Retention/Blockage
Renal Calculi

Renal Calculi/Urolithiasis: Renal calculi are the presence of calculi (stones) in the urinary tract where high levels of minerals and chemicals in the urine form into crystals. When they become large enough to form stones it is called *nephrolithiasis*. Stones can also form in the ureter or the bladder as well. Calcium phosphate stones represent 75–80% of all stones and are associated with high levels of calcium in blood or urine. Approximate 15–20% are struvite stones that are very large and are associated with urinary tract infections caused by urease-producing bacteria (i.e., Proteus). Only 5–10% are uric acid stones that occur when uric acid is high, common in individuals with gout. The etiology is unknown but the risk factors include that males are more likely to have stones with family history as a contributing factor. Other risk factors include: immobility, dehydration, diet, local water supply (may be high in minerals), infection, urinary stasis or retention. **Hydronephrosis** is when the urine backs up into kidney because of partial blockage of the ureters. Renal calculi can lead to renal obstruction and progress to acute renal failure. It then becomes essential that the stone(s) be removed (Lewis, Dirksen, Heitkemper, Bucher & Camera, 2011).

Renal calculi (stones) are extremely painful as they travel through the ureter. It is important to monitor the renal function because stones can lead to acute renal failure if they block urine output. Kidney stones in about 85% of the clients are small enough (5 mm) to pass during normal urination. This usually occurs within 2–3 days, but it can take months to pass. The healthcare provider usually provides a collection kit with a filter and asks the client to save any passed stones for analysis of the stone content. If the stone has not passed in 2–3 days, additional treatment will be needed. In some severe cases, hospitalization may be necessary. Alpha-blockers such as tamsulosin (Flomax) can relax muscles in the urinary tract, helping kidney stones pass.

Exceptions and Additions by Diseases

Pathophysiology: Retention/Blockage
Renal Calculi

FIRST-DO PRIORITY INTERVENTIONS

SYSTEM-SPECIFIC ASSESSMENTS / DIET	EQUIPMENT	PLANS/INTERVENTIONS "RELIEF"	HEALTH PROMOTION
PAIN ASSESS "PQRST" **Use Appropriate Pain Scale for Age** **P**rovokes: what causes pain, what makes it better? **Q**uality: Severe & disabling Pain: intensifies as stone moves (flank pain if stone is in kidney or ureter) **R**adiates: to abdomen, scrotum, testes or vulva (stone maybe in ureter or bladder) **S**everity of pain (use pain scale) **T**ime: When pain started, assess anxiety, VS, nonverbal cues. Assess, monitor and trend: VS, renal function (BUN & Creatinine), frequency, dysuria, hematuria & oliguria/anuria, signs of infection. **DIET** • Nutrition counseling needed on what foods to avoid based on the analysis of the components of the stones. • Diet restrictions for calcium phosphate and/or oxalate include limiting foods high in calcium and oxalate, increase foods that acidify urine. • Refer to Concept on Nutrition for specifics.	• Urine strainer for stones. • Collect & send to lab for analysis.	• **Report** and review trends in VS indicative of pain, ↑ HR, ↑ RR. • **Evaluate** pain frequently, use pain scales appropriate for age. Document behaviors that indicate pain (may range from stillness to restlessness & constant mobility, facial expressions, crying, decreased attention span). • **Look** for stones in urine, use filter to strain urine. • **Initiate** & give pain meds, use non-pharmacologic interventions when possible. • **Evaluate** VS after pain med given especially with opioid medications, monitor for ↓ HR, RR, BP, ↓ LOC. Assess if pain relieved within 30 minutes. Document if no relief & notify HCP. • **Fluids** plenty, drink 2–3 liters a day if not contraindicated by health history (i.e., heart failure, renal failure, etc.).	Teach client/family about: • How to strain urine for stones & save for lab analysis. • Importance of ambulating & drinking 2–3 L/day (unless contraindicated) to help pass stone(s). • Diet instructions on what foods to avoid based on type of stone.

PRIORITIES

PRIORITY

MONITOR URINE OUTPUT

RENAL STONES CAN BLOCK URINE OUTFLOW → LEAD TO ACUTE RENAL FAILURE!!

Emergency: report immediately to HCP. Prepare the client for removal of stone.

Pathophysiology: Retention/Blockage
Benign Prostatic Hypertrophy

Benign Prostatic Hypertrophy (BPH) can reduce flow of urine from the bladder. There are two processes that occur: hyperplasia that narrows the lumen of the urethra that goes through the prostate gland and hypertrophy (enlargement) of the prostrate that can cause obstruction at the neck of the bladder. The retention of urine can lead to infection and a reflux of urine back into the kidney. This in turn can dilate the ureter that may further lead to infection. Prolonged obstruction can lead to decreased renal function or even failure. BPH is very common in the elderly male (LeMone, Burke & Bauldoff, 2011).

Exceptions and Additions by Diseases

SYSTEM-SPECIFIC ASSESSMENTS Remember, Symptoms begin "SLOW"	DIET	FIRST-DO PRIORITY INTERVENTIONS		
		EQUIPMENT	PLANS/INTERVENTIONS "PEE"	HEALTH PROMOTION
Slowly symptoms of BPH begin with urinary retention. (↑ PSA count may indicate malignancy.) **L**eaking of urine, urgency and voiding small amounts frequently; monitor the renal function (BUN & Creat). **O**ften hard to start urinating and urine stream may be hesitant and interrupted. **W**aking in night (nocturia) to void.	• Avoid bladder stimulants like caffeine and alcohol.	• Refer to continuous bladder irrigation following surgery in this chapter.	**P**ee when feel the urge. **E**liminate drinking large amounts of fluid at one time & medications that decrease bladder tone (i.e., anticholinergics, decongestants, antihistamines, etc.). **E**jaculation has been found to release prostatic fluid, decreasing size of prostate. Prepare for surgery if client requires a Transurethral Resection of the Prostate (TURP) or other similar procedures.	Teach client/family about: • Diet. • Some medications can take 6 months to a year to improve symptoms. • Side effects (i.e., impotence, decrease in libido, and retrograde ejaculation) are possible side effects of the medications and may contribute to non-compliance.

Pathophysiology: Retention/Blockage

Benign Prostatic Hypertrophy
Procedure: Continuous Bladder Irrigation (CBI) following
Prostate or Bladder Surgery

"IRRIGATION"

Continuous Bladder Irrigation (CBI) consists of a three-way closed irrigation system; one port is connected to a catheter to drain urine & solution, one port is used for continuous bladder irrigation with irrigating solution as prescribed, and one port is for inflation of a large balloon on catheter (35–45 mL) that keeps pressure to prevent bleeding (Nettina, 2013).

"IRRIGATION"

Irrigation used & adjusted to keep fluid return pink or lighter or may be irrigated with 50 mL of irrigation solution using aseptic technique as prescribed.

Rate of irrigation ↑ if return is bright red or if clots or tissue are observed.

Rate of irrigation ↓ if no drainage, check for possible obstruction.

If obstructed with clots, use 50 mL syringe & irrigate with 50 mL of irrigating solution per protocol.

Get HCP if no urine; **NEVER** remove a catheter without consulting HCP.

Assess patency of catheter & flow of urine, color & amount
    Intake = Amount of irrigation instilled
    Output = Take amount of fluid instilled minus the output
        collected
    Difference = Urine output should be (at least 0.5 mL/kg/hr.)

Trend for complications of bleeding: bright red bleeding from catheter or large clots that will not clear with irrigation; notify HCP immediately. Output should become pink within 24 hours.

Instruct client to notify the nurse if voiding around the catheter (may occur with bladder spasms that can be caused by clots in the drainage). Irrigate with irrigation solution if clots noted; administer pain medication as prescribed.

Observe for signs of infection, (i.e., cloudy urine, ↑ WBCs, ↑ Temp), document & report.

Need to instruct client if catheter remains in place on discharge that it normally is removed within 8–10 days. Instruct on what symptoms to report, leakage around catheter. Instruct to drink 8–10 glasses of water/day unless contraindicated. Call HCP if no urine drainage (Nettina, 2013).

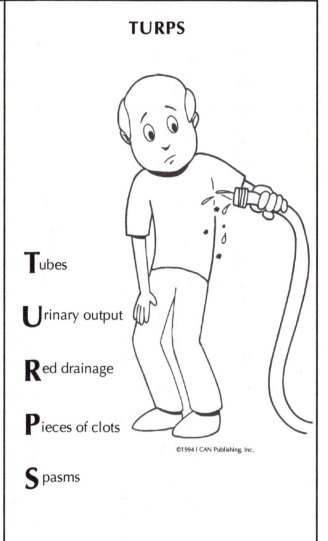

TURPS

Tubes

Urinary output

Red drainage

Pieces of clots

Spasms

©1994 I CAN Publishing, Inc.

It is all about the Concept of Fluid Balance!!!
(Refer to Concept Fluid Balance for specifics.)

Pathophysiology: Infections
Urinary Tract Infections

Urinary System

Urinary Tract Infections (UTI): The most common cause of urinary tract infections is Escherichia coli. Other organisms include enterobacteriaceae microorganisms (Klebsiella, Proteus), Pseudomonas aeruginosa, and Serratia marcescens). Urosepsis is a serious complication of untreated urinary tract infections.

Lower UTI:

Cystitis is an infection and inflammation of the lower urinary tract and bladder that results in lower abdominal pain, tenderness over bladder. Untreated UTIs can result in urosepsis, which can cause septic shock and death. The earliest sign and may be the only clinical finding with elderly clients is often confusion or decreased level of consciousness (LOC). The lack of apparent clinical findings puts the elderly client at risk for urinary tract infections to go undiagnosed until late in the infectious process.

Urethritis is an inflammation of the urethra and is caused by bacteria entering the opening of the urethra. Clinical findings include pain and burning on urination with a sense of urgency to void.

Upper UTI:

Pyelonephritis is a bacteria invasion of upper urinary tract leading to interstitial inflammation of kidneys and renal pelvis, tubular cell necrosis and abscess formation in the capsule, cortex or medulla of the kidney. Infection usually begins in lower urinary tract & progresses up the urinary tract. Chronic infections can lead to inflammation & scarring that alters the blood flow to the kidney, glomerulus and tubular structure. It can be acute or chronic and can lead to a decrease in renal function (Osborn, Wraa, Watson & Holleran, 2014).

Vesicoureteral Reflux is when the urine flows back (reflux) from the bladder into one or both ureters. It may also reflux back into the kidneys. It is most common in infants and children but may also occur in adults.

Exceptions and Additions by Diseases

Pathophysiology: Infections
Urinary Tract Infections

FIRST-DO PRIORITY INTERVENTIONS

System-Specific Assessments "URINE"	Diet	Equipment	Plans/Interventions "UTIS"	Health Promotion
Urine characteristics: Color of urine, frequency, nocturia, and incontinence. Obtain a clean catch urine specimen for routine analysis and culture and sensitivity. **R**eport pain: Dysuria. **I**ncrease WBCs and Temp, assess. **N**ausea & vomiting may occur. **E**valuate mental status.	• Increase intake of cranberry juice to help acidify the urine and prevent bacteria from adhering to the mucosa of the urinary tract.	• Indwelling catheters • Intermittent catheters	**U**rinary assessment, strict I & O, daily weights, compare, contrast & trend; note color, smell of urine, frequency and/or complaint of pain & burning. Give Pyridium or other pain medications as prescribed (note: if client is taking Pyridium, it is important to instruct the client that their urine may be orange in color and it is not harmful). **T**emperature ↑ & WBC ↑, report. Assess VS (↑HR & RR). Obtain clean catch urine specimen for a urine culture and sensitivity test as prescribed to determine the bacteria causing the infection. Administer antibiotics as prescribed. **I**ncrease fluids ↑ 3 L/day if not contra-indicated (i.e., heart failure, renal failure, etc.). Instruct to void q 3–4 hours instead of waiting until the bladder is full. **S**ystem-specific assessments: monitor electrolytes; assess for costovertebral angle tenderness, a possible indication the infection has moved up the urinary tract to the kidneys (pyelonephritis).	Teach client/family about: • Instruct to increase fluid 3L/day if not contra-indicated (i.e., heart failure, renal failure, etc.). • Take all of antibiotics as instructed. • Good body hygiene, bathe daily. • Wear cotton absorbent undergarments; avoid synthetics (less absorbent). • Empty bladder every 3–4 hours, do not wait until bladder is full. • Urinate before and after intercourse. • Instruct female clients to wipe perineal area from front to back, avoid bubble baths, sitting in wet bathing suits and wearing tight fitting clothes.

↓ **LOC early sign of a UTI with the elderly client.**

Pathophysiology: Infections
Urinary Tract Infections

System-Specific Assessment Comparisons for Lower and Upper Urinary Tract Infections

Assessments "URINE"	Lower Urinary Tract Infections Cystitis, Urethritis	Upper Urinary Tract Infections Pyelonephritis	ELDERLY Clinical Findings
Urine: Color of urine	Red-tinged, smoky, coffee colored, cloudy	Dark in color, cloudy	X
Odor	X (foul odor)	X (foul odor)	May not have
Frequency	X	X	May not have
Nocturia	X	X	May not have
Report pain: Dysuria	Burning with voiding, bladder spasms, lower back pain	Costovertebral Angle Tenderness (Flank pain)	May not complain of pain
Increase WBCs, Temp	X	X	May not have ↑ WBC, ↑ Temp, ↑ HR, ↑ RR; if elevated may indicate urosepsis
Evaluate Mental Status ↓ LOC	Late sign in non-elderly clients	Late sign in non-elderly clients	↓ LOC may be the only sign for elderly clients

INSANELY EASY TIP for Upper and Lower UTI Assessments!!

**Remember the Differences are
the Type and Location of the Pain.**

The Rest of the Assessments are the Same!

Remember: ELDERLY MAY ONLY HAVE ↓ LOC.

Clinical Decision-Making Exercises

1. Which one of these clinical assessments for a client who is post-prostatic resection (TURP) would require intervention by the nurse?

   ① Urine output is light red to red during the first postoperative day.

   ② Urine output has 2 blood clots during the 1st post-op day.

   ③ Urine output is very dark red 2nd post-op day.

   ④ Urine output is pale pink during the 3rd post-op day.

2. Which of these systems-specific assessments would indicate the client might have a lower urinary tract infection (cystitis)? *Select all that apply.*

   ① Burning and dysuria.

   ② Costovertebral tenderness.

   ③ Bladder cramping.

   ④ Foul smelling urine.

   ⑤ Inability to void.

3. Which of these actions would be appropriate for the RN delegate to the UAP for a client with ureteral stones?

   ① Encourage client to remain in bed until the renal calculi has passed.

   ② Remind client about the need to restrict fluid.

   ③ Provide client with a glass of milk for the snack.

   ④ Strain and record urine output.

4. The appropriate response for a client with calcium oxalate stones who asks why he needs to see the dietician before he goes home, would be?

   ① "Reducing your weight and salt intake will decrease the incidence of stones."

   ② "Your kidney stone was a calcium oxalate stone and requires a high calcium diet."

   ③ "Diet instructions based on the analysis of your kidney stones may help prevent future stones."

   ④ "You would need to follow high protein diet to prevent renal calculi."

5. What would be the priority to report to the healthcare provider for a client with a renal calculus who is receiving 1000 mL of 0.9% normal saline IV at a rate of 125 mL/hour, has a HR that was 76 BPM four hours ago and is now 98 BPM?

   ① Client reports of feeling "sweaty."

   ② Flank pain that radiates to the lower abdomen.

   ③ No urine output for 4 hours.

   ④ Nausea that is controlled with prescribed medication.

6. Which statement would be of most concern stated by the daughter who brought her 88-year-old mother to the urgent care center?

   ① "My mother has been complaining of constipation."

   ② "My mother has been very hungry lately."

   ③ "My mother has not been herself lately, she is never confused."

   ④ "My mother has been complaining of itching."

7. Which one of these clinical findings indicates the development of a potential complication for a client in a long-term care facility with urinary incontinence?

   ① Three incontinent episodes in 24 hours.

   ② A 2 cm red circular area on the thigh that does not blanch.

   ③ A foul strong odor of soaked linens.

   ④ The client who refuses to accept assistance from the UAP.

8. Which one of these interventions is appropriate to implement for an ambulatory client who is receiving bladder training?

   ① Offer a bedpan or urinal at regular intervals.

   ② Instruct client about the importance of a regular routine for elimination.

   ③ Teach client to increase intake of caffeine.

   ④ Instruct the client to increase fluid intake at bedtime.

9. What is the priority nursing action for a client with an indwelling catheter whose system specific assessments include oral temperature of 102.2° F, has hot flushed skin, and dark, cloudy urine in the collection bag?

   ① Limit PO fluid intake to 1000 mL per day.

   ② Document and continue to monitor the client.

   ③ Irrigate the catheter immediately.

   ④ Obtain urine specimen for culture and sensitivity as ordered.

10. Which of the following statements by a 25-year-old female being discharged following a urinary tract infection (UTI) indicates an understanding of how to prevent future UTIs?

    ① "I should take frequent baths to avoid re-infection."

    ② "I will change all my undergarments to synthetic as this is a part of the problem."

    ③ "I will be sure to void both before and after intercourse."

    ④ "I will avoid fluids like cranberry juice that can contribute to an UTI."

1. Which one of these **clinical assessments** for a client who is **post-prostatic resection (TURP)** would **require intervention** by the nurse?

   ① INCORRECT: Urine output is light red to red during the first postoperative day. The urine would be light red to red in the first 24 hours post-op.

   ② INCORRECT: Urine output has 2 blood clots during the 1st post-op day. A few clots the first day would be expected and would not be a concern.

   ③ **CORRECT: Urine output is very dark red 2nd post-op day. This would be a concern as the expected outcome for 48 hours following a TURP would be the urine should be pink in color, not dark red.**

   ④ INCORRECT: Urine output is pale pink during the 3rd post-op day. This would be desired outcome.

The strategy for answering this question is to know the potential complications following a TURP, and to compare, contrast and trend the clinical findings. This is one of your strategies in prioritizing care (*refer to the Prioritization chart in Chapter 1*). The expected outcome for a client 2nd day post-op from a TURP would be the urine should be pink in color. Urine that is very dark red in color indicates the client is most likely bleeding and it would be important for you to notify the healthcare provider. In addition you would be monitoring the client's vital signs for ↑ HR and RR, and the amount of output compared to the intake. See how you are linked the priority care of a client who has had a TURP procedure to the priority care for any client with the potential for fluid volume deficit regardless if it was for post partum bleeding, bleeding from a traumatic injury to any other surgical procedure. It's all about the concept of Fluid Balance!!

Reduction of Risk: Recognize signs and symptoms of complications and intervene appropriately when providing care.

Reduction of Risk: Manage the care of a client with fluid and electrolyte imbalance.

2. Which of these **systems-specific assessments** would **indicate** the client might have a **lower urinary tract infection (cystitis)**? *Select all that apply.*

   ① **CORRECT: Burning and dysuria. This is an assessment finding for a UTI.**

   ② INCORRECT: Costovertebral tenderness. This would be an assessment finding for pyelonephritis indicating a potential complication or the lower UTI was moving up the urinary tract to the kidneys.

   ③ **CORRECT: Bladder cramping. This is an assessment finding for a UTI.**

   ④ **CORRECT: Foul smelling urine. This is an assessment finding for a UTI.**

   ⑤ INCORRECT: Inability to void. This would indicate a problem that may be found with kidney stones that are blocking the ureters or with BPH, not with a lower UTI.

The strategy for answering is to understand the pathophysiology of urinary tract infections and the resulting clinical findings. As you progress, you will begin to differentiate between clinical findings that define a disorder to the clinical findings that indicate a potential complication or an increase in the severity of the disease process. Even if you do not know the disease process, by doing your focused assessment you will be able to compare, contrast and trend changes that need intervention.

Physiological Adaptation: Identify pathophysiology related to acute or chronic conditions (i.e., signs and symptoms).

Physiological Adaptation: Perform focused assessment.

3. Which of these **actions** would be **appropriate** for the **RN delegate to the UAP** for a client with **ureteral stones**?

① INCORRECT: Encourage client to remain in bed until the renal calculi has passed. Ambulation is encouraged to help the client pass the kidney stone.

② INCORRECT: Remind client about the need to restrict fluid. Increased fluids are needed to help pass renal calculi.

③ INCORRECT: Provide client with a glass of milk for the snack. This is not correct as the client has a history of calcium oxalate renal calculi and foods or beverages high in calcium would be restricted.

④ **CORRECT: Strain and record urine output. This would be a correct intervention to see if the stone(s) had passed and to send it for analysis of the composition.**

The strategy for answering this question is to understand the plan of care for a client with renal calculi. It also required an understanding of the pathophysiology of renal calculi and the composition of the most common stones. This knowledge helped you prioritize the plan of care that would assist the client to pass the stone by ambulating, drinking plenty of fluids, straining the urine and implementing dietary restrictions. You linked the concepts of fluid balance and nutrition together to provide a quality plan of care! Even if you were not sure about what a UAP could do, you were able to select appropriate option for the care of this client as you knew the other options were incorrect regardless who was providing the care! Good job!

Basic Care and Comfort: Assess and manage a client with alteration in elimination.

Management of Care: Assign and supervise care provided by others.

4. The **appropriate response** for a client with **calcium oxalate stones** who asks **why he needs to see the dietician** before he goes home, would be?

① INCORRECT: "Reducing your weight and salt intake will decrease the incidence of stones." This is not correct.

② INCORRECT: : "Your kidney stone was a calcium oxalate stone and requires a high calcium diet". A low calcium diet would be needed, not a high calcium diet.

③ **CORRECT: "Diet instructions based on the analysis of your kidney stones may help prevent future stones." This would be correct. An analysis of the kidney stone content can help the client plan with the dietician what foods should be avoided to help prevent future stones from forming.**

④ INCORRECT: "You would need to follow high protein diet to prevent renal calculi." A high protein diet is not indicated to prevent renal calculi.

The strategy for answering this question is to understand the need for client teaching and health promotion to help prevent readmission to the acute care setting. This requires a collaborative approach by the nurse to involve the dietician in helping the client with a diet that can help prevent future stones from forming. In addition, you would know that teaching the client to drink plenty of fluids, exercise are also important preventive measures. Collaboration with the appropriate healthcare team members provides a comprehensive approach to client care and enhances the desired outcomes. As the nurse you may play a lead role in bringing the healthcare team members together! Job Well Done!!

Management of Care: Collaborate with healthcare members in other disciplines when providing client care.

Physiological Adaptation: Educate client regarding an acute or chronic condition.

Health Promotion and Maintenance: Provide information about healthy behaviors and health promotion and maintenance recommendations.

5. What would be the **priority** to **report** to the healthcare provider for a client with a **renal calculus** who is receiving **1000 mL of 0.9% normal saline IV at a rate of 125 mL/hour, has a HR that was 76 BPM four hours ago and is now 98 BPM?**

   ① INCORRECT: Client reports of feeling "sweaty". This would not be the priority to report.

   ② INCORRECT: Flank pain that radiates to the lower abdomen. Clients with renal calculus do have flank pain but this would not be the priority over option 3.

   ③ **CORRECT: No urine output for 4 hours. This would be a concern and should be reported as it may indicate a renal stone is blocking the ureters and preventing urine output.**

   ④ INCORRECT: Client reports seeing a small 1 cm size stone in the urine strainer four hours ago. This would be reported but it is not the priority over option 3.

The strategy for answering this question should look very familiar to you. You guessed it, alteration in fluid balance! It was important to link each of the distractors in this question to the stem of the question. An important link to make was with the pathophysiology of renal calculi and the potential complication of one or more of the stones blocking urinary output. This is strategy from the Prioritization chart from chapter one to trend for potential complications. You see in the stem of the question, the client is receiving IV fluids at 125mL/hour times 8 hours; this amounts to 1000mL of fluid. Then in option 3 it indicates that there has been no urine output for 4 hours ...this is a problem! In addition, the client is now having signs and symptoms of fluid volume excess indicated by the increased heart rate. Notifying the healthcare provider is a priority! Great job linking the concept of fluid balance with prioritizing care to the pathophysiology of renal calculi!!! You are mastering key concepts ... excellent job!!! Genius!!!!

Reduction of Risk: Assess client and respond to changes in vital signs.

Physiological Adaptation: Manage the client with fluid and electrolyte imbalance.

6. Which **statement** would be of **most concern** stated by the **daughter who brought her 88-year-old mother to the urgent care center?**

   ① INCORRECT: "My mother has been complaining of constipation." This could be a concern, but there is no specific information about if the constipation is new or how long it has been occurring. This would not be a priority over option 3.

   ② INCORRECT: "My mother has been very hungry lately." This would not be a priority.

   ③ **CORRECT: "My mother has not been herself lately, she is never confused." This would be a concern as new changes in mental status; confusion and level of consciousness are often early signs of UTIs in elderly clients.**

   ④ INCORRECT: "My mother has been complaining of itching." This could be a concern but would not take priority over option 3.

The strategy for answering this question is linking signs and symptoms to how clinical findings may manifest in the elderly client. After this chapter, you understand that a decrease in LOC or confusion can be early signs for the elderly, particularly with UTIs. You also linked this information to the fact that elderly have a decreased thirst mechanism and are at risk for dehydration. Knowing the pathophysiology of UTIs, and the increase risk of infection with dehydration, you were able to make a sound clinical judgment linking pathophysiology with changes that occur with aging. Great Connect!!

Health Promotion and Maintenance: Provide care and education for adults over 85.

Reduction of Risk: Recognize trends and changes in client condition and intervene as needed.

Physiological Adaptation: Identify pathophysiology related to acute or chronic conditions (i.e., signs and symptoms).

7. Which one of these **clinical findings** indicates the **development of a potential complication** for a client in a **long-term care facility** with **urinary incontinence**?

   ① INCORRECT: Three incontinent episodes in 24 hours. The client has urinary incontinence, so this would not be a change in condition.

   ② CORRECT: A 2 cm red circular area on the thigh that does not blanch. This would be a concern as it indicates a potential skin breakdown.

   ③ INCORRECT: A foul strong odor of soaked linens. Soaked linens do have a foul smell and it would not indicate a potential complication.

   ④ INCORRECT: The client who refuses to accept assistance from the UAP. This is not correct.

The strategy for answering this question was to link the concept of tissue/skin integrity with urinary incontinence (*refer to the Concept Tissue/Skin Integrity for specifics*). Clients who are incontinent have an increased risk for skin/tissue breakdown. It takes vigilant assessments and preventive interventions to prevent skin breakdown particularly with elderly clients who often do not drink enough to maintain fluid balance or eat enough to maintain adequate nutrition to help prevent skin breakdown. Great job in assessing this early sign of potential skin breakdown so preventive interventions can be implemented!!

Basic Care and Comfort: Perform skin assessment and implement measure to maintain skin integrity and prevent skin breakdown.

Reduction of Risk: Recognize trends and changes in client condition and intervene as needed.

8. Which one of these **interventions** is **appropriate to implement** for an ambulatory client who is **receiving bladder training**?

   ① INCORRECT: Offer a bedpan or urinal at regular intervals. The client is ambulatory, so a bedpan would not be appropriate.

   ② CORRECT: Instruct client about the importance of a regular routine for elimination. This is an important part of a bladder training program.

   ③ INCORRECT: Teach client to increase intake of caffeine. This is not correct; caffeine intake should be decreased.

   ④ INCORRECT: Instruct the client to increase fluid intake at bedtime. This is not correct; fluids should be limited at bedtime.

The strategy for answering this question was to understand the importance of establishing a regular routine with bladder training. As a nurse, one of your key roles is client education for health promotion. This role is essential to help the client maintain independence and to prevent unnecessary acute care admissions. Helping clients maintain bladder control as they age contributes not only to their physical health but their quality of life as well. See what you can do as a nurse!!!

Health Promotion and Maintenance: Provide information about healthy behaviors and health promotion and maintenance recommendations.

9. What is the **priority nursing action** for a client with an **indwelling catheter** whose system-specific assessments include oral **temperature of 102.2° F, has hot flushed skin, and dark, cloudy urine in the collection bag?**

    ① INCORRECT: Limit PO fluid intake of 1000mL per day. Fluid intake should be increased with a temperature.

    ② INCORRECT: Document and continue to monitor the client. Documentation and continuing monitoring would be done, but this is not the priority intervention over option 4.

    ③ INCORRECT: Irrigate the catheter immediately. This would not be a correct intervention.

    ④ **CORRECT: Obtain a urine specimen for culture and sensitivity as ordered. This would be a priority assessment to determine the origin of a potential infection so the healthcare provider can prescribe an effective antibiotic for the organism involved.**

The strategy for answering this question is to link the pathophysiology of infections with the potential risk that occurs when clients have indwelling catheters. Although, minimizing the need for Foley catheters is a priority, sometimes the client's condition requires it. When that happens, it is the nurse's responsibility to maintain aseptic technique and to monitor for potential signs of infection. In this question you linked the assessment findings of the increased temperature, the hot flushed skin and the color of the urine to a possible infections. As a part of the collaborative team with the healthcare provider, it is important to obtain a urine specimen for culture and sensitivity so the correct antibiotic treatment can be initiated. You were able to rule out option 1 by knowing that fluid intake should be increase, not decreased. Option 2 to document and continue to monitor would be done, but it would not take priority over option 4. There is no indication for the need for option 3. Infections in the acute care setting are primary reasons for extended stays that are costly to the client and to the facility. Good job!!!

Reduction of Risk Potential: Obtain specimens for diagnostic testing.

Reduction of Risk: Recognize trends and changes in client condition and intervene as needed.

10. Which of the following **statements** by a **25-year-old female** being **discharged** following a **urinary tract infection (UTI)** indicates an **understanding of how to prevent future UTIs?**

    ① INCORRECT: "I should take frequent baths to avoid re-infection." Showers are recommended over baths to prevent UTIs.

    ② INCORRECT: "I will change all my undergarments to synthetic as this is a part of the problem." Cotton undergarments are recommended, as they are more absorbent.

    ③ **CORRECT: "I will be sure to void both before and after intercourse." This is correct.**

    ④ INCORRECT: I will avoid fluids like cranberry juice that can contribute to an UTI. Juices like cranberry juice have been found to be beneficial in preventing UTIs because they help keep the urine acetic and bacteria from adhering to the tissue walls.

The strategy for answering this question was to link the pathophysiology of UTIs, with once again, health promotion and prevention! Are you seeing a pattern in this chapter? Client teaching that helps clients maintain their health and prevent admission to an acute care facility is a priority of care with every client. (*Refer to Bladder Training in this chapter for specifics*).

Health Promotion and Maintenance: Provide information about healthy behaviors and health promotion and maintenance recommendations.

Decision-Making Analysis Form

Use this tool to help identify why you missed any questions. As you enter the question numbers in the chart, you will begin to see patterns of why you answered incorrectly. This information will then guide you toward what you need to focus on in your continued studies. Ultimately, this analytical exercise will help you become more successful in answering questions!!!

Questions to ask:

1. Did I have the knowledge to answer the question? If not, what information do I need to review?
2. Did I know what the question was asking? Did I misread it or did I miss keywords in the stem of the question?
3. Did I misread or miss keywords in the distractors that would have helped me choose the correct answer?
4. Did I follow my gut reaction or did I allow myself to rationalize and then choose the wrong answer?

	Lack of Knowledge (Concepts, Systems, Pathophysiology, Medications, Procedures, etc.)	Missed Keywords or Misread the Stem of the Question	Missed Keywords or Misread the Distractors	Changed My Answer (Second-guessed myself, i.e., my first answer was correct.)
Put the # of each question you missed in the column that best explains why you think you answered it incorrectly.				

If you changed an answer because you talked yourself out of the correct answer, or you second-guessed yourself, this is an **EASY FIX: QUIT changing your answers**!!! Typically, the first time you read a question, you are about 95% right! The second time you read a question, you start talking yourself into changing the answer. The third time you read a question, you do not have a clue—and you are probably thinking "Who in the heck wrote this question?"

On the other hand, if you read a question too quickly and when you reread it you realize you missed some key information that would impact your decision (i.e., assessments, lab reports, medications, etc.), then it is appropriate to change your answer. When in doubt, go with the safe route: your first thought! Go with your gut instinct!

As you gain confidence in answering questions regarding specific nursing concepts, you will be able to successfully progress to answering higher-level questions about prioritization. Please refer to the *Prioritization Guidelines* in this book for a structure to assist you with this process.

You CAN do this!

> *"An ounce of prevention*
> *is worth a pound of cure."*
> BENJAMIN FRANKLIN

References for Chapter 16

Black, J M. and Hawks, J. H. (2009). *Medical surgical nursing: Clinical management for positive outcomes (8th ed.)*. Philadelphia: Elsevier/Saunders.

Daniels, R. & Nicoll, L. (2012). *Contemporary medical-surgical nursing*, (2nd ed.). Clifton Park, NY: Delmar Cengage Learning.

Eliopoulos, C. (2014). *Gerontological nursing* (8th ed.), Philadelphia: Lippincott Williams & Wilkins.

Giddens, G. F. (2013). *Concepts for nursing practice*. St. Louis, MO: Mosby, an imprint of Elsevier.

Hogan, M. A. (2014). *Pathophysiology: Reviews and rationales* (3rd ed.) Boston, MA: Pearson.

Ignatavicius, D. D. and Workman, M. L. (2010). *Medical-surgical nursing: Patient-centered collaborative care* (6th ed.). Philadelphia: Elsevier/Saunders.

LeMone, P., Burke, K. M., and Bauldoff, G. (2011). *Medical-surgical nursing: Critical thinking in patient care* (5th ed.). Upper Saddle Road, NJ: Pearson/Prentice Hall.

Lewis, S., Dirksen, S., Heitkemper, M., Bucher, L., and Camera, I. (2011). *Medical surgical nursing: Assessment and management of clinical problems* (8th ed.). St. Louis: Mosby.

Manning, L. and Rayfield, S. (2014). *Nursing made insanely easy* (7th ed.). Duluth, GA: I CAN Publishing, Inc.

Manning, L. and Rayfield, S. (2013). *Pharmacology made insanely easy* (4th ed.). Duluth, GA: I CAN Publishing, Inc.

Mauk, K. (2013). *Gerontological nursing: competencies for care* (3rd ed.) Boston: Jones & Bartlett Publishers.

National Council of State Boards of Nursing, INC. (NCSBN) 2012. *Research brief: 2011 RN practice analysis: linking the NCLEX RN® examination to practice*. Retrieved from https://www.ncsbn.org/index.htm

Nettina, S. L. (2013). *Lippincott manual of nursing practice* (10th ed.). Philadelphia, PA: Walters Kluwer Health/Lippincott Williams & Wilkins.

North Carolina Concept Based Learning Editorial Board (2011). *Nursing a concept based approach to learning*, Upper Saddle Road, NJ: Pearson/Prentice Hall.

Osborn, K. S., Wraa, C. E., Watson, A. S., and Holleran, R. S. (2014). *Medical surgical nursing: Preparation for practice* (2nd ed.). Upper Saddle Road, NJ: Pearson.

Pagana, K. D. and Pagana, T. J. (2014). *Mosby's manual of laboratory and diagnostic tests* (5th ed.). St. Louis, MO: Mosby, an imprint of Elsevier.

Porth, C. (2011). *Essentials of pathophysiology* (3d ed.). Philadelphia, PA: Lippincott Williams ad Wilkins.

Porth, C. M. and Grossman, S. (2013). *Pathophysiology: Concepts of altered health states* (9th ed.). Philadelphia, PA: Lippincott Williams & Wilkins.

Potter, P. A., Perry, A. G., Stockert, P., and Hall, A. (2013). *Fundamentals of nursing* (8th ed.). St. Louis, MO: Pearson/Prentice Hall.

Smeltzer, S. C., Bare, B. G., Hinkle, J. L., and Cheever, K. H. (2010). *Brunner & Suddarth's Textbook of medical-surgical nursing* (12th ed.). Philadelphia: Lippincott Williams & Wilkins.

University of Maryland (2012). Kidney stones. Retrieved from http://umm.edu/health/medical/reports/articles/kidney-stones

Wagner, K. D. and Hardin-Pierce, M. C. (2014). *High-Acuity nursing* (6th ed.). Boston: Pearson.

CHAPTER 17

Renal System
Linking Concepts to Pathophysiology of Diseases
Concept Perfusion Renal

A Snapshot of Renal Perfusion

Chronic renal disease is a progressive, irreversible reduction in renal function such that the kidneys are no longer able to maintain the body environments. The glomerular filtration rate (GFR) gradually decreases as the nephrons are destroyed. The nephrons left intact are subjected to an increased workload, resulting in hypertrophy and inability to concentrate urine. Serum creatinine has a gradual increase over months to years for chronic renal failure (CRF) exceeding 4 mg/dL. Blood urea nitrogen (BUN) gradually increase with elevated serum creatinine over months to years for CRF, 180–200 mg/dL (CRF). Glomerular Filtration Rate (GFR) is less than 60 mL/min for longer than 3 months. GFR less than 15 mL/min indicates kidney failure.

Older adult clients are an increased risk for chronic renal disease due to the normal aging process that includes a decrease in the number of functioning nephrons, decreased GFR. Older adults on bed rest, confused, and have a lack of thirst with minimal access to water are an increased risk for dehydration. This can result in chronic renal disease.

Chronic renal disease (CRD), chronic renal failure (CRF), and chronic kidney disease (CKD) will be referred to in this chapter as the medical diagnoses that result in alteration in renal perfusion. While there are five stages of Chronic Kidney Disease, this is NOT going to be the focus for this chapter. The good news is that the focus for this chapter will be on multiple concepts interrelated as a result of an alteration in renal perfusion from chronic renal failure. Each of these concepts will not only be linked in this chapter, but will also be reviewed again in their own specific chapters. This is one of the benefits of "Conceptual Learning"! For example, once you have an understanding of the concept: fluid volume excess, the nursing assessments and plan of care will be the same for renal perfusion, cardiac perfusion, the diagnosis of Syndrome of Inappropriate Antidiuretic Hormone, etc. This approach will also simplify the complexity of this concept by linking the multiple concepts to pathophysiology. Repetition is the mother of learning!

Let's get started by reviewing the pathophysiology for the multiple concepts! The mnemonic "FAILURE" will provide the structure for organizing these concepts!

The Pathophysiology Behind an Alteration in Renal Perfusion

Renal Perfusion–Chronic Renal "FAILURE": Multiple Concepts

Fluid Volume Excess	**A**ltered Electrolyte Balance	**I**mmobility/ Integumentary	**L**ook for Infection	**U**nderstand Client's Need to Cope	**R**eview Nutrition	**E**valuate Oxygenation
• Hypervolemia/ Hypernatremia. but dilutional • Hypertension • Heart failure • Pericardial effusion • Uremic pericarditis • Atherosclerotic heart disease • Pulmonary Edema • Pleural Effusions	• Hyperkalemia = dysrhythmias • Hyponatremia (dilutional) = Seizures • Accumulation of lactic acid = metabolic acidosis • Hyperphos-phatemia = hypocalcemia = broken bones	**Immobility (musculoskeletal)** • Mineral and bone disorder • Vascular calcifi-cation • Osteomalacia **Integumentary** • Yellow/gray • Discoloration of skin • Pruritus, Uremic Frost • Ecchymosis • Risk for decubitus • Impaired wound healing	• Infection • Leuko-cytosis	• Emotional lability • Depression • Psychosis • Personality Changes • Reproductive changes	• Hypoparathy-roidism • Hyperphos-phatemia • Hyperglycemia/ ↑ Lipids • Gastritis • PUD • Anemia ↓ Protein = Anasarca (due to altered osmotic pressure) =Impaired skin integrity • ↓ Metabolism of vitamin D = Bone mineral disease	• ↓ O_2 due to ↓ Erythropoietin • Anemia • Heart Failure • Altered platelet function leading to bleeding tendencies

Linking Pathophysiology to System-Specific Assessments for an Alteration in Renal Perfusion from Chronic "RENAL" Failure

Pathophysiology "RENAL"	System-Specific Assessments "RENAL"
Respiratory Status: Accumulation of lactic acid may result in metabolic acidosis. The respiratory system will compensate/correct by increasing respiratory rate (RR) and depth of RR to blow off CO_2 and increase the pH. Fluid volume excess can result in adventitious breath sounds and/or respiratory infections. Altered renin-angiotensin system can lead to ↑ BP. Leukocytosis leads to ↑ Temp.	**R**espiratory status: RR ↑ (Kussmaul respirations); dyspnea; breath sounds. Monitor for ↑ BP, I & O, weight. ↑ Temp.
Electrolyte imbalances: Decrease in glomerular filtration rate-leads to electrolyte imbalances, which can result in cardiac dysrhythmias. Edema is from sodium and fluid retention from renal failure. Sodium is dilutional from the fluid retention. Renal disease affects the parathyroid hormone (PTH) from the parathyroid glands and the calcitonin from the thyroid. Calcitonin moves Ca^{++} into bone; PTH shifts Ca^{++} from bone into the ECF. ↑ P = ↓ Ca^{++} + ↑ PO_4 = bone demineralization (renal osteodystrophy). **E**motional: Physical changes can lead to anxiety.	**E**lectrolyte imbalances: (K^+, Ca^{++}, PO_4, Na^+); check for muscle cramps; evaluate for broken bones. **E**motional: Assess coping skills and family/social support.
Neurologic changes: Accumulation of acid waste products due to renal failure. **N**utrition: (*Refer to concept Nutrition in this chapter.*) Abdominal girth and the characteristics of the abdomen such as is it soft, hard, distended, etc. will indicate if there are any trends with bleeding.	**N**eurological changes: CNS depressed; headache, weakness, seizures. **N**utrition: Review nutritional intake. Does client understand the nutritional needs for CRF? Assess bowel sounds, abdominal girth; signs of a GI bleed (i.e., stool color, ↑ HR, ↑ RR, ↓ BP, abdominal distention, etc.).
Anemia and bleeding: Impairment in oxygen transport due to a decreased erythropoietin production. Impairment in perfusion is due to increased workload from the chronic state of anemia.	**A**nemia and bleeding: (↑ HR, ↓ Hgb and Hct), check emesis for bleeding, and abdominal girth for internal bleeding; check for malnutrition. Monitor HR, BP, pulses, color of skin/ mucous membranes for trends.
Look at skin for dryness, flakiness, ecchymosis, yellow-gray due to toxins and/or uremic frost; pruritus.	**L**ook at skin for dryness, flakiness or ecchymosis; color: yellow-gray; pruritus.

Alteration with Renal Perfusion

Labs and Diagnostic Tests and Procedures

Labs	Diagnostics Tests/Procedures
Urinalysis: Hematuria, proteinuria	Ultrasound
Serum creatinine: Gradual ↑ over months to years for CKD exceeding 4 mg/dL. May be as high as 15 to 30 mg/dL	Kidneys, ureter and bladder (KUB)
BUN: Gradual ↑ with increased serum creatinine over months to years for CKD. May be as high as 180 to 200 mg/dL	Computerized tomography (CT)
Serum electrolytes: ↓ sodium (dilutional), ↓ Calcium, Increased potassium, phosphorus, and magnesium	Magnetic resonance imaging (MRI) without contrast dye
CBC: ↓ hemoglobin and hematocrit from anemia secondary to loss of erythropoietin in CRF	Cystoscopy
↓ Urinary creatinine clearance	Aortorenal angiography
	Retrograde pyelography
	Kidney biopsy

INSANELY EASY TIP!

Increase: Potassium, Phosphorus, Magnesium, BUN, Creatinine, Sodium high but is (dilutional)

Decreased: Calcium, Hemoglobin/Hematocrit

Phosphorus and Calcium are **inversely related:**
when **Phosphorus is** ↑, **Calcium is** ↓!

Alteration with Renal Perfusion

Renal Lab Review

The kidneys regulate fluid, acid-base, and electrolyte balance, while also eliminating wastes from the body. The filtration occurs in the glomerulus via a semipermeable membrane. When the pressure gradients from the glomerular capillaries across the semipermeable membrane to the glomerulus are altered, changes in the glomerular filtration rate (GFR) occur. GFR < 15 mL/min indicates kidney failure. Refer to the image of the trampoline below. *Notice, the majority of the semi-permeable membrane (top of the trampoline) is colored in, indicating it is not working effectively. This will result in the lack of ability to regulate the acid-base and fluid and electrolyte balance.*

As a result of changes in the semipermeable membrane, these values are jumping up which can lead to physiological complications from the changes in the acid-base balance and electrolyte imbalance. While the sodium does increase, the value may appear low due to the extra fluid making it dilutional. The calcium and hemoglobin/hematocrit look as if they are falling off the trampoline. Calcium got low. Hyperparathyroidism causes hyperphosphatemia resulting in hypocalcemia. A tip to remember is that calcium and phosphorus are inversely related. The outcome could be broken bones! The hemoglobin and hematocrit are low due to the lack of production of the erythropoietin. The image below will illustrate these to assist you in transferring this into your long-term memory.

Lab Changes With Chronic Renal Failure

SAFETY: Concept Renal Perfusion
Chronic Renal "FAILURE": Multiple Concepts

System-Specific Assessment "RENAL"	First-Do Priority Interventions "FAILURE"	Evaluation of Expected Outcomes "RENAL"

Respiratory status: ↑ RR, (Kussmaul respirations), ↑ BP, Temp, dyspnea
 	
Electrolyte imbalances: (K⁺, Ca⁺⁺, PO₄, Na⁺); check for muscle cramps; evaluate metabolic acidosis; ECG; edema; fluid overload
 	
  Emotional: assess coping skills and family/social support
 	
Neurological changes: CNS depressed; headache, weakness, seizures
Nutrition review
 	
Anemia and bleeding: (↑ HR, color of skin/lips, mucous membranes, ↓ Hgb and Hct), check emesis for bleeding, and abdominal girth for internal bleeding; check for malnutrition
 	
Look for dryness, flakiness, ecchymosis, yellow-gray due to toxins and/or uremic frost; pruritus
	Fluid overload (*Refer to Fluid Overload in this chapter*).
	
	Anemia, fatigue (*Refer to Oxygenation in this chapter*).
	
	Immobility complications (*Refer to concept Mobility for specifics*).
	  Integumentary (*Refer to concept Tissue Integrity for specifics*).
	
	Look for infection—T, HR, RR, color of secretions, ↑ WBC, etc. (*Refer to concept Infection Control for specifics*). Adhere to meticulous cleaning of areas on skin that are not intact and access sites to control infections.
	
	Understand need for emotional support! Look for depression, etc. (*Refer to concept Coping for specifics.*)
	
	Review nutritional needs (*Refer to Nutrition in this chapter*). Review importance of managing diabetes mellitus if client has medical condition. Uncontrolled diabetes is a major risk for developing chronic renal disease.
	
	Electrolyte imbalances (*Refer to Electrolyte Imbalances in this chapter*).
		Respirations WDL for client with no Temp, no dyspnea, or Kussmaul respirations.
		
		Electroytes are analyzed and evaluated based on the client's normal baseline. Trends are not indicating any major changes or complications out of the client's normal baseline; free of muscle cramps and/or bone pain.
		
		Neurological assessments are stable and within the norm for the client. Client is coping.
		Nutrition: weight is WDL for client
		
		Anemia (Hgb, Hct, VS) within client's norm, no active bleeding noted. Color of skin/lips, mucous membranes is pink.
		
		Looking at skin indicates no complications with ecchymosis, dryness, and/or pruritus.

Alteration with Renal Perfusion
Chronic Renal Failure Medication Review

<table>
<tr><td>

Medications for Clients with Renal Disease

Digoxin (Lanoxin)

Erythropoietin alfa (Epogen, Procrit)

Ferrous Sulfate (Feosol)

Aluminum hydroxide gel (Amphogel)

Furosemide (Lasix)

Kayexalate

</td><td>

Medications to Avoid with Renal Disease

Ace Inhibitors (PRILS)

Angiotensin II Receptor Blockers (ARBS)

Aldactone

Potassium Supplements

NSAIDS

Avoid antimicrobial medications that are nephrotoxic
Aminoglycosides (Streptomycin, Gentamycin, etc.)
Amphotericin

Avoid sedatives and hypnotics due to decrease ability to metabolize and excrete.

Avoid contrast dyes, which are nephrotoxic. Tests that end in "**GRAM**" require dyes.

</td></tr>
</table>

Concept Fluid & Electrolyte Imbalance from Chronic Renal Failure

Hypervolemia (Extracellular Fluid Volume Excess)	Hyperkalemia > 5.0 mEq/L	Hyponatremia < 135 mEq/L (dilutional)	Hyperphosphatemia/ Hypocalcemia	Hypermagnesemia	BUN and Creatinine are elevated Metabolic Acidosis
• Altered renin-angiotensin system. • GFR < 15 mL/min. **1 kg = 2.2 lbs. daily weight increase is approximately 1 L of fluid retained**	• Acidosis accentuates hyper-kalemia • Decreased urinary excretion	• Sodium low due to being diluted from fluid retention	• Hyperpara-thyroidism results in hypocalcemia and an increase in the phosphorus level. • Renal disease affects the parathyroid hormone (PTH) from the para-thyroid glands and calcitonin from the thyroid. Calcitonin moves Ca^{++} into bone; PTH shifts Ca^{++} from bone into the ECF. • ↑ Phosphate (PO_4) $= ↓ Ca^{++}$; bone demineralization (renal osteodystrophy). • Hypothyroidism.	• Mildly elevated levels are found early in the disease. Client does not reach a dangerous level unless the client is receiving magnesium-containing laxatives or antacids.	• BUN and serum creatinine increase as waste products of protein metabolism accumulate in the blood. The serum creatinine is the most accurate measure of renal function. • Kidneys lose ability to compensate for acid overload; thus, H^+ ions are not excreted, nor is HCO_3 retained in normal amounts. • Accumulation of acid waste products. • Compensation/ Correction: respiratory system increases rate and depth of RR to blow off CO_2 and increase the pH.

Concept Fluid and Electrolytes:

Fluid Volume Exesss (Hypervolemia) from Chronic Renal Failure

First-Do Priority Interventions

"RESTRICT"

An **INSANELY EASY** approach to remember the priority care for clients with hypervolemia is to begin with **AIRWAY**! If fluid gets in those lungs, this will not be a good thing. It would be best to prevent this from occurring by **reducing the IV flow rate**, monitoring the **I & O and daily weight**. To promote optimal **oxygenation**, position in the **semi-Fowler's position** and assess those breath sounds on going along with the HR and RR. If the fluid retention continues to increase, there will be extra workload on the heart that may result in hypertension. This may be the time that the client needs a little extra help in diuresing, so it may be appropriate to get a prescription for **a diuretic**.

Skin integrity could also be a major challenge to this client due to the extra fluid and low protein. There may also be peripheral edema. The client may feel so poorly that he/she does not have energy to move in bed. It may be important for the nurse to provide this assistance. Assess the skin for any color or **circulation** changes or edema. The last thing any client needs is to develop a decubitus. Remember **to turn and reposition** and always assess!!!

There you have it in the nutshell! "**ABCDEF**"!

Airway

Breath sounds, BP

Control I & O

Decrease risk for complications with alteration in skin integrity; **D**aily weight

Electrolyte: Sodium will be dilutional (< 135 mEq/L) due to the extra fluid

Fluid restriction!

Reduce IV flow rate.

Evaluate breath sounds, HR, RR, BP, and ABGs, LOC.

Semi-Fowler's position.

Treat with oxygen, diuretics, antihypertensives; dialysis as ordered. Teach about meds.

Reduce fluid and sodium intake; Restrict fluid to 600 to 1000 mL/day; adjust to urinary output and/or dialysis.

I & O and daily weight.

Circulation, color, and presence of edema–assess.

Turn and position (promote skin integrity) per protocol. Teach how to distribute fluid over the day.

Concept Fluid and Electrolytes: Hyponatremia (Dilutional) from Chronic Renal Failure ↑ Fluid Volume = ↓ Na⁺ (due to dilutional factor) Na⁺ < 135 mEq/L		
System-Specific Assessments "EDEMA"	**First-Do Priority Interventions "RESTRICT"**	**Evaluation of Expected Outcomes "EDEMA"**
Edema (pitting) **D**ecrease in the hematocrit **E**levated weight; I & O; elevated BP, HR, RR **E**valuate serum Na⁺ **M**entation decreased (lethargic, seizures) **A** flushing of the skin	**R**estrict fluid based on output and sodium intake. **E**valuate for cerebral changes such as headache, nausea; evaluate for seizures. **S**eizure precautions (*Refer to Concept Intracranial Regulation for specifics*); fall precautions. **T**he blood pressure is elevated (fluid excess); the VS need to be monitored; I & O. **R**educe fluid and sodium intake; Restrict fluid to 600 to 1000 mL; adjust to urinary output and/or dialysis; low-sodium diet (nothing in a bag, bottle, can, or box)! **I** & O (strict); due to risk of constipation include bran / fiber in diet; stool softener. Include oral hygiene. **C**heck daily weight. **T**he excess fluid may be removed by diuretics/dialysis; teach client foods low in Na⁺.	**E**dema (pitting)–**none** **D**ecrease in the hematocrit– Hematocrit WDL **E**levated weight; elevated BP, HR, RR; serum Na⁺ 135-145 mEq/L–All are within defined limits **M**entation decreased (lethargic, seizures)–no changes; WDL **A** flushing of the skin–**none**

Concept Fluid and Electrolytes: Hyperphosphatemia/Hypocalcemia from Chronic Renal Failure Serum Phosphorus > 4.5mg/dL(or 2.6mEq/L) Serum Calcium < 9.0 mg/dL		
System-Specific Assessments "TWITCH"	**First-Do Priority Interventions "SAFE"**	**Evaluation of Expected Outcomes "TWITCH"**
Trousseau's Sign (hand/finger spasms)	**S**eizure precautions; environmental stimuli ↓.	**T**rousseau's Sign (hand/finger spasms). **NO Trousseau's sign**
Watch for dysrhythmias (pulse, prolonged ST segment, prolonged QT interval on ECG)	**A**dminister calcium supplements; phosphate binders (stool softener since Amphogel can lead to constipation). Teach to take with meals to bind phosphate in food and stop phosphate absorption. Teach client about constipation.	**W**atch for dysrhythmias (pulse, prolonged ST segment and QT interval on ECG); **NO dysrhythmias**
Increase in anorexia, nausea and/or vomiting		**I**ncrease in anorexia, nausea, vomiting; **No anorexia, nausea, or vomiting**
Tetany, twitching, seizures	**F**oods high in calcium (i.e., dairy, green); educate.	**T**etany, twitching, seizures. **NONE**
Chvostek's sign (facial twitching)	**E**mergency equipment on standby; evaluate for bone disorder (osteomalacia); careful with bones.	**C**hvostek's sign (facial twitching)– **NONE**
Hypotension, hyperactive DTR		**H**ypotension, hyperactive DTR. **No hypotension or hyperactive DTR**

Concept Acid-Base Imbalance: Metabolic Acidosis from Chronic Renal Failure pH < 7.35; HCO$_3$ < 22 mmHg		
System-Specific Assessments "Ds"	**First-Do Priority Interventions "RESPIRATE"**	**Evaluation of Expected Outcomes "Ds"**
Deep, rapid respirations (Kussmaul)– compensatory action by the lungs **D**iarrhea, nausea, vomiting **D**ecreased BP **D**ysrhythmias related to hyperkalemia **D**rowsiness, disorientation, headache, seizures	**R**eview initially to determine underlying problem in order to manage. Review ABGs and keep HCP informed. HCP may need to start dialysis if client becomes to acidotic and/or electrolytes elevate to a dangerous level. Review weight ongoing. **E**valuate RR and support to promote compensation for the metabolic acidosis. **S**aO$_2$, pH, and HCO$_3$ levels should be monitored; seizure precautions. **P**lace on ECG monitor and evaluate for dysrhythmias from hyperkalemia. **I**ntake and output records should be maintained. **R**eview weight of client. **A**ssess renal function and hydration status. If client has diabetes mellitus, evaluate for ketoacidosis, and administer insulin accordingly. **T**each client rationale for nursing care and meds. **E**valuate lab values for hyperkalemia; renal function tests; ketones.	**D**eep, rapid respirations (Kussmaul)–compensatory action by the lungs. **NO Kussmaul** **D**iarrhea, nausea, vomiting–**None** **D**ecreased BP. **BP WDL** **D**ysrhythmias related to hyperkalemia. **No dysrhythmias** **D**rowsiness, disorientation, headache, seizures. **No symptoms**

Concept Altered Oxgenation (Anemia) from Chronic Renal Failure

Anemia is defined as an abnormally low number of circulating red blood cells (RBCs), low level of hemoglobin, or both. There are three causes of anemia, but the focus here is the cause from a reduction in the amount of erythropoietin, which normally stimulates the bone marrow to produce red blood cells. Chronic renal failure is a common cause of decreased erythropoietin production. The kidneys are involved in producing red blood cells. As a result, clients can develop anemia that does not respond to iron intake due to the insufficient erythropoietin levels, a protein based hormone. Due to the loss of carrier proteins, iron deficiency anemia may also be experienced with clients who have CKD. As a result of anemia, there is an increase workload on the heart because of less oxygenated blood.

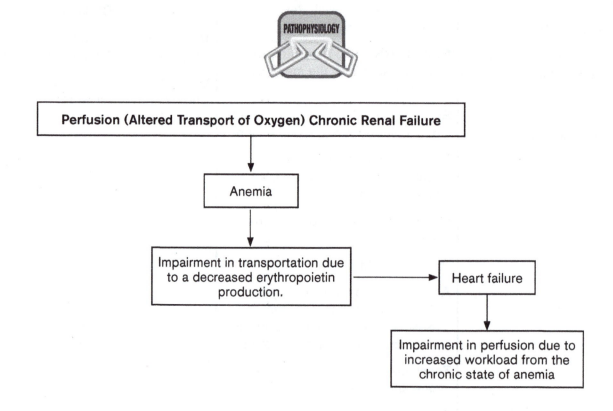

Concept Oxygenation (Altered Transport) from Chronic Renal Failure

Concept Oxygenation (Altered Transport of Oxygen) from Chronic Renal Failure		
System-Specific Assessments "TIRED"	**First-Do Priority Interventions "ENERGY"**	**Evaluation of Expected Outcomes "TIRED"**
Tachycardia **I**rritable (anxious) **R**espirations increased **E**valuate for bleeding **D**ecrease in color (pale), O_2 sat, BP	**E**rythropoietin (Epogen, Procrit, Aranesp). **N**ote any signs of bleeding (GI, bruising, etc.). **E**ncourage intake of folic acid (1 mg daily); iron supplement (stool softener; take with food); evaluate hemoglobin and hematocrit, BP. **R**eview vital sigs for signs of hypoxia from decrease in perfusion. **G**ive blood transfusions if ordered and per protocol; give iron supplement (stool softener to ↓ constipation; take with food). **Y**es, support client if anxious and organize care around client's activity tolerance.	**T**achycardia **No tachycardia, HR WDL** **I**rritable (anxious) **No irritability** **R**espirations increased **RR WDL** **E**valuate for bleeding–**No bleeding** **D**ecrease in color (pale), O_2 sat, BP **Color pink, O_2 sat > 95%, BP WDL**

Concept Nutrition for Chronic Renal Failure

Nutrition is altered because of the organ damage that affects the metabolism of nutrients; for example, in the common condition of chronic kidney disease (CKD), nutritional status is adversely impacted through a variety of mechanisms. Protein is lost through the urine and can cause hypoalbuminemia that, in turn, can lead to impaired skin integrity, impaired wound healing, suppressed immunity, sarcopenia, and generalized edema (such as with anasarca), leading to altered osmotic pressure. As CKD progresses, phosphorus levels can increase, resulting in hypocalcemia. Renal disease will further reduce nutrient levels, such as vitamin D due to an impaired ability to metabolize vitamin D_2 into the active D_3 form. With the decrease in the vitamin D status, bone health is impacted because vitamin D is required to absorb calcium into bones. Bone-mineral disease (BMD) is common with CKD. Medical nutrition therapy (MNT) that is used to manage CKD can have adverse nutritional consequences attributable to limitations on food intake and corresponding nutrients with protein and potassium restrictions. This is especially true when CKD is compounded with an acute illness (Dumler, 2011). (*Refer to chapter on Nutrition regarding specific foods for each dietary need.*)

Concept: NUTRITION for CRF (High Carbohydrates and Moderate in Fat)						
Hypoalbuminemia	↑ Phosphorus ↓ Calcium	Low Vitamin D	↓ Erythropoietin	Constipation	↑ Serum, Glucose & Lipids	Medical Nutrition Therapy due to pathophysiology of the CKD
• Impaired skin integrity • Impaired wound healing • Suppressed immunity • Anasarca (due to altered osmotic pressure)	• Ca^{++} shift from ECF into Bone or physiologically unavailable form. • Hyperphosphatemia leads to ↓ Ca = bone disease.	• Impaired ability to metabolize vitamin D • Decrease in bone health • (Bone mineral disease)	• Anemia	• Antacids, Ferrous Sulfate, & Amphogel can result in constipation	• Monitor and ↓ foods ↑ glucose and lipids	• ↓ Sodium • ↓ Phosphate • ↓ Potassium • ↓ Magnesium • RESTRICT Protein
Dietary Needs						
Protein should be RESTRICTED; may vary from just a decrease in protein intake to a specific restriction of 20 to 40 g/day. Protein should be of a high biologic value (1.2 to 1.3 g/kg); this assists with the utilization of the amino acids and results in formation of fewer nitrogen waste products. Increase carbohydrates and moderate in fat.	INCREASE calcium intake. RESTRICT phosphorus-rich foods; take aluminum hydroxide gel (Amphogel) to bind phosphate in food and stop phosphate absorption.	INCREASE foods rich in Vitamin D.	INCREASE foods rich in Folic Acid.	INCREASE bran and fiber diet. Administer stool softeners.	DECREASE glucose/ lipids.	RESTRICT foods high in sodium, phosphate, potassium (avoid salt substitutes), magnesium. Avoid antacids containing magnesium. Protein should be restricted; may vary from just a decrease in protein intake to a specific restriction of 20 to 40 g/day. Protein should be of a high biologic value (1.2 to 1.3 g/kg); this assists with the utilization of the amino acids and results in formation of fewer nitrogen waste products.

Summary: Alteration in Renal Perfusion from Chronic Renal "FAILURE"

Concepts	Increased	Decreased	Nursing Care
Fluid Volume Excess			
Fluid volume excess due to alteration in the elimination from renal failure	X		Weigh, Intake and output, neurological assessments, and vital signs. Review importance of monitoring fluid intake. Remember a 1 Kg or 2.2 lbs weight gain is 1 Liter of fluid retained! Limit the fluid and sodium intake. (*Refer to chapter on concept for Fluid Balance for more specific interventions.*)
Altered Electrolyte Balance			
Hyponatremia (Dilutional)			Refer to above for managing fluids. Limit sodium intake.
Hyperkalemia	X		Monitor cardiac monitor for tall or peaked T waves/dysrhythmias; diarrhea; and/or any muscle twitching. Refer to medication and nutrition chart regarding medications and foods to limit with chronic renal failure. Teach client importance of not using salt substitutes with food due to high potassium.
Metabolic Acidosis			Monitor for dysrhythmias. May need to start dialysis per protocol for progression of acidosis. Evaluate RR and support to promote compensation due to metabolic acidosis. Place on ECG monitor and evaluate for dysrhythmias from hyperkalemia. Evaluate labs for hyperkalemia. Monitor BUN, creatinine, and arterial blood gases. Monitor for signs of gout due to elevated uric acid. (*Refer to chapter on Concept for Acid Base Balance for more specific interventions.*)
Immobility	X		Range of motion. Provide protective devices to prevent injury. Stool softeners due to risk of constipation from immobility. Due to a reduction of calcium from the increase phosphate in clients with renal disease, this bone demineralization results in a risk for bone injury.
Integrity, Tissue/Skin	X		Decrease irritation from pruritus. Keep fingernails clipped to prevent injury to the skin from scratching. Assess for skin breakdown due to fluid retention from and uremic frost. (Refer to the chapter Tissue/Skin Integrity for specific care.)
Look for Infection Leukocytosis	X		Monitor for signs of infection. Infection control precautions! (Transmission-based precautions.)
Understand Client's Need to Cope	X		Emotional support! Encourage client to ventilate thoughts and feelings.
Review Nutrition			Carbohydrates may need to be increased for energy. (Refer to chapter on Nutrition Balance for specifics.) Will require a low sodium, potassium, and protein diet.
Evaluate Oxygenation Fluid Retention (risk for progression to pulmonary edema) Heart failure (Due to fluid overload) Anemia (Erythropoietin) Risk for GI bleeding from ulcers		X	Assess breath sounds q 4 hours or per hospital protocol; O_2 saturation, RR. Could progress to pulmonary edema. Assist with turning, coughing and deep breathing. Assess ↑ HR, ↑ BP, ↑ RR, ↑ CVP, ↑ PAWP (*Refer to chapter on Perfusion/Shock for specifics on CVP and PAWP*) weights, Intake and & Output. Assess cardiac sounds. S3 may be present. (*Refer to chapter on Concept for Cardiac/Perfusion for more specific interventions.*) Administer erythropoietin due to a decrease in the renal system's ability to manufacture red blood cells. Assess for bleeding. Support risk for ulcers with appropriate food (Refer to chapter on Nutrition/Balance). **Avoid magnesium-based antacids** due to risk for toxicity from renal disease. (*Refer to chapter Gastrointestinal/Biliary System for specific management.*)

Insanely Easy Summary of Concept: Alteration in Renal Perfusion from Chronic Renal Failure

The image below is a fun, easy tool to assist you in remembering many of the body systems affected by chronic renal failure. The image to have in your mind is that with renal failure the semipermeable membrane in the glomerulus is no longer effective. When the pressure gradients from the glomerular capillaries across the semipermeable membrane to the glomerulus are altered, changes in the glomerular filtration rate (GFR) occur. GFR < 15 mL/min indicates kidney failure. Now refer to the trampoline below. Notice, the semi-permeable membrane (top of the trampoline) is colored in, indicating it is not working effectively. This will result in the lack of ability to regulate the acid-base and fluid and electrolyte balance.

As a result of these changes in the semipermeable membrane, multiple body systems are affected by chronic renal failure requiring specific nursing care. While the majority of the care was discussed in the previous chart, we thought it would be fun to link this to a simple image. This content can seem overwhelming; however, if you can move it into the long-term memory by using an image, it will remain in your memory bank for both future nursing practice and nursing exams. *The next page provides you with a review of this concept. See how many blanks you are able to complete. Remember, the key to learning is to link nursing care to pathophysiology.*

Let's Practice What You Have Learned!
Refer to the image on page 480.

1. Do you see the image of the ECG monitor? The cardiac assessment is important because of ___
_____! (*Answer: Remember, hyperkalemia can result in peaked T waves resulting in lethal dysrhythmias.*) Fluid overload can result in an elevation in the heart rate and workload, which can lead to heart failure causing decrease in perfusion (*this represents the broken heart under the trampoline—see page 480*).

2. Let's move to the image with fluid in the lungs. Pulmonary edema can result from fluid overload from renal failure. This may also indicate a complication with left sided heart failure (a complication with afterload). What nursing care would be important with this alteration in oxygenation?_____ (*Answer: Remember, some of the basic care such as deep breathing, moving, coughing; assessing those breath sounds; assessing the O$_2$ saturation; limiting fluid intake, diuretic, etc.*) Does this sound familiar? *It is all about the concept of altered oxygenation! In realty, this is nothing new!*

3. Did you see the swollen ankles on the top right side of the image? What is the pathophysiology for this edema?_____ (*Answer: Absolutely, fluid retention from the renal system not working.*) *Skin care is important!*

4. The swollen big toe is due to the increase in uric acid crystals resulting in gout.

5. Why is there a hand scratching the arm?_____
(*Answer: The uremic frost that can occur from renal disease can result in pruritus.*) *Skin care is also important here to prevent skin breakdown.*

6. What is the reason for the broken bone on the trampoline?_____
(*Answer: The hyperparathyroid results in hypocalcemia. This lack of calcium can contribute to broken bones! Safety is a priority in preventing complications!*)

7. Let's move directly under the broken bone on the trampoline to the Bran Cereal. Why would this be included in the care for a client with renal failure?_____
(*Answer: Immobilization can result in constipation. Bran is important to assist in preventing this complication.*)

8. What is the reason for orange juice, salt substitutes, salt image?_____
(*Answer: Clients with renal failure should be on a low potassium and sodium diet.*) *While the sodium level may be dilutional, it would be unsafe to add sodium to the diet since this may contribute to additional fluid retention.*

Look how you are linking the concepts!

Pathophysiology: Glomerular Inflammatory Reaction
Glomerulonephritis

Glomerulonephritis has many types to include nephrotic syndrome. The specific type is diagnosed through clinical findings and a renal biopsy. The elderly client is at greater risk for renal damage. **Acute Glomerulonephritis** occurs when immune complexes are trapped in glomerular capillary loop, which leads to obstruction, edema, and vasospasm. Then an antigen-antibody reaction occurs from infectious agent (most often group A beta-hemolytic streptococcal) and activates the WBCs increasing the inflammation of the glomerular capillary wall. Immune complexes then develop and become trapped in the glomerular capillary loop resulting in swelling and in a decrease in the glomerular filtration rate (GFR). The GFR is the ability of the glomerular filter to remove wastes and excess fluids. The renal clinical findings usually occur 10–21 days after original infection. Most individuals recover completely, but recurrence may occur and it can be acute, chronic, or latent. Individuals at risk have histories of systemic lupus erythematous, hypertension, diabetes, or have taken nephrotoxic drugs (Black & Hawk, 2009).

    Chronic Glomerulonephritis can occur without any previous history of acute glomerulonephritis. It is a slow progressive destruction of the glomeruli and hardening. It is one of the major causes of end-stage renal disease.

	FIRST-DO PRIORITY INTERVENTIONS			
SYSTEM-SPECIFIC ASSESSMENTS "TEAS"	DIET	EQUIPMENT	PLANS/INTERVENTIONS "FILTER"	HEALTH PROMOTION
Tea or cola-colored urine from hematuria **E**dema (facial and periorbital) **E**levated BP; I & O **A**cute glomerulonephritis may be mild with proteinuria and/or asymptomatic hematuria; alteration (decrease) in urine output. Azotemia: presence of nitrogenous waste products in the blood **S**ymptoms with chronic glomerulonephritis reflect progressive renal failure; more common in adults	• Decrease in sodium intake. • Protein restriction if client is azotemic. • During oliguric phase, foods containing large amount of potassium are frequently restricted.	• Catheter • Dipstick for urine tests	**F**luid balance: monitor I & O; BP; check proteinuria, specific gravity, and color of urine; weigh client daily; if has hypertension, check blood pressure q 2 to 4 hours. **I**nfection: antibiotic therapy if cultures are positive. When client does not feel well, then he/she will restrict own activity. **L**ethargic; limit activity and encourage rest. **T**o protect from infections. **E**ducate client/family how to prevent UTIs & respiratory infections; diet, fluid needs, and medication therapy. Teach how to dipstick urine to monitor for protein. Evaluate serum K+ levels. **R**eassure and provide comfort to client and/or family; review progress. Many times the first sign of improvement is an increase in the urine output that may progress to profuse diuresis.	• Avoid drugs that are nephrotoxic such as aminoglycosides. • Dietary changes. • Infection control precautions. • Teach skin care, importance of a daily weight. Report weight gains of greater than 2 lbs. per day or 5 lbs. per week. Discuss the importance of ongoing blood pressure checks and when to report. • Watch for signs of infection, increased temperature, ↑ WBCs (*Refer to Concept Infection Control for specifics*). • Educate regarding importance of taking full prescription of antibiotics if client has an infection to prevent glomerulonephritis.

Pathophysiology: Protein Wasting Secondary to Glomerular Damage

Nephrotic Syndrome

Nephrotic Syndrome is a group of clinical manifestations caused by protein wasting due to glomerular damage. The damaged glomerular capillaries now permeable to the protein, results in increased serum protein in the urine and hypoabuminemia. This in turn causes decreased serum osmotic pressure and fluid moves from the vascular system into the interstitial spaces resulting in edema. This movement of fluids stimulates the renin system with increased production of aldosterone. This adds to the extracellular fluid volume as the kidneys hold on to sodium and water. The causes of nephrotic syndrome are many to include diabetes, immunological disorders, chronic illnesses, reactions to medications and decrease renal function that comes with age. The major challenge is the edema that becomes massive with protein losses in the urine as high as 4–30 grams per day (Black & Hawk, 2009).

SYSTEM-SPECIFIC ASSESSMENTS "EDEMA"	DIET	EQUIPMENT	PLANS/INTERVENTIONS "PROTEINS"	HEALTH PROMOTION
Edema: periorbital edema, more in A.M. and subsides during the day; generalized edema of the lower extremities may increase during the day. May progress to more generalized edema (anasarca)	Need high calories, low Na+. Proteins consumed should have high biologic value (low to moderate protein diet). The degree of protein and Na+ restriction will depend on amount client is excreting.	• Dipstick for checking urine for protein and the specific gravity	**P**rotect from protein loss—determine weight daily; measure abdominal girth/test urine with dipstick for protein; check specific gravity.	• Dietary changes.
Decrease in urine output (foamy and tea colored)			**R**eview fluid and electrolytes; Monitor cardiac functions for complications from edema while still being hypovolemic.	• Infection control precautions.
Elevation in the weight			**O**utput and Intake—monitor.	• Teach skin care, importance of a daily weight. Report weight gains of greater than 2 lbs. per day or 5 lbs. per week.
Malnourishment: child may have a decrease intake and loss of protein (edema may mask the malnutrition)			**T**hrombosis: Due to risk of renal vein thrombosis, some clients may be given anticoagulation therapy. Teach how to monitor for hemorrhage and carry identification that lists the drugs.	• Watch for signs of infection, increased temperature, WBCs (*Refer to Concept Infection Control for specifics*).
Mood–Irritable, fatigue, lethargic			**E**dema (reduced) by: salt-poor albumin; monitor for circulatory overload when administering.	
An infection can result in morbidity or mortality			**I**nfection is prevented. Client is highly susceptible to infection due to a compromised immune state in addition to being on steroids. Assess breath sounds; perform good pulmonary hygiene; protect from respiratory infections.	
			Nutrition–promote: encourage low to moderate protein intake of high biologic value; serve frequent small quantities of food to client. Decrease sodium intake.	
			Skin care and keep opposing surfaces on skin dry; alter client positions frequently.	

FIRST-DO   PRIORITY   INTERVENTIONS

Exceptions and Additions by Diseases

Similarities between Glomerulonephritis and Nephrotic Syndrome

System-Specific Assessments: Although the pathophysiological reasons are different, the system-specific assessments are similar for these two medical diagnoses. The concepts of maintenance of fluid and electrolyte balance and nutrition are important in both. Below is a way to remember the assessments for these two disorders. The diets and plans of care that are similar are included in the chart.

SYSTEM-SPECIFIC ASSESSMENTS "RENAL"	FIRST-DO PRIORITY INTERVENTIONS			
	DIET	EQUIPMENT	PLANS/INTERVENTIONS	HEALTH PROMOTION
Renal Symptoms: ↓ GFR, ↓ urine, urine smoky and coffee colored, dysuria, hematuria, proteinuria, electrolyte imbalance, report oliguria to HCP ASAP **E**dema from Fluid Volume Excess, ↑ NA⁺, ↓ albumin: periorbital, lower extremities, ascites, distended neck veins, adventitious lung sounds, SOB **N**ote ↑ BP (due to increase extracellular fluid), ↑ RR, (fluid in lungs) dyspnea, orthopnea, ↑ Temp with acute (AGN) **N**euro status: Adults– changes in level of consciousness, (children: behavior changes) **N**eed skin assessment due to massive edema **A**ppetite decrease, anorexia, diet restrictions difficult to comply with **A**ssess coping and emotional status of dealing with long term illness **L**ethargic, decrease activity, irritable, pale in color	• Monitor Albumin and pre-albumin for nutritional state. • Need high calories, low Na⁺ and low protein while kidneys are recovering, (the degree of protein and NA⁺ restriction will depend on amount client is excreting. • Monitor ↓ GFR and ↑ BUN, Creatinine (azotemia) • Refer to concept on Nutrition for specifics	• IV pump • Urinary catheter	• Plan: Implement interventions for Fluid Volume Excess. (*Refer to concept on Fluid and Electrolytes: Fluid Volume Excess for specifics.*) • Treat pain per orders. (*Refer to concept on Pain for specifics.*) • **Strict bed rest during acute stage** to decrease metabolic demands and reduce catabolic activity, hematuria and proteinuria. Skin care: turn and change position to prevent breakdown. (*Refer to concept Skin and Tissue Integrity for specifics.*)	• Instruct client to reduce fluids, (24 hour output + 500 ml or per protocol), weigh daily and compare weight, report weight gains of greater than 2 lbs. per day or 5 lbs. per week. (*Refer to concept on Fluid and Electrolytes: Fluid Volume Excess for specifics.*) • Watch for signs of infection, increased temperature, WBCs. (*Refer to concept on Infection Control for Specifics.*)

Exceptions and Additions by Diseases

Hemodialysis for Chronic Renal Failure

HEMODIALYSIS: Shunts the blood of the client through a dialyzer and returns back into circulation. **Vascular access must be established.** Hemodialysis is a process to initiate the passage of particles (ions) from an area of increased concentration to an area of lower concentration across the semi-permeable membrane. In hemodialysis, the semipermeable membrane used as pores that are large enough for waste products and water to transport through. These pores are, however, too small for blood cells and protein molecules to pass through.

INDICATIONS	PRE-PROCEDURE	EDUCATION	HOMEOSTASIS AFTER HEMODIALYSIS "VASCULAR"	COMPLICATIONS "CHAIR"
• BUN > 120 mg/dL • Uncontrolled hypertension, uremia, and metabolic acidosis • GFR < 15 mL/min • Serum potassium level > 6 mEq/L • Serum fluid volume overload	• Check for an informed consent. Use the temporary dual- or triple-lumen catheter, or subcutaneous device until a long-term device is inserted and able to be accessed for procedure. • Patency of a long-term device—arteriovenous (AV) fisula or arteriovenous graft—can be assessed by palpating a thrill or hearing a bruit, assessing distal pulses, and circulation. • **Remember:** Hear a bruit or feel a thrill! If present, shunt is patent. **No blood pressures, medication administration, venipunctures or insertion of IV sits on arm with an access site. Elevate extremity after the procedure of the AV fistula to decrease edema.** • Assess base line vital signs, weight, laboratory values (i.e., BUN, serum creatinine, Hct, serum Na^+, K^+, Phosphorus) • Hold meds prior to to dialysis, which include dialyzable meds, antihypertensive meds and/or diuretics.	• Review with client that hemodialysis is typically done three times/week. The sessions may last for 3–5 hrs.	**V**ascular access site assess **A**ssess weight **S**ounds: heart **C**ommon side effects: ↓ BP, headache, muscle cramps **U**nusual bleeding from access site **L**ung sounds **A**ssess electrolytes and trend changes **R**eview and support client's emotions	Think of a "dialysis **CHAIR.**" **C**lotting/infection of site **H**ypotension **A**nemia **I**nfectious Diseases **R**apid ↓ of BUN/volume **Clotting/infection** may occur due to the anticoagulants that may be given to prevent blood clots from forming. Infections may occur at the site during cannulation. Surgical aseptic technique should be used with cannulation. **Hypotension** may occur as a result of rapid fluid depletion during dialysis. Replace volume with transfusion of IV fluids or colloid as prescribed. Decrease the dialysate exchange rate. Lower the HOB for client. If client becomes unresponsive, then discontinue dialysis. **Anemia** may occur as a result of loss of blood and folate removal during dialysis. Client already has anemia from ↓ erythropoietin secretion. **Infectious disease** such as HIV and Hepatitis B and C, sepsis may occur from frequent blood access for hemodialysis. Maintain sterility of equipment. **Rapid decrease** in BUN and volume: This may result in cerebral edema and increased intracranial pressure (also referred to as Disequilibrium syndrome. Early assessments include: nausea, vomiting, change in LOC, seizures.) To prevent, use a slow dialysis exchange rate.

INSANELY EASY TIP!
Hear a bruit or feel a thrill is a great way to remember how to evaluate the patency of the access site for an arteriovenous shunt.

Exceptions and Additions by Diseases

Peritoneal Dialysis for Chronic Renal Failure

PERITONEAL DIALYSIS: Infusion of hypertonic dialysate solution into the peritoneal cavity. This fluid will dwell in the peritoneal cavity as prescribed. The dialysate will then be drained which will include the waste products. The peritoneum serves as the membrane for filtration. The peritoneal membrane should be without adhesions from infection or surgeries.

INDICATIONS	PRE-PROCEDURE	INTRAPROCEDURE "PERITONEAL"	POST-PROCEDURE "TEACHES"	COMPLICATIONS "HOP"
• Adults who are older–treatment of choice • Anticoagulants–client is unable to tolerate • Access with vascular site is difficult • A chronic infection/unstable	• Assess weight (assess when dialysate is drained), serum electrolytes, creatinine, serum glucose, and BUN. • Assess ability of client to perform self-peritoneal dialysis. (alert, experience with dialysis, knowledge) • Assess knowledge about procedure and instruct as needed. Explain about the feeling of fullness when dialysis is the phase of dwelling. There may be some discomfort initially. • Continuous ambulatory peritoneal dialysis (CAPD) is typically done 7 days a week for 4 to 8 hours. Continuation of normal activities are encouraged during CAPD. • Continuous-cycle peritoneal dialysis (CCPD) is a 24-hour dialysis. When client is sleeping is when exchange occurs. Final exchange dwells throughout the day. • Automated peritoneal dialysis (APD) is a 30-minute exchange repeated over 8 to 10 hours while sleeping.	**P**rovide emotional support. **E**valuate vital signs. **R**eview the serum glucose inflow; record amount compared to outflow of dialysate. **I**ntake and output–monitor. **T**he color/amount of dialysate; assess. **O**bserve for complications: abdominal pain, respiratory complications, discolored outflow, decreased outflow. **N**ote if site dressing is wet. **E**valuate if fibrin clot has formed and if so, carefully milk peritoneal dialysis catheter. **A**void use of microwaves when warming the dialysate; asepsis of the catheter insertion site and when accessing catheter. **L**ook to follow prescribed times for infusing, dwelling, and outflowing. Lower the outflow bag below the client's abdomen (drain by gravity).	**T**each about home care of site. **E**ducate how to perform peritoneal dialysis; emotional support. **A**ssess weight, electrolytes, creatinine, BUN, serum glucose. **C**ognitive or physical deficits may prevent older client from performing peritoneal dialysis. **H**as body image changes from bloating (may occur). **E**ssential minerals and vitamins with supplements of phosphorus, calcium, sodium, potassium. **S**eek information from the National Kidney Foundation for local support groups.	**H**yperglycemia/Hyperlipidemia **O**utflow/inflow of dialysate is poor **P**eritonitis/Protein loss **Hyperglycemia** can result from the hyperosmolarity of the dialysis. Glucose may be absorbed from the dialysate. **Hyperlipidemia** may occur from long time in therapy with a result of hypertension. Nursing Action: Monitor serum glucose; administer insulin and antilipemic meds for triglycerides. **Outflow/inflow** may become a problem if the tubing becomes obstructed. Constipation can also cause outflow / inflow problems. Reposition client. Check for kinks. Use a stool softener/fiber in diet. **Peritonitis** from micro-organisms in the peritoneum. Use surgical asepsis and monitor for infection. Protein may be lost from the blood along with excess fluid, wastes, & electrolytes. Monitor serum albumin.

Clinical Decision-Making Exercises

1. Which nursing actions should the nurse delegate to the unlicensed assistive personnel (UAP) for a client with renal failure who has a complication of "Fluid Volume Excess" related to compromised regulatory mechanisms? *Select all that apply.*

   ① Record vital signs every 4 hours.

   ② Weigh client every morning using standing scale.

   ③ Listen to breath sounds daily.

   ④ Teach client the importance of eating oranges and bananas.

   ⑤ Remind client to save all urine for intake and output record.

2. Which of these should be included in the plan of care for a client who has chronic kidney disease? *Select all that apply.*

   ① Assess for a flat T wave on the ECG monitor.

   ② Discuss the importance of using salt substitutes.

   ③ Encourage taking an NSAID for discomfort.

   ④ Review the importance of taking Aluminum hydroxide gel (Amphogel) with meals.

   ⑤ Review the importance of monitoring and reporting trends in weight gain.

3. Which of these lab reports should receive priority attention for a school-age-child with a diagnosis of secondary hyperparathyroidism following treatment for chronic renal disease?

   ① Serum glucose and sodium.

   ② Blood urea nitrogen.

   ③ Calcium and phosphate.

   ④ Urine specific gravity and weight.

4. Which of these statements regarding anemia indicate the teaching was effective for a client with chronic kidney disease?

   ① "I may have anemia due to my poor iron intake, since I have been ill."

   ② "If I increase iron in my diet, I should get a good report on my hemoglobin during the next visit."

   ③ "There is a decrease in the erythropoietin production, which is the reason for my anemia."

   ④ "My heart should not have to work as hard, since there is less blood to pump from my anemia."

5. Which one of these clinical findings would be a priority for the nurse to report for a client with chronic renal failure?

   ① An inverted T-wave on the ECG monitor.

   ② Depressed reflexes.

   ③ The presence of Chvostek's sign.

   ④ The Glasgow Coma Scale going from 7 to 12.

6. Which one of these statements indicates the nurse understands the physiological change that can cause hyponatremia in a client with chronic renal disease?

  ① "The client is not taking in enough sodium to replace what is lost during dialysis."

  ② "The client needs to replace the fluids lost due to the inability for the kidneys to compensate."

  ③ "The sodium is low due to being diluted from fluid retention."

  ④ "The sodium is low due to hypokalemia."

7. Which one of these interventions indicates safe practice for a client with chronic renal disease?

  ① Administers Milk of Magnesisa for complications with GERD.

  ② Administers Lisinopril for BP 160/90.

  ③ Administers Aldactone for the increase in edema.

  ④ Encourages client to include green leafy vegetables in diet.

8. Which of these actions by the unlicensed assistive personnel (UAP) would require intervention from the charge nurse for a client with chronic renal failure?

  ① Performs oral hygiene routinely.

  ② Encourages client to drink fluids hourly.

  ③ Refuses to give client the fruit salad with oranges for a snack.

  ④ Takes the weight daily and records it.

9. What is the priority of care for a 74-year-old client with diabetes mellitus and chronic renal failure who has an order for an intravenous pyelogram (IVP)?

  ① Assess for allergies to dyes.

  ② Educate client regarding the procedure,

  ③ Obtain consent from the client.

  ④ Verify appropriateness for procedure with healthcare provider.

10. What would be the priority of care for a client with chronic renal failure who presents with lethargy, pulse oximeter SaO_2 of 84%, and HR–100 bpm?

  ① Complete a physical assessment.

  ② Assess breath sounds and position in the semi-Fowler's position.

  ③ Increase the O_2 flow rate and suction the client.

  ④ Immediately check the ABG's and report to healthcare provider.

Answers and Rationales

1. Which nursing actions should the nurse **delegate to the unlicensed assistive personnel** (UAP) for a client with renal failure who has a complication **"Fluid Volume Excess"** related to compromised regulatory mechanisms? Select all that apply.

    ① **CORRECT: Record vital signs every 4 hours. Vital signs are important to monitor for trends (i.e., ↑ BP, ↑ HR, ↑ RR). These will be all be ↑ with fluid excess (overload).**

    ② **CORRECT: Weigh client every morning using standing scale. Weight is a reliable client assessment for fluid excess.**

    ③ INCORRECT: Listen to breath sounds daily. Due to risk of adventitious breath sounds, this should be done more frequently. This would not be done by the UAP, but if you have not reviewed delegation, you can still get this correct by understanding safe care for clients in renal disease is to monitor for complications from fluid overload. While you may need more review on delegation, using the strategy of pathophysiology will assist you with this question. (Refer to the book, *Nursing Made Insanely Easy*, Manning & Rayfield, 2014 for specific strategies for delegation.)

    ④ INCORRECT: Teach client the importance of eating oranges and bananas. This is unsafe, since these are ↑ in K⁺.

    ⑤ **CORRECT: Remind client to save all urine for intake and output record. This is important to monitor for trends.**

The strategy is to understand the concept of Fluid Volume Excess (*Refer to concept Fluid Balance for specifics*). Notice a link simplifying this concept is to recognize that when there is a volume excess for any reason such as renal disease, fluid overload, high intake of sodium, corticosteroid therapy, Cushing's disease etc. the vital signs and CVP will be increased. Link = Increased fluid = Increased vital signs. In order to understand the care such as monitoring weight, I & O, vital signs, etc., it is crucial to understand that one of the complications from renal disease is an excess in the fluid volume.

Management of Care: Assign and supervise care provided by others (i.e., LPN/VN, assistive personnel, etc.).

Physiological Adaptation: Manage the care of the client with a fluid and electrolyte imbalance.

2. Which of these should be included in the **plan of care for a client who has chronic kidney disease?** Select all that apply.

    ① INCORRECT: Assess for a flatten T wave on the ECG monitor. This indicates hypokalemia. It would be a tall peaked T wave.

    ② INCORRECT: Discuss the importance of using salt substitutes. This would be high in potassium.

    ③ INCORRECT: Encourage taking an NSAID for discomfort. These can cause hyperkalemia.

    ④ **CORRECT: Review the importance of taking Aluminum hydroxide gel (Amphogel) with meals. These will bind to phosphate in food and stop phosphate absorption.**

    ⑤ **CORRECT: Review the importance of monitoring and reporting trends in weight gain. Weight is a reliable client assessment for evaluating fluid excess from chronic renal failure.**

The strategy to answer this correctly is to understand that labs such as potassium and phosphate increase with chronic renal disease. It is also important to understand the medications that can result in elevated potassium levels. Refer to list in this chapter. In addition to these links, it is important to understand that Amphogel will bind to phosphate to assist in stopping the phosphate absorption. In the last option, there is also the concept of fluid excess that makes monitoring and reporting trends in the weight one of the priority plans of care. This is another example of one way to evaluate the concept of fluid excess. (*Refer to concept Fluid Balance for more specifics.*)

Physiological Adaptation: Recognize trends and changes in client condition and intervene as needed.

Pharmacological and Parenteral Therapies: Prepare and administer medications.

3. Which of these **lab reports** should receive **priority** attention for a school-age-child with a diagnosis of **secondary hyperparathyroidism** following treatment for chronic renal disease?

    ① INCORRECT: Serum glucose and sodium. These are not linked to the parathyroid; glucose would be linked with the pancreas.

    ② INCORRECT: Blood urea nitrogen. This rises in CRD, but is not connected to the parathyroid.

    ③ **CORRECT: Calcium and phosphate. Hyperparathyroidism is characterized by excessive secretion of PTH, resulting in hypocalcemia. Normal functions of PTH are for maintenance of serum calcium and phosphate levels. Excessive PTH results in an elevated phosphorus and a decrease in the calcium level resulting in risk for injury to the bones.**

    ④ INCORRECT: Urine specific gravity and weight. This would be a concern with the posterior pituitary.

The strategy is to link the function of the parathyroid with the lab values. It doesn't matter if the function of the parathyroid gland is altered from a tumor, trauma, or from renal disease, etc.; the changes in the lab values will be the same due to the pathophysiology involved with the parathyroid gland.

Reduction of Risk Potential: Monitor the results of the diagnostic testing (labs) and intervene as needed.

Physiological Adaptation: Identify pathophysiology related to an acute or chronic condition (i.e., signs and symptoms).

4. Which of these statements **regarding anemia** indicate the **teaching was effective** for a client with chronic renal disease?

    ① INCORRECT: "I may have anemia due to my poor iron intake, since I have been ill." Not accurate due to physiology.

    ② INCORRECT: "If I increase iron in my diet, I should get a good report on my hemoglobin on the next visit." Not focused on the actual cause.

    ③ **CORRECT: "There is a decrease in the erythropoietin production, which is the reason for my anemia." This is correct based on the pathophysiology for clients with chronic renal disease.**

    ④ INCORRECT: "My heart should not have to work as hard, since there is less blood to pump from my anemia." This is the opposite of what actually happens. Due to the lack of hemoglobin, the heart works harder to assist with the lack of oxygen.

The strategy is to link the anemia with the lack of erythropoietin production that occurs with renal disease. Erythropoietin is developed in the kidneys. Understanding the pathophysiology is a great strategy to assist you in remembering the cause. Understanding the "WHYS" is the key to success!

Health Promotion: Educate client about treatments and procedures.

Physiological Adaptation: Identify pathophysiology related to an acute or chronic condition (i.e., signs and symptoms).

5. Which one of these **clinical findings would be a priority** for the nurse to **report for a client with chronic renal failure**?

    ① INCORRECT: An inverted T wave on the ECG monitor. The answer would be tall peaked T wave ($\uparrow K^+$) for this client.

    ② INCORRECT: Depressed reflexes. This would be if client had hypokalemia.

    ③ **CORRECT: The presence of Chvostek's sign (facial twitching). This is indicative of hypocalcemia and requires further assessment and intervention.**

    ④ INCORRECT: The Glasgow Coma Scale going from a 7 to a 12. This is going up which means client is more alert and oriented. (No need to report.)

The strategy is to understand and link the concept of hypocalcemia to this condition. The Chvostek's sign indicates hypocalcemia. (*Refer to the chapter on Calcium Balance for details on how to perform this test.*) Options 1 and 2 address hypokalemia which is not what happens with chronic renal failure. Option 4 is a sign of improvement of verbal, eye, and motor assessments, so there is not a need to report this. The scale ranges from 3–15, with the lower range representing less responsiveness and the higher range more responsiveness. This test would be appropriate for a client with neurological changes affecting the level of consciousness.

Physiological Adaptation: Recognize signs and symptoms of complication and intervene appropriately when providing care.

6. Which one of these statements indicates the **nurse understands** the physiological change that can cause **hyponatremia** in a client with **chronic renal disease**?

① INCORRECT: "The client is not taking in enough sodium to replace what is lost during dialysis." Not a true statement.

② INCORRECT: "The client needs to replace the fluids lost due to the inability for the kidneys to compensate." Not a true statement. This would be appropriate if client had diabetes insipidus.

③ **CORRECT: "The sodium is low due to being diluted from fluid retention." With the fluid retention, the sodium is dilute.**

④ INCORRECT: "The sodium is low due to hypokalemia." The sodium is low due to being diluted with the extra fluid retention.

The strategy is to link this concept with the physiology of hyponatremia being dilutional. This concept applies to any clinical situation where there is too much fluid on board, such as SIADH (*Refer to Concept Sodium Balance for specifics*). Understanding "WHY" will help move this concept into your long-term memory!

Physiological Adaptation: Identify pathophysiology related to an acute or chronic condition (i.e., signs and symptoms).

7. Which one of these **interventions indicates safe practice** for a client with **chronic renal disease**?

① INCORRECT: Administers Milk of Magnesisa for complications with GERD. This is unsafe, since magnesium can be elevated.

② INCORRECT: Administers Lisinopril for BP 160/90. This would be contraindicated due to risk of hyperkalemia.

③ INCORRECT: Administers Aldactone for the increase in edema. This should not be administered due to risk for hyperkalemia.

④ **CORRECT: Encourages client to include green leafy vegetables in diet that are high in folic acid; important due to lack of erythropoietin.**

The strategy is to understand the need for folic acid due to the lack of erythropoietin. Then it is important to understand the foods high in folic acid. While we are discussing chronic renal disease and the need for these foods, these foods could also apply to a pregnant client or a young female wanting to become pregnant. A client who is an alcoholic also can have a folic acid deficiency. The causes for these additional clients are not about the erythropoietin production, but about other physiological changes that make the need for folic acid a priority. Our goals at this time are for you to recognize the foods high in folic acid (green leafy vegetables) and understand that in clients with renal disease the need is due to a lack of erythropoietin. You CAN do this!!! (*Refer to Concept Nutrition for more specifics.*)

Basic Care and Comfort: Manage client's nutritional intake.

8. Which of these **actions by the unlicensed assistive personnel** (UAP) would **require intervention from the charge nurse for a client with chronic renal failure?**

    ① INCORRECT: Performs oral hygiene routinely. This is safe practice, and requires no further intervention.

    ② **CORRECT: Encourages client to drink fluids hourly. This is unsafe with CRF; fluid restriction is important!**

    ③ INCORRECT: Refuses to give client the fruit salad with oranges for a snack. Oranges are high in potassium; should not be given to a client in renal failure. This requires no intervention since it is within the standard of practice for these clients.

    ④ INCORRECT: Takes the weight daily and records it. This is safe practice and does not require intervention.

The strategy is to understand the incorrect options for this client. Clients in CRF need to have fluid intake carefully monitored. This is linked to the concept of fluid balance: excess. The more fluid the client takes in, the more dilutional the sodium will get. This can lead to a risk for seizures. Also, extra fluid can lead to hypertension, tachycardia, and adventitious lung sounds. All of this adds extra work on the heart!!! Remember SAFETY is a priority!

Management of Care: Recognize unsafe care of healthcare personnel and intervene as appropriate (i.e., improper care)

9. What is the **priority of care for a 74-year-old client with diabetes mellitus and chronic renal failure** who has an order for an **intravenous pyelogram (IVP)?**

    ① INCORRECT: Assess for allergies to dyes. Due to age and diagnoses, the dyes in the IVP could present a problem with not being able to be excreted.

    ② INCORRECT: Educate client regarding the procedure. This procedure may be inappropriate for client, so teaching is not the immediate priority.

    ③ INCORRECT: Obtain consent from the client. Not appropriate until HCP is notified.

    ④ **CORRECT: Verify appropriateness for procedure with healthcare provider. This exam may be unsafe due to the dyes which will need to be excreted in**

the urine. This can be a problem for a client in CRF. It is also an issue with an older client due to the decrease in the glomerular filtration rate as individuals age.

The strategy is to understand that as individuals age the glomerular filtration rate decrease. Diabetes mellitus can also affect the renal system. The client is already in renal failure, so dyes would not be appropriate due to risk of not being able to eliminate the dye. This would be unsafe care if the nurse did not notify the HCP to verify this order!

Management of Care: Verify appropriateness and/or accuracy of treatment order.

10. What would be the priority of care for a client with chronic renal failure who presents with lethargy, pulse oximeter SaO_2 of 84%, and HR–100 bpm?

    ① INCORRECT: Complete a physical assessment. The system involved is the respiratory system.

    ② **CORRECT: Assess breath sounds and position in the semi-Fowler's position. Client may be in fluid overload in the lungs.**

    ③ INCORRECT: Increase the O_2 flow rate and suction the client. Client should be assessed initially and repositioned.

    ④ INCORRECT: Immediately check the ABGs and report to healthcare provider. This may not be necessary.

The strategy for answering this question is to link the concept of altered oxygenation with these system specific assessments. You may not be certain of the cause, but a good guess would be it is from fluid overload. Of course, there are no assessments of the breath sounds, so you have to make decisions based on only what you have in the question and the options. Let's approach this from first looking at the options. Option 1 is unnecessary since the stem only focuses on signs of altered oxygenation. Option 3 would not be the priority of care without additional assessments and repositioning first. Option 4 may not be necessary. Option 2 is appropriate due to risk of fluid overload. More assessments are necessary. (*Remember to refer to the "Prioritizing Algorithm" in chapter 1 to assist with the guide for prioritizing. The strategy that you could use here is the "ABCs".*)

Management of Care: Prioritize delivery of care.

Decision-Making Analysis Form

Use this tool to help identify why you missed any questions. As you enter the question numbers in the chart, you will begin to see patterns of why you answered incorrectly. This information will then guide you toward what you need to focus on in your continued studies. Ultimately, this analytical exercise will help you become more successful in answering questions!!!

Questions to ask:

1. Did I have the knowledge to answer the question? If not, what information do I need to review?

2. Did I know what the question was asking? Did I misread it or did I miss keywords in the stem of the question?

3. Did I misread or miss keywords in the distractors that would have helped me choose the correct answer?

4. Did I follow my gut reaction or did I allow myself to rationalize and then choose the wrong answer?

	Lack of Knowledge (Concepts, Systems, Pathophysiology, Medications, Procedures, etc.)	Missed Keywords or Misread the Stem of the Question	Missed Keywords or Misread the Distractors	Changed My Answer (Second-guessed myself, i.e., my first answer was correct.)
Put the # of each question you missed in the column that best explains why you think you answered it incorrectly.				

If you changed an answer because you talked yourself out of the correct answer, or you second-guessed yourself, this is an **EASY FIX: QUIT changing your answers**!!! Typically, the first time you read a question, you are about 95% right! The second time you read a question, you start talking yourself into changing the answer. The third time you read a question, you do not have a clue—and you are probably thinking "Who in the heck wrote this question?"

On the other hand, if you read a question too quickly and when you reread it you realize you missed some key information that would impact your decision (i.e., assessments, lab reports, medications, etc.), then it is appropriate to change your answer. When in doubt, go with the safe route: your first thought! Go with your gut instinct!

As you gain confidence in answering questions regarding specific nursing concepts, you will be able to successfully progress to answering higher-level questions about prioritization. Please refer to the *Prioritization Guidelines* in this book for a structure to assist you with this process.

You CAN do this!

*"You are never to old to set a new goal
or to dream a new dream!"*

C. S. LEWIS

References for Chapter 17

Black, J M. and Hawks, J. H. (2009). *Medical surgical nursing: Clinical management for positive outcomes (8th ed.).* Philadelphia: Elsevier/Saunders.

Daniels, R. & Nicoll, L. (2012). *Contemporary medical-surgical nursing,* (2nd ed.). Clifton Park, NY: Delmar Cengage Learning.

Dumler, F. Body composition modifications in patients under low protein diets. *Journal of Renal Nutrition* 21 (1): 76-81 2011.

Eliopoulos, C. (2014). *Gerontological nursing* (8th ed.), Philadelphia: Lippincott Williams & Wilkins.

Giddens, G. F. (2013). *Concepts for nursing practice.* St. Louis, MO: Mosby, an imprint of Elsevier.

Hogan, M. A. (2014). *Pathophysiology: Reviews and rationales* (3rd ed.) Boston, MA: Pearson.

Ignatavicius, D. D. and Workman, M. L. (2010). *Medical-surgical nursing: Patient-centered collaborative care* (6th ed.). Philadelphia: Elsevier/Saunders.

LeMone, P., Burke, K. M., and Bauldoff, G. (2011). *Medical-surgical nursing: Critical thinking in patient care* (5th ed.). Upper Saddle Road, NJ: Pearson/Prentice Hall.

Lewis, S., Dirksen, S., Heitkemper, M., Bucher, L., and Camera, I. (2011). *Medical surgical nursing: Assessment and management of clinical problems* (8th ed.). St. Louis: Mosby.

Manning, L. and Rayfield, S. (2014). *Nursing made insanely easy* (7th ed.). Duluth, GA: I CAN Publishing, Inc.

Manning, L. and Rayfield, S. (2013). *Pharmacology made insanely easy* (4th ed.). Duluth, GA: I CAN Publishing, Inc.

National Council of State Boards of Nursing, INC. (NCSBN) 2012. *Research brief: 2011 RN practice analysis: linking the NCLEX RN® examination to practice.* Retrieved from https://www.ncsbn.org/index.htm

Nettina, S. L. (2013). *Lippincott manual of nursing practice* (10th ed.). Philadelphia, PA: Walters Kluwer Health/Lippincott Williams & Wilkins.

North Carolina Concept Based Learning Editorial Board (2011). *Nursing a concept based approach to learning,* Upper Saddle Road, NJ: Pearson/Prentice Hall.

Osborn, K. S., Wraa, C. E., Watson, A. S., and Holleran, R. S. (2014). *Medical surgical nursing: Preparation for practice* (2nd ed.). Upper Saddle Road, NJ: Pearson.

Pagana, K. D. and Pagana, T. J. (2014). *Mosby's manual of laboratory and diagnostic tests* (5th ed.). St. Louis, MO: Mosby, an imprint of Elsevier.

Porth, C. (2011). *Essentials of pathophysiology* (3d ed.). Philadelphia, PA: Lippincott Williams ad Wilkins.

Porth, C. M. and Grossman, S. (2013). *Pathophysiology: Concepts of altered health states* (9th ed.). Philadelphia, PA: Lippincott Williams & Wilkins.

Potter, P. A., Perry, A. G., Stockert, P., and Hall, A. (2013). *Fundamentals of nursing* (8th ed.). St. Louis, MO: Pearson/Prentice Hall.

Smeltzer, S. C., Bare, B. G., Hinkle, J. L., and Cheever, K. H. (2010). *Brunner & Suddarth's Textbook of medical-surgical nursing* (12th ed.). Philadelphia: Lippincott Williams & Wilkins.

Wagner, K. D. and Hardin-Pierce, M. C. (2014). *High-Acuity nursing* (6th ed.). Boston: Pearson.

CHAPTER 18

Musculoskeletal System
Linking Concepts to Pathophysiology of Diseases
Concept Mobility

A Snapshot of Mobility

"Mobility is the state or quality of being mobile or movable" (Venes, 2014). The scope ranges from full to partial mobility with part of body to the full body being involved. The state of mobility may be on a continuum that ranges from temporary to permanent immobility and may occur with a slow or sudden onset. Immobility can cause potential complications without intervention. Changes in mobility can impact many of the body systems. Mobility is also related to body changes from aging. Loss of muscle mass, reduction in muscle strength and function, stiff, less mobile joints, and gait changes affect balance and can lead to mobility issues for the geriatric client (Giddens, 2013). Elderly clients have an increased risk of complications from immobility. Disease, trauma, injuries and surgeries (i.e., scoliosis repair, arthroscopic procedures, open and/or closed reduction of fractures with or without traction, amputations, laminectomy, and joint replacements, etc.) can each impact the client's mobility status. The goal of nursing care with clients with partial or full immobility is help the client maintain functional ability, prevent additional impairment of physical activity, prevent potential complications of immobility and ensure client safety from further injury.

The Pathophysiology Behind An Alteration in Mobility

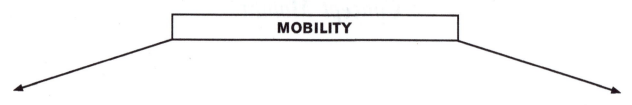

Skeletal Dysfunction	Neuromuscular Dysfunction	Muscular Dysfunction	Joint and Connective Dysfunction and/or Inflammation
• Fractures • Amputation • Osteoporosis	• Guillain-Barre Syndrome • Multiple Sclerosis • Myasthenia Gravis • Amyotrophic Lateral Sclerosis (ALS) • Stroke • Spinal Cord injury • Parkinson's disease • Refer to Concept Intracranial Regulation for specifics	• Fibromyalgia	• Osteoarthritis • Osteomyelitis • Gout • Rheumatoid Arthritis • Systemic Lupus Erythematosus

System-Specific Assessments for Mobility

Use the following to help guide your assessments for clients with impaired mobility. The nmeumonic **"IMMOBILE"** will help you remember priority assessments.

System-Specific Assessments Mobility
"IMMOBILE"

Important to obtain a history of injury, progression of symptoms to include neurovascular and circulatory status. Assess for pain (i.e., pain in calf, pain at site of injury, etc.) Assess the **6 Ps**: **P**ain, **P**aresthesia (temporary/intermittent), **P**allor, **P**aralysis, **P**ulseless, **P**oikilothermia (extremity same temperature as environment).

Musculoskeletal assessment of strength, flexibility, joint movement & ability to walk, sit in chair, do activities of daily living. What is the client's degree of independence or do they need assistance?

Mentation: boredom, decrease in communication, assess need for mental health, physical, occupational, and/or social work consultations.

Oxygenation: RR, breath sounds, SaO_2, cough, sputum (i.e., color, odor, thickness, amount secretions, etc.), and use of accessory muscles.

Bone demineralization; assess risk for fractures, Ca^{++} level, history of osteoporosis, menopause, etc.

Intake: assess labs for protein, calcium, protein, pre-albumin, albumin levels and dietary intake. Assess resources & ability to prepare meals.
Integumentary System: risk for skin breakdown, assess of non-blanchable areas, pressure points, dryness, lesions.

Lack or decrease in cardiac capacity; assess vital signs, strength of peripheral pulses, & skin color; assess VS lying, sitting and standing; assess for risk of falls due to possible orthostatic hypotension. Look for redness, swelling, pain in legs for signs of deep vein thrombosis (DVT).

Elimination: assess bladder and bowel patterns & bowel sounds. Encourage fluids and (residue) fiber to prevent constipation. Monitor I & O, urine and stool. Provide privacy to help encourage elimination.

Linking Pathophysiology to System-Specific Assessments of Mobility

Pathophysiology	System-Specific Assessments "IMMOBILE"
Important to obtain history of injury and assessment. A complete assessment of pain needs to be done to include the site of the injury or surgery along with assessing for potential complications, (i.e., pain in calf from a deep vein thrombosis (DVT) or pain in chest from atelectasis, etc.). The 6 Ps gives a baseline of where the client is and the extent of the injury and if circulation is compromised (*Refer to concept Perfusion Cardiac/Peripheral for specifics*). Remember, when clients are in pain, recovery takes longer and the potential for complications increases because of (i.e., shallow breathing: atelectasis; not moving: lead to DVT, etc.).	Important to obtain a history of injury, progression of symptoms to include neurovascular and circulatory status. Assess for pain (i.e., pain in calf, pain at site of injury, etc.). Assess the 6 Ps: Pain, Paresthesia (temporary/intermittent), Pallor, Paralysis, Pulseless, Poikilothermia (extremity same temperature as environment.
Musculoskeletal complications; ↓ in muscle mass & muscle atrophy from immobility, joint contractions from improper alignment; motor capability; can contribute to the ability of the client to move. It ↑ the client's risk for falls and ↓ the chance of a full recovery. Maintaining muscle mass and avoiding contractures helps keep the client mobile preventing complications (i.e., atelectasis, deep vein thrombosis, risk for falls, etc.).	Musculoskeletal assessment of strength, flexibility, joint movement & ability to walk, sit in chair, do activities of daily living. What is the client's degree of independence or will they need assistance?
Mentation: boredom, grieving loss of function or limb, disturbed body image and ↓ in communication can all be challenges for the client with acute or chronic immobility to improve. The client may not be able to work or have their social network for support, resulting in a sense of social isolation. Physical and occupational therapy help maintain physical function and ability to perform activities of daily living.	Mentation: boredom, ↓ in communication, assess need for mental health, physical, occupational, and/or social work consultations. Assess availability of diversional activities particularly if on bedrest (i.e., traction, cervical spine injuries, etc.).
Oxygenation can ↓ due to a lack of physical activity which ↓ the ability for full lung expansion leading to atelectasis. Secretions can collect and if the client has less ability to cough up the secretions, it may ↑ the risk for respiratory infections like pneumonia. A client with co-morbidities, like asthma or COPD is at a greater risk. Pain keeps clients from breathing deeply and from moving which can = "TERRIBLE" (*Refer to in this chapter*).	Oxygenation: RR, breath sounds, SaO_2, cough, (i.e., color, odor, thickness, & amount secretions, etc.), & use of accessory muscles.
Bone demineralization is due to decrease, loss or removal of the mineral constituents of bones. Temporary loss of bone mineral content is especially associated with extended immobilization. This can lead to osteoporosis increasing the client's risk for fractures particularly with the elderly and postmenopausal women due to decreased calcium intake and weight bearing exercise. Bones store the calcium for the body and are a factor in the production of red blood cells.	Bone demineralization; assess risk for fractures, Ca^{++} level, history of osteoporosis, menopause, etc.
Intake of adequate fluids, protein, calories & vitamins are needed for healing (i.e., fractures, post joint replacement) and for energy. Integumentary system; at risk from the sustained pressure on the tissues from prolonged bedrest, sitting or immobility. The shearing forces of moving the client in the bed, incontinence, and poor nutritional intake all lead to an increase risk for skin breakdown. Clients with peripheral vascular disease, diabetes, etc. are at an increase risk of skin breakdown due to ↓ circulation.	Intake: assess labs: protein, Ca^{++}, protein, pre-albumin, albumin levels, & dietary intake. Assess resources & ability to prepare meals. Integumentary System: risk for skin breakdown, assess for non-blanchable areas, pressure points, dryness, lesions.
Lack or ↓ in cardiac capacity due to decreased physical activity is a result of ↓ muscle mass and strength and force of the contraction = ↓ cardiac output and ↓ perfusion to the organs and tissues. The blood pools in the extremities contributing to a ↑ risk for deep vein thrombosis and a ↑ risk of falls from orthostatic hypotension.	Lack or ↓ in cardiac capacity, assess VS, strength of peripheral pulses, & skin color; assess VS lying, sitting and standing; assess risk for falls due to possible orthostatic hypotension. Look for redness, swelling, pain in legs for signs of DVT.
Elimination: bladder and bowel. Immobile clients are at risk for constipation due to decrease in peristaltic activity or not being able to assume an upright position conducive for a bowel movement. Urinary stasis, loss of bladder tone may lead to urinary tract infections and renal calculi.	Elimination: assess bladder and bowel patterns & bowel sounds. Encourage fluids & residue (fiber) to prevent constipation. Monitor I & O, urine and stool. Provide privacy to help encourage elimination.

Alteration with Mobility

Common Lab/Diagnostic Tests/Therapeutic Procedures/Surgery

Labs	Diagnostics Tests/Procedures	Invasive Procedures/ Surgery
• CBC • Electrolytes • Antinuclear antibody (ANA) • C-Reactive Protein • Erythrocyte sedimentation rate (ESR) • Rheumatoid factor (RF) • Calcium • Phosphorus • Alkaline phosphatase • Creatinine kinase • Protein levels • Pre-albumin • Albumin	• X-ray used to detect skeletal abnormalities • Magnetic Resonance Imaging (MRI) used to detect abnormalities of tendons, ligaments and muscles and conditions like avascular necrosis • Computed Axial Tomography (CAT) used to detect bone tumors and spinal fractures • Dual-Energy X-Ray Absorptiometry (DEXA) used for diagnosis of osteoporosis • Bone Scans	• Arthrocentesis • Arthrogram • Arthroscopy • Electromyelogram • Nerve Conduction Test **Surgeries** • Joint Arthroplasty Replacement (partial or total) • Amputations • Reduction and/or repair of fractures

Alteration with Mobility

Medications for Mobility

ANTI-INFLAMMATORY AGENTS
Nonsteroidal Anti-Inflammatory (NSAIDS)
• Diclofenac (Voltaren)
• Ibuprofen (Advil, Motrin)
• Indomethacin (Indocin)
• Ketorolac (Toradol)
• Meloxicam (Mobic)
• Naproxen (Aleve, Naprosyn)

Nonsteroidal Anti-Inflammatory (Cox$_2$ Inhibitors)
• Celecoxib (Celebrex)
• Valdecoxib (Bextra)

Acetaminophen (Tylenol)

Antigout
• Allopurinol (Zyloprim)
• Colchicine (Colchicine)
• Febuxostat (Uloric)

RHEUMATIC ARTHRITIS AGENTS
• Abatacept (Orencia)
• Adalimumab (Humira)
• Etanercept (Enbrel)
• Infliximab (Remicade)
• Rituximab (Rituxan)

GLUCOCORTICOIDS
• Prednisone (Deltasone)

SKELETAL MUSCLE RELAXERS (SMRS)
• Cyclobenzaprine (Flexeril)
• Diazepam (Valium)
• Methocarbamol (Robaxin)

INTRA-ARTICULAR INJECTIONS FOR OSTEOARTHRITIS
• Hyaluronic acid (Hyalgan, Synvisc)

COMPLEMENTARY AGENTS
• Glucosamine (2-amino-2-deoxyglucose sulfate, chitosamine)

BONE HEALTH
Biophosphonates
• Alendronate (Fosamax)
• Risedronate (Actonel)

RECLAST
• Zoledronic acid (Reclast, Zometa)

BONE RESORPTION INHIBITOR
• Ibandronate (Boniva)

SELECTIVE ESTROGENT RECEPTOR MODULATOR (SERM)
• Raloxifene (Evista)

ESTROGEN
• Esterified estrogens (Estratab, Estratest, Menest)
• Conjugated estrogens (Premarin, Premphase, Prempro)

PAIN MANAGEMENT NARCOTIC ANALGESICS
• Codeine
• Fentanyl (Sublimaze)
• Hydrocodone (Hycodan)
• Hydromorphone (Dilaudid)
• Morphine (Roxanol, MS Contin)
• Oxycodone (Roxicodone)
• Propoxyphene (Darvon)

ANALGESIC (CENTRALLY ACTING)
• Tramadol (Ralivia, Ultram, Ultram ER)

TOPICAL ANALGESICS
• Trolamine salicylate (Aspercreme)
• Capsaicin (Axsain, Capsin)

NONOPIOID ANALEGESIC
• pregabalin (Lyrica)

First Do Priority Interventions
"ACTIVE"

A   Alignment: Position body in alignment, Reposition minimally every 2 hours. Teach to use assistive devices (i.e., cane, crutches, wheel chair).

C   Cough & deep breathe, use incentive spirometer every 1–2 hours while awake. Position client in an upright position to assist with lung expansion. Collaboration with dietician to ($\uparrow$ protein, calories, Ca^{++} & Vitamin D), dietary supplements may be needed for healing. May need to increase residue (fiber) in meals to prevent constipation

T   Transfer out of bed. Referrals to occupational therapy (OT) & physical therapy, (PT), interdisciplinary team members, to help teach the client how to dress, (start with affected then unaffected extremity) and maintain mobility within physical limitations.

I   Increase fluids to 2000mL to 3000mL/day unless contraindicated (i.e., heart failure, renal failure).
Intervene for pain, medications as prescribed, assess for effectiveness of pain relief; try hot & cold therapy.

V   deVices for immobilization: know care of (i.e., casts, traction, etc.). Prevent DVT (sequential compression device, elastic stockings). Encourage use of unaffected limb. May need anticoagulants (i.e., low weight molecular heparin: Lovenox, etc.).

E   Exercise in bed, passive and/or active ROM; sit on side of bed or chair and promote weight bearing when able. Encourage isometric exercises for abdomen and gluteal muscles unless contraindicated. Encourage diversional activities to help relieve boredom from immobility, (i.e., clients on traction, cervical spine injuries, etc.) Encourage visitors.
Educate client about:
  Primary prevention: diet include $\uparrow$ calcium, protein, vitamins C and D, regular exercise.
  Secondary prevention: assess for osteoporosis, fall risks, mobility screening.
  Tertiary prevention: may need a long-term rehab center (i.e., spinal cord injuries, stroke, etc.).

Linking Pathophysiology to
First-Do Priority Interventions for Mobility

Pathophysiology	First-Do Priority Interventions "ACTIVE"
Alignment: Correct alignment is needed to prevent contractures and to promote circulation. Need to avoid constriction that impairs circulation and perfusion. Safety is a PRIORITY in teaching and assisting clients how to use assistive devices to keep them mobile.	**A**lignment: Position body in alignment, Reposition minimally every 2 hours. Teach to use assistive devices (i.e., cane, crutches, wheel chair, etc.).
Cough & deep breathe and use of incentive spirometer helps open the airway and prevent shallow breathing that occurs with immobility. This helps prevent atelectasis that can lead to infections. (*Refer to concept Oxygenation for specifics*). **C**ollaboration: dietary (↑ protein, calories, calcium & Vitamin D) to help ensure nutrition essential for healing. Supplemental feeding may be needed to meet the increased needs. The client also needs additional residue (fiber) in the diet to prevent constipation that can occur with immobility or limited mobility; this helps keep "TERRIBLE" away (*Refer to later in this chapter*). Remember to encourage fluids to go with the fiber.).	**C**ough & deep breathe, use incentive spirometer every 1–2 hours while awake. Position client in an upright position to assist with lung expansion. **C**ollaboration with dietician to (↑ protein, calories, Ca^{++} & Vitamin D), dietary supplements may be needed for healing. May need to increase residue (fiber) in meals to prevent constipation.
Transferring out of bed safely helps prevent additional injuries. Occupational and physical therapist can help the client establish an appropriate exercise plan and provide valuable instruction and assistive devices for maintaining independence with activities of daily living (i.e., teach the client how dress, (start with affected then unaffected extremity), assist with occupational skills and physical therapy to help client maintain and/or improve mobility, contribute to the safety and quality of life, etc.). Hot & cold therapy helps decrease inflammation and pain in the injured tissue and joints and provides some pain relief (*Refer to hot & cold therapy later in this chapter*).	**T**ransfer out of bed. Referrals to occupational therapy (OT) & physical therapy, (PT), interdisciplinary team members, to help teach the client how to dress, (start with affected then unaffected extremity) and maintain mobility within physical limitations.
Increase fluids & residue (fiber) promotes elimination in immobile clients, and helps prevent constipation and urine retention. Urine retention can lead to a ↑ risk of renal calculi. The immobility can result in decreased peristaltic activity. The risk of a DVT is ↑ due to inactivity and a potential decrease in fluids in the vascular system. Intervening for pain management is very important so the client can deep breathe and move. However, remember, narcotic analgesics can contribute to constipation as does stress and depression. A stool softener may be needed while taking pain medications that can cause constipation along with increased fluids. Encourage a regular schedule for elimination (*Refer to Concept Elimination for specifics*).	**I**ncrease fluids to 2000mL to 3000mL/day unless contraindicated (i.e., heart failure, renal failure, etc.) Intervene for pain, medications as prescribed, assess for effectiveness of pain relief; try hot & cold therapy.
de**V**ices for immobilization: need (sequential compression device, elastic stockings), and encourage use of unaffected limb help maintain perfusion and prevent stasis of the blood that can lead to deep vein thrombosis. Adequate fluid intake prevents concentration of the circulating volume that also increases the risk for DVTs. May need anticoagulants (i.e., low weight molecular heparin–Lovenox, etc.) to prevent DVTs.	de**V**ices for immobilization: know care of (i.e., casts, traction, etc.). Prevent DVT (sequential compression device, elastic stockings). Encourage use of unaffected limb. May need anticoagulants (i.e., low weight molecular heparin: Lovenox, etc.).
Exercises in bed, passive &/or active ROM or promotion of weight bearing exercises prevents loss of muscle strength. Ambulating or sitting in the chair or the side of the bed is best, but if bed ridden, turn the client to prevent skin breakdown and to increase circulation. Active or passive range of motion exercises should be done to promote circulation and maintain muscle tone. Isometric exercise of the abdomen and gluteal muscles can help with strength and decreased constipation. The remodeling process that occurs with bone healing requires adequate nutrition and blood supply. Encourage diversional activities to help the client cope with the boredom that can be associated with immobility. Boredom can lead to depression, and decrease the client's motivation to do activities necessary for healing. **E**xplore family and friend support systems; refer to counselors, religious/ spiritual advisors as needed. Educate for Health Promotion through an interdisciplinary approach: Primary Prevention interventions are aimed at preventing the occurrence of disease, injury, or disability, risk reduction and specific protection, (i.e., diet, exercise, etc.). Secondary Prevention interventions are directed detecting disease early enough to allow effective treatment and prevent disease progression (i.e., screening for osteoporosis, mobility screening, etc.). Tertiary Prevention interventions help decrease the limitation of disability through an appropriate rehabilitation process.	**E**xercise in bed, passive &/or active ROM; sit on side of bed or chair and promote weight bearing when able. **E**ncourage isometric exercises for abdomen and gluteal muscles unless contraindicated. Encourage diversional activities to help relieve boredom from immobility, (i.e., clients on traction, cervical spine injuries, etc.) Encourage visitors. Educate client about: Primary prevention: diet include ↑ calcium, protein, vitamins C & D, regular exercise. Secondary prevention: assess for osteoporosis, fall risks, mobility screening. Tertiary prevention: may need a long-term rehab center (i.e., spinal cord injuries, stroke, etc.).

Safety: Concept Mobility

System-Specific Assessment "IMMOBILE"	First-Do Priority Interventions "ACTIVE"	Evaluation of Expected Outcomes Not "IMMOBILE"
Important to obtain a history of injury, progression of symptoms to include neurovascular and circulatory status. Assess for pain (i.e., pain in calf, pain at site of injury, etc.). Assess the 6 Ps: Pain, Paresthesia (temporary/intermittent), Pallor, Paralysis, Pulseless, Poikilothermia (extremity same temperature as environment).	Alignment: Position body in alignment, Reposition minimally every 2 hours. Teach to use assistive devices (i.e., cane, crutches, wheel chair).	Important to obtain history of injury, progression of symptoms: include neurovascular status: evaluate circulation (6 Ps). Circulation WDL, no progression of symptoms and/or symptoms resolving.
Musculoskeletal assessment of strength, flexibility, joint movement & ability to walk, sit in chair, do activities of daily living. What is the client's degree of independence or will they need assistance?	Cough & deep breathe, use incentive spirometer every 1–2 hours while awake. Position client in an upright position to assist with lung expansion.	Musculoskeletal NO complications: Motor skills WDL of client ability, In alignment, able to demonstrate how to safely use assistive devices: able to transfer out of bed; how to dress. Able to do ADL.
Mention: boredom, ↓ in communication, assess need for mental health, physical, occupational, and/or social work consultations. Assess availability of diversional activities particularly if on bedrest (i.e., traction, cervical spine injuries, etc.).	Collaboration with dietician to (↑ protein, calories, Ca++ & Vitamin D). dietary supplements may be needed for healing. May need to increase residue (fiber) in meals to prevent constipation.	Mention: participates in care & ADL, talks about emotions, participates in activities within capability.
Oxygenation: RR, breath sounds, SaO2, cough, (i.e., color, odor, thickness, & amount secretions, etc.), & use of accessory muscles.	Transfer out of bed. Referrals to occupational therapy (OT) & physical therapy, (PT), interdisciplinary team members, to help teach the client how to dress, (start with affected then unaffected extremity) and maintain mobility within physical limitations.	Oxygenation: RR and SaO2, WDL, BS clear.
Bone demineralization; assess risk for fractures, Ca++ level, history of osteoporosis, menopause, etc.	Increase fluids to 2000mL to 3000mL/day unless contraindicated (i.e., heart failure, renal failure, neuro, etc.). Intervene for pain, medications as prescribed, assess for effectiveness of pain relief; try hot & cold therapy.	Bone: NO fractures, healing with minimal muscle loss.
Intake: assess labs: protein, Ca++, protein, pre-albumin, albumin levels, & dietary intake. Assess resources & ability to prepare meals.	deVices for immobilization: know care of (i.e., cast, traction, etc.). Prevent DVT (sequential compression device, elastic stockings). Encourage use of unaffected limb. May need anticoagulants (i.e., low weight molecular heparin: Lovenox, etc.).	Intake & output WDL: nutritional needs met.
Integumentary System: risk for skin breakdown, assess for non-blanchable areas, pressure points, dryness, lesions.	Exercise in bed, passive &/or active ROM; sit on side of bed or chair and promote weight bearing when able. Encourage isometric exercises for abdomen and gluteal muscles unless contraindicated.	Integumentary System: risk for skin breakdown: No skin breakdown or pressure ulcers.
Lack or ↓ in cardiac capacity, assess VS, strength of peripheral pulses, & skin color; assess VS lying, sitting and standing; assess risk for falls due to possible orthostatic hypotension. Assess for redness, swelling, pain in legs for signs of DVT.	Encourage diversional activities to help relieve boredom from immobility, (i.e., clients on traction, cervical spine injuries, etc.) Encourage visitors.	Lack cardiac compromise: VS WDL, no cardiac compromise.
Elimination: assess bladder and bowel patterns & bowel sounds. Encourage fluids & residue (fiber) to prevent constipation. Monitor I & O, urine and stool. Provide privacy to help encourage elimination.	Educate client about: Primary prevention: diet include ↑ calcium, protein, vitamins C and D, regular exercise. Secondary prevention: assess for osteoporosis, fall risks, mobility screening. Tertiary prevention: may need a long-term rehab center (i.e., spinal cord injuries, stroke, etc.).	Elimination: urine and bowels WDL.

Muscular/Skeletal System: Concept Mobility
Trend for Potential Complications: Immobility

The **PRIORITY** for Clients with Mobility Disorders/Diseases is to
Prevent Complications of Immobility!!!
Because complications are "**TERRIBLE**"

Thrombus formation (risk)
Elimination (fluid and electrolyte imbalance)
Risk of atelectasis
Reduced cardiac output
Integumentary compromise
Bone loss
Loss of muscle endurance
Emotional status changes

Priority assessments and interventions for the immobile client focus on how to
Prevent "**TERRIBLE**"!!!

Insanely Easy Tip for Immobile Clients, is they need "M and M"!!!!

Manage Pain & "MO$_2$VE" the Client!

Move the clients within their ability: assist to ambulate, sit, turn, ROM, etc.

O$_2$xygenate: assess need by checking SaO$_2$ sat, RR; cough, deep breathe & incentive spirometry

Vital signs, evaluate trends for altered oxygenation & intervene

Eliminate pain, if clients are in pain, they won't deep breathe or move!

(Refer to Concept Oxygenation for specifics)

Exceptions and Additions by Diseases

Pathophysiology: Skeletal Dysfunction
Fractures

Fractures are a break in the bone. This can occur because of bone disease, such as osteoporosis, a fall or traumatic injury, physical abuse or metastatic disease. Fractures are classified according to the type of break: complete break is where the bone is broken all the way through; an incomplete break is where the bone is only partially broken or splintered. The break can be an open or compound fracture where the bone is protruding through the skin or a closed break with no penetration of the skin. The pathophysiology of a break starts when the bone is broken and a hematoma occurs from the ruptured blood vessels within and around the bone. The clotting factors then form a fibrin mesh around the fracture site. The granulation process starts within 48-72 hours with the proliferation of osteoblasts that are responsible for forming the new bone. The granulation tissue then becomes callus that is composed of new cartilage, calcium, phosphorus and osteoblasts. Ossification is when the callus is then replaced with new bone (Osborn, Wraa, Watson & Holleran, 2014). The fractures are named accordingly:

Comminuted: Bone is shattered into pieces.

Compression: Bone is crushed

Impacted: Ends of bones are jammed together

Spiral: Bone twists and have jagged breaks

Greenstick: Incomplete break

Transverse: Complete break at right angle to the long axis of the bone

The goal of treating fractures is to control hemorrhage, provide pain relief, prevent ischemia, and remove potential sources of contamination. The fracture is then reduced and maintained, which helps the fracture to heal and prevent potential complications. Non-operative treatment includes casts, traction, (skin and/or skeletal traction). Surgery may be needed.

Pathophysiology: Skeletal Dysfunction
Fractures

SYSTEM-SPECIFIC ASSESSMENTS "PAIN"	FIRST-DO PRIORITY INTERVENTIONS			
	DIET	EQUIPMENT	PLANS/INTERVENTIONS	HEALTH PROMOTION
Pain: Assess with **PQRST**, note if pain is worse or unrelieved with pain medication (risk for compartment syndrome). (*Refer to Concept Pain for specifics*). **A**nalysis & observation of injury site for protrusion of bone, swelling. **A**nalysis of **6 PS**: Pain, Paresthesia (temporary/ intermittent), Pallor, Paralysis, Pulseless, Poikilothermia (extremity same temperature as environment). **I**mmobility of affected limb as prescribed. **N**eed to confirm fracture with X-Ray.	• Increase protein • Increase calories • Vitamin D • Calcium • Refer to Concept on Nutrition for specifics	• Assistive devices • Traction • Casts • Refer to information in this chapter on traction & casts	• Pain control, be proactive, and administer pain medication as prescribed. • Cleanse site of injury if needed. • Immobilize injury, (prevents further injury & helps control pain). • Elevate extremity and/or apply ice packs as prescribed to reduce swelling. • May need to prepare for surgery. • Consult with physical and occupational therapy per protocol.	Teach client/family: • How to care for cast • How to use assistive devices, (i.e., crutches, walker, etc.) • Signs of fat emboli or signs of compartment syndrome (*Refer to the next page*).

Pathophysiology: Skeletal Dysfunction
Fractures: POST-OP CARE: Cast Care

"CAST"

Cast care first 24 hours, elevate with ice over fracture site; allow cast to dry. Fiberglass casts are most common: allow 5 to 30 minutes to dry; plaster casts are used less often, require 10–72 hours to dry.

Always report increased pain, change in color, coolness of extremity, numbness or tingling in fingers or toes.

Stay dry: protect plaster casts from moisture at all time (plastic over cast during bathing); fiberglass casts: dry thoroughly after getting wet.

Teach how to do self-care and use assistive devices for mobility during recovery.

PRIORITIES

TREND POTENTIAL COMPLICATIONS OF FRACTURES			
Fat Emboli Can occur with all fractures but higher risk with large bone fractures. Fat droplets act as emboli and become impacted in the pulmonary and other microvasculature beds, (i.e., brain).		**Compartment Syndrome** Hemorrhage and edema following fracture leads to inability of fascia to accommodate the excessive edema impairing circulation that can result in an ischemia and death of tissue.	
System-Specific Assessments	**First-Do Priority Interventions**	**System-Specific Assessments**	**First-Do Priority Interventions**
• Early Sign: ↓ SaO_2 • Respiratory distress, ↑ RR, shortness of breath, rapid shallow respirations • ↑ HR • Altered mental status, ↓ LOC, or drowsiness or coma • Petechial rash on chest, axilla, conjunctiva, and neck	• **Notify HCP immediately** • Administer high flow O_2; may need ventilator and PEEP (*Refer to Concept Oxygenation for specifics*) • Adequate IV fluids to prevent hypovolemic shock • Albumin may be given (helps bind with fatty acids) • Administer high dose steroids as prescribed **Prevention: Reduce long bone fractures as soon as possible after injury.**	• Pain: **unrelieved** with elevation and pain medications • Analysis of 6 Ps: Pain, Paresthesia (temporary/ intermittent), Pallor, Paralysis, Pulseless, Poikilothermia (extremity same temperature as environment)	• Notify HCP immediately: delay can result in tissue ischemia & necrosis • Loosen constrictive dressings • Elevate extremity and apply ice • May have to cut cast on one side • May need to prepare for fasciotomy: surgical incision through subcutaneous tissue and fascia to relieve pressure & improve circulation

Pathophysiology: Skeletal Dysfunction
Fractures: Traction

Types of Traction	Purpose of Traction
MANUAL	Manual is a temporary pulling force applied with hands used with immobilization device.
SKIN TYPES • **BUCKS** • **BRYANT**	Bucks is used intermittently: pulling force is applied by weights attached by cables to the client. Bryant traction used with pediatrics only.
DUNLAP TRACTION	Dunlap traction is used to immobilize the upper arm in the treatment of contracture or supracondylar fracture of the elbow. The mechanism uses a system of traction weights, pulleys, and cables and may be accompanied by skin traction.
SKELETAL TYPES: • **SKELETAL TONGS** • **HALO** • **CRUTCHFIELD TONGS**	Skeletal tongs are used continuously with pulling force applied directly to bone through weights attached by rod/screw in bone. Halo is a ring around the head is secured to the skull bone with screws, and then attached to rod, secured to non-removable vest worn by client. Crutchfield tongs are inserted in skull, traction works to fatigue neck muscles, relieves cord "pinching" between vertebrae.
INTERNAL FIXATION	Internal fixation: rods and screws are utilized to immobilize the part of the body internally.
EXTERNAL FIXATION	External fixation: rods and screws will be attached to an external source that immobilizes the client.

Plan of Care for Client in Traction
Use "TRACTION" to Remember the Priority Plan of Care

Try to do ROM per protocol; maintain body alignment.

Respiratory complications prevented.

Assess neurovascular: analysis of 6 Ps: Pain, Paresthesia (temporary/intermittent), Pallor, Paralysis, Pulseless, Poikilothermia.

Care of pin site (skeletal or external fixation methods): 1 cotton swab/pin q 8 hrs. with peroxide & iodine or per protocol.

Trapeze to help move, with halo traction, move as a unit so as not to apply pressure to the rods to avoid loosening of pins.

Infection prevent: monitor temperature, WBCs, observe color, smell, amount of drainage around pin sites.

Ongoing assessment: traction weights are as prescribed, hang freely, & pulley cables are free of knots. Avoid lifting or removing weights.

Need wrench to release rods from vest used with Halo traction (taped to front of vest for emergency).
Notify the provider for severe pain not relieved by medications and/or repositioning or for muscle spasms.

Pathophysiology: Skeletal Dysfunction
Amputations

Amputations can be traumatic or are used to treat injuries, cancers, limb gangrene and limb-threatening arterial disease. The public's awareness has grown about amputees with the number of soldiers returning home with one or more limbs amputated. Peripheral vascular disease and diabetes are also major reasons for amputations in the elderly because of arterial occlusion. The technology of new prostatic wear and the support to help amputees return to a normal life over the past decade has been significant.

There are two types of planned surgical amputations, both of which are done as distally as possible.

Closed amputation: allows skin flap to close site.

Open amputation: used with active infections and may need reconstructive surgery later.

Plan of Care for Client with an Amputation
Use "AMPUTATE" to help you remember the Priority Plan of Care

Assess neurovascular signs for potential complications; analysis of 6 Ps: Pain, Paresthesia (temporary/intermittent), Pallor, Paralysis, Pulseless, Poikilothermia.

Monitor for infection (record drainage from wound site, color, smell); note temperature, WBC count.

Position stump ↑ on pillow during first 24 hours to ↓ edema; then position in dependent position to promote blood flow or per protocol.

U need to implement shrinkage interventions (↓ edema and prepare for prosthetic; may use stump shrinker sock). Keep stump clean with soap and water.

Treat pain. Interventions for phantom pain: (i.e., range of motion exercises, visual imaging, nerve-stabilizing and pain medications, etc.).

Avoid prolonged sitting.

Try to prevent contractures: correct positioning, ROM , and have client lie prone several times per day to avoid flexion contractures.

Encourage and support grieving process, refer to support groups, physical and occupational health to achieve maximal function. Designing a prosthetic is usually started 2–3 weeks after client begins wearing an elastic wrap or a shrinker sock.

Do you see the similarities in priority concepts with clients in traction and clients who have had an amputation? You got it: Prevent "TERRIBLE" and "M and M"!

"M and M" Prevents the
"TERRIBLE" of Immobility!

Pathophysiology: Skeletal Dysfunction
Osteoporosis

Osteoporosis is a loss of bone mass that predisposes clients to bone fractures. It begins with bone demineralization due to decrease, loss or removal of the mineral constituents of bones. Temporary loss of bone mineral content is especially associated with extended immobilization. Osteoporosis develops as the rate of bone reabsorption exceeds the rate of bone formation. The outer cortex of the bone becomes thinner which increases the risk for fractures (LeMone, Burke & Bauldoff, 2011). There are two types of osteoporosis:

Type I is associated with postmenopausal estrogen deficiency.

Type II is associated with calcium deficiency called senile osteoporosis.

Plan of Care "BONES"	
Bone density scan result reported to HCP. **O**ut of calcium: assess Ca⁺⁺ & Vitamin D levels, supplements as needed; may need referral to dietician (*Refer to Concept on Nutrition for specifics*). **N**eed drugs to prevent further deterioration: administer Selective Estrogen Receptor Modulators (SERM), Bisphosphonates (i.e., Fosamax), etc. as prescribed; (if taking medications, advise dentist prior to dental procedures (*Refer to the medication list in this chapter*). **E**strogen may help decrease incidence of osteoporosis. **E**xercise (weight bearing) program with weight bearing exercises implement. **E**xercise fall precautions. **S**tress fractures assess for: low back pain, fractures of forearm, spine, and hip. Select assistive devices as needed.	Josephine is on the treadmill getting some weight bearing exercise to help prevent osteoporosis. On the table are medications (i.e., Fosamax and calcium) to help prevent osteoporosis. **JOSEPHINE BONE-A-PART** 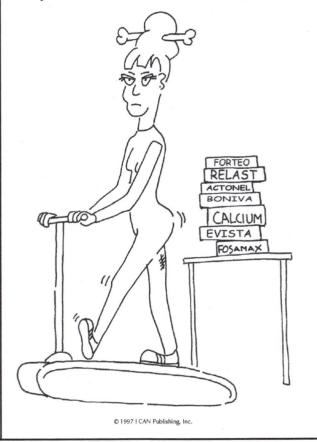 © 1997 I CAN Publishing, Inc.

Exceptions and Additions by Diseases

Pathophysiology: Neuromuscular Dysfunction

The diseases listed below often result in partial to full paralysis from neurological disorders of the neurons to extreme muscle wasting and deterioration. Information about neuromuscular dysfunction disease processes will be covered in the Neurovascular System chapter (*Refer to Concept Intracranial Regulation for specifics*).

- Guillian–Barre Syndrome: ascending paralysis
- Multiple Sclerosis: progressive muscle spasticity, extreme weakness
- Myasthenia Gravis: extreme muscular weakness
- Amyotrophic Lateral Sclerosis (ALS): progression of extreme muscle weakness, atrophy to paralysis, descending paralysis
- Stroke: muscle weakness to paralysis of affected side
- Spinal Cord injury: paralysis partial (paraplegic) to complete (quadriplegic) depending on level of spinal cord injury

Pathophysiology: Muscular Dysfunction

Fibromyalgia is a syndrome of chronic pain of the muscles, joints, and complaint of fatigue. The onset is usually gradual, but can be acute. Clients complain of tender points on the body that hurt with pressure. The etiology is unknown but it is often associated with disturbances in sleep, endocrine disorders, and affective disorders. It is most common in middle age and elderly women. Clients with histories of rheumatoid arthritis and other autoimmune diseases are at a higher risk of developing fibromyalgia (Osborn, Wraa & Watson, 2014).

Fibromyalgia

SYSTEM-SPECIFIC ASSESSMENTS "PAIN"	FIRST-DO PRIORITY INTERVENTIONS			
	DIET	EQUIPMENT	PLANS/INTERVENTIONS	HEALTH PROMOTION
Pain: assess (use the "**PQRST**") muscle pain, spasms, local or generalized, most often neck, shoulders, lower back and hips, headache, stiffness; tingling or numbness in hands & feet (*Refer to Concept Pain for specifics*) **A**ltered mood, depression; assess for sources of stress, trouble thinking **I**rritable bowel syndrome often associated with it **N**eed for sleep because of sleep disturbances	• Well balanced diet • Refer to Concept on Nutrition for specifics	• Assistive devices if needed	• Pain control (NSAIDS), pregabalin (Lyrica) • Suggest alternative pain control methods, (i.e., music, pet therapy, TENS units, etc.) (*Refer to concept Pain for specifics*) • Encourage activity with a low impact exercise program, (i.e., walking, swimming, biking, etc.) • May need antidepressants for mood and sleep • Need well balanced diet	Teach client/ family: • Available support groups • Need for adequate rest • Refer for stress management

Pathophysiology: Joint and/or Connective Tissue Dysfunction or Inflammation
Osteoarthritis

Osteoarthritis or degenerative joint disease is a progressive deterioration of the articular cartilage. The new tissue is produced to replace the damaged cartilage but cannot keep up and the bone and cartilage erode. The pain, caused by bone spurs (osteophytes) that develop in the joint spaces, leads to immobility and muscle spasms. Osteoarthritis is usually non-inflammatory, unless it is systemic. It is the most common type of arthritis. It can be idiopathic (no history of joint injury, disease or systemic illness) or secondary occurring from previous trauma or other inflammatory joint disease like avascular necrosis or a neuropathic disorder such as Legg-Calve-Perthes disease. Traumatic arthritis can develop after a fracture or joint injury. Arthritis can also develop from repetitive injury, like sports. It can be severe enough to require joint(s) replacement (Eustice, 2014).

Risk factors include: age, > 60, women > risk than men, obesity, smoking, genetic link and history of repetitive stress on joints (i.e., running, tennis, golf, etc.).

"ARTHUR" Has Osteoarthritis

Assess pain, administer analgesic medications as prescribe, ROM, ability to do ADL.

Remind to use proper body mechanics, splinting for joint protection.

Teach to use assistive devices (i.e., elevate toilet seat, etc.) as needed.
Try complementary & alternative therapies, (i.e., acupuncture, **TENS** unit*, music, etc.).

U need to rest between exercising.

Referrals to OT, PT & dietary (well balanced diet, weight loss if needed).

*TENS: Transcutaneous Electric Nerve Simulation Unit

ARTHUR ITIS

I sure am achy and stiff in the mornin's.

Pathophysiology: Joint and/or Connective Tissue Dysfunction or Inflammation

Total Joint Arthroplasty/Replacement

Joint replacement, arthroplasty, is the surgical removal of diseased joint and replacement with an artificial joint. The most common joint replacements are knee and hip but other joints can be replaced as well (i.e., shoulder, ankle, etc.). The decision to do a joint replacement is primarily decided by the client's functional ability and the intensity and debilitation resulting from the pain. The desired outcomes of joint replacement surgery are to eliminate pain, restore joint motion and improve client's functional status and quality of life. Clients' requiring joint replacements early in life may need a 2nd or 3rd replacement during their lifetime (Osborn, Wraa, Watson & Holleran, 2014).

"ACT NOW"	General "POST-OP CARE"
Assess for all allergies (i.e., shellfish, iodine, anesthetic agents & any prior experience with sedation). **A**ssess ID of client. **C**onsent required (informed). **T**each, give explanation for post op care & importance of pain management & movement post-op. **N**eed to assess baseline VS, pulses, BUN/Creatinine p**O**sition as prescribed (i.e., hip, knee) for comfort preoperatively. **W**atch and assess for risks (i.e., recent infection, arterial impairment to affected extremity, unstable co-morbidities, & history or risk for DVT, etc.); notify surgeon of concerns.	**P**atency of airway assess, lung sounds, SaO_2 sat, encourage cough & deep breathing & incentive spirometer every 1–2 hours. **O**bserve incision site for bleeding, monitor CBC, and check clotting factors. **S**kin color, lips & mucous membranes note, evaluate surgical wound for healing, note any redness, swelling, drainage (i.e., color, odor, amount, etc.). **T**rend VS, signs of infections, (i.e., ↑ temp or WBCs), bowel sounds, note if present, hypo or hyperactive; neurovascular assessment of affected extremity every 2-4 hours or per protocol. **O**utput (I & O) monitor; J tube, T tube, monitor, evaluate & trend output and drainage if applicable. **P**ain management, be proactive, offer pain medication on schedule (bone pain is severe), assess IV site and ensure Patient Controlled Analgesia (PCA) pump is working adequately if used. Instruct client on use. **C**ardiac monitor if needed; monitor level of consciousness (LOC). **A**nesthesia response, (i.e., VS, LOC, etc.), administer pain medications as prescribed. **R**enal function, BUN & Creatinine evaluate post operatively. **E**lectrolyte & fluids monitor closely, I & O record. **E**ncourage movement within client's ability (referral to physical therapy).

Pathophysiology: Joint and/or Connective Tissue Dysfunction or Inflammation

Joint Replacement

Care of the Post-Op "Joint" Replacement Client

"JOINT"

Joints need exercise; early ambulation, get out of bed on unaffected side.

Observe and monitor for bleeding, hypovolemia; prevent and monitor for DVT.

Infection: monitor WBCs, temperature; assess incision for color, incision edges approximated; drainage: amount, color, odor.

Need correct positioning post-op:
  Hip replacement: avoid internal rotation, abduction for hip; avoid flexion of hip > 90 degrees.
    Use elevated toilet and chair seating, use abduction pillow while in bed and when turning.
    DO NOT cross legs.
  Knee replacement: avoid flexion of the knee for knee replacement.
    Use Continuous Passive Motion (CPM) machine as prescribed.

Treat pain, assess frequently and if pain is relieved; instruct client how to use a patient controlled analgesia pump.
  Teach how to use assistive devices, consult with physical therapy, home health for a comprehensive risk assessment, home care 6 weeks or greater may be needed.

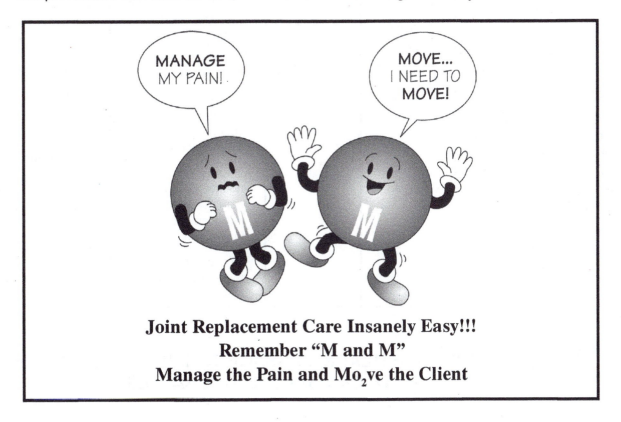

Joint Replacement Care Insanely Easy!!!
Remember "M and M"
Manage the Pain and Mo$_2$ve the Client

Exceptions and Additions by Diseases

Pathophysiology: Joint and/or Connective Tissue Dysfunction or Inflammation

Osteomyelitis

Osteomyelitis is inflammation within the bone secondary to penetration by an infectious organism. The most common organism is Staphylococcus aureus. The bone can be infected by three different routes: 1) blood stream (carry infection from one part of body to the bones); 2) direct invasion via open fractures, surgery or penetrating objecting into the bone; or 3) infections in nearby structures, (i.e., natural or artificial joints or soft tissue). When the bone is infected, the bone marrow swells and presses against the rigid outer wall of the bone thus compressing the blood vessels in the bone marrow. This can result in decreased blood supply to the bone. The infection can spread from the bone to form abscesses in nearby soft tissue like the muscles. If the infection becomes chronic, bone cells become necrotic and break which provides a medium for further spread of the bacteria. When new bone formation develops around the necrotic cells, sinus tracts may develop to the skin which allows pus to drain (Porth & Grossman, 2013).

SYSTEM-SPECIFIC ASSESSMENTS	FIRST-DO PRIORITY INTERVENTIONS			
	DIET	EQUIPMENT	PLANS/INTERVENTIONS	HEALTH PROMOTION
Infections of leg & arm bones • Pain in infected bone • Area over bone, sore, red, warm & swollen • Movement painful • Fever • May have fatigue & weight loss **Infections of the vertebrae** • Persistent back pain • Tenderness over area when touched • Pain worse with movement • Not relieved by rest or analgesics • Fever often absent	**Nutrition for Healing** • Increase protein • Increase calories • Vitamin C • Refer to Concept on Nutrition for specifics	• Assistive devices • Refer to information in this chapter	• May need strict bed rest to prevent spread of bacteria • Pain control • Antibiotics (may take weeks & months of antibiotic therapy) • Immobilize affected site if needed • May need to debride wound, then need wound care with aseptic technique • Chronic infections may require debridement of dead tissue and bone, area then packed with healthy tissue & skin • May need hyperbaric oxygen treatments for healing	Teach client/family: • Signs of infection • How to use aseptic technique • Importance of taking complete prescription of antibiotics (may be long term) • Signs and symptoms to report to the HCP, (i.e., ↑ temp, weight loss, fatigue, etc.)

CAUTION WITH HEAT & MASSAGE TO THE AFFECTED AREA: BOTH CAN SPREAD THE BACTERIA.

Pathophysiology: Joint and/or Connective Tissue Dysfunction or Inflammation

Gout

Gout is a metabolic bone disorder where purine (protein metabolism) is altered by uric acid accumulation. Urate crystals form when there are high levels of uric acid in the blood. The body produces uric acid when purines are broken down. The sharp urate crystals accumulate in the joints where there is rapid swelling and pain in the affected joint, most often the big toe, but it can be in any joint, (i.e., ankles, knees, etc.). Normally uric acid dissolves and is excreted by the kidneys.

SYSTEM-SPECIFIC ASSESSMENTS	FIRST-DO PRIORITY INTERVENTIONS			
	DIET	EQUIPMENT	PLANS/INTERVENTIONS "GOUT"	HEALTH PROMOTION
• Redness, swelling & tenderness of joint (great toe is common site) • May be acute in onset with severe pain • Fever • Tachycardia • Can be asymptomatic for years • Late changes result in multiple joints affected with restriction of movement • Risk for atherosclerosis • May cause renal calculi	**Avoid foods high in purines** • Organ meats, shell fish, salmon, choose low fat meat and fish • Alcohol • High fructose (i.e., soft drinks, fruit drinks) **Include in diet:** • Increase whole grains • Eat low fat dairy • Refer to Concept on Nutrition for specifics	• Immobilize the joint	**G**ulp 3 liters fluid/day unless contraindicated (i.e., heart failure, renal disease, etc.) **O**rgan meats, alcohol, shell fish avoid **U**rine output ↑ 2 L/day to excrete uric acid & prevent kidney stones **T**each about medications & to avoid salicylates • During acute attack, immobilize the joint • Weight reduction if needed	Teach client/family: • Diet avoiding high purine foods • Need for increase fluid intake • Medications (i.e., colchicine, indomethacin (Indocin) or naproxen (Naprosyn) • Avoid salicylates

Exceptions and Additions by Diseases

Pathophysiology: Joint and/or Connective Tissue Dysfunction or Inflammation

Rheumatoid Arthritis

Rheumatoid arthritis is a chronic progressive autoimmune disease. It can be systemic with inflammation of the joints that may result in deformity. The inflammatory response may be initiated by an exposure to a virus. The immunoglobulin G (IgG) is formed in response to antigens, but the body produces autoantibodies (rheumatoid factors) against the IgG for unknown reasons. This results in chronic inflammation and destruction of articular cartilage and the surrounding joint structures. The synovial fluid that lubricates the joint structures hypertrophies and thickens due to the chronic inflammation. The blood supply is then occluded and cellular necrosis results. This causes the formation of pannus (vascular granulation tissue), which extends from the synovial membrane into the joint capsule and subchondral bone causing the bone destruction. Then fibrous adhesion and bony ankylosis (joint immobility or fixation) occurs as the bone is destroyed. This process extends to the support structures of the bone, tendons and ligaments and results in joint instability and deformity results. Pacing activity with rest periods helps the client prevent an increase in joint pain or stiffness related to swelling and fatigue (American Rheumatism Association, 2012).

SYSTEM-SPECIFIC ASSESSMENTS "ARTHY"	FIRST-DO PRIORITY INTERVENTIONS			
	DIET	EQUIPMENT	PLANS/INTERVENTIONS	HEALTH PROMOTION
A.M. stiffness, vague symptoms first, anorexia, weight loss **R**educed ability to do ADL **T**enderness of multiple joints, inflammation, swelling **H**ands, feet, wrists, elbows with decreased range of motion, knees and spine as it progresses **Y**ou need to use the American Rheumatism Association for assessment & diagnostic criteria (American Rheumatism Association, 2012)	**Foods that help REDUCE inflammation:** • Olive oil • Nuts • Fresh herbs (i.e., basil, oregano, thyme, etc.) • Chocolate • Tea • Avoid red meat	• Assistive devices • Refer to information in this chapter	• Administer as prescribed: NSAIDS, systemic corticosteroids, disease modifying drugs (DMARDs) • Refer to *Pharmacology Made Insanely Easy* book in reference list • Use heat and cold applications as indicated	Teach client/family: • Support groups like Arthritis Foundation • Referral to physical therapy to teach client how to decrease joint stress and range of motion activity • Pace activities with rest (rest helps to decrease pain and joint swelling) • Refer to occupational therapy for assistive devices for ADLs • How to avoid complications from immobility • Guided imagery • Relaxation techniques

Insanely Easy Way to Remember Priorities for Use of Heat and Cold Therapies:

Heat = Vasodilation = ↓ Pain

Cold = Vasoconstriction = ↓ Bleeding, Swelling & Pain

Remember **DO NOT USE HOT OR COLD IF THERE ARE ALTERATIONS IN PERFUSION**
(i.e., diabetes, peripheral vascular disease, etc.)

Pathophysiology: Joint and/or Connective Tissue Dysfunction or Inflammation

Systemic Lupus Erythematosus (SLE)

Systemic Lupus Erythematosus (SLE) is multisystem chronic inflammatory, rheumatic, autoimmune disease, characterized by remission and exacerbations. It often occurs in young women. The body produces antibodies against the body that combines with antigens to form immune complexes. The complexes accumulate in the connective tissue and trigger an inflammatory response. This chronic inflammation destroys connective tissue and can involve multiple organs (i.e., skin, joints, kidneys, lungs, etc.). The symptoms may vary depending on the organ involved. Clients need to pace their activity with rest to avoid an increase in achiness and fatigue (LeMone, Burke, & Bauldoff, 2011).

SYSTEM-SPECIFIC ASSESSMENTS "LUPUS"	FIRST-DO PRIORITY INTERVENTIONS			
	DIET	EQUIPMENT	PLANS/INTERVENTIONS "GOUT"	HEALTH PROMOTION
Lesions, painless in mouth **U** have a butterfly rash on cheeks (malar rash), and/or red rash with raised round patches (discord rash) and/or rash on skin exposed to the sun **P**olyarthralgia of musculoskeletal system **U** may have an increase in fever, malaise, fatigue, weight loss, painful swollen joints **S**clerosis of skin on fingers • Others symptoms vary depending on organ involvement: (i.e., pericarditis, pleural effusion, glomerulonephritis, renal failure, seizures, CVA, anemia, leukopenia, thrombocytopenia, infections, etc.)	• Well balanced diet with plenty of fruits, vegetables, and whole grains • Other diet recommendations based on organ or system involved	• As indicated	Administer as prescribed: • NSAIDS • Antidepressants • Corticosteroids during exacerbations • Immunosuppressive drugs • Use application of heat to joints • Exercise program • Assess factors that may trigger exacerbations	Teach client/family: • How to pace activity with rest • Referral to dietary for nutritional needs • Good oral care • Stress management • Refer to support groups • Instruct on undesired effects of medications • Prevention of infection • Protection from UV exposure • Need to avoid birth control pills, sulfonamides, & penicillin

Pathophysiology: Joint and/or Connective Tissue Dysfunction or Inflammation

Mobility Equipment: Assistive Devices

Immobilizers limit movement of the affected extremity or joint. Immobilizers are made for shoulders, arms, legs, etc. Casts, splints, and braces are also considered immobilizers.

"CANE"–The Strong Side Leads

C ane is used on the side opposite the affected leg.

A ffected leg and cane move together.

N ote that the cane should be advanced simultaneously with the opposite affected lower limb.

E valuate for correct size...measure from wrist to the floor.

Cane is on the **O**pposite side of the affected leg and cane is advanced with the **A**ffected **L**eg! Another approach to remembering this is to remember "**COAL**"!

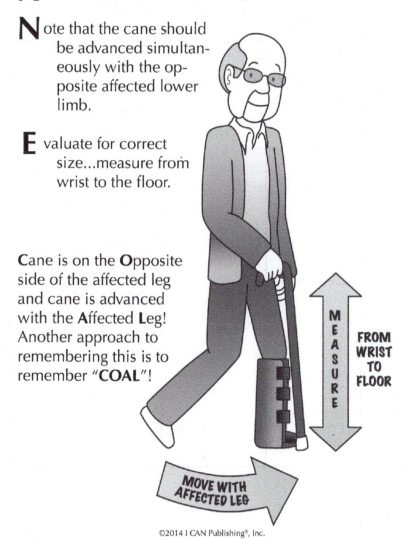

MEASURE

FROM WRIST TO FLOOR

MOVE WITH AFFECTED LEG

Pathophysiology: Joint and/or Connective Tissue Dysfunction or Inflammation
Crutch Walking

"MEASURE" for Crutches

Measurement may be taken with client supine or standing.

Evaluate in supine position: measure the distance from the client's axilla to a point 6 inches lateral to the heel.

Adjust hand bars so client's elbows are flexed at approximately 30 degrees.

Standing: evaluate distance from client's axilla to a point 4 to 6 inches to side and 4 to 6 inches in front of the foot.

U should be able to put 2 of your fingers between client's axilla and crutch bar.

Remember, if client was measured while supine, assist to stand with crutches.

Evaluate distance between client's axilla and arm.

Four-Point Alternate Gait:

P artial weight on both feet

A rthritis or cerebral palsy are some examples of who would benefit from this gait

R eal safe gait, in that there are 3 points of support on the floor at all times

T he gait provides a normal walking pattern and makes some use of the muscles of the lower extremities

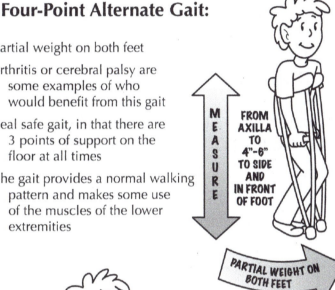

MEASURE FROM AXILLA TO 4"-6" TO SIDE AND IN FRONT OF FOOT

PARTIAL WEIGHT ON BOTH FEET

Three-Point Alternate Gait:

O ne foot should be able to bear weight on

N on-weight bearing for the affected foot or leg

E ducate to move both crutches forward together with the affected leg while the weight is being borne by the client's hands on the crutches. The unaffected leg is then advanced forward.

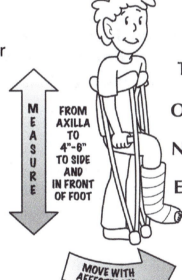

MEASURE FROM AXILLA TO 4"-6" TO SIDE AND IN FRONT OF FOOT

MOVE WITH AFFECTED LEG

Pathophysiology Joint and/or Connective Tissue Dysfunction or Inflammation

Instructions for Crutch Walking

Insanely Easy Way to Remember
How to Use Crutches on Stairs!!!

The good leg goes up the stairs first:
"GOOD GOES TO HEAVEN!"

The bad leg goes down the stairs first
"BAD GOES TO YOU KNOW WHERE!"

© 2001 I CAN Publishing, Inc.

Pathophysiology: Joint and/or Connective Tissue Dysfunction or Inflammation

Instructions for the use of the Walker: "WALK"

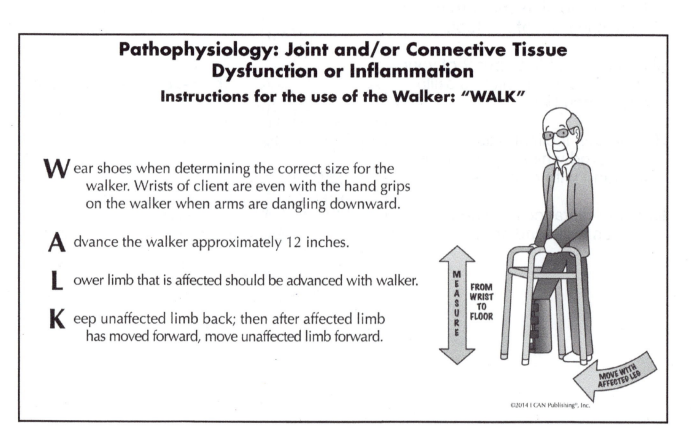

W ear shoes when determining the correct size for the walker. Wrists of client are even with the hand grips on the walker when arms are dangling downward.

A dvance the walker approximately 12 inches.

L ower limb that is affected should be advanced with walker.

K eep unaffected limb back; then after affected limb has moved forward, move unaffected limb forward.

©2014 I CAN Publishing®, Inc.

Musculoskeletal System: Concept Mobility

Let's review the key main concepts for all of the musculoskeletal disorders!! Can you name all the Concepts?

The nursing care of clients with altered mobility revolves around the concepts and

Preventing "TERRIBLE"!

- **Oxygenation**: Immobile clients need help to **MO$_2$VE** & encouraged to deep breathe to **PREVENT ATELECTASIS**!

- **Pain**: Clients with pain won't breathe deeply or move. **MANAGE THE PAIN** so clients will **MO$_2$VE** (The **"M and M"s**)!

- **Perfusion**: Clients who have alteration with mobility, need assistance to **MO$_2$VE** to **PREVENT DVTs**!

- **Fluid Balance**: Clients **NEED FLUIDS** for healing and to **PREVENT CONSTIPATION**!

- **Tissue/Skin Integrity**: Immobile clients need help to **MO$_2$VE to PREVENT SKIN BREAKDOWN**!

- **Nutrition Balance**: Need adequate **NUTRITION FOR HEALING**.

- **Infection Control**: Watch WBCs, temp, incision/pin sites for redness, swelling or drainage to **PREVENT INFECTION**!

- **Coping**: Immobility can lead to boredom & depression, use diversion & support to **Maintain Emotional Health.**

(Refer to Concepts: Oxygenation, Pain, Perfusion, Fluid Balance, Tissue/Skin Integrity, Nutrition, Infection Control, Coping for specifics.)

THE "M and M"s are the Key to Prevent "TERRIBLE"!

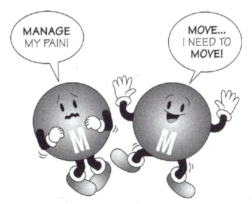

You Got This!!! Another Genius Award for You!

Clinical Decision-Making Exercises

1. Which of these nursing interventions are important to prevent complications of immobility in a client with a fractured femur? *Select all that apply.*
   ① Use incentive spirometer every 2 hours while awake.
   ② Limit caloric intake to avoid weight gain while immobile.
   ③ Administer stool softener as ordered.
   ④ Adjust weights to maintain traction.
   ⑤ ROM on the unaffected extremities 2–3 times per day.

2. Which statement made by the new nurse who is giving a class on assistive devices would indicate to the charge nurse that the nurse needs additional instruction?
   ① "When using crutches to climb stairs, the crutch and the good leg are placed on the next step, followed by the affected leg."
   ② "When using crutches to climb stairs, the affected leg and the crutch are placed on the next step, followed by the good leg."
   ③ "When using a cane, it is positioned on the unaffected side and advanced with the affected extremity."
   ④ "When using a walker, the walker is moved forward with the affected leg."

3. What is the priority action for a client with a long leg cast on the right leg whose assessment reveals: right foot is pale and cool to touch and the right leg pain is still severe with no relief from the given pain medication 45 minutes ago?
   ① Apply a heating pad to the right toes.
   ② Repeat the dose of analgesic stat.
   ③ Remove the cast immediately.
   ④ Notify the HCP immediately.

4. Which of these clients would be highest risk for the development of a DVT?
   ① A 50-year-old client who is post-op for hernia repair.
   ② A 60-year-old client in traction for fractured hip.
   ③ A 70-year-old client who is post bronchoscopy.
   ④ An 80-year-old client who has osteoarthritis.

5. Which of the food selections made by the client with an acute episode of gout indicates an understanding of the dietary needs to help prevent exacerbations of gout?
   ① Salmon, milk and canned peaches.
   ② Fried chicken, carrots and dinner rolls.
   ③ Lean steak, green beans and skim milk.
   ④ Bean soup, cornbread and a beer.

6. Which of these clinical findings would be appropriate to report with a client in skeletal traction? *Select all that apply.*
   ① Client is using incentive spirometer every 1–2 hours.
   ② Redness at the pin site.
   ③ Respiratory rate was 16, is now 21.
   ④ Adventitious lung sounds in left lower lung.
   ⑤ Pedal pulses are 1+ and equal bilaterally.

7. What is a priority intervention for a client with left knee replacement surgery 24 hours ago that is to attend a physical therapy session in 30 minutes?

   ① Administer pain medication as ordered.

   ② Instruct the client to empty their bladder.

   ③ Administer pain medication only if the client is currently complaining.

   ④ Hold pain medication until after the physical therapy.

8. Which of these statements made by the client with a new diagnosis of rheumatoid arthritis indicates there is a need for further teaching?

   ① "I understand that I will have morning stiffness and pain in my affected joints."

   ② "I should constantly remain active throughout the day to avoid joint pain and stiffness."

   ③ "I understand that this disease may affect the joints of my extremities."

   ④ "I should prepare myself for the deformities that I will experience as my disease progresses."

9. Which clinical finding would be a priority to report to the healthcare provider about an 80-year-old client who is immobile due to a fractured hip 3 days ago?

   ① Pulse 95 bpm

   ② Potassium–4.9 mEq/L

   ③ No stools for 3 days

   ④ Calcium 9.6 mEq/L

10. What is the priority intervention that should be included in the plan of care to prevent complications of immobility in an elderly client?

    ① Obtain orders for therapeutic elastic stockings (TED hose).

    ② Determine the need for assistive devices to move the client.

    ③ Turn, cough and deep breathe every two hours.

    ④ Do a comprehensive skin assessment every other week to check for breakdown.

Answers and Rationales

1. Which of these **nursing interventions are important to prevent complications of immobility** in a client with a fractured femur? Select all that apply.

    ① **CORRECT: Use incentive spirometer every 2 hours while awake. Helps keep the lungs expanded.**

    ② INCORRECT: Limit caloric intake to avoid weight gain while immobile. Need additional calories for healing.

    ③ **CORRECT: Administer stool softener as ordered. Immobility makes it difficult for elimination and pain medications can be constipating. Stool softeners help prevent the client from straining.**

    ④ INCORRECT: Adjust weights to maintain traction. The nurse never adjusts the weights on tractions; this is done by the HCP or physical therapy as prescribed.

    ⑤ **CORRECT: ROM on the unaffected extremities 2–3 times per day. This helps the client maintain muscle tone and mobility of joint. It helps promote circulation, which decreases risk for DVT, contractures.**

The strategy for answering this question is to be knowledgeable about the potential complications of immobility and the PRIORITY nursing interventions needed to prevent complications of immobility. The incentive spirometer, along with deep breathing, and elevating the head of the bed to expand the airway, prevents atelectasis and potential infections. Stool softeners, in addition to adequate fluid intake of 2,000 mL/day, unless contraindicated (i.e., heart failure, renal disease, neuro, etc.) and increased residue (fiber) in the diet, help prevent the complication of constipation. The ROM exercises help prevent the potential complication of deep vein thrombosis and help the keep muscles toned and maintain strength. The ROM exercises also help with perfusion to increase the return of the circulating blood back to the heart. **Remember, Immobility Care Made Insanely Easy:** Just "MO$_2$VE" to Prevent "Terrible"!!!

Physiological Adaptation: Use precautions to prevent injury and/or complications associated with diagnosis

Basic Care and Comfort: Assess and manage client with alteration in elimination (i.e. bowel).

Basic Care and Comfort: Implement measures to promote circulation (i.e. range of motion).

Physiological Adaptation: Provide pulmonary hygiene (i.e., incentive spirometry).

2. Which **statement** made by the new nurse who is giving a **class on assistive devices** would **indicate** to the charge nurse that the **nurse needs additional instruction**?

    ① INCORRECT: When using crutches to climb stairs, the crutch and the good leg are placed on the next step, followed by the affected leg. Remember the good leg goes up to Heaven!! Start with the good leg.

    ② **CORRECT: When using crutches to climb stairs, the affected leg and the crutch are placed on the next step, followed by the good leg. This is not correct, start with good leg.**

    ③ INCORRECT: When using cane, position on the unaffected side and advance with the affected side. There is no need for further intervention. This is the correct procedure.

    ④ INCORRECT: When using a walker, the walker is moved forward with the affected leg. Then move the unaffected limb forward. This is a correct statement and does not need any intervention.

The strategy for answering this question is to be knowledgeable about assistive devices so you can assist the client in learning how to use them safely to improve their mobility. Knowing the correct use of assistive devices is a SAFETY issue to prevent falls and further injury.

Safety and Infection Control: Assure appropriate and safe use of equipment in performing client care.

Safety and Infection Control: Use ergonomic principles when providing care (i.e. assistive devices).

Safety and Infection Control: Protect client from injury (i.e. falls).

3. What is the **priority action** for a client with a **long leg cast on the right leg whose assessment reveals: right foot is pale** and cool to touch and the right leg **pain is still severe with no relief from the given pain medication 45 minutes ago?**

① INCORRECT: Apply a heating pad to the right toes. This intervention would not be appropriate based on the clinical findings in the stem of the question.

② INCORRECT: Repeat the dose of analgesic stat. This would not be correct because the severe unrelieved pain is a sign of decreasing perfusion to the affected leg.

③ INCORRECT: Remove the cast immediately. This would not be the first action to take; the cast might be cut, but not removed.

④ **CORRECT: Notify the HCP immediately. These clinical findings indicate a possible compartment syndrome, requiring immediate intervention and guidance from the healthcare provider to ensure circulation is restored to the affected limb.**

The strategy for answering this question is to be vigilant in your system specific assessments with a client with the potential complications of compartment syndrome. Clients with casts, due to bleeding and/or increased edema at the fracture site and the enclosed environment of the cast are at risk for compartment syndrome. The decreasing circulation to the right foot indicated by the cool skin temperature and paleness in color and particularly the unrelieved pain, are classic clinical findings for this complication. The healthcare provider needs to be notified immediately so that circulation can be restored to the limb without damage.

Physiological Adaptation: Use precautions to prevent injury and/or complications associated with diagnosis.

Management of Care: Collaborate with health care members with other disciplines when providing care.

4. Which of these clients would be **highest risk for the development of a DVT?**

① INCORRECT: A 50-year-old client who is post-op for hernia repair. Hernia repair has short recovery with minimal limitations on mobility.

② **CORRECT: A 60-year-old client in traction for fractured hip. This causes long term immobility because of the traction and decrease ability to move and turn. The long term immobility increases the chance of venous pooling in the extremities leading to formation of clots.**

③ INCORRECT: A 70-year-old client who is post bronchoscopy. This is minimal risk due to the short time of immobility.

④ INCORRECT: An 80-year-old client who has osteoarthritis. Although elderly with osteoarthritis may have some mobility limitations, the distractor does not state the client is unable to move.

The strategy for answering this question is to know the pathophysiology of the increased risk of deep vein thrombosis in clients with immobility. The traction and fracture limit the venous return to the heart and the increases stasis of the blood in the veins which increases the risk of clots. It would be Priority with this client to turn, and do ROM on the unaffected limb, increase fluid intake unless contraindicated (i.e., heart failure, renal disease, neuro, etc.). The client may be put on a low weight molecular heparin, like Lovenox to decrease the risk of clots.

Reduction of Risk Potential: Recognize trends and changes in the clients condition and intervene appropriately.

5. Which of the **food selections** made by the client with an **acute episode of gout** indicates an understanding of the **dietary needs to help prevent exacerbations of gout?**

① INCORRECT: Salmon, milk and canned peaches. Salmon is a high fat fish and is high in purines), whole milk high in fat (saturated fat lowers the body's ability to eliminate uric acid) and peaches are high in fructose syrup all contraindicated with a low purine diet.

② INCORRECT: Fried chicken, carrots and dinner rolls. Fried chicken is high in fat, carrots are fine but bread needs to be whole grain.

③ **CORRECT: Lean steak, green beans and skim milk. All of these foods are low in fat and in purines.**

④ INCORRECT: Bean soup, cornbread and a beer. The cornbread and the beer make this an unhealthy choice (sounds like a great meal, but not a good choice for gout)!!!!

The strategy for answering this question is to know the pathophysiology of what contributes to gout. Although, the diet is not the only intervention the client needs, it can help the client take an active role in their care by choosing the right foods that could lessen the chance for painful exacerbations from gout (*Refer to Concept Nutrition for specifics*).

Health Promotion and Maintenance: Provide the client and family with information about their condition/ illness or outcomes.

Basic Care and Comfort: Intervene with client who has an alteration in nutritional intake.

6. Which of these **clinical findings** would be appropriate to **report** with a **client in skeletal traction**? Select all that apply.

① INCORRECT: Client is using incentive spirometer every 1–2 hour. This is a desired activity for a client in traction to help promote deep breathing and lung expansion.

② **CORRECT: Redness at the pin site. Redness at the pin site could indicate a potential infection. As the nurse you would want to investigate this further with the healthcare provider to be proactive in preventing a possible infection. Infections in an immobile client prevent a risk to the client in their recovery.**

③ **CORRECT: Respiratory rate was 16, is now 22. Although the respiratory rate is only slightly above normal, it is trending up and with the assessment of the adventitious lung sounds. As a nurse, you want to be proactive in preventing respiratory infections that can prolong the hospitalization and negatively impact desired outcomes.**

④ **CORRECT: Adventitious lung sounds in left lower lung. This is another indicator of a potential infection and encouragement of coughing and deep breathing would be needed along with an incentive spirometer. Repositioning**

elevate the head of the bed to encourage lung expansion would also be a PRIORITY intervention.

⑤ INCORRECT: Pedal pulses are 1+ and equal bilaterally. Although the pulses are only 1+ in strength, they are palpable and equal. It would be important to compare with baseline assessments.

The strategy to answer this question is to know the pathophysiology of the potential complications of immobility as well as recognizing signs of infection (*Refer to Concept Infection Control for specifics*). It is a PRIORITY for the nurse to intervene early to minimize the potential complications (*Refer to chapter 1 Prioritization for specifics*). The redness at the pin site with the increased respiratory rate and adventitious lungs sounds are all pointing to a potential infection. Think of "**TERRIBLE**", and remember immobile clients are an increased risk for infection because of their immobility.

Physiological Adaptation: Use precautions to prevent injury and/or complications associated with diagnosis

Physiological Adaptation: Provide pulmonary hygiene (i.e., incentive spirometry.

7. What is a **priority intervention** for a client with **left knee replacement surgery** 24 hours ago that is to attend a physical therapy session in 30 minutes?

① **CORRECT: Administer pain medication as ordered. Pain medication 30 minutes prior to physical therapy will help the client participate more actively and the session will be more beneficial than if the client is in pain and is reluctant to move. The client is only 24 hours post-op, and pain control is a priority.**

② INCORRECT: Instruct the client to empty their bladder. It is fine, but it is not the priority prior to physical therapy.

③ INCORRECT: Administer pain medication only if the client is currently complaining. With joint replacement surgeries, pain management needs to be proactive and maintained on a schedule particularly prior to exercise that might illicit pain. It is easier to relieve pain before it becomes intense.

④ INCORRECT: Hold pain medication until after the physical therapy. Without pain medication, the physical therapy session will be less effective because the client will be reluctant to participate because of the pain.

The strategy to answer this question is Insanely Easy ... Clients who Hurt don't MO$_2$VE and they need to move. **Remember the "M and Ms" ... you need to Manage Pain and MO$_2$VE the Client!!!**

Pharmacological and Parenteral Therapies: Use pharmacological measure for pain management PRN.

8. Which of these **statements made by the client** with a new diagnosis of rheumatoid arthritis **indicates there is a need for further teaching?**

    ① INCORRECT: "I understand that I will have morning stiffness and pain in my affected joints". This is a true statement.

    ② CORRECT: **"I should constantly remain active throughout the day to avoid joint pain and stiffness." Activity is important and necessary with rheumatoid arthritis, but the activity needs to be paced with rest periods** (*Refer to Concept Cardiac/ Peripheral Perfusion for specifics on activity intolerance*).

    ③ INCORRECT: "I understand that this disease may affect the joints of my extremities." This is true.

    ④ INCORRECT: "I should prepare myself for the deformities that I will experience as my disease progresses. This is true.

The strategy for this question is to pace activity with rest. This is true for clients with SLE and osteoarthritis. The activity is good to maintain joint function and mobility, but without resting in between, the swelling in the joints increase which leads to increased pain and fatigue. This is a quality life issue with these clients and an important nursing intervention. Can you remember other clients, where pacing activity with rest was important? Think about clients who have pain or shortness of breath and need to rest between activities, (*Refer to Concept Cardiac/ Peripheral Perfusion for specifics on activity intolerance*).

Basic Care and Comfort: Assist client with performance of activities of daily living.

Basic Care and Comfort: Assess client for need for sleep/rest and intervene.

9. Which **clinical finding** would be a **priority to report** to the healthcare provider about an **80-year-old client who is immobile due to a fractured hip 3 days ago?**

    ① INCORRECT: Pulse 95 bpm. This is ok, no trend indicated the pulse has increased.

    ② INCORRECT: Potassium–4.5 mEq/L. This is at the high end of normal but not a priority to report.

    ③ CORRECT: **No stools for 3 days. This is a priority; the client is immobile and elderly and most likely has been taking pain medication, which can increase the risk of constipation. Constipation leads to a decrease in fluid and food intake because the client feels full. As the fluid and intake decrease, the constipation increases. With severe cases of constipation, the kidneys can fail because the client decreases their fluid intake significantly.**

    ④ INCORRECT: Calcium 9.6 mEq/L. The level is within normal range.

The strategy to answer this question is to recognize the complication of constipation with an immobile client especially in an elderly client. The constipation would require immediate intervention. This was an illustration of the "**TERRIBLE**" in immobility. The take away is to assess the client's normal bowel routine and to intervene early to prevent constipation with immobile clients through adequate fluid, residue (fiber), and mobility within client's ability. It is also important to be an advocate for your client and make sure there is an order for a stool softener. Constipation is never good, and particularly for an elderly client who has a fractured hip.

Basic Care and Comfort: Assess and manage client with an alteration in elimination (i.e. bowel).

10.   What is the **priority intervention** that should be **included in the plan of care** to **prevent complications of immobility in an elderly client?**

① INCORRECT: Obtain orders for therapeutic elastic stockings (TED hose). Although TED hose can be used, sequential compression devices or intermittent pneumatic compression are more effective because of the pumping action that helps return blood back to the heart. Elastic stocking cannot do that and are very difficult to get on a client, particularly an elderly client. This involved a higher level of thinking, although it was a potential right answer, it was not the best answer compared to option 3!

② INCORRECT: Determine the need for assistive devices to move the client. This question was asking about the priority intervention and not an assessment, assessing the need for assistive devices would not prevent the complication.

③ **CORRECT: Turn, cough and deep breathe every two hours. This is a must in preventing immobility complications. The deep breathing helps expand the lungs and the cough helps move secretions.**

④ INCORRECT: Do a comprehensive skin assessment every other week to check for breakdown. The skin assessment needs to be done every day as you bathe or turn the client to assess early for any potential skin breakdown particularly with an elderly client that is already at a greater risk (*Refer to Concept Tissue/Skin Integrity for specifics*).

The strategy for answering this question is again, knowing the pathophysiology of the complications of immobility! Sounding familiar? This time you needed to apply the information to select the **PRIORITY** nursing intervention. Remember, the "M and Ms" and you will be the GENIUS nurse of immobility!!!

Physiological Adaptation: Use precautions to prevent injury and/or complications associated with diagnosis.

Basic Care and Comfort: Implement measures to promote circulation (i.e., ROM, positioning).

Basic Care and Comfort: Apply and maintain devices used to promote venous return (i.e., sequential compression devices).

Basic Care and Comfort: Perform skin assessment and implement measure to maintain skin integrity an prevent skin breakdown (i.e., turning, repositioning).

Decision-Making Analysis Form

Use this tool to help identify why you missed any questions. As you enter the question numbers in the chart, you will begin to see patterns of why you answered incorrectly. This information will then guide you toward what you need to focus on in your continued studies. Ultimately, this analytical exercise will help you become more successful in answering questions!!!

Questions to ask:

1. Did I have the knowledge to answer the question? If not, what information do I need to review?
2. Did I know what the question was asking? Did I misread it or did I miss keywords in the stem of the question?
3. Did I misread or miss keywords in the distractors that would have helped me choose the correct answer?
4. Did I follow my gut reaction or did I allow myself to rationalize and then choose the wrong answer?

	Lack of Knowledge (Concepts, Systems, Pathophysiology, Medications, Procedures, etc.)	Missed Keywords or Misread the Stem of the Question	Missed Keywords or Misread the Distractors	Changed My Answer (Second-guessed myself, i.e., my first answer was correct.)
Put the # of each question you missed in the column that best explains why you think you answered it incorrectly.				

If you changed an answer because you talked yourself out of the correct answer, or you second-guessed yourself, this is an **EASY FIX: QUIT changing your answers**!!! Typically, the first time you read a question, you are about 95% right! The second time you read a question, you start talking yourself into changing the answer. The third time you read a question, you do not have a clue—and you are probably thinking "Who in the heck wrote this question?"

On the other hand, if you read a question too quickly and when you reread it you realize you missed some key information that would impact your decision (i.e., assessments, lab reports, medications, etc.), then it is appropriate to change your answer. When in doubt, go with the safe route: your first thought! Go with your gut instinct!

As you gain confidence in answering questions regarding specific nursing concepts, you will be able to successfully progress to answering higher-level questions about prioritization. Please refer to the *Prioritization Guidelines* in this book for a structure to assist you with this process.

You CAN do this!

"Determine that the thing can and shall be done and then … find the way."

ABRAHAM LINCOLN

References for Chapter 18

American Rheumatism Association (2012). *Diagnostic criteria for rheumatism.* Retrieved form http://www.wheelessonline. com/ortho/american_rheumatism_association_diagnostic_criteria_for_ra

Black, J M. and Hawks, J. H. (2009). *Medical surgical nursing: Clinical management for positive outcomes (8th ed.).* Philadelphia: Elsevier/Saunders.

Daniels, R. & Nicoll, L. (2012). *Contemporary medical-surgical nursing,* (2nd ed.). Clifton Park, NY: Delmar Cengage Learning.

Eliopoulos, C. (2014). *Gerontological nursing* (8th ed.), Philadelphia: Lippincott Williams & Wilkins.

Eustice, C. (2014). *What defines an arthritis flare? An increase in symptoms.* Retrieved from http://arthritis.about.com/od/ arthritislearnthebasics/f/flare.htm

Giddens, G. F. (2013). *Concepts for nursing practice.* St. Louis, MO: Mosby, an imprint of Elsevier.

Hogan, M. A. (2014). *Pathophysiology: Reviews and rationales* (3rd ed.) Boston, MA: Pearson.

Ignatavicius, D. D. and Workman, M. L. (2010). *Medical-surgical nursing: Patient-centered collaborative care* (6th ed.). Philadelphia: Elsevier/Saunders.

LeMone, P., Burke, K. M., and Bauldoff, G. (2011). *Medical-surgical nursing: Critical thinking in patient care* (5th ed.). Upper Saddle Road, NJ: Pearson/Prentice Hall.

Lewis, S., Dirksen, S., Heitkemper, M., Bucher, L., and Camera, I. (2011). *Medical surgical nursing: Assessment and management of clinical problems* (8th ed.). St. Louis: Mosby.

Manning, L. and Rayfield, S. (2014). *Nursing made insanely easy* (7th ed.). Duluth, GA: I CAN Publishing, Inc.

Manning, L. and Rayfield, S. (2013). *Pharmacology made insanely easy* (4th ed.). Duluth, GA: I CAN Publishing, Inc.

Mayo Clinic (2012). *Gout diet, what's allowed, what's not.* Retrieved from http://www.mayoclinic.org/gout-diet/art-20048524

National Council of State Boards of Nursing, INC. (NCSBN) 2012. *Research brief: 2011 RN practice analysis: linking the NCLEX RN® examination to practice.* Retrieved from https://www.ncsbn.org/index.htm

Nettina, S. L. (2013). *Lippincott manual of nursing practice* (10th ed.). Philadelphia, PA: Walters Kluwer Health/Lippincott Williams & Wilkins.

North Carolina Concept Based Learning Editorial Board (2011). *Nursing a concept based approach to learning,* Upper Saddle Road, NJ: Pearson/Prentice Hall.

Osborn, K. S., Wraa, C. E., Watson, A. S., and Holleran, R. S. (2014). *Medical surgical nursing: Preparation for practice* (2nd ed.). Upper Saddle Road, NJ: Pearson.

Pagana, K. D. and Pagana, T. J. (2014). *Mosby's manual of laboratory and diagnostic tests* (5th ed.). St. Louis, MO: Mosby, an imprint of Elsevier.

Porth, C. (2011). *Essentials of pathophysiology* (3d ed.). Philadelphia, PA: Lippincott Williams ad Wilkins.

Porth, C. M. and Grossman, S. (2013). *Pathophysiology: Concepts of altered health states* (9th ed.). Philadelphia, PA: Lippincott Williams & Wilkins.

Potter, P. A., Perry, A. G., Stockert, P., and Hall, A. (2013). *Fundamentals of nursing* (8th ed.). St. Louis, MO: Pearson/Prentice Hall.

Shaikh, N. (2009). *Emergency management of fat embolism syndrome.* Retrieved from http://www.ncbi.nlm.nih.gov/pmc/ articles/PMC2700578/

Smeltzer, S. C., Bare, B. G., Hinkle, J. L., and Cheever, K. H. (2010). *Brunner & Suddarth's Textbook of medical-surgical nursing* (12th ed.). Philadelphia: Lippincott Williams & Wilkins.

Venes, D. (2014). *Tabor's online cyclopedic medical dictionary (22nd ed.).* Philadelphia: FA Davis. Retrieved from http://www. tabers.com/tabersonline/view/Tabers-Dictionary/756143/0/mobility.

Wagner, K. D. and Hardin-Pierce, M. C. (2014). *High-Acuity nursing* (6th ed.). Boston: Pearson.

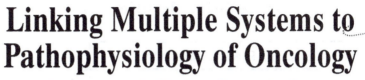

CHAPTER 19

Linking Multiple Systems to Pathophysiology of Oncology
Concept Cellular Regulation

A Snapshot of Cellular Regulation

Cellular Regulation is a term that refers to all functions carried out within the cells to maintain homeostasis, including their response to extracellular signals (i.e., neurotransmitters, hormones) and the way the cells produce an intracellular response (Rosenberg, 2005). Cellular replication and growth are included within these functions and are described by the terms, proliferation and differentiation.

Proliferation is the term for reproduction of new cells through cell division. Differentiation is the term used to describe the acquisition of a specific cell function.

Neoplasia is another term associated with an abnormal and progressive multiplication of cells, resulting in a neoplasm (tumor). This refers to new and abnormal tissue growth that is uncontrolled and progressive. This concept will focus on these two categories of neoplasms, benign and malignant.

Benign neoplasms arise from normal differentiated cells. They retain most of the morphologic and functional characteristics of the normal cells from which they arose. Benign tumors typically do not invade adjacent tissue or metastasize. However, benign tumors can result in health consequences if they obstruct or press on other body structures, resulting in dysfunction, pain, or even death if allowed to continue to grow.

A malignant neoplasm (cancer) is a disease of the cell that presents with abnormal function, growth, and dissemination of affected cells. Due to the alteration in the cell cycle, there is an excessive cell proliferation, poor differentiation, and longer than normal cell lifespan.

531

The Pathophysiology Behind Alterations in Cellular Regulation

CELLULAR REGULATION

MALIGNANT TUMORS

Benign Tumors	Carcinoma and Adenocarcinoma	Lymphomas	Leukemia	Cellular Immunity
	Originates from skin, glands, mucous membrane lining of respiratory, gastrointestinal, and genitourinary tracts	Originates from Lymph System	Originates from Hematopoietic System	Human immunodeficiency virus (HIV)
• Benign Prostate Hypertrophy	• Breast Cancer • Colon Cancer • Lung Cancer • Prostate Cancer	• Hodgkin's lymphoma • Non-Hodgkin's lymphoma	• Chronic lymphocytic leukemia (CLL) • Chronic myeloid leukemia (CML) • Acute lymphocytic leukemia (ALL) • Acute myeloid leukemia (AML)	• HIV/AIDs

These cancer cells are out of control. Due to the alteration in the cell cycle, there is an excess in cell proliferation and poor differentiation. These cancer cells are being fought off by rest, exercise, good nutrition, meditating, etc.

Once cancer has developed; however, surgery, chemotherapy, radiation, and/or target therapy are essential to fight the cancer cells.

Our goal is to promote health to prevent cancer from occurring.

Multiple Systems: Cellular Regulation

System-Specific Assessments: Risk Factors
"CAUTION"

Change in bowel/bladder habits

A sore throat that doesn't heal

Unusual bleeding or discharge

Thickening or lump in breast somewhere

Indigestion or difficulty swallowing

Obvious changes in moles or warts

Nagging cough or hoarseness

(American Cancer Society, 7 *Warning Signs*)

Additional Signs:

- Fatigue

- Weight loss

- Unexplained pain

Multiple Systems: Cellular Regulation
System-Specific Assessments

Using the risk factors outlined by the American Cancer Society, we have adapted the mnemonic "**DIETS**" to connect together the guidelines from Healthy People 2020 (Healthy People 2020, 2014), with the nursing care. After completing the initial assessment, primary preventative nursing care should be incorporated throughout the plan of care.

Cancer prevention	**D**iet is balanced including fresh fruits and vegetables, adequate fiber and whole grains, and decrease fats and preservatives; avoid smoked and salt-cured foods containing increased nitrates.
	Intake of alcohol should be limited.
	Exercise at least 30 minutes of moderate to vigorous exercise 5 days a week.
	Try to avoid carcinogens (i.e., cigarette smoking, sun exposure, etc.).
	Sleep and rest at least 6–8 hours per night; stress needs to be decreased or change perception; improve ability to cope with stress.
Assess history	Assess abnormal findings that can suggest a complication with a neoplasm including: visible lesions, physical asymmetry, palpable masses, and presence of blood such as with a guaiac test for occult blood or pelvic exam (Wilson, 2009).
Nutrition	**N**utrition: Assess for protein and calorie malnutrition.
Chemotherapy	**C**hemotherapy effect: Remember "**NAUSEA.**"
	Non-productive cough, fever, tachypnea (pneumonitis, referred to as pulmonary toxicity)
	Anemia: (anemia, thrombocytopenia, leukopenia)
	Uricemia is increased (hyperuricemia); ulceration from infusion therapy
	Stomatitis (mucositis)
	Elimination (anorexia, nausea, vomiting, constipation)
	Alopecia
Examination	Examination (*Refer to chart, Labs and Diagnostic Tests/Procedures/Diagnostics in this chapter*).
Radiation Reactions	Radiation reactions: Remember "**SKIN.**"
	Skin reactions: erythema, followed by dry desquamation of the skin in the treatment field; blistered skin; wet desquamation, particularly in skinfolds (axillary, breast); loss of hair on skin in location of radiation; discoloration of skin pigmentation.
	Keep assessing for signs of cystitis if radiation is near the urinary tract.
	Intestinal (GI) disturbances are more prevalent when radiation is delivered to area close to GI tract.
	Note pericarditis may occur when chest wall receives radiation.

Alteration with Cellular Regulation

Labs and Diagnostic Tests/Therapeutic Procedures

Labs	Diagnostic Tests/Therapeutic Procedures
• CBC • PT, PTT, INR • Platelets • BUN • Creatinine • Electrolytes • Serum Glucose • Hormones • Lipids • Proteins • UA • Tumor Markers • CA125-ovarian, digestive tract, uterus, cervix, pancreas, liver, colon, breast and lung • Prostate Specific Antigen- (PSA) • Prostatic Acid Phosphatase (PAP) • Neuron-Specific Enolase (NSE) • CA 27–29: breast, colon, stomach, kidney, lung, ovary pancreas, uterus and liver • Lactate dehydrogenase (LDH) • CA19–9 colon, stomach and bile duct • Human Chorionic Gonadotropin (HCG) • Alpha-Fetoprotein (AFP) • Carcinoembryonic antigen (CEA) • CA 15–3 breast, ovary, lung, prostate	• X-ray • Barium Enema • Biopsy • Digital Rectal Exam (DRE) • Fecal Occult Blood Tests • Sigmoidoscopy • Bone Marrow Aspirations and Biopsy • Ultrasound • Tumor Marker Tests • Bone Scan • Upper Endoscopy • Breast MRI • Colonoscopy • Multigated Acquisition (MUGA) Scan • Integrated PET-CT Scan • Computed Tomography (CT) Scan • Magnetic Resonance Imaging (MRI) • Endoscopies • Mammography • PAP Test • Positron Emission Tomography (PET) Scan

Alteration with Cellular Regulation
Common Antineoplastic Agents

The goal is to refer back to the concept addressing the concerns with the side effects of chemotherapy. You are not expected to become an expert with each of these drugs. We do want you to become familiar with several of these examples and understand the safety involved in administration of these medications.

ALKYLATING AGENTS
(Nitrogen Mustard)
- Cyclophosphamide (Cytoxan)
- Busulfan (Gusulfex, Myleran)
- Chlorambucil, (Leukeran)

TOPOISOMERASE INHIBITOR
- Topotecan (Hycamtin)

MITOTIC INHIBITORS
- Paclitaxel (Taxol)
- Vincristine (Oncovin)

INTERFERON
- Interferon-alfa (Roferon-A)
- Interfereon-gamma (Actimmune)

IMMUNOSUPPRESSIVE AGENT
- Azathioprine (Imuran)

GRANULOCYTE COLONY-STIMULATING FACTOR
- Filgrastim (Neupogen)
- Pegfilgrastim (Neulasta)

PROTEASE INHIBITORS
- Tipranavir (Aptivus)
- Indinavir (Crixivan)
- Saquinavir Mesylate (Invirase)
- Atazanavir Sulfate (Reyataz)
- Ritonavir (Norvir)

ANTIMETABOLITES
- Fluorouracil (5-Fluorouracil (5-FU)
- Capecitabine (Xeloda)

ANTIBIOTICS
- Doxorubicin (Adriamycin)
- Methotrexate (Rheumatrex)

SERMS: SELECTIVE ESTROGEN RECEPTOR MODULATORS
- Tamoxifen (Tamoxifen, Nolvadex)
- Raloxifene (Evista)
- Toremifene (Fareston)

AROMATASE INHIBITOR
- Anastrozole (Arimidex)
- Letrozole (Femara)
- Exemestane (Aromasin)

COLONY STIMULATING FACTORS
- Epoetin (Epogen, Procrit)

GRANULOCYTE MACROPHAGE COLONY-STIMULATING FACTOR
- Sargramostim (Leukine)

NUCLEOSIDE/NUCLEOTIDE REVERSE TRANSCRIPTASE INHIBITORS (NRTI'S)
- Zidovudine (Retrovir)

Alteration with Cellular Regulation
Linking the Concepts with Pathophysiology to the Plan of Care

"**CANCERS**" is a mnemonic to represent all of the concepts associated with alterations in cellular regulation.
The concepts include:

Coping

Altered Oxygenation, anemia

Nutrition

Concern with infection

Evaluate pain
  Elimination

Review Fluid and Electrolyte Balance

Skin/Tissue Integrity
  Support Health Promotion

Alteration with Cellular Regulation

Linking the Concepts with Pathophysiology to the Plan of Care

CONCEPTS	PATHOPHYSIOLOGY	PLAN OF CARE
Coping Diagnosis of cancer. Effects of chemotherapy, radiation, & surgery (i.e., body image: alopecia, mastectomy, colostomy, etc.) Fear of dying	Due to the psychosocial impact from the changes in body image associated with the cancer and treatment, there is a major need for emotional support. The effect from chemotherapy can result in alopecia. Some of the cancers can result changes in the image from specific surgical procedures. With any cancer, clients immediately become concerned with dying.	• Encourage verbalization of thought and feelings (*Refer to Concept Coping chapter for specifics*). • Educate client/family on disease process. Assist client to cope with alopecia. • Explain hair will grow back in at a different texture. • Recommend shopping for a wig prior to losing hair or for a hat or scarf based on personal preference. • Recommend shaving head versus waiting for hair to fall out. • Avoid exposure of scalp to sunlight. • Do not rub scalp, use hair rollers, hair dryers, or curling irons. • Avoid excessive shampooing, combing or brushing hair. • Encourage support groups based on personal needs.
Altered **O**xygenation **A**nemia (fatigues, activity intolerance)	Chemotherapy affects both cancer and healthy cells, resulting in decreased red blood cells. The outcome is a decrease in hemoglobin, causing a decrease in the oxygenation (*Refer to Concept Oxygenation chapter for specifics*). • Decrease hemoglobin = ↓ oxygenation • Decrease oxygenation = fatigue, activity intolerance, color pale • Decrease oxygenation = ↑ HR, ↑ RR	• Fatigue is expected with chemotherapy; instruct client to report any significant increase. Fatigue increase may indicate additional decrease in RBCs. • Encourage diet high in iron, protein and calories. • Administer iron supplement as needed. • Administer erythropoietin as prescribed based on Hgb and Hct. • Monitor hemoglobin & hematocrit levels.
Nutrition **N**eed for ↑ nutrients, protein, calories, vitamins Loss of appetite from chemotherapy, radiation	Adequate protein, calories and vitamins are essential for healing and to fight infections. Cancerous cells rob nutrients from the body to assist in the rapid cellular growth, resulting in clients undergoing treatment losing weight from reduced or lost appetite, nausea, stomatitis, or just a lack of eating. Third spacing can occur from a decrease in the serum albumin level from poor nutrition.	• Need adequate fiber in diet (particularly with constipation or bowel involvement). • Follow prescribed diet, supplements as needed. • Evaluate nutritional status: protein albumin, pre-albumin, Hgb, Hct, calcium, iron (*Refer to Concept Nutrition for specifics*).
Concern with **INFECTION** Leukopenia (Decrease white blood cells)	Chemotherapy affects both cancer and healthy cells, resulting in decreased white blood cells. The decrease in WBCs to fight infection, leads to an increase risk for infection. Decrease WBCs = ↑ risk for infection • ↑ risk for infection = Temperature = ↑ HR, ↑ RR	• ↑ Temperature: advise healthcare provider regarding any fever > 100°F or any signs of infection. • Protect client from infections (i.e., hand hygiene, location of room, etc.). • Use protective precautions for immunosuppression (i.e., cancer, chemotherapy, bone marrow transplant, etc.). • Use appropriate personal protective equipment (PPE) when handling bodily fluids, (urine, stool). • Monitor WBC count, especially neutrophil levels & ↑ adventitious lung sounds. • Obtain urine & stool cultures & sensitivity as ordered. • Document amount, color, smell in urine and stool. (*Refer to Concept Infection Control for specifics*.)

Continued on next page

Alteration with Cellular Regulation—cont'd.

Linking the Concepts with Pathophysiology to the Plan of Care

CONCEPTS	PATHOPHYSIOLOGY	PLAN OF CARE
Evaluate Pain from cancer and metastasis treatment, surgery **Elimination** Diarrhea Constipation	Pain can occur from the disease, treatment, and complications. • Hyperuricemia (Increased levels of uric acid). This can occur in the advanced cancer in addition to an adverse effect from chemotherapy. Mitotic Inhibitors such as vincristine (Oncovin) can cause increase in uric crystals. • The effect of chemotherapy and radiation can result in diarrhea. Also bowel obstruction can occur as a result of the disease (i.e., colorectal cancer) or the urinary flow can be blocked from an enlarged prostate (*Refer to Concept Elimination chapter for specifics*).	**Pain:** • Assess Pain with "**PQRST**". • Give pain medication as prescribed (*Refer to Concept Pain chapter for specifics*). • Pain meds can ↑ constipation, administer with stool softeners & laxatives as needed (elderly particularly), encourage fluid intake. **Elimination:** • If appropriate for client and not contraindication, encourage fluid intake up to 3000 mL daily. • Allopurinol (Zyloprim) may be used as prevention or as treatment. • Monitor I & O and trend. • If experiencing diarrhea, encourage fluids, low-residue/fiber diet. • If prone to constipation, maintain a diet high in residue/fiber and fluids; use stool softeners as needed.
Review Fluid & Electrolyte Balance Bleeding from decreased platelets (thrombocytopenia) Nausea & vomiting from side effects of chemotherapy and radiation Stomatitis (mucositis)	Bleeding can be the result of decreased platelets from chemotherapy. The outcome is an increase risk for bleeding (Refer to Concept Fluid Deficit chapter for specifics). • Decrease platelets = ↑ risk for bleeding • ↑ risk for bleeding = ↑ HR, ↑ RR, ↓ BP • ↑ risk for shock = hypovolemia Several imbalances can occur from cancer and the treatment. Dehydration occurs from vomiting and GI complications. Stomatitis (mouth sores) is a result of the chemotherapy). Dehydration (fluid loss) = weight loss **Vital signs:** **Early:** ↑ HR & ↑ RR, (↓ LOC in elderly) **Late:** ↓ BP, oliguria	• Implement bleeding precautions (i.e., ↓ invasive procedures, ↓ injections). • Assess gums for bleeding, ↑ bruising, and hematuria. • Monitor platelet count. • Document amount, signs of bleeding in urine and stool. • Monitor for signs of dehydration such as: ↑ HR & ↑ RR, ↓ LOC in elderly, ↓ BP, I & O and trend for a decrease. • Encourage adequate fluid intake: PO fluids (if tolerated 2500-3000 mL/day). • IV fluids if needed or unable to take adequate PO fluids. • May need electrolyte replacement. • Fluid volume overload: ↑ HR & ↑ RR, ↑ BP, bounding pulses. **Oral Hygiene:** • Encourage good oral hygiene and frequent oral checks. • Keep mucous membranes moist with frequent rinses of saline solutions. • Brush teeth with every meal and at bed time. • Avoid alcohol or spicy foods. • Stomatitis can impact on the client's nutrition due to the pain of the mouth ulcers making it difficult to eat (*Refer to Concept for Fluid Balance chapter for more specific interventions*).

Alteration with Cellular Regulation—cont'd.
Linking the Concepts with Pathophysiology to the Plan of Care

CONCEPTS	PATHOPHYSIOLOGY	PLAN OF CARE
Skin/Tissue Integrity Urinary & Bowel Incontinence Colostomies/ Ileostomies Radiation effects Skin cancers	Increased risk for alteration if the albumin level is decreased due to decreased nutritional intake. This can result in skin breakdown and complications with healing. In addition to these physiological changes, if the client does not move and continues with ongoing pressure with minimal relief, a compromise in circulation may also contribute to an alteration in skin/tissue integrity.	• Monitor for non-blanchable areas. • Keep skin dry, protect skin when client is incontinent. • Turn & reposition q 2 hrs. or more frequently if needed. • Position to avoid pressure points, particularly if client is edematous. • Ambulation, up in chair, ROM to promote circulation (*Refer Concept Tissue/Skin Integrity for specific care*).
	Tissue irritation, necrosis, ulceration can occur from chemotherapy infusion, especially with vesicant medications.	• A central line should be used when infusing vesicant medications to promote dilution of medication. • Monitor the site for infection. • Flush in between each medication administration if client is receiving multiple medications. • If extravasation occurs with a vesicant medication in the peripheral site: "**STOP**": **S**top the infusion; remove other drugs in the needle or tubing. **T**alk to HCP and review hospital protocol and precautions. **O**rder for antidote may be directly instilled into infiltrated skin.
Support Health Promotion		**P**ut ice or heat on site; may need to elevate extremity for 24 to 48 hours based on specific medication.
Primary—Prevention	Research shows that the risk factors below account for nearly 60% of all cancers (*Guidelines from Healthy People 2020*) Remember "**DIETS**" **D**iet is balanced including fresh fruits and vegetables, adequate fiber & whole grains, and decrease fats and preservatives; avoid smoked & salt cured foods containing increased nitrates.	**Primary Prevention** • Educate client regarding the importance of eating a balanced diets in nutrients, limit intake of alcohol, exercise for 30 minutes 5 times a week. • Avoid smoking and the sun. • Discuss the need for rest and sleep. • Refer to CAUTION in this chapter for the signs of cancer.
Secondary— Screening	**I**ntake of alcohol should be limited. **E**xercise at least 30 minutes of moderate to vigorous exercise 5 days a week. **T**ry to avoid carcinogens (i.e., cigarette smoking, sun exposure, etc.). **S**leep and rest at least 6–8 hours per night; stress needs to be decreased or change perception; improve ability to cope with stress.	**Secondary** • Secondary Screening (*Refer to Diagnostic Procedures in this chapter*). **Home Care:** • Review the importance of decreasing or limiting exposure to infection (*Refer to Concept Infection Control chapter for specifics*). • Review the importance of effective management of pain to provide optimal rest and relief.

Alteration with Cellular Regulation

Concerns of the Elderly with Cancer Treatment

Cancer is a Disease of Aging
Goal: Best Treatment while Maintaining Quality of Life

Elderly Concerns
"QUALITY"

Quantity of medications taken is great and medications increase risk of drug interactions with treatment.

Understand that other comorbidities may be more serious or life threatening than cancer.

Ability to manage physical and mental challenges of cancer symptoms, side effects of treatments, and potential complications may be decreased.

Limited immunity increases risk of infection with chemotherapy, radiation and surgery.

Inability to make good choices with cancer management may be limited due to decrease in cognitive ability.

Treatment options must involve a holistic approach that is individualized for each client.

You have to balance treatment options with quality of life and their needs.

Exceptions and Additions by Diseases

Pathophysiology: Breast Cancer

Breast cancers are malignant tumors that typically begin in the ductal-lobular epithelial cells of the breast and spread via the lymphatic system to the axillary lymph nodes. The tumor may metastasize to the other areas of the body (i.e., lungs, liver, bone, and brain). The finding of breast cancer in the axillary lymph nodes is an indicator of the tumor's ability for potential distant spread and is not merely contiguous growth into the adjacent region of the breast. Most primary breast cancers are adenocarcinomas located in the upper outer quadrant of the breast (Black& Hawks, 2009).

Breast cancer is the second leading cause of cancer in women in the U.S. Breast self-exam (BSE) and clinical breast exam (CBE) and mammography are effective in detecting cancer and reducing mortality rates. The recommendations to begin screening with mammography is age 40 according to the American Cancer Society, however, mammography should be performed earlier for women at increased risk for breast CA.

	FIRST-DO PRIORITY INTERVENTIONS			
SYSTEM-SPECIFIC ASSESSMENTS	DIET	EQUIPMENT	ACTIVITY/POSITION/ PROCEDURE	HEALTH PROMOTION
• Skin changes (peau d'orange) • Dimpling • Increased vascularity • Nipple retraction or ulceration • Enlarged lymph nodes • Breast pain or soreness	• Diet as tolerated • Increase in protein, calories, vitamins as needed to maintain nutritional balance • Supplements as needed • Referral to dietician	• Maintain surgical asepsis of dressings, incision, drains • Support arm on operative side with sling while ambulating • Proper fitting prosthesis • Report numbness, pain, heaviness, impaired motor function	• Monitor for signs and symptoms • Assess clients risk factors, FH, PMH, breast self-exam and mammograms • Circulatory status of affected arm • Discuss client preference for prosthesis • Nursing care of client with cancer • Encourage client to lie on unaffected side post-op to relieve pain • Early arm exercises, avoid dependent position • Avoid injections, VS, phlebotomy to affected side	Teach client/family: • Perform breast self-exam • Mammogram • Not to use talc powder or deodorant before procedures • Best when done in the first 2 weeks of menstrual cycle (minimal cystic changes are present) **Screening Guidelines** • > 20 years of age for monthly BSE, annual CBE • Need baseline screening for mammogram by 40 years of age, then yearly • Biopsy • No constrictive clothing to affected side, avoid injury • BSE, home care

Exceptions and Additions by Diseases

Pathophysiology: Lung Cancer

Lung cancer develops when the cells in the lungs mutate and reproduce excessively. It is a bronchogenic carcinoma because the tumor usually stems from the bronchial mucosa. There are several classifications of lung cancer: non-small cell lung cancer (NSCLC); squamous cell carcinomas, large cell carcinomas, and adenocarcinoma. Others include small-cell lung cancer (SCLC): oat cell; asbestos lung cancer and mesothelioma, cancer of the lining of the lungs. The most common cause is tobacco smoke where the polycyclic hydrocarbons are mutagenic and transform normal cells into malignant ones. Exchange of oxygen and carbon dioxide is limited due to the cancerous cells that can no longer adequately perform. The tumor cells grow, invading other lung tissue. This limits the expansion of the lungs and further limits the exchange of oxygen and carbon dioxide. As the tumor cells continue to grow, they invade the airways, lymph nodes and the thoracic duct. Lung cancer is often not diagnosed until in advanced stages. The major risk factors are tobacco use of second-hand smoke and exposure to radon (American Cancer Society, 2014).

SYSTEM-SPECIFIC ASSESSMENTS	FIRST-DO PRIORITY INTERVENTIONS			
	DIET	EQUIPMENT	PLANS/INTERVENTIONS	HEALTH PROMOTION
• Client history of smoking: pack-year history = (# packs smoked per day x # years smoked) • Persistent cough • Rust-colored or blood-tinged sputum • Dyspnea • Unilateral wheezing • Chest wall pain • Muffled heart sounds • Fatigue • Weight loss • Anorexia	• Diet as tolerated • Increase in protein, calories, vitamins as needed to maintain nutritional balance • Supplements as needed • Referral to dietician	• Oxygen equipment • Humidified O_2	• Maintain patent airway: suction, position upright or high-Fowler's. • Check cough reflexes, swallowing ability. • Monitor VS, respiratory status. • Administer medications as prescribed: chemotherapy, bronchodilators, corticosteroids. • Pain management. • Prepare for thoracentesis as needed to remove fluid to ease breathing. • Refer to hospice care, social work, home health as needed.	Teach client/family: • Smoking cessation • Checking for levels of radon in the home or work place • Limiting exposure to known cancer causing chemicals

Pathophysiology: Prostate Cancer

Prostate cancer forms in tissues of the prostate. Adenocarcinomas represent 90% of the cancers that originate in the peripheral zone of the prostate gland in comparison to the benign prostate hypertrophy that originates in the transitional zone. Prostate cancer usually grows slowly and initially remains confined to the prostate gland. Localized prostate cancer has few clinical symptoms. The benefit of screening for prostate cancer is controversial as to the benefit. Some of the screening methods used are digital rectal exam (DRE) and prostate-specific antigen (PSA) test. PSA is naturally produced by the prostate gland, but elevated levels may indicate cancer or infection, inflammation or enlargement. If prostate cancer metastasis, the tumor cells invade and interrupt the function of the urinary tract and travel via blood supply or lymph nodes to other surrounding tissue and organs (Prostate Cancer Foundation, 2014).

Risk factors include: age over 65, family history of prostate or breast cancer, obesity, and/or race (African American men have increased risk).

	FIRST-DO PRIORITY INTERVENTIONS			
SYSTEM-SPECIFIC ASSESSMENTS	**DIET**	**EQUIPMENT**	**ACTIVITY/POSITION/ PROCEDURE**	**HEALTH PROMOTION**
• Painless hematuria • Urinary hesitancy • Recurrent bladder infections • Urinary retention	• Diet as tolerated • Increase in protein, calories, vitamins as needed to maintain nutritional balance • Supplements as needed • Referral to dietician	• Patient-controlled analgesia (PCA) pump	• Administer hormone therapy: Lupron • Prepare for possible surgery • Radiation therapy; external beam or implanted seeds **Post-operative care:** • Assess and treat pain as ordered • PCA pump for pain management • Elevate scrotum & penis, intermittently apply ice • SCDs, anti-embolism stockings • Instruct client in catheter care • Medications: antispasmodics • Monitor I & O	Teach client/family: • Emotional support for diagnosis, possible sexual/erectile dysfunction • Monitor client coping • Refer to counseling • Antidepressants as needed as prescribed

Exceptions and Additions by Diseases

Pathophysiology: Cancers form the Lymph System

The lymphatic system is a network of nodes connected by vessels whose function is to filter foreign organisms and cells and then drain the fluid and waste products from the body. The lymphatic system produces white blood cells (lymphocytes) that protect the body from infections cause by bacteria, viruses and fungi.

Hodgkin's Disease is a cancer of the lymph or lymphoma that most commonly affects the lymph nodes in the neck, the area between the lungs and behind the breast bone. The Epstein-Barr virus (EBV) is thought to be one of the causative agents. The cancer transformation occurs within the lymph node and eventually replaces the entire node with area of necrosis. It spreads through the lymphatic system to adjacent tissues and organs. Clients are generally asymptomatic and are diagnosis on examination with enlarged lymph nodes (Osborn, Wraa, Watson, & Holleran, 2014).

Non-Hodgkin's lymphoma comprises a group of malignancies with a common origin in the lymphoid cells. Abnormal proliferation of neoplastic lymphocytes occurs with the cells remaining at one state of development and then proliferating. This eventually obstructs the lymph nodes. It occurs 60% more times in clients with AIDS than in the general population with an increased incidence after age 50.

	FIRST-DO PRIORITY INTERVENTIONS			
System-Specific Assessments	**Diet**	**Equipment**	**Plans/Interventions**	**Health Promotion**
Hodgkin's lymphoma • Painless swelling of one or more lymph nodes. • Swelling, fluid accumulation, or pain in the abdomen. • Shortness of breath, wheezing, or coughing. • Bloody stool or vomit. • Swelling of the face, neck, and arms. • Blockage of urine flow. • Bone pain.	• Diet as tolerated • Increase in protein, calories, vitamins as needed to maintain nutritional balance • Supplements as needed • Referral to dietician	• Supplemental O_2 as needed	• Monitor for signs of infection (i.e., ↑ temp & WBCs, adventitious lung sounds, etc.) as a result of chemotherapy • Monitor vital signs for decreased cardiac output due to thrombocytopenia from chemo (i.e., ↑ HR, RR) • Pace activities with rest due to fatigue from anemia from treatment • Prepare for possible bone marrow transplant	Teach client/family: • Monitor client coping • Refer to counseling • Antidepressants as needed as prescribed • Signs & symptoms to report to the HCP, (i.e., ↑ temp & WBCs, productive cough, increase in fatigue, etc.)

Pathophysiology: Hematopoietic System

Leukemia

Leukemia is a malignant disease of the blood forming tissues and organs (bone marrow, spleen and lymph system). Leukemia results from abnormal proliferation of immature white blood cells (WBCs or leukocytes). Fewer normal WBCs are produced and the abnormal cells continue to proliferate causing damage to the bone marrow, spleen, lymph nodes, liver, kidneys, lungs, skin and central nervous system. Approximate half of the diagnosis of leukemia is acute and will result in death if not treated within days or months. Chronic leukemia has an insidious onset with a prolonged clinical course and clients may be asymptomatic early in the disease process. There are several types of leukemia. The type of WBC affected, granulocytic, lymphocytic and monocytic categorizes them. Lymphocytic/lymphoblastic (ALL) proliferates in the bone marrow and is most common in children, ages 2–10. Acute myelogenous or myelocytic (AML) or acute granulocytic leukemia (AGL) generally occurs in those over age 50. Immature granulocytes proliferate and accumulate in the bone marrow. Chronic myelogenous leukemia (CML) is the proliferation of abnormal incompetent lymphocytes that spread to other lymphatic tissue and is most common age 50–70 years of age. Abnormal stem cells lead to uncontrolled proliferation of granulocyte cells in chronic myelogenous leukemia (CML). This causes in increase in the circulating blast cells, which leads to leukostasis and intracerebral hemorrhage. The abnormality of chromosome 22 (Philadelphia chromosome) is often present.

	FIRST-DO	PRIORITY	INTERVENTIONS	
SYSTEM-SPECIFIC ASSESSMENTS "CANCERS"	**DIET**	**EQUIPMENT**	**PLANS/INTERVENTIONS**	**HEALTH PROMOTION**
Coping: assess coping strategies **A**ltered Oxygenation: assess for activity intolerance and fatigue assess for thrombocytopenia, signs of bleeding **N**utrition: assess weight, note trends in weight loss **C**oncern with Infection **E**valuate Pain, joint pain **E**limination **R**eview Fluid & Electrolytes **S**kin/Tissue Integrity **S**upport Health Promotion	• High-calorie • High-protein • Avoid foods or beverages that cause oral, esophageal irritation • Dietary supplements • Referral to dietician	• Supplemental oxygen • IV infusion pump	• Refer to **"CANCERS"** in this chapter • Medications for pain as prescribed • Monitor for signs of infection (i.e., ↑ temp, WBCs, productive cough, adventitious lung sounds, etc.) • Initiate Protective Precautions as needed (*Refer to Concept Infection Control for specifics*) • Pace activities with rest • **Monitor for signs of bleeding** (i.e., ↑ HR & RR, hemoptysis, blood in stools, etc.) • Use soft toothbrush; falls prevention; electric razor only **Interdisciplinary Collaboration:** • Infectious diseases • Respiratory services • Nutritional services • Rehabilitation services • Hospice services • Home Health	Teach client/family: **Infection Prevention** • Good hand hygiene • Avoid crowded area • Avoid raw foods, such as meats and vegetables • Avoid cleaning litter boxes to reduce toxoplasmosis • Well-balanced diet **Medication** • administration • education (safety) **Coping:** Encourage verbalizing concerns (*Refer to concept Coping chapter*)

Exceptions and Additions by Diseases

Pathophysiology: Cellular Immunity
Human Immunodeficiency Virus (HIV)

Human Immunodeficiency Virus (HIV): A condition resulting from severe impairment of the immune system's ability to respond to invading pathogens, ultimately it affects all of the body systems. Human Immunodeficiency Virus is a retrovirus that is transmitted through blood and body fluids (i.e., semen, vaginal secretions). HIV targets CD4+ lymphocytes, also known as T-cells or T-lymphocytes. T-cells work with B-lymphocytes. Both are parts of specific acquired (adaptive) immunity. HIV integrates its RNA into host cell DNA through reverse transcriptase, reshaping the host's immune response. The client who becomes infected will harbor the virus for the rest of his or her life. HIV cannot be transmitted by animals or insects; dishes or silverware handled by an infected person; objects such as doorknobs, bathtubs, or toilet seats; nonsexual contact such as kissing, holding hands, or hugging.

SYSTEM-SPECIFIC ASSESSMENTS "SAFE SEX"	FIRST-DO PRIORITY INTERVENTIONS			
	DIET	EQUIPMENT	PLANS/INTERVENTIONS	HEALTH PROMOTION
Safe sex practices **A**ssess daily weight; analgesics **F**luid & electrolytes; I & O, ↑T **E**valuate lung sounds; O$_2$ PRN **S**kin integrity; status of pain **E**valuate neuro status (LOC), **X** out IV drug use	• High-calorie • High-protein • Avoid foods or beverages that cause oral, esophageal irritation • Dietary supplements • Referral to dietician	• Supplemental oxygen • IV infusion pump	**Interdisciplinary Collaboration:** • Infectious diseases • Respiratory services • Nutritional services • Rehabilitation services • Hospice services • Home Health	Teach client/family: **Health Promotion** **Infection Prevention:** • Good hand hygiene • Avoid crowded area • Avoid raw foods, such as meats and vegetables • Avoid cleaning litter boxes to reduce toxoplasmosis • Safe sex practices • Well balanced diet **Medication** • administration • education (safety) **Coping:** Encourage ventilating concerns (*Refer to concept Coping chapter*)

Clinical Decision-Making Exercises

1. Which of these statements made by the nurse indicates an understanding of the pathophysiology of a malignant tumor?

    ① "Malignant tumors retain most of the morphologic and functional consequences."

    ② "Malignant tumors arise from normal differentiated cells."

    ③ "Malignant tumors have poor differentiation and longer than normal cell lifespan."

    ④ "Malignant tumors always obstruct or press on other body structures."

2. What is the priority of care for a client who has a diagnosis of leukemia and has developed thrombocytopenia from the chemotherapy?

    ① Encourage ambulation and oxygen supplement.

    ② Assess temperature every 4 hours per protocol.

    ③ Encourage periodic rest periods while pacing activity during day.

    ④ Question a medication order for an intramuscular injection.

3. Which of these statements made by a client who is receiving external radiation therapy for cancer indicates a need for further teaching?

    ① "I must leave the skin markings on my skin."

    ② "I will not use lotions while I am receiving external radiation."

    ③ "I will fast prior to the treatment."

    ④ "I will swim laps after the first treatment."

4. Which of these statements indicate that the nurse understands how to appropriately administer erythropoietin (Procrit)?

    ① "I will administer this medication daily as ordered."

    ② "I will administer this medication IM."

    ③ "I will evaluate frequent WBC counts to determine effectiveness."

    ④ "I will monitor the hematocrit frequently for dosage adjustments."

5. The nurse is planning discharge education for a client diagnosed with colon cancer about the side effects of chemotherapy. The nurse understands that it is important to stress which of the following? *Select all that apply.*

    ① Side effects can occur anywhere in the gastrointestinal track.

    ② Chemotherapy may have lasting effects on heart and lung function.

    ③ Chemotherapy can cause alopecia.

    ④ Chemotherapy can cause an increased absolute neutrophil count (ANC).

    ⑤ Few to no side effects typically occur.

6. What would be the priority of care for a client who is receiving chemotherapy and has a Hgb 9 gm/dL and a Hct 27%?

    ① Initiate protective infection control precautions.

    ② Report HR- 120 bpm, RR-28/min, and feels more fatigue than previous day.

    ③ Initiate bleeding protocol.

    ④ Recommend client to pace activities and organize these based on energy level.

7. Which of these clients should be seen immediately after shift report?

① A client complaining of discomfort at the IV insertion site of the chemotherapy transfusion.

② A client complaining of a feeling of fatigue following chemotherapy.

③ A client complaining of nausea and vomiting following chemotherapy.

④ A client with a temperature of 99.0°F.

8. What information from the UAP indicates the charge nurse needs additional information on making out assignments for a client who is neutropenic from chemotherapy?

① The UAP does not prefer to take care of clients in protective isolation.

② The UAP has had diarrhea for 24 hours.

③ The UAP is in the second trimester of pregnancy.

④ The UAP reports only taking care of 2 other clients with neutropenia.

9. Which of these documentations indicate an early side effect after starting external radiation?

① A gradual weight gain.

② Constipation.

③ Insomnia.

④ Skin erythema.

10. Which of these nursing actions by the LPN for a client who is in protective isolation following chemotherapy indicates a need for immediate intervention by the charge nurse?

① The LPN delivers a fruit tray including apples, pears, and bananas to the client.

② The LPN refuses to take in a moist potted plant to the client.

③ The LPN notifies the healthcare provider that the client's temperature is 100.8° F.

④ The LPN requires the UAP to practice effective.

Answers and Rationales

1. Which of these **statements made by the nurse** indicates an understanding of the **pathophysiology of a malignant tumor?**

   ① INCORRECT: "Malignant tumors retain most of the morphologic and functional consequences." This describes benign tumors.

   ② INCORRECT: "Malignant tumors arise from normal differentiated cells." This describes benign tumors.

   ③ **CORRECT: "Malignant tumors have poor differentiation and longer than normal cell lifespan." This is correct.**

   ④ INCORRECT: "Malignant tumors always obstruct or press on other body structures." This describes benign tumors. They can obstruct or press on other structures, but not always!

The strategy for answering this question is to understand the pathophysiology of malignant tumors. Due to the alteration in the cell cycle, there is an excessive cell proliferation, poor differentiation, and longer than normal cell lifespan. The benign tumors arise from normal differentiated cells. They retain most of the morphologic and functional characteristics of the normal cells from which they arose. Benign tumors typically do not invade adjacent tissue or metastasize. However, benign tumors can result in health consequences. These tumors can obstruct or press on other body structures, resulting in dysfunction, pain, or even death if allowed to continue to grow.

Physiological Adaptation: Identify pathophysiology related to an acute or chronic condition.

2. What is the **priority of care for a client who has a diagnosis of leukemia** and has developed **thrombocytopenia** from the chemotherapy?

   ① INCORRECT: Encourage ambulation and oxygen supplement. This would be priority if client had anemia.

   ② INCORRECT: Assess temperature every 4 hours per protocol. This would be priority for neutropenia.

   ③ INCORRECT: Encourage periodic rest periods while pacing activity during day. This would be priority for anemia.

   ④ **CORRECT: Question a medication order for an intramuscular injection. This is appropriate since the client is at risk for bleeding due to thrombocytopenia. The priority is to minimize bleeding; no need for IM or any unnecessary needle sticks.**

The strategy is to organize the care around thrombocytopenia (perfusion or volume issues due to bleeding). If platelets are decreased, there is a risk for bleeding. This concept is all about risk for bleeding. Can you think of other clinical situations that would require this same type of answer "Bleeding Precautions"? How about liver disorders, the use of Coumadin or any anticoagulants, etc., or any condition that would result in a decrease in the platelets. *See you CAN do this! It is all about organizing concepts in your brain!*

Management of Care: Verify appropriateness and/or accuracy of order.

3. Which of these **statements made by a client** who is receiving **external radiation therapy** for cancer indicates a need for **further teaching?**

    ① INCORRECT: "I must leave the skin markings on my skin." No need for further teaching.

    ② INCORRECT: "I will not use lotions while I am receiving external radiation." No need for further teaching.

    ③ INCORRECT: "I will fast prior to the treatment." No need for further teaching.

    ④ **CORRECT: "I will swim laps in the sun after the first treatment." The skin markings are used by the radiotherapist to determine the exact area to be radiated. Swimming may cause the marks to fade, and the skin should not be exposed to the sun.**

The strategy for answering this question is to review the Insanely Easy Tip about external radiation therapy. It is all about the "**SKIN**" (*Refer to the tip earlier in this chapter*). The mnemonic of "**SKIN**" reminds you of the priority care for these clients. Even if you do not remember the details, you can get this correct simply by thinking about skin.

Reduction of Risk Potential: Educate client about treatments and procedures.

4. Which of these statements indicate that the **nurse understands** how to appropriately **administer erythropoietin** (Procrit)?

    ① INCORRECT: I will administer this medication daily as ordered." Should only be administered 3 times/week.

    ② INCORRECT: "I will administer this medication IM." It should be Subcutaneous or IV.

    ③ INCORRECT: "I will evaluate frequent WBC counts to determine effectiveness." Should be Hgb/Hct.

    ④ **CORRECT: "I will monitor the hematocrit frequently for dosage adjustments." Correct!**

The strategy is to know how to safely administer erythropoietin (Procrit). It is given to help with RBC production. Erythropoietin (Procrit) should decrease fatigue, weakness, SOB. RBCs should increase. Should only be administered IV or SQ and 3 times per week.

Pharmacological and Parenteral Therapies: Evaluate client response to medication.

5. The nurse is planning **discharge education for a client diagnosed with colon cancer about the side effects of chemotherapy.** The nurse understands that it is important to stress which of the following? Select all that apply.

    ① **CORRECT: Side effects can occur anywhere in the gastrointestinal track. True.**

    ② **CORRECT: Chemotherapy may have lasting effects on heart and lung function. True.**

    ③ **CORRECT: Chemotherapy can cause alopecia. True.**

    ④ INCORRECT: Chemotherapy can cause an increased absolute neutrophil count (ANC). It would decrease.

    ⑤ INCORRECT: Few to no side effects typically occur. Not true.

The strategy is to know the concepts related to chemotherapy and cancer. It is all about safety. There are many side effects from chemotherapy; neutrophils can be decreased. "CANCERS" will help you organize these concepts.

Pharmacological and Parenteral Therapies: Educate client about medications.

6. What would be the **priority of care** for a client who is receiving **chemotherapy** and has a **Hgb 9 gm/dL and a Hct 27%?**

    ① INCORRECT: Initiate protective infection control precautions. This would be if WBCs were low.

    ② **CORRECT: Report HR–120 bpm, RR–28/min, and feels more fatigue than previous day. Refer to strategy below.**

    ③ INCORRECT: Initiate bleeding protocol. This would be appropriate if it were about thrombocytopenia.

    ④ INCORRECT: Recommend client to pace activities and organize these based on energy level. This is important, but not a priority over option 2 which is indicating with the elevated HR, RR, and fatigue the low hemoglobin is a result of low oxygen.

The strategy is to know the following:

Decrease hemoglobin = ↓ oxygenation

Decrease oxygenation = fatigue, activity intolerance, color pale

Decrease oxygenation = ↑ HR, ↑ RR

This concept of oxygenation applies to any client with any disease that results in alteration in oxygenation, for example: anemia, pneumonia, asthma, stress, etc. In this situation the hypoxia is from low hemoglobin from the chemotherapy; however, in the respiratory diseases the hypoxia is from lack of oxygen exchange due to the infection or constricted alveoli. The pathophysiology is different, but the concept is the same! Take a minute to reflect over this statement! Before you know it, you will be an expert with chemotherapy! After all, this is all about linking the priority concepts. In this question, the concept is oxygenation.

Reduction of Risk Potential: Recognize signs and symptoms of complications and intervene appropriately when providing care.

7. Which of these **clients** should be seen **immediately after shift report?**

    ① **CORRECT: A client complaining of discomfort at the IV insertion site of the chemotherapy transfusion. This may indicate extravasation has occurred with a vesicant mediation and needs to be discontinued to prevent further tissue damage.**

    ② INCORRECT: A client complaining of a feeling of fatigue following chemotherapy. Expected.

    ③ INCORRECT: A client complaining of nausea and vomiting following chemotherapy. Expected.

    ④ INCORRECT: A client with a temperature of 99.0°F. Not a priority over option 1.

The strategy is to understand safe IV administration. Whenever a chemotherapeutic agent is infusing and it is a vesicant, there is a risk for extravasation. This would require immediate intervention to prevent further tissue damage.

Management of Care: Prioritize deliver of care.

8. What **information from the UAP** indicates the charge nurse needs additional information on making out **assignments for a client who is neutropenic** from chemotherapy?

    ① INCORRECT: The UAP does not prefer to take care of clients in protective isolation. Does not require additional information.

    ② **CORRECT: The UAP has had diarrhea for 24 hours. This is a sign of an infection and would not be appropriate to assign to a client on neutropenic precautions.**

    ③ INCORRECT: The UAP is in the second trimester of pregnancy. No contraindication for assignment.

    ④ INCORRECT: The UAP reports only taking care of 2 other clients with neutropenia. No contraindication for assignment.

The strategy is to understand the care for a client who is neutropenic and link to concept of infection control. The UAP who has diarrhea should never be assigned to this client due to risk for infection. Remember the following strategy: Neutropenic = Infection control; Thrombocytopenia = Bleeding; Decrease in erythrocytes = Anemia.

Management of Care: Recognize limitations of self/others.

9. Which of these documentations indicate an **early side effect after starting external radiation**?

    ① INCORRECT: A gradual weight gain. It should be weight loss to be correct.

    ② INCORRECT: Constipation. More about the skin.

    ③ INCORRECT: Insomnia. More about the skin.

    ④ **CORRECT: Skin erythema. Correct since the priority assessments focus on "SKIN."**

The strategy is to focus on how to remember side effects from external radiation. Use "**SKIN**" to help organize these facts.

Pharmacological and Parenteral Therapies: Evaluate client response to medications (i.e., side effects).

10. Which of these **nursing actions by the LPN** for a client who is in **protective isolation** following chemotherapy indicates a need for immediate intervention by the charge nurse?

    ① **CORRECT: The LPN delivers a fruit tray including apples, pears, and bananas to the client. This violates the standard of care for protective isolation and requires immediate intervention.**

    ② INCORRECT: The LPN refuses to take in a moist potted plant to the client. Appropriate care.

    ③ INCORRECT: The LPN notifies the healthcare provider that the client's temperature is 100.8°F. Appropriate care.

    ④ INCORRECT: The LPN requires the UAP to practice effective hand hygiene when providing care to the client. Appropriate care.

The strategy for answering this question is to understand the standard of care for clients receiving chemotherapy. Option 1 indicates the charge nurse needs to intervene due to inappropriate care. The other options indicate safe practice and do not require further intervention.

Management of Care: Recognize limitations of others and intervenes.

Decision-Making Analysis Form

Use this tool to help identify why you missed any questions. As you enter the question numbers in the chart, you will begin to see patterns of why you answered incorrectly. This information will then guide you toward what you need to focus on in your continued studies. Ultimately, this analytical exercise will help you become more successful in answering questions!!!

Questions to ask:

1. Did I have the knowledge to answer the question? If not, what information do I need to review?
2. Did I know what the question was asking? Did I misread it or did I miss keywords in the stem of the question?
3. Did I misread or miss keywords in the distractors that would have helped me choose the correct answer?
4. Did I follow my gut reaction or did I allow myself to rationalize and then choose the wrong answer?

	Lack of Knowledge (Concepts, Systems, Pathophysiology, Medications, Procedures, etc.)	Missed Keywords or Misread the Stem of the Question	Missed Keywords or Misread the Distractors	Changed My Answer (Second-guessed myself, i.e., my first answer was correct.)
Put the # of each question you missed in the column that best explains why you think you answered it incorrectly.				

If you changed an answer because you talked yourself out of the correct answer, or you second-guessed yourself, this is an **EASY FIX: QUIT changing your answers**!!! Typically, the first time you read a question, you are about 95% right! The second time you read a question, you start talking yourself into changing the answer. The third time you read a question, you do not have a clue—and you are probably thinking "Who in the heck wrote this question?"

On the other hand, if you read a question too quickly and when you reread it you realize you missed some key information that would impact your decision (i.e., assessments, lab reports, medications, etc.), then it is appropriate to change your answer. When in doubt, go with the safe route: your first thought! Go with your gut instinct!

As you gain confidence in answering questions regarding specific nursing concepts, you will be able to successfully progress to answering higher-level questions about prioritization. Please refer to the *Prioritization Guidelines* in this book for a structure to assist you with this process.

You CAN do this!

> *"There are two ways to spread the Light: to be a candle or the mirror that reflects it."*
>
> EDITH WHARTON

References for Chapter 19

American Cancer Society (2014). Retrieved from http://www.cancer.org

Black, J M. and Hawks, J. H. (2009). *Medical surgical nursing: Clinical management for positive outcomes* (8th ed.). Philadelphia: Elsevier/Saunders.

Daniels, R. & Nicoll, L. (2012). *Contemporary medical-surgical nursing*, (2nd ed.). Clifton Park, NY: Delmar Cengage Learning.

Eliopoulos, C. (2014). *Gerontological nursing* (8th ed.), Philadelphia: Lippincott Williams & Wilkins.

Giddens, G. F. (2013). *Concepts for Nursing Practice*. St. Louis, MO: Mosby, an imprint of Elsevier.

Healthy People 2020. (2014). Retrieved from http://healthypeople.gov/2020/default. aspx

Hogan, M. A. (2014). *Pathophysiology, Reviews and Rationales*, (3rd Edition) Boston, MA: Pearson.

Ignatavicius, D. D. and Workman, M. L. (2010). *Medical-Surgical Nursing: Patient-Centered Collaborative Care* (7th ed.). Philadelphia: Elsevier/Saunders.

LeMone, P. Burke, K. M. and Bauldoff, G. (2011). *Medical-surgical nursing: Critical thinking in patient care* (5th edition). Upper Saddle Road, NJ: Pearson/Prentice Hall.

Lewis, S., Dirksen, S., Heitkemper, M., Bucher, L., and Camera, I. (2011). *Medical surgical nursing: Assessment and management of clinical problems* (8th ed.). St. Louis: Mosby.

Manning, L. and Rayfield, S. (2014). *Nursing made insanely easy* (7th ed). Duluth, GA: I CAN Publishing, Inc.

Manning, L. and Rayfield, S. (2013). *Pharmacology made insanely easy* (4th ed.). Duluth, GA: I CAN Publishing, Inc.

National Council of State Boards of Nursing, INC. (NCSBN) 2012. *Research brief: 2011 RN practice analysis: linking the NCLEX RN® examination to practice.* Retrieved from https://www.ncsbn.org/index.htm

Nettina, S. L. (2013). *Lippincott manual of nursing practice* (10th ed.). Philadelphia, PA: Walters Kluwer Health/Lippincott Williams & Wilkins.

North Carolina Concept Based Learning Editorial Board. (2011). *Nursing a Concept Based Approach to Learning.* Upper Saddle Road, NJ: Pearson/Prentice Hall.

Osborn, K. S., Wraa, C. E., Watson, A. S., and Holleran, R. S. (2014). *Medical surgical nursing: preparation for practice* (2nd ed.). Upper Saddle Road, NJ: Pearson.

Pagana, K. D. and Pagana, T. J. (2014). *Mosby's manual of laboratory and diagnostic tests* (5th ed.). St. Louis, MO: Mosby, an imprint of Elsevier.

Porth, C. (2011). *Essentials of pathophysiology* (3rd edition). Philadelphia, PA: Lippincott Williams ad Wilkins.

Porth, C. M. and Grossman, S. (2013). *Pathophysiology, Concepts of altered health states* (9th edition). Philadelphia, PA: Lippincott Williams & Wilkins.

Potter, P. A., Perry, A. G., Stockert, P., and Hall, A. (2013). *Fundamentals of nursing* (8th ed). St. Louis, MO: Pearson/Prentice Hall.

Prostate Cancer Foundation. (2014). Retrieved from http://www.pcf.org/site/c.leJRIROrEpH/b.5699537/k.BEF4/Home.htm

Rosenberg, S. (2005). *The principles of surgical oncology: General issues.* Philadelphia: Lippincott, Williams & Wilkins.

Smeltzer, S. C., Bare, B. G., Hinkle, J. L., and Cheever, K. H. (2010). *Brunner & Suddarth's Textbook of medical-surgical nursing* (12th ed.). Philadelphia: Lippincott Williams & Wilkins.

Wagner, K. D. and Hardin-Pierce, M. C. (2014). *High-Acuity nursing* (6th ed.). Boston: Pearson.

Wilson, S. & Giddens, J. (2009). *Health assessment for nursing practice* (4th ed.). St. Louis: Mosby/Elsevier.

CHAPTER 20

Integumentary System
Linking Concepts to Pathophysiology of Diseases
Concept Tissue/Skin Integrity

A Snapshot of Tissue/Skin Integrity

The concept of tissue/skin integrity is described as the integrity of the levels of structural and/or function in muscle, neural, connective and epithelial (skin), corneal and mucous membranes. Damage to the skin and/or tissue can result from trauma or an injury, from an infectious process, loss of perfusion, and thermal, radiation or chemical burns. Injury to the skin and/or tissue can also be the result of benign and cancerous lesions. Impaired tissue and skin integrity may range from superficial to deep penetrating wounds.

The Pathophysiology Behind Alterations in Cellular Regulation

TISSUE/SKIN INTEGRITY							
Trauma/ Injury	Infection				Loss of Perfusion	Thermal/ Radiation	Premalignant, Benign & Skin Cancer
	Bacterial	Fungal	Viral	Infestations			
• Surgical incision • Abrasion • Laceration • Avulsion • Blister • Ecchymosis • Hematoma • Chemical irritant	• Cellulitis • Impetigo	• Tinea: • Capitis • Cruris • Pedis (athlete's foot)	• Herpes Simplex Virus Type 1 (HSV) (oropharyngeal) • Herpes Simplex Virus Type 2 (HSV)– (genitalia) • Herpes Zoster– (shingles) • Verruca (warts)	• Lice • Scabies	• Pressure Ulcers • Diabetic foot ulcer • Peripheral Vascular Disease (arterial & venous) ulcers	• Hypothermia (Frostbite) • Burns (sunburn, thermal, chemical, electrical, and radiation)	• Actinic keratosis • Benign tumors • Squamous cell carcinoma • Basal cell carcinoma • Malignant melanoma

System-Specific Assessments for Tissue/Skin Integrity

"SKIN"

S Skin assessment: turgor (not accurate for elderly), color, (redness, pallor, purple in dark skin clients), and check for non-blanching areas; check for dryness; note color & shape of any lesions. Use tests (i.e., Woods lamp, Tissue biopsy, Wound culture, Patch test, etc.) to check skin. Note with any lesion variation that may indicate positive for disease.

K Know and assess any allergies (i.e., meds, food, allergens, etc.); note bowel or urinary incontinence.

I Inspect bony prominences for: skin color changes, assess wounds; pressure ulcers: measure depth, width, signs of granulation.

N Norton or Braden scale to assess:
- **Norton Scale:** measures physical and mental condition, activity, mobility, and incontinence
- **Braden Scale:** measures sensory perception, moisture, activity-mobility, nutrition, friction, and shear
- **Pressure Ulcer Scale for Healing (PUSH Tool):** categorize ulcers according to size of the wound, exudates, and type of tissue
- **Dermatome** (light touch, pinprick): complete loss, $\downarrow$ or $\uparrow$ sensation.
- **Doppler ultrasonography & ultrasound:** determine quality of blood flow

Nutrition status: (i.e., serum protein, albumin levels $<$ 3.5 mg/dL, = high risk for skin breakdown & potential $\downarrow$ in healing & $\uparrow$ risk for infection). Assess iron levels & CBC.

Linking Pathophysiology to System-Specific Assessments of Tissue/Skin Integrity

Pathophysiology	System-Specific Assessments "SKIN"
Skin Assessment needs to be head to toe at a minimum of once a month by the individual to detect changes in the appearance of moles, lesions, or new lesions. Any questionable spot, exam by HCP; may need biopsy. Skin cancers may be small on the surface, but may have tunneled down and spread to the underlying tissues below. Color, temperature of the skin, pulses, and capillary refill indicate if there is perfusion to the area. Areas with ↓ perfusion will not blanch and healing will be impaired. The other tests, (i.e., Woods lamp: test for tinea; tissue biopsy: cancer; wound culture: infection and Patch test: allergies) provide information to determine the plan of care.	**S**kin assessment: turgor (not accurate for elderly), color, (redness, pallor, purple in dark skin clients), and check for non-blanching areas; check for dryness; note color & shape of any lesions. Use tests (i.e., Woods lamp, Tissue biopsy, Wound culture, Patch test, etc.) to check skin. Note with any lesion variation that may indicate positive for disease.
Know or ask the client about their allergies to help determine the cause of unknown rashes. Allergies can develop at any time during the life span. Refer for allergy testing for unknown allergy or severe cases. Bowel or urinary incontinence can be a source of irritation to the skin, causing skin & tissue breakdown.	**K**now & assess any allergies (i.e., meds, food, allergens, etc.); note bowel or urinary incontinence.
Inspection: bony prominences are an area that is the source of skin/tissue breakdown because of pressure points when the client is lying or sitting. Measuring and documenting the size, depth, width, and amount of granulation on an open wound, provides the information necessary to compare, contrast, and trend wound healing. Assessment should include amount, color, and odor of any drainage to include any indication of tunneling or pockets within the wound that are not healing.	**I**nspect bony prominences for: skin color changes, assess wounds or pressure ulcers: measure depth, width, and signs of granulation.
Norton or Braden scales provide an objective method of assessment to determine the risk of skin/tissue breakdown in clients. The PUSH tool helps to categorize the ulcers to help determine the best course of action for treatment. The surface of the skin is divided into specific areas called dermatomes that are derived from the somite cell. A dermatome is an area of the skin where the sensory nerves come from a single spinal nerve root. The Dermatome detects increase of loss of sensation and can be used when applying skin grafts. The Doppler ultrasonography determines the quality of the blood flow to the wounds with adequate oxygen and nutrients necessary for healing.	**N**orton or Braden scale to assess: • **Norton Scale**: measures physical and mental condition, activity, mobility, and incontinence • **Braden Scale**: measures sensory perception, moisture, activity-mobility, nutrition, friction, and shear • **Pressure Ulcer Scale for Healing (PUSH Tool)**: categorize ulcers according to size of the wound, exudates, and type of tissue • **Dermatome** (light touch, pinprick): complete loss, ↓ sensation. • **Doppler ultrasonography & ultrasound**: determine quality of blood flow.
Nutritional intake of fluids, protein, calories & vitamins are essential for healing of wounds or ulcers. Due to the hypermetabolic state of burns, a significant ↑ in the number of calories & protein is required. Serum albumin levels < 3.5 mg/dL = high risk for skin breakdown & potential ↓ in healing. Decrease in healing contributes to a ↑ risk for infection. Monitor serum protein levels, iron, CBC, vitamin levels & client's weight to ensure adequate nutrition needs are met.	**N**utrition status (i.e., serum protein, serum albumin levels < 3.5 mg/dL = high risk for skin breakdown & potential ↓ in healing and ↑ risk for infection); assess iron, CBC.

Alteration with Tissue/Skin Integrity

Common Lab/Diagnostic Tests/Therapeutic Procedures/Surgery

Labs	Diagnostic Tests/Procedures	Therapeutic Procedures/Surgery
• CBC	• Tzanck smear (Herpes Simplex)	• Biopsy: tissue or bone
• Electrolytes	• Culture of lesion	• Skin scraping (cells from a lesion)
• Calcium	• Immunofluorescent studies of tissues	• Cryotherapy or freezing
• Phosphorus	• Potassium hydroxide smear– (identify fungi)	
• Serum protein levels	• Patch Test (test for allergies)	
• Prealbumin	• X-ray	
• Albumin	• Bone scan	
• Erythrocyte sedimentation rate (ESR)	• Magnetic resonance imaging (MRI)	
• Transferrin		
• Urinalysis and culture		
• Stool examination		
• Blood cultures if bacteremia or sepsis		

PRIORITIES

Of the lab values, the most important one to know is:

Serum albumin levels < 3.5 mg/dL = High risk for skin breakdown

Multiple Systems: Concept Tissue/Skin Integrity
Common Medications

ORAL ANTIBIOTICS
- Erythromycin (E-Mycin, Erytab, Erythrocin)
- Tetracycline (Achromycin)
- Dicloxacillin (Dynapen, Pathocil)

TOPICAL ANTIBIOTICS
- Polymixin B
- Neomycin (Mycifradin, Neobiotic)

ANTIFUNGAL AGENTS
- Ketoconazole (Nizoral)
- Fluconazole (Diflucan)
- Nystatin (Mycostatin)
- Miconazale (Lotrimin)
- Griseofulvin (Fulsovin)
- Itraconazole (Sporanox)

BURN CARE MEDICATIONS
Antimicrobial Ointments
- Silver Sulfadizine (Silvadene, Thermazene)
- Mafenide (Sulfamylon)
- Silver Nitrate
- Povidone-iodine (Betadine, Tridine)

ANTIBIOTICS
- Oxacillin (Bactocill, Prostaphilin)
- Mezolcillin (Mezlin)
- Gentamicin (Garamycin, Jenamicin)

ANABOLIC STEROIDS
- Oxandrolone (Oxandrin)

ANTIVIRAL AGENTS
- Valacyclovir (Valtrex)
- Acyclovir (Zorivax)
- Famciclovir (Famvir)

ANTIHISTAMINES
- Diphenhydramine (Benadryl)
- Loratadine (Claritin)
- Fexofenadine (Allegra)

ANTI-INFLAMMATORY
- Alclometasone (Acolvate)
- Beclomethasone (Beclovent, Beconase, QVAR)
- Hydrocortisone (Cort-Dome, Cortef, Hydrocortone)
- Triamcinolone (Azmacort, Kenalog, Nasacort)

PRESSURE-SORE NON-SURGICAL MANAGEMENT
- Hyaluronic Acid (Hyaluronan)
- Silver Sulfadizaine
- Propylene Glycol
- Cadexomer Iodine
- Hydrocolloid (Duoderm)
- Hydrogel
- Alginate
- Silver impregnated dressings
- Honey impregnated dressings
- Impregnated Gauze

First-Do Priority Interventions
Keep Clients a "TURNIN"

T Turn and reposition q 1–2 hours, maintain head of bed at or below 30° of elevation. Use silicone gel pads placed under the buttocks of clients in wheelchairs; sheepskin pads to protect skin. Maintain clean, dry skin and wrinkle-free linens; sun protection factor (SPF) 15 or >. Use padded and corrective devices, T-shirt (cotton) under braces.

U Use assistive devices as ordered (i.e., wheelchair, tilt table, etc.); use therapeutic bed/mattress for long term (provides continuous change in pressure across mattress); use eggcrate style or other foam mattress for circulation under the body to keep area dry.

R ROM (active/passive) as needed; OT & PT consults as needed.

N Nutritional intake needed for healing, ↑ protein and ↑ calories within restrictions. Continue to assess protein, albumin, zinc, iron, and CBC; call HCP with abnormal values. Promote fluid intake: (2,000 to 3,000 mL/day) if not contraindicated (i.e., heart failure, renal disease, neuro, etc.).

I Inspect skin every 2 hrs. Document changes, skin color, blanching, position, re-moisturize after bathing with lotion or protective moisturizer. Remember do not rub excessively and avoid hot water with skin care.

N Need to keep dry; use barrier ointments as prescribed. No strong detergents. No skin products with alcohol. Give skin and perineal care as needed.

"Just keep them a TURNIN, TURNIN, TURNIN!"

Multiple Systems: Concept Tissue/Skin Integrity

First-Do Priority Interventions

Pathophysiology	First-Do Priority Interventions Keep Client a "TURNIN"
Turning, positioning, and avoid sheering are essential to maintain skin and tissue integrity. Correct alignment is needed to prevent contractures and to promote circulation. Avoid constriction that impairs circulation and perfusion. Implement preventative skin and tissue measures for all clients at risk based on the Norton or Braden Scale Risk Assessment Tool.	**T**urn & reposition q 1–2 hours, maintain head of bed at or below 30° of elevation. Use silicone gel pads placed under the buttocks of clients in wheelchairs; sheepskin pads to protect skin. Maintain clean, dry skin & wrinkle free linens; sun protection factor (SPF) 15 or >. Use padded & corrective devices, T-shirt (cotton) under braces.
Use of assistive devices help promote safety for the client and for the health-care team. Correct moving of clients avoids unnecessary shearing of skin or tissue. A therapeutic bed or mattress helps avoid long-term contact with pressure points on the body. The client still needs to be turned and repositioned minimally every 2 hours even if on therapeutic bed/mattress.	**U**se assistive devices as ordered (i.e., wheelchair, tilt table, etc.); use therapeutic bed/mattress for long term (provides continuous change in pressure across mattress); use eggcrate style or other foam mattress for circulation under the body to keep area dry.
ROM helps promote circulation to damage tissue if the client is unable to get out of bed. The movement also helps prevent complications of deep vein thrombosis or atelectasis. Encourage deep breathing when moving the client to promote oxygenation. If the client can ambulate, it should be encouraged. Clients with ulcers on their feet can be up in a chair and can do active ROM. Isometric exercise of the abdomen and gluteal muscles can help with strength and with constipation. Occupational and physical therapists help the client establish an appropriate exercise plan and provide valuable instruction and assistive devices for maintaining independence with activities of daily living.	**R**OM (active/passive) as needed; OT & PT consults as needed.
Nutritional intake requirements increase for clients with wounds, ulcers or burns, (i.e., ↑ protein, calories, calcium, vitamins, zinc, etc.) to help ensure nutrition essential for healing. Collagen is responsible for repair of tissue. Collagen & granulation tissue grow to form a scar. Production of collagen depends on adequate perfusion to deliver O_2 and protein to the wound. Collagen is essential for healing, forming granulation tissue & blood vessel development. Supplemental feeding (i.e., hyperalimentation, albumin, fat emulsion, etc.) may be recommended. Increase fluid intake to 2,000–3000mL/day if not contraindicated due to (i.e., heart failure, renal failure, neuro, etc.).	**N**utritional intake needed for healing, ↑ protein & calories within restrictions. Continue to assess protein, albumin, zinc, iron, and CBC; call HCP with abnormal values. Promote fluid intake: (2,000 to 3,000 mL/day) if not contraindicated (i.e., heart failure, renal disease, neuro, etc.).
Inspect skin every 2 hours to detect early potential skin/tissue breakdown or to compare, contrast and trend ↑ or ↓ in tissue healing. Check skin for blanching, an indication of the blood supply to the area. Non-blanching areas should be noted and reported to the wound care team for early intervention to prevent breakdown.	**I**nspect skin every 2 hrs. Document changes, skin color, blanching, position; re-moisturize after bathing with lotion or protective moisturizer. Remember to not rub excessively & avoid hot water with skin care.
Need to keep skin dry using barrier ointments to prevent skin breakdown from irritation (i.e., urine or feces). Eliminate detergents and skin products with alcohol that are dying to the skin. **Elderly alert:** Elderly skin may be rough, scaly, flaky, or cracked, indicating xerosis (abnormal drying of the skin). Age-related dermal changes (i.e., thinner epidermal layer, a reduction in skin cell turnover, and a ↓ in the skin's capacity to retain moisture) require skin be moisturized after bathing to prevent further drying or ↑ risk for breakdown.	**N**eed to keep dry, use barrier ointments as prescribe. No strong detergents. No skin products with alcohol. Give skin & perineal care as needed.

Multiple Systems: Concept Tissue/Skin Integrity

Skin/Tissue Changes in the Elderly Clients

Causes of Changes in Skin & Tissue of Elderly		Recommendations for "SKIN CARE" for Elderly
• Thinner epidermal layer. • A reduction in skin cell turnover results in thinner, fragile skin. • Natural oil-producing sebaceous glands ↓ ability to moisturize the skin and retain moisture leads to xerosis (abnormal drying of the skin). • Loss of elasticity with ↓ production of collagen & elastin. • Decrease in lean body mass. • Hyaluronic acid ↓ in production = imbalance between production of hyaluronic acid & its breakdown by enzymes. • Multiple conditions (i.e., renal, cardiovascular, thyroid, etc.) and medications i.e., diuretics ↓ production of moisturizing sebaceous oils. • Exfoliants, harsh cleansers, and alcohol-based products such as astringents further dry aging skin.		**S**kin gently pat dry skin with cotton towel after a bath or shower. **K**eep skin moist; use thicker fragrance free moisturizers because they better help skin retain its moisture. **I**ncrease fluid & water intake; increase protein as needed for healing. **N**eed to apply a liberal amount of emollient moisturizing lotion within three minutes of taking a bath or shower; apply it several times per day. **C**otton and natural fiber clothing best; avoid wool clothing. **A**void hot baths (hot water strips away natural oils produced by the skin), frequent showering or bathing, and excessive skin scrubbing; drink plenty of water. **R**educe sun exposure. Use a humidifier in the home when necessary. **E**liminate drying creams avoid (i.e., antibacterial cleansers that contain alcohol, some anti-aging creams, etc.) (Lazare, 2012).

SAFETY
Concept: Tissue/Skin Integrity

System-Specific Assessments "SKIN"	First-Do Priority Interventions Keep Clients a "TURNIN"	Evaluation of Expected Outcomes No "SKIN"
Skin assessment: turgor (not accurate for elderly), color, (redness, pallor, purple in dark skin clients), and check for non-blanching areas; check for dryness; note color & shape of any lesions. Use tests (i.e., Woods lamp, Tissue biopsy, Wound culture, Patch test, etc.) to check skin. Note with any lesion variation that may indicate positive for disease. **K**now & assess any allergies (i.e., meds, food, allergens, etc.); note bowel or urinary incontinence. **I**nspect bony prominences for: skin color changes, assess wounds or pressure ulcers: measure depth, width, signs of granulation tissue. **N**orton or Braden scale to assess: • Norton Scale: measures physical and mental condition, activity, mobility, and incontinence • Braden Scale: measures sensory perception, moisture, activity-mobility, nutrition, friction, and shear • Pressure Ulcer Scale for Healing (PUSH Tool): categorized ulcers according to size of the wound, exudates, and type of tissue • Dermatome (light touch, pinprick): complete loss, ↑ or ↓ sensation. • Doppler ultrasonography & ultrasound: determine quality of blood flow. **N**utrition status: (i.e., serum protein, serum albumin levels < 3.5 mg/dL, = high risk for skin breakdown & potential ↓ in healing & ↑ risk for infection). Assess iron levels & CBC.	**T**urn & reposition q 1–2 hours, maintain head of bed at or below 30° of elevation. Use silicone gel pads placed under the buttocks of clients in wheelchairs; sheepskin pads to protect skin. Maintain clean, dry skin & wrinkle free linens; sun protection factor (SPF) 15 or >. Use padded & corrective devices T-shirt (cotton) under braces. **U**se assistive devices as ordered (i.e., wheelchair, tilt table, etc.); use therapeutic bed/mattress for long term (provides continuous change in pressure across mattress); use eggcrate style or other foam mattress for circulation under the body to keep area dry. **R**OM (active/passive) as needed; OT & PT consults as needed. **N**utritional intake needed for healing, ↑ protein & calories within restrictions. Continue to assess protein, albumin, zinc, iron, and CBC; call HCP with abnormal values. Promote fluid intake: (2,000 to 3,000 mL/day) if not contraindicated. **I**nspect skin every 2 hrs. Document changes, skin color, blanching, position, re-moisturize after bathing with lotion or protective moisturizer. Remember to not rub excessively & avoid hot water with skin care. **N**eed to keep dry, use barrier ointments as prescribe. No strong detergents. No skin products with alcohol. Give skin & perineal care as needed.	**S**kin assessment: WDL with **NO** (redness, pallor, purple in dark skin clients), or non-blanching areas; skin dry **K**now if any med allergies, note bowel/urinary incontinence; **NOT** Present **I**nspect bony prominences for: skin color changes, wounds; pressure ulcers: **NOT** present or healing **N**orton or Braden scale to assess. **NO** loss sensation or skin breakdown. **N**utritional status **WDL** and/or improving.

Exceptions and Additions by Disease/Injury

Pathophysiology: Tissue/Skin Integrity

Trauma/Injury to Skin and Tissue is damage to the skin and/or tissue that can result from thermal, chemical, radiation, and loss of perfusion, infection or surgical intervention. Injury to the skin and/or tissue can also be the result of benign and cancerous lesions. Impaired tissue and skin integrity skin may range from superficial to deep penetrating wounds. Assess the history and source of the injury, (i.e., surgery, trauma, abrasions, bites, etc.).

Terms to Know:

Surgical Incision is a cut through the skin, to the tissues, muscles or into the body organs. It is referred to as a surgical wound. The wound is then closed with sutures, staples, and surgical glue or it may be left open if there is an active infection. **Wound dehiscence** is when the margins of the wound separate.

Abrasion is superficial damage to the skin or epidermis where the skin is missing or separated.

Laceration is a torn or jagged wound often caused by sharp objects where there is a separation of the connective tissue. The term cut may be used to describe the same wound. Gash may be used to describe a longer or deeper cut.

Avulsion is a wound where the tissue of the body is torn away.

Ecchymosis is a flat, skin discoloration caused by blood leaking into the tissues from ruptured blood vessels. It can also occur in mucous membranes.

Hematoma is a collection of blood, not in the blood vessel, that can occur because of injury to the blood vessel, which allows blood to leak into the tissues.

Petechiae are small red or purple spots that do not blanch with pressure.

Purpura is hemorrhage into tissues and causes a bruise.

Blister is a fluid filled bump that develops on the skin. A blister may occur from rubbing, exposure to heat, electricity, chemical, and radiation from the sun, cold injuries, spider bites or a blood blister if capillaries are damaged. Blisters are seen with chicken pox and herpes simplex viruses.

Chemical irritants can cause contact dermatitis, redness, blisters, scales or crusts. It can also result in an allergic contact dermatitis, because of an allergic response to the material. Chemical irritants can be as common as soap, disinfectants to more serious irritants like acid. The factors that contribute are the properties of the chemical substance, the amount and concentration and the length and frequency of the exposure (Hogan, 2014).

Types of Wound Closure

Primary intention is a method of surgical wound closure that joins the wound edges together by (i.e., sutures, staples, steri-strips, and/or surgical glue, etc.) before granulation occurs.

Secondary intention is a method of wound closure by allowing adhesion of granulating surfaces when the edges of the wound cannot be brought together. The granulation process heals the wound from the base and sides to the surface of the wound.

Third intention or delayed primary closure is a method of wound closure used when the wound is contaminated or infected. The wound is left open until the infection is resolved or the contamination is reduced and/or the inflammation has subsided. The wound is then generally closed by first intention.

Skin grafts (human or animal) may be used to cover damaged or missing skin that results from burns, injury, chronic wounds, excision of cancerous lesions or wounds that will not heal. The graft can be skin from another part of the body or from a donor. The graft must acquire blood supply to survive (Wagner & Hardin-Pierce, 2014).

Exceptions and Additions by Disease/Injury

Pathophysiology: Tissue/Skin Integrity

Plan of Care for Wounds from Trauma or Injury

SYSTEM-SPECIFIC ASSESSMENTS	FIRST-DO PRIORITY INTERVENTIONS			
	DIET	EQUIPMENT	PLANS/INTERVENTIONS "WOUND"	HEALTH PROMOTION

Assess:
 	
• History of injury, source of injury (i.e., trauma, abrasions, bites, etc.).
 	
• Wound: width, depth, length; note color, smell & amount of drainage.
 	
• Tetanus immunization status. If wound is due to animal bite, assess if rabies prophylaxis is needed.
 	
• If deep tissue injury, assess if skin intact above injury and if there is blood supply.
 	
• For type of wound injury: (i.e., trauma, abrasions, lacerations, blisters or damage of underlying soft tissue, etc.).
 	
• Pain level (i.e., PQRST or other appropriate pain scale).
 	
• Neuro status if injury was to head, scalp, neck, or back.
 	
May need to prepare for surgical debridement.
	• High protein, zinc, Vitamins A & C
	
	• Increase calories as needed
	
	• Refer to Concept on Nutrition for specifics
		• May need vacuum-assisted wound-closure system
		
		• Wound and dressing material
			Wound cleaning: clean with direct pressure using a 20–30 mL syringe with minimum of 100mL of saline to remove debris & exudates.
			
			Wound assessment: note width, depth and length; note color, smell & amount of drainage; note signs of healing, granulation; compare, contrast & trend findings.
			
			Offer pain medication or anesthetization as needed prior to debridement or closing of wound; may need to elevate extremity (reduce swelling) as prescribed and/or apply ice packs (reduce swelling).
			
			U (you) leave wound open for abrasion injuries or wounds with active draining; may need vacuum-assisted closure systems with negative pressure for draining large amounts of exudates.
			
			Need tetanus & Rabies vaccine prophylaxis: tetanus for injury from dirty, contaminated surfaces, (i.e., burns, rusty nails, rocks, etc.), and Rabies vaccine for bites from un-vaccinated animals, (report animal bites to animal control).
			
			Dressing applied for protection and/or healing per protocol.
			  Debridement for wounds with dry, leathery eschar.
			  Diet for healing: (protein, vitamins A & C, zinc, calories as needed and intake of 2,000–3,000 mL/fluid/day unless contradicted (i.e., heart failure, renal disease, neuro, etc.).
			
			Referrals to wound care, dietician, OT & PT as needed.
				Teach client/family:
				• About diet recommen-dations
				
				• Activity level
				
				• Pain manage-ment
				
				• Wound care and dressing changes
				
				• Medication instructions for ointments, antibiotics, etc. as needed.

Pathophysiology: Tissue/Skin Integrity

Plan of Care for Wounds from Trauma or Injury

Insanely Easy Way to Remember Plan of Care for Injury to skin and tissue is:
"INJURY"

I   Investigate VS and assess wound: (cause, type, size, depth, etc.).

N   Need to assess indicators of infection (↑temp, ↑WBCs, purulent drainage, etc.).

    Need to assess if tetanus or rabies vaccinations are needed. Report animal bites to authorities.

J   Just give pain medications as prescribed and assess effectiveness.

U   U clean and dress wound per protocol using appropriate PPE.

R   Requirements met for adequate fluid & nutrition for healing.

Y   You teach client/family how to care for wound, about meds and prevention of further injury.

It's about Promoting Healing & Preventing Infection!!!!!

Refer to Concept Infection for specifics.

Exceptions and Additions by Disease/Injury

Pathophysiology: Tissue/Skin Integrity
Infections

There are several predisposing factors for skin and soft tissue infections (SSTI), which include infections of skin, subcutaneous tissue, fascia, and muscle. Some of the infections include impetigo, cellulitis, to severe infections like necrotizing fasciitis. Predisposing factors for clients may be an opening in the epidermis, dry, irritated skin, being in an immunocompromised status (i.e., malnutrition, burns, diabetes, AIDS, etc.), and or a history of peripheral vascular disease or chronic lymphatic insufficiency. These infections can be uncomplicated and respond well to antibiotic treatment, debridement or wound care while others are very complicated by the client's underlying disease processes and may involve needing to save a limb or life with surgical intervention. Some of the infecting organisms are: *Staphylococcus aureus* (the most common pathogen), *Streptococcus pyogenes*, site-specific infections (i.e., gram-negative bacilli in perianal abscesses), *Pseudomonas aeruginosa, beta-hemolytic streptococci*, and *Enterococcus* (National Institutes of Health, 2014).

Bacterial:

Cellulitis: infection of the dermis and subcutaneous tissue layers. Caused by Staphylococcus aureus or Group A beta-hemolytic streptococcus.

Impetigo: infection of the dermis. Caused by Streptococcus (strep), Staphylococcus (staph), or Methicillin-resistant staph aureus (MRSA).

Fungal:

Tinea: (ringworm), can be from different types of Tinea and locations on skin will vary based on type.
Tinea Capitis: scalp and hair follicle
Tinea Cruris: groin area
Tinea Pedis: feet (athlete's foot)
Tinea Corporis: trunk and limbs

Viral:

Herpes Simplex Virus Type 1 (HSV) (oropharyngeal) caused by the herpes virus.
Herpes Simplex Virus Type 2 (genitalia) caused by the herpes virus.
Herpes Zoster (shingles) caused by the latent varicella-zoster.
Verruca (warts) caused by the human papillomavirus.

Infestations:

Lice caused by parasitic insects; pediculus humonius or pthiras pubis.
Scabies caused by Sarcoptes scabiei.

Pathophysiology: Tissue/Skin Integrity

System-Specific Assessments for Types of Infecting Organisms

Bacterial	Fungal	Viral	Infestations
Cellulitis • A rash with painful, red, tender skin that may blister and scab over • Fever and chills **Impetigo** • Blisters filled with pus, yellow or honey colored, ooze & then crust over surrounded by redness • Rash, begin as a single spot, or sore & spreads by scratching, most commonly on face. **Common Symptoms:** • Blisters • Swollen glands or lymph nodes	• **Tinea:** red skin rash that forms a ring around normal-looking skin • **Tinea Capitis** (scalp & hair): red patches, bald spots • **Tinea Pedis** (athlete's foot): scaly rash with cracked skin between toes that itches & burns • **Tinea Cruris** (groin, jock itch): red, raised, scaly patches, may blister & ooze **Common Symptoms:** • Burning • Itching	• **Herpes Simplex Virus Type 1 & 2:** Vesicles with erythematous base, appear in groups • **Herpes Zoster:** erythematous vesicles scattered over skin along 1 or 2 dermatomes, occurring in clusters, proceeded by fever, pain, itching & burning, may have lasting neuralgia pain long after • **Verruca (warts):** epidermal eruptions, flesh-colored papules flat or dome shaped with back dots on surface **Common Symptoms:** • Herpes–vesicles	• **Lice:** Tickly feeling in hair, itching • **Scabies:** Itching, thin, irregular burrow tracks of tiny blisters or bumps on skin **Common Symptoms:** • Itching at night

Exceptions and Additions by Disease/Injury

Pathophysiology: Tissue/Skin Integrity
Infections

	FIRST-DO PRIORITY INTERVENTIONS			
SYSTEM-SPECIFIC ASSESSMENTS	**DIET**	**EQUIPMENT**	**PLANS/INTERVENTIONS**	**HEALTH PROMOTION**
• Refer to preceding chart • Assess vital signs and associated symptoms (i.e., fever, ↑ WBCs, etc.). • Palpate lesions and adjacent lymph nodes. • Location, appearance (i.e., redness, swelling, drainage, onset and duration of lesions, etc.). • Analysis of symptoms: location, onset, duration, distribution and presence; previous treatments. • Underlying chronic condition. • Examination of scalp, skin & nails for type and distribution of lesion(s). • Identify clinical stage, primary (2–14 days after inoculation, lesion grouped vesicles that may have ruptured) for herpes viruses. • Ask about previous occurrence and exposures to infected people. • Assess client's coping, self-esteem, body image.	• High protein, zinc, Vitamins A & C • Increase calories as needed • Refer to Concept on Nutrition for specifics	• Wound and dressing material as prescribed	• Pain: administer pain medication as prescribed. • Antibiotics as prescribed. *Note: with impetigo, important to take full prescription of antibiotic to prevent glomerulonephritis or mitral value involvement.* • Topical ointments applied as prescribed. • Gently wash to help remove crusts. • Position to avoid pressure, assess & apply topical dressings and medications for itching as prescribed. • Wear appropriate personal protective precautions: Standard Precautions/ Contact Precautions. • Psychological support as needed.	Teach client/family: • Diet • Activity • Importance of taking complete course of antibiotics as prescribed • Ways to prevent spread of infection or virus as applicable to the organism • **Lice treatment:** wash hair, then leave on permethrin 1% liquid (Nix) for 10 minutes, repeat in 7 days. Treat all family member & close contacts. Use contact precautions (*Refer to Concept Infection Control for specifics*)

Exceptions and Additions by Disease/Injury

Pathophysiology: Loss of Perfusion to Skin and/or Tissue
Pressure/Diabetic and Peripheral Vascular Disease Ulcers

Pressure ulcer is "an area of unrelieved pressure over a defined area, usually over a bony prominence, resulting in ischemia, cell death, and tissue necrosis," as defined by The National Pressure Ulcer Advisory Panel in 1992. These wounds are also known as decubitus but pressure ulcer is the accepted term.

Diabetic foot ulcer (neurotrophic) is one of the most common reasons for hospital admissions with people with diabetes. Often painless, they develop from pressure on the bottom of the feet. They occur from a combination of factors, poor circulation from vascular disease resulting in ischemia, cell death and tissue necrosis. The client due to peripheral neuropathy, (lack of feeling), often does not recognize the pressure, pain or injury to the foot (*Refer to Concept Glucose Metabolism for specifics*).

Peripheral vascular disease (arterial & venous) ulcers can be caused by decreased circulation from atherosclerosis, venous insufficiency or arterial embolism that leads to ischemia of the skin, an eventually becomes an ulcer. Often peripheral vascular disease is a compounding factor for pressure and diabetic foot ulcers and are seen together.

Risk factors for ulcers include: clotting disorders, renal failure, lymphedema, inflammatory diseases, rheumatological condition, smoking, immobility, infections and cancer.

System-Specific Assessments: Comparison of Ulcers

	Arterial Ulcers	Venous Ulcers	Neurotrophic (Diabetic) Foot Ulcers	Pressure Ulcers
Locations	Bottom of feet, between toes	Lower leg, ankle	Bottom of feet	**Anywhere on body, predominately at pressure points, (buttocks, heals, etc.)**
Appearance	**Regular borders, round**	Irregular shape	Center punched out, edges callused	Deep, irregularly shaped area
Color	Pale, gray or yellowish, brown	Beefy red, covered with yellow fibrous tissue	Variable, may be pink, red or brown	Depends on stage of ulcer (Refer to stages of ulcers in this chapter)
Pain	Burning, throbbing; dangling leg relieves pain	When leg is dependent, dull, heavy and achy	**May not have pain due to neuropathy**	Burning, throbbing
Drainage	Small amount of drainage to none.	Exudative wounds	Drainage if become infected or is also associated with a venous ulcer	May bleed, exudative wounds

INSANELY EASY TIP!!
Note the similarities in the different type of ulcers …
The tip: Remember the differences!
Arterial ulcers: regular borders and round
Diabetic ulcers: may not have pain due to neuropathy
Pressure ulcers: occur anywhere on the body.

Staging an Ulcer

The **Braden Scale for Risk Predictors for Skin Breakdown** assessment tool is a widely accepted tool for assessing risk predictors for skin breakdown that was developed by Barbara Braden and Nancy Bergstrom in 1988 (National Institutes of Health U.S. National Library of Medicine, 2013). An ultrasound may be done to help determine the blood flow around the ulcer; adequate blood flow is necessary for healing. Many facilities and clinics now have certified wound and ostomy nurses that can be consulted or may actually manage the wound care. These nurses are experts and are excellent resources. Another tool used is **The Pressure Ulcer Scale for Healing (PUSH Tool)** developed by the National Pressure Ulcer Advisory Panel (NPUAP) in 2007, categorizes ulcers according to size of the wound, exudates, and type of tissue. The goal of care is to prevent skin breakdown by identifying risk factors or to identify the ulcer in Stage 1 where the outcome is highly successful (Osborn, Wraa, Watson, & Holleran, 2014).

Braden Scale Risk Predictors for Skin Breakdown		PUSH Tool "WET"	
Sensory–perception Activity–mobility Moisture Nutrition Friction Shear	**Range of Score: 6–23** No Risk: 19–23 Mild Risk: 15–18 Moderate Risk: 13–14 High Risk: 10–12 Very High Risk: ≤ 9	Wound Size Exudates Type of Tissue	**Score of 0 = Wound Healed** **Score of 17= Wound not Healed**

The Four Stages of Pressure Ulcers:

Stage 1: Skin intact with non-blanchable redness over a localized area typically over a bony prominence.

Stage II: Partial-thickness with loss of dermis presenting as a shallow open ulcer with a red-pink wound bed.

Stage III: Loss of the full thickness of the tissue. Subcutaneous tissue and fat may be visible; bone, tendon, and/or muscle are not exposed. May include undermining and tunneling.

Stage IV: Full-thickness tissue loss with exposed bone, tendon, or muscle. Slough or eschar may be present on some parts of the wound. Often includes undermining and tunneling.

Unstageable: Full-thickness tissue loss in which the base of the ulcer is covered by slough (yellow, tan, gray; green, or brown) and/or eschar (tan, brown, or black) in the wound bed (National Pressure Ulcer Advisory Panel, 2007).

Exceptions and Additions by Disease/Injury

Pathophysiology: Loss of Perfusion to Skin and/or Tissue
Ulcer Care

| | FIRST-DO | PRIORITY | INTERVENTIONS | |
SYSTEM-SPECIFIC ASSESSMENTS	**DIET**	**EQUIPMENT**	**PLANS/INTERVENTIONS**	**HEALTH PROMOTION**

• Refer to preceding chart.
 	
• Use the Braden Scale for Risk Predictors for Skin Breakdown.
 	
• Ultrasound for blood flow. Determine stage of ulcer.
 	
• Medical history: (i.e., diabetes, peripheral vascular disease, etc.).
 	
• Assess vital signs, associated symptoms, signs of infection (i.e., fever, ↑ WBCs, etc.).
 	
• Palpate lesions and adjacent lymph nodes.
 	
• Location, appearance (i.e., redness, swelling, drainage, onset and duration of ulcers, wounds etc.).
 	
• If ulcer or wound present, identify clinical stage.
 	
• Assess client's coping, self-esteem, body image.
	• High protein, zinc, Vitamins A & C
	
	• Increase calories as needed
	
	• Refer to Concept on Nutrition for specifics
		• Wound and dressing material as prescribed
		
		• Vacuum-assisted wound closure system or negative-pressure wound system as prescribed
			• Referrals to wound care nurse for care & treatment of ulcer as prescribed, referral to dietician for nutrition assessment and diet plan.
			
			• Increase fluid intake: 2,000 to 3,000 mL/fluid/day if not contraindicated.
			
			• Dressing types (depend on type of ulcer) per protocol. May include:
			  • Moist to moist dressings
			  • Hydrogels/hydrocolloids
			  • Alginate dressings
			  • Collagen wound dressings
			  • Debriding agents
			  • Antimicrobial dressings
			  • Composite dressings
			  • Synthetic skin substitutes.
			
			• Use vacuum-assisted wound closure system or negative-pressure wound systems as prescribed.
			  • Pulls fluid from the wound, decreasing edema.
			  • Allows the wound to compress down.
			  • Encourages new healthy tissue growth and blood vessels to form.
			  • Wounds may heal faster & shorten length of stay.
			
			• Specialty mattresses as pre-scribed: Note still important to turn the client at least every 2 hours or per protocol.
				Teach client/family:
				• About need for ↑ protein & calories in diet.
				
				• Exercise.
				
				• Stop smoking.
				
				• Importance of taking complete course of antibiotics.
				
				• Instruction on ways to prevent skin breakdown: avoid sitting or lying in one place for extended periods of time, protect feet with shoes, seek attention immediately when ulcer begins: reddened area, will not blanch.

Elderly clients may need to ↑ dietary protein for healing.

Tips for increasing protein in the diet:
- Add protein powder or small pieces of meat to soups, salads or casseroles
- Add milk powder in mashed potatoes, scrambled eggs, cereal
- Eat desserts with eggs (i.e., custards, bread pudding)

Pathophysiology: Tissue/Skin Integrity
Thermal/Radiation

Tissue and Skin

Hypothermia can lead to frostbite, which is defined as freezing of body tissue that occurs when blood flow and oxygen is reduced from constricted blood vessel and microvascular stasis (LeMone, Burke & Bauldoff, 2011). It generally affects the skin and occurs most often in fingers, toes, nose and ears where color and sensation are decreased. Frostbite may be superficial or deep and there are three categories: frostnip, superficial frostbite and deep frostbite. The symptoms include: skin is white or grayish yellow in color, hard, waxy or numb. It may have blisters or become dark or black in color. Rewarming should begin as soon as the client is removed from the cold environment. The process is painful requiring pain medication. Affected area is wrapped in loose sterile bulky dressings and changed daily or per protocol (Black & Hawk, 2009).

Burn Injuries

Burn injuries result when energy from a heat source is transferred to the tissues of the body. It is caused by thermal, electrical, chemical or nuclear radiation. Burns are categorized accordingly:

Superficial burns: affect outer layer (epidermis) of the skin, (i.e., sunburn).

Superficial partial-thickness burns: damage is sustained to the epidermis and the superficial layer of the dermis.

Deep partial-thickness burns: involves the epidermis and deep layer of the dermis.

Full-thickness burns: involves the epidermis, dermis, and subcutaneous layers of skin and tissue.

Deep full-thickness burns usually involve all layers of the skin and may include injury to muscle, tendons or bone (Wagner & Hardin-Pierce, 2014).

Types of Burns

Thermal burns are caused from exposure or contact with heat source, (i.e., flame, steam, hot objects, etc.) and cause microvascular and inflammatory responses immediately. This causes histamine and serotonin to be released from the damaged cells increasing the vascular permeability. Fluid, electrolytes and proteins leak from the intravascular space into the interstitial spaces resulting in a hypovolemic state that can progress to shock. Severity of the burn depends on the amount, location and depth of the burn.

Chemical burns are caused from items like alkalis, acids or organic compounds found in the home or workplace. Severity depends on the type, duration of exposure and the concentration of the chemical.

Electrical burns result from electrical energy as it goes through the body. Sources can be electrical wiring, lightening or high voltage power lines. The severity depends on the duration of the contact, the amount and type of voltage, the path of the current through the body and the resistance of the tissues.

Radiation burns result from exposure to a radioactive source. Sunburns are considered to be radiation burns from the ultra violet rays of the sun (Wagner & Hardin-Pierce, 2014).

Inhalation injury or burns can result from exposure to carbon monoxide or smoke inhalation from the burns or the chemicals. Inhalation injury contributes to the severity and mortality of the client.

Pathophysiology: Tissue/Skin Integrity

System-Specific Assessments for Thermal/Radiation

The assessment begins with the client's history to determine cause of burns, (i.e., thermal, chemical, electrical, and or radiation). Early burn classification is very important in guiding the resuscitative plan. This involves determining the depth of the burn and the percentage of total body surface area (TBSA) burned. The most accurate guide is the Lund and Browder Chart, which adjusts the TBSA for age. The Rule of Nines is a quick and easy guide but less accurate particularly for children (Wagner & Hardin-Pierce, 2014). It is always very important to assess if there was any type of inhalation injury that would increase the risk for impaired oxygenation.

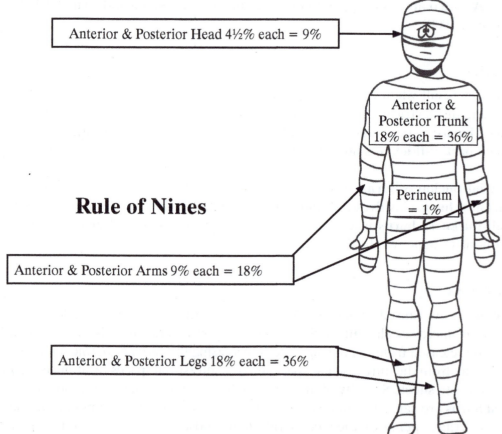

Anterior & Posterior Head 4½% each = 9%

Anterior & Posterior Trunk 18% each = 36%

Perineum = 1%

Rule of Nines

Anterior & Posterior Arms 9% each = 18%

Anterior & Posterior Legs 18% each = 36%

Burn clients are ideally transferred to burn centers that are equipped to care for the very complex needs of the client. The basics of the resuscitative phase will be discussed in this chapter. The resuscitative phase begins from the time of the burn to 48–72 hours post burn injury. As discussed previously, the first challenge is the hypovolemia that occurs as the fluid and electrolytes shift from the intravascular space to the interstitial spaces. There are a number of formulas used to guide fluid resuscitation. One of the most frequently used is the Parkland Formula. You are not expected to be an expert at burn care, but the following mnemonic "**BURNS**" can help you remember the priorities of care for the burn client in the first 72 hours. Notice as you review this mnemonic for "**BURNS**", the numerous concepts that are linked to the care for these clients: *Oxygenation, Fluid & Electrolyte Balance, Perfusion, Infection Control, Nutrition, Pain, Tissue/Skin Integrity, and Coping.*

Pathophysiology: Tissue/Skin Integrity

Thermal/Radiation
System-Specific Assessments (first 24 hours)

Oxygenation: First PRIORITY (if there are burns to the face, neck, upper body, inhalation); airway support as needed.

Fluid Volume Deficit: PRIORITY The heart rate may increase to 100–125 bpm as the heart tries to compensate for the decreased circulating volume (perfusion). Does this sound familiar? Once again fluid volume deficit is a Priority!!! The expected outcome of effective fluid replacement will be measured by trends of improvement in the: urine output, vital signs, peripheral pulses, and level of consciousness.

Priority Plan of Care of a Client with Burns
"BURNS"

Breathing, keep airway open, ↑ risk of respiratory distress with facial, inhalation burns; monitor for ↑ RR, shallow and labored breathing, bloody sputum, and hoarseness.

Urine output best indicator of fluid status. Desire minimum urine output of (30–45 mL/hour)
   Ulcer (gastric) risk because of stress; administer IV H_2 Blockers or proton pump inhibitors as prescribed

Rule of Nine is a quick way to estimate the degree of surface burns; for accuracy based on age, use Lund & Browder Chart, to calculate the TBSA.
   Replacement of Fluids: 2–4 mL x kg body weight x (% burn); Give ½ fluids in the first 8 hours, Give last ½ fluids in the next 16 hours per the Parkland Formula. Isotonic crystalloid solutions (i.e., NS & LR) are used in the 1st 24 hrs. Colloid solutions (i.e., albumin, plasma expanders, etc.) may be used after 24 hours. Fluids given using large bore needles. Fluid shifts can continue for 24 to 36 hour. Mobilization of fluid & diuresis begin to occur 48–72 hours after burn.
   Require infection control measures: PROTECTIVE (see next page in this chapter). (*Refer to Concept Infection Control for specifics*).
   Relief of pain; administer IV, not orally, subcutaneously or IM due to ↓ absorption.

Nutrition: need high calories, protein (determine using daily caloric expenditure estimate); supplemental feedings or hyperalimentation may be used. Daily weights, lab values will be used to evaluate status.

Signs of Shock: monitor closely vital signs, LOC, pulses, capillary refill, & renal function.
   Signs of Infection: (i.e., ↑ WBCs, temp and drainage from burn wounds, lung sounds, etc.).
   Skin & Tissue Integrity impaired due to the loss and/or damage to the skin & tissues.
   Support for coping with body image; make appropriate referrals, as needed.

Pathophysiology: Tissue/Skin Integrity

Thermal/Radiation
Infection Prevention with Burns

Clients who have burns are at a high risk for infection because the client's first line of defense, the skin, has been damaged. Protective isolation precautions will also minimize complications of infection by other organisms. The image below: "Positive Pressure: Positive Paul" can help you remember important information needed in caring for clients with burns. See Paul, he is using **POSITIVE PRESSURE** to keep the organisms out of the room!

Positive Pressure "PROTECT"

Private room with efficiency particulate air (HEPA) Filtration.

Requires PPE, not beyond what is indicated for Standard & Transmission-Based Precautions.

Orient client transport to minimize taking client out of the room if there is construction with the risk of fungal spores. Severely immunocompromised should wear a N95 respirator mask.

Things like flowers with standing water should not be in the room.

Eliminate sharing any equipment with other clients.

Close assessments for any signs of infection (i.e., ↑ Temp, ↑ WBCs, burns wounds with purulent drainage or foul odor, etc.).

Teach client, family & visitors the importance of following the Standard and Transmission-Based Precautions (Manning & Rayfield, 2014). (*Refer to concept Infection Control for specifics*).

POSITIVE PRESSURE: POSITIVE PAUL

©2008 I CAN Publishing, Inc.

P ositive

P ressure

P ositively

P revents

P atient infection by

P ushing air out

Concept Link Exercise!

The care of a Client with Burns is complex. It is multiple systems with multiple concepts. Can you list the concepts involved? There are at least 9 different concepts!!!

Give it a try, we bet you can! You may even think of more than 8!!!

1.	2.	3.
4.	5.	6.
7.	8.	9.

Priority Exercise for Burn Clients:

10. What is the first priority if a client has sustained a burn to the face and neck? _____
_____

11. What is a priority for all clients who have sustained burns in the first 24–48 hours? _____
_____

12. What is a potential complication that can result if not prevented with clients who have suffered burn injuries to the skin and tissue? _____

Great job!
Aren't you amazed at how easy that was to
pull the concepts together with the priority of care?

Pathophysiology: Tissue/Skin Integrity
Premalignant, Benign/Skin Cancer

Skin cancer is the most common type of cancer in the United Sates. Of the seven most common cancers, it is the only cancer growing in the rate of occurrence. The risk factors are from prolonged exposure to ultraviolet light from the sun. The key with skin cancer is prevention with the use of sunscreens, limiting time in the sun and regularly examining the skin for changes (Skin Cancer Foundation, 2014).

Actinic Keratosis is a precancerous lesion that is scaly or crusty and generally is red in color, but can be tan or flesh colored in appearance. The ultraviolet rays are the primary cause. It usually appears on exposed areas of the face, scalp, back of hands or lips. Actinic keratosis, if not treated, can advance to squamous cell carcinoma.

Squamous cell carcinoma is the second most common skin cancer. It develops in the epidermal keratinocytes and is more difficult to identify as the edges blend into the surrounding tissue. It grows more rapidly and can invade surrounding tissue and structures.

Basal cell carcinoma is the most common. It is rarely metastatic but the recurrence rate is high. The tumor grows slowly and is usually painless. It is predominately on the face, ears, neck or hands but may occur on the upper back and chest. Although it is not metastatic, it can be destructive if not treated will grow into the tissue and underlying structures.

Malignant melanoma is a deadly form of skin cancer with an ever-increasing rate of occurrence. The mortality rate from melanoma is also rising. Exposure to ultra violet light continues to be the major cause. There are multiple risk factors to include: fair complexion, excessive exposure to UV rays, bad sunburns as a child, increased number of moles, family history, and the presence of a changing mole on the skin (Skin Cancer Foundation, 2014).

Benign Skin Tumors or Lesions

Seborroeic keratosis are brown or black spots which appear on surface of the skin and increase in number with age. They are usually asymptomatic but may itch. It there is any doubt in diagnosis, a biopsy should be done.

Sebacceous (senile) hyperplasia is very common in middle age and elderly clients. They are soft yellow, dome shaped papules and occur mainly on the face.

Dermatofibroma are benign tumors that often represent a fibrous reaction to minor trauma or insect bites. The raised papules or nodules vary in color from brown, purple or red. They may occur anywhere but are more common on the legs. The lesions may resemble melanomas, so a biopsy may be needed to confirm the diagnosis.

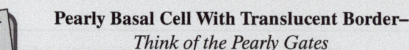

Insanely Easy Way
to Distinguish Between Basal Call Carcinoma and Melanoma!

Pearly Basal Cell With Translucent Border–
Think of the Pearly Gates

Versus

Dark Brown Or Black Melanoma–
Think of a Black Hole that Progressively Gets Bigger

Pathophysiology: Tissue/Skin Integrity

Premalignant, Benign/Skin Cancer
Prevention through Health Promotional Activities

The role of the nurse in health promotion is invaluable in promoting the prevention of skin cancer. It is an area that all nurses can engage in, whether it is in the acute care setting or in a public meeting, church, or a health bazaar. The opportunities are limitless! It will be important as you progress in nursing school that you recognize the differences in benign skin lesions and those that need immediate follow-up with a healthcare provider. Practice looking at pictures and begin to learn the distinguishing differences in the appearance of lesions. However, here are some key teaching points about skin cancer prevention you can start sharing now with your clients, your family and perhaps you might need to implement yourself. It is all about **PREVENTION**!

Insanely Easy Way to Remember

"SUN CARE"

Seek shade from 10am to 4pm when the sun's rays are the strongest.

U need sunscreen 15 or higher; apply every day and more often when in sun or water.

Note changes in skin of any kind; know the **Skin Cancer Warning Signs: ABCDEs** (Skin Cancer Foundation, 2014).

    Asymmetrical (draw line through the lesion & 2 sides do not match.

    Borders are uneven, notched

    Color variety of colors

    Diameter, melanomas (may be larger i.e., size of the eraser on a pencil, 1/4 inch or 6 mm)

    Evolving (change in size, shape, color, elevation, or another trait, or any new symptom such as bleeding, itching or crusting)

Cover up with clothes, a broad rimmed hat, and 100% UV sunglasses when outside.

Avoid tanning in UV tanning booths.

Refrain from having infants in direct sunlight.

Examine skin, head to toe once a month.

Clinical Decision-Making Exercises

1. Which of these represents the correct fluid replacement schedule using the Parkland Baxter Formula requiring 4000 mL during the first 24 hours for a client with severe burns?
    ① 160 mL/hr x 8 then 190 mL/hr x 8, and then 200 mL/hr x 8.
    ② 250 mL/hr x 8, then 125 mL/hr x 8, and then 22 mL/hr x 8 x 3.
    ③ 245 mL/hr x 8 then 190 mL/hr x 8, and then 100 mL/hr x 8.
    ④ 167 mL/hr x 8 167 mL/hr x 8 and then 167 mL/hr x 8.

2. Which of these assessments indicates the expected outcome of the fluid resuscitation for a client with a burn injury?
    ① HR increased from 58 to 110.
    ② Urine out was 28 mL/hr now 60 mL/hr.
    ③ Decreased level of consciousness.
    ④ Peripheral pulses 1+ bilaterally.

3. Which of the actions by the LPN requires the RN to intervene immediately while caring for a client on protective isolation for a burn injury?
    ① The LPN is providing the client with clean sheets and linens.
    ② The LPN is performing strict hand washing technique.
    ③ The LPN is delivering a vase of flowers to the client.
    ④ The LPN is wearing gloves and a gown when assisting with wound dressing changes.

4. Which of these clients is a priority to assess immediately after shift report?
    ① A client admitted with an abnormal skin lesion that has grown in size over the last month.
    ② A client who was in a house fire 2 hours ago who is resting quietly.
    ③ The client who is scheduled for their dressing changes for a pressure ulcer.
    ④ A client with full thickness burns to his chest and is complaining of shortness of breath and chest pain.

5. Which of these clinical findings would be of concern for a client with stage 3 wound?
    ① Hgb 12%, Hct 34%.
    ② Decreased prealbumin level.
    ③ Appearance of red tissue in the wound.
    ④ Small amount of serous drainage on dressing.

6. Which of these clinical findings would be of greatest concern for a client with urinary incontinence in a long-term care facility?
    ① Three incontinent episodes in 24 hours.
    ② A 2cm red circular area on the left buttocks that does not blanch.
    ③ A foul strong odor of urine on soaked linens.
    ④ The client is combative and refuses to accept assistance from the UAP.

7. Which information is appropriate for the nurse to include at a community health fair about early warning signs of skin cancer? ***Select all that apply.***

    ① Changes in size of mole or skin lesion.

    ② Lesion is all one color.

    ③ Asymmetrical in size.

    ④ Small diameter lesion, unchanged.

    ⑤ Lesions borders are irregular.

8. Which of these nursing actions is appropriate for a client at risk for skin breakdown?

    ① Reposition client carefully using the draw sheet.

    ② Decrease client's fluid intake.

    ③ Position pillows under knees for comfort when client is in bed.

    ④ Turn the client every 4 hours while awake.

9. Which clinical assessment findings would be an early indication of hypovolemia?

    ① BP was 147/70 now is 160/ 90, RR was 18/min now is 24/min.

    ② Urine output 40 now 30 mL/hr, HR was 96 BPM now is 88 BPM.

    ③ RR was 18/min now 28/min, HR was 78 BPM now is 99 BPM.

    ④ HR was 70 BPM now is 52 BPM, client c/o of restlessness.

10. What information should be included in an unit inservice on how to provide skin care for an incontinent client?

    ① Turn the client every 4 hours.

    ② Skin that does not blanch is the desired outcome.

    ③ Decrease protein intake in a client at risk for impaired skin/tissue integrity.

    ④ Inspect the skin every 2 hours and document skin color, blanching.

Answers and Rationales

1. Which of these represents the **correct fluid replacement schedule** using the **Parkland Baxter Formula** requiring **4000 mL during the first 24 hours for a client with severe burns?**

    ① INCORRECT: 160 mL/hr x 8 then 190 mL / hr x 8, and then 200 mL/hr x 8. This is not correct.

    ② **CORRECT: 250 mL/hr x 8, then 125 mL/ hr x 8, and then 125 mL/hr x 8. This option uses the correct formuala that requires the client to receive half of the total amount of fluid in the first 8 hours and the remaining amount of fluid divided over the next 16 hours.**

    ③ INCORRECT: 245 mL/hr x 8 then 190 mL/hr x 8, and then 100 mL/hr x 8. This is not correct.

    ④ INCORRECT: 167 mL /hr x 8 167 mL/hr x 8 and then 167 mL/hr x 8. This is not correct.

The strategy for answering this question is to understand the Parkland Baxter Formula and the pathophysiology for the need for fluid replacement during the first 24 hours of a burn injury. Thermal burn injuries result in microvascular and inflammatory responses immediately. This causes histamine and serotonin to be released from the damaged cells increasing the vascular permeability. Fluid, electrolytes and proteins leak from the intravascular space into the interstitial spaces resulting in a hypovolemic state that can progress to shock if fluid replacement is not done immediately. In this question you were able to link the concept of fluid balance with the pathophysiology of burn injuries. Fluid balance is the **PRIORITY** concept in the first 24 hour. Oxygenation would be of equal priority if the client had inhalation injury or burns to the face, neck, or upper chest resulting in a compromised airway. Using the Prioritization chart from chapter

1, oxygen and fluid balance are critical physiological needs for a client with severe burns. Great job in pulling together concepts with physiology and to be able to schedule fluid replacement!!!!

Physiological Adaptation: Identify pathophysiology related to an acute or chronic condition.

Physiological Adaptation: Manage the care of the client with fluid and electrolyte imbalance.

2. Which of these **assessments** indicates the **expected outcome** of the **fluid resuscitation** for a client with a **burn injury?**

    ① INCORRECT: HR increased from 58 to 110. The desired outcome of the fluid replacement would be an increase in the circulating volume requiring the heart not to have to pump as hard with a decrease in heart rate.

    ② **CORRECT: Urine out was 28mL/hr now 60 mL/hr. This is the expected outcome and the best indicator of adequate fluid replacement is when the urine output is 30–45 mL/hour minimally for clients with burn injuries.**

    ③ INCORRECT: Decreased level of consciousness. The expected outcome from the fluid replacement would be adequate perfusion to the vital organs to include cerebral perfusion with an increase in the level of consciousness, not a decrease (*Refer to the Concept Intracranial Regulation for specifics*).

    ④ INCORRECT: Peripheral pulses 1+ bilaterally. Not the correct answer over option 2.

The strategy for answering this question is to link the pathophysiology of burn injury to the concept of fluid replacement and the expected outcomes from the fluid replacement. With burn clients in the first 24-48 hours, urine output is the best indicator of the fluid status. The goal is to maintain the urine output at a minimum of 30–45 mL/hours. This is a better indicator than using hemodynamic monitoring until the fluid shifts stabilize. In this question you were able to use the **TRENDING** strategy from the Prioritization chart in chapter 1 to assist you with this decision along with your knowledge of fluid balance with burn injuries. You are really doing great and pulling concepts together with pathophysiology and then prioritizing the care!!!!

Physiological Adaptation: Identify pathophysiology related to an acute or chronic condition.

Physiological Adaptation: Manage the care of the client with fluid and electrolyte imbalance.

Reduction of Risk Potential: Evaluate responses to procedures and treatments.

3. Which of the **actions by the LPN** requires the **RN to intervene immediately** while caring for a client on **protective isolation for a burn injury?**

    ① INCORRECT: The LPN is providing the client with clean sheets and linens. This would be appropriate.

    ② INCORRECT: The LPN is performing strict hand washing technique. This would be appropriate.

    ③ **CORRECT: The LPN is delivering a vase of flowers to the client. This is not allowed with protective isolation because of the risk of bacteria growing in the standing water of the vase.**

    ④ INCORRECT: The LPN is wearing gloves and a gown when assisting with wound dressing changes. This would be appropriate standard based plus contact precautions.

The strategy for answering this question is to know what infection control measures and personal protective equipment is needed for a client with a burn injury. (*Refer to concept infection control for specifics*). **Prevention of infection in a burn client is a priority** because the burn has destroyed the body's first line defense, the skin. Protective isolation would be needed using a room with positive pressure. Remember **Positive Paul** pushing the bad organism

out of the room! An infection can significantly increase the length of stay and increase the mortality rate for a burn client. **Infection Control is the Priority!!!**

Safety and Infection Control: Apply principles of infection control (i.e., hand hygiene, room assignment, isolation, aseptic/sterile technique, universal/standard precautions).

4. Which of these clients is a **priority to assess** immediately **after shift report?**

    ① INCORRECT: A client admitted with an abnormal skin lesion that has grown in size over the last month. This is not priority over option 4.

    ② INCORRECT: A client who was in a house fire 2 hours ago who is resting quietly. This is not a priority over option 4.

    ③ INCORRECT: The client who is scheduled for their dressing changes for a pressure ulcer. This is not a priority over option 4.

    ④ **CORRECT: A client with full thickness burns to his chest that is complaining of shortness of breath and chest pain. This is a priority to the location of the burns and the client's complaints of respiratory involvement.**

The strategy for answering this question is linking Prioritization to the pathophysiology of the client's clinical situation. In this question, a good question to ask is, "What is the worst thing that could happen if I do not go see this client first?" This can be a great prioritizing strategy to use. An abnormal skin lesion is not an immediate life-threatening event. Option 2, you probably considered and put it on your possible answers column. Option 3 is not life threatening, a dressing change can wait, and then you got to option 4 and you knew it was the answer because of the risk of respiratory distress due to the location of the burns and the clients complaints. You now disregard, option 2 and you have your answer! Wasn't that easy!

Reduction of Risk Potential: Recognize trends and changes in client condition and intervene as needed.

5. Which of these **clinical findings** would be of **concern** for a client with **stage 3 wound?**

   ① INCORRECT: Hgb 12%, Hct 34%. This is within the normal defined limits.

   ② **CORRECT: Decreased prealbumin level. This would be a concern indicating the client's nutritional status is not adequate to help promote healing.**

   ③ INCORRECT: Appearance of red tissue in the wound. This would not be a concern in a wound.

   ④ INCORRECT: Small amount of serous drainage on a peripheral venous ulcer dressing. This would be an expected finding for venous ulcers that produce a large amount of drainage.

The strategy for answering this question is to apply the information you know about the pathophysiology of the stages of wounds to what is expected clinical findings and what is needed for healing. Option 1 is within defined range of normal, option 3 is an expected finding in a wound, and option 4 would be an expected finding with peripheral venous ulcer. The only possible option is the decrease in the pre albumin level. Albumin & protein are required for collagen production essential for wound healing. Decrease in albumin and protein would indicate the wound may not be getting adequate protein needed for healing. This would require intervention (i.e., consultation with a dietician and/or HCP) to increase the protein in the diet. Great job of linking together the concept of nutrition with pathophysiology of wound healing!!!! Another great connection is made... Yes!!!!

Basic Care and Comfort: Manage the client's nutritional intake

Physiological Adaptation: Identify pathophysiology related to an acute or chronic condition.

6. Which of these **clinical findings** would be of **greatest concern** for a **client with urinary incontinence** in a long-term care facility?

   ① INCORRECT: Three incontinent episodes in 24 hours. The client has urinary incontinence, so this would not be a change in condition.

   ② **CORRECT: A 2 cm red circular area on the thigh that does not blanch. This would be a concern as it indicates a potential skin breakdown.**

   ③ INCORRECT: A foul strong odor of soaked linens. Soaked linens do have a foul smell and it would not indicate a potential complication.

   ④ INCORRECT: The client who refuses to accept assistance from the UAP. This is not correct.

The strategy for answering this question was to link the concept of tissue/skin integrity with urinary incontinence. Clients who are incontinent have an increased risk for skin/tissue breakdown. It takes vigilant assessments and preventive interventions to prevent skin breakdown particularly with elderly clients who often do not drink enough to maintain fluid balance or eat enough to maintain adequate nutrition to help prevent skin breakdown. Great job in assessing this early sign of potential skin breakdown so preventive interventions can be implemented!! **Remember it is all about prevention so identifying early signs is a PRIORITY!**

Basic Care and Comfort: Perform skin assessment and implement measure to maintain skin integrity and prevent skin breakdown.

Reduction of Risk: Recognize trends and changes in client condition and intervene as needed.

7. Which **information is appropriate** for the nurse to include at a community health fair about **early warning signs of skin cancer?** Select all that apply.

   ① **CORRECT: Changes in size of mole or skin lesion. This is one of the ABCDEs of skin cancer warning signs.**

   ② INCORRECT: Lesion is all one color. Not correct because most often, cancerous skin lesions may have a variety of colors. It would important to continue to monitor lesion.

   ③ **CORRECT: Asymmetrical in size. This is one of the ABCDEs of skin cancer warning signs.**

④ INCORRECT: Small diameter lesion, unchanged in size. Not correct because normally lesions are larger in size, particularly with melanomas and have changed in size. It would important to continue to monitor lesion.

⑤ **CORRECT: Lesions borders are irregular. This is one of the ABCDEs of skin cancer warning signs.**

The strategy to answer this question was to know the warning signs of skin cancer. This is an important role nurses can take in health promotion and education for the clients you care for and other people you encounter on a daily basis. Take opportunities to participate in health fairs, organizational or social meetings to help educated the public about the risks of skin cancer. Prevention is the key!

Health Promotion and Maintenance: Assess and teach client about health risks based on family, population and/or community characteristics

Health Promotion and Maintenance: Plan or participate in community health education.

8. Which of these **nursing actions** is **appropriate** for a client at **risk for skin breakdown?**

    ① **CORRECT: Reposition client carefully using the draw sheet. Using a draw sheet can help prevent shearing when moving a client in bed.**

    ② INCORRECT: Decrease the client's fluid intake. Not correct, fluid intake should be increased not decreased to prevent skin/ tissue breakdown.

    ③ INCORRECT: Position pillows under knees for comfort when client is in bed. Not correct, this position can decrease perfusion to the lower extremity. Adequate perfusion is necessary to carry oxygen and nutrients to the skin and tissue.

    ④ INCORRECT: Turn the client every 4 hours while awake. Not correct, the client should be turned at least every 2 hours, not every 4 hours to prevent skin/tissue breakdown.

The strategy for answering this question was to understand and know the risk factors that can contribute to skin/tissue breakdown and what preventative measure were needed. Clients at risk for skin

breakdown need to protect the skin from shearing forces that could tear the skin. Pulling a client up in bed without a draw sheet causes a shearing force on the skin. This is a simple but effective way to prevent injury to the skin and tissue.

Basic Care and Comfort: Perform skin assessment and implement measure to maintain skin integrity ad prevent skin breakdown.

9. Which **clinical assessment findings** would be an **early indication of hypovolemia?**

    ① INCORRECT: BP was 147/70, now is 160/ 90, RR was 18 /min, now is 24/min. BP would not be the early indicator of hypovolemia.

    ② INCORRECT: Urine output 50, now 40 ml/hr, HR was 96 BPM, now is 88 BPM. Although the urine decreased some, the heart rate did as well, so this would not be the correct option over option 3.

    ③ **CORRECT: RR was 18/min, now is 28/min, HR was 78 BPM, now is 99 BPM. These are early signs of potential for hypovolemia, an increasing respiratory rate and heart rate.**

    ④ INCORRECT: HR was 70 BPM now is 52 BPM, RR was 20/min now is 16/min. A decrease in heart rate or respiratory rate would not be the clinical findings for hypovolemia.

The strategy for answering this question was to understand the pathophysiology of hypovolemia and to recognize early system specific assessments indicating possible hypovolemia. Early signs of hypovolemia are an increasing heart rate because the heart is trying to compensate for the decrease in the circulating volume. The respiratory rate increases because of the decreased perfusion needed to bring adequate oxygen to the tissues. The other options had one or more of the parts of the distractor incorrect. Remember, a great test taking strategy is that all parts of the distractor have to be correct for it to be the correct answer.

10.   What information **should be included** in an unit **inservice on how to provide skin care for an incontinent client?**

①   INCORRECT: Turn the client every 4 hours. Need to turn every 2 hours at a minimum.

②   INCORRECT: Skin that does not blanch is the expected outcome. Skin that blanches is the expected outcome. Skin that does not blanch is an early sign of potential skin/tissue breakdown.

③   INCORRECT: Decrease protein intake in a client at risk for impaired skin/tissue integrity.

④   **CORRECT: Inspect the skin every 2 hours and document skin color, blanching.**

The strategy to answer this question is once again about **prevention of skin/tissue breakdown ...** are you seeing a pattern?!!! Preventing skin breakdown not only saves the client from an extended stay in the acute care setting and further potential complications that can result, like an infections; it saves the institution money. Today's healthcare environment requires that all healthcare team members practice preventative care. Doing an in-service is one part of that requirement to ensure all team members are adequately prepared to give quality care. This should have been an easy question for you now that you have completed this chapter ... Excellent job!! .

Management of Care: Participate in providing cost effective care.

Basic Care and Comfort: Perform skin assessment and implement measure to maintain skin integrity and prevent skin breakdown.

Decision-Making Analysis Form

Use this tool to help identify why you missed any questions. As you enter the question numbers in the chart, you will begin to see patterns of why you answered incorrectly. This information will then guide you toward what you need to focus on in your continued studies. Ultimately, this analytical exercise will help you become more successful in answering questions!!!

Questions to ask:

1. Did I have the knowledge to answer the question? If not, what information do I need to review?

2. Did I know what the question was asking? Did I misread it or did I miss keywords in the stem of the question?

3. Did I misread or miss keywords in the distractors that would have helped me choose the correct answer?

4. Did I follow my gut reaction or did I allow myself to rationalize and then choose the wrong answer?

	Lack of Knowledge (Concepts, Systems, Pathophysiology, Medications, Procedures, etc.)	Missed Keywords or Misread the Stem of the Question	Missed Keywords or Misread the Distractors	Changed My Answer (Second-guessed myself, i.e., my first answer was correct.)
Put the # of each question you missed in the column that best explains why you think you answered it incorrectly.				

If you changed an answer because you talked yourself out of the correct answer, or you second-guessed yourself, this is an **EASY FIX: QUIT changing your answers**!!! Typically, the first time you read a question, you are about 95% right! The second time you read a question, you start talking yourself into changing the answer. The third time you read a question, you do not have a clue—and you are probably thinking "Who in the heck wrote this question?"

On the other hand, if you read a question too quickly and when you reread it you realize you missed some key information that would impact your decision (i.e., assessments, lab reports, medications, etc.), then it is appropriate to change your answer. When in doubt, go with the safe route: your first thought! Go with your gut instinct!

As you gain confidence in answering questions regarding specific nursing concepts, you will be able to successfully progress to answering higher-level questions about prioritization. Please refer to the *Prioritization Guidelines* in this book for a structure to assist you with this process.

You CAN do this!

> *"A pessimist sees the difficulty in every opportunity;*
> *An optimist sees the opportunity in every difficulty."*
> SIR WINSTON LEONARD SPENCER-CHURCHILL

References for Chapter 20

Black, J M. and Hawks, J. H. (2009). *Medical surgical nursing: Clinical management for positive outcomes* (8th ed.). Philadelphia: Elsevier/Saunders.

Cleveland Clinic (2014). Retrieved from http://my.clevelandclinic.org/heart/disorders/vascular/legfootulcer.aspx

Daniels, R. & Nicoll, L. (2012). *Contemporary medical-surgical nursing*, (2nd ed.). Clifton Park, NY: Delmar Cengage Learning.

Eliopoulos, C. (2014). *Gerontological nursing* (8th ed.), Philadelphia: Lippincott Williams & Wilkins.

Giddens, G. F. (2013). *Concepts for nursing practice.* St. Louis, MO: Mosby, an imprint of Elsevier.

Hogan, M. A. (2014). *Pathophysiology, reviews and rationales*, (3rd Edition) Boston, MA: Pearson.

Ignatavicius, D. D. and Workman, M. L. (2010). *Medical-Surgical nursing: Patient-Centered collaborative care* (7th ed.). Philadelphia: Elsevier/Saunders.

Lazare, J. (2012). *Careful attention to aging skin.* Retrieved from http://www.todaysgeriatricmedicine.com/archive/091712p18. shtmlLeMone, P., Burke, K.M., & Bauldoff, G. (2011). Medical-surgical nursing: Critical thinking in patient care (5th ed.). Upper Saddle Road, NJ: Pearson/Prentice Hall.

Lewis, S., Dirksen, S., Heitkemper, M., Bucher, L., and Camera, I. (2011). *Medical surgical nursing: Assessment and management of clinical problems* (8th ed.). St. Louis: Mosby.

Manning, L. and Rayfield, S. (2014). *Nursing made insanely easy* (7th ed). Duluth, GA: I CAN Publishing, Inc.

Manning, L. and Rayfield, S. (2013). *Pharmacology made insanely easy* (4th ed.). Duluth, GA: I CAN Publishing, Inc.

National Council of State Boards of Nursing, INC. (NCSBN) 2012. *Research brief: 2011 RN practice analysis: linking the NCLEX RN® examination to practice.* Retrieved from https://www.ncsbn.org/index.htm

National Institutes of Health. (2014). *Skin infections.* Retrieved from http://www.nlm.nih.gov/medlineplus/skininfections.html

National Institutes of Health National Library of Medicine. (2013). *Braden scale source information.* Retrieved from http://www.nlm.nih.gov/research/umls/sourcereleasedocs/current/LNC_BRADEN/

Nettina, S. L. (2013). *Lippincott manual of nursing practice* (10th ed.). Philadelphia, PA: Walters Kluwer Health/Lippincott Williams & Wilkins.

North Carolina Concept Based Learning Editorial Board. (2011). *Nursing a concept based approach to learning.* Upper Saddle Road, NJ: Pearson/Prentice Hall.

Osborn, K. S., Wraa, C. E., Watson, A. S., and Holleran, R. S. (2014). *Medical surgical nursing: Preparation for practice* (2nd ed.). Upper Saddle Road, NJ: Pearson.

Pagana, K. D. and Pagana, T. J. (2014). *Mosby's manual of laboratory and diagnostic tests* (5th ed.). St. Louis, MO: Mosby, an imprint of Elsevier.

Porth, C. (2011). *Essentials of pathophysiology* (3rd edition). Philadelphia, PA: Lippincott Williams ad Wilkins.

Porth, C. M. and Grossman, S. (2013). *Pathophysiology, Concepts of altered health states* (9th edition). Philadelphia, PA: Lippincott Williams & Wilkins.

Potter, P. A., Perry, A. G., Stockert, P., and Hall, A. (2013). *Fundamentals of nursing* (8th ed). St. Louis, MO: Pearson/Prentice Hall.

Prevention Plus. Retrieved http://www.bradenscale.com/

Skin Cancer Foundation. (2014). *The abcde of melanoma.* Retrieved from http://www.skincancer.org/skin-cancer-information/melanoma/melanoma-warning-signs-and-images/do-you-know-your-abcdes#panel1-5

Skin Cancer Foundation (2014). *Skin cancer facts.* Retrieved from http://www.skincancer.org/skin-cancer-information/skin-cancer-facts

Smeltzer, S. C., Bare, B. G., Hinkle, J. L., and Cheever, K. H. (2010). *Brunner & Suddarth's Textbook of medical-surgical nursing* (12th ed.). Philadelphia: Lippincott Williams & Wilkins.

The National Pressure Ulcer Advisory Panel. *NPUAP Pressure Ulcer Stages/Categories*, Retrieved from http://www.npuap.org/resources/educational-and-clinical-resources/npuap-pressure-ulcer-stagescategories/

Wagner, K.D. & Hardin-Pierce, M.C. (2014). *High-Acuity nursing* (6th ed.). Boston: Pearson

CHAPTER 21

Visual and Auditory Systems
Linking Concepts to Pathophysiology of Diseases
Concept Sensory Perception

A Snapshot of Sensory Perception

Sensory Perception can be defined as the ability to receive sensory input, and through various physiologic processes in the body, translate the stimulus or data into meaningful information (Giddens, 2013). The ability to perceive stimulation through one's sensory organs such as the eyes, ears, and nose is known as sensation. This stimulation can be internal, from within the body, or external, from outside the body. This includes temperature, light, and feelings of pain. External stimuli are typically received and processed with the five senses: vision, hearing, taste, smell, and touch. Perception is defined as the process by which we receive, process, and interpret the sensation.

PATHOPHYSIOLOGY The Pathophysiology Behind Sensory Perception

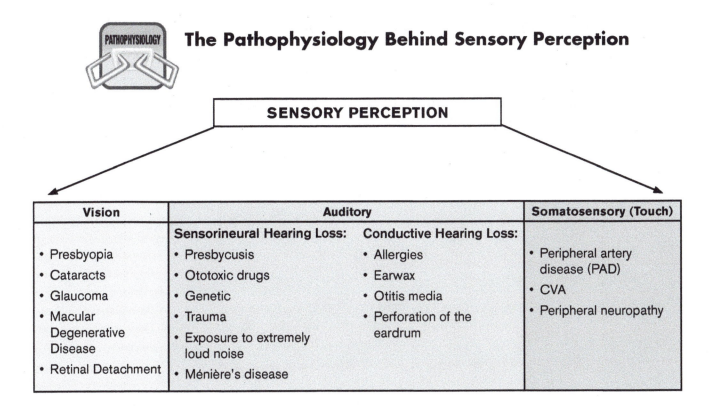

	SENSORY PERCEPTION	

Vision	Auditory	Somatosensory (Touch)
• Presbyopia • Cataracts • Glaucoma • Macular Degenerative Disease • Retinal Detachment	**Sensorineural Hearing Loss:** • Presbycusis • Ototoxic drugs • Genetic • Trauma • Exposure to extremely loud noise • Ménière's disease	**Conductive Hearing Loss:** • Allergies • Earwax • Otitis media • Perforation of the eardrum	• Peripheral artery disease (PAD) • CVA • Peripheral neuropathy

System-Specific Assessments Sensory Perception

"VISION"

V   Visual acuity

I   Internal eye–examine with an ophthalmoscope

S   Sensory assessment–begin with history, past medications, surgery, etc.

I   Inspect external eye–eyebrows, lashes, lids, etc.

O   Observe movement of the eyes

N   Note list of meds and sensory perception symptoms regardless of vision

Linking Pathophysiology to System-Specific Assessments of Vision

Pathophysiology	System-Specific Assessments "VISION"
Visual acuity: Visual acuity refers to the clarity of vision and is basically a measure of how well a person sees. This is typically done with a Snellen chart. Due to the many changes that occur with the aging process, the American Optometric Association (AOA) recommends adults up to age 40 receive an eye exam at least every 2 years. The same is true for up to age 60 unless clients have complications with diabetes, heart disease, and hypertension and then these clients should receive special attention. During middle age there is a decrease in the ability to focus on near objects due to the reduction in the elasticity of the lens, referred to as presbyopia.	**V**isual acuity: Use a Snellen chart. Record as a fraction on which the numerator shows the distance that the client was from the chart, typically 20 feet, and the denominator represents the distance that the average eye can read that same line of the chart. For example, 20/40 means a client can see clearly at 20 feet what the average eye sees at 40 feet.
Internal eye: This is done to evaluate for unexpected findings such as hemorrhages, swelling of the optic disc (also known as papilledema); or cotton wool spots (poorly defined yellow areas on the retina), that is often related to the damage of the nerve fibers. Pupillary response to light should be evaluated.	**I**nternal eye: examine with an ophthalmoscope.
Sensory assessment: Due to the potential adverse effects with medications, it is important to get a list of all medications (both over-the-counter and prescription). For example, if client is taking anticoagulants, there may be an increased risk for a bleed.	**S**ensory assessment: Begin with history, past medications, surgery, social history.
Inspect external eye: Start with examining the eyebrows, lashes, and lids. Then the eyes should be palpated (both the eyelid and the eye) and inspect the conjunctiva for signs of irritation or infection (redness, drainage). If the sclera is not predominantly white and/or the lens is not transparent, it could indicate a complication.	**I**nspect external eye: Inspect eyebrows, lashes, lids, etc.
Observe movement of the eyes: The cranial nerves III, IV, and VI and six extraocular muscles typically control the eye movement. If the client is unable to follow through all of the six cardinal fields of gaze, then this could indicate a host of visual disorders. A rapid movement of the eye that is involuntary, known as nystagmus, can be evaluated during this part of the assessment.	**O**bserve movement of the eyes by having the client follow a finger, with no head movement.
Note list of medications and sensory perception symptoms regardless of vision. This is important due to risk involved physiologically with many medications.	**N**ote list of medications and sensory perception symptoms regardless of vision.

System-Specific Assessments
Alteration with Sensory Perception
Common Lab/Diagnostic Tests/Therapeutic Procedures

VISION

Myopia is a term for nearsigntedness: vision for objects up close is better than vision for distant objects.

Hyperopia is a term for farsightedness: vision for distant objects is better than vision for near objects.

Presbyopia is a term for decreasing accommodation and focus for near vision.

Dry Eye Syndrome is an imbalance or alteration of the tear flow system of the eye. This imbalance can lead to: blurred vision, sensitivity to light, burning, itching, or scratchy feeling.

Ophthalmic Diagnostics

Snellen (typical eye chart ... letters)
Rosenbaum (numeric, much like DMV eye test)
Ophthalmoscopy
Biomicroscopy
Refractive error evaluation
Tonometry

Alteration with Sensory Perception

Common Ophthalmology Medications

ANTIBIOTICS
- Azithromycin (AzaSite)
- Besifloxacin Opthalmic (Besivance)
- Levofloxacin (Quixin)
- Gatifloxacin Ophthmalmic (Zymaxid)
- Erythromycin Ointment
- Ciprofloxacin (Ciloxan)
- Gentamycin Eye Drops (OcuMycin, Genoptic, Garamycin Ophthalmic)

ANTI-INFLAMMATORY AGENTS
- Ketorolac Tromethamine (Acuvail)
- Prednisolone Ophthalmic (Pred Forte)

GLAUCOMA MEDICATIONS
- Brimondine (Alphagan)
- Bimatoprost Ophthalmic (Lumigan)
- Unoprostone Isopropyl Ophthalmic (Rescula)
- Travoprost Ophthalmic (Travatan)
- Levobunolol Ophthalmic (AKBeta, Betagan)
- Metipranolol Ophthalmic (OptiPranolol)
- Xalatan Eye Drops (Latanoprost)

ANTIVIRAL
- Cidofovir (Vistide)
- Valganciclovir HCL (Valcyte)

ANALGESIC
- Difluprednate (Durezol)
- Diclofenac Ophthalmic (Voltaren)

MACULAR DEGENERATION
- Verteporfin (Visudyne)
- Ranibizumab (Lucentis)
- Aflibercept (Eylea)
- Pegaptanib (Macugen)

ALLERGIES
- Optivar (Astelin, Azelastine)
- Olopatadine Ophthalmic (Patanol)
- Ketorolac Ophthalmic (Acular)

ARTIFICIAL TEAR PRODUCTION
- Ciclosporin (Restasis)

Concept: Sensory Perception

Age-Related Changes in the Eye for Elderly Clients

Causes of Changes in Sensory Perception	Significance	Expected Outcomes for Altered Sensory Perception
The Lens: • ↓ elasticity, decreasing accommodation and focus for near vision (presbyopia) • ↓ size and density, lens becomes more stiff and opaque • Color perception is altered due to the yellowing of the lens and changes in the retina **The Cornea:** • ↓ corneal sensitivity • Throughout the cornea there are fat deposits around the periphery **The Pupil:** • ↓ size and response to light; sphincter is hardening **The retina and visual pathways:** • Visual fields narrow • Cells are lost for photophobia • Depth perception distortion • Longer to adapt to dark and light **The lacrimal apparatus:** • ↓ tear production • ↓ reabsorption of intraocular fluid **The posterior cavity:** • Condensation and debris become visible • Vitreous body may be pulling away from retina	• Most older adults require corrective lenses to accommodate work that is detailed and close up. Increased opacity leads to the development of cataracts. As cataracts develop, they increase sensitivity to glare and alter night vision. • An arcus senilis, which is a partial or total white circle that may form around the cornea. The lipid deposits in the cornea result in blurred vision. Alteration in sensitivity increases risk of injury to eye. • Due to the difficulty seeing in dim light or at night and the increase in light perception; increase in light is necessary to see adequately. • Central vision and peripheral vision may be lost due to macular degeneration. There is an increased risk for falls due to the changes in depth perception and adaptation to changes in the light. Vision progressively declines with age. • Increase risk of developing glaucoma; eyes feel and look dry. • Vision is blurred and distorted. The older client can see "Floaters".	**S**ocial interaction maintained. **O**verload in social interactions are prevented. **C**ommunication: an effective method is developed. **I**njury is prevented (No falls). **A**ctivities of daily living are performed independently. Safe medication administration. **L**earn how to promote and maintain the function of existing senses.

SAFETY Summary

Concept: Sensory Perception "VISION"

System-Specific Assessments "VISION"	First-Do Priority Interventions "PREVENTS"	Evaluation of Expected Outcomes "VISION"
Vision acuity: Questions to ask: • How would you rate your vision (excellent, good, fair, or poor)? • Do you wear glasses or contact lenses? • Do you have difficulty seeing near or far items? • Do you have any difficulty seeing at night? • Have you experienced any blurred vision, double vision, spots moving in front of your eyes, blind spots, light sensitivity, flashing lights, or halos around objects? • When did you last have your eyes examined? **I**nternal eye inspect (assessment) **S**ensory assessment: Is it a safe environment? **I**nspect external eye **O**bserve movement of the eyes **N**ote list of medications	**P**rotect and prevent injury and disease to the eyes; wear protective devices for the eyes. Client education: SAFETY and prevention of injury. • Uncluttered environment • Clear pathways for safe ambulation • Organize self-care activities within reach of client **R**eview how to prevent or reduce further loss 　**R**eview Healthy People 2020 for ongoing protocols **E**ye protection with safety goggles; support with glasses and/or contact lenses **V**ision screening–after 40, eye exam every 2 years **E**valuate for chronic diseases such as diabetes **N**ursing skills – eye irrigation, administering eye medications **T**ests to evaluate vision and sensation **S**ocial Support; sensory aids for visual deficits: • Eyeglasses with the correct prescription; clean & repaired • Room lighting is adequate; night lights • Reduce glare with sunglasses or shades • Bright contrasting colors in the environment • Phone with large numbers to see when dialing • Watch and clock with large numbers • Large print with reading materials	• Client's vision deficits will be supported with visual aids such as glasses and/or contact lenses. Vision will remain WDL for client. • Client will protect eyes with safety goggles when participating in dangerous activities. • Client will participate in ongoing eye (based on client's age) examinations to support and minimize ongoing loss. • Client will be able to perform ADL's with minimal limitations. • Client will engage in ongoing social support.

System-Specific Assessments Sensory Perception
"HEARING"

H earing aid: Assess what client knows and then develop teaching plan on identified needs, including how to use and maintain

E valuate how to remove ear wax if impacted cerumen is a problem; may need an ear irrigation

A ssess for dizziness, nausea, and vomiting if had a stapedectomy

R eassure client during communication by standing in front of client at eye level to speak; speak slowly

I nstruct client not to wear hearing aid while bathing or swimming

N o hair spray, cosmetics, or oils around ear

G ive hearing aid a rest at night and turn it off and open the battery compartment to prevent battery drain

Linking Pathophysiology to System-Specific Assessments
HEARING

Pathophysiology	System-Specific Assessments "External Ear Assessment"
• Any drainage or redness may indicate an inflammatory response to an infection or trauma. Skin lesions or scales around the rim of the auricle may indicate skin cancer. Small, raised lesions on the rim of the ear may indicate gout. These are known as tophi.	• Inspect the auricle. External ears are typically bilaterally equal in size, of equal color with the client's face. There should be no redness or lesions.
• Purulent drainage, redness, or lesions may indicate an infection. Cerumen varies in color and texture. If it is hardened, dry and/or has a foul odor, this may indicate an infection or an impaction of cerumen that may require removal.	• Inspect the external auditory canal with the otoscope. The walls of the ear canal should remain pink and smooth with no lesions. Cerumen is normally present in small, odorless amounts.
• White, opaque areas on the tympanic membrane are often scars from previous perforations. Inconsistent color and texture may be from scarring after previous perforations resulting from allergies, trauma, or infection. Bulging membranes are indicated by a loss of bony landmarks and a distorted light reflex. These bulges may be from otitis media or auditory tubes that are not functioning. If there is a distortion in the light reflex and the bony landmarks are accentuated, then the tympanic membranes may be retracted. This can be due to an obstructed auditory membrane.	• Inspect the tympanic membrane. It should be pearly gray, shiny, and translucent with no bulging or retraction.

Alteration with Sensory Perception

Common Lab/Diagnostic Tests/Therapeutic Procedures: System-Specific Assessments

Hearing Diagnostics

Whisper test

Weber (tuning fork 256 Hz)

Rinne test (tuning fork 512 Hz)

Tympanogram

Otoscopy

Audiometry

For fun and easy ways to organize the facts about diagnostic tests, refer to the book *Nursing Made Insanely Easy!* by Manning and Rayfield.

Alteration with Sensory Perception

Common Ear Medications

ANTIBIOTICS
- Ofloxacin (Floxin)
- Cefuroxime (Ceftin)
- Clarithromycin (Biaxin)
- Azithromycin (Zithromax)
- Amoxicillin (Amoxil, Polymax)

ANTIBIOTICS + CORTICOSTEROIDS
- Chloroxylenol +Pramoxine HCL + Hydrocortisone (Cortic)
- Ciprofloxacin + Hydrocortisone (Cipro HC Otic)

CERUMINOLYTICS
- Carbamide Oerixude 6.5% (Auro, Debrox, Murine Ear Drops)

INNER EAR VERTIGO
- Meclizine Bonine, Antivert)
- Diazepam (Valium)
- Dimenhydrinate

OTIC ANESTHETICS
- Benzocaine (Benzotic, Otocain, Pinnacaine)

STEROIDS
- Fluoccinolone Acetonide 0.01% (Dermotic Oil)

Concept: Sensory Perception

Age-Related Changes in Hearing for Elderly Clients

Causes of Changes in Sensory Perception	Significance	Expected Outcomes for Altered Sensory Perception
Inner Ear: • ↓ blood supply, decrease in the hair cells, basilar membrane is less flexible, spinal ganglion cells degenerate, and ↓ production of endolymph causing a progressive loss of hearing with age. **Presbycusis from the following:** • Cochlear degeneration • Progressive hearing loss • Begins in early adulthood • Higher-pitched tones and conversation speech **Middle ear:** • Muscles and ligaments weaken and stiffen causing the acoustic reflex to be decreased **External ear:** • The cerumen has a higher keratin content, resulting in an increased cerumen in the ear canal	• Hearing aids may be required to assist in hearing. • With the loss of high frequency sounds, middle and low-frequency sounds may be also decreased or lost. • One's own body sounds (i.e., heart beat, breathing, etc.) and speech are louder and many interfere with speech, hearing, and communication. • Accumulated cerumen may impair hearing.	**S**ocial interaction maintained. **O**verload in social interactions are prevented. **C**ommunication: an effective method is developed. **I**njury is prevented (No falls). **A**ctivities of daily living are performed independently. Safe medication administration. **L**earn how to promote and maintain the function of existing senses.

SAFETY Summary

Concept: Sensory Perception "HEARING"

System-Specific Assessments "HEARING"	First-Do Priority Interventions "PREVENTS"	Evaluation of Expected Outcomes
Hearing aid: teach how to use and maintain. **E**valuate and intervene for impacted cerumen; may need an ear irrigation. **A**ssess for dizziness, nausea, and vomiting if had a stapedectomy. Assess for vertigo. Assess auditory functioning. *How would you rate your hearing? Do you wear a hearing aid? Describe any recent changes in your hearing? Can you locate the direction of sounds and distinguish various sounds of voices? How is your balance? Do you ever have any vertigo or dizziness? Have you ever experienced any humming, ringing, or fullness in the ears? Are you around loud music and/ or noise on a regular basis? If so, how often and how much?* **R**eassure client during communication by standing in front of client at eye level to speak; speak slowly. **I**nstruct client to determine whether their hearing aid can remain in place while bathing or swimming. **N**o hair spray; cosmetics, or oils around ear. **G**ive hearing aid a rest at night; turn it off and open the battery compartment to prevent battery drain.	**P**rotect and prevent injury and disease to the eyes; wear protective devices for the eyes. Client education: SAFETY and prevention of injury. • Uncluttered environment • Clear pathways for safe ambulation • Organize self-care activities within reach of client **R**eview Healthy People 2020 for ongoing protocols. **R**eview how to prevent or reduce further loss. **E**ar protection with loud noises. **V**isual sense can compensate for hearing deficit. **E**valuate home safety. Provide devices that will amplify sounds or respond with flashing lights to sounds such as a baby crying, a smoke detector, a doorbell or a burglar alarm. **N**ursing skills: ear irrigation, administering ear medications. **T**ests to evaluate hearing and sensation. **S**ocial Support; sensory aids for hearing deficits: • Hearing aid in good order • Lip reading • Amplified telephones • Flashing alarm clocks • Flashing smoke detectors • Telecommunication device for the deaf • Refer to next page for Communication Strategies for clients who have a hearing deficit	• Client's hearing deficits will be supported with hearing aids. Hearing will remain WDL for client. • Client will protect ears with earplugs when participating in activities that produce a loud sound. • Client will participate in ongoing hearing (based on client's age) examinations to support and minimize ongoing loss. • Client will be able to perform ADL's with minimal limitations. • Client will engage in ongoing social support.

Concept Sensory Perception: Hearing

Insanely Easy Tip on Communication Strategies
for Clients Who Have a Hearing Deficit

"CLARITY"

Convey your presence to client before initiating the conversation. Move to a position you can be seen or gently touch the client.

Longer phrases tend to be easier to understand than shorter ones.

Always speak as clearly and accurately as possible. Clearly articulate consonants. Address the client directly. Do not turn away while talking.

Remove background noises (i.e., loud music, television, etc.) prior to speaking.

Identify a new subject at a slower rate, making sure that the person follows the change in subject. A key word at the beginning of a new topic is helpful.

Talk at a moderate rate and with a normal tone of voice. Shouting makes understanding more difficult.

Yes, empty your mouth of any chewing gum or candy, etc., prior to talking. Avoid covering your mouth with your hand.

Concept Sensory Perception

System-Specific Assessments: "TOUCH"

The mnemonic represents the priority assessments, including both tactile and alterations in gait that are included with somatosensory.

The gait: assess for shuffling, staggering, and asymmetric stride.

Observe for balance: assess using Romberg test.

Use (identify) stimuli affecting the major peripheral nerves including the arms, hands, feet, legs, & abdomen. Cranial Nerve VII (trigeminal nerve) is most closely associated with sensory function. Client should be able to correctly identify if a stimulus feels sharp or dull and the location of the sensation. Assess for sensory nerve damage: numbness, pain, shooting pair or burning, and/or impaired touch, temperature and/or pain sensation.

Can use the monofilament testing to assess peripheral neuropathies. Assess for motor nerve damage: muscle weakness, cramps, and muscle loss. Monofilaments are single-fiber threads that can be positioned on the skin of the client (typically feet).

Have client detect the presence of the filament which is the single-fiber nylon threads that are placed on the client's skin, typically the feet. Help client with safety protocol such as "Fall Prevention".

Linking Pathophysiology to System-Specific Assessments
"TOUCH"

Pathophysiology	System-Specific Assessments "TOUCH"
• Sense of touch, or the somatosensory system, is controlled by a large network of touch receptors and nerve endings in the skin. The sense of pain, pressure, temperature change, and itching are transmitted by the receptors to the brain for processing. • There are major risks involved associated with an impaired somatosensory system. These would include the decreased ability to sense pain, potentially leading to injury and possible wound infections associated with injury. • In addition, decreased sensitivity to heat and cold could result in hypothermia and burns.	**T**he gait: assess for shuffling, staggering, and asymmetric stride **O**bserve for balance: assess using Romberg test **U**se (identify) stimuli affecting the major peripheral nerves including the arms, hands, feet, legs, & abdomen. Cranial Nerve VII (trigeminal nerve) is most closely associated with sensory function. Client should be able to correctly identify if a stimulus feels sharp or dull and the location of the sensation. Assess for sensory nerve damage: numbness, pain, shooting pair or burning, and/or impaired touch, temperature and pain sensation. **C**an use the monofilament testing to assess peripheral neuropathies. Assess for motor nerve damage: muscle weakness, cramps, and muscle loss. Monofilaments are single-fiber threads that can be positioned on the skin of the client (typically feet). **H**ave client detect the presence of the filament which is the single-fiber nylon threads that are placed on the client's skin, typically the feet. Help client with safety protocol such as "Fall Prevention".

Alteration with Sensory Perception

Common Lab/Diagnostic Tests/Therapeutic Procedures:
System-Specific Assessments

Peripheral Neuropathy

Complete blood count (CBC)
Electromyography
Metabolic panel
Nerve biopsy
Serum levels for B_{12} and thiamine
Thyroid function tests
Urine screening

Concept: Sensory Perception

Age-Related Changes in Touch (Somatosensory) for Elderly Clients

Causes of Changes in Sensory Perception	Significance	Expected Outcomes for Altered Sensory Perception
• Research shows evidence that tactile recognition tends to decrease with age. • Sensation at the fingertips and toes tends to decline faster, especially with heat and cold.	• There would be a delay in the process of sensing a stick from the needle, which can result in potential injuries. • This change in sensation of hot and cold at the fingertips and toes can lead to potential burns and frostbite.	**S**ocial interaction maintained. **O**verload in social interactions are prevented. **C**ommunication: an effective method is developed. **I**njury is prevented (No falls). **A**ctivities of daily living are performed independently. Safe medication administration. **L**earn how to promote and maintain the function of existing senses.

INSANELY EASY TIP on Teaching Topics
for Clients Who Have an Alteration with Sensory Perception!

"PERCEPTION"

Pain management; prevent falls; promote SAFETY.

Exercise is important.

Referral as appropriate (i.e., occupational/physical therapist, support group, etc.).

Care for the feet; client may not feel injuries to the feet especially with diabetes.

Eliminate smoking.

Prolonged pressure should be avoided!

Toxic chemicals should be avoided.

Improve circulation through massage which will stimulate nerves and reduce pain.

Omit repetitive motion.

Nutrition, review the need for sources of B_{12}.

SAFETY Summary

Concept: Sensory Perception "TOUCH"

System-Specific Assessments "TOUCH"	First-Do Priority Interventions "PREVENTS"	Evaluation of Expected Outcomes
The gait: assess for shuffling, staggering, and asymmetric stride. **O**bserve for balance. assess using Romberg's sign. **U**se stimuli affecting the major peripheral nerves including the hands, arms, feet, legs, & abdomen. CN VII (trigeminal nerve) is most closely associated with sensory function. Client should be able to correctly identify if stimulus feels sharp or dull and the location of the sensation. **C**an use the monofilament testing to assess peripheral neuropathies. Assess for motor nerve damage: numbness, tingling, muscle weakness, cramps, muscle loss. **H**ave client detect the presence of the filament which is the single-fiber nylon threads that are placed on the client's skin, typically the feet. Have client describe any pain and the characteristics; any anxiety or depression; challenges performing self-care; ask about any over-the-counter medications.	**P**rotect and prevent injury from the disturbed sensory perception. Client education: SAFETY and prevention of injury. Prevent falls! **R**eview Healthy People 2020 for ongoing protocols. **E**valuate for anxiety or depression. **E**valuate sensory/motor assessments and cranial nerves. **V**erify if client is on a healthy, well-balanced diet (vitamin supplements may be necessary), regular exercise, smoking cessation, limit on alcohol, and engages in daily foot care. **E**valuate home safety to prevent injury and falls. (*Refer to PERCEPTION on page 601 for specific teaching topics.*) **E**valuate for pain and anxiety. Promote non-pharmacological interventions to reduce pain prior to pharmacological agents. **N**ote to help client encourage to discuss feelings and concerns related to the sensory loss. **T**ests (Diagnostic) to evaluate sensory changes. **S**ocial support.	• Client's pain will be under control and will allow for comfort and rest. • Client will review a list of plans to decrease the risk of injury and promote safety. • Client will experience no shuffling, staggering, and/or asymmetric stride. • Client will be able to maintain balance. • Client will be able to recognize the stimuli while examining the hands, arms, feet, legs, & abdomen. • Client will not experience any falls. • Client will participate in ongoing diagnostic tests (based on client's needs) and examinations and treatment plan to support and minimize ongoing loss of function. • Client will be able to perform ADL's with minimal limitations. • Client will engage in ongoing social support.

Pathophysiology: Visual Deficit
Concept: Sensory Perception

Cataracts are a partial or complete opacity of the lens that occurs when protein clumps compromise the clarity of images on the retina. This may occur at birth (congenital cataract). Cataracts occur most frequently in the older adult past middle age, and are known as senile cataracts.

Age-Related Macular Degenerative Disease (AMD) is the most common cause of loss in the central vision for clients over 40 years of age. It is a response to the aging of the retina.

Glaucoma is a group of disorders characterized by an increase in the intraocular pressure and progressive vision loss. It is either an acute or chronic condition that is a leading cause of blindness.

Primary open-angle glaucoma (POAG) is chronic and is the most common form. It is slow in the onset and is caused by the obstruction of the flow of aqueous humor. The flow can be slow or actually stop, resulting in an increase in the intraocular pressure. Late in the disease there will be a chronic and progressive peripheral vision loss.

Primary angle-closure glaucoma (PACG) is acute. There is a rapid increase in the intraocular pressure from a reduction in the aqueous humor outflow. This may also occur in the client with prolonged pupil dilation. Symptoms can occur suddenly mandating immediate medical intervention and treatment. This may result in total blindness within hours to a day.

Retinal Detachment is the separation of the sensory retina and the underlying epithelium. This epithelium allows the fluid to collect in the space. If this condition is untreated, retinal detachment will almost always result in the loss of vision in the eye.

Exceptions and Additions by Disease/Injury

Pathophysiology: Comparisons of Sensory Perception (Vision)
"SAFE"

Sensory Loss: Vision	Cataracts *No Emergency*	Macular Degeneration *No Emergency*	Open Angle Glaucoma *No Emergency*	Angle closure Glaucoma *Emergency*	Retinal Detachment *Emergency*
System-Specific Physiology	• Opacity of lens in eye impairs • No pain • Progressive • Blurred vision vision	• Deterioration of macular that affects central vision • Most common loss of vision in those over 60 • No pain • Progressive • Blind spots center vision • Peripheral vision maintained	• Intraocular pressure ↑ from Aqueous humor • Optic fibers destroyed • Progressive tunnel vision • Eventual blindness • No pain • Progressive • Tunnel vision • ↑ IOP > 21mm Hg	• Less common • Unilateral • Intermittent • Severe pain • Abrupt onset • See halos • Rapid ↑ IOP • Pupils do not react • Photophobia	• Painless separation of retina from epithelium • Abrupt onset • No pain • Abrupt onset • Veil over eyes– loss of vision • Flashes of light/ floating dark spots
Analysis of the Concepts	SAME FOR ALL Medical Diagnoses! • Safety/Prevention of Injury • Altered Sensory Perception (vision) • Health Promotion				
Sensory Loss: Vision	Cataracts *No Emergency*	Macular Degeneration *No Emergency*	Open Angle Glaucoma *No Emergency*	Angle closure Glaucoma *Emergency*	Retinal Detachment *Emergency*
First-Priority Inter-ventions	• Comprehensive risk assessment to prevent injury • Post-op care • Wear dark glasses • Report yellow/ green drainage • No activity that increases IOP • Limit sports and driving • Report sudden change in vision • Antibiotic steroid eye drops	• Comprehensive risk assessment to prevent injury • Supportive care • Maintain safe environment at home to prevent injuries	• Comprehensive risk assessment to prevent injury • Client teaching on importance of taking medications • Cholinergic agonists: Miotics–constrict (for ↑ IOP) • Beta-blockers • Occular steroids	• Less common • Unilateral • Intermittent • Severe pain • Abrupt onset • See halos • Rapid ↑ IOP • Pupils do not react • Photophobia	• Comprehensive risk assessment to prevent injury • Scleral Buckling • Restrict activity • Cover both eyes with patch • No activity that increases IOP anticholinergic: • Mydriatics – (atropine) dialate • Cycloplegia • Anagesics
Evaluation of Expected Outcomes	SAME FOR ALL Medical Diagnoses! • Safety/Prevention of Injury–No injury • Coping with Sensory Perception Alteration • Knowledgeable of Care				

Alteration in Sensory Perception

INSANELY EASY TIP on Comparing Visual Changes:

Glaucoma

Cataracts

Retinal detachment

Macular degeneration BLACK SPOT

Exceptions and Additions by Disease/Injury

Pathophysiology: Hearing/Auditory Deficit

Ménière's Disease is an inner ear disorder caused by excess endolymph in the semicircular and vestibular canals. The vestibular system of the inner ear maintains the coordination and balance.

Otitis externa is inflammation of the ear canal (also referred to as swimmer's ear).

Otitis internal, also called **Inner Ear Labyrinthitis** is an inflammation of the cochlear and/or vestibular portion of the inner ear.

Otitis media is inflammation of the middle ear.

Hearing Aids: Refer to System-Specific Assessments Sensory Perception **"HEARING"** reviewed previously in this chapter.

Cochlear Implants may be the only plan for restoring sound perception. The cochlear implant has a microphone, speech processor, transmitter, and receiver/stimulator, and electrodes. While the cochlear implants provide sound perception, there is no normal hearing. The client is able to recognize warning sounds such as sirens, telephones, and opening doors. Clients with hearing impairment may receive assistance from speech therapy.

Stapedectomy is a reconstructive surgery of the middle ear to help restore hearing with a conductive hearing loss. Stapedectomy is the removeal and replacement of the stapes. The procedure is used to treat hearing loss related to otosclerosis

Pathophysiology: Comparisons of
Sensory Perception (Hearing/Auditory)
"SAFE"

Sensory Loss: Hearing	Inner Ear Ménière's Disease	Inner Ear Labyrinthitis	Hearing Aids

System-Specific Physiology	• Triad of symptoms
	  • Vertigo
	  • Tinnitus
	  • Progressive unilateral hearing loss
	• Cause is unclear
	• Adults between ages of 35 and 60
	• Women and men equally
		• Infection of labyrinth often secondary to otitis media	• Fits into ear or just outside of ear

System-Specific Assessment Signs & Symptom	• Tinnitus–ringing in the ear • Signs of vertigo • Nausea • Vomiting • Falls	• Sudden onset of tinnitus and vertigo • May resolve 3–6 days or longer	
Analysis of the Concepts	SAME FOR ALL Medical Diagnoses! • Safety/Prevention of Injury • Altered Sensory Perception (vision) • Health Promotion		
Sensory Loss: Hearing	**Inner Ear Ménière's Disease**	**Inner Ear Labyrinthitis**	**Hearing Aids**
First Priority Interventions	• Rest in quiet, dark environment • Bed rest • Avoid tobacco, alcohol, caffeine • May need sedatives, valium, Benadryl. Diuretics to help decease fluid. Antivert for prevention and treatment of "motion sickness" symptoms. Antiemetics. Diet low in sodium. **Risk for Injury:** • Comprehensive Risk assessment needed to maintain safe environment at home to prevent injuries **Surgery**	• Supportive care. • Change positions slowly. • Minimize stimulation and sudden position changes. • Remind client as a safety precaution to lie down immediately if an attack feels imminent! **Risk for Injury:** • Comprehensive Risk assessment needed to maintain safe environment at home to prevent injuries. • Assess where client is and individual needs and current situation. **May need surgery**	Health Promotion: • Check battery regularly • Turn off hearing aid when not in use • Always have extra battery available
Evaluation of Expected Outcomes	SAME FOR ALL Medical Diagnoses! • Safety/Prevention of Injury–No injury • Coping with Sensory Perception Alteration • Knowledgeable of Care		

Clinical Decision-Making Exercises

1. What is the priority plan of care for fall prevention in the older adult?
    ① Recommend removing all the rugs in the home.
    ② Encourage installment of appropriate lighting in the home.
    ③ Review the normal aging changes that place the client at risk.
    ④ Complete a comprehensive risk assessment.

2. Which of these nursing plans would be priority for a client admitted with Ménière's disease?
    ① Assess the frequency and intensity of the attacks.
    ② Encourage visitors to come.
    ③ Encourage listening to music on the client's iPod.
    ④ Verify the accuracy of an order for a diuretic.

3. What would be the priority nursing action for a client who is ambulating in the hall and begins to present with vertigo?
    ① Assess to determine if the client is experiencing syncope or vertigo.
    ② Assist the client to lie down.
    ③ Take client back to the well-lit room.
    ④ Encourage client to increase fluid intake.

4. Which of these clients should be assessed immediately following shift report?
    ① A client with discomfort in the right ear from otitis media.
    ② A client who needs eye drops for Primary Open-Angle Glaucoma (POAG).
    ③ A client with a cataract on the right eye who is having challenges reading the paper.
    ④ An older adult client who is complaining of floaters in the visual field and an abrupt sensation of a curtain over eye.

5. Which of these clinical findings would be a priority to incorporate in the plan of care for an elderly client who is being admitted to a long-term care facility?
    ① Presbycusis.
    ② Presbyopia.
    ③ Inability to recognize sharp touch on lower extremities.
    ④ Increase in the cerumen in the ear canal.

Answers and Rationales

1. What is the **priority plan** of care for **fall prevention** in the older adult?

   ① INCORRECT: Recommend removing all the rugs in the home. Appropriate, but NOT the most inclusive.

   ② INCORRECT: Encourage installment of appropriate lighting in the home. Appropriate, but NOT most inclusive.

   ③ INCORRECT: Review the normal aging changes that place the client at risk. Appropriate but NOT most inclusive.

   ④ **CORRECT: Complete a comprehensive risk assessment. It is the answer because it is MOST inclusive.**

The strategy is to recognize that option 4 includes all of the other options. Each of these would be a part of performing a complete comprehensive assessment. The great connect is that this applies to any of the alterations with sensory perception. The Prioritization Algorithm in chapter 1 will assist you with this decision, since one of the first steps in planning is to assess.

You are catching on! Even if you missed it; as long as you understand why, this is the key!

Health Promotion and Maintenance: Perform a comprehensive health (risk) assessment.

2. Which of these nursing plans would be **priority for a client admitted with Ménière's disease?**

   ① **CORRECT: Assess the frequency and intensity of the attacks. This will assure a safe plan.**

   ② INCORRECT: Encourage visitors to come. Stimulation needs to be minimized not maximized.

   ③ INCORRECT: Encourage listening to music on the client's iPod. Stimulation needs to be minimized not maximized.

   ④ INCORRECT: Verify the accuracy of an order for a diuretic. No need to, since this will assist in fluid excretion.

The strategy for answering this question is to review the Prioritization Algorithm in chapter 1. The first step is to assess when planning the care for a client. Of course, you need to determine if the option is correct for the client! The assessment must be correct for the presenting medical condition. We also want you to understand the pathophysiology, so you will be able to apply this information to a clinical situation. In order to assure client safety, the nurse must assess the frequency and intensity of the attacks to best plan for the client. Options 2 and 3 are incorrect, since visitors, stimulation, loud noises, etc. need to be minimized. Client needs to be in a quiet and dark room to decrease stimuli. Option 4 would be a correct order to assist with removing the extra endolymph fluid.

Basic Care: Provide non-pharmacological comfort measures.

Basic Care: Assess client need for rest and intervene as needed.

3. What would be the **priority nursing action** for a client who is **ambulating** in the hall and begins to present with **vertigo?**

① INCORRECT: Assess to determine if the client is experiencing syncope or vertigo. Safety is the priority!

② **CORRECT: Assist the client to lie down. Yes, due to safety.**

③ INCORRECT: Take client back to the well lit room. Not correct due to not answering the immediate need for safety.

④ INCORRECT: Encourage client to increase fluid intake. Not appropriate, but also it is not addressing the immediate need.

The strategy is to recognize that safety is the priority for a client who is getting ready to fall. It does not matter if the question is asking about "an alteration in sensory perception, or a cardiac dysrhythmia that is not allowing adequate perfusion, or a client who is experiencing hypovolemia due to fluid loss, etc."; the priority remains the same, SAFETY! If you were only answering this with a strategy versus a strategy and understanding of the necessary nursing care, then you may have answered option 1. Assessment was the reason the previous question was correct. The key is to compare and contrast the options! This is the reason it is so important to be able to learn how to think like a nurse NOW (and like the NCLEX®) versus waiting until the end of school! You are starting to wire your brain with NCLEX® standards and strategies that will serve you well both on the NCLEX® and in clinical practice.

Safety and Infection Control: Protect client from injury (i.e., falls).

4. Which of these **clients should be assessed immediately** following shift report?

① INCORRECT: A client with discomfort in the right ear from otitis media. Expected assessment.

② INCORRECT: A client who needs eye drops for Primary Open-Angle Glaucoma (POAG). Important, but it is not an emergency.

③ INCORRECT: A client with a cataract on the right eye who is having challenges reading the paper. Expected due to blurred vision from the cataract.

④ **CORRECT: An older adult client who is complaining of floaters in the visual field and an abrupt sensation of a curtain over eye. Symptoms of a retinal detachment and requires immediate intervention to prevent further damage.**

The strategy for answering this question is to recognize which of these clinical presentations is an emergency. The Insanely Easy Tip and the chart in this section on comparisons of the visual disorders will assist you in organizing these facts. Option 4 is presenting with signs of retinal detachment. This is an emergency and requires immediate intervention.

Management: Prioritize delivery of care.

Reduction of Risk: Recognize signs of complication and intervene appropriately when providing care.

5. Which of these **clinical findings** would be a **priority** to incorporate in the plan of care for **an elderly client who is being admitted to a long-term care facility?**

① INCORRECT: Presbycusis. Expected with aging.

② INCORRECT: Presbyopia. Expected with aging.

③ **CORRECT: Inability to recognize sharp touch on lower extremities. Creates an increase risk for injury.**

④ INCORRECT: Increase in the cerumen in the ear canal. Expected with aging.

The strategy for answering this question is to identify the normal signs of aging, and then prioritize the care within "SAFETY". Options 1, 2, and 4 are all normal changes. Yes, these need to be integrated into the care; however, "SAFETY" is the priority due to not being aware the pain is present.

Health Promotion: Provide care and education for adults over 85 year.

Decision-Making Analysis Form

Use this tool to help identify why you missed any questions. As you enter the question numbers in the chart, you will begin to see patterns of why you answered incorrectly. This information will then guide you toward what you need to focus on in your continued studies. Ultimately, this analytical exercise will help you become more successful in answering questions!!!

Questions to ask:

1. Did I have the knowledge to answer the question? If not, what information do I need to review?
2. Did I know what the question was asking? Did I misread it or did I miss keywords in the stem of the question?
3. Did I misread or miss keywords in the distractors that would have helped me choose the correct answer?
4. Did I follow my gut reaction or did I allow myself to rationalize and then choose the wrong answer?

	Lack of Knowledge (Concepts, Systems, Pathophysiology, Medications, Procedures, etc.)	Missed Keywords or Misread the Stem of the Question	Missed Keywords or Misread the Distractors	Changed My Answer (Second-guessed myself, i.e., my first answer was correct.)
Put the # of each question you missed in the column that best explains why you think you answered it incorrectly.				

If you changed an answer because you talked yourself out of the correct answer, or you second-guessed yourself, this is an **EASY FIX: QUIT changing your answers**!!! Typically, the first time you read a question, you are about 95% right! The second time you read a question, you start talking yourself into changing the answer. The third time you read a question, you do not have a clue—and you are probably thinking "Who in the heck wrote this question?"

On the other hand, if you read a question too quickly and when you reread it you realize you missed some key information that would impact your decision (i.e., assessments, lab reports, medications, etc.), then it is appropriate to change your answer. When in doubt, go with the safe route: your first thought! Go with your gut instinct!

As you gain confidence in answering questions regarding specific nursing concepts, you will be able to successfully progress to answering higher-level questions about prioritization. Please refer to the *Prioritization Guidelines* in this book for a structure to assist you with this process.

You CAN do this!

> *"The difference in winning and losing is most often ... not quitting."*
>
> WALT DISNEY

References for Chapter 21

Black, J M. and Hawks, J. H. (2009). *Medical surgical nursing: Clinical management for positive outcomes* (8th ed.). Philadelphia: Elsevier/Saunders.

Daniels, R. & Nicoll, L. (2012). *Contemporary medical-surgical nursing,* (2nd ed.). Clifton Park, NY: Delmar Cengage Learning.

Eliopoulos, C. (2014). *Gerontological nursing* (8th ed.), Philadelphia: Lippincott Williams & Wilkins.

Giddens, G. F. (2013). *Concepts for nursing practice.* St. Louis, MO: Mosby, an imprint of Elsevier.

Hogan, M. A. (2014). *Pathophysiology, reviews and rationales,* (3rd Edition) Boston, MA: Pearson.

Ignatavicius, D. D. and Workman, M. L. (2010). *Medical-Surgical nursing: Patient-Centered collaborative care* (7th ed.). Philadelphia: Elsevier/Saunders.

Lewis, S., Dirksen, S., Heitkemper, M., Bucher, L., and Camera, I. (2011). *Medical surgical nursing: Assessment and management of clinical problems* (8th ed.). St. Louis: Mosby.

Manning, L. and Rayfield, S. (2014). *Nursing made insanely easy* (7th ed). Duluth, GA: I CAN Publishing, Inc.

Manning, L. and Rayfield, S. (2013). *Pharmacology made insanely easy* (4th ed.). Duluth, GA: I CAN Publishing, Inc.

National Council of State Boards of Nursing, INC. (NCSBN) 2012. *Research brief: 2011 RN practice analysis: linking the NCLEX RN® examination to practice.* Retrieved from https://www.ncsbn.org/index.htm

Nettina, S. L. (2013). *Lippincott manual of nursing practice* (10th ed.). Philadelphia, PA: Walters Kluwer Health/Lippincott Williams & Wilkins.

North Carolina Concept Based Learning Editorial Board. (2011). *Nursing a concept based approach to learning.* Upper Saddle Road, NJ: Pearson/Prentice Hall.

Osborn, K. S., Wraa, C. E., Watson, A. S., and Holleran, R. S. (2014). *Medical surgical nursing: preparation for practice* (2nd ed.). Upper Saddle Road, NJ: Pearson.

Pagana, K. D. and Pagana, T. J. (2014). *Mosby's manual of laboratory and diagnostic tests* (5th ed.). St. Louis, MO: Mosby, an imprint of Elsevier.

Porth, C. (2011). *Essentials of pathophysiology* (3rd edition). Philadelphia, PA: Lippincott Williams ad Wilkins.

Porth, C. M. and Grossman, S. (2013). *Pathophysiology, concepts of altered health states* (9th edition). Philadelphia, PA: Lippincott Williams & Wilkins.

Potter, P. A., Perry, A. G., Stockert, P., and Hall, A. (2013). *Fundamentals of nursing* (8th ed). St. Louis, MO: Pearson/Prentice Hall.

Schiffman, S. (2009). *Sensory impairment: taste and smell impairments with aging.* In Wales C., Ritchie C. editors: Handbook of clinical nutrition and aging (2nd ed.). Totowa, NJ: Humana Press.

Smeltzer, S. C., Bare, B. G., Hinkle, J. L., and Cheever, K. H. (2010). *Brunner & Suddarth's textbook of medical-surgical nursing* (12th ed.). Philadelphia: Lippincott Williams & Wilkins.

SECTION TWO

Concepts that are Inter-Related throughout the Systems

Linking Multiple Systems and Concepts
to the Pathophysiology of Diseases

NOTES

CHAPTER 22

Linking Multiple Systems and Concepts
Safety/Prevention of Injury

A Snapshot of Safety/Prevention of Injury

Safety is the priority in today's healthcare environment. The volume of information, resources, and priority this topic has received over the past decade is significant. When the Institute of Medicine published its work on patient safety with the 2000 publication of *To Err is Human: Building a Safer Health System*, a campaign was launched for safety that continues today. Safety has been defined by numerous sources but a synopsis of the definitions is the prevention and freedom from accidental injury, minimizing errors, injury and/or complications errors, and intercepting errors when they occur (Institute of Medicine, 2000, Institute of Medicine, 2004, & National Patient Safety Foundation, 2014). This chapter will provide an overview of the components of safety. The reference list will contain websites (i.e., IOM, Joint Commission, QSEN, Institute of Heath, Institute of Safe Medicine Practice, Agency of Healthcare Quality and Research, Healthy People 2020 and National Patient Safety Foundation). All of the websites have a plethora of information and resources for you as a student and as a new graduate.

While in nursing school, you are learning about the importance of safety in the workplace for both the clients and yourself. This chapter should serve as a resource and even more importantly help you see that SAFETY is not a recommendation, but an expectation. The chart on the next page provides you examples of all of the aspects of a safe working environment. Take a moment to see how many areas it covers and reflect on how it is operationalized in practice.

The Components of a Safe Patient-Care Environment

Injury to Self	Environmental	Ergonomics	Pharmacological/ Parenteral Therapies	Equipment/ Medical Procedures	Biohazard
Self-Inflicted • Tobacco use • Alcohol abuse • Drug abuse • Prescription abuse • Suicide • Vehicle collisions • Self-mutilation (Cutting) **Inflicted by others** • Sexually transmitted infections, HIV/ AIDS • Domestic violence • Child abuse • Vehicle collisions • Crime (i.e., homicide, sexual assault, assault & battery, etc.)	• Infection exposure • Fall prevention (i.e., elderly, delirium from medical condition, pain, infection, electrolyte imbalance, etc.) • Institutional securities, (i.e., newborn nursery, bomb threats, etc.) • Home & institutional safety (i.e., stairs, electrical hazards, lights, rugs, etc.) • Suicide prevention (i.e., no ropes, cords, belts, etc.) • Confined safe environment for "wanders" (elderly with delirium, dementia) and "crawlers" (toddlers)	• Lifting devices • Assistive devices (i.e., crutch and cane walking, walker, etc.) • Proper lifting • Correct body mechanics for lifting and moving	• Prevention of errors in healthcare (i.e., safe medication administration, and blood products' administration guidelines, elderly with drug/drug interaction, etc.) • Safe intravenous infusions and site maintenance, (i.e., central lines, PICC, epidural, venous access devices, etc.) • Safe administration of parenteral nutrition (i.e., TPN, etc.) • Safe access of venous access devices, (i.e., tunneled, implanted, & central lines, etc.)	• Equipment safety (i.e., education, maintenance, appropriate operation, etc.) • Restraints • Pharmacology (Safe Med Administration) • Safe performance of diagnostic testing, (i.e., O$_2$ sat, ECG, glucose monitoring, blood specimens, etc.) • Safety with invasive medical procedures, (i.e., thora-centesis, lumbar punctures, bronchoscopy, etc.) • Safety when obtaining specimens for diagnostic testing (i.e., blood, wound, stool, and urine, etc.)	• Radiation, radium implants • Biohazard materials (i.e., chemical, biological & neurological agents, etc.)

Multiple Systems
Concept Safety/Prevention of Injury
Preparation to be a Safe Practicing Nurse

The Quality and Safety Education for Nurses (QSEN) project developed competencies to assist you while you are in school. There are competencies for patient-centered care, teamwork and collaboration, evidence based practice, quality improvement, informatics and, of course, safety! All of the QSEN competencies are very important and are interlinked to practice. For this chapter, however, the focus will be on the safety competency. The goal is that as a new graduate nurse you will be able to contribute to the improvement of the quality and safety of the healthcare system where you work (QSEN Institute, 2014).

The QSEN Safety competencies include that you are able to safely use equipment, communicate effectively, avoid unsafe abbreviations, and if errors occur, look for the cause. A safe nurse is always vigilant of the care provided. Errors or hazards should be reported and measures taken to ensure safe care is provided to the client (QSEN Institute, 2014). The safety standards are also reflected in the NCLEX-RN® activities for management of care. It is all about applying the patient safety standards that have been covered throughout this book.

As you review the current patient-safety standards on the next page, you quickly see how important this competency is for you to develop and master.

Multiple Systems
Concept Safety/Prevention of Injury

The reality according to the Institute of Medicine report in 2007 death statistics,
PREVENTABLE MEDICATION ERRORS caused:
7,000 deaths/year or 583 deaths/month or 134 deaths/week or 19 deaths/day!!
Do you see how important SAFETY Is????
Look at the Similarities of the Safety Standard Priorities

	The Joint Commission Hospital 2014 National Safety Standards Priorities (Joint Commission, 2014)	Institute for Safe Medication Practice 2014-2015 Targeted Medication Safety Best Practices for Hospitals (Institute for Safe Medication Practice 2014)	The National Patient Safety Foundation: 2014-2015 Major Patient Safety Issues (National Patient Safety Foundation, 2014)	NCLEX-RN® (National Council for State Boards of Nursing 2012)
Medications	• Safely give meds: label meds, correct blood to correct client • Know other meds client is taking • Closely monitor high-risk drugs (i.e., heparin, Coumadin, etc.). • Identify the client using two methods	• Medication Errors (Most could have been prevented)	• Use only metric system (i.e., mL, kg, etc.,)	• Safe medication administration • Client identification (two methods) • Evaluation accuracy of medication orders • Review for drug/drug interactions • High risk drugs
Equipment	• Alarms must be on for equipment and loud enough to be heard	• Use syringes for oral medicine prepared by pharmacy if not supplied through unit dose system	• Oral liquid meds must be unit dose or be in a syringe prepared by pharmacy	• Protect client from injury (i.e., equipment, alarms, etc.) • Assess ability to manage at home equipment safety
Infections	• Reduce the risk of health care–associated infections (2013 Goal)		• Catheter-related bloodstream infections • Hospital-acquired pneumonia • Surgical site infections	• Recognize trends & changes in client condition indicating an infection • Apply principles of infection control • Educate client & staff regarding infection control measures

continued on next page

Multiple Systems
Concept Safety/Prevention of Injury (cont'd.)

	The Joint Commission Hospital 2014 National Safety Standards Priorities (Joint Commission, 2014)	Institute for Safe Medication Practice 2014-2015 Targeted Medication Safety Best Practices for Hospitals (Institute for Safe Medication Practice 2014)	The National Patient Safety Foundation: 2014-2015 Major Patient Safety Issues (National Patient Safety Foundation, 2014)	NCLEX-RN® (National Council for State Boards of Nursing 2012)
Falls/Safety	• Clients at risk for suicide • Clients at risk for falls		• Impaired memory • Muscle weakness > 60 years old • Affect gait, mobility • Confusion • Altered elimination (fall on way to bathroom)	• Protect client from injury (i.e., falls, etc.) • Assess potential for violence & use safety precautions (i.e., suicide, homicide, & self-destructive behavior, etc.) • Recognize signs & symptoms of complications & intervene appropriately (i.e., risk for falls from fluid deficit, cardiac arrhythmias, hypotension, undesirable effects of medications, etc.)
Readmissions	• Effective transition/continuation of care (i.e., communication, patient education, planning, risk management, etc.)		• Poor quality care • Discharged prematurely	• Participate in performance improvement/quality improvement process • Initiate, evaluate, & update plan of care (i.e., care map, clinical pathway, etc.) • Perform procedures necessary to admit, transfer or discharge a client • Provide care & education about treatment & procedures • Assess client's ability to manage care in home environment & plan care accordingly (i.e., equipment, community resources, etc.)
Communication	• Right information to right person in the right time (i.e., lab results, etc.) • Correct surgery/correct client, in correct place		Poor transition between providers & care setting • Did not receive adequate information or resources	• Collaborate with healthcare members in other disciplines when providing client care • Verify appropriates of treatment/medication order • Recognize need for referrals & obtain necessary orders • Manage conflict between clients and healthcare staff

Multiple Systems
Concept Safety/Prevention of Injury

Concept – Safety – Prevention of Injury		
System-Specific Assessments	**First-Do Priority Interventions Primary Goal: "PREVENT"**	**Evaluation of Expected Outcomes**
Assess for Risks/Cause: **Guided by Risk Management Protocols** • Injury to self • Self-inflicted • Inflicted by other • Environment hazards • Ergonomic principal violations • Pharmacological/parenteral therapies risks/errors • Equipment/medical procedures risks/errors • Biohazard agents risks/errors	Interventions appropriate for cause of injury. Refer to specific protocols and guidelines. **P**rotocols: Point of care (safety standards) must be followed, (i.e., fall prevention protocols, safe administration of medication, blood products' administration guidelines, invasive lines protocols, handling of bio-hazardous materials & ergonomic guidelines, etc.) **R**isks assessed and appropriate protocols put in place to protect from harm (i.e., suicide precautions, safe environment for "wanderers & crawlers", etc.) **E**ducate staff safe & proper use of equipment, prevention of injury, appropriate safety protocols **V**ent and address concerns of client & family, and members of the healthcare team. **E**valuate & document the effectiveness of safety procedures and protocols. **N**eed to coordinate and communicate at a system level care with the interdisciplinary health care team. **T**each client and family appropriate safety measures with respect to prevention of injury, (i.e., home environment, child safety, safe medications, etc.)	Client will remain safe and free from injury.

Multiple Systems

Concept Safety/Prevention of Injury

Conditions That Must Be Reported as Required by the Law

The picture and the mnemonic below will help you remember how to "Comply with state and/or federal regulations on reporting client conditions (communicable disease, abuse, animal bites, accidents resulting in death, gunshot/knife wound or evidence of neglect)." It is one of the NCLEX RN® standards (NCLEX RN®, 2012).

Remember in the picture, the **Banged up Bird** in "CAGE" (see below). The bird has black eye from abuse, a hole from a gunshot wound, trying to catch the communicable disease and it certainly looks like there is evidence that the bird is neglected (Manning & Rayfield, 2013).

Be sure you know your state and federal laws when you begin your practice as a new graduate nurse.

C ommunicable diseases

A buse; animal bites; accidents resulting in death

G unshot/knife wounds

E vidence of neglect

Multiple Systems

Concept Safety/Prevention of Injury

References and Websites for Additional Information on Safety/Prevention of Injury

Subjects	Agencies	Resources
Fall Precautions	**Agency for Healthcare Research and Quality** http://www.ahrq.gov/legacy/research/ltc/fallpxtoolkit/fallpxtk3.htm **Local facilities, acute, long-term care, rehabilitation centers will have policies**	Falls Protocols
Suicide Precautions	**American Foundation for Suicide Prevention** http://www.afsp.org/preventing-suicide	Suicide prevention protocols, identifying clients at risk
Medication Administration Safety Protocols **Administration of Blood Protocols**	**Institute of Safe Medicine Practices** https://www.ismp.org/ **Local facilities, acute, long-term care, rehabilitation centers will have policies** **Joint Commission**	Information on medication and blood products' safety protocols
Invasive lines Protocols **Invasive Procedures Protocols**	**Institute for Clinical Systems Improvements** https://www.icsi.org/_asset/1hht9h/NonOR-Interactive0912.pdf	Protocols for non-OR high-risk procedures
Biohazard Materials Protocols	**Joint Commission** http://www.jointcommission.org/assets/1/18/TJC-ImprovingPatientAndWorkerSafety-Monograph.pdf	Standards and strategies
Ergonomics	**Joint Commission** http://www.jointcommission.org/assets/1/18/TJC-ImprovingPatientAndWorkerSafety-Monograph.pdf	Standards and strategies
Injury & Violence Across the Life Stages	**Healthy People 2020** http://healthypeople.gov/2020/LHI/injuryViolence.aspx?tab=determinants	Recommendations and resources

Clinical Decision-Making Exercises

1. What would be the most important nursing actions to prevent back injury to the nurse when assisting a client out of bed to the standing position with no weight bearing to the left leg? *Select all that apply.*

    ① Apply an immobilizer to the left leg as prescribed and position client on side of bed.

    ② Position nurse's feet close together to assist with stability.

    ③ Instruct client to position arms around the waist of the nurse.

    ④ Instruct client to lean slightly forward and bear weight on the right foot as the left foot and leg are held forward.

    ⑤ Apply a transfer belt around client's waist.

2. Put in chronological order the steps for transferring an older client from the bed to chair? *Use all of the options.*

    ① Lower the bed to the lowest setting.

    ② Instruct client how to assist when possible.

    ③ Assist the client to stand, and then pivot.

    ④ Position the bed or chair, so that the client is moving toward the strong side.

    ⑤ Assess if client understands the steps of getting up from bed to chair.

    1. _____
    2. _____
    3. _____
    4. _____
    5. _____

3. Which of these nursing plans should be a priority to include in discharge teaching for an elderly client who has just started taking amitriptyline (Elavil) for depression?

    ① Assess the client daily for a fever.

    ② Eat a diet high in residue (fiber).

    ③ Review the importance of reporting symptoms of hypertension such as a headache.

    ④ Review importance of taking medication 15 minutes after taking Nardil (phenelzine).

4. What would be the priority of care for an elderly client who lives at home alone and is beginning to show signs of failing to thrive?

    ① The nurse should notify the neighbors and church members to check on client.

    ② The nurse should contact the neighborhood community center for further information.

    ③ The nurse should contact the ambulance to have client taken to the hospital.

    ④ The nurse should discuss observations with the case manager employed by the home care agency.

5. What would be the priority nursing action for a client who reports to the nurse, "Please do not tell anyone this information, but I have a gun under my mattress to protect myself from my roommate, who is not mentally healthy. I also have a gunshot wound on my lower leg."

    ① Report the incident, but do not inform the client of the intent.

    ② Utilize therapeutic communication to convince client to share this information.

    ③ Understand the importance of keeping this confidential, but observe roommate hourly.

    ④ Inform client that this will need to be reported to health care staff due to being a safety issue and the law.

Answers and Rationales

1. What would be the most important nursing actions to prevent back injury to the nurse **when assisting a client out of bed to the standing position with no weight bearing to the left leg?** Select all that apply.

    ① **CORRECT: Apply an immobilizer to the left leg as prescribed and position client on side of bed. This is correct practice.**

    ② INCORRECT: Position nurse's feet close together to assist with stability. May contribute to a fall.

    ③ INCORRECT: Instruct client to position arms around the waist of the nurse. Results in a lack of balance.

    ④ **CORRECT: Instruct client to lean slightly forward and bear weight on the right foot as the left foot and leg are held forward. Provides a safe transfer.**

    ⑤ **CORRECT: Apply a transfer belt around client's waist. Minimizes risk for falls.**

The strategy is that the nurse should make certain the immobilizer is applied as prescribed and the client is positioned to the side of the bed to assist with the transfer. If the client has been in the supine position for an extended period of time, this will also facilitate decreasing the risk of orthostatic hypotension. Option 4 is correct. To assist with the client's center of gravity, have the client lean slightly forward from the hips. This will assist in positioning the trunk and head in the same direction as the transfer. The nurse should remain in front of the client positioning one foot forward and one back while flexing the hips, knees, and ankles. The nurse should use the leg muscles to assist the client to the standing position. Option 5: To assist with holding onto the client, the transfer belt will provide this security by providing a way for the nurse to control the movements. Option 2 is incorrect since the nurse should be positioned in a broad stance. The narrow stance will only provide the nurse with a narrow base of support. Option 3 may result in the nurse losing balance.

Safety and Infection Control: Use ergonomic principles when providing care (i.e., proper transfer from bed to chair).

2. Put in chronological order the **steps for transferring an older client from the bed to chair?** Use all of the options.

    ① Lower the bed to the lowest setting.

    ② Instruct client how to assist when possible.

    ③ Assist the client to stand, and then pivot.

    ④ Position the bed or chair, so that the client is moving toward the strong side.

    ⑤ Assess if client understands the steps of getting up from bed to chair.

    1. (5)Assess if client understands the steps of getting up from bed to chair. Assessment is a great place to begin! Helps the nurse know what information to include when teaching.

    2. (2)Instruct client how to assist when possible. Remember, nurses must educate prior to interventions.

    3. (1)Lower the bed to the lowest setting. Remember client safety is always important prior to moving ahead with intervention!

    4. (4)Position the bed or chair, so that the client is moving toward the strong side. Now focuses on the equipment or chair, and the side it must be on (strong side leads).

    5. (3)Assist the client to stand, and then pivot. This is to the goal!

The strategy is to remember principles of ergonomics when transferring clients. The NCLEX® is not just about client safety, but it also evaluates a standard on the use of safe ergonomic principles.

Safety and Infection Control: Use ergonomic principles when providing care (i.e., proper transfer from bed to chair).

3. Which of these **nursing plans should be a priority** to include in **discharge teaching for an elderly client** who has just started **taking amitriptyline** (Elavil) for depression?

① INCORRECT: Assess the client daily for a fever. There is no assessment to indicate this assessment would be a priority.

② **CORRECT: Eat a diet high in residue (fiber). Elavil has anticholinergic properties which can lead to constipation. Elderly clients who are depressed contributes to this complication even more.**

③ INCORRECT: Review the importance of reporting symptoms of hypertension such as a headache. The effect may be hypotension versus hypertension.

④ INCORRECT: Review importance of taking medication 15 minutes after taking Nardil (phenelzine). Does not address the question.

The strategy is to consider safe medication practice with the elderly, especially because of the changes in pharmacokinetics for the elder clients. Option 2 is correct. An undesirable effect from this medication may be the anticholinergic effect, which is constipation. Option 1 is incorrect. Option 3 is incorrect. The client may experience a complication of hypotension versus hypertension. Option 4 is incorrect since Nardil (phenelzine) is a MAOI, and they should never be taken together or this close due to the risk of a potentially fatal adverse reaction. Remember, it takes an oral medication approximately 30-60 min. to be absorbed.

An easy way to remember this information can be found in the book, *Pharmacology Made Insanely Easy* by Manning and Rayfield. "TinaTricycle"is the image that will assist you in moving testing facts from your working memory into your long-term memory. In this question, if you remember anticholinergic effects include: "can't pee, can't see, can't spit, can't sh*t", then you will remember the strategies for answering these type of questions! You CAN do this! I bet you will get the next question correct when you come across this on the NCLEX®. The beauty in all of this is that we have just reviewed several types of questions with this one concept. For example, if you have a cardiac or neuro client on these meds, would you ever want them to be constipated? What about a client with a T6 or higher spinal cord injury or a client with cirrhosis of the liver and has esophageal varices? In other words, the answer is "no" for all of

these. A diet high in residue (fiber) would be great for any of these questions! Good JOB!! You are starting to link the concept of "elimination/constipation" to SAFETY and throughout nursing! You are on your path to SUCCESS!

Pharmacological and Parenteral Therapies: Review pertinent data prior to medication administration (i.e., potential undesirable effects).

4. What would be the **priority of care** for an elderly client who lives at home alone and is **beginning to show signs of failing to thrive?**

① INCORRECT: The nurse should notify the neighbors and church members to check on client. Violation of HPPA.

② INCORRECT: The nurse should contact the neighborhood community center for further information. Not an appropriate plan.

③ INCORRECT: The nurse should contact the ambulance to have client taken to the hospital. There is no emergency.

④ **CORRECT: The nurse should discuss observations with the case manager employed by the home care agency. This is appropriate based on the responsibility of the case manage.**

The strategy for answering this question is to familiarize yourself with the multidisciplinary team that is crucial for coordinating safe care after discharge. This is all about SAFE care!

Option 4 is correct. The priority of care for this client would be to consult with the case manager employed by the home care agency. Home care agencies have a group of multidisciplinary team members such as therapists, dieticians, etc. Case managers are excellent for coordinating and assisting with appropriate placement of clients with additional physical, emotional, etc. needs. Option 1 is not appropriate due to client confidentiality. Option 2 is not the priority action, since this is not their expertise when it comes to planning and coordinating care for an elderly client who is having a change in physical assessment findings. The case manager is the resource that will provide the best support. Option 3 is incorrect. This would be appropriate if client was in an emergency, but the nurse is not concerned with an emergency but with signs of failing to thrive.

Management of Care: Collaborate with healthcare members in other disciplines when providing client care.

5. What would be the **priority nursing action** for a client who reports to the nurse, "Please do not tell anyone this information, but I have a gun under my mattress to protect myself from my roommate, who is not mentally healthy. I also have a **gunshot wound on my lower leg**."

    ① INCORRECT: Report the incident, but do not inform the client of the intent. Not appropriate standard.

    ③ INCORRECT: Utilize therapeutic communication to convince client to share this information. Not appropriate standard.

    ④ INCORRECT: Understand the importance of keeping this confidential, but observe roommate hourly. Not appropriate standard.

    ② **CORRECT: Inform client that this will need to be reported to health care staff due to being a safety issue and the law. The appropriate standard of practice.**

The strategy for answering this is to understand the law regarding what is imperative to report. Option 4 is correct. This is evaluating the activity "Report client conditions as required by law (i.e., abuse/neglect, gunshot wound, communicable disease, etc.)." This is a priority response to this clinical situation. Option 1 is not being truthful to the client, which is NEVER acceptable. Option 2 is not a priority over 4. It is imperative to be truthful and up front with client, so client will understand the responsibility of the nurse based on the protocol and law. Option 3 is incorrect.

Insanely Easy Tip: "CAGE" will assist you in remembering conditions that must be reported as required by the law. Remember, it is illegal not to report these, so if we do something illegal we may go to prison behind bars. (*Refer to "CAGE" in this chapter*).

Psychosocial Integrity: Report client conditions as required by law i.e., abuse /neglect, gunshot wound, communicable disease, etc.

Decision-Making Analysis Form

Use this tool to help identify why you missed any questions. As you enter the question numbers in the chart, you will begin to see patterns of why you answered incorrectly. This information will then guide you toward what you need to focus on in your continued studies. Ultimately, this analytical exercise will help you become more successful in answering questions!!!

Questions to ask:

1. Did I have the knowledge to answer the question? If not, what information do I need to review?
2. Did I know what the question was asking? Did I misread it or did I miss keywords in the stem of the question?
3. Did I misread or miss keywords in the distractors that would have helped me choose the correct answer?
4. Did I follow my gut reaction or did I allow myself to rationalize and then choose the wrong answer?

	Lack of Knowledge (Concepts, Systems, Pathophysiology, Medications, Procedures, etc.)	Missed Keywords or Misread the Stem of the Question	Missed Keywords or Misread the Distractors	Changed My Answer (Second-guessed myself, i.e., my first answer was correct.)
Put the # of each question you missed in the column that best explains why you think you answered it incorrectly.				

If you changed an answer because you talked yourself out of the correct answer, or you second-guessed yourself, this is an **EASY FIX: QUIT changing your answers**!!! Typically, the first time you read a question, you are about 95% right! The second time you read a question, you start talking yourself into changing the answer. The third time you read a question, you do not have a clue—and you are probably thinking "Who in the heck wrote this question?"

On the other hand, if you read a question too quickly and when you reread it you realize you missed some key information that would impact your decision (i.e., assessments, lab reports, medications, etc.), then it is appropriate to change your answer. When in doubt, go with the safe route: your first thought! Go with your gut instinct!

As you gain confidence in answering questions regarding specific nursing concepts, you will be able to successfully progress to answering higher-level questions about prioritization. Please refer to the *Prioritization Guidelines* in this book for a structure to assist you with this process.

You CAN do this!

> *"To have meaningful work is a tremendous happiness."*
>
> RITA MAE BROWN

References for Chapter 22

Agency for Healthcare Research and Quality. Retrieved from http://www.ahrq.gov/

Agency for Healthcare Research and Quality. (2012). A decade of evidence, design, and implementation: Advancing patient safety. Retrieved from http://www.ahrq.gov/professionals/quality-patient-safety/patient-safety-resources/resources/advancing-patient- safety/index.html

Changing the built environment to prevent injury; p. 257-76. Examination to practice. Retrieved from https://www.ncsbn.org/index.htm

Daniels, R. & Nicoll, L. (2012). *Contemporary medical-surgical nursing*, (2nd ed.). Clifton Park, NY: Delmar Cengage Learning.

Eliopoulos, C. (2014). *Gerontological nursing* (8th ed.), Philadelphia: Lippincott Williams & Wilkins.

Giddens, G. F. (2013). *Concepts for nursing practice*. St. Louis, MO: Mosby, an imprint of Elsevier.

Healthy People 2020. (2014). Retrieved from http://www.healthypeople.gov/2020/default.aspx

Health People 2020. (2014). Injury and violence across life stages. Retrieved from http://healthypeople.gov/2020/LHI/injuryViolence.aspx?tab=determinants

Institute for Clinical Systems Improvements (2012). Health care protocol: Non-OR procedural safety. Retrieved from https://www.icsi.org/_asset/1hht9h/NonOR-Interactive0912.pdf

Institute of Medicine. (2010). The future of nursing: Leading change, advancing health Retrieved from http://www.iom.edu/Reports/2010/the-future-of-nursing-leading-change-advancing-health.aspx

Institute of Medicine. (2006). Preventing medication errors. Retrieved from http://www.iom.edu/~/media/Files/Report%20Files/2006/Preventing-Medication-Errors-Quality-Chasm-Series/medicationerrorsnew.pdf

Institute of Safe Medication Practices. (2014). 2104-15 Targeted medication safety best practices for hospitals. Retrieved from https://www.ismp.org/Tools/BestPractices/TMSBP-for-Hospitals.pdf

Institute of Healthcare Improvement http://www.ihi.org/explore/PatientSafety/Pages/default.aspx

Joint Commission Patient Safety Goals (2014). Hospital: 2104 National patient safety goals. Retrieved from http://www.jointcommission.org/hap_2014_npsgs/

Joint Commission (2012). Improving patient and worker safety: Opportunities for synergy, collaboration and innovation. Retrieved from http://www.jointcommission.org/assets/1/18/TJC-ImprovingPatientAndWorkerSafety-Monograph.pdf

Manning, L. and Rayfield, S. (2014). *Nursing made insanely easy* (7th ed). Duluth, GA: I CAN Publishing, Inc.

Manning, L. and Rayfield, S. (2013). *Pharmacology made insanely easy* (4th ed.). Duluth, GA: I CAN Publishing, Inc.

National Council of State Boards of Nursing, INC. (NCSBN) 2012. *Research brief: 2011 RN practice analysis: linking the NCLEX RN® examination to practice*. Retrieved from https://www.ncsbn.org/index.htm

National Patient Safety Foundation (2014). Definitions and hot topic. Retrieved form http://www.npsf.org/for-healthcare-professionals/resource-center/definitions-and-hot-topics/

Premier, Transforming Healthcare Together. (2014). Medical errors and the institute of medicine (IOM). Retrieved from https://www.premierinc.com/safety/topics/patient_safety/index_1.jsp

QSEN (2014). QSEN institute pre-licensure KSAS competencies. Retrieved from http://qsen.org/competencies/

CHAPTER 23

Linking Multiple Systems and Concepts
Concept Infection Control

A Snapshot of Infection Control

The goals of infection control prevention and control measures are to ensure the protection of those who might be vulnerable to acquiring an infection, both in the general community and while receiving care due to health problems, in a variety of settings. The World Health Organization's goals are quality promotion of health care, which is safe for clients, health care workers and others, in the health care setting and to prevent spread of infectious disease through evidence-based infection control measures (World Health Organization, 2014).

Standard Precautions are the minimum infection prevention practices that apply to all client care, regardless of suspected or confirmed infection status of the client, in any setting where healthcare is delivered. The CDC has added to the Standard Precautions the following: **Hygiene/Cough Etiquette, Safe injection practices, and Use of masks for insertion of catheters or injection of material into spinal or epidural spaces via lumbar puncture procedures** (i.e., myelogram, spinal or epidural anesthesia). These new elements of Standard Precautions focus on **protection of clients**. Most elements of the Standard Precautions evolved from Universal Precautions that had originally been developed for protection of healthcare personnel.

Airborne transmission: "Occurs by dissemination of either airborne droplet nuclei or small particles (droplets smaller than 5 micrometers) in the respirable size range containing infectious agents that remains infective over time and distance" (Centers for Disease Control, 2007).

Droplet transmission: "It is technically, a form of contact transmission, and some infectious agents transmitted by the droplet route also may be transmitted by the direct and indirect contact routes. However, in contrast to contact transmission, respiratory droplets (droplets larger than 5 micrometers) carry infectious pathogens that transmit infection when they travel directly from the respiratory tract of infectious individuals to the susceptible mucosal surfaces of the recipient, generally over short distances, necessitating facial protection" (Centers for Disease Control, 2007).

Contact: Direct transmission: "Occurs when microorganisms are transferred from one infected person to another person without a contaminated intermediate object or person" (Centers for Disease Control, 2007).

Contact: Indirect transmission: "Involves the transfer of an infectious agent through a contaminated intermediate object or person. In the absence of a point-source outbreak, it is difficult to determine how indirect transmission occurs. However, extensive evidence cited in the *Guideline for Hand Hygiene in Health-Care Settings*, suggests that the contaminated hands of healthcare personnel are important contributors to indirect contact transmission" (Centers for Disease Control, 2007).

629

Concept: Infection Control (continued)

The individual categories of transmission will be reviewed in this chapter regarding the specific transmission-based precautions.

Protective Precautions: This category includes clients who are experiencing a decrease in their WBCs, are immunocompromised or have (i.e., burn injury, undergone chemotherapy, bone marrow transplants, etc.) requiring neutropenic precautions. According to the CDC website, protective environment does not include the use of barrier precautions beyond those indicated for standard and transmission based precautions. No published reports support the benefit of placing solid organ transplants or other immunocompromised clients in a protective environment. Barrier precautions (i.e., masks, gowns and gloves, etc.) are not required for healthcare personal in the absence of suspected or confirmed infections in the client or if they are not indicated according to standard precautions (Centers for Disease Control, 2007).

Immunocompromised: Client has an immune system that has been impaired by disease or medical treatment.

Immunocompetent: The body is able to elicit an immune response; able to recognize antigens and act against them.

INSANELY EASY TIP!

The role of the nurse is to be able to correctly make room assignments with another client.

It is a priority to understand the importance of not putting a client in a room with a client who has different organisms requiring a different type of infection control precautions.

A client can be in a room with a client who has the same organism or who requires the same type of infection control precautions, since the organism is transmitted the same.

You need to know your organisms for the infections, viruses, etc. and you will have this mastered!!!

Standard Precautions Used for Every Client Include:

Hand hygiene and use of personal protective equipment (PPE) such as gloves, gowns, masks.

Hand "HYGIENE"	Personal Protective Equipment Recommendations for Specific Nursing Care
Hand hygiene procedures include use of alcohol-based hand rubs (containing 60-95% alcohol) &/or use of antibacterial soap & water using friction for at least 15 seconds. **Y**es, hygiene is important after contact with blood, body fluids or excretions, or wound dressings. **G**ood hygiene prior to performing an aseptic task (i.e., accessing a port, preparing an injection, etc.). **I**f hands will be moving from a contaminated-body site to a clean-body site during client care then hand hygiene is necessary. **E**ach time gloves are removed, hand hygiene must be performed. **N**ote prior to touching a client, even if gloves will be worn hand, hygiene is required. **E**ntering and exiting (before) the client's care area, after touching the client or the immediate environment the nurse should perform hand hygiene.	**Gloves** • Whenever you come in contact with body secretions. **Gowns** • Wear a gown to protect skin and clothing during procedures or activities where contact with blood or body fluids is anticipated. • Gown should only be worn when providing care for one client only. Change gowns between clients. • Remove gown and perform hand hygiene before leaving the client's environment (i.e., exam room, etc.). • Refer to Steps for Donning and Removing PPE for recommended order in this chapter. **Facemasks** • Wear a facemask when there is potential contact with respiratory secretions and sprays of blood or body fluids. **Goggles, Face Shields** • Wear eye protection for potential splash or spray of blood, respiratory secretions, or other body fluids. • Personal eyeglasses and contact lenses are not adequate eye protection.

For fun and easy ways to organize the facts about infection control, refer to the book *Nursing Made Insanely Easy!* by Manning and Rayfield.

Use Standard Precautions Reviewed on the Previous Page
PLUS
Precautions Below Based on the Organism

Droplet	Contact	Airborne
• Streptococcal (group A) pharyngitis • Diphtheria • Mycoplasma pneumonia • Meningococcal disease (until therapy for 24 hrs.) • Neisseria meningitides (until therapy for 24 hrs.) • Mumps • Pandemic influenza (human influenza) • Haemophilus influenza • Pertussis • Pneumonia or scarlet fever in infants & young children • Rubella (**+ Contact**) (until 7 days after rash onset)	• Hepatitis A virus (until 7 days after jaundice onset) • Hepatitis B, C, D or E virus (extent of illness) • Herpes Simplex (recurrent, oral, skin, genital) (until lesions are crusted over) • Herpes zoster (shingles) (**+ Airborne**) (until visible lesions are gone or extent of illness) • Human immunodeficiency virus (HIV) (extent of illness) • Clostridium difficile (C. Diff) (extent of illness) • Vancomycin-resistant enterococci (VRE) (until 3 negative cultures from infectious site done 1 week apart) • Methicillin-resistent (Staphylococcus aureus (MRSA) (extent of illness) • Methicillin-sensitive (Staphylococcus aureus (MSSA) (extent of illness) • Meningitis Viral (for infants and young children) • Salmonella (extent of illness) • Respiratory Syncytial Virus (RSV) (extent of illness) • Staphylococcus aureus (extent of illness) • Rotavirus (contact precautions required if wear diapers) • Shigellosis (Dysentery) (extent of illness) **Major abscesses:** • Cellulitis, Decubitus, Pediculosis **Sexually Transmitted:** • HIV, Human papillomavirus (HPV), Candidiasis, gonorrhea,	• Varicella zoster (Chickenpox) (**+ Contact**) (until lesions crust over) • SARS–Associated coronavirus (**+ Eye protection**) • Rubeola (Measles) • Mycobacterium tuberculosis (TB) (until 3 negative sputum smears) • Small pox (**+ Contact**) • Pneumonia from resistant organisms (i.e., MRSA, MSSA, etc.) use airborne (**+ Contact**)
DROPLET (The Ps) Put on your Surgical Facemask –distance 6–10 ft. from client. For the **Ps**: • Stre**P**tococcal (group A) **P**haryngitis • Di**P**htheria • Myco**P**lasma pneumonia • **P**ertussis • **P**neumonic plague • **P**neumonia or scarlet fever in infants & young children	**CONTACT–"PRIVATE"** **P**rivate room or cohort with same organisms **R**emove gown, gloves/perform hand hygiene between clients **I**solation procedures-use CONTACT PRECAUTIONS **V**isibly soiled from contaminants (i.e. stool, blood)–change gloves immediately **A**lcohol is not sporicidal! (Must do hand washing with C Diff) **T**he clients with VRE/MRSA/MSSA–NOT in room with clostridium difficile **E**quipment: Do NOT share! Remember C. diff is located on many surfaces including toilet seats, stethoscopes, linens, shared toys among pediatric patients etc.	**AIRBORNE–"AIIR"** **A**irborne Infection Isolation Room (AIIR) (Negative pressure) **I**nfections included in this Isolation are TB, smallpox, etc. **I**nsist that client wear a surgical mask if they must be transported (transports should be limited). **R**espiratory protection mask should always be worn. (N95) mask recommended, required for (i.e.,TB, smallpox, etc.).

Put on your Surgical Facemask—distance 3–6 ft. from client for the P's

AIRBORNE PRECAUTIONS

©2014 I CAN Publishing®, Inc.

Multipe Systems and Concepts

Safety Concept: Infection Control

SAFETY Concept: Infection Control		
General Infection Control Concept for All Clients *(Refer to Standard Precautions and Appropriate PPE for Contact, Airborne, Droplet, and Protective Precautions)*		
System-Specific Assessments "TEMPS"	**First-Do Priority Interventions "HANDS"**	**Evaluation of Expected Outcomes**

Temperature ↑, HR ↑.
 	
Evaluate WBC ↑.
 	
Mucous (thickness, quantity, color odor).
  Monitor incision site: redness, excessive tenderness, purulent drainage.
  Monitor wound drains.
 	
Pulmonary: auscultate breath sounds for adventitious sounds, RR, SaO$_2$ sat.
 	
Signs of infection at peripheral IV site or central lines, wounds, etc.
	Hand washing, PPE, HR, T, WBC – monitor & report changes & trends to HCP.
	
	Appropriate suctioning.
	  Antibiotics as prescribed.
	  Auscultate breath sounds q 2–4 hrs.
	
	Note: importance of oral care q 2hrs & encourage fluids as tolerated.
	
	Drains , sputum, dressings–Document & monitor changes in drainage. (Note amount, color, & consistency of sputum, mucous color, & breath sounds); report changes/trends to HCP.
	  Diet–↑ calories, protein, vitamin C.
	
	Sterile, aseptic technique; (dressing changes).
		• No "**TEMPS**"
		
		• No signs of infection: WBCs WDL
		
		• No drainage
		
		• No odor, healing
		
		• WBC WDL
		
		• VS WDL
		
		• Lungs clear
		
		• IV sites without s/s of infection

Nursing Care
Recommended Personal Protective Equipment

	Hand Hygiene	Gloves	Mask/Goggles/ Face Shield	Gowns	Mask N(95)
STANDARD PRECAUTIONS					
Vital Signs	X				
Start an IV	X	X			
Bathing the client	X	X			
Cleaning a client who is incontinent	X	X		X	
Coming in contact with respiratory secretions or sprays of body secretions or projectile secretions (i.e., coughing, vomiting, diarrhea, etc.)	X	X	X (eye protection)	X	
CONTACT PRECAUTIONS	Plus (Add STANDARD PRECAUTIONS ABOVE BASED ON NURSING CARE)				
Walk in the room for a client requiring Contact Precautions	X	X		X	
DROPLET PRECAUTIONS	Plus (Add STANDARD PRECAUTIONS ABOVE BASED ON NURSING CARE)				
Any nursing care within a distance of < 3 feet is currently viewed as an example of a "short distance from client. Recommended donning a mask within 6–10 feet from client or entry into client's room with exposure to emerging or highly virulent pathogens is likely	X		X (face mask)		
Transport client out of room	X		X (mask on client)		
AIRBORNE PRECAUTIONS	Plus (Add STANDARD PRECAUTIONS ABOVE BASED ON NURSING CARE)				
Any nursing care for a client requiring Airborne Precautions	X				X
Transport client out of room	X		X (mask on client)		

* Face mask and mask are used interchangeably. The N95 is separate and the Face Shield is separate

Infection Prevention for Clients Requiring Neutropenic or Immunocomprised Precautions

Clients who require neutropenic precautions or are at a high risk for developing an infection from burns will need protection from all types of organisms. The image below illustrates this by "**Positive Paul**" attempting to push any organism out the door by positive pressure

INFECTION PREVENTION: POSITIVE PRESSURE "PROTECT"	POSITIVE PRESSURE "POSITIVE PAUL"
Private room with a positive pressure airflow & high-efficiency particulate air (HEPA) filtration. **R**espiratory PPE as indicated for standard & transmission based precautions. **O**rient client & transport team about the need for the N95 mask on the severely immunocompromised client during transport when it is anticipated the client could inhale fungal spores during construction. **T**hings such as flowers and potted plants with standing water should never be in the room. **E**nsure client has dedicated equipment in the room that is not shared. **C**lose assessments for any signs of infection; control precautions based on the individual client. **T**each client/family, visitors, and/or staff about infection precautions based on the individual client.	PATIENT'S ROOM ©2008 I CAN Publishing, Inc. **P** ositive **P** ressure **P** ositively **P** revents **P** atient infection by **P** ushing air out

Procedures for Donning and Removing
Personal Protective Equipment (PPE) (Reference CDC.gov)

Sequence for Donning PPE

Step 1: Put on gown

Step 2: Put on mask

Step 3: Put on goggles

Step 4: Put on gloves

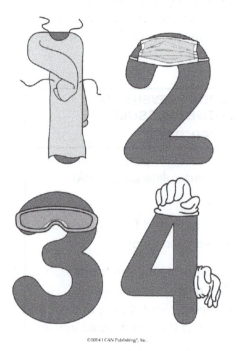

©2014 I CAN Publishing®, Inc.

Sequence for Removing PPE

Step 1: Take off gloves

Step 2: Take off goggles

Step 3: Take off gown

Step 4: Take off mask

©2014 I CAN Publishing®, Inc.

Summary of Category of Precautions

(Reference CDC.gov)

Infectious Agent	Standard	Air-borne	Droplet	Contact	Duration of Precautions
All Clients	S				
Rotavirus	S			Diapers	Extent of illness
Measles (Rubeola Virus)	S	A			Extent of illness
Tuberculosis (TB) Pulmonary	S	A			Three negative sputum smears
Meningococcal disease	S		D		Until therapy for 24 hours
Rubella	S		D	C	7 days after rash onset
AIDS/HIV	S			C	Extent of illness
Clostridium difficile	S			C	Extent of illness
Hepatitis A	S			C	7 days after jaundice onset
Hepatitis B	S			C	Extent of illness
Hepatitis C	S			C	Extent of illness
Herpes Simplex (Recurrent, oral, skin, genital)	S			C	Until lesions crust over
Methicillin–resistant Staphylococcus aureus (MRSA)	S			C	Extent of illness
Salmonella	S			C	Extent of illness
Shigellosis (dysentery)	S			C	Extent of illness
Staphylococcus aureus (infection or colonization)	S			C	Extent of illness
Vancomycin-resistant enterococci (VRE) (infection or colonization)	S			C	Until 3 negative cultures from infectious site (1 week apart)
Varicella Zoster (chickenpox)	S	A		C	Until lesions crust over
Herpes Zoster (shingles) Disseminated or localized if immunocompromised*	S	A*		C	Visible lesions or extent of illness
Respiratory Syncytial Virus (RSV)	S			C	Extent of illness

Management of clients with herpes zoster: Infection-control measures depend on whether the client with herpes zoster is immunocompromised or immunocompetent and whether the rash is localized or disseminated. In all cases, standard infection-control precautions should be followed.

Immunocompromised: Client has an immune system that has been impaired by disease or medical treatment.

- If the client is immunocompromised with localized herpes zoster, standard precautions plus airborne and contact precautions should be followed until disseminated infection is ruled out. The standard precautions should be followed until lesions are dried and crusted.

- If the client is immunocompromised with disseminated herpes zoster, then standard precautions plus airborne and contact precautions should be followed until lesions are dried and crusted.

Immunocompetent: The body is able to elicit an immune response; able to recognize antigens and act against them.

- If the client is immunocompetent with localized herpes zoster, then standard precautions should be followed and lesions should be completely covered.

- If the client is immunocompetent with disseminated herpes zoster (defined as appearance of lesions outside the primary or adjacent dermatomes), then standard precautions plus airborne and contact precautions should be followed until lesions are dried and crusted (Centers for Disease Control, 2014).

Clinical Decision-Making Exercises

1. Which staff nurse may need further instruction regarding wearing the appropriate personal protective equipment (PPE)?
    ① The RN wears a gown and gloves when entering the room for a client with Clostridium Difficile.
    ② The RN wears a N95 mask for a client in airborne precautions with TB.
    ③ The LPN wears sterile gloves when bathing an infant with Respiratory syncytial virus (RSV).
    ④ The LPN removes gloves and washes hands with soap and water after care for a client with Clostridium Difficile.

2. Which of these clinical situations should the charge nurse intervene with due to not following the appropriate standard of practice?
    ① The LPN reinforces the instruction with a client who has Hepatitis A that this can be transmitted through infected food handlers.
    ② The LPN puts on gloves to administer an injection with a client who has Hepatitis B.
    ③ The RN discusses the need to avoid sexual activity for a client with Hepatitis A.
    ④ The UAP puts on a gown and mask prior to giving a bath to a client with Hepatitis B.

3. What would be the most important for the nurse to include in a teaching plan for a child diagnosed with varicella?
    ① Instruct to keep fingernails short.
    ② Isolate child until all the vesicles have crust.
    ③ Provide quiet activities to keep child occupied.
    ④ Recommend bathing the child in warm baths with a mild soap.

4. Which nursing actions indicate the nurse understands how to prevent the spread of active pulmonary tuberculosis? *Select all that apply.*
    ① Place client in a negative airflow room.
    ② Wear gown and gloves at all times.
    ③ Apply an N95 mask when in direct contact with client.
    ④ Apply a surgical mask on client when transported outside of negative-airflow room.
    ⑤ Precautions may be discontinued following two negative sputum smears.

5. The client with a spinal cord injury has been diagnosed with Clostridium Difficile. Which of these nursing actions indicate the nurse understands how to safely provide care for this client? *Select all that apply.*
    ① Place a client in a room with another client who has MRSA.
    ② Wash hands with hand sanitizer outside the client's room.
    ③ Put on a gown when in contact with the client.
    ④ Put on gloves when in contact with the client.
    ⑤ Refuses to share blood pressure cuff with the LPN who needs one for another client.

Answers and Rationales

1. Which staff nurse may need **further instruction** regarding wearing the **appropriate personal protective equipment** (PPE)?

    ① INCORRECT: The RN wears a gown and gloves when entering the room for a client with Clostridium Difficile. Correct standard of care, so there is no need for further instruction.

    ② INCORRECT: The RN wears a N95 mask for a client in airborne precautions with TB. Correct standard of care, so there is no need for further instruction.

    ③ **CORRECT: The LPN wears sterile gloves when bathing an infant with Respiratory syncytial virus (RSV). No need for sterile gloves.**

    ④ INCORRECT: The LPN removes gloves and washes hands with soap and water after care for a client with Clostridium Difficile. Correct standard of care, so there is no need for further instruction.

    The strategy to successfully answer this question is to recognize the standards of care for infection control. This is a frequently tested concept on the NCLEX® because it is a frequent part of providing safe nursing care. Remember SAFETY is the key to quality care. Option 3 is incorrect. The staff nurse does need further discussion regarding the appropriate PPE to wear, since an infant with RSV does not require the nurse to wear sterile gloves. This infant is not immunocompromised. This infant with RSV would require the nurse to wear a mask when entering the room of the infant. If the nurse is bathing the infant, then gloves would be appropriate based on the Standard Precaution Guidelines for Infection Control; however, there is not a need for sterile gloves.

    Safety and Infection Control: Apply principles of infection control.

2. Which of these **clinical situations** should the **charge nurse intervene** with due to not following the **appropriate standard of practice**?

    ① INCORRECT: The LPN reinforces the instruction with the client who has Hepatitis A that it can be transmitted through infected food handlers. Correct, so no need for intervention.

    ② INCORRECT: The LPN puts on gloves to administer an injection with a client who has Hepatitis B. Correct, so no need for intervention.

    ③ INCORRECT: The RN discusses the need to avoid sexual activity for a client with Hepatitis A. Correct, so no need for intervention.

    ④ **CORRECT: The UAP puts on a gown and mask prior to giving a bath to a client with Hepatitis B. No need for a mask in this clinical situation.**

    The strategy for answering this question correctly is to understand that hepatitis requires the infection control guidelines of standard precautions which include blood and body fluids. Option 4 is the answer. Standard precautions are the appropriate type of infection control for all clients with hepatitis. Droplet precautions are not necessary for these clients. There is no need for a mask to be placed on the nurse due to how Hepatitis B is transmitted which is by blood and blood products. The nurse would need to put on gloves while giving a bath as outlined in the infection control protocol for Standard precautions from the CDC. The UAP needs to put on gloves and review the appropriate infection control standards for this infection. Options 1, 2, and 3 do not require further intervention, since they are following the appropriate standards of care.

    Safety and Infection Control: Apply principles of infection control.

3.   What would be the **most important** for the nurse to include in a teaching plan for a child diagnosed with varicella?

①   INCORRECT: Instruct to keep fingernails short. This is important, but not a priority over option 2.

②   **CORRECT: Isolate child until all the vesicles have crust. Standard of practice.**

③   INCORRECT: Provide quiet activities to keep child occupied. This is important, but not a priority over option 2.

④   INCORRECT: Recommend bathing the child in warm baths with a mild soap. The baths should be tepid with no soap.

The strategy for answering this type of question is evaluating higher-level thinking. This level of thinking will help you to recognize the other options are not incorrect; they are simply just not the priority. Remember, you are learning to think at a higher level versus responding to simple facts. Option 2 is the correct answer. The key to answering this question is to understand the diagnosis of varicella (chickenpox) and the process for transmission. Varicella is transmitted via contact and airborne. The incubation period is 14 to 16 days. Varicella is highly contagious, usually occurring in children under 15 years of age and presenting with maculopapular rash with vesicular scabs in multiple stages of healing. The duration for transmission is 1 day prior to the lesions appearing to the time when all lesions have formed crusts. The child should be isolated, and family members, health care providers, etc. need to follow the appropriate infection control precautions in order to prevent others from being exposed to the infection. Option 1, while it is important to keep fingernails short to prevent scratching, it is not a priority over Option 2 due to the risk for others being exposed and possibly resulting in an infection. Option 3 is also important, but not a priority over Option 2. Option 4 is incorrect; the water would be cool-tepid and no soap would be used.

Safety and Infection Control: Apply principles of infection control.

4.   Which nursing actions indicate the **nurse understands** how to prevent the spread of active pulmonary **tuberculosis**? Select all that apply.

①   **CORRECT: Place client in a negative airflow room. Correct standard of care.**

②   INCORRECT: Wear gown and gloves at all times. Not necessary based on the standard of care.

③   **CORRECT: Apply an N95 mask when in direct contact with client. Correct standard of care.**

④   **CORRECT: Apply a surgical mask on client when transported outside of negative-airflow room. Correct standard of care.**

⑤   INCORRECT: Precautions may be discontinued following two negative sputum smears. Not standard of care.

The strategy is to understand the concept of Airborne precautions. Options 1, 3 and 4 are correct for the infection control precautions for a client who is in Airborne/Standard precautions. Airborne precautions are for diseases known to be transmitted by air for infectious agents smaller than 5 mcg (measles, varicella, pulmonary or laryngeal tuberculosis). PPE per protocol include: gloves, mask and/or (N95 respirator for known or suspected TB). In addition to the gloves and mask, the client will be in a private room with monitored negative airflow (air exchange and air discharge through HEPA filter). The door should be kept closed. The nurse must be fitted for the N95 respirator. The nurse should apply a small surgical mask to the client if the client needs to leave the room for medical necessity. Option 2 is incorrect. A gown does not need to be worn routinely unless the nurse will come in contact with blood, body secretions and/or fluids as outlined in the Standard precautions for infection control. Option 5 is incorrect. The standard for discontinuing the precautions would require three negative sputum smears to rule out TB.

Safety and Infection Control: Apply principles of infection control.

5. The client with a spinal cord injury has been diagnosed with **Clostridium Difficile**. Which of these nursing actions indicate the nurse understands how to safely provide care for this client? Select all that apply.

① INCORRECT: Place a client in a room with another client who has MRSA. Not standard of care.

② INCORRECT: Wash hands with hand sanitizer outside the client's room. Not standard of care.

③ **CORRECT: Put on a gown when in contact with the client. Standard of care.**

④ **CORRECT: Put on gloves when in contact with the client. Standard of care.**

⑤ **CORRECT: Refuses to share blood pressure cuff with the LPN who needs one for another client. Standard of care.**

The strategy is to understand the type of infection precautions for Clostridium Difficile. Options 3, 4, and 5 are correct. This diagnosis requires Contact/Standard Precautions. This includes hand hygiene, personal protective equipment (gloves and gown) if in contact with client, disposal of infectious dressing material into a nonporous bag. Dedicated equipment for the client or disinfect after each use. Option 5 is correct since the equipment should not be shared with clients if one of the clients is on contact precautions. Option 1 is incorrect. These clients should not be placed with a client with Clostridium Difficile. Option 2 is incorrect since this is not a sporicidal. Hands should be washed with soap and water.

Safety and Infection Control: Apply principles of infection control.

Decision-Making Analysis Form

Use this tool to help identify why you missed any questions. As you enter the question numbers in the chart, you will begin to see patterns of why you answered incorrectly. This information will then guide you toward what you need to focus on in your continued studies. Ultimately, this analytical exercise will help you become more successful in answering questions!!!

Questions to ask:

1. Did I have the knowledge to answer the question? If not, what information do I need to review?

2. Did I know what the question was asking? Did I misread it or did I miss keywords in the stem of the question?

3. Did I misread or miss keywords in the distractors that would have helped me choose the correct answer?

4. Did I follow my gut reaction or did I allow myself to rationalize and then choose the wrong answer?

	Lack of Knowledge *(Concepts, Systems, Pathophysiology, Medications, Procedures, etc.)*	Missed Keywords or Misread the Stem of the Question	Missed Keywords or Misread the Distractors	Changed My Answer *(Second-guessed myself, i.e., my first answer was correct.)*
Put the # of each question you missed in the column that best explains why you think you answered it incorrectly.				

If you changed an answer because you talked yourself out of the correct answer, or you second-guessed yourself, this is an **EASY FIX: QUIT changing your answers**!!! Typically, the first time you read a question, you are about 95% right! The second time you read a question, you start talking yourself into changing the answer. The third time you read a question, you do not have a clue—and you are probably thinking "Who in the heck wrote this question?"

On the other hand, if you read a question too quickly and when you reread it you realize you missed some key information that would impact your decision (i.e., assessments, lab reports, medications, etc.), then it is appropriate to change your answer. When in doubt, go with the safe route: your first thought! Go with your gut instinct!

As you gain confidence in answering questions regarding specific nursing concepts, you will be able to successfully progress to answering higher-level questions about prioritization. Please refer to the *Prioritization Guidelines* in this book for a structure to assist you with this process.

You CAN do this!

> *"Patience and perseverance have a magical effect before which difficulties disappear and obstacles vanish."*
>
> JOHN QUINCY ADAMS

References for Chapter 23

Centers for Disease Control. (2010). *2007 Guideline for isolation precautions: Preventing transmission of infectious agents in healthcare settings.* Retrieved from http://www.cdc.gov/hicpac/2007IP/2007isolationPrecautions.html

Centers for Disase Control. (2009). *Guideline for isolation precautions: Preventing transmission of infectious agents in healthcare settings: Appendix A.* Retrieved from http://www.cdc.gov/hicpac/2007IP/2007ip_appendA.html

Centers for Disease Control. (2011). *Guide to Infection Prevention for Outpatient Settings: Minimum Expectations for Safe Care.* Retrieved from http://www.cdc.gov/HAI/settings/outpatient/outpatient-care-gl-standard-precautions.html

Centers for Disease Control. (2009). 2007 Guideline for isolation precautions: Preventing transmission of infectious agents in healthcare settings: Table 2, clinical syndromes for conditions warranting empiric transmission-based precautions in addition to standard precautions pending confirmation of diagnosis. Retrieved from http://www.cdc.gov/hicpac/2007ip/2007ip_table2.html

Centers for Disease Control. (2014). *Preventing varicella-zoster virus (VZV) transmission from zoster in healthcare settings.* Retrieved from http://www.cdc.gov/shingles/hcp/HC-settings.html

Daniels, R. & Nicoll, L. (2012). *Contemporary medical-surgical nursing*, (2nd ed.). Clifton Park, NY: Delmar Cengage Learning.

Eliopoulos, C. (2014). *Gerontological nursing* (8th ed.), Philadelphia: Lippincott Williams & Wilkins.

Giddens, G. F. (2013). *Concepts for nursing practice.* St. Louis, MO: Mosby, an imprint of Elsevier.

Manning, L. and Rayfield, S. (2013). *Pharmacology made insanely easy* (4th ed.). Duluth, GA: I CAN Publishing, Inc.

National Council of State Boards of Nursing, INC. (NCSBN) 2012. *Research brief: 2011 RN practice analysis: linking the NCLEX RN® examination to practice.* Retrieved from https://www.ncsbn.org/index.htm

Nettina, S. L. (2013). Lippincott manual of nursing practice (10th ed.). Philadelphia, PA: Walters Kluwer Health / Lippincott Williams & Wilkins.

Pagana, K.D. & Pagana, T.J. (2014). Mosby's manual of laboratory and diagnostic tests (5th ed.). St. Louis, MO: Mosby, an imprint of Elsevier

World Health Organization. (2014). Retrieved from http://www.who.int/topics/infection_control/en/

NOTES

CHAPTER 24

Linking Multiple Systems and Concepts
Concept Nutrition

A Snapshot of Nutrition

Nutrition is adequate intake or metabolism of nutrients for the metabolic needs of the body. It is the nutrition requirements needed for tissue and organ maintenance, growth, and provision of energy for metabolism and activity. Adequate nutrition is essential for the growth and development of children. Macronutrients are the Kilocalorie (kcal or energy source) that is obtained from carbohydrates, proteins and fats. Micronutrients are vitamins and minerals. Water is essential for the physiological processes to be effective. According to Healthy People 2020, diet and body weight are linked to health status. Healthy diets can help reduce the risks for many health conditions to include: heart disease, diabetes, obesity, malnutrition and some cancers (Healthy People 2020, 2014). Factors contributing to the adherence of a healthy diet include: age and social factors (i.e., knowledge, attitudes, skills, social support and cultural norms, food assistance programs and economic status, etc.).

NUTRITION HEALTHY BODY MASS INDEX = 18.5 - 24.9						
Insufficient Nutrition–(BMI < 17)					Excess Nutrition (BMI >25)	
Starvation	**Eating Disorders**	**Deficiencies**	**Deficiencies & Metabolism**	**Metabolism**	**Excess**	**Obesity**
•Protein-calorie malnutrition/ Marasmus •Malabsorption syndromes •Kwashiorkor	•Anorexia nervosa •Bulimia nervosa	•Ulcerative colitis and Crohn's Disease •Post GI surgery (i.e., Billroth I or II; (partial or total removal of colon, gastric bypass, etc.) •HIV •Cancer •Alcoholism / Drug Addiction	•Celiac Disease •Diabetes •Burns	•Celiac Disease •Hypothyroidism (Myxedema) •Hyperthyroidism (Graves Disease) •Diabetes •Pregnancy & Breast Feeding •Burns (hypermetabolic state)	•Cardiac Disease •Hypertension	•> Body Mass Index (BMI

Safety Concept/Nutrition

SAFETY–Concept: Nutrition–Less than Requirements		
System-Specific Assessments "NUTRITIONAL"	**First-Do Priority Interventions "DIETS"**	**Evaluation of Expected Outcomes "NUTRITIONAL"**
Nutritional intake: Need to ↑ **U**nusual appetite changes–anorexia **T**he med history, Body Mass Index **R**estrictive diet NOT NEEDED; weigh & compare; trend weight loss and prevent malnutrition **I**dentify allergies, family & social history **T**eeth: no cavities; oral tissues pink & moist; skin integrity, hair brittle **I**dentify c/o; signs and symptoms, interpersonal communication (emotions) **O**ther signs and symptoms: I & O; pain; GI: N/V, diarrhea; wound healing **N**ote changes in client's condition **A**lbumin or pre-albumin level **L**abs: LDL, HDL, triglycerides; Hb A$_{1c}$, electrolytes; iron; vitamin deficiencies; PO$_4$, ammonia levels	**D**ietary supplement (↑ calorie, protein, vitamins, supplements). **I**nterventions collaborative , (i.e., dietary, surgery, pharmacology, (if taking > 3 drugs, nutritional status is complex and may be difficult to measure). **E**valuate weight regularly, evaluate need for anti-nausea and/or pain meds prior to meals to help enhance client's appetite. **T**each healthy dietary facts, support with vitamin & mineral supplements. **S**upport: calm and inviting environment while eating. Give appetite stimulants per order. Tube feedings if needed: gastrostomy , nasogastric, jejunostomy tube; TPN.	• Body weight increased or maintained • Lab values, electrolytes, iron studies, Hgb/Hct, protein and albumin WDL • Wounds (if any) healing • Knowledgeable of dietary needs

Safety Concept/Nutrition

SAFETY–Concept: Nutrition–More than Requirements		
System-Specific Assessments "NUTRITIONAL"	**First-Do Priority Interventions "DIETS"**	**Evaluation of Expected Outcomes "NUTRITIONAL"**
Nutritional intake: Need to ↓ **U**nusual appetite changes–always hungry **T**he med hx, take Body Mass Index (BMI) **R**estrictive diet; weigh and compare; trend **I**dentify allergies, family & social history **T**eeth: no cavities; oral tissues pink & moist; skin integrity hair brittle **I**dentify c/o; signs & symptoms, interpersonal communication (emotions) **O**ther signs and symptoms: I&O; pain; GI: N/V, diarrhea; wound healing **N**ote changes in client's condition **A**lbumin or pre-albumin level **L**abs: LDL, HDL, triglycerides; HbA_{1c}, electrolytes; iron; vitamin deficiencies; PO_4, ammonia levels	**D**ietary: Implement dietary restrictions (low calorie, low fat). **I**nterventions collaborative, (i.e., dietary, surgery, pharmacology); (if taking > 3 drugs, nutritional status is complex and may be difficult to measure). Increase fiber and fluids. **E**valuate weight regularly, evaluate need for anti-nausea and/or pain meds prior to meals. **T**each healthy dietary facts, support with vitamin & mineral supplements if needed. **S**upport (nursing): Medication administration, support client in selecting low calorie, low fat snacks.	• Body weight decreased or maintained • Lab values, electrolytes, iron studies, Hgb/Hct, protein and albumin WDL • Wounds (if any) healing • Knowledgeable of dietary restrictions

Concept Nutrition: Snapshot of Macronutrients
PROTEIN

FUNCTION

Building Blocks: Amino acids comprise protein and give structural integrity to body

Enzymes for (i.e., digestion, etc.)

Fight infection with antibiodies

Maintain osmotic pressure (albumin), acts as buffer to maintain normal acid-base balance

SYSTEM-SPECIFIC ASSESSMENTS

Decreased Amounts
- Muscle wasting, weakness
- Edema
- Growth limitied
- Infections
- Tired, moody
- **Alert: If jaundiced or if ↑ ammonia level: ↓ protein to no protein as prescribed**

NUTRITIONAL COMPARISON WITH MEDICAL CONDITIONS
NUTRITIONAL GUIDELINES (DIETS)

Increase Need for Protein
- Healing
- Burns
- Post operative
- Kwashiorkor
- Marasmus
- Cystic fibrosis
- Nephrotic syndrome
- Prolonged illness
- Diet low in protein

Decrease Need for Protein
- Liver disease
- Renal disease
- Genetic disorders (i.e., Sickle cell disease, Phenylketonuria {PKU})

FOOD SOURCES
"PROTEIN"

Peanut butter

Remember beans

Offer cottage cheese, yogurt, soy milk

Tuna, tofu

Eggs

Include meat, chicken

Nuts and seeds

Happy   =   Hamburger

To   =   Tuna

Consume =   Chicken

My   =   Milk

Calories   =   Cottage Cheese

Sanely   =   Soy Beans

Concept Nutrition: Snapshot of Macronutrients
CARBOHYDRATES

FUNCTION

Structural: component of cell membranes and walls

Energy: major source

Cellular: prevent ketosis and regulate blood glucose levels

Insoluble: ↓ CA risk, ↑ regularity

Soluble: ↓ cholesterol, regulate blood sugar

FOOD SOURCES

"CARB"

Cereal, Oatmeal (soluble)

Apples, strawberries, blueberries

Real whole grains (soluble)

Beans, nuts & seeds (insoluble)

SYSTEM-SPECIFIC ASSESSMENTS

Decreased Amounts

• Changes in blood sugar

• Decrease energy, fatigue

• Depression

• Ketosis

• Constipation

NUTRITIONAL COMPARISON WITH MEDICAL CONDITIONS
NUTRITIONAL GUIDELINES (DIETS)

Increase Need for Carbohydrates

• Renal disease

• Liver disease

Decrease Need for Carbohydrates

• Diabetes Mellitus

Concept Nutrition: Snapshot of Macronutrients
Lipid (Fats)/Cholesterol

FUNCTION

Energy and absorption of nutrients

Provides cushion for vital organs, insulation

Transport: Lipoproteins (proteins + lipid): Carry triglycerides from bloodstream to liver

Low-density (LDL): carry cholesterol to cell ($\uparrow$ LDL = heart disease)

High density liproteins (HDL): carry fat in bloodstream to tissue or liver to be excreted ("good" cholesterol)

FOOD SOURCES

"LO FAT"

Limited organ meats

Omit high saturated fat, trim visible fat

Fiber (soluble) legumes, whole grains

Add seafood, lean meat and chicken

Try fruits and vegetables

SYSTEM-SPECIFIC ASSESSMENTS

Decreased Amounts
* *Note: Fat amount $\uparrow$ for protein/calorie or other diseases causing malnutrition*

Increased Amounts
* $\uparrow$ Body weight
* $\uparrow$ Cholesterol and triglyceride levels
* Low energy
* Depression

NUTRITIONAL COMPARISON WITH MEDICAL CONDITIONS
NUTRITIONAL GUIDELINES (DIETS)

Increase Lipid (Fats)
* Increase fat with protein calorie malnutrition

Decrease Lipid (Fats)
* Cardiac disease
* Obesity
* Gall bladder
* Malabsorpton of fat
* Chronic Pancreatitis
* Clients with increased cholesterol

Concept Nutrition: Snapshot of Minerals
SODIUM (NA⁺)

FUNCTION

Involved in **fluid balance** (maintaining osmolality)

Neurological function

Cellular response, edema to shrinkage

Altered acid base

SYSTEM-SPECIFIC ASSESSMENTS

Decreased Levels of Na⁺
- ↓ Cerebral function
- ↓ LOC; risk for seizures
- ↓ Muscle strength
- ↓ Deep Muscle Reflexes (DTR)
- ↓ Volume = fast HR (thready pulse)
- ↓ Blood Pressure; orthostatic hypotension
- ↓ Urine output
- ↓ Weight

Increased Levels of Na⁺ (Fluid Excess)

Edema (pitting)

Decrease in hematocrit; diet ↑ Na⁺

Elevated weight; ↑ BP & HR

Mentation ↓ (lethargic)

Assess serum Na⁺ > 145 mEq/L; flushing of the skin

Increased Levels (Na⁺)
Hemoconcentrated from "DRIED"

Dryness of mucous membranes ↑

↑ concentration in urine

Red, flushed skin, ↑ restless

Increased temperature

Elevated HR ↑

Decreased weight; ↓ BP and CVP

FOOD SOURCES
"SODIUM"

Salt limit–eating/cooking

Omit salty snacks

Do use spices/herbs–↑ taste

Include fresh fruits and vegetables

Use lemon juice for flavor

Minimize canned foods, ketchup, sodas

NUTRITIONAL COMPARISON WITH MEDICAL CONDITIONS
NUTRITIONAL GUIDELINES (DIETS)

Increase Need for Sodium
- Addison's Disease
- Cystic Fibrosis
- Clients only receiving D_5W
- Nasogastric tube to low suction

Decrease Need for Sodium
- Cardiac disease
- Hypertension
- Renal disease
- Aldosteronism
- Fluid deficit (dehydration hypovolemia)
- Hypernatremia
- Cushing's Disease/Syndrome
- Neurological clients with head injuries or IICP (cerebral edema)
- Note: due to ↓ in body fluid, Na⁺ may need to be ↓ for elderly

Concept Nutrition: Snapshot of Minerals
Potassium (K⁺)

FUNCTION

Involved in **acid-base balance**

Nerve conduction

Cardiac muscle contraction

SYSTEM-SPECIFIC ASSESSMENTS

Decreased Levels of K⁺
"CRAMPS"

Complications with GI losses (diarrhea)

Reflexes, RR ↓ and shallow

Arrhythmias: ↓ T waves; abdominal distention; alkalosis; anxiety, confusion

Muscle cramps; weakness

Pulse weak, irregular

Serum K⁺ < 3.5 mEq/L

Increased Levels of K⁺
"DEATH"

Dysrhythmias (Arrhythmias) ↓ HR

ECG changes: tall peaked T waves

Abdominal cramping; diarrhea

The muscles twitch, cramp

Hypotension; irritability/restlessness

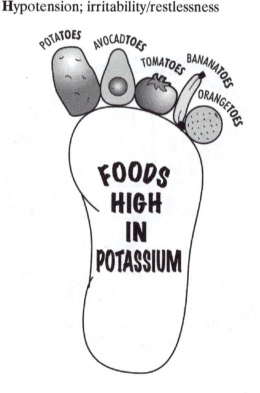

FOOD SOURCES

"TOES"

- Pota**TOES**
- Toma**TOES**
- Avocad**TOES**
- Banana**TOES**
- Orange**TOES**

NUTRITIONAL COMPARISON WITH MEDICAL CONDITIONS
NUTRITIONAL GUIDELINES (DIETS)

Increase Potassium

- Severe burns
- Cushing's Disease/Syndrome
- Long-term steroid therapy
- Potassium excreting diuretics and/or digitalis
- Diet lacking potassium-rich foods
- Anorexia
- Vomiting and/or acute/chronic diarrhea
- Laxative abuse
- Nasogastic suction without replacement
- Chronic heart failure
- Cirrhosis
- Primary hyperaldosteronism
- Alkalosis
- Excessive use of insulin

Decrease Potassium

- Hypo-secretion of the adrenal cortex (Addison's Disease)
- Renal disease
- Severe oliguria
- Potassium-sparing diuretics (Aldactone)
- Angiotensin-converting enzyme (ACE) inhibitors
- Metabolic acidosis
- Lack of insulin
- Crushing injuries
- Tissue lysis
- Excessive blood transfusions

Concept Nutrition: Snapshot of Minerals
Calcium (Ca⁺⁺)

FUNCTION

Normal **formation of bone and teeth**

Muscle contraction, especially the heart

Clotting factors

Normal **nerve conduction**

SYSTEM-SPECIFIC ASSESSMENTS

Decreased Levels of Ca⁺⁺
The "Ds"
Drowsy
Decrease in muscle tone
Depressed CNS
Decreased QT interval
Decreased ST segment
Decrease in bowel movement (constipation)

Increased Levels of Ca⁺⁺
"TWITCH"
Trousseau's Sign, tingling
Watch for dysrhythmias: ↑ HR
Increased bowel sounds; diarrhea
Tetany, twitching, tingling seizures; spasms at rest
Chvostek's sign
Hypotension, hyperactive DTR

FOOD SOURCES

"CALCIUM"

Cheese

d**A**iry yogurt

Leafy green vegetable

Cottage cheese

Intake of whole grains

t**U**na and salmon

Milk

NUTRITIONAL COMPARISON WITH MEDICAL CONDITIONS
NUTRITIONAL GUIDELINES (DIETS)

Increase Calcium
- Osteoporosis
- Post-thyroidectomy
- Renal disease
- Hyperphosphatemia
- Hpocalcemia
- Multiple blood transfusions
- Crohn's Disease
- Acute pancreatitis
- Chronic diarrhea
- Hyperaldosteronism
- Diet low in calcium
- Hypoparathyroidism
- Alkalosis
- Lack of Vitamin D

Decrease Calcium
- Thiazide Diuretics
- Cancers that secrete bone-resorbing factors
- Vitamin D or Calcium overdose
- Paget's disease
- Chronic immobility
- Hyperparathyroidism
- Renal calculi
- Hypercalcemia
- Adrenal insufficiency
- Hyperthyroidism

Concept Nutrition: Snapshot of Water-Soluble Vitamins
Vitamin B$_6$

FUNCTION

Stimulates heme production for red blood cells, necessary for antibody formation

Nervous system function

Protein metabolism

FOOD SOURCES

- Organ meats
- Wheat, corn cereal
- Soybeans
- Tuna and salmon
- Chicken

SYSTEM-SPECIFIC ASSESSMENTS

Decreased Levels
- Increased inflammation
- Depression
- Cognitive problems
- Anemia ($\downarrow$ Hgb, Hct)

NUTRITIONAL COMPARISON WITH MEDICAL CONDITIONS
NUTRITIONAL GUIDELINES (DIETS)

Increase Need for Vitamin B$_6$
- Pyridoxine deficiency
- Isoniazid

Decrease Need for Vitamin B$_6$
- Levodopa

I N H (Isoniazid)

I
N
C
R
E
A
S
E   ANTI-TUBERCULIN

Levodopa

L
O
W
E
R   ANTI-PARKINSONISM

Concept Nutrition: Snapshot of Water-Soluble Vitamins
Vitamin B$_9$ (Folic Acid)

FUNCTION

Stimulates production of red and white blood cells and platelets necessary for maintenance of erythropoiesis.

NUTRITIONAL COMPARISON WITH MEDICAL CONDITIONS
NUTRITIONAL GUIDELINES (DIETS)

Increase Need for Vitamin B$_9$
- Inadequate dietary intake
- Macrocytic anemia associated with pregnancy
- Infancy, childhood

Decrease Need for Vitamin B$_9$
- Pernicious Anemia
- Aplastic anemia
- Normocytic anemia

SYSTEM-SPECIFIC ASSESSMENTS (DECREASED)

- Fatigue, poor growth
- Mouth sores
- Gray hair
- Swollen tongue

FOOD SOURCES

- Green leafy vegetables
- Wheat germ
- Liver
- Legumes

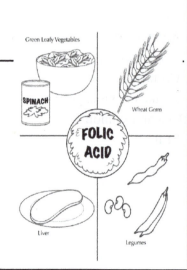

Green Leafy Vegetables

SPINACH

Wheat Germ

FOLIC ACID

Liver

Legumes

Concept Nutrition: Snapshot of Water-Soluble Vitamins
Vitamin B$_{12}$ (Cobalamin)

FUNCTION

Formation of RBCs

Nerve function

Helps make **DNA**

SYSTEM-SPECIFIC ASSESSMENTS

Decreased Levels
- Weakness
- Light-headedness
- ↑ HR and RR
- Sore tongue
- Bruising, bleeding
- Diarrhea or constipation
- Weight loss

NUTRITIONAL COMPARISON WITH MEDICAL CONDITIONS
NUTRITIONAL GUIDELINES (DIETS)

Increase Need for Vitamin B$_{12}$
- Pernicious anemia/lack of intrinsic
- Vitamin B$_{12}$ deficiency
- Thyrotoxicosis
- Hemorrhage
- Renal and/or liver disease

Decrease Need for Vitamin B$_{12}$
- History of allergy to cobalamin
- Folate deficient anemia

FOOD SOURCES
"FISH"

Fish, salmon, tuna

Include milk, soy milk, cheese, eggs

Should eat meat, liver

High-fortified cereals

Concept Nutrition: Snapshot of Water-Soluble Vitamins
Vitamin C (Ascorbic Acid)

FUNCTION

Biosynthesis of collagen (needed for connective tissue for wound healing)

Protein metabolism

Antioxidant, may regenerate other antioxidants

Immune function

Absorption of Iron

SYSTEM-SPECIFIC ASSESSMENTS

Decreased Levels

- Signs of infection, ↑ temp and WBCs
- Bruising
- Fatigue
- Mood swings
- Joint and muscle aches
- Dry skin and hair

NUTRITIONAL COMPARISON WITH MEDICAL CONDITIONS
NUTRITIONAL GUIDELINES (DIETS)

Increase Need for Vitamin C

- Iron supplement (Increases absorption)
- Bleeding tendency/scurvy

Decrease Need for Vitamin C

- Urinary stones

FOOD SOURCES

- Red and green peppers
- Oranges
- Strawberries, Kiwi
- Broccoli, Brussels sprouts

Concept Nutrition: Snapshot of Fat-Soluble Vitamins
Vitamin A

FUNCTION

Need for **vision** (night)

Cell growth in vital organs, skin, hair, and tissues

Immune function

SYSTEM-SPECIFIC ASSESSMENTS

Decreased Levels

- Vision: night blindness
- Dry skin and hair
- Risk for infection ($\uparrow$ Temp, WBCs)

NUTRITIONAL COMPARISON WITH MEDICAL CONDITIONS
NUTRITIONAL GUIDELINES (DIETS)

Increase Need for Vitamin A

- Cystic Fibrosis
- Hepatitis

FOOD SOURCES

- Vitamin B_9 (Folic Acid)
- Diet + don't forget the orange! (Orange: veggies and fruit: sweet potato, carrots, cantaloupe, etc.)

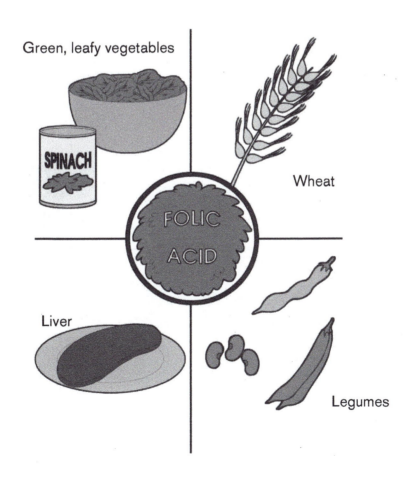

Green, leafy vegetables

SPINACH

Wheat

FOLIC ACID

Liver

Legumes

Concept Nutrition: Snapshot of Fat-Soluble Vitamins
Vitamin D

FUNCTION

Promotes **absorption** and **use of calcium and phosphate** for bones and teeth.

SYSTEM-SPECIFIC ASSESSMENTS

Decreased Levels

- Muscular weakness
- ↑ risk of cardiovascular disease
- ↑ risk periodontal disease (gums, teeth)
- ↓ Cognition, depression

NUTRITIONAL COMPARISON WITH MEDICAL CONDITIONS
NUTRITIONAL GUIDELINES (DIETS)

Increase Need for Vitamin D

- Infants need 400 IU supplements every day, starting at birth.
- Renal disease; hypocalcemia

Decrease Need for Vitamin D

- Hypercalcemia
- Renal stones
- Calcification of soft tissues

FOOD SOURCES

"BONES"

Beef
Organ meat, calf liver
Need cheese
Egg yolks
Salmon, can tuna, soy milk fortified with Vitamin D

Concept Nutrition: Snapshot of Fat-Soluble Vitamins
Vitamin E

FUNCTION

Need for **platelet aggregation**

Immune function

SYSTEM-SPECIFIC ASSESSMENTS

Decreased Levels
- Muscle weakness
- Dry hair and skin
- Decreased healing of wounds
- Leg cramps
- GI upset

NUTRITIONAL COMPARISON WITH MEDICAL CONDITIONS
NUTRITIONAL GUIDELINES (DIETS)

Increase Need for Vitamin E
- Preterm infant may need supplement
- Supplement when used as antioxidant
- Production of normal red blood cells

FOOD SOURCES

- Vitamin B_9 (Folic Acid) diet
- Don't forget the nuts and seeds!

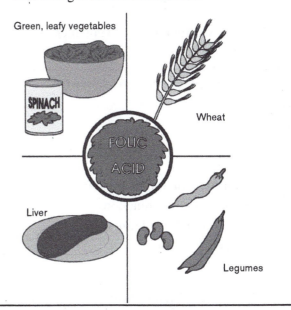

Green, leafy vegetables
SPINACH
FOLIC ACID
Wheat
Liver
Legumes

Concept Nutrition: Snapshot of Fat-Soluble Vitamins
Vitamin K

FUNCTION

Production of prothrombin and **conversion of fibrinogen to fibrin**

Synthesis of proteins found in plasma, bone, and kidneys

SYSTEM-SPECIFIC ASSESSMENTS

Decreased Levels
- Anemia, risk for bleeding
- ↑ Clotting times

FOOD SOURCES
"LEAF"

Leafy green vegetables (spinach, Brussels sprouts)

Eggs

Asparagus

Fiber: Beans and soybeans

NUTRITIONAL COMPARISON WITH MEDICAL CONDITIONS
NUTRITIONAL GUIDELINES (DIETS)

Increase Need for Vitamin K
- Neonate to prevent complications with hemorrhagic disease
- Hypoprothrombinemia
- Vitamin K malabsorption

Decrease Need for Vitamin K
- Warfarin (Coumadin)
- Severe liver disease

BZZZ

Concept Nutrition: Snapshot of Minerals & Therapeutic Diets
Iron

FUNCTION

Synthesis of hemoglobin: prevent anemia

SYSTEM-SPECIFIC ASSESSMENTS

Decreased Levels

- Tired and weak
- Slow cognitive and social development during childhood
- Difficult to maintain body temp
- Decreased immune function
- Glossitis (an inflamed tongue)
- Altered CBC results

NUTRITIONAL COMPARISON WITH MEDICAL CONDITIONS
NUTRITIONAL GUIDELINES (DIETS)

Increase Iron

- Hemodilutional anemia (pregnancy)
- Poor dietary intake
- Iron deficient anemia
- Surgery on gastrointestinal tract
- IV therapy for an extended time

Decrease Iron

- Hemolytic anemia
- Peptic ulcer
- Ulcerative colitis

FOOD SOURCES

"IRON"

Include fish, chicken, eggs, and green leafy vegetables

Raisins, sunflower seeds, and legumes

Organ meats; liver and red meats

Need Vitamin C to absorb iron in diet

Concept Nutrition: Snapshot of Minerals & Therapeutic Diets
Purine

FUNCTION

Key component of DNA

SYSTEM-SPECIFIC ASSESSMENTS

Increased Levels
- Kidney stones
- Gout (high levels of uric acid)

NUTRITIONAL COMPARISON WITH MEDICAL CONDITIONS
NUTRITIONAL GUIDELINES (DIETS)

Do not need to increase Purine

Decrease Purine
- Gout
- High levels of uric acid

FOOD SOURCES

Substitute:
Soy, Almond, Coconut milk

GOUT

Gulp 3 liters fluid per day

Organ meats or wines

Urine output increased to 2 liters per day

Teach

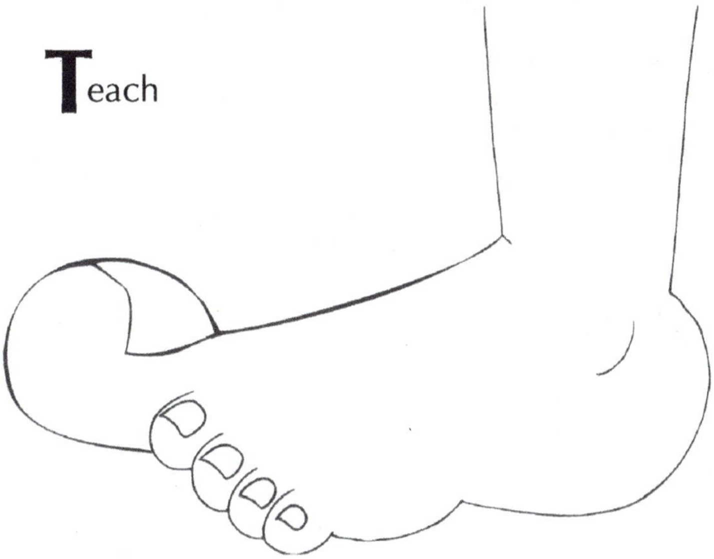

Concept Nutrition: Snapshot of Minerals & Therapeutic Diets
Residue (Fiber)—High

FUNCTION

Assists to move food through the digestive system and prevent constipation.

SYSTEM-SPECIFIC ASSESSMENTS

Increased Levels
- Gas
- Bloating
- Decrease absorption of minerals

FOOD SOURCES
"Hi Res"

High intake of lentils, split peas, beans
Include artichokes

Raspberries, pears, apples
Eat whole grains, bran
Sunflower seeds

Note: With Diverticulosis, stay away from foods with indigestible fibers (i.e., celery, whole corn; seeds: sesame & poppy; foods with small seeds).

NUTRITIONAL COMPARISON WITH MEDICAL CONDITIONS
NUTRITIONAL GUIDELINES (DIETS)

Increase Residue
- Constipation
- Diverticulosis
- Irritable bowel (IBS)
- Taking Iron supplement
- Anticholinergics,
- Antidepressants
- Many medications Calcium channel blockers
- Diverticulosis: Stay away from foods with indigestible fibers (i.e., celery, whole corn; seeds: sesame & poppy; foods with small seeds)

Decrease Residue
- Use with Diverticulitis, *refer to chart below!*

Concept Nutrition: Snapshot of Minerals & Therapeutic Diets
Residue (Fiber)—Low

FUNCTION

Slow down digestive process, bowel rest.

SYSTEM-SPECIFIC ASSESSMENTS

Decreased Levels
- Frequent stools and diarrhea
- Constipation
- Weight gain

FOOD SOURCES
"LO RES"

Limited fat
Omit milk

Real fresh fish, ground meat
Eggs boiled
Strained foods

NUTRITIONAL COMPARISON WITH MEDICAL CONDITIONS
NUTRITIONAL GUIDELINES (DIETS)

Increase Residue
- Diverticulosis: Stay away from foods with indigestible fibers (i.e., celery, whole corn; seeds: sesame & poppy; foods with small seeds)

Decrease Residue
- Crohn's disease
- Gastric intestinal irritations or infections
- Before and/or after surgery
- Diverticulitis
- Ulcerative colitis

Concept Nutrition: Snapshot of Minerals & Therapeutic Diets
Lactose-Free

FUNCTION

Prevent GI effects of lactose intolerance.
Develops when small intestine does not make
enough lactase enzyme needed to digest lactose.

SYSTEM-SPECIFIC ASSESSMENTS

- Bloating, pain or cramps in the lower belly.
- Abdominal pain occurs 30 minutes to 2 hours
  after eating or drinking any food that contains
  lactose.

FOOD SOURCES

Nonmilk products, yogurt

NUTRITIONAL COMPARISON WITH MEDICAL CONDITIONS
NUTRITIONAL GUIDELINES (DIETS)

Increase Lactose

Decrease Lactose

- Prevent GI effects of lactose intolerance

Concept Nutrition: Snapshot of Minerals & Therapeutic Diets
Gluten-Free

FUNCTION

Gluten is a protein composite found in wheat,
barley, and rye.

SYSTEM-SPECIFIC ASSESSMENTS

- Diarrhea
- Abdominal pain
- Bloating

FOOD SOURCES

NO Barley, Rye, Oat, Wheat

Corn and Rice okay

NUTRITIONAL COMPARISON WITH MEDICAL CONDITIONS
NUTRITIONAL GUIDELINES (DIETS)

Increase Gluten

Decrease Gluten

- Want client on a Gluten FREE Diet:
- Celiac Disease
- Gastritis

CELIAC DIET

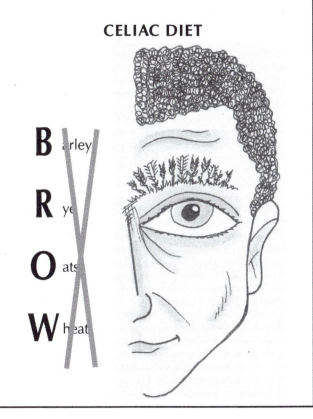

B arley
R ye
O ats
W heat

System/Diseases Specific Diet Needs	
RENAL DIET	**Monitor** • Sodium • Potassium • Protein level (*Refer to concept Renal Perfusion chapter for specifics*).
HEALTHY HEART DIET	**Monitor and Maintain to keep levels WDL or lower as prescribed:** • Fat • Sodium • Triglycerides • Cholesterol (*Refer to concept Cardiac/Peripheral Perfusion for specifics*)
LIVER DIET	**Monitor & base on individual nutritional deficits.** • Malnourishment can be comprehensive, nutritional analysis needed • Monitor labs and weight • Clinical findings (*Refer to concept Liver Metabolism chapter for specifics*)

Protein / Calorie Malnutrition		
	System-Specific Physiology	**Outcomes**
MARASMUS • Result of deficiency of caloric and protein intake	• **Carbohydrates** used first • Depleted within 18 hours • **Amino Acids** used by liver for formation of glucose. Also used as energy source • Puts person in negative nitrogen balance that lasts about 5–9 days	• Synthesis of new plasma proteins is $\downarrow$ • Albumin $\downarrow \rightarrow \downarrow$ in osmotic pressure • Edema becomes visible • *Ascites (contains large amounts of protein) (classic sign in Kwashiorkor) • $NA^+ - K^+$ pump fails results:
	Body Fat Mobilized After 5–9 Days • 97% of calories are provided by fat, in prolong starvation used up in 4–6 weeks (depending on amount of fat there was to start with)	• Liver becomes infiltrated with fat • Death will occur without needed nutrients
KWASHIORKOR • Deficiency of protein superimposed on a catabolic stress event	**Protein Is Used When Fat Is Gone** • Used up rapidly for energy • Liver function becomes impaired	

A Snapshot of What You Need to Know for Other Therapeutic Diets
Eating Disorder: Anorexia Nervosa

DESCRIPTION

An eating disorder that occurs from an intense fear of gaining weight and/or becoming obese. The client has a need of perfectionism and control and has a disturbance of body image.

SYSTEM-SPECIFIC ASSESSMENTS

Decreased Levels
- Weight and electrolyte balance are the best assessment tools for this disorder.
- With malnourishment, electrolyte imbalance, particularly hypokalemia, is a frequent cause of death with this disease.
- Assess self-image, and family interactions & support.
- Refeeding syndrome can result if system is replenished too quickly, leading to cardiovascular collapse

FOODS

- If client is unable or unwilling to maintain adequate oral intake, a liquid diet may be administered through a nasogastric tube.
- Consult with dietician and determine number of calories required to provide adequate nutrition and realistic weight.
- Limit of 30 minutes should be allotted for time for meals.
- Observe 1 hour after meals. Offer reinforcement and support for obvious improvements in eating behaviors.

S imply won't eat

T ype A personality

A menorrhea

R un–extreme exercise

V icious cycle–lifetime

E lectrolyte imbalance; (low–blood hemoglobin test)
↓ Na
↓ K
↓ Ca
↓ Cl

A Snapshot of What You Need to Know for Other Therapeutic Diets
Eating Disorder: Bulimia Nervosa

DESCRIPTION

Recurrent episodes of binge eating. Secretive binge eating and purging behaviors (diuretics, laxatives, excessive exercise).

Recurrent episodes of binge eating. Russell's sign-calluses of bruises on the thumb or hand caused by trauma from self-induced vomiting.

Erosion of tooth enamel or pharyngitis may occur.

Self-induced vomiting and depressed mood after eating binge.

SYSTEM-SPECIFIC ASSESSMENTS

Decreased Levels
- Auscultate breath sounds and check for edema.
- If syrup of ipecac is used to induce vomiting, the absorption of the ipecac can lead to cardiotoxcity and heart failure.
- Weight and electrolyte balance are the best assessment tools for this disorder.
- With malnourishment, electrolyte imbalance, particularly hypokalemia, is a frequent cause of death with this disease.

FOODS

- The problem is far more than about food. It is typically about a low self-esteem and body image.
- Help client develop realistic perceptions of body image and relationship with food.
- Encourage feeling of control within environment.
- Assist client to understand perfection is a myth.

S hove it in

T ooth enamel is destroyed

U pchuck

F ull weight

F ear of fat

Clinical Decision-Making Exercises

1. Which of these statements, if made by a client with oliguric renal failure, would indicate a need for further teaching?
   ① "I will only drink 2 glasses of canned tomato juice per day."
   ② "I must limit the amount of salt I eat."
   ③ "I won't eat pickles and green olive anymore."
   ④ "I will eat fresh fruits and vegetables."

2. During a teaching session, which of these foods should the nurse include when discussing foods that are good sources of iron. *Select all that apply.*
   ① Beans
   ② Dried fruit
   ③ Spinach
   ④ Tuna fish
   ⑤ Yogurt

3. Which food selection by the client would indicate to the nurse that the client needs further education regarding meal planning and menu selections about important restriction in chronic renal failure (CRF)?
   ① Jell-O
   ② Baked potato
   ③ Angel food cake
   ④ Oreo cookies

4. Which food selection indicates compliance for a client with cardiac disease?
   ① Baked fish, vegetable casserole, avocado salad.
   ② Baked ham, rice, and fruit cup.
   ③ Hamburger, cup of canned soup, and lettuce salad.
   ④ Baked chicken, green vegetables, and fresh fruit.

5. Which statement made by a client with a diagnosis of diverticulosis who is recovering from an episode of diverticulitis indicates a need for further teaching prior to discharge?
   ① "I will eat more raw fruits and vegetables in my diet."
   ② "I will eat more whole corn and celery in my diet."
   ③ "I will decrease my intake of fat and red meat."
   ④ "I will increase my activity such as more walking and exercise."

Answers and Rationales

1. Which of these statements, if made by a client with oliguric **renal failure**, would indicate a need for **further teaching**?

    ① INCORRECT: "I will eat fresh fruits and vegetables." Correct; no need for action.

    ② INCORRECT: "I must limit the amount of salt I eat." Correct statement.

    ③ INCORRECT: "I won't eat pickles and green olives anymore." Correct statement.

    ④ **CORRECT: "I will only drink 2 glasses of orange juice per day." High in K⁺.**

The strategy is to understand that in renal failure the sodium and potassium should be decreased. Option 4 is correct. Canned orange juice is high in potassium and could lead to hyperkalemia in clients with renal failure. This must be clarified with the client and more teaching must occur. Options 1, 2, and 3 indicate an understanding by the client of the need to limit sodium intake. Refer to the memory tool, **"TOES"** that will help in transferring the foods high in potassium into your long-term memory! This will apply to any client who needs low potassium diet. *Refer to chart reviewing "A Snapshot of What You Need to Know for Nutrition".*

Basic Care and Comfort: Manage the client's nutritional intake.

2. During a teaching session, which of these foods should the nurse include when discussing foods that are **good sources of iron**. Select all that apply.

    ① **CORRECT: Beans. High in iron.**

    ② **CORRECT: Dried fruit. High in iron.**

    ③ **CORRECT: Spinach. High in iron.**

    ④ **CORRECT: Tuna fish. High in iron.**

    ⑤ INCORRECT: Yogurt. Low in iron.

The strategy is to remember the foods high in iron. Refer to image on the chart, "Reviewing system-specific assessments that reflect nutritional deficits/excess and illustrated images" to assist you in remembering these foods. Options 1, 2, 3 and 4 are correct. These are high in iron. Option 5 is not high in iron. This strategy will apply to any client who needs a diet high in iron. *Refer to chart reviewing "A Snapshot of What You Need to Know for Nutrition".* A few additional examples may include: poor dietary intake and iron deficient anemia.

Basic Care and Comfort: Manage the client's nutritional intake.

3. Which **food selection** by the client would indicate to the nurse that the client needs **further education** regarding meal planning and menu selections about important restriction in chronic **renal failure** (CRF)?

    ① INCORRECT: Jell-O. No need for further teaching.

    ② **CORRECT: Baked potato. High in potassium.**

    ③ INCORRECT: Angel food cake. No need for further teaching.

    ④ INCORRECT: Oreo cookies. No need for further teaching.

The strategy is to know that clients in renal failure should not eat foods high in potassium. This can be remembered by reviewing the **"TOES"**. Remember : pota**TOES**, avocad**TOES**, tomoa**TOES**, banana**TOES**, and orange**TOES** (We stretched the spelling, but you get the point!) This will apply to any client who needs a low potassium diet. *Refer to chart reviewing "A Snapshot of What You Need to Know for Nutrition".* Notice the similarity with question #1; just a different food. Remember, repetition is the mother of learning.

Basic Care and Comfort: Manage the client's nutritional intake.

4. Which **food selection indicates** compliance for a client with **cardiac disease?**

    ① INCORRECT: Baked fish, vegetable casserole, avocado salad. A food ↑ in fat.

    ② INCORRECT: Baked ham, rice, and fruit cup. A food ↑ in sodium.

    ③ INCORRECT: Hamburger, cup of canned soup, and lettuce salad. Soup ↑ sodium.

    ④ **CORRECT: Baked chicken, green vegetables, and fresh fruit. Low sodium.**

The strategy is to remember foods high in sodium should not be included in the diet for client with cardiac disease. Remember these foods high in sodium can be anything in a bag, box, can or bottle. If it is natural, most likely it is low in sodium. Option 4 is correct. A cardiac diet is low cholesterol/fat, and low sodium. These foods are fresh, baked, and not high in fat, cholesterol, and/or sodium Option #1 is incorrect since the avocado is high in fat (150 Gms serving has 22 Gms of fat). Option 2 is incorrect due to the ham being high in sodium. Option 3 is incorrect since the hamburger is red meat, which is high in cholesterol, and canned soup is high in sodium. This will apply to any client who needs a low sodium diet. *Refer to chart reviewing "A Snapshot of What You Need to Know for Nutrition".* A few additional examples may include: renal disease, hypernatremia, Cushing's disease/syndrome, etc.

Basic Care and Comfort: Manage the client's nutritional intake.

5. Which **statement** made by a client with a diagnosis of **diverticulosis** who is recovering from an episode of diverticulitis indicates a **need for further teaching** prior to discharge?

    teaching.

    ① INCORRECT: "I will eat more raw fruits and vegetables in my diet."

    ② **CORRECT: "I will eat more whole corn and celery in my diet."**

    ③ INCORRECT: "I will decrease my intake of fat and red meat."

    ④ INCORRECT: "I will increase my activity such as more walking and exercise."

The strategy in answering this question is to link the diverticulitis with the dietary need for high residue (fiber) and the importance of not eating indigestible fibers and foods with seeds. Option 2 is correct. The goal for diverticulosis is to prevent constipation with the high fiber diet and prevent acute diverticulitis. Foods restricted for prevention of acute diverticulitis include: indigestible fibers; celery, whole corn; seeds such as sesame and poppy; foods with small seeds. These may precipitate diverticulitis, but they do not contribute to the development of diverticula. This statement indicates a need for further teaching. Option 1 is incorrect. There is no need to do further teaching since this would indeed be included in the care of this medical condition. High-carbohydrate foods that are high in residue (fiber) are included in the plan of care for clients with diverticulosis. Option 3 is incorrect since this is part of the management of uncomplicated diverticulum. Option 4 is incorrect since this is also included in the management.

The stem of the question asks, "Which statement indicates a need for further teaching". If you misread the question, your clue was that several of these options include the appropriate diet for this medical condition. Since this is not a select all that apply question, then you would know that there is only one correct answer. Another key to answering this question is to remember the foods that are restricted on the diet for these clients with diverticulosis.

Basic Care and Comfort: Manage the client's nutritional intake.

Decision-Making Analysis Form

Use this tool to help identify why you missed any questions. As you enter the question numbers in the chart, you will begin to see patterns of why you answered incorrectly. This information will then guide you toward what you need to focus on in your continued studies. Ultimately, this analytical exercise will help you become more successful in answering questions!!!

Questions to ask:

1. Did I have the knowledge to answer the question? If not, what information do I need to review?
2. Did I know what the question was asking? Did I misread it or did I miss keywords in the stem of the question?
3. Did I misread or miss keywords in the distractors that would have helped me choose the correct answer?
4. Did I follow my gut reaction or did I allow myself to rationalize and then choose the wrong answer?

	Lack of Knowledge (Concepts, Systems, Pathophysiology, Medications, Procedures, etc.)	Missed Keywords or Misread the Stem of the Question	Missed Keywords or Misread the Distractors	Changed My Answer (Second-guessed myself, i.e., my first answer was correct.)
Put the # of each question you missed in the column that best explains why you think you answered it incorrectly.				

If you changed an answer because you talked yourself out of the correct answer, or you second-guessed yourself, this is an **EASY FIX: QUIT changing your answers**!!! Typically, the first time you read a question, you are about 95% right! The second time you read a question, you start talking yourself into changing the answer. The third time you read a question, you do not have a clue—and you are probably thinking "Who in the heck wrote this question?"

On the other hand, if you read a question too quickly and when you reread it you realize you missed some key information that would impact your decision (i.e., assessments, lab reports, medications, etc.), then it is appropriate to change your answer. When in doubt, go with the safe route: your first thought! Go with your gut instinct!

As you gain confidence in answering questions regarding specific nursing concepts, you will be able to successfully progress to answering higher-level questions about prioritization. Please refer to the *Prioritization Guidelines* in this book for a structure to assist you with this process.

You CAN do this!

> *"We are kept from our goal, not by obstacles but by a clear path to a lesser goal."*
>
> ROBERT BRAULT

References for Chapter 24

American Heart Association. (2014). *Sodium and salt.* Retrieved from http://www.heart.org/HEARTORG/GettingHealthy/NutritionCenter/HealthyDietGoals/Sodium-Salt-or-Sodium-Chloride_UCM_303290_Article.jsp

American Heart Association (2014). The american heart association's diet and lifestyle recommendations. Retrieved from http://www.heart.org/HEARTORG/GettingHealthy/HealthyEating/Diet-and-Lifestyle-Recommendations_UCM_305855_Article.jsp

Black, J M. & Hawks, J.H. (2009). *Medical surgical nursing: Clinical management for positive outcomes* (8th ed.). Philadelphia: Elsevier/Saunders.

Daniels, R. & Nicoll, L. (2012). *Contemporary medical-surgical nursing,* (2nd ed.). Clifton Park, NY: Delmar Cengage Learning.

Eliopoulos, C. (2014). *Gerontological nursing* (8th ed.), Philadelphia: Lippincott Williams & Wilkins.

Giddens, G. F. (2013). *Concepts for nursing practice.* St. Louis, MO: Mosby, an imprint of Elsevier.

Healthy People 2020. (2014). Retrieved from http://www.healthypeople.gov/2020/topicsobjectives2020/overview.aspx?topicid=29

Hogan, M. A., Gingrich, M. M., Willcutts, K. & DeLeon, E. (2006). *Nutrition and diet therapy* (2nd ed). Upper Saddle River, New Jersey: Prentice Hall.

Manning, L. & Rayfield, S. (2013). *Nursing made insanely easy.* Duluth, GA.: ICAN Publishing, Inc.

Manning, L. and Rayfield, S. (2013). *Pharmacology made insanely easy* (4th ed.). Duluth, GA: I CAN Publishing, Inc.

National Council of State Boards of Nursing, INC. (NCSBN) 2012. *Research brief: 2011 RN practice analysis: linking the NCLEX RN® examination to practice.* Retrieved from https://www.ncsbn.org/index.htm

North Carolina Concept Based Learning Editorial Board (2011). *Nursing a concept based approach to learning,* Upper Saddle Road, NJ: Pearson/Prentice Hall.

Tucker, S.B. & Dauffenbach, V. (2011). *Nutrition and diet therapy for nurses.* Upper Saddle River, New Jersey: Pearson.

NOTES

CHAPTER 25

Linking Multiple Systems and Concepts
Concept Pain

A Snapshot of Pain

Pain, as defined by the American Pain Society, is "an unpleasant sensory and emotional experience associated with actual or potential tissue damage" (2010). Pain can be classified according to timeline (acute or chronic) or cause (nociceptive or neuropathic). Acute pain can be directly related to tissue damage and generally dissipates when the tissue damage is resolved. Chronic pain is pain that extends past the reasonably expected timeline based on an injury, (generally lasts longer than six months). Some disorders may have characteristics of both chronic and acute pain (i.e., back pain, etc.). The nociceptive pain comes from the Latin word *nocere*, 'to injure,' and results from injury to tissues. Neuropathic pain occurs when the sensory nerves themselves are damaged or dysfunctional (Porth, 2011). Intractable pain (i.e., nerve compression, malignancy, etc.) is resistant to pain treatment or management (Daniels & Nicoll, 2012). Below is a chart of the most frequent disorders that result in "Pain."

The Pathophysiology Behind Pain

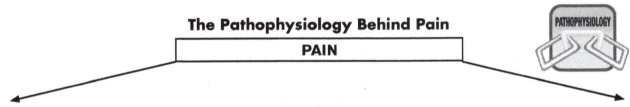

Nociception Pain		Neuropathic Pain Pain when there is direct injury to a peripheral nerve, the spinal cord or brain.		
Somatic Pain when nerves from skin, tissue, bones, muscle & blood vessels are activated	**Visceral** Pain involving the internal organs or body cavity lings, (i.e., lungs, heart, abdomen, organ metastasis, etc.)	**Centrally Generated Pain**	**Peripherally Generated Pain**	**Mixed Pain**
•Arthritic pain •Surgical pain •Wound pain •Burn pain	•Inflammatory bowel diseases (i.e., Crohn's, ulcerative colitis, etc.) •Cancer pain involving organs •Biliary diseases (i.e., pancreatitis, cholecystitis, etc.)	•Injury to spinal cord •Peripheral nerve injury (resulting in phantom pain) •Pain following a cerebral vascular accident	•Neuropathies (i.e., nutritional deficits from alcohol, diabetes, etc.) •Neuralgia (postherpetic from shingles caused by varicella zoster virus) •Cranial nerve 5 (Trigeminal pain) •Guillain-Barré syndrome	•Some headaches •Some types of neck, shoulder and back pain •Fibromyalgia •Myofascial pain •Pain associated with human immunodeficiency virus (HIV)

Multiple Systems: Pain

System-Specific Assessments: Pain

"PQRST"

It is well established that the client's report of pain is the best information the healthcare team can use in managing the client's pain. Below are questions to obtain information needed to develop an effective individualized plan of care for pain management (American Society for Pain Management Nursing, 2010).

Assess:

- Pain history (i.e., prior experience with pain, what has relieved pain in the past, etc.)
- Vital signs
- Non-verbal cues (i.e., restlessness, verbal moaning, muscle tension, facial expression, etc.)

"PQRST"

Provokes: What causes pain? What alleviates the pain?

Quality: How does it feel? What is effect of pain on function & quality of life?

Radiates: Where is the pain and does the pain radiate to another location?

Severity/Intensity: How severe is the pain based on age appropriate pain scale? (i.e., Visual Analog Scale, Numeric Rating Scale, FACES Pain Scale, etc.).

Time: When did the pain start? Is it constant or intermittent?

Multiple Systems: Pain

System-Specific Assessments: Pain

Types of Pain Scales

Pain scales are an objective way to help the client describe their pain to facilitate a plan of care for effective pain management. The pain scale should be chosen that will best fit the individual needs and developmental age of the client.

VISUAL ANALOG SCALE (VAS)	NUMERIC RATING SCALE (NRS)	FACES PAIN SCALE REVISED FACES PAIN RATING SCALE:	THE BEHAVIOR PAIN RATING SCALE (BPS)
It is a line (10 cm) in length with the words "No Pain" at one end and at the other end, the words "Worst Pain Imaginable." The client indicates where on the line their pain is. The line can have numeric value points on it. No Pain_____ Worst Pain Imaginable	A scale of 0–10. 0 = no pain 10 = the most intense, worst pain	Word descriptions under 6 faces. Smiling face = no pain Frowning tearful face = worst pain The faces are numbered 0, 2, 4, 6, 8 and 10. The faces with 0 = no pain to 10 = worst pain. Pain scale is reliable for use with children and adults.	A reliable assessment tool for moderately to deeply sedated clients because the three measurements do not require client cooperation or communication. Behaviors are: • Restlessness • Muscle tension • Facial expression • Vocalization • Wound guarding Behaviors are given a 0 to 2 rating with 2 being the worst.

(Wagner & Hardin-Pierce, 2014)

Linking Pathophysiology to System-Specific Assessments

PAIN

Pathophysiology	System-Specific Assessments "PQRST"
Assessment of pain, as stated by the client is subjective. Objective data is from specific questions, assessments and numeric scales. The client's pain history provides information of how the client has handled pain in the past and what has been effective. It is important to know if there were negative experiences that could increase anxiety and lessen the effect of the pain medication and or other alternative pain relief measures. Some clients are stoic and do not want to admit they are in pain, or are afraid of becoming "*addicted*" to the pain medication. The vital signs provide a physiological measure of pain; HR, RR and BP may all ↑ with pain. Other clinical findings may be diaphoresis, restlessness, altered facial expressions, withdrawal, and/or refusal to interact. The client's family/friends can provide insight if this is the client's normal behavior.	**Assess:** • Pain history (i.e., prior experience with pain, what has relieved pain in the past, etc.) • Vital signs • Non-verbal cues (i.e., restlessness, verbal moaning, muscle tension, facial expression, etc.)
Provokes: what provokes or causes pain helps to know how to prevent pain. Pain medication should be given prior to a painful intervention, such as burn care. All pain medications do not work the same on everyone; asking what has worked in the past is helpful in planning care. Alternative methods, (i.e., listening to music, meditation, prayer, etc.) can help with pain relief and may be used with pain medication.	**Provokes:** what causes pain? What alleviates the pain?
Quality of pain can only be described and answered by the client. It is a subjective, but very important part of the pain assessment. The impact of pain on the quality of life can decrease the client's response to treatment, decrease the client's mood, and lead to depression which further decreases the chance of a positive response to pain treatments; it can become a viscous cycle.	**Quality:** How does it feel? What is effect of pain on function & quality of life?
Radiation of the pain description by the client helps determine if the pain is localized or is following a nerve route. Nerve root pain comes from a nerve in the spine and carries messages about the pain to the muscles and can cause numbness and weakness of the muscle. The pain can be felt in other areas of the body supplied by that nerve.	**Radiates:** Where is the pain and does the pain radiate to another location?
Severity of the pain varies in clients because of the neuro-biopsychological nature of pain. Self-reporting of pain is necessary to manage pain effectively. It is also a subjective measure because clients have different perspectives about the severity level of their pain. Pain assessment tools add an objective perspective about the pain.	**Severity/Intensity:** How severe is the pain based on age appropriate pain scale? (i.e., Visual Analog Scale, Numeric Rating Scale, FACES Pain Scale, etc.)
Time when the pain started again is a subjective measure given by the client. The client can describe if the pain is constant, never lets up or is intermittent. Vital sign changes provide objective data, (i.e., ↑ HR, RR, & BP, etc.).	**Time:** When did the pain start? Is it constant or intermittent?

Pain

Common Labs, Diagnostic Tests, Therapeutic Procedures/Surgeries

Labs	Diagnostic Tests	Therapeutic Procedures
• CBC • Electrolytes • Liver enzymes • BUN & Creatinine • Urinalysis • ESR	• X-rays • Computerized Tomography Exam (CT) • Magnetic Resonance Imaging (MRI) • Myelogram • Ultrasounds • Electromyelogram (EMG)	• Lumbar puncture • Thoracentesis • Paracentesis • Biopsy • Diagnostic nerve block

Medications and the Elderly

"CONFUSION"

Elderly clients require careful monitoring with pain medication. Remember the mnemonic "**CONFUSION**" because that may be the result! It is all about **SAFETY**!!

CNS depressants should be used with caution.

Often require less medication to achieve pain relief.

Need to take history of all prescription medications, over-the-counter medications (OTC), alcohol, caffeine, and tobacco use.

Fluids: ↓ body water = ↓ blood level of water-soluble drugs.

Use and take more medications, increasing the risk of drug-drug interactions.

Sustained and prolonged effects of fat-soluble drugs due to ↓ body fat and distribution of fat tissue.

Impaired vision and memory increase chance of incorrect dosage.

Observe for drug toxicity because the elderly vary in capacity to absorb, metabolize and excrete drugs.

Need easy to open medication bottles due to impaired agility.

Multiple Systems: Concept Pain
Common Medications for Pharmacologic Pain Management

The list below includes some of the more commonly prescribed pain medications. We recommend you learn these more-commonly prescribed medications (refer to the book *Pharmacology Made Insanely Easy* for specifics). It is always a priority to know potential adverse effects prior to administering the drug.

ANTI-INFLAMMATORY AGENTS
Nonsteroidal Anti-Inflammatory (NSAIDS)
- Diclofenac (Voltaren)
- Ibuprofen (Advil, Motrin)
- Indomethacin (Indocin)
- Ketorolac (Toradol)
- Meloxicam (Mobic)
- Naproxen (Aleve, Naprosyn)
- Oxaprozin (Daypro)
- Piroxicam (Feldene)
- Etodolac (Lodine)

Nonsteroidal Anti-Inflammatory (Cox$_2$ Inhibitors)
- Celecoxib (Celebrex)
- Valdecoxib (Bextra)

Acetaminophen (Tylenol)

CORTICOIDSTEROIDS
- Prednisone (Deltasone)
- Cortisone
- Dexamethasone
- Methylprednisolone (Medrol, Depo Medrol, Solu Medrol)

Muscle Relaxants
- Baclofen (Lioresal)
- Carisoprodol (Soma)
- Cyclobenzaprine (Flexeril)
- Chlorzoxazone (Parafon Forte)

OPIOID ANALGESICS
- Acetaminophen with Codiene (Tylenol 2, 3,4)
- Fentanyl Transdermal Patches (Duragesic)
- Hydrocodone with Acetaminophen (Lortab Elixir, Vicodan)
- Hydrocodone with Ibuprofen (Vicoprofen)
- Meperidine (Demerol, Merpergan)
- Morphine and Morphine Sustained Release (MS-Contin)
- Oxycodone (Roxicodone)
- Oxycodone Sustained Relief (MS-Contin)
- Oxycodone with Aspirin (Percodan)
- Oxycodone with Acetomenophen (Percocet)
- Pentazocine (Talwin)
- Propoxyphene (Darvon)

ANALGESIC (CENTRALLY ACTING)
- Tramadol (Ralivia, Ultram, Ultram ER)

TOPICAL ANALGESICS
- Trolamine salicylate (Aspercreme)
- Capsaicin (Axsain, Capsin)

NONOPIOID ANALEGESIC
- Pregabalin (Lyrica)

Anxiolytics
- Alprazolam (Xanax)
- Diazepam (Valium)
- Lorazepam (Ativan)
- Triazolam (Halcion)

OPIOID REVERSAL AGENT
- Naloxone (Narcan)

Pain: First-Do Priority Interventions

"RELIEF"

The Joint Commission standard on pain management states:

- "Recognize the right of patients to appropriate assessment and management of pain.
- Screen patients for pain during their initial assessment and, when clinically required, during ongoing, periodic re-assessments.
- Educate patients suffering from pain and their families about pain management." (Joint Commission, 2014).

Pain management is a PRIORITY!

R   Report and review trends in vital signs indicative of pain, ↑ HR, ↑ RR, ↑ BP. Document evaluation of pain.

E   Evaluate pain every hour or per protocol, use pain scales appropriate for age. Document evaluation of pain.

L   Look & document behaviors that may indicate pain, (i.e., stillness, restlessness, constant mobility, altered facial expressions, crying, and/or ↓ attention span, etc.).

I   Intervene with appropriate medications for pain as prescribed.

Initiate use of non-pharmacologic interventions when appropriate; ice for damaged tissues that are inflamed, red, hot and swollen; heat for mild pain relief, muscles, muscle spasms or knots. Mind-body therapies (i.e., music, prayer, relaxation techniques, pet therapy, etc.).

E   Evaluate vital signs after pain medication is given, especially with opioid medications. Monitor for ↓ HR, BP, RR, and quality of respirations (i.e., depth & regularity, etc.) & for ↓ SaO_2 sat. Administer Naloxone (Narcan) as prescribed if severe respiratory depression develops; have emergency equipment at bedside.

F   Follow-up to see if pain is relieved within 30 minutes. If not, report to HCP; document pain medication administration and client's response to the pain medication or non-pharmacologic intervention.

First-Do Priority Interventions

PAIN

Pathophysiology	First-Do Priority Interventions "RELIEF"
Report and Review Trends: The vital signs provide a physiological measure about the pain; heart rate, respiratory rate and blood pressure may all elevate with pain; assess associated diaphoresis, restlessness, and facial expression changes.	**R**eport and review trends in vital signs indicative of pain, ↑ HR, ↑ RR, ↑ BP. Document evaluation of pain.
Evaluate pain frequently is a proactive approach to pain management. Clients who are in pain often do not move in an attempt to control the pain. The immobility leads to decreased perfusion that can result in deep vein thrombosis or pulmonary complications (i.e., atelectasis or pneumonia, etc.).	**E**valuate pain every hour or per protocol, use pain scales appropriate for age. Document evaluation of pain.
Look for behaviors that can indicate pain. It is particularly important for non-verbal clients or clients who do not want to admit they are experiencing pain.	**L**ook & document behaviors that may indicate pain, (i.e., stillness, restlessness, constant mobility, altered facial expressions, crying, and/or ↓ attention span, etc.).
Intervene with a preventive approach where analgesics are given before the client complains is effective when pain is occurring regularly over a 24-hour period. An around the clock approach (ATC) is more effective than administering pain meds PRN. Offering pain medication is also more effective than the client having to request pain medication because the client may wait until the pain is severe before requesting medication. Effective pain management can be enhanced with combination of opioid and nonopioid therapy, i.e., acetaminophen, aspirin and NSAIDS particularly. Adjuvant therapy can also assist in reducing certain types of pain by decreasing other symptoms associated with the underlying condition (Wagner & Hardin-Pierce, (2014). Remember to ask the client about the effectiveness of alternative methods, (i.e., listening to music, meditation, prayer, etc.).	**I**ntervene with appropriate medications for pain as prescribed. **I**nitiate use of non-pharmacologic interventions when appropriate; ice for damaged tissues that are inflamed, red, hot and swollen; heat for mild pain relief, muscles, muscle spasms or cramps. Mind-body therapies (i.e., music, prayer, relaxation techniques, pet therapy, etc.)
Evaluate vital signs for decreasing respiratory rate and quality of respirations (i.e., depth and regularity, etc.), SaO$_2$ sat, heart rate or blood pressure. The observation should focus on the client's response to the opioid medication, as sedation usually develops before respiratory depression. Monitoring for oversedation is a better guide for respiratory depression especially with the first dose. Any oversedation should be documented and reported to the HCP. The use of a standard assessment for opioid oversedation is best practice. Commonly used scales are the Pasero Opioid-Induced Sedation Scale (POSS), the Richmond Agitation and Sedation Scale (RASS) and the Aldret (a scale used often in postoperative care units). Document evaluation.	**E**valuate vital signs after pain medication is given, especially with opioid medications. Monitor for ↓ HR, BP, RR, and quality of respirations (i.e., depth & regularity, etc.) & ↓ SaO$_2$ sat. Administer Naloxone (Narcan) as prescribed if severe respiratory depression develops; have emergency equipment at bedside.
Follow-up assessment to see if pain is relieved is a required intervention. This also allows the nurse to be an advocate for a client in pain if the pain medication is not effective. It also provides an opportunity to teach the client and/or family about effective pain management.	**F**ollow-up to see if pain is relieved within 30 minutes. If not, report to HCP; document pain medication administration and client's response to the pain medication or non-pharmacologic intervention.

SAFETY Concept: Pain

System-Specific Assessments "PQRST"	First-Do Priority Interventions "RELIEF"	Evaluation of Expected Outcomes
Assess: • Pain history (i.e., prior experience with pain, what has relieved pain in the past, etc.) • Vital Signs • Non-verbal cues (i.e., restlessness, verbal moaning, muscle tension, facial expression, etc.) **P**rovokes: what causes pain? What alleviates the pain? **Q**uality: How does it feel? What is effect of pain on function & quality of life? **R**adiates: Where is the pain and does the pain radiate to another location? **S**everity/Intensity: How severe is the pain based on age appropriate pain scale? (i.e., Visual Analog Scale, Numeric Rating Scale, FACES Pain Scale, etc.) **T**ime: When did the pain start? Is it constant or intermittent?	**R**eport and review trends in vital signs indicative of pain, ↑HR, ↑RR, ↑BP. Document evaluation of pain. **E**valuate pain every hour or per protocol, use pain scales appropriate for age. Document evaluation of pain. **L**ook & document behaviors that may indicate pain, (i.e., stillness, restlessness, constant mobility, altered facial expressions, crying, and/or ↓ attention span, etc.). **I**ntervene with appropriate medications for pain as prescribed. **I**nitiate use of non-pharmacologic interventions when appropriate; ice for damaged tissues that are inflamed, red, hot and swollen; heat for mild pain relief, muscles, muscle spasms or cramps. Mind-body therapies (i.e., music, prayer, relaxation techniques, pet therapy, etc.) **E**valuate vital signs after pain medication is given, especially with opioid medications. Monitor for ↓HR, BP, RR, and quality of respirations (i.e., depth & regularity, etc.) & ↓ SaO_2 sat. Administer Naloxone (Narcan) as prescribed if severe respiratory depression develops; have emergency equipment at bedside. **F**ollow-up to see if pain is relieved within 30 minutes. If not, report to HCP; document pain medication administration and client's response to the pain medication or non-pharmacologic intervention.	NO Pain or pain managed with pain medication or alternative therapies: • Communicates "**PQRST**" and/or other pain score assessment • Pain score decreased/relieved • VS within WDL • Behavior appropriate for age; able to demonstrate alternative therapies or activities for pain relief

Insanely Easy Way to remember when to use hot and cold therapy! **Heat** causes **vasodilation and relieves pain.** **Cold** causes **vasoconstriction, stops bleeding, and reduces swelling.**

Never USE HOT or COLD when there is **altered circulation** (i.e., diabetes, peripheral vascular disease, etc.)

Exceptions and Additions by Disease/Injury

Multiple Systems: Concept Pain

Pain Management

	FIRST-DO PRIORITY INTERVENTIONS			
SYSTEM-SPECIFIC ASSESSMENTS "PQRST"	DIET	EQUIPMENT	PLANS/INTERVENTIONS "RELIEF"	HEALTH PROMOTION
Assess: • Pain history (i.e., prior experience with pain, what has relieved pain in the past) • Vital Signs • Non-verbal cues (i.e., restlessness, verbal moaning, muscle tension, facial expression, etc.) **P**rovokes: what causes pain? What alleviates the pain? **Q**uality: How does it feel? What is the effect of pain on function & quality of life? **R**adiates: Where is the pain and does the pain radiate to another location? **S**everity/Intensity: How severe is the pain based on age appropriate pain scale? (i.e., Visual Analog Scale, Numeric Rating Scale, FACES Pain Scale, etc.). **T**ime: When did the pain start? Is it constant or intermittent?	• Diet as tolerated based on physio-logical condition	• IV pumps, patient controlled analgesia • O_2 (with chest pain, pneumonia, as needed for ↓ SaO_2 sat etc.)	**R**eport and review trends in vital signs indicative of pain, ↑ HR, ↑ RR. Document evaluation. **E**valuate pain q hour or per protocols, use pain scales appropriate for age. Document evaluation. **L**ook & document behaviors that indicate pain, (may range from stillness to restlessness & constant mobility, altered facial expressions, crying, ↓ attention span). **I**ntervene with appropriate ordered medications for pain. Initiate use of non-pharmacologic interventions when appropriate; ice for damaged tissues that are inflamed, red, hot and swollen; heat for mild pain relief, muscles, muscle spasms or cramps. Mind-body therapies (i.e., music, prayer, relaxation techniques, pet therapy, etc.). **E**valuate vital signs after pain medication is given, especially with opioid medications. Monitor for ↓ RR, HR or BP and quality of respirations (i.e., depth & regularity, etc.) & SaO_2 sat. Administer Naloxone (Narcan) if severe respiratory depression develops as prescribed. **F**ollow-up to see if pain is relieved within 30 minutes. If not, report to HCP; document pain medication administration and client's response to the pain medication or non-pharmacologic intervention.	Teach client/family: • About the importance of pain management with healing, (i.e., participate in activity, prevention of complications, (DVT, pneumonia). • Effect of pain on the client's mobility, functional ability and the client's mood and affect. • What to report: (i.e., break through pain or any side effects, allergies, extreme drowsiness, etc.).

Pharmacological Agents—Analgesics

There are three classes of analgesics (nonopioids, opioids, narcotics) and adjuvants that are the mainstays for relieving and managing pain.

Nonopioid Used for treating mild to moderate pain. Includes: • Salicylates • Acetaminophen • Non-steroidal anti-inflammatory drugs (NSAIDS) • Pregbalin (Lyrica) *Mr. Lyrica is singing because chronic pain is gone, but he has a dry mouth and is dizzy!*	 (Lyrica)	• Administer medication with antacids/ food to prevent gastric upset. • Monitor for salicylism (vertigo, tinnitus, decreased hearing acuity). • NSAIDs: monitor for signs of bleeding, (i.e., ↑ HR, ↓ Hgb and Hct, etc.). • Monitor liver function with acetaminophen, & NSAIDS. With acetaminophen, take no more than 4g/ day. • Monitor renal function with Lyrica.
Opioid Analgesics Used to reverse effects of opioid agonist (narcotic analgesic) by competing for the receptor sites. • Codeine • Morphine sulfate • Fentanyl (Sublimaze) *Droopy is drooping from too much morphine.*	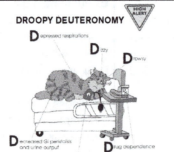	• For acute pain, parenteral route is most effective for immediate short-term relief. • Around the clock administration of opioids (24 to 48 hours) is preferred to manage acute severe pain, versus PRN schedule. • Dosing and consistent timing of opioids helps provide consistent pain management. • Monitoring, assessing and intervening for adverse effects of opioid use are essential.
Narcotic Antagonists Used for reversing the effect of opiod narcotics. Includes: • Naloxone (Narcan) • Nalmefena (Revex) *Notice "Perky," everything is ↑ to reverse the narcotic, but he is experiencing the undesirable effects of these drugs.*	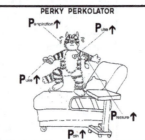	• Monitor carefully; when Narcan wears off, the Opioid may still be present & client may go into respiratory arrest. • Have emergency equipment at the bedside. • Prepare to administer pain meds, as pain may return with intensity.
Adjuvant Analgesics Used to help alleviate other symptoms that aggravate pain: (i.e. inflammation, seizures, depression, etc.).	Includes: • Glucocoritoids: dexamethasone (Decadron) • Antiemetics: ondansetron (Zofran) • Anticonvulsants: carbamazepine (Tegretol) • Antihistamine: hydroxyzine (Vistaril) • Antianxiety agents: diazepam (Valium)	• Enhance the effect of nonopioids. • Are useful in treating neuropathic pain.
Patient-Controlled Analgesics (PCA) • Self-administered to manage pain • Consistent plasma levels are maintained through small frequent dosing • Increases clients sense of control of pain management (may decrease the amount of medication needed)	Typical opioids for PCA delivery include: • Morphine sulfate • Hydromorphone (Dilaudid)	• The client should control the PCA button to prevent over medication. • Instruct client to inform the nurse if the PCA is not effectively managing the pain. • Equipment check prior to starting and the beginning of each shift for safety (Manning & Rayfield, 2013).

Multiple Systems: Concept Pain

First-Do Priority Interventions

Nonpharmacological Pain Management

The following methods of nonpharmacological pain management (alternative pain management) can provide very effective pain relief, individually or in conjunction with pharmacological pain management.

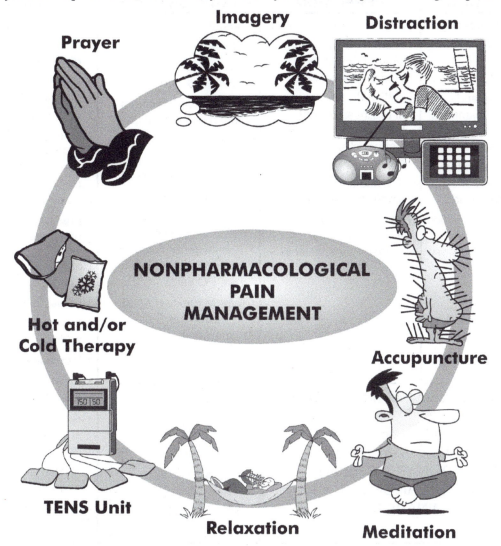

Definitions of Nonpharmacological Pain Management

Acupuncture: the use of needles in conjunction with vibration or electrical stimulation, being inserted into very specific points in the skin or subcutaneous tissue.

Cutaneous Stimulation of the Skin: the use of heat, cold, massage, therapeutic touch or TENS (transcutaneous nerve stimulation).

    Heat to increase the blood flow and to reduce stiffness
    Cold to treat areas of inflammation
    TENS to interrupt the pain pathways

Relaxation: modalities such as progressive muscle relaxation, yoga and meditation.

Imagery: Cognitive ability to concentrate to focus on a pleasant thought to divert the focus of the pain

Distraction: Modalities can include music, television, Internet, deep breathing, ambulation and interaction with people or pets (National Centers for Complementary and Alternative Medicine, 2013).

Multiple Systems: Concept Pain

Trend for Potential Complications of Pain Management

Linking Concepts to Help Prevent Potential Complications

OXYGENATION	PERFUSION	FLUID BALANCE	ELIMINATION
Respiratory depression	**Orthostatic hypotension**	**Nausea/vomiting**	**Urinary retention**
Early Indication: Sedation:	• Instruct clients to move slowly from a lying or sitting position to standing.	• Monitor I & O.	• Assess for bladder distension.
• Assess level of consciousness and take safety precautions; sedation often precedes respiratory depression.	• If dizziness or light-headedness does occur, instruct client to sit or lie down.	• Daily weights, compare, contrast & trend.	• Monitor I & O & urine output: > 30mL/hr minimally.
• Assess the respiratory rate prior to and after administering opioids.	• Provide assistance with ambulation as needed.	• Administer antiemetic with pain medication.	• If needed, administer bethanechol (Urecholine) as prescribed.
• If respiratory depression and sedation occur a reduction of opioid dose is generally the initial treatment.	*(Refer to concept Perfusion Cardiac/ Peripheral for specifics)*	• Eliminate odors.	• Catheterize as prescribed for continued urinary retention.
		• Instruct the client to lie still or move slowly.	
		• If severe/diarrhea occur, monitor fluid & electrolyte balance.	**Constipation**
• Have Naloxone (Narcan) available as needed.		• Administer IV fluids as prescribed if unable to take PO fluids.	• Monitor and record bowel movements.
(Refer to concept Oxygenation for specifics)		*(Refer to concept Fluid and Electrolyte Balance for specifics)*	• Increased residue (fiber) in diet.
			• Increase fluid intake.
			• Promote activity as tolerated.

Remember what IMMOBILITY from pain can do!

Use "M and M" to help prevent complications of decreased OXGENATION, PERFUSION, FLUID BALANCE, and ELIMINATION!

MANAGE MY PAIN!

MOVE... I NEED TO MOVE!

• Administer stool softeners, stimulants as prescribed.

• Laxative and/or enema may be needed.

(Refer to concept Elimination for specifics)

SAFETY—Remember the Ds

Clients can become DIZZY, DROWSY AND DOPEY on Pain Meds!!!!

May Need FALL PRECAUTIONS!!!!

Clinical Decision-Making Exercises

1. Which of these nursing interventions would be a priority when administering the narcotic antagonist Naloxone (Narcan)?

   ① Have resuscitation equipment available.

   ② Be prepared to re-administer pain medications if pain becomes too intense.

   ③ Be prepared to intervene if the client has a decreased heart rate or pulse from administration of this medication.

   ④ Have cool compresses available since this medication may make the client perspire.

2. Which of these clinical assessments would be important to monitor in a client receiving Morphine (MS Contin) for pain? *Select all that apply.*

   ① Respiratory rate and depth.

   ② BUN and bilirubin levels.

   ③ Monitor the number of stools.

   ④ Dietary intake for last two days.

   ⑤ Able to arouse and level of drowsiness.

3. What is the priority of care for a client who has Ibuprofen (Advil) ordered every 6 hours for pain around the clock post a laparoscopic cholecystectomy 2 days ago whose HR was 77 bpm pre surgery, is now 98 bpm, Hct was 31%, is now 26%, and Hgb was 13 g/dL, is now 10g/dL?

   ① Recheck the laboratory reports for liver enzymes.

   ② Substitute the Advil for Motrin.

   ③ Hold the Advil and notify the healthcare provider.

   ④ Assess the client's dietary intake post operatively.

4. What is the priority action for the nurse to take for a one-day post-operative client who is on a PCA pump and demonstrates through objective behavior that pain is not under control?

   ① Deliver the second order for a bolus dose per prescription.

   ② Assess the pain for quality, if it is radiating, and severity.

   ③ Notify the HCP for an order for a new medication.

   ④ Use an alternative therapy such as yoga.

5. What would be the initial action from the charge nurse for a client with chronic pain who reports that the nurse has not been following through with their many requests for pain medication?

   ① Check the MAR and nurses' notes for the past 72 hours.

   ② Request that a quality assurance program is immediately started on the unit.

   ③ Meet with the nurse who is responsible and review the standard of care for pain management.

   ④ Complete a pain assessment history and share with the nurse.

Answers and Rationales

1. Which of these nursing **interventions** would be a **priority** when **administering the narcotic antagonist Naloxone** (Narcan)?

    ① **CORRECT: Have resuscitation equipment available. Narcan is short acting, so the respiratory depression can reappear.**

    ② INCORRECT: Be prepared to re-administer pain medications if pain becomes too intense. This would not be a priority over option 1, because of the respiratory depression.

    ③ INCORRECT: Be prepared to intervene if the client has a decreased heart rate or pulse from administration of this medication. Narcan will cause the heart rate to increase.

    ④ INCORRECT: Have cool compresses available since this medication may make the client perspire. This is not a priority over option 1.

The strategy for answering this question is to know the effects of Narcan. As you saw the image "Perky Perkolator," the pulse, perspiration, pain and pressure can all go up as it reverses the respiratory depression from a opioid (narcotic). Narcan is short acting, and the pain can return to the client suddenly. The drug should be administered slowly as prescribed to help avoid the return of sudden onset of pain. The **PRIORITY** is to have the respiratory equipment at the bedside because the client may go back into a respiratory arrest. This is because the opioid is longer acting than Narcan. (*Refer to the book Pharmacology Made Insanely Easy for specifics*). Now you are ready for an emergency but remember the goal is to trend potential complications before they occur. Sedation of the client can be an early sign of impending respiratory depression. Monitor the sedation level of the client, the respiratory rate and depth and the SaO_2 sat and you will be on top of it!!

Pharmacological and Parenteral Therapies: Evaluate the client response to medication (i.e., therapeutic effect, side effects, adverse reactions)

Reduction of Risk Potential: Recognize trends and changes in client condition and intervene as needed.

2. Which of these clinical **assessments** would be **important to monitor** in a client receiving **Morphine (MS Contin)** for pain? Select all that apply.

    ① **CORRECT: Respiratory rate and depth. Monitoring respiratory rate and depth is important to detect early any signs of respiratory depression.**

    ② INCORRECT: BUN and bilirubin levels. The BUN would be appropriate but not the bilirubin level.

    ③ **CORRECT: Monitor the number of stools. One of the complications with narcotics is the risk of constipation.**

    ④ INCORRECT: Dietary intake for last two days. Not important related to this question about Morphine.

    ⑤ **CORRECT: Able to arouse and level of drowsiness. Priority assessment to detect early signs of respiratory depression when giving opioids like Morphine.**

The strategy for answering this question is to know the priority assessments for the administration of opioids. Respiratory rate and depth and the level of drowsiness are priority assessments to detect early any signs of respiratory depression. Also very important is the number of stools due to the constipating affect of narcotics. Encouraging fluids and residue (fiber) in the diet and offering a stool softener as prescribed can prevent constipation. You may need to be an advocate for your client and work with the healthcare provider to be proactive in preventing constipation. That is a complication a client in pain does not need! This was similar to question #1, but added the potential complication of constipation, that can be a problem, particularly with the elderly clients. Good job!

Pharmacological and Parenteral Therapies: Assess client need for pain management.

Pharmacological and Parenteral Therapies: Evaluate the client response to medication (i.e., therapeutic effect, side effects, adverse reactions).

3. What is the **priority of care** for a client who has **Ibuprofen (Advil) ordered every 6 hours** for pain around the clock post a laparoscopic cholecystectomy **2 days ago** whose **HR was 77 bpm pre surgery, is now 98 bpm, Hct was 31%, is now 26%, and Hgb was 13g/dL, is now 10g/dL?**

    ① INCORRECT: Recheck the laboratory reports for liver enzymes. Although Advil, an NSAID, is metabolized in the liver, this is not the priority of care over option 3.

    ② INCORRECT: Substitute the Advil for Motrin. Motrin is another NSAID and would not be appropriate.

    ③ **CORRECT: Hold the Advil and notify the healthcare provider. This would be the priority because of the vital signs and lab reports indicating possible bleeding.**

    ④ INCORRECT: Assess the client's dietary intake post operatively. Not a priority.

The strategy for answering this question is to know the potential side effects of administering NSAIDS. Nonopioids can be used independently or with opioids. The potential risk for bleeding must be monitored closely. In this case the increased heart rate was the result of the heart was working harder to pump blood to the tissues and organs due to a decreased blood volume. (Remember the concept Perfusion Cardiac/Peripheral!!!) The Hgb and the Hct were both decreased, another clinical finding for bleeding. Linking the clinical findings to the fact the client had been taking Advil around the clock every 6 hours for 2 days, the **PRIORITY** is to hold the Advil and notify the healthcare provider. Superb clinical decision-making!!!

Pharmacological and Parenteral Therapies: Review pertinent data prior to medication administration (i.e., contraindications, lab results, allergies, potential interactions).

Pharmacological and Parenteral Therapies: Evaluate the client response to medication (i.e., therapeutic effect, side effects, adverse reactions).

4. What is the **priority** action for the nurse to take for a **one-day post-operative** client who is on a **PCA pump** and demonstrates through objective behavior that **pain is not under control?**

    ① INCORRECT: Deliver the second order for a bolus dose per prescription. Not the priority over option 2.

    ② **CORRECT: Assess the pain for quality, if it is radiating, and severity. These assessments are part of the PQRST. Since the information in the stem of the question is indicating the pain has not been relieved, further assessment is needed.**

    ③ INCORRECT: Notify the HCP for an order for a new medication. Need to have more information about the pain prior to notifying the HCP.

    ④ INCORRECT: Use an alternative therapy such as yoga. This would not be an option 1 day post-op.

The strategy for answering this question is when pain is not relieved, further assessment is needed to better improve the plan for pain management. With a PCA pump, it would be important to assess how much pain medication the client has actually used. Often, post operatively, the client is very drowsy from the anesthesia and has not access the PCA pump as often as they could. It would also be important to establish where the pain is located, the severity of the pain and has the client had any relief from the pain. Another important assessment to make is does the client know how to work the PCA pump and is the PCA pump working correctly. With a PCA pump, you are not only managing the clients pain, but must remember to make sure the equipment is in working order at the beginning of each shift and other times as required. Remember, the client's perspective on pain is the most important assessment!

Pharmacological and parenteral Therapies: Assess client need for pain medication

Safety and Infection Control: Facilitate appropriate and safe use of equipment.

5. What would be the **initial action** from
    the charge nurse for a client with **chronic
    pain** who **reports that the nurse has not
    been following through with their many
    requests for pain medication?**

    ① INCORRECT: Check the MARs and nurses'
       notes for the past 72 hours. Not the initial
       action to take over option 3.

    ② INCORRECT: Request that a quality
       assurance program is immediately started
       on the unit. Would not be the initial action.

    ③ **CORRECT: Meet with the nurse who is
       responsible and review the standard of
       care for pain management. It is always
       important when you receive complaints
       to go to the source to get the information
       first. In this scenario, it was the nurse
       who the client said was not meeting their
       requests for pain medication.**

    ④ INCORRECT: Complete a pain assessment
       history and share with the nurse. Not the
       initial action to take.

The strategy for answering this question is just
like with your clients, you need to assess all of the
information first. It could be there was a sound reason,
or the client had perceived their needs were not
being met or there could be an actual challenge that
the nurse had not administered the pain medication.
Either way, the client's perception is that their needs
are not being met. Once the charge nurse has all of
the information, a plan of action can be taken. Pain
management is a priority for all clients; however,
each client's pain must be managed individually. It is
important to include the client in the plan of care.
Communication is the key!

Management of Care: Manage conflict among clients
and healthcare staff.

Management of Care: Advocate for client rights and
needs.

Decision-Making Analysis Form

Use this tool to help identify why you missed any questions. As you enter the question numbers in the chart, you will begin to see patterns of why you answered incorrectly. This information will then guide you toward what you need to focus on in your continued studies. Ultimately, this analytical exercise will help you become more successful in answering questions!!!

Questions to ask:

1. Did I have the knowledge to answer the question? If not, what information do I need to review?

2. Did I know what the question was asking? Did I misread it or did I miss keywords in the stem of the question?

3. Did I misread or miss keywords in the distractors that would have helped me choose the correct answer?

4. Did I follow my gut reaction or did I allow myself to rationalize and then choose the wrong answer?

	Lack of Knowledge (Concepts, Systems, Pathophysiology, Medications, Procedures, etc.)	Missed Keywords or Misread the Stem of the Question	Missed Keywords or Misread the Distractors	Changed My Answer (Second-guessed myself, i.e., my first answer was correct.)
Put the # of each question you missed in the column that best explains why you think you answered it incorrectly.				

If you changed an answer because you talked yourself out of the correct answer, or you second-guessed yourself, this is an **EASY FIX: QUIT changing your answers**!!! Typically, the first time you read a question, you are about 95% right! The second time you read a question, you start talking yourself into changing the answer. The third time you read a question, you do not have a clue—and you are probably thinking "Who in the heck wrote this question?"

On the other hand, if you read a question too quickly and when you reread it you realize you missed some key information that would impact your decision (i.e., assessments, lab reports, medications, etc.), then it is appropriate to change your answer. When in doubt, go with the safe route: your first thought! Go with your gut instinct!

As you gain confidence in answering questions regarding specific nursing concepts, you will be able to successfully progress to answering higher-level questions about prioritization. Please refer to the *Prioritization Guidelines* in this book for a structure to assist you with this process.

You CAN do this!

"Find a place inside where there's joy, and the joy will burn out the pain."

JOSEPH CAMPBELL

References for Chapter 25

American Society for Pain Management Nursing, 2010). *Optimizing the Treatment of Pain in Patients with Acute Presentations.* Retrieved from http://www.aspmn.org/Organization/documents/OptimizingPositionPaper.pdf

Black, J M. and Hawks, J. H. (2009). *Medical surgical nursing: Clinical management for positive outcomes (8th ed.).* Philadelphia: Elsevier/Saunders.

Daniels, R. & Nicoll, L. (2012). *Contemporary medical-surgical nursing,* (2nd ed.). Clifton Park, NY: Delmar Cengage Learning.

Eliopoulos, C. (2014). *Gerontological nursing* (8th ed.), Philadelphia: Lippincott Williams & Wilkins

Giddens, G. F. (2013). *Concepts for nursing practice.* St. Louis, MO: Mosby, an imprint of Elsevier.

Hogan, M. A. (2014). *Pathophysiology: Reviews and rationales* (3rd ed.) Boston, MA: Pearson.

Ignatavicius, D. D. and Workman, M. L. (2010). *Medical-surgical nursing: Patient-centered collaborative care* (6th ed.). Philadelphia: Elsevier/Saunders.

Joint Commission (2014). Facts about pain management. Retrieved from http://www.jointcommission.org/pain_management/

LeMone, P., Burke, K.M., & Bauldoff, G. (2011). *Medical-surgical nursing: Critical thinking in patient care* (5th ed.). Upper Saddle Road, NJ: Pearson/Prentice Hall.

Lewis, S., Dirksen, S., Heitkemper, M., Bucher, L., and Camera, I. (2011). *Medical surgical nursing: Assessment and management of clinical problems* (8th ed.). St. Louis: Mosby.

Manning, L. and Rayfield, S. (2014). *Nursing made insanely easy* (7th ed.). Duluth, GA: I CAN Publishing, Inc.

Manning, L. and Rayfield, S. (2013). *Pharmacology made insanely easy* (4th ed.). Duluth, GA: I CAN Publishing, Inc.

National Council of State Boards of Nursing, INC. (NCSBN) 2012. *Research brief: 2011 RN practice analysis: linking the NCLEX RN® examination to practice.* Retrieved from https://www.ncsbn.org/index.htm.

Osborn, K. S., Wraa, C. E., Watson, A. S., and Holleran, R. S. (2014). *Medical surgical nursing: Preparation for practice* (2nd ed.). Upper Saddle Road, NJ: Pearson.

Pagana, K. D. and Pagana, T. J. (2014). *Mosby's manual of laboratory and diagnostic tests* (5th ed.). St. Louis, MO: Mosby, an imprint of Elsevier.

Porth, C. (2011). *Essentials of pathophysiology* (3d ed.). Philadelphia, PA: Lippincott Williams ad Wilkins.

Porth, C. M. and Grossman, S. (2013). *Pathophysiology: Concepts of altered health states* (9th ed.). Philadelphia, PA: Lippincott Williams & Wilkins.

Potter, P. A., Perry, A. G., Stockert, P., and Hall, A. (2013). *Fundamentals of nursing* (8th ed.). St. Louis, MO: Pearson/Prentice Hall.

Smeltzer, S. C., Bare, B. G., Hinkle, J. L., and Cheever, K. H. (2010). *Brunner & Suddarth's Textbook of medical-surgical nursing* (12th ed.). Philadelphia: Lippincott Williams & Wilkins.

Wagner, K. D. and Hardin-Pierce, M. C. (2014). *High-Acuity nursing* (6th ed.). Boston: Pearson.

CHAPTER 26

Linking Multiple Systems and Concepts
Concept Thermoregulation

A Snapshot of Thermoregulation

Thermoregulation is defined as the process of maintaining a core body temperature at a constant value. The normal range of body temperature, also referred to as *Normothermia,* is from 36.2° to 37.6°C (97.0° to 100°F), or an average of 37°C (98.6°F) (Braine, 2009). Changes outside this range are a result of a disease process, an unusual activity that may be strenuous, or an exposure to an extreme environmental temperature. The regulation of the body temperature is crucial for maintaining physiologic function. This concept of thermoregulation is essential for nurses to apply throughout nursing practice (Giddens, 2013).

Hypothermia occurs when the body temperature decreases below 36.2°. These ranges can be further classified as mild (34° to 36°C or 93.2° to 96.8°F); moderate (30° to 34°C or 86° to 93°F); or severe (<30°C or <86°F). Hypothermia can result accidentally or be therapeutic. Accidental hypothermia can result from exposure to low environmental temperature or from a complication of a serious systemic disorder. Therapeutic hypothermia can occur intentionally as a result of a systemic disorder attempting to decrease the metabolism, consequently preserving tissue through prevention of tissue ischemia (Giddens, 2013).

Hyperthermia refers to a body temperature above normal range (greater than 37.6°C) with an unchanged hypothalamic set point (Giddens, 2013). When there is an interruption of the body's natural ability to dissipate heat, heat conditions can occur with the body, resulting in an elevation of the body temperature that exceeds heat loss. Several factors may be involved with the environment (i.e., humidity, temperature, etc.), pharmacological agents, trauma to the hypothalamus, and/or a genetic abnormality. A fever also represents an increase in the body temperature; however, it is different from hyperthermia because it is associated with an elevation in the hypothalamic set point caused by the release of interleukin-1 and tumor necrosis factor from the white blood cells. A fever is typically associated with an inflammatory process, but can also result from drugs and tumors. Fever is one of the most frequent symptoms seen in clinical practice. The underlying cause of the temperature elevation is the differentiation between fever and hyperthermia; it is not the body temperature that defines the difference (Giddens, 2013).

Thermoregulation is all about balancing heat gain and heat loss. The adjustments for alteration in the thermoregulation are controlled by the hypothalamus, often referred to as the thermostat center of the body. This book will focus on medical surgical concepts and related diseases with respect to body temperature ranges from lower (hypothermia) or higher (hyperthermia) than normal. Neonates and infants will be included in another book on maternity and newborn concepts. However, guidelines specific to the older child for temperature management are reviewed in this book.

The Pathophysiology Behind Thermoregulation

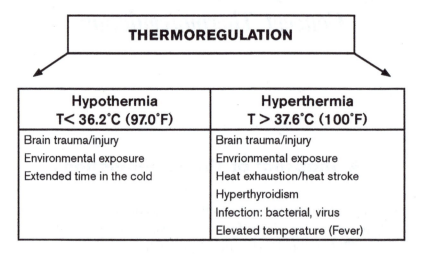

THERMOREGULATION	
Hypothermia T< 36.2°C (97.0°F)	**Hyperthermia** T > 37.6°C (100°F)
Brain trauma/injury	Brain trauma/injury
Environmental exposure	Envrionmental exposure
Extended time in the cold	Heat exhaustion/heat stroke
	Hyperthyroidism
	Infection: bacterial, virus
	Elevated temperature (Fever)

Concept Thermoregulation

The Physiological Processes for Optimal Thermoregulation

As long as the heat production and heat loss are balanced, the body temperature remains constant. The factors contributing to heat production and conservation (increase of temperature) are outlined on the left side of the scale. The physiology of heat loss is outlined on the right side of the scale.

ABCs of the Physiology of Heat Production	The Physiology of Heat Loss
Activity of the muscle contraction produces heat through muscle tone and shivering.	**Conduction**: Transfer of heat from a direct contact of one surface to another. Warmer surfaces can lose heat to a cooler one.
Basal metabolism will be increased by the epinephrine release.	**Convection**: The dispersion of heat by air currents. Movement of body heat to cool air (a result of a fan).
Conserves heat by the body through peripheral vasoconstriction.	**Evaporation (vaporization)**: Ongoing evaporation of moisture from the respiratory tract, the mucosa of the mouth, and perspiration from the skin.
Driving effects on heat production is food consumption, physical activity and hormone levels.	**Radiation**: The transfer of heat from the surface of one object (body) to the surface of another without contact between the 2 objects.
	Vasodilation: Brings blood volume to body surface. Increased heat loss occurs by conduction as reviewed above.
	Perspiration: Evaporation from moisture from the skin. Typically in an adult, the heat loss accounts for 600 mL of water loss per day.
	Respirations: Cool air is inhaled and warmed in the respiratory tract. The warmed air then will be exhaled. Clients with a fever will typically have elevated respiratory rates.

Linking Priority System-Specific Assessments to Multiple Concepts

Concept Thermoregulation

Concepts	System-Specific Assessments "TEMP"
Temperature of skin: Assessments for hyperthermia: fever, flushing, warm, or hot skin are due to an increase in the metabolic rate. As a result, there is an increased need for fluids. If fluid is not replaced, the outcome will be fluid imbalance. Does this concept sound familiar? Tachycardia, tachypnea, dry lips and mucous membranes, and/or poor skin turgor may result from this imbalance. (*Concept*: Fluid Balance)	**T**emperature assessment; assess for infection such as a rash, color of secretions, breath sounds, neck pain, etc. Assess vital signs–↑ HR & RR in hyperthermia and ↓ with hypothermia; BP changes. Assess for signs of dehydration (i.e., lips and mucous membranes for dryness/moistness; skin turgor if appropriate for developmental stage; peripheral pulses; etc.).
Elimination: Due to the potential loss of fluids from the elevated temperature, nausea and vomiting, diarrhea, and/or a decrease in the appetite, the client may experience weight loss. Which concept would you say this reflects in addition to the concept of Fluid Balance reviewed in the above statement? (*Concept*: Nutrition) **E**valuate for cardiac dysrhythmias: Due to potential vomiting, diarrhea, and/ or poor appetite, there is a risk for loss of electrolytes, which can result in metabolic complications leading to cardiac dysrhythmias. Several concepts would be a priority with this complication. What are you thinking? (*Concepts*: Fluid and Electrolyte Balance, Acid-Base Balance, Cardiac Perfusion)	**E**limination: monitor I & O, daily weights. Assess for nausea and vomiting; diarrhea; poor appetite. **E**valuate fluid and electrolytes. Monitor for cardiac dysrhythmias.
Mental (capacity): Due to the risk for an infection involving the neurological system (i.e., meningitis, etc.) or any condition causing an alteration in fluid and electrolytes, these may result in difficulty with concentrating, fatigue, malaise, weakness, and/or decrease in responsiveness. What concept are we focusing on now? (*Concept*: Intracranial Regulation)	**M**ental (capacity): assess the level of consciousness; fatigue; ability to concentrate; muscle coordination, etc. Monitor for seizures if there is an alteration in the electrolytes (i.e., sodium), or if the client is a neonate or infant. (For example if the client is an infant or neonate, both will be high risk for seizures from the elevated temperature. The older client will be high risk for seizures from the alteration in the electrolytes resulting from the elevated temperature.)
Physical exam: Although much of the exam focused on the physical findings, it is always important to consider the social and family history. It is important to determine if the alteration in the temperature is a result of the environment, a change in physical activity, and /or from the type of clothing worn by the client. This concept should be included with each system, concept, and/or diagnosis. (*Concept*: Health Promotion)	**P**hysical exam: health, family, and/or social history; assess physical activity, clothing worn, shelter, environmental exposure and/or control (i.e., for both heat and cold).

HYPOthermia: Linking Plan of Care to Pathophysiology

"WARM" the client who is experiencing HYPOthermia!

Concept Thermoregulation

The mnemonic "WARM" will assist in organizing the plan of care to help increase the temperature!

Pathophysiology	Plan of Care
Warm client: The compensatory mechanism of the body initially is to shiver to produce heat from the activity of the muscles.	**W**arm client: If the client has been outside in cold weather, warm with blankets. Maintain environmental control of heat. Minimize any drafts or exposure to cold/cool environment to assist in preventing any shivering.
Assess color of skin: A reduction in the peripheral circulation is caused by vasoconstriction, resulting in a pale skin color. Decreased metabolic rate and decreased organ demands can result in a decrease in the RR and HR. A reduction in the HR can cause a decrease in the cardiac output. This decrease in perfusion can result in a safety issue from falls. A decrease in the blood flow to the kidneys can result in a decrease in the urinary output.	**A**ssess color of skin (may range from being pale to cyanotic). Watch those vital signs for a HR & RR ↓ with hypothermia; monitor and trend for a decrease in BP. Due to risk for hypotension, implement fall precautions! Dysrhythmias need to be monitored due to the alteration in cardiac output. Monitor I & O and report trends with a decreased output to HCP.
Reduce risk: Due to the hypothermia, vasoconstriction occurs decreasing the flow of the circulating bloodstream.	**R**educe risk through education (of all ages) regarding safe care in regards to environmental temperature. Review topics (i.e., shelter, clothing; rewarming by applying warm blankets or heating pads, warm bath, etc.) Discuss importance of regulating environmental temperature, for clients with frostbite of toes, nose, and fingers. Rewarm affected area for 20-30 minutes. Do not rub or massage areas. Manage with warm drinks; monitor for muscle rigidity or shivering.
Mentation: Decrease in the metabolic rate and decrease in the cardiac output will result in a decrease in the blood flow to the brain. Decrease in muscle coordination.	**M**entation (cognition): Monitor level of consciousness. Implement fall precautions due to decrease in muscle coordination.

Summary Concept Thermoregulation: HYPOthermia

"WARM" the client who is experiencing HYPOthermia!

The mnemonic "**WARM**" will assist in organizing the plan of care to help increase the temperature!
Let's put all of this together!

SAFETY
Concept Thermoregulation: HYPOthermia

System-Specific Assessments "TEMP"	First-Do Priority Interventions "WARM"	Evaluation of Expected Outcomes
Temperature assessment; assess for infection such as a rash, color of secretions, breath sounds, neck pain, etc. Assess vital signs– ↑ HR & RR in hyperthermia and ↓ with hypothermia; BP changes. Assess for signs of dehydration (i.e., lips and mucous membranes for dryness/moistness; skin turgor if appropriate for developmental stage; peripheral pulses; etc.).	**W**arm client: If the client has been outside in cold weather, warm with blankets. Maintain environmental control of heat. Minimize any drafts or exposure to cold/cool environment to assist in preventing any shivering.	• Temperature will remain within the normal range 36.2° to 37.6°C (97°–100°F).
	Assess color of skin (may range from being pale to cyanotic). Watch those vital signs for a HR & RR ↓ with hypothermia; monitor and trend for a decrease in BP. Due to risk for hypotension, implement fall precautions! Dysrhythmias need to be monitored due to the alteration in cardiac output. Monitor I & O and report trends with a decreased output to HCP.	• Skin color pink
Elimination: monitor I & O, daily weights. Assess for N/V, diarrhea; poor appetite. Evaluate fluid and electrolytes. Monitor for cardiac dysrhythmias.		• HR, RR, BP will remain WDL.
		• No dysrhythmias.
		• Intake and output will remain WDL.
Mental (capacity): assess the level of consciousness; fatigue; ability to concentrate; muscle coordination, etc. Monitor for seizures if there is an alteration in the electrolytes (i.e., sodium), or if the client is an infant or neonate. (The infant or neonate will be high risk for seizures from the elevated temperature. The older client will be high risk for seizures from the alteration in the electrolytes resulting from the elevated temperature).	**R**educe risk through education (of all ages) regarding safe care in regards to environmental temperature. Review topics (i.e., shelter, clothing; rewarming by applying warm blankets or heating pads, warm bath, etc.) Discuss importance of regulating environmental temperature for clients with frostbite of toes, nose, and fingers. Rewarm affected area for 20–30 minutes. Do not rub or massage areas. Manage with warm drinks; monitor for muscle rigidity or shivering.	• Daily weight WDL.
		• Lab values will remain WDL.
		• LOC WDL.
Physical exam: health, family, and/ or social history; assess physical activity, clothing worn, shelter, environmental exposure and/ or control (i.e., for both heat and cold)	**M**entation (cognition): Monitor level of consciousness. Implement fall precautions due to decrease in muscle coordination.	

HYPERthermia: Linking Plan of Care to Pathophysiology

"COOL" the client who is experiencing HYPERthermia!

Concept Thermoregulation

The mnemonic "**COOLS**" will assist in organizing the plan of care to help decrease the temperature!

Pathophysiology	Plan of Care
Cool the warm skin. As the temperature of the body increases, the blood vessels vasodilate to begin to assist in causing more blood flow to go to the surface of the body. Result=skin feels warm secondary to warmth of the flow of blood.	**C**ool by a tepid bath; antipyretic. Remove clothing and skin covering. Cool washcloths to axilla, groin, forehead and nape of neck. Use cooling blanket. If client has malignant hyperthermia, keep emergency equipment close to the client.
Observe core body temperature because as the temperature increases, there is an increase in the metabolic rate causing the respiratory rate and heart rate to increase.	**O**bserve core body temperature; assess for weakness, nausea, vomiting, syncope; change in cognition; muscle cramps; assess vital signs for a ↓ BP, ↑ RR, ↑ HR, ↓ CO. Monitor overall skin color and capillary refill to evaluate perfusion.
Observe for and monitor insensible water loss increases as a result of perspiration, increase in the metabolic rate, and tachypnea. The problem of dehydration can occur quickly, especially in young children and older adults if client is not adequately rehydrated.	**O**bserve for and monitor characteristics of pulses. Monitor intake and output and report trending if there is a decrease in the output. Increase fluid intake 2000 mL/day** unless contraindicated by (i.e., cardiac, neurological, and or renal complications, etc.).
Look for flushing because as the temperature increases, there is an insensible water loss due to an increase in the perspiration. This can also result with an increase in metabolic rate and tachypnea. Dehydration can occur quickly, especially in young children and older adults if client is not being adequately rehydrated	**L**ook for flushing and skin temperature (dry or diaphoretic); look for signs of dehydration. Monitor labs: Na+, Hct, BUN, urine specific gravity. With fluid loss, the labs will be increased.Monitor hydration status and increase fluid intake and output. Monitor the daily weight and note trends in a decrease in the weight. With fluid loss, the lab values will increase.
Seizure precautions are important for the infant and young child due to risk for seizures from the elevated temperature. Older clients with an alteration in the sodium level will also be high risk for seizures due to electrolyte imbalance.	**S**eizure precautions for a febrile infant/child; an adult with hypernatremia. **Keep in mind that the 2000 mL is a generic value for the increase in fluid intake because if the client is a neonate, infant, young child, and/or older adult this amount would NOT be correct. This value would need to be determined based on the weight of the client.*

Summary Concept Thermoregulation: HYPERthermia

The mnemonic "**COOLS**" will assist in organizing the plan of care to help decrease the temperature!
Let's put all of this together!

SAFETY		
Concept Thermoregulation: HYPERthermia		
System-Specific Assessments "TEMP"	**First-Do Priority Interventions "COOLS"**	**Evaluation of Expected Outcomes**
Temperature assessment; assess for infection such as a rash, color of secretions, breath sounds, neck pain, etc. Assess vital signs– ↑ HR & RR in hyperthermia and ↓ with hypothermia; BP changes. Assess for signs of dehydration (i.e., lips and mucous membranes for dryness/moistness; skin turgor if appropriate for developmental stage; peripheral pulses; etc.).	**C**ool by a tepid bath; antipyretic. Remove clothing and skin covering. Cool washcloths to axilla, groin, forehead and nape of neck. Use cooling blanket. If client has malignant hyperthermia, keep emergency equipment close to the client.	• Temperature will remain within the normal range 36.2° to 37.6°C (97°–100°F). • Skin color pink • HR, RR, BP will remain WDL. • No dysrhythmias. • Intake and output will remain WDL. • Daily weight WDL. • Lab values will remain WDL. • LOC WDL. Client experiences no seizures.
Elimination: monitor I & O, daily weights. Assess for N/V, diarrhea; poor appetite. Evaluate fluid and electrolytes. Monitor for cardiac dysrhythmias.	**O**bserve core body temperature; assess for weakness, nausea, vomiting, syncope; change in cognition; muscle cramps; assess vital signs for a ↓ BP, ↑ RR, ↑ HR, ↓ CO. Monitor overall skin color and capillary refill to evaluate perfusion.	
Mental (capacity): assess the level of consciousness; fatigue; ability to concentrate; muscle coordination, etc. Monitor for seizures if there is an alteration in the electrolytes (i.e., sodium), or if the client is an infant or neonate. *(The infant or neonate will be high risk for seizures from the elevated temperature. The older client will be high risk for seizures from the alteration in the electrolytes resulting from the elevated temperature).*	**O**bserve for and monitor characteristics of pulses. Monitor intake and output and report trending if there is a decrease in the urine output. Increase fluid intake 2000 mL/ day** unless contraindicated by (i.e., cardiac, neurological, and or renal complications, etc.).	
	Look for flushing and skin temperature (dry or diaphoretic); look for signs of dehydration. Monitor labs: Na^+, Hct, BUN, urine specific gravity. With fluid loss, the labs will be increased. Monitor hydration status and increase fluid intake and output. Monitor the daily weight and note trends in a decrease in the weight. With fluid loss, the labs will be increased.	
Physical exam: health, family, and/ or social history; assess physical activity, clothing worn, shelter, environmental exposure and/ or control (i.e., for both heat and cold).	**S**eizure precautions for a febrile infant/ child; an adult with hypernatremia.	
	**Keep in mind that the 2000 mL is a generic value for the increase in fluid intake because if the client was younger or an older adult this amount would NOT be correct. This value would need to be determined based on the weight of the client.*	

Physiological Changes in the Older Adult Client that Result in Altered Thermoregulation

1. Decreased in the ability to regulate body temperature.

2. Decrease in the number of sweat glands.

3. Decrease in the circulation.

4. Decrease vasoconstrictive response.

5. Decrease shivering response.

6. Decrease in the metabolic rate.

7. Decrease in physical activity.

8. Decrease in the perceptions of heat and cold.

9. Decrease in the resources to stay warm or cool in environment extremes.

10. Decrease in the level of consciousness (acute confusion) is the typical clinical assessment.

INSANELY EASY TIP!

for remembering the changes that occur with the older adult client with **Thermoregulation.**

Everything is **DECREASED**!! Try it out! It will work.
Oh no, there is one thing that increases with age! Do you know what it is? One guess!

FAT!!! No fair, but it is reality!

Guidelines for Treating Children with a Temperature

Expected Outcome = "AFEBRILE"

A Assess temperature ongoing as per protocol (i.e., q 4–6 hours).

F Fever: If child does not look sick and immune system is effective in fighting the virus within the body's natural defenses, do NOT intervene with antibiotics.

Fluids: encourage to increase intake.

E Evaluate behavior and response to infection. The medication may decrease fever, but it will return until the infection is gone.

B Bathe in tepid water after antipyretic has been administered. NEVER use cold water, since this may increase shivering and discomfort! NEVER use alcohol for bathing.

R Rise of temperature again 4 hours after medicated with an antipyretic may occur. Check temperature and give another dose. Follow directions regarding maximum dose.

I Ibuprofen or acetaminophen are given to lower temperature. Identify right dosage; drops and syrups do NOT have the same concentrations.

L Layer of light clothing only; remove all other layers.

E Educate parents when to call healthcare provider.

INSANELY EASY TIP!

to Summarize Thermoregulation!

The key for you to remember about priority nursing interventions
for thermoregulation is:

If Hyperthermic, "**COOL**" the client. If Hypothermic, "**WARM**" the client.

It is all about balance between *heat production* and *heat loss*!

Isn't that what life is all about? Balance!

HYPERthermia		**HYPO**thermia
The key for you to remember regarding priority nursing interventions with this concept is that if the client is *hyperthermic*: "**COOL**" the client!	As you can see, the brain is in the middle of the two images to illustrate the role it has in regulating the temperature. The hypothalamus is also referred to as the body's thermostat.	The key for you to remember regarding priority nursing interventions with this concept is that if the client is *hypothermic*: "**WARM**" the client!
Remember, in the **D**esert the vessels will **DILATE** in an attempt to **DECREASE** the temperature.	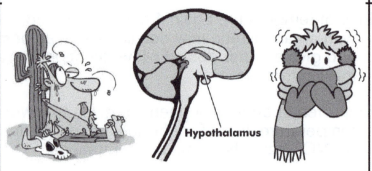 Hypothalamus	In the **C**old, the vessels will **CONSTRICT** in an attempt to **CONSERVE** heat! See the earmuffs and scarf, along with shivering? Shivering is an attempt to produce heat.

Clinical Decision-Making Exercises

1. During a health promotion program at a long-term care facility, what would be the priority information to include in the teaching plan about the prevention of hypothermia in the geriatric client?

   ① Discuss the benefits of drinking a warm cup of tea 20 minutes prior to going to bed.

   ② Discuss the importance of putting on a sweater when client starts to feel cold and begins shivering.

   ③ Review the importance of keeping the room cool due to the increase in sensitivity to temperature.

   ④ Review the importance of using more blankets in the winter due to decrease in circulation.

2. What is the priority of care for a client who is brought to the emergency room with an increased blood alcohol level and a temperature of 88.6° F?

   ① Review the importance of decreasing the intake of alcohol.

   ② Perform a complete head to toe physical assessment.

   ③ Provide a warm environment; warm blankets prior to placing on client.

   ④ Immediately provide client with oxygen via the mask.

3. Which of these nursing actions for a young child with a temperature of 102.4° F by the LPN would be a priority for the charge nurse to intervene?

   ① Bathes a young child in cold water to assist with decreasing the temperature.

   ② Uses tepid water for bathing the child.

   ③ Initiates seizure precautions.

   ④ Encourages the child to drink fluid every hour.

4. Which of these statements made by the nurse indicates a need for additional information regarding the pathophysiology of thermoregulation?

   ① "A client who is febrile may look flushed because as the temperature increases, the blood vessels vasodilate to bring more blood to the surface of the body."

   ② "Clients experiencing hyperthermia will have constricted vessels to assist in contracting the skeletal muscles in an attempt to remove the heat."

   ③ "There may be an elevated heart rate for a client who has a temperature due to the increase in the metabolic rate."

   ④ "Due to the physiological changes that occur with aging such as a decrease in the vasoconstrictive response, the older adult will experience a decrease in ability to regulate temperature."

5. Which of these clinical assessment findings would be a priority for a client who has a temperature of 101.8 °F?

   ① A flushed color of the skin.

   ② A warm feeling of the skin.

   ③ BUN 28 mg/dL; specific gravity 1.030.

   ④ Hemoglobin–12 g/dL; hematocrit–36%.

Answers and Rationales

1. During a health promotion program at a long-term care facility, what would be the **priority information** to include in the teaching plan about the prevention of hypothermia in the **geriatric client**?

   ① INCORRECT: Discuss the benefits of drinking a warm cup of tea 20 minutes prior to going to bed. The caffeine will keep client awake, so is not a good choice. Warm fluid is great, but no caffeine.

   ② INCORRECT: Discuss the importance of putting on a sweater when client starts to feel cold and begins shivering. The geriatric client has a decrease in the shivering response. Care needs to be proactive.

   ③ INCORRECT: Review the importance of keeping the room cool due to the increase in sensitivity to temperature. The room should be kept warm. There is a decrease in perception of hot and cold.

   ④ **CORRECT: Review the importance of using more blankets in the winter due to decrease in circulation. Due to the many physiological changes that occur with the aging process, it is important to educate the geriatric client, family, and/ or staff of the importance of preventing hypothermia by using blankets, sweaters, environmental control, etc. It is important to prevent the problem, since the geriatric client has a decrease in perception of heat and cold.**

The strategy for answering this question is to understand the physiological changes that occur with the geriatric client. Remember, most physiological responses to maintaining thermoregulation are decreased!

Health Promotion and Maintenance: Provide care and education for adults over 85 years.

Physiological Adaptation: Maintain optimal temperature of client.

2. What is the **priority of care** for a client who is brought to the emergency room with an **increased blood alcohol level and a temperature of 88.6° F**?

   ① INCORRECT: Review the importance of decreasing the intake of alcohol. This is not the priority in the emergency room. The physical needs are the priority. (*Refer to Prioritizing algorithm in the first chapter for review.*)

   ② INCORRECT: Perform a complete head to toe physical assessment. This is not the priority.

   ③ **CORRECT: Provide a warm environment; warm blankets prior to placing on client. Due to the vasodilating effect of alcohol, the client will continue to lose heat. This priority is to conserve the heat to assist with an increase in the temperature. This will also assist the metabolic rate.**

   ④ INCORRECT: Immediately provide client with oxygen via the mask. The priority is the hypothermia.

The strategy is to understand the physiology of hypothermia and the effect on the body. The alcohol will work against the body's natural physiological response for vasoconstriction to decrease heat loss. As long as the client remains hypothermic, the metabolic rate will not increase. The cardiac output may also be decreased with this low temperature. It will also be important for the client to be rewarmed slowly due to risk for dysrhythmias if temperature is increased too quickly.

Management: Prioritize delivery of care.

Reduction of Risk: Recognize signs and symptoms of complications and intervene appropriately when providing care.

Physiological Adaptation: Maintain optimal temperature of client.

3. Which of these **nursing actions** for a **young child with a temperature of 102.4° F** by the LPN would be a **priority for the charge nurse to intervene?**

    ① **CORRECT: Bathes a young child in cold water to assist with decreasing the temperature. Should be tepid. This is not the standard of practice, so would require further management. Cold water may increase shivering and further discomfort. This may result in a further increase in the temperature.**

    ② INCORRECT: Uses tepid water for bathing the child. Correct standard of practice. No need for intervention.

    ③ INCORRECT: Initiates seizure precautions. Correct standard of practice. No need for intervention. Due to the age of the child, a risk for seizures is a potential problem and requires seizure precautions to be included in the plan of care.

    ④ INCORRECT: Encourages the child to drink fluid every hour. Correct standard of practice. No need for intervention. With this high temperature, there is a high risk for fluid and electrolyte imbalance. Fluids are an important part of care for these clients with a high temperature as long as there are no contraindications such as the client having a cardiac or neurological condition.

The strategy for this question is to recognize the standard of practice for the child with a fever. Refer to "AFEBRILE" previously in the chapter that will review the care for febrile clients. Option 1 should not be done due to the risk for increasing shivering to produce heat from muscle activity, so would require further intervention by the charge nurse in order to assist child. This shivering may cause the fever to increase further. The charge nurse would also need to review the correct care, so the LPN can learn to provide safe care within the standard of practice.

Management: Recognize limitations of others and assist as needed.

Physiological Adaptation: Maintain optimal temperature of client.

4. Which of these **statements** made by the nurse **indicates a need for additional information** regarding the **pathophysiology of thermoregulation?**

    ① INCORRECT: "A client who is febrile may look flushed because as the temperature increases, the blood vessels vasodilate to bring more blood to the surface of the body." Correct statement.

    ② **CORRECT: "Clients experiencing hyperthermia will have constricted vessels to assist in contracting the skeletal muscles in an attempt to remove the heat." Incorrect. Shivering is to increase heat production. This requires further information.**

    ③ INCORRECT: "There may be an elevated heart rate for a client who has a temperature due to the increase in the metabolic rate." Correct statement. No need for additional information.

    ④ INCORRECT: "Due to the physiological changes that occur with aging such as a decrease in the vasoconstrictive response, the older adult will experience a decrease in ability to regulate temperature." Correct statement. No need for additional information.

The strategy is to understand the pathophysiology for both hyper and hypothermia. The chart "Linking Physiology to Thermoregulation" reviews "Constrict" and "Dilate", and will assist you in this process. Clients who are hypothermic will constrict their vessels to decrease heat loss. They may also shiver in an attempt to increase heat production. Clients who are hyperthermic will dilate their vessels to increase heat loss.

Physiological Adaptation: Identify pathophysiology related to an acute or chronic condition

Physiological Adaptation: Maintain optimal temperature of client.

5.   Which of these **clinical assessment** findings would be a **priority** for a **client who has a temperature of 101.8 °F?**

     ① INCORRECT: A flushed color of the skin. This is an expected assessment with a fever.

     ② INCORRECT: A warm feeling of the skin. This is an expected assessment with a fever.

     ③ **CORRECT: BUN 28 mg/dL; specific gravity 1.030. This indicates a fluid deficit.**

     ④ INCORRECT: Hemoglobin–12 g/dL; hematocrit–36%. This is WDL. Hematocrit should be 3x the Hgb.

The strategy is to recognize the laboratory findings that indicate a complication with fluid volume deficit. Remember, the concept of fluid volume deficit; lab values increase as the fluid volume decreases. These labs will be the same no matter what the cause is due to the fluid volume deficit. Do you remember any of the other lab values that increase too? *Repetition is the mother of learning!* A few others include serum sodium, osmolality, and the urine sodium, and osmolality. Thermoregulation is interrelated with fluid and electrolytes (*Refer to Concept Fluid and Electrolyte Balance for specifics*).

Physiological Adaptation: Manage the care of a client with a fluid and electrolyte imbalance.

Reduction of Risk: Monitor the results of the labs/ diagnostic testing and intervene as needed.

Decision-Making Analysis Form

Use this tool to help identify why you missed any questions. As you enter the question numbers in the chart, you will begin to see patterns of why you answered incorrectly. This information will then guide you toward what you need to focus on in your continued studies. Ultimately, this analytical exercise will help you become more successful in answering questions!!!

Questions to ask:

1. Did I have the knowledge to answer the question? If not, what information do I need to review?

2. Did I know what the question was asking? Did I misread it or did I miss keywords in the stem of the question?

3. Did I misread or miss keywords in the distractors that would have helped me choose the correct answer?

4. Did I follow my gut reaction or did I allow myself to rationalize and then choose the wrong answer?

	Lack of Knowledge (Concepts, Systems, Pathophysiology, Medications, Procedures, etc.)	Missed Keywords or Misread the Stem of the Question	Missed Keywords or Misread the Distractors	Changed My Answer (Second-guessed myself, i.e., my first answer was correct.)
Put the # of each question you missed in the column that best explains why you think you answered it incorrectly.				

If you changed an answer because you talked yourself out of the correct answer, or you second-guessed yourself, this is an **EASY FIX: QUIT changing your answers**!!! Typically, the first time you read a question, you are about 95% right! The second time you read a question, you start talking yourself into changing the answer. The third time you read a question, you do not have a clue—and you are probably thinking "Who in the heck wrote this question?"

On the other hand, if you read a question too quickly and when you reread it you realize you missed some key information that would impact your decision (i.e., assessments, lab reports, medications, etc.), then it is appropriate to change your answer. When in doubt, go with the safe route: your first thought! Go with your gut instinct!

As you gain confidence in answering questions regarding specific nursing concepts, you will be able to successfully progress to answering higher-level questions about prioritization. Please refer to the *Prioritization Guidelines* in this book for a structure to assist you with this process.

You CAN do this!

"To be kind is more important than to be right. Many times what people need is not a brilliant mind that speaks, but a special heart that listens."

AUTHOR UNKNOWN

References for Chapter 26

Black, J M. and Hawks, J. H. (2009). *Medical surgical nursing: Clinical management for positive outcomes (8th ed.)*. Philadelphia: Elsevier/Saunders.

Braine, M. (2009). *The role of the hypothalamus, part 1: The regulation of temperature and hunger*, Br J Neurosci Nurs, 66-72.

Daniels, R. & Nicoll, L. (2012). *Contemporary medical-surgical nursing*, (2nd ed.). Clifton Park, NY: Delmar Cengage Learning.

Eliopoulos, C. (2014). *Gerontological nursing* (8th ed.), Philadelphia: Lippincott Williams & Wilkins

Ellis, K.M. (2012). *EKG: Plain and simple* (3rd ed.). Upper Saddle Road, NJ: Pearson.

Giddens, G. F. (2013). *Concepts for nursing practice*. St. Louis, MO: Mosby, an imprint of Elsevier.

Hogan, M. A. (2014). *Pathophysiology: Reviews and rationales* (3rd ed.) Boston, MA: Pearson.

Ignatavicius, D. D. and Workman, M. L. (2010). *Medical-surgical nursing: Patient-centered collaborative care* (6th ed.). Philadelphia: Elsevier/Saunders.

LeMone, P., Burke, K.M., & Bauldoff, G. (2011). *Medical-surgical nursing: Critical thinking in patient care* (5th ed.). Upper Saddle Road, NJ: Pearson/Prentice Hall.

Lewis, S., Dirksen, S., Heitkemper, M., Bucher, L., and Camera, I. (2011). *Medical surgical nursing: Assessment and management of clinical problems* (8th ed.). St. Louis: Mosby.

Manning, L. and Rayfield, S. (2014). *Nursing made insanely easy* (7th ed.). Duluth, GA: I CAN Publishing, Inc.

Manning, L. and Rayfield, S. (2013). *Pharmacology made insanely easy* (4th ed.). Duluth, GA: I CAN Publishing, Inc.

National Council of State Boards of Nursing, INC. (NCSBN) 2012. *Research brief: 2011 RN practice analysis: linking the NCLEX RN® examination to practice*. Retrieved from https://www.ncsbn.org/index.htm.

Nettina, S. L. (2013). *Lippincott manual of nursing practice* (10th ed.). Philadelphia, PA: Walters Kluwer Health / Lippincott Williams & Wilkins.

North Carolina Concept Based Learning Editorial Board (2011). *Nursing a concept based approach to learning*, Upper Saddle Road, NJ: Pearson/Prentice Hall.

Osborn, K. S., Wraa, C. E., Watson, A. S., and Holleran, R. S. (2014). *Medical surgical nursing: Preparation for practice* (2nd ed.). Upper Saddle Road, NJ: Pearson.

Pagana, K. D. and Pagana, T. J. (2014). *Mosby's manual of laboratory and diagnostic tests* (5th ed.). St. Louis, MO: Mosby, an imprint of Elsevier.

Porth, C. (2011). *Essentials of pathophysiology* (3d ed.). Philadelphia, PA: Lippincott Williams ad Wilkins.

Porth, C. M. and Grossman, S. (2013). *Pathophysiology: Concepts of altered health states* (9th ed.). Philadelphia, PA: Lippincott Williams & Wilkins.

Potter, P. A., Perry, A. G., Stockert, P., and Hall, A. (2013). *Fundamentals of nursing* (8th ed.). St. Louis, MO: Pearson/Prentice Hall.

Smeltzer, S. C., Bare, B. G., Hinkle, J. L., and Cheever, K. H. (2010). *Brunner & Suddarth's Textbook of medical-surgical nursing* (12th ed.). Philadelphia: Lippincott Williams & Wilkins.

SECTION THREE

Guides to Linking Multiple Systems and Concepts

NOTES

CHAPTER 27

Linking Multiple Systems and Concepts
Concept Health Promotion

A Snapshot of Health Promotion

Health promotion, according to the World Health Organization, is "the process of enabling people to increase control over their health and to improve their health" (World Health Organization, 2014). This concept will include client/family teaching and health maintenance, primary, secondary and tertiary prevention and Healthy People 2020 recommendations. Health promotion involves the individual, family, community, populations and the environment.

Client Teaching is an integral part of nursing and essential to achieving quality client outcomes. Client teaching is providing knowledge and skills needed to maintain or improve health. Client teaching is part of Primary, Secondary and Tertiary Prevention. It includes the client, their family and significant others.

Primary Prevention are interventions aimed at preventing the occurrence of disease, injury, or disability, risk reduction and specific protection.

Secondary Prevention are interventions aimed at screening and detecting disease early enough to allow effective treatment and prevent disease progression.

Tertiary Prevention are interventions that are focused on the rehabilitation and the limitation of disability.

The Organization of All Aspects of Health Promotion

HEALTH PROMOTION

↓

CLIENT TEACHING

Considerations include:

- Learner needs, motivation and style of learning
- Plan of education, individual, group, self-directed
- Developmental and cognitive level
- Cultural and spiritual needs
- Communication style, language
- Family dynamics

Primary Prevention Remember P for "Primary" as Prevention	Secondary Prevention Remember S for "Secondary" as Screening	Tertiary Prevention Remember R for "teRtiary" as Rehabilitation
Considerations include: - Immunizations - Individual genetic counseling - Individualize nutritional health, (i.e., folic acid when pregnant, etc.) - Injury prevention (i.e., toddlers: poisoning; adolescents: accidents; & elderly: falls, etc.) - Information for medication safety: (i.e., impact on individuals physical condition, nutritional status, injury, depression, hearing, drug/drug interactions, over-the-counter medications (OTC), etc.) - Information for (i.e., addiction cessations: smoking, alcohol, abuse of prescribed drugs, accident prevention, seat belt use, child seats, etc.) - Information on oral health care - Information on occupational safety & health	*Considerations include:* - **Screening:** (i.e., Rh factor, sexually transmitted infections (STI), weight, body mass index (BMI), developmental, hearing, vision, BP, cancer screening, depression, substance abuse, etc.) - Early treatment: appropriate referrals	*Considerations include:* - **Restoration/Rehabilitation** - Physical therapy - Speech therapy - Occupational therapy - Social work - Stress management - Mental health

Multiple Systems

Concept: Health Promotion

Client Teaching

The client-teaching template below provides a guideline that can be used for client teaching regardless of the subject matter being taught. It will help remind you of the important points to include in client teaching sessions. Remember that client teaching is an essential part of care for many reasons; to help the client improve or manage their disease, to prevent complications, and to help them stay at home and avoid being readmitted to the acute care setting. Client teaching is also linked to reimbursement for hospitals. If health teaching and the appropriate referrals are not done, the healthcare facility may not be reimbursed for services provided (Centers for Medicare and Medicaid Services, 2014). Client teaching is one of the most rewarding and long lasting benefits nurses can provide their clients. So, let's get teaching!

HEALTH PROMOTION		
Concept–Client Teaching Template		
System-Specific Assessments "LEARN"	**First-Do Priority Interventions "TEACH"**	**Evaluation of Expected Outcomes**
Learning: assess needs and style **E**valuation of client's cognitive and motivation level, family dynamics, cultural and spiritual concerns **A**ssess need for individual, group or self-directed learning and resources needed **R**eferral need; assess for interdisciplinary team members or outside organizations, (i.e. ,home health, rehab, skilled nursing facility, etc.) **N**eed for follow-up for mastery of content **N**eed to document appropriately	**T**each about: • Medications • Diet • Symptoms to report • Infection control • Stress management techniques • Follow-up appointments **E**quipment needs and teach or referrals for safe use **A**ssessment of current status per protocol–document **A**ssess pain level–document **C**onsults and referrals as needed to other interdisciplinary team members (i.e., smoking cessation, occupational health, physical therapy, home health, etc.) **H**ealth promotion needs to promote healthy lifestyle, (i.e., referrals for vaccines, screening tests, weight loss, etc.)	• Client and/or family or significant others will verbally repeat information and be able to appropriately answer questions about the information taught (may need a translator for non-English speaking clients) • Teach back/Return demonstration • Maintenance or change in assessment parameters

Multiple Systems

Concept: Health Promotion

Client Teaching

Important Components of Client/Family Teaching				
Types of Client/Family Education	**Assessment of Learners' Needs**	**Hierarchy of Needs**	**Blocks to Learning**	**Evaluation of Learning**
• Formal classes: (i.e., nutritional classes, wound care, diabetes management, etc.) • Informal encounters during care • Self-Directed: (i.e., instructional videos, computer programs, pamphlets, internet resources, etc.) • Formal community classes: (i.e., cardiac rehab, stress management, child birth classes, etc.)	• Education level of client • Literacy level: ability to understand written and verbal information • Stage of Development: child versus adult • Generational Considerations: Need for feedback: the elderly require less feedback about how they are doing than the younger generations who expect immediate feedback	• Social economic status • Resources available, time, money, support • Need to know what information is important to the client right now	• Cultural & ethnical differences • Financial resources • Time: both for the client and the nurse (who may have conflicting priorities) • Motivation level to learn • Non-compliance: desire to learn, but faces barriers of financial, literacy, support, etc.	• Teach back: client or significant other teaches the information back to the instructor, or takes a quiz, or answers questions • Return demonstration needed for skills

All client/family teaching must be documented!

As nurses say, Not Documented–Not Done!!

Multiple Systems: Concept Health Promotion

Document the Teaching and the Evaluation of the Client Teaching

The health promotion template below provides a guideline that can be used for all health promotion needs. It will help remind you of the important aspects of health promotion to include in acute, long-term care, rehab centers, home health or community settings. As discussed in the Tissue/Skin Integrity Concept chapter about the need to take every opportunity to teach clients and the public about the prevention of skin cancer, you can do the same with any health promotion topic. The nurse's role is to provide referral to support groups or classes on health promotion (i.e., quit smoking, healthy diet, importance of exercise, etc.). Look for opportunities to promote health, in the acute care settings, public meetings, organizations, community and church health fairs, or develop a new venue! Remember the public trusts nurses more than any other profession; let's use that for the good of the public (Advance Healthcare Network for Nurses, 2013).

Concept–Health Promotion Template **System-Specific Assessments**		
Assess Individual as Client Prenatal, Infants, Children, Adolescents, Adults, & Elderly	**Assess Family as Client as Appropriate**	**Assess the Community as Client as Appropriate**
FIRST-DO PRIORITY INTERVENTIONS		
Primary Prevention	**Secondary Prevention**	**teRtiary Prevention**
Interventions aimed at preventing the occurrence of disease, injury, or disability including risk reduction and specific protection: • Infection control principles • Immunizations • Individual genetic counseling • Individualized nutritional health, (i.e., folic acid when pregnant, etc.) • Injury prevention (i.e., toddlers: poisoning; adolescents: accidents; & elderly: falls, etc.) • Information for medication safety: (i.e., impact on individuals physical condition, nutritional status, injury, depression, hearing, drug/drug interactions, over-counter medications (OTC), etc.) • Information for (i.e., addiction cessations: smoking alcohol, abuse of prescribed drugs, accident prevention, seat belt use, child seats, etc.) • Information on oral health care • Information on occupational safety & health • Include growth & developmental milestones (education based upon developmental needs)	Interventions aimed at detecting disease early enough to allow effective treatment and prevent disease progression **Screening:** (i.e., Rh factor, sexually transmitted infections (STI), weight, body mass index (BMI), development level, hearing, vision, BP, cancer screening, depression, substance abuse, etc.) **Early Treatment:** appropriate referrals **Safety Medication:** (i.e., importance of adhering to medication regimen, impact on individuals physical condition, nutritional status, injury, depression, hearing, drug/drug interactions, over-counter medications, herbals, vitamins, etc.)	Interventions aimed at the limitation of disability and rehabilitation **Restoration/ Rehabilitation** (i.e., CVA with physical therapy, speech therapy, occupational therapy, social skills training, etc.)
EVALUATION OF EXPECTED OUTCOMES Evaluate the outcomes from the preventative interventions and the follow-up from consultations & referrals.		

Insanely Easy Tip

To remember the LEVELS OF PREVENTION!!

Primary	Secondary	TeRtiary
P in Primary	**S** in Secondary	**R** in Te **R**tiary
Think of **P**rior to onset of disease. PrImary has an **I**. Think of **I**nfection Control, **I**mmunizations, **I**nformation	Think of **S**creening (Pap smear, colonoscopy, etc.)	Think of **R**ehabilitation (Physical therapy for a hip replacement, cardiac rehabilitation post myocardial infarction, etc.)

Answer these questions to see what you know about the levels of Health Promotion and Prevention.

1. What level of prevention is done prior to the onset of a disease?
2. What level includes a referral to have a mammogram done?
3. What level would include referring a client for physical therapy?
4. What level would include recommending a client get the Hepatitis B vaccine?
5. What level includes teaching a client about how to manage their risk factors for heart disease?

We Bet You Got Them All Right!! Great Job!
Remember: Health Promotion Is A Priority In The Plan of Care For The Client!

Answers:
1. Primary 2. Secondary 3. Tertiary 4. Primary 5. Primary

Multiple Systems: Concept Health Promotion

Client Teaching: Planning for Discharge

Discharge planning begins with the admission of the client. Immediately begin assessing what the discharge needs may be while doing the initial admission assessment. Remember, discharge planning and implementation requires the involvement of the interdisciplinary team to help meet all of the client's needs.

The mnemonic "DISCHARGE" will help you remember the priorities to consider.

COLLABORATING WITH THE INTERDISCIPLINARY TEAM FOR DISCHARGE PLANNING "DISCHARGE"	"DISCHARGE"
Do refer/collaborate if there are any physiological complications (i.e., breathing (need of O_2, blood sugar (glucose monitor equipment) or pain (prescriptions for pain management), etc.)	©2014 I CAN Publishing®, Inc.
Interdisciplinary Care (i.e., dietary, physical or occupational therapy, counselor, social services, etc.)	**D**o refer/collaborate if there are any physiological complications
Safety (i.e., home health assessment for environmental safety, stairs to climb, lighting, etc.)	**I**nterdisciplinary care
Community Resources (i.e., family members that need CPR training, support groups, etc.)	**S**afety
Health Promotion Activities (i.e., Primary: immunizations; Secondary: mammogram; Tertiary: Rehab center, etc.)	**C**ommunity resources
Activity (i.e., physical therapy, walking program, etc.)	**H**ealth Promotion activities
Routine Follow-up (i.e., appointments for follow-up with HCP, etc.)	**A**ctivity
Guidelines for meds and notifying the HCP, etc. (i.e., signs & symptoms of infections, adverse side effects of meds, etc.)	**R**outine follow-up
Equipment education (i.e., safe operation of oxygen equipment, suctioning equipment, etc.) (Manning & Rayfield, 2014)	**G**uidelines for meds, and notifying HCP, etc.
	Equipment Education

References for Chapter 27

Advance Healthcare Network for Nurses. (2013). Nurses once again top gallup's annual survey of most trusted professionals. Retrieved from http://nursing.advanceweb.com/News/National-News/Nurses-Once-Again-Top-Gallups-Annual-Survey-of-Most-Trusted-Professionals.aspx

Black, J M. and Hawks, J. H. (2009). *Medical surgical nursing: Clinical management for positive outcomes (8th ed.).* Philadelphia: Elsevier/Saunders.

Centers for Medicare & Medicaid Services. (2014). Accountable care organization 2014 program analysis quality performance standards narrative measure specifications. Retrieved from https://www.cms.gov/Medicare/Medicare-Fee-for-Service-Payment/sharedsavingsprogram/Downloads/ACO-NarrativeMeasures-Specs.pdf

Daniels, R. & Nicoll, L. (2012). *Contemporary medical-surgical nursing,* (2nd ed.). Clifton Park, NY: Delmar Cengage Learning.

Eliopoulos, C. (2014). *Gerontological nursing* (8th ed.), Philadelphia: Lippincott Williams & Wilkins

Giddens, G. F. (2013). *Concepts for nursing practice.* St. Louis, MO: Mosby, an imprint of Elsevier.

HealthyPeople 2020. (2014). Education and community- based programs. Retrieved from http://www.healthypeople.gov/2020/topicsobjectives2020/overview.aspx?topicid=11

Ignatavicius, D. D. and Workman, M. L. (2010). *Medical-surgical nursing: Patient-centered collaborative care* (6th ed.). Philadelphia: Elsevier/Saunders.

LeMone, P., Burke, K.M., & Bauldoff, G. (2011). *Medical-surgical nursing: Critical thinking in patient care* (5th ed.). Upper Saddle Road, NJ: Pearson/Prentice Hall.

Lewis, S., Dirksen, S., Heitkemper, M., Bucher, L., and Camera, I. (2011). *Medical surgical nursing: Assessment and management of clinical problems* (8th ed.). St. Louis: Mosby.

Manning, L. and Rayfield, S. (2014). *Nursing made insanely easy* (7th ed.). Duluth, GA: I CAN Publishing, Inc.

National Council of State Boards of Nursing, INC. (NCSBN) 2012. *Research brief: 2011 RN practice analysis: linking the NCLEX RN® examination to practice.* Retrieved from https://www.ncsbn.org/index.htm.

North Carolina Concept Based Learning Editorial Board (2011). *Nursing a concept based approach to learning,* Upper Saddle Road, NJ: Pearson/Prentice Hall.

Osborn, K. S., Wraa, C. E., Watson, A. S., and Holleran, R. S. (2014). *Medical surgical nursing: Preparation for practice* (2nd ed.). Upper Saddle Road, NJ: Pearson.

Potter, P. A., Perry, A. G., Stockert, P., and Hall, A. (2013). *Fundamentals of nursing* (8th ed.). St. Louis, MO: Pearson/Prentice Hall.

Smeltzer, S. C., Bare, B. G., Hinkle, J. L., and Cheever, K. H. (2010). *Brunner & Suddarth's Textbook of medical-surgical nursing* (12th ed.). Philadelphia: Lippincott Williams & Wilkins.

World Health Organization. (2012). Health education. Retrieved from http://www.who.int/topics/health_education/en/

CHAPTER 28

Linking Multiple Systems and Concepts
Concept Coping

A Snapshot of Coping

Coping is related to the concept of stress and involves the ability to cognitively and/or behaviorally manage internal or external situations (stressors). Coping can range from effective to ineffective/ maladaptive. Coping is considered maladaptive when conflicts go unresolved or intensify (Townsend, 2012) and adaptive when the person (family or community) manages stress using a variety of positive coping strategies (i.e., active problem solving, accessing social support, maintaining healthy exercise, etc). Coping relates to the individual, family or community and is required throughout the lifespan. A variety of stressors (events, situations or illnesses) require individuals to utilize coping mechanisms. Potential stressors include but are not limited to, chronic, acute or terminal illnesses and impending death, life style changes, psycho-social events or diseases, death of family member. Coping mechanisms can be overwhelmed by stressors leading to poor outcomes and thus require nursing intervention.

Stress is a "condition that is characterized by symptoms of physical or emotional tension. It is a reaction to a situation where a person feels threatened or anxious" (Centers for Disease Control and Prevention, 2014). Stress can be positive (i.e., preparing for a wedding) or negative (i.e., dealing with a terminal illness). Clients have a variety of reasons and situations while in the healthcare setting that are "stressors" (i.e., an unknown, diagnosis, stress of worrying about who is taking care of things at home, being away from their place of employment, undergoing painful procedures, etc.). How individual clients and/or their family or significant others cope with the different stressors, can impact their physical, mental and emotional well-being and may be an asset to their healing process or a detriment (Center for Disease Control and Prevention, 2014).

Crisis is an "experience of being confronted by a stressful event in which an individual is unable to cope or solve problems" (Hogan, 2013). Any healthcare situation, diagnosis, treatment, managing a chronic disease, or facing a life-threatening acute event can be a crisis to a client based on his/her ability to cope and their past experiences with coping.

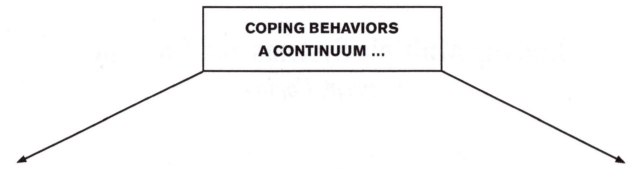

Adaptive Coping	Maladaptive Coping				
POSITIVE COPING STRATEGIES/ STRESS MANAGEMENT	**SUBSTANCE ABUSE**	**ANXIETY**	**ACTIVITIES OF DAILY LIVING**	**DEPRESSION**	**VIOLENCE**
• Counseling (i.e., cognitive behavior therapy, dialectical behavior therapy, etc.) • Journaling • Therapy (i.e., art, music, imagery, relaxation breathing, mindfulness, etc.) • Cognitive approaches (i.e., prioritizing demands, active problem solving, reframing negative thoughts; assertiveness, etc.) • Diversional activities (i.e., reading, TV, etc.) • Physical exercise • Therapeutic communication	• Alcohol abuse • Dependency • Drug abuse • No adherence to treatment plan	• Somatic complaints/pain • Anxiety • Bullying • Emotional outbursts • Dissociation • Decreased learning capacity • Fear • Role performance problems • Trauma responses • Denial • Developmental delay	• Impaired functional status (i.e., grooming, hygiene, etc) • Excessive eating • Inadequate nutrition	• Social withdrawal & isolation • Low self esteem • Ineffective problem solving • Negativity: cognitive distortions • Suicidal ideation • Psychomotor & cognitive slowing • Hyper/ hyposomnia • Hopelessness • Role performance problems	• Violence towards others (i.e., homicide, assault, & battery, etc.) • Violence towards self (suicide, self-mutilation/ cutting) • Hostility

Multiple Systems: Concept Coping

Risk Factors

All individuals have a variety of coping strategies that they use in life for a variety of life's situations or dilemmas. Individuals vary, however in the strengths of their coping skills based on the situation and how they perceive the stressful situation. Risk factors for ineffective coping skills include:

"POOR COPING"

Psychosocial resources, poor self esteem, depression and lack of motivation can lead to poor coping skills

Older adults may lack the social support, resources, or have less resilience because of multiple health conditions

Oblivious to stressors, avoidance of stressful situations

Report of poor past experiences in handling stressful situations

Chronic health conditions often lead to poor coping styles depending on the individual's perception of the health conditions

Obvious changes in cognition can impact individual's ability to assess the stressful situation

Perceived lack of control over the situation

Inability to accurately determine what the stressor is

No experience in dealing with stressful situations

Growth, development and age contribute to perception of stressful situations

Multiple Systems: Concept Coping

SAFETY: Concept Coping		
System-Specific Assessments "ANXIOUS"	**First-Do Priority Interventions "CALMER"**	**Evaluation of Expected Outcomes**
Altered sleep patterns; assess anxiety with coping measurement instruments. **N**onverbal behavior (i.e., pacing, frowning, etc.). e**X**press (i.e., communication, process random thoughts, etc.) uses odd wording. **I**nterest in eating changes; identify current medications client is taking. **O**utlook to client is dismal. **U**nderstanding: Does client understand care? What are their questions about immediate and long term management; use of alcohol or drugs. **S**tressed about need for equipment used during nursing care. ***Additional Assessments May be Needed:*** • CAGE AID (substance abuse screening tool) assessment • Mental status assessment • Suicide/homicide risk assessment • Nutritional assessment	**C**alm demeanor when providing care. **C**ollaborative interventions. **A**llow and encourage client to ventilate thoughts & feelings. Assist with therapeutic communication (i.e., active listening, empathy, etc.). **L**ook for community resources to support family. **M**onitor & teach coping mechanisms for life: • Relaxation techniques • Increase exercise • Encourage 8 hrs of sleep each night • Make appropriate life-style changes • Use positive coping: diversional activities (i.e., reading, games, TV, outings, imagery, journaling, massage, meditation, music therapy, physical therapy, etc.) • Reframe irrational negative cognitions with with more positive ones **E**valuate & confront substance use and denial. **R**eview strategies to link thoughts-feelings-actions to consequences. Generate new & alternative approaches to problems & discuss potential outcomes.	• Free from injury to self or others • Verbalizes alternative approaches to problem resolution • Verbalizes realistic appraisal of stressors & ways to decrease exposure to stressors when possible • Demonstrates use of alternative, positive coping skills (relaxation skills, accesses social support etc.) • Engages appropriately with staff and peers (assertive versus hostile or passive) • Abstains from substance use

Multiple Systems: Concept Coping

Resources to Help with Coping

"SELF-HELP" for Clients

Socially connect with others, do not isolate yourself.

Eat a healthy, well-balanced diet.

Learn to relax, take a break (i.e., get a massage, play tennis, cards, etc.).

Find support: (i.e., seek help from a partner, family member, friend, counselor, doctor, clergy, spiritual guide, etc.).

Help a neighbor, volunteer, take the dog for a walk.

Exercise regularly.

Learn to take care of yourself, avoid drugs and alcohol.

Plenty of sleep you need.

Collaborative Interventions

Problem-focused coping strategies

- Used when stressors can be modified, changed or controlled.

Emotion-focused coping strategies

- Examining the feeling associated with the stressor(s).

- Develop an actual plan with the individual that identifies coping strategies the client can use.

- Determining what resources are available to use.

- Examine the stressor from a different perspective; positive outlook about the stressor can increase the clients coping ability (Giddens, 2013).

Resources

AARP Grief and Loss
http://www.aarp.org/griefandloss

Alternative Medicine
http://www.alternativemedicine.com

American Cancer Society
http://www.cancer.org

The American Psychological Association
http://www.apahelpcenter.org/

American Society of Clinical Oncology
http://www.oncology.com

Cancer Care Inc.
http://www.cancercare.org

CancerLinks.org Web
http://www.cancerlinks.org

Cancer Survivors Network
http://www.acscsn.org

The Compassionate Friends
http://www.compassionatefriends.org

Crisis, Grief & Healing
http://www.webhealing.com

Grief, Loss & Recovery
http://www.grieflossrecovery.com

Hospice Foundation of America
http://www.hospicefoundation.org

References for Chapter 28

Black, J M. and Hawks, J. H. (2009). *Medical surgical nursing: Clinical management for positive outcomes (8th ed.)*. Philadelphia: Elsevier/Saunders.

Centers for Disease Control and Prevention. (2014). Coping with stress. Retrieved from http://www.cdc.gov/violenceprevention/pub/coping_with_stress_tips.html

Daniels, R. & Nicoll, L. (2012). *Contemporary medical-surgical nursing*, (2nd ed.). Clifton Park, NY: Delmar Cengage Learning.

Eliopoulos, C. (2014). *Gerontological nursing* (8th ed.), Philadelphia: Lippincott Williams & Wilkins

Giddens, G. F. (2013). *Concepts for nursing practice*. St. Louis, MO: Mosby, an imprint of Elsevier.

Hogan, M.A. (2013). *Mental health nursing: Reviews and rationales* (3rd ed.) Upper Saddle River: Pearson.

Hogan, M.A. (2014). *Pathophysiology: Reviews and rationales* (3rd ed.) Upper Saddle River: Pearson.

Ignatavicius, D. D. and Workman, M. L. (2010). *Medical-surgical nursing: Patient-centered collaborative care* (6th ed.). Philadelphia: Elsevier/Saunders.

Kneisl, C.R. & Tigoboff, E. (2013). *Contemporary psychiatric-mental health nursing*, 3rd ed. Pearson: Boston, MA.

LeMone, P., Burke, K.M., & Bauldoff, G. (2011). *Medical-surgical nursing: Critical thinking in patient care* (5th ed.). Upper Saddle Road, NJ: Pearson/Prentice Hall.

Lewis, S., Dirksen, S., Heitkemper, M., Bucher, L., and Camera, I. (2011). *Medical surgical nursing: Assessment and management of clinical problems* (8th ed.). St. Louis: Mosby.

Manning, L. and Rayfield, S. (2014). *Nursing made insanely easy* (7th ed.). Duluth, GA: I CAN Publishing, Inc.

Manning, L. & Rayfield, S. (2013). *Pharmacology made insanely easy* (4th ed.). Duluth, GA: I CAN Publishing, Inc.

National Council of State Boards of Nursing, INC. (NCSBN) 2012. *Research brief: 2011 RN practice analysis: linking the NCLEX RN® examination to practice*. Retrieved from https://www.ncsbn.org/index.htm.

North Carolina Concept Based Learning Editorial Board (2011). *Nursing a concept based approach to learning*, Upper Saddle Road, NJ: Pearson/Prentice Hall.

Osborn, K. S., Wraa, C. E., Watson, A. S., and Holleran, R. S. (2014). *Medical surgical nursing: Preparation for practice* (2nd ed.). Upper Saddle Road, NJ: Pearson.

Potter, P. A., Perry, A. G., Stockert, P., and Hall, A. (2013). *Fundamentals of nursing* (8th ed.). St. Louis, MO: Pearson/Prentice Hall.

Smeltzer, S. C., Bare, B. G., Hinkle, J. L., and Cheever, K. H. (2010). *Brunner & Suddarth's Textbook of medical-surgical nursing* (12th ed.). Philadelphia: Lippincott Williams & Wilkins.

Townsend, M.C. (2012). *Psychiatric mental health nursing* (7th ed.) Philadelphia, PA: F.A. Davis.

Wagner, K.D. & Hardin-Pierce, M.C. (2014). *High-Acuity nursing* (6th ed.). Boston: Pearson.

INDEX

Organized around concepts.

ACID BASE BALANCE
Arterial Blood Gases
Interpretation the easy 1, 2, 3 approach, 103–111
Procedure, 101
Referee approach, 114
ROME approach to ABG interpretation, 112–113
assessments, 97–100
decision-making analysis form, 121
definitions, 95, 102
interventions, 97–100
labs and diagnostic tests, 102
metabolic acidosis, 99
metabolic alkalosis, 100
pathophysiology, 96
respiratory acidosis, 97
respiratory alkalosis, 98
safety, plan of care, 97–100

CELLULAR REGULATION
assessments, 533–534
decision-making analysis form, 553
definitions, 531
geriatrics, concerns of, 540
interventions, 537–539
labs and diagnostic tests, 535
medications, 536
Medical Diagnoses
Breast Cancer, 541
Cellular Immunity: Human Immunodeficiency Virus (HIV), 546
Colon Cancer
Leukemia, 545
Lung Cancer, 542
Lymphomas, 544
Prostate Cancer, 543
pathophysiology, 532, 537–539

COPING
assessments 720
coping behaviors
adaptive, 718
maladaptive, 718
definitions, 717
interventions, 720
resources to help with coping, 721
risk factors for poor coping, 719
safety, plan of care, 720

ELIMINATION
decision-making analysis form, 463
definition, 439
geriatric risk factors, 440, 446, 454
interconnected concepts, 441
labs, diagnostic tests, and procedures, 443
Medical Diagnoses
Benign Prostatic Hypertrophy, 451
Continuous Bladder Irrigation (CBI), 452
Bowel Incontinence/Constipation, 447–448
Lower Urinary Tract Infections, 453–455
Cystitis, 453, 455
Urethritis, 453, 455
Renal Calculi, 449–450
Upper Urinary Tract, 453–455
Pyelonephritis, 453–455
Urinary Incontinence/Retention, 445–446
medications, 444
pathophysiology, 440–441
plan of care, 441

FLUID & ELECTROLYTES
CALCIUM IMBALANCE
assessment, 74, 76
decision-making analysis form, 83
definition, 69
foods high in calcium, 77
geriatrics: physiological changes, 75
interventions, 74, 76
labs and diagnostic tests, 71
safety, plan of care, 74, 76
summary, 78
Medical Diagnoses
Hypercalcemia
safety: plan of care, 76
Hypocalcemia
safety: plan of care, 74
medications, 75, 77
pathophysiology, 70
physiology, 72–73

FLUID BALANCE
assessment, 24–26
decision-making analysis form, 33
definition, 21
interventions, 24, 25
labs and diagnostic procedures, 22, 24, 26
Medical Diagnoses
Fluid Volume Deficit (hypovolemia), plan of care, 24
Fluid Volume Excess (hypervolemia), plan of care, 25
pathophysiology, 22
risk for dehydration, 23
safety, plan of care, 24–25

MAGNESIUM IMBALANCE
assessment, 87–88
decision-making analysis form, 92
definition, 85
foods high in magnesium, 87
interventions, 87–88
labs and diagnostic procedures, 86
Medical Diagnoses
Hypermagnesemia safety: plan of care, 88
Hypomagnesemia safety: plan of care, 87
pathophysiology, 86
safety, plan of care, 87–88

POTASSIUM IMBALANCE
assessments, 59–60
decision-making analysis form, 66
definition, 57
foods high in potassium, 60
geriatrics: physiological changes, 61

interventions, 59–60
Medical Diagnoses
　Hyperkalemia safety: plan of care, 60
　Hypokalemia safety: plan of care, 59
medications affecting potassium, 59, 61
pathophysiology, 58
safety, plan of care, 59–60
summary, 62

SODIUM IMBALANCE
assessment, 43, 45
decision-making analysis form, 54
definition, 35
fluid types, 38–42
foods high in sodium, 46
geriatric changes, 36
hypernatremia, plan of care, 45
hypertonic, 39, 41, 42
hyponatremia, plan of care, 43–44
hypotonic, 40–42
interventions, 43, 45
isotonic, 38, 41, 42
labs and diagnostic tests, 46
pathophysiology, 36
safety, plan of care, 43–45
song, 37
summary, 47

HEALTH PROMOTION
assessments, 711, 713
client teaching, 710–713
definitions, 709
discharge teaching, 715
interventions, 711, 713
primary prevention, 710–711, 713–714
safety, plan of care, 711
secondary prevention, 710-711, 713–714
tertiary, 710–711, 713–714

INFECTION CONTROL
assessments, 629
category of precautions (summary), 637
decision-making analysis form, 642
definitions, 629-630
interventions, 631–635
pathophysiology, 632
personal protective equipment, 631–636
procedure for donning and removing, PPE, 636
safety, plan of care, 633

Transmission Precautions
　Airborne Precautions, 632
　Contact Precautions, 632
　Droplet Precautions, 632
　Protective Precautions, 635
　Standard Precautions, 629, 631

INTRACRANIAL REGULATION
assessments, 247, 250–255, 261
　Comparison of VS for Shock and IICP, 255
　Complications, 255–257
　　Cushing's Triad, 256
　　Syndrome of Inappropriate Antidiuretic Hormone, 257
　Cranial Nerves, 252–254
　Glasgow Coma Scale, 251
　PEERLA, 251
decision-making analysis form, 292
definitions, 245–246
geriatrics: neurological changes, 248–249
interdisciplinary team for clients with "alteration in intracranial regulation", 286
interventions, 259–261
labs and diagnostic tests, 258
Medical Diagnoses
　Alzheimer's Disease, 278–279, 284
　Amyotrophic Lateral Sclerosis (ALS), 283–284
　Autonomic Dysreflexia, 270
　Brain Neoplasm, 276
　Cerebral Vascular Accident (CVA), 262–263
　Craniotomy, 277
　Guillain Barré, 275
　Head Injury, 264
　Meningitis, 285
　Multiple Sclerosis, 280–281, 284
　Myasthenia Gravis, 273–274
　　cholinergic crisis, 274
　　myasthenic Crisis, 274
　Parkinson's Disease, 282, 284
　Seizures, 271–272
　Spinal Cord Injury, 265–269
　　Bowel and bladder retraining, 269
medications, 258
pathophysiology, 246, 260
safety, plan of care, 261

METABOLISM
GASTROINTESTINAL/BILIARY SYSTEM
assessments, 298–299, 304
associated concepts, 297

decision-making analysis form, 334
definitions, 295
interventions, 302–304
labs and diagnostic tests, therapeutic procedures/surgery, 300
linking system with associated concepts, 297
Medical Diagnoses
　Cholecystitis/Cholelithiasis, 319
　Gastroesophageal Reflux Disease (GERD), 305
　Gastrointestinal Surgery Post-Op Care, 308
　　Dumping Syndrome, 309
　Hernias, 311
　Hirschsprung's Disease, 310
　Infections (Bacteria, Viruses and Parasites)
　　Diarrhea (Clostridium d-Difficile, Escherichia coli, etc.), 312–313
　Inflammatory Bowel Disease (IBD) 314–315,
　Acute IBD
　　Gastroenteritis, 314–315
　　Appendicitis, 314–315
　　Peritonitis, 314–315
　Chronic IBD
　　Crohn's Disease, 316–318
　　Ulcerative Colitis, 316–318
　　Diverticular Disease, 316–318
　Intestinal Obstructions, 321–323
　　Colon Cancer (Colostomy/ Ileostomy Care), 324–325
　　Perforations, 323
　　Pyloric stenosis, 322
　Irritable Bowel Syndrome (IBS), 310
　Pancreatitis, 320
　Peptic Ulcer Disease (PUD), 306–309
　　Dumping Syndrome, 309
　　Post-op care, 308
medications, 301
pathophysiology, 296, 299, 303
safety, plan of care, 304
tubes and drains, 326

METABOLISM
LIVER FAILURE
concept connections, 342–343
decision-making analysis form, 363
definition, 337
labs and diagnostic tests, 339
medications, 340
nutritional imbalances, 344–345
pathophysiology, 338, 341
plan of care, 341

Medical Diagnoses
Cirrhosis of the Liver, 350–355
paracentesis, 353
esophagogastric balloon
tamponade, 354
esophageal varices, 353–354
hepatic encephalopathy, 355
Hepatitis (A,B, C, D, and E),
346–347
hepatitis immunizations, 348
transmission of hepatitis, 349

**METABOLISM PITUITARY,
THYROID, AND ADRENAL**
assessments, 366
decision-making analysis form, 397
definitions, 365
labs, diagnostic tests, procedures, 367
medications, 367
pathophysiology, 366

ADRENAL GLAND
Addison's Disease, 385–389
assessments, 387
Cushing's Syndrome, 385–389
definitions, 384
interventions, 388
labs, diagnostic tests, procedures,
366–367
medications, 367
pathophysiology, 366, 385–386

PITUITARY
assessments, 370, 372–375
concept connections, 369-375
definitions, 368
Diabetes Insipidus (DI), 369–373
interventions, 371, 373–375
labs, diagnostic tests, procedures,
367, 369
medications, 367
pathophysiology, 366, 368–369
safety, plan of care, 372–375
song to connect assessments/
interventions, 376
Syndrome of Inappropriate
Antidiuretic Hormone
(SIADH), 369–371, 374–375

THYROID
assessments, 378
definitions, 377
geriatrics, 379
Hyperthyroidism (Graves
Disease), 378
Radioactive Iodine Therapy,
380
interventions, 379
labs, diagnostic tests, procedures,
367

medications, 367
pathophysiology, 377
safety, plan of care, 382
Thyroidectomy, 381
complication, hypocalcemia,
382
Thyroid Storm, 383
Hypothyroidism (Myxedema),
378
Myxedema Coma, 383

**METABOLISM PANCREAS;
GLUCOSE**
Diabetes Mellitus (Type 1)
Hyperglycemia
assessments, 403, 406, 408–409
complications, chronic long-term,
415-417
decision-making analysis form, 437
definitions, 399
do's and don'ts of foot care, 407
geriatrics, plan for administration of
insulin, 407
health promotion for nutrition, 408
insulin administration, teaching plan,
409
insulin therapy, complications, 415
dawn phenomenon, 415–416
somogyi effect, 415
insulin guidelines for sliding scale,
413–414
interventions, 400, 406, 408–409
labs/diagnostic tests/procedures, 401
Medical Diagnoses
Diabetic Ketoacidosis (DKA),
421–426
Diabetes Mellitus (Type 2),
427–428
Gestational Diabetes, 428–430
Hyperosmolar Hyperglycemic
Nonketotic Syndrome
(HHNS), 421–426
Hypoglycemia, 419–426
medications, 411–414, 417
pathophysiology, 400, 402, 404–405
safety, plan of care, 404, 406, 408–409
self-monitoring of blood glucose, 410
"sick day" guidelines, 418

MOBILITY
assessments, 497, 502
assistive devices
Cane, 518
Crutch walking, 519–520
Walker, 520
complications of immobility, 503, 521
decision-making analysis form, 529
definition, 495
interventions, 498, 500–502
labs and diagnostic tests, 499

Medical Diagnoses
Amputations, 508
Fibromyalgia, 510
Fractures, 504–505
Cast Care, 506
Complications (Fat Emboli
and Compartment
Syndrome), 506
Traction Care, 507
Gout, 515
Osteoarthritis, 511
Joint Replacement Care,
512–513
Osteomyelitis, 514
Osteoporosis, 509
Post-Op Care: Cast Care, 506
Rheumatoid Arthritis, 516
hot and cold therapy, 516
Systemic Lupus Erythematous,
517
Total Arthroplasty/Replacement,
512–513
medications, 499
pathophysiology, 496, 498, 501
safety, plan of care, 502

NCLEX® Questions and Rationales
Acid-Base Balance, 115–120
Calcium Imbalance, 79–82
Cellular Regulation, 547–552
Elimination, 456–462
Fluid Imbalance, 27–32
Infection Control, 638–641
Intracranial Regulation, 287–291
Magnesium Imbalance, 89–91
Metabolism
Gastrointestinal/biliary System,
327–333
Glucose, 431–436
Liver, 356–362
Pituitary, Thyroid, and Adrenal,
390–396
Mobility, 522–528
Nutrition, 667–669
Oxygenation (Respiratory System),
147–151
Pain, 685–688
Perfusion
Cardiac/Peripheral, 212–219
Renal, 487–492
Shock, 237–242
Potassium Imbalance, 63–65
Prioritization, 16–19
Safety/Prevention of Injury, 623–626
Sensory Perception, 608–610
Sodium Imbalance, 48–53
Thermoregulation, 701–704
Tissue/Skin Integrity, 580–586

NUTRITION BALANCE
Decision-Making Analysis Form, 670
Definition, 645
Nutritional Comparison Guidelines
Fat Soluble Vitamins (A, D, E, K), 657–659
Macronutrients (Protein, Carbohydrates, Fat), 648–650
Minerals (Sodium, Potassium, Calcium), 651–653
Other Therapeutic Diets (Anorexia Nervosa, Bulimia Nervosa), 665–666
System/Diseases Nutritional/Diet Needs, 664
Therapeutic Diets (Iron, Residue, Purines, Lactose-Free, Gluten), 660–663
Water Soluble Vitamins (B$_6$, B$_9$, B$_{12}$, C), 654–656
Pathophysiology, 645
Safety, plan of care, 646–647

OXYGENATION
assessments, 124–125, 127
decision-making analysis form, 152
definitions, 123
geriatric physiological changes with respiratory system, 132
interventions, 129–131, 146
labs and diagnostic tests, procedures, 128
Medical Diagnoses
Acute Respiratory Distress Syndrome (ARDS), 142
Acute Respiratory Failure (ARF), 142
Anemia, 144
Asthma, 134
COPD (Emphysema/Bronchitis), 133
Cystic Fibrosis, 135
Epiglottitis/Croup, 136
Hemothorax, 139
Pneumonia, 138
Pneumothorax, 139
Pulmonary Emboli, 141
Severe Acute Respiratory Syndrome (SARS), 138
Sickle Cell Anemia, 145
Tension pneumothorax, 139
Tonsillitis, 137
Tuberculosis, 137
medications, 128
pathophysiology, 124–126, 130, 142
safety, plan of care, 131
ventilator care, 143
water-sealed chest drainage, 140

PAIN
assessments, 674–675, 680–681
concepts linked, 684
decision-making analysis form, 689
definition, 673
geriatrics, monitoring, 676
interventions, 678–681
labs and diagnostic tests, therapeutic procedures, 676
medications, 677
pathophysiology, 673, 675, 679
safety, plan of care, 680
pain management, types of
Nonpharmacological Pain Management, 683
Pharmacological Pain Management, 682

PERFUSION CARDIAC/ PERIPHERAL
Arrhythmias
asystole, 206
atrial fibrillation, 199–200
atrial flutter, 199–200
bradycardia, 194
heart blocks, 201–202
pacemakers, 202–203
premature ventricular contractions, 204
sinus arrhythmia, 197
sinus bradycardia, 198
sinus tachycardia, 198
tissue death or ischemia, 207
ventricular tachycardia, 205
assessments, 158–160, 165
associated concepts, 157
cardiac catheterization, 176
cardiac conduction system, 192–193
cardiac monitoring, 191
cardiac rhythm analysis, 194–197
cardiac sounds, 159
cardioversion, 208
decision-making analysis form, 220
defibrillation, 208
definition, 155–156
geriatrics, age related changes, 178
interventions, 163–165, 186
labs and diagnostic tests, 161, 175
Medical Diagnoses
Acute Myocardial Infarction, 177-181
Angina, 173–174, 177
Atherosclerosis, 156, 169
Cardiac Conduction/ Dysrhythmias, 187–203
Cardiogenic Shock, 190, 223, 225, 227, 231
Cardiac Tamponade, 211
Congenital Heart Defects, 188

Coronary Bypass Surgery (CABG), 182
Deep Vein Thrombosis (DVT), 172
Endocarditis, 210–211
Heart Failure, 183–185
Hypertension, 166–168
Hypertensive Crisis, 168
Myocarditis, 210–211
Pericarditis, 210–211
Peripheral Vascular Disease, 169–170
arterial and venous ulcers, 171
Pulmonary Edema, 187
Rheumatic Heart Disease, 210–211
Valvular Heart Disease, 156–157, 189
medications, 162, 180
normal sinus arrhythmia, 197
pacemakers, 202–203
pathophysiology, 156, 160, 164
risk factors, 157
safety, plan of care, 165
summary: interactive exercise about arrhythmias, 209

PERFUSION RENAL
CHRONIC RENAL DISEASE
assessments, 467, 470, 473–475, 477
concept review, 470–471, 473–478
concept summary, 479–481
decision making analysis form, 493
definition, 465
interventions, 470, 472–475, 477
labs and diagnostic tests, diagnostic procedures, 468–469
Medical Diagnoses
Glomerulonephritis, 482
Nephrotic Syndrome, 483–484
Hemodialysis, 485
Peritoneal Dialysis, 486
medications, 471
nutrition review, 478
pathophysiology, 466–467, 476
safety, plan of care, 470, 473–475, 477
summary of chronic renal failure, 479–481

PERFUSION/SHOCK
assessments, 226–229, 234
decision making analysis form, 243
definition, 223–224
interventions, 232–234, 235-236
hemodynamic monitoring, 233
labs and diagnostic tests, 230
medications/fluids comparison, 231
pathophysiology, 223–225

safety, plan of care, 232, 234
types of shock, 223, 225, 227, 231
    Cardiogenic Shock,190, 223, 225, 227, 231
    Distributive Shock, 223, 225, 227, 231
        Anaphylactic, 223, 225, 227, 231
        Neurogenic, 223, 225, 227, 231, 266
        Septic, 219, 221, 223, 227
    Hypovolemic Shock, 223–236
    Obstructive Shock, 223, 225, 227, 231

PRIORITIZATION, 11-12
Algorithm, 13
Strategies, 14–19

SAFETY PREVENTION OF INJURY
components of a safe patient-care environment, 616
comparison of patient safety standards, 618–619
conditions that must be reported by law, 621
decision-making anaylsis form, 627
definitions, 615
resources and web sites, 622
safety, plan of care, 620
safety QSEN competencies for the nurse, 617

SENSORY PERCEPTION
decision-making anaylsis form, 611

HEARING
assessments, 595–596, 598
communication strategies for clients who have a hearing deficit, 599
definition, 589
diagnostic tests, 596
geriatric, age-related changes in hearing, 597
interventions, 598
Medical Diagnoses
    Ménière's Disease, 606–607
    Labyrinthitis (Otitis internal), 606–607
medications, 597
pathophysiology, 589, 596
safety, plan of care 598

SOMATOSENSORY (TOUCH)
assessments, 599 , 600, 602
definition, 589
geriatric, age-related changes in the touch, 601
interventions, 602

labs and diagnostic tests, 600
pathophysiology, 589, 600
safety, plan of care, 602
teaching topics for clients who have an alteration in sensory perceptions, 601

VISION
assessments, 590–591, 598
definition, 589
diagnostic tests, 596
geriatric, age-related changes in the eye, 597
interventions, 598
Medical Diagnoses
    Cataracts, 603–605
    Macular Degeneration, 603–605
    Glaucoma, 603–605
    Retinal Detachment, 603–605
medications, 597
pathophysiology, 589, 596
safety, plan of care, 598

THERMOREGULATION
assessment, 693, 695, 697
decision-making analysis form, 705
definitions, 691
geriatric, age-related changes that result in altered thermoregulation, 698
guidelines for treating children with a temperature, 699
hyperthermia, 696–697, 700
hypothermia, 694–695, 700
interventions, 695, 697
pathophysiology, 692, 694, 696
physiological processes for optimal thermoregulation, 692
safety, plan of care, 695, 697

TISSUE INTEGRITY
assessments, 556–557
concept link exercise, 577
decision-making analysis form, 587
definition, 555
geriatrics, skin/tissue changes, 562
interventions, 560–561
labs/diagnostic tests/procedures, 558
medications, 559
pathophysiology, 555, 561, 557
preventative care, 556–557, 560–561
safety, plan of care, 563
Medical Diagnoses
    Benign and Premalignant Skin Cancer, 578–579
    Burn Care, 570
    Infections, 567, 569
    Bacterial (Cellulitis), 568

    Fungal (Tinea) Viral (Herpes Simplex Type 1 and 2), 567–568
    Infestations (Lice and Scabies, 567–568
    Thermal/Radiation Injuries, 573-576
    Trauma/Injury to skin, 564–566
Types of Wounds
Wound Care, 565–566

ULCERS
care of, 572
stages of ulcers, 571
types of (Pressure, Diabetic, Arterial and Venous), 570